FIFTY CARIBBEAN WRITERS

FIFTY CARIBBEAN WRITERS

A BIO-BIBLIOGRAPHICAL CRITICAL SOURCEBOOK

EDITED BY
DARYL CUMBER DANCE

GREENWOOD PRESS
New York • Westport, Connecticut • London

Library of Congress Cataloging-in-Publication Data

Main entry under title:

Fifty Caribbean writers:

Bibliography: p.
Includes index.
1. Caribbean literature (English)— Bio-Bibliography.
2. Caribbean literature (English)— History and criticism. 3. Authors, Caribbean— Biography— Dictionaries. I. Dance, Daryl Cumber.
PR9205.A52F54 1986 810′.9′9729 85-10008
ISBN 0-313-23939-8 (lib. bdg. : alk. paper)

Library of Congress Catalog Card Number: 85-10008
ISBN: 0-313-23939-8

First published in 1986

Greenwood Press, Inc.
88 Post Road West
Westport, Connecticut 06881

Printed in the United States of America

The paper used in this book complies with the Permanent Paper Standard issued by the National Information Standards Organization (Z39.48-1984).

10 9 8 7 6 5 4 3 2 1

COPYRIGHT ACKNOWLEDGMENTS

The editor is grateful to the following for permission to reproduce copyrighted material:

To Curtis Brown Group Limited on behalf of Phyllis Shand Allfrey, for two poems, copyright by Phyllis Shand Allfrey.

To Louise Bennett and Sangster's Book Stores, for permission to quote poems from *Selected Poems*, published by Sangsters Book Stores in 1982, copyright by Louise Bennett.

To Williams-Wallace Publishers, for poems from Dionne Brand's *Chronicles of the Hostile Sun*, copyright 1984 by Dionne Brand; *Primitive Offensive*, copyright 1982 by Dionne Brand; and *Winter Epigrams and Epigrams to Ernesto Cardenal in Defense of Claudia*, copyright 1983 by Dionne Brand.

To Wayne Brown and to Andre Deutsch, Ltd., for permission to quote excerpts from *On the Coast*, copyright 1972 by Wayne Brown.

To Jan Carew and to A. J. Seymour for excerpts from Carew's poetry, published in *A Treasury of Guyanese Poetry*, ed. A. J. Seymour (Georgetown, Guyana: Author, 1980).

To Lawrence & Wishart Ltd., for permission to quote excerpts from *Poems of Resistance*, copyright 1954 and 1979 by Martin Carter.

To Mrs. Ellice Collymore (Literary Executor for the estate of Frank Collymore) and to The Advocate Company Limited for permission to quote from *Collected Poems*, copyright 1959 by Frank Collymore, published by The Advocate Co., Bridgetown, Barbados.

To John J. Figueroa and to Three Continents Press for permission to quote excerpts from *Ignoring Hurts*, published by Three Continents Press, copyright 1972 by John J. Figueroa.

To Anthony McNeill and to Savacou Publications for permission to quote poems from *Reel from "The Life-Movie*," copyright 1975 by Anthony McNeill (published by Savacou Publications).

To Anthony McNeill and The Institute of Jamaica Publications Limited for permission to quote poems from *Credences at the Altar of Cloud*, copyright 1979 by Anthony McNeill (published by The Institute of Jamaica).

To Anthony McNeill and to Institute of Jamaica Publications Limited for permission to reprint "Chinaware" from the *Jamaica Journal* (1970).

To Anthony McNeill and to Hamish Hamilton Limited for permission to quote an extract from "The Crack" from *Breaklight*, ed. Andrew Salky (first published by Hamish Hamilton, 1971).

To Jonathan Cape Ltd. and to Mrs. Jessie Taylor (Executrix of the estate of Roger Mais) for permission to quote excerpts from *The Three Novels of Roger Mais* (London: Jonathan Cape), copyright 1966.

To Mervyn Morris and Sangster's Book Stores for permission to quote poems from *On Holy Week*, copyright 1976 by Mervyn Morris (published by Sangster's Book Stores).

To Mervyn Morris and New Beacon Books Ltd., for permission to quote poems from *The Pond*, copyright 1973 by Mervyn Morris (published by New Beacon Books Ltd.).

To my children, Warren, Allen, and Daryl Lynn

Contents

Acknowledgments

I am grateful to Virginia Commonwealth University for granting me a leave during the 1984–85 school year, which allowed me the time to prepare and edit this collection. I also wish to thank Dr. Elske v.P. Smith, Dean of the College of Humanities and Sciences, for making the resources of her office available to me in the preparation of this manuscript. I am particularly indebted to Ms. Dianne Marshall and Mr. Gene Dunaway for their help in typing the essays. Special kudos are due Mrs. Barbara Hobson and Mrs. Norma Middleton, who typed, and photocopied, and filed, and telephoned, and provided all manner of clerical assistance. I am also indebted to numerous librarians for special assistance: I especially wish to thank Mrs. Susan Bass and Miss Arlene Best of the Interlibrary Loan Staff, Virginia Commonwealth University, and Mr. Samuel Washington of the Library of Congress. The encouragement, support and understanding of my Departmental Chairman, Dr. Dorothy Scura, sustained me throughout.

I am grateful to all of my friends and colleagues who offered encouragement, advice, and assistance during the three years I have been working on this book. It is impossible to list all of them, but I must especially thank Mr. Mervyn Morris, who consulted with me extensively in the selection of writers to be included in this volume and who assisted me in soliciting contributors, and Mrs. Jean D'Costa, who also advised and aided me in contacting contributors and who offered critiques, advice, information, and materials that were of critical help in the preparation of this work.

Finally, I wish to thank the many scholars who worked so hard to prepare the essays which constitute this volume.

FIFTY CARIBBEAN WRITERS

Introduction

Sailors, saltfish merchants, displaced criminals, yellow-fever victims, slaves in the canefields, Maroons in the bush: such were the men and women who laid the foundations of Caribbean societies in the 16th and 17th centuries. From such groups emerge rumor and legend, but rarely a formal literature. Indeed, the literature of the Caribbean, like that of most colonial societies, passed through the usual stages, moving from apparent silence to assimilation, imitation, and apology, and on to innovation, affirmation, and transformation. Today it is possible to chart the movement of Caribbean literature, tracing it from the derivative writings of the 18th and 19th centuries—much of it composed by visitors to the region, all of it firmly Eurocentric—to the strikingly innovative art of a Derek Walcott or a Wilson Harris.

The beginnings of Caribbean literature lie hidden in the folklore of the plantation era and in the prim, condescending travelogues, the exotic novels, and the apparently naive slave narratives—often authored by Whites—that began to appear as early as the 18th century. (Helpful reviews of this early literature may be found in Anthony Boxill, "The Beginnings to 1929," in *West Indian Literature*, ed. Bruce King, 1979, pp. 30–44; and Edward Brathwaite, "Creative Literature of the British West Indies During the Period of Slavery," *Savacou* 1 [June 1970], 46–73). Among the early writers, a few voices ring a prophetic note. Francis Williams, the classically educated Black poet of 18th century Jamaica, used conventional Augustan poetics to protest racism and assert the common humanity of mankind. The diction is of England, but the vision draws from Caribbean life. By the 19th century some Black poets (notably those of

Guyana) began to write of their own concerns and experiences. A few took the critical step of writing in the local vernacular, masking this revolutionary shift behind comic and nonserious verse forms. (For a useful review of this early poetry, see Arthur Drayton, "West Indian Consciousness in West Indian Verse," *Journal of Commonwealth Literature* 9 [July 1970], 66–88; for examples of some of the early poetry, see Norman Cameron's anthology, *Guianese Poetry: 1831–1931* [Georgetown, Guyana: Argosy, 1931].)

Despite the fact that there is this large body of early writings produced in the West Indies, most scholars do not consider that a corpus that can accurately be denoted Caribbean literature—a literature which reflects the themes and concerns, the language and culture, the perspective and ambience of the Caribbean and its people—evolved until the 20th century. In a 1960 publication (*The Pleasures of Exile*) George Lamming declared, "The West Indian novel, by which I mean the novel written by the West Indian about the West Indian reality, is hardly twenty years old" (p. 68). In his seminal study of West Indian fiction, Kenneth Ramchand asserts that "the earliest known work of West Indian prose fiction" that can be called distinctively West Indian appeared in 1903 (*The West Indian Novel and its Background*, 1970, p. 3). Like Ramchand, Michael Gilkes dates the beginning of "a recognizable West Indian literature" from Tom Redcam's 1903 novel, *Becka's Buckra Baby*, and considers the novels of Herbert G. de Lisser as representing "the beginning of a genuine awareness of . . . the realities of everyday West Indian life" (*The West Indian Novel, 1981, p. 11)*. Lloyd Brown, author of the definitive study of West Indian poetry, describes the first 180 years of West Indian poetry (1760–1940) as "downright unpromising" (*West Indian Poetry*, 1978, p. 19) and acclaims Claude McKay (whose first work appeared in 1912) the first major poet.

These promising beginnings came to fruition in the critical period of the 1930s and 1940s, the period of focused nationalism and political self-determination. During these decades appeared native literary journals such as *The Beacon* (which appeared in Trinidad in 1931), *Bim* (started in Barbados in 1942); *Focus* (started in Jamaica in 1943); *Kyk-Over-Al* (started in Guyana in 1945); and the *Caribbean Quarterly* (begun in Jamaica in 1949). These journals were to play a crucial role as stimulants to debate, as sources of information, and, importantly, as a literary forum for young, developing writers. In their pages appeared the first works of most of the Caribbean authors who achieved prominence during the ensuing decades. The radio series *Caribbean Voices*, which the BBC began in 1946, also helped to introduce many of the writers. Among those who began to publish during these decades were the Trinidadians Alfred H. Mendes and C. L. R. James, the White Dominican Jean Rhys, the Guyanese Edgar Mittelholzer and A. J. Seymour, the Jamaicans Roger Mais and Vic Reid, and the Barbadian Frank Collymore. The literary movement spanned the range of the area, from continental Guyana all along the island chain.

The period from 1950 to 1965 was one of such extensive and outstanding publications by West Indian writers that Edward Brathwaite has labeled it the

West Indian Renaissance ("The Love Axe: Developing a Caribbean Aesthetic 1962–1974," in *Reading Black: Essays in the Criticism of African, Caribbean, and Black American Literature*, ed. Houston A. Baker [Ithaca: Cornell University African Studies and Research Center, 1976]. During these years there appeared the first novels and volumes of poetry by writers who have earned distinguished reputations in 20th century literature, among them George Lamming, Samuel Selvon, V. S. Naipaul, Wilson Harris, and Derek Walcott.

The ensuing years, including Brathwaite's "Revolutionary Period" (1968–1972)—and beyond—have witnessed the publication of major works by a phenomenal number of exceptionally talented writers, some of whom have already established an international reputation for themselves. The poets Edward Brathwaite, Mervyn Morris, and Dennis Scott and the fiction writers Michael Anthony and Earl Lovelace have set a stamp on this period which belongs equally to the as yet lesser-known talents of Tony McNeill, Erna Brodber, and Jamaica Kincaid (it is worth noting that there is an increasing number of women among this latter group).

The most notable Caribbean writers are prominent not only within the context of Caribbean letters; a remarkable number of them are clearly among the truly outstanding writers of the world. C. L. R. James was guilty neither of exaggeration nor of nationalism when he declared, "I do not know at the present time any country writing in English which is able to produce a trio of the literary capacity and effectiveness of Wilson Harris, George Lamming, and Vidia Naipaul" (Ian Munro and Reinhard Sander, "Interview with C. L. R. James," in *Interviews with Three Caribbean Writers in Texas, Kas-Kas* [Austin: African and Afro-American Research Institute, University of Texas, 1972], p. 24). There are a number of other names that James and others would obviously insist upon adding to that list today, authors whose contributions clearly reflect the quality of contemporary Caribbean literature, names such as Derek Walcott, to whom poet Joseph Brodsky referred when he insisted, "the great poet of the English language is a black man" ("On Derek Walcott," *New York Review of Books*, November 10, 1983, p. 39).

This study of fifty Caribbean writers comes at a crucial time, for there is nothing more fascinating than studying the works of a "nation" during its efflorescence and focusing on writers who have a sense of themselves as, on the one hand, continuing a long literary and cultural tradition (largely Western and African) and, on the other hand, being a part of the beginning of an exciting new cultural development, writers who often view themselves as New Adams in a New World Eden. This fact is symbolically reinforced by Walcott's insistence that

> there are so many places that are virginal, really primal, in the Caribbean, . . . so many places in St. Lucia where there has never been a human footprint, . . . and if one can lift one's foot up sharply and put it down on that place the resonances of that are the same

> as the resonances that it meant for Adam to put his foot down in Eden. (interview with Daryl Cumber Dance, Richmond, Virginia, March 3, 1981)

Like Walcott they recognize how blessed they are to inherit ''a virginal, unpainted world'' and to have the task, like Adam, of ''giving things their names'' (*Another Life* [London: Jonathan Cape, 1973], p. 152).

To appreciate fully the pleasure of ''giving things their names'' one must understand the special meaning that naming has traditionally in Africa and especially in the Caribbean, where, as is suggested in Walcott's statement, the West Indian's sense of himself as new man stems from the force of the *Word*, which he has inherited, and the awareness that through the *Word* he possesses the supreme power of naming and identifying and giving meaning to—in effect, indeed *creating*—his universe. In his poem ''Naming'' (*The Arrivants*, 1973; originally published in *Islands*, 1969), Edward Brathwaite suggests that the act of naming bestows the life force on the object: it is imperative, he insists, to name the tree, for it is the naming which ''gives it fruit / issues its juices'' (p. 217). The idea that the Word is their inheritance was reinforced by Martin Carter, who declared ''the major art form [in the Caribbean] is rhetoric, . . . *rhetoric*!'' He observed that a visitor to Guyana commented to him, ''Man, all you got is *words*'' (interview with Daryl Cumber Dance, Georgetown, Guyana, March 20, 1980). A similar sentiment is voiced by Walcott's Shabine in *The Star-Apple Kingdom*: ''But that's all them bastards have left us: words'' (1977, p. 9). That may be *all* that they've been left, but as heirs to *that* heritage, Caribbean writers assume a divine task as New World Adams. Thus, in the penultimate poem of his epic, Edward Brathwaite admonishes the Caribbean man to write on his broken ground, for it is there that the word is transformed into a god that walks among them (*The Arrivants*, pp. 265–66).

While most of these writers might agree on the significance of the Word, there is considerable controversy about the question of *which* word, for there are many language forms available to them. As Kenneth Ramchand has noted,

> We have had so many different notions of what our language is: it should be Standard English or it should be some African language, or it should be Hindi, or it should be deep-level dialect, or. . . . There are so many versions of what our language should be, that it is a challenge to the West Indian writer, not to say I am choosing *one*, but what can I take from all of these. (interview with Daryl Cumber Dance, Port of Spain, Trinidad, March 18, 1979)

Novelist Jean D'Costa, who asserts that for the writer ''the choice is both liberating and exacting'' (letter to Daryl Cumber Dance, March 12, 1985), has written extensively about this matter of the choice of language (see her ''The West Indian Novelist and Language: A Search for a Literary Medium,'' in *Studies in Caribbean Language*, ed. Laurence Carrington [St. Augustine, Trinidad: Society for Caribbean Linguistics, 1983], pp. 252–65; and ''Expression and Communication: Literary Challenges to the Caribbean Polydialectal Writer,'' *Journal of Commonwealth Literature* 19 [August 1984], 123–41). A sensitive issue in evaluating the work of writers such as Vic Reid, Louise Bennett, and Samuel Selvon has been their use of dialect, which has been variously applauded and condemned. Other writers have been accused of sacrificing the vitality and originality of the folk speech for a staid Standard English. The controversy rages; indeed Edward Baugh devotes one full section of his *Critics on Caribbean Literature: Readings in Literary Criticism*(1978) to this issue—part 4, ''A Language of One's Own.''

Language and identity are inseparable. The quest for identity is another prevalent concern in Caribbean literature. In this quest the West Indian author and his dramatis personae generally make three journeys, starting with the journey to England (or, more recently, to the United States or Canada), the journey, in other words, into the White Western world. This involves both the trauma of sailing away from all that is familiar and the agony of lonely exile; generally this journey reinforces the fact that the cold and alien land is not home and that the traveler must divest himself of his Europeanization or his Westernization, which is antithetical to his sense of himself as a West Indian. It is important to note that despite the fact that he grew up in a West Indian society where both worlds existed, it is generally not until he experiences exile that he becomes aware of how diverse his consciousness is, how at odds is his Caribbeanness to the metropolitan world. Second, there is a journey to Africa (or, for Naipaul, to India), where most find that the Middle Passage has irreparably severed them from their roots in the homeland. And finally, there is a return journey to the home island, a return which many find is impossible because their European trek, especially their European education, has taken them too far away from their people, their roots, and thus themselves. As Dennis Scott writes, ''To travel / is to return / to strangers'' (''Exile,'' *Uncle Time*, p. 5). Upon his return home Walcott's narrator finds nothing is the same as it was—''it was a book / you'd read a life ago''; and, disillusioned, he leaves, taking one last look ''at things that would not say what they once meant'' (*Another Life*, p. 113). For many of the younger writers, the journey in quest of identity takes place within the island itself, with the characters moving from the provinces into the modernized, industrialized, Westernized urban society. The challenge to maintain a sense of self and of tradition and culture is no less great in this journey, and the intra-island traveler frequently finds himself beset in the New World Babylon with some of the same problems and some of the same threats to self-realization that beset his earlier counterparts in England (or Canada or the United States).

The effects of metropolitan culture on Caribbean youth hamper, in many ways, the development of a healthy self-image. Such is the peril of constant exposure to American mass media in this generation, just as British education threatened those of earlier generations. To counter these influences, a number of novelists have set out to write for the young Caribbean audience. Writers such as Vic Reid, Jean D'Costa, and Andrew Salkey deliberately create a fictive world which emphasizes and reinforces a positive Caribbean identity centered in Caribbean youth. Numerous other writers, although they address themselves to an adult audience, are no less dedicated to the task of leading their countrymen to a greater appreciation of their past, their heritage, their culture, their nations, and thus themselves. Notable among this group are Edward Brathwaite, Earl Lovelace, Michael Thelwell, Dennis Scott, Wilson Harris, and Orlando Patterson.

It is interesting also to observe that while a great many of this group of (often younger) writers pursued advanced degrees abroad, as did their predecessors, several of them received more of their education at home, some of them being among the first to study at the new University College of the West Indies, Mona, Kingston, the forerunner of the University of the West Indies. Mervyn Morris, like those who came before him, aspired to win a scholarship to a British university; instead, "A crucial thing happened to me which I should probably be eternally grateful for" (Interview with Pamela Mordecai, Kingston, Jamaica, December, 1983): he won a grant to the University College of the West Indies. Other budding and developing writers either studying or teaching at Mona at some point during this early period (from the early 1950s to the early 1960s) were Slade Hopkinson, Derek Walcott, Orlando Patterson, Jean D'Costa, Garth St. Omer, Velma Pollard, Pamela Mordecai, Dennis Scott, Sylvia Wynter, John Hearne, Neville Dawes, and Edward Brathwaite. Clearly, the coming together of so many bright young artists on their own turf at a period when their nations were gaining independence had an impact on their development as writers, as well as on their image of themselves as Caribbean men and women. Furthermore the younger writers enjoyed the active encouragement of established older scholars, especially John Figueroa and Philip Sherlock, who for long periods were associated with the University of the West Indies. Jean D'Costa recalls particularly their soirees, where one might meet visiting notables such as George Lamming, whom she first met at Figueroa's home.

The Mona group and several other of their peers, such as Michael Anthony and Earl Lovelace in Trinidad, tend generally more often to address themselves to a West Indian audience than to a foreign (usually British) audience to which their predecessors often addressed (and explained and justified) themselves. Their major concern seems to be helping their West Indian brothers discover themselves within the context of the West Indies.

The relatively new and fascinating body of Caribbean literature is just beginning to produce the criticism it deserves and requires. Among the early noteworthy studies of the literature are George Lamming's *The Pleasures of Exile* (1960); Wilson Harris's *Tradition the Writer & Society* (1967); Louis James's *The Islands in Between: Essays in West Indian Literature* (1968); and Gerald Moore's *The Chosen Tongue* (1969). These general studies were complemented in the 1970s with commentaries on distinct genres, such as Kenneth Ramchand's seminal *The West Indian Novel and its Background* (1970); and Lloyd Brown's definitive *West Indian Poetry* (1978). During the 1980s thematic analyses, in such works as Selwyn R. Cudjoe's *Resistance and Caribbean Literature* (1980), have enlarged the scope of Caribbean criticism. Beginning with pamphlets such as C. L. R. James's *Wilson Harris—a Philosophical Approach* (1965), full-length studies focusing on individual authors and even on specific works now proliferate, especially examinations of V. S. Naipaul, Wilson Harris, Jean Rhys, Derek Walcott, Claude McKay, George Lamming, and Edward Brathwaite. With the exception of Ivan Van Sertima's pioneering effort (*Caribbean Writers: Critical Essays*, 1968), useful reference guides to the study of West Indian literature did not begin to appear until the late 1970s, including most notably Donald E. Herdeck's *Caribbean Writers: A Bio-Bibliographical-Critical Encyclopedia* (1979); Michael Hughes's *A Companion to West Indian Literature* (1979); and Jeannette B. Allis's *West Indian Literature: An Index to Criticism 1930–1975* (1981).

Unfortunately, serious and intensive critical attention has tended to focus on only a handful of the Caribbean writers. Many authors whose contributions to Caribbean literature are widely recognized have received little or no extended treatment, having been accorded only general mention in broad surveys or brief commentaries in largely inaccessible, small regional newspapers and journals. Among the notables who have suffered this neglect are C. L. R. James, Martin Carter, Mervyn Morris, Louise Bennett, Michael Anthony, Jan Carew, Austin Clarke, Denis Williams, Jean D'Costa, and Earl Lovelace. Many of the newer writers have received no attention at all, save for newspaper reviews. This is the case with talented writers who have excited rave reviews with their first works, such as Erna Brodber, Jamaica Kincaid, and Michael Thelwell.

The essays included in this book are intended to introduce the reader to the wide range of important Caribbean writers, from the pioneers to the contemporaries. Each essay provides significant biographical information, an extended critical review of the major works and themes, an evaluative survey of selected scholarship, and a listing of major honors and awards. A bibliography of primary and secondary works, with full publication data, concludes each essay. Frequently cited general references are not detailed in each bibliography, but the reader is referred to the relevant item in the General Bibliography.

In addition to providing the first extended studies of several important Caribbean authors, *Fifty Caribbean Writers* significantly updates, supplements, and expands the biographical, critical, and bibliographical information available on most of those writers who have been considered elsewhere. Not only does this collection provide a convenient introduction to the authors and a handy overview of their works and critiques, such as the beginning researcher might require, but it also provides challenging and provocative critical commentaries which even the most advanced scholar will find indispensable. Furthermore the range of concerns in Caribbean literature and the varied approaches of the critics to individual authors will provide material of interest to students from a variety of fields other than literature, including politics, sociology, religion, economics, history, music, art, folklore, and linguistics.

Contributors to *Fifty Caribbean Writers* include leading scholars of Caribbean literature from throughout the world, many of whom have produced several of the seminal and definitive studies of Caribbean literature (see Contributors). A small majority of the essays were prepared by critics from the Caribbean, including Caribbean writers themselves (some of whom are also treated separately in this volume). Within this group is represented a diverse range of backgrounds and experiences and ethnic groups. The scholars hail from a number of different islands. Although all of them have received some part of their education outside the West Indies, a large number of them have spent most of their professional lives in the Caribbean, for the most part associated with one of the colleges of the University of the West Indies. Several others are affiliated with major American, Canadian, or European universities. Racially, they include Blacks, Whites, Chinese, and Indians. The remaining essays were prepared by European, Canadian, Indian, and American scholars, a number of whom have connections with the Caribbean beyond their research interests, a few being descendants of emigrants from the Caribbean and others having taught, traveled, and lived in the area. Many of the essayists are personally acquainted with their subjects and were able to make use of interviews, correspondence, and long associations to enhance their studies and add new perspectives to their analyses.

Looking at the range of Caribbean writing treated in the following essays, the reader can begin to assess for himself the richness of this emerging literature, the uniqueness of the Caribbean experience it captures, and the fascinating promise it holds for the future. The Caribbean writer who, like Derek Walcott, "entered the house of literature as a houseboy" (*Another Life*, 1973, p. 77), has earned the right to partake freely of whatever sacraments of that sacred house he desires: indeed, Mervyn Morris, making use of a similar image in a poem which also considers the subject of the Caribbean writer educated in an alien tradition, declares, "And these are my rooms now" (*The Pond*, 1973, p. 16). Not only have the Caribbean writers appropriated what they require from their European heritage, but they seize upon their rich African and Indian traditions as well. These people who (to paraphrase Martin Carter) come "from the nigger yard of yesterday" (*Poems of Resistance*, 1979, p. 41), these "sweepers of an ancient sky" and "discoverers of new planets" (p. 33) are creating a remarkable canon that firmly enshrines them in the international arena of world literature, one that captivates, challenges, and inspires us all.

ELAINE CAMPBELL

Phyllis Shand Allfrey (1915–)

BIOGRAPHY

Phyllis Shand Allfrey lives with her husband, Robert, in a tiny stone house next to a stream quite a long walk from Roseau. Born in Dominica, West Indies, she speaks with a mixture of British and West Indian intonations, but her frequent interjection of the West Indianism "man" suggests the dominance of the latter. Of her heritage, she volunteers that a visitor once asked her sister if she were racially mixed and her sister replied, "After so many hundreds of years here, who's to say what blood lines our family incorporates?" Phyllis Allfrey, in recognition of her complex heritage, entitled a collection of her poetry *Palm and Oak* to identify what she calls "the tropical and Nordic strains in my ancestry" (unless otherwise indicated, quotations from Allfrey throughout this biography are from various letters written to Elaine Campbell, some of them undated).

Donald Herdeck's *Caribbean Writers: A Bio-Bibliographical-Critical Encyclopedia* (1979) cites her birthdate as October 24, 1915. Born Phyllis Byam Shand, she was the second of four daughters of Francis Byam Berkeley Shand, a young barrister from Antigua, and his wife Elfreda, daughter of Doctor H. A. A. Nicholls (later Sir Henry Alford Nicholls) of Dominica. Through the female antecedents of Francis Shand, Phyllis Allfrey is descended from Byams, Berkeleys, and Warners. (Thomas Warner came to St. Kitts in 1624, and Père Labat writes at length about the Amerindian mother of Warner's children, Mme. Ouvenarde.) Doctor Nicholls, on Phyllis Allfrey's mother's side, was the only English-born progenitor for over 200 years, and he married Dominican Marion Crompton, after whose family Crompton Point in Dominica was named. Marion's family was from Martinique; consequently, Phyllis looks to Antigua, St. Kitts, and Martinique as well as to Dominica and England for her heritage.

Phyllis had no formal education. She learned from "a series of tutors, some splendid and some eccentric." Of these she remembers best her mother's elder sister, Aunt Mags, known as a bluestocking, Anglican Rector Martin Turnell, Mlle. B., and Mrs. Scully. She remembers Mrs. Scully being very angry with her when "she heard her translating a Beethoven sonata into calypso rhythm" at the piano. "There was a convent school in Dominica [familiar to readers of Jean Rhys's *Wide Sargasso Sea*] and I could never understand why we four girls were kept away from it." Despite her lack of a formal education, Phyllis "gobbled up scores of books" as a child. "I started writing poems and short stories very young. Sold my first short story to the now defunct *Tiger Tim's Weekly* at age thirteen for enough money to buy a camera. Never tried to publish my poems until years later. I wrote short plays too, and I and my sisters acted them."

Phyllis had three sisters: Marion (who died in 1960), Celia, and Rosalind. "We were rather poor, but Mother had inherited a Crompton house [Moss Lodge, "La Maison Rose" in *Orchid House* (1953)], where now the Cable and Wireless office is. My sisters were good at sewing and were better-looking than me. I never put needle to cloth (refused), used to climb into trees and think of poems instead." After a while Celia left for England and then wrote from London that she was getting married, asking if Phyllis could come. As a result, Phyllis made what is now recognized as the traditional West Indian writer's voyage to England. Celia married Jack Richmond Allfrey and Phyllis met Jack's younger brother, Robert. Robert and Phyllis were later married, and they then migrated to the United States, where their daughter, Josephine, and their son, Philip, were born. But the United States during the depression did not offer a favorable job market, and after living poorly in New York State for several years, the Allfreys returned to England. Phyllis got a job as secretary to the novelist-historian Naomi Mitchison—a job that plunged her into politics. According to Herdeck, "She met some of the world's great writers and politicians and became a socialist; she became involved in the Fabian Society, the British Labour Party, and the Parliamentary Committee for West Indian Affairs" (p. 19). During the war she kept open house for Dominicans and worked as a London County Council welfare officer to the bombed. After the war she gained additional political experience working with the Fabian Colonial Bureau and was active in the Fulham Labour Party. During her period of political activity in London she wrote mostly poems and short stories, but after winning an international award for a poem ("While the Young Sleep") she started work on her first novel, *The Orchid House*. The novel was written and published quickly with a British edition (Constable, 1953), an American edition (Dutton, 1953), and a French edition (Librarie Stock, 1954). Writing the novel, according to Phyllis, "drove me towards my home island," and she and Robert returned to Dominica in 1954. Finding herself caught up in the social and economic realities of Dominica, she called upon her Labour Party experience and cofounded the Dominica Labour Party to help the island's underpaid tropical fruit workers.

In his historic overview of Dominica's movement toward self-government, Lennox Honychurch explains that after its founding the Dominica Labour Party flourished under the direction of Edward LeBlanc, and the subsequent formation of an opposition nonlabor party (the Dominican United People's Party) encouraged the growth of Dominican political sophistication. LeBlanc and Allfrey were Dominica's candidates for the Federation government ministry when all-island elections were held in 1958, and Phyllis won the portfolio of Minister of Labour and Social Affairs in the Federal Government of the West Indies. She moved to Federation headquarters in Trinidad until 1961, when Federation failed. Then she returned to Dominica, where she and her husband at first ran *The Dominica Herald* and then, in 1965, founded the weekly newspaper the *Star*.

Back in Dominica the Allfreys adopted an Afro-Caribbean girl, Sonia, and two Carib boys, David, now grown up and living in London, and their teenage son, Robbie, who has just left Dominica for the nearby French Island of Marie Galante. Josephine (''Phina'') was killed in Botswana in April, 1977, and Phyllis, emotionally shattered by the death of her only natural daughter, gave up her novel-in-progress, *In the Cabinet*.

During her newspaper years, Phyllis Allfrey continued writing poetry and short stories in addition to political essays and editorials for the *Star*. Some of her varied work is now becoming recognized. For example, Alan McLeod plans to include Allfrey's Federation departure speech in his collection of West Indian oratory, Robert Ross plans to include some of her Dominican poetry in his anthology of writing by Commonwealth women, and Virago Press has included two of her poems (''Cunard Liner 1940'' and ''Young Lady Dancing with Soldier'') in an anthology of World War II poetry. Poor health and poverty caused the Allfreys to give up the *Star* at the end of February, 1982, allowing time for the completion of *In the Cabinet*, on which Constable holds a first option. With the possible publication of *In the Cabinet*, with the new Virago Press paperback edition of *The Orchid House*, and with the slowly growing critical recognition of Phyllis Allfrey's fiction, poetry, and essays, she, like Jean Rhys, may enjoy an overdue appreciation of her role as one of the few West Indian women to participate in the early growth of West Indian literature.

MAJOR WORKS AND THEMES

Although written by a woman with a highly developed political sense and with long experience in practical politics, *The Orchid House's* political message is never overt. Well integrated into the narrative level of the novel, Allfrey's vision of the transfer of power from the colonizer to the colonized does not disrupt the story of L'Aromatique's family. Both the subtlety with which the political elements are rendered and the early date of the novel's political commitment combine to make it a significant example of West Indian fiction from the period immediately following World War II. Retaining some aspects of colonialist literature—clues to a literature in transition—*The Orchid House* nevertheless promotes assumption of political responsibility by the young Black Creole, Baptiste, and his friend Joan, the middle sister from L'Aromatique. It is the women of the orchid house who effect the family's survival and the island's regeneration. Thus, they serve as the liaison between the ailing White Creole men and the new leadership-to-be.

The Orchid House story is narrated by Lally, the elderly Black nurse who pits her Methodism and Creole English against the Catholicism and patois French of those around her. Lally comes close to the stereotype of the Black mammy faithful to her White family, but she is not lacking insight into the quality of her loyalty. Speaking of Bill Buffon, the boatman, she says, "He truly loves the family. The family is everything to a man like Buffon and to a woman like me. I suppose that in coming years poor people won't take such stock of families. . . . But it's a comfort to have a family to tend and admire, at least I have found it so" (p. 27). Her narration, in fact, shows two Lallys—the young woman who first came to L'Aromatique and the old woman who comes back to care for the children of the returning sisters. Lally's double vision enables her older self to look back upon the unquestioning loyalty of her younger self: "I did not even pay any attention to my own people, the black people, in those days, but now I am observing them and seeing what is happening to them. I am seeing how poor they are, and how the little babies have stomachs swollen with arrowroot and arms and legs spotted with disease" (pp. 8–9). Lally, written as an individual character rather than as a racial symbol, is more faithful to the idea of the old, colonial order than she is to a new, revolutionary order, but she both recognizes and acknowledges her point of view.

Intruding into the family's personal concerns with all the imperturbability of a secure retainer, Lally as narrator is skillfully worked. Gossiping, eavesdropping, participating, judging, she is able to convey convincingly her story of Mr. Lilipoulala's hold over the family's fate. She adroitly synthesizes the novel's events, sorting out the background material and integrating it into the account of present-day action. The action is precipitated by the return of the three daughters of L'Aromatique. Coming from New England, London, and Trinidad, they bring with them winds of change which initiate the demise of Mr. Lilipoulala, "the Master," and the old order. Challenging their father's drug-induced torpor, revolting against the hold of the Roman Catholic clergy, struggling against the family's poverty, and undermining the political hegemony of a privileged White minority, Stella, Joan, and Natalie are not unlike the riders of the Apocalypse.

The three sisters are, as Anthony Boxill has pointed out in his doctoral dissertation, "well distinguished and contrast well with each other. Stella's romantic passion, Joan's strength and practicality and Natalie's vivacity give interesting changes of mood to the novel" ("The Novel in English in the West Indies 1900–1962," 1966, p. 256). Following Lally's long memorial reconstruction of the past in "The Days Before," the novel is broken into three sections, one devoted to each sister: "Miss Stella Comes Home," "Miss Joan Returns," and "Miss Natalie Arrives." The sisters, markedly different one from the other, are bound together symbolically by the confirmation dress that each wears in turn upon returning to L'Aromatique. After effecting radical family changes (Stella murders the drug dealer Lilipoulala, and Natalie flies her invalided father to his death), Stella and Natalie return to their adopted countries. Joan, however, does not return to the slums of Balham but instead remains on the island to help Baptiste with its political reorganization. Eliminated from direct participation in political activity by a bargain with the Roman Catholic priest, who suspects Stella's hand in the mysterious death of Mr. Lilipoulala, Joan sends for her husband, a guerrilla fighter from the Spanish Civil War. Lally returns to the solace of her Bible, while the political future of the island is left open-ended.

Frequently interrupted by political involvement, personal tragedies and illness, the as-yet-unpublished novel *In the Cabinet* is prefaced with a sample of Phyllis Allfrey's trenchant verse:

In the cabinet of life
poverty, achievement, strife

In the cabinet of heart
embedded deep a nuclear dart

Cabinet of politics:
noble aims and dirty tricks

Cabinet of eternity:
I and I and you and me.

Opening with the chapter heading "Why Are We Still Alive?" *In the Cabinet* begins in a pessimistic key. The physical hardships and emotional sufferings through which Phyllis Allfrey has passed since writing *The Orchid House* inform the subject and the tone of the new novel. The setting is again the West Indian island that we know to be Dominica. Here it is named Anonica. But it is not the brilliantly beautiful island to which Louis James referred when writing about *The Orchid House* in *The Islands in Between* (1968): "The house at the centre of the action is called L'Aromatique. The island around it is drowsy with humming-birds, jewelled flowers, and the glow of jewelled flowers" (p. 45). In Anonica, the hummingbirds, jewelled flowers, and even the green are gone. It is not a post-nuclear world that explains Anonica's devastation. It is a post-hurricane world. The high green mountains stripped of their foliage are a true-to-life portrait of Dominica/Anonica following David, the worst hurricane of modern Caribbean history.

The natural devastation underscores the man-made devastation of Joan's political idealism. Sitting in her island wasteland, Joan reviews her past life. Unlike Lally's double focus of past and present in *The Orchid House*, however, Joan's review is all of one piece—decidedly downhill. The body of the novel is Allfrey's thinly disguised fictionalization of her services in the West Indian Federation cabinet, showing the failure of the multi-island dream to create a common political identity from which to negotiate with the outside world. From this core material emerge two outstanding points: Allfrey's distaste for the destructive sniping of Trinidadian politicians and her deep affection for the Federation prime minister. Especially painful are her fictionalized references to the tragedy of young Philip (Ned) and to the death of beautiful Phina (Andrina). The pain of three decades is poured into this nihilistic picture of Anonica—the nation symbolized by a young Black mother sitting with her dying baby.

Constructed largely out of old Federation records and long speeches, *In the Cabinet* is probably too tedious for any reader not greatly interested in modern West Indian political history. For the Caribbeanist, however, there is considerable fascination offered by anecdotes about identifiable political figures from the Federation period. Following Joan's mental review of Federation collapse—on the public level—and Andrina's death—on a personal level—only the matter of an appropriate resolution remains. Allfrey's first choice was to have the hurricane survivors embark on a long suicide swim to Marie Galante. As of December, 1983, however, she writes, "I decided to change the ending which was to have been very sad . . . and now they will be stopped on the shore by a Carib boat which takes them over" (Letter, December 7, 1983).

The poetry of Phyllis Allfrey is widely scattered, representing diverse life experiences in different countries. For example, "Maine," in *Palm and Oak II*, is a lovely memento of the Allfreys' early married life in New England. Of the wartime poems that Virago Press unearthed in England, Phyllis has little recollection. A comprehensive collection of poetry by Allfrey would represent a difficult research project. Partial collections, according to Herdeck, are *In Circles*, printed in England in 1940 by Raven Press; *Palm and Oak I*, privately printed in London in 1950; *Contrasts*, printed in Barbados in 1955 by Advocate Press, and *Palm and Oak II*, printed in Dominica in 1974 by the Star Printery.

From *Palm and Oak II*, the most accessible collection, although limited to an edition of 300 copies, come poems of consistently high quality addressing a broad range of subject matter. It includes the poem for which Vita Sackville-West awarded Allfrey second prize in an international poetry contest for women, and it includes two touching commentaries on the plight of the West Indian emigrant in London: "The True-Born Villager" and "Expatriates." There is the militant "Resistance" and the lyric "Love for an Island," the first verse of which Lennox Honychurch used to preface his history of Dominica, *The Dominica Story*. And there is the poem written many years ago for Jean Rhys, "The Child's Return":

> I remember a far tall island
> floating in cobalt paint

The thought of it is a childhood dream
torn by a midnight plaint

There are painted ships and rusty ships
that pass the island by,
and one dark day I'll board a boat
when I am ready to die

The timbers will creak and my heart will break
and the sailors will lay my bones
on the stiff rich grass, as sharp as spikes
by the volcanic stones.

There is presently no collection of Allfrey's short stories, although several stories will appear in *The Whistling Bird*, an anthology of writing by West Indian women forthcoming from Three Continents Press. *Caribbean Writers* lists Argosy, The Windmill, Pan-Africa, Writers Guild, and Heinemann as past publishers of Allfrey short stories, and there are, at present, efforts being made to publish a collection of twenty short stories by Allfrey which were recently brought to the United States by a researcher in West Indian literature.

CRITICAL RECEPTION

The first major critical attention to *The Orchid House* appeared in Kenneth Ramchand's *The West Indian Novel and its Background* (1970). In his chapter "Terrified Consciousness," Ramchand focuses on three White Creole novelists: Jean Rhys, Geoffrey Drayton, and Phyllis Shand Allfrey. Ramchand gave the novel the boost it needed to prevent it from becoming lost in the avalanche of novels by male West Indian writers publishing in the 1950s and 1960s. Ramchand calls her writing "politically conscious" and "tough-minded" (p. 227); however, he feels that the language of the novel "is not equal to the sensuous task she sets it" (p. 226). He explains that there are "too many laboured passages of passionate declaration" (p. 226). Ramchand's approval of "tough-mindedness" and his disapproval of "passionate declaration" probably display some degree of gender bias, but he does, in the long run, come out in Allfrey's favor.

In the March-June, 1965, issue of *Caribbean Quarterly*, W. I. Carr of the University of the West Indies wrote, "The only West Indian novel which provides an analysis in depth of a society is Phyllis Allfrey's *The Orchid House*. The novel is set in Dominica, a society frozen into its past. With rich and careful nostalgia, and a penetrating but unobtrusive symbolism, Mrs. Allfrey establishes the society and the attempt of three young people both to understand it and break away from it. In political terms the novel supplies the means of its own betrayal" ("The West Indian Novelist: Prelude and Context," p. 77).

In "The Novel in English in the West Indies 1900–1962," Anthony Boxill's doctoral dissertation written in 1966 for the University of New Brunswick, Boxill devotes six pages to a discussion of *The Orchid House*. Boxill spotlights the anti-church aspect of the novel, claiming that "this prolonged criticism of an established church is new in the West Indian novel" (p. 264). He decides that Allfrey "handles her material fairly confidently" (p. 264), and he then praises the characterization of the three sisters but finds the characterization of Lally, the narrator, flawed. He concludes, "In spite of this flaw, however, the novel is pleasing in its evocation of the physical beauty of the island, and in its genuine concern for human beings" (p. 265).

Louis James's *The Islands in Between* has already been cited as a source of critical comment on *The Orchid House*. James calls the novel "in some ways . . . the dark reverse side of Selvon's book [*Turn Again Tiger*]," explaining that Lally's "heavy, slow-moving speech rhythms reflect the atmosphere of the book." James's primary point is the success with which the novel's imagery supports the theme that the island is simultaneously "fascinating and diseased" and that "the very beauty of an island . . . can imprison and corrupt" (p. 45).

Two full-length articles have appeared in *World Literature Written in English* regarding Allfrey's novel: Barrie Davies' "Neglected West Indian Writers: No. 1. Phyllis Allfrey. *The Orchid House*" (1972); and Elaine Campbell's "Report from Dominica, B.W.I." (1978). Davies is singularly positive. He opens his article with the claim that Allfrey's novel

> is a memorable one in several ways. Not the least of these are the absence of self-conscious West Indian detail and her refusal to purvey the cliches of race, colour, and class. Instead she offers something more subtle and enduring, a sustained and sensitive analysis of Dominican Society. She pursues her theme with a single-mindedness which does not exclude the feeling for a whole society, economically caught in the rich metaphor of her prose." (pp. 81–82)

Davies analyzes the various characters of the novel, and he brings new insight to the novel's criticism: an explanation of the central motif of the orchid. He ends his analysis of the novel with the judgment that "the world of *Orchid House* has a metaphorical intensity and is convincing because it is all-pervasive. It enlarges our understanding of human frailty. There is nothing hackneyed, no comment, no moralizing, no bitter flourish. Instead there is quiet pathos for people matched against an inscrutable and inexorable historical process" (p. 82–83).

Campbell's essay compares Allfrey's novel with Jean Rhys's *Wide Sargasso Sea*, but she contests Ramchand's statement that the "elements of continuity between them" result "not from the authors' knowledge of one another or of one another's work, but involuntarily from the natural stance of the White West Indian" (p. 224). Campbell maintains that the two women were conscious of each other's writing (Allfrey had sent Rhys a copy of *The Orchid House*) and that such consciousness is as likely an explanation for continuities between the two books as is any stereotypic stance based on race and nationality. Considering the two novels along with Brontë's *Jane Eyre*, Campbell finds the plantation house/manor house image to be "an almost cynical doubling" (p. 313).

Especially useful for biographical background is Donald Herdeck's illustrated entry on Allfrey in his *Caribbean Writers*; also useful biographically and critically is Campbell's introduction to the Virago Press reprint of *The Orchid House* (1982). Two noteworthy reviews occasioned by the paperback reprint are Robert Ross's in *Commonwealth Novel in English* (1983) and Maria Quinn's in the *Morning Star* ("Fight for Rights in Caribbean Classic," 1982). *Kunapipi*, the journal of the European Association of Commonwealth Literature and Language Studies, carried in 1980 an interesting piece by Allfrey about Hurricane David and in 1979 a tribute to Jean Rhys by Allfrey written shortly after Rhys's death. The Jean Rhys commemorative issue of *Kunapipi* (1, no. 2, 1979) carried an article on Rhys which contains information about her relationship with Allfrey ("From Dominica to Devonshire: A Memento of Jean Rhys"). Passing references to *The Orchid House* can be found in Edward Brathwaite's articles in *Bim* (January-June 1961; July-December 1963; and July-December 1968), in Rhonda Cobham's "The Background," and in Cheryl M. L. Dash's "Jean Rhys." (The last two essays form chapters in Bruce King's *West Indian Literature*, 1979.)

BIBLIOGRAPHY

Works by Phyllis Shand Allfrey

Palm and Oak I. London: Author, 1950.

The Orchid House. London: Constable, 1953; New York: Dutton, 1953; Paris: Librarie Stock, 1954; London: Virago Press, 1982.

Contrasts. Barbados: Advocate Press, 1955.

Palm and Oak II. Roseau: The Star Printery, 1974.

In the Cabinet. Forthcoming.

Studies of Phyllis Shand Allfrey

Boxill, Anthony. "The Novel in English in the West Indies 1900–1962." Doctoral dissertation. University of New Brunswick, 1966.

Campbell, Elaine. "From Dominica to Devonshire: A Memento of Jean Rhys." *Kunapipi* 1 (1979), 6–22.

———. Introduction to *The Orchid House*. London: Virago Press, 1982.

———. "Report from Dominica, B.W.I." *World Literature Written in English* 17 (April 1978), 305–16.

Carr, W. I. "The West Indian Novelist: Prelude and Context." *Caribbean Quarterly* 11 (March-June 1965), 71–84.

Davies, Barrie. "Neglected West Indian Writers. No. 1. Phyllis Allfrey. *The Orchid House*." *World Literature Written in English* II (November 1972), 81–83.

Honychurch, Lennox. *The Dominica Story*. Barbados: Letchwood Press, 1975.

James, Louis. *The Islands in Between*. London: Oxford University Press, 1968.

Labat, Père. *The Memoirs of Père Labat 1693–1705*. London: Frank Cass, 1931, 1970.

Pattullo, Polly. "Caribbean Chronicle." *Observer Magazine*, July 22, 1984, 22–24.

Quinn, Maria. ''Fight for Rights in Caribbean Classic.'' *Morning Star*, May 6, 1982.
Ross, Robert. ''Review of *The Orchid House*, by Phyllis Shand Allfrey.'' *Commonwealth Novel in English* 2 (July 1983).
See also General Bibliography: Allis, Herdeck, Hughes, King, Ramchand (1970).

DARYL CUMBER DANCE

Michael Anthony (1932–)

BIOGRAPHY

Michael Anthony was born in Mayaro, Trinidad, on February 10, 1932. After receiving an education in the primary schools in his hometown and the Junior Technical School of San Fernando, he worked as a molder in an iron foundry in Pointe à Pierre, Trinidad. In December, 1954, he migrated to England, where he worked in factories, on the railways, and as a telegraphist, while pursuing his writing career. He left England in 1968 for Rio de Janeiro, Brazil, and served there in diplomatic service for two years. Since 1970 he, his wife, and their four children (all born abroad—three in England, one in Brazil) have lived in his native Trinidad, where the novelist has worked with the National Cultural Council of Trinidad and Tobago, produced radio shows, and continued his writing.

When he first started writing, he wrote poetry, much of which was published in the local paper in Trinidad, but he was discouraged from pursuing a career as a poet when he submitted some poems to the BBC's *Caribbean Voices*, which V. S. Naipaul was producing at the time. Anthony observed: "I realized too around the time when Naipaul discouraged me that I wasn't writing *vital* poetry, . . . and I began to feel like poetry wasn't really my line" (interview with Daryl Cumber Dance, Port of Spain, Trinidad, March 18, 1980; further quotes from Anthony are also from this interview). After that, with the encouragement of *Caribbean Voices*, he focused on the short story; but in 1960 when he attempted to publish a collection, he was told that because short stories did not sell well he should first write a novel, after which the publisher would consider a volume of short stories. Thus Anthony began work on *The Year in San Fernando* (1965). That novel and many of his other works focus upon a young man in a closely knit family, often one where the father is ill or dead, a situation which is motivated by his own childhood, where he recalls his close attachment to his mother and his father, the latter of whom died, following a long illness, when Michael Anthony was ten. Anthony commented: "The close family relationships [which appear in my works result from] a little bit of nostalgia because my father died when I was very young. I loved him very much and I really *missed* the fact that he wasn't *there*, and I thought that our relationship would have been a very meaningful one, and so I believe that I have projected this into my work."

Anthony's works, particularly *The Year in San Fernando* and *King of the Masquerade* (1974), are frequently used in schools in Trinidad and several of the other Caribbean nations.

MAJOR WORKS AND THEMES

Michael Anthony has published six novels: *The Games Were Coming* (1963); *The Year in San Fernando* (1965); *Green Days by the River* (1967); *King of the Masquerade* (1974; a novel for children); *Streets of Conflict* (1976); and *All That Glitters* (1981). He has also done two collections of short stories, *Sandra Street and Other Stories* (1973) and *Cricket in the Road* (1973; an expanded collection which includes all of the *Sandra Street* stories and eleven additional stories), and a collection of tales: *Folk Tales and Fantasies* (1976). Anthony has written several historical works: *Glimpses of Trinidad and Tobago: With a Glance at the West Indies* (1974); *Profile Trinidad: A Historical Survey from the Discovery to 1900* (1975); *The Making of Port of Spain* (1978); and *Bright Road to El Dorado* (1981). Indeed, he has noted that his several volumes of history, coupled with his emphasis on Trinidadian history in his radio programs, have resulted in a situation where "within Trinidad *now* people see me more as a historian than as a writer of fiction."

Michael Anthony's novels, as well as many of his short stories, center upon a brief but critical period in the lives of children or young adults. The events upon which he focuses our attention in the novels admittedly seem slight on one level (a bicycle race, one uneventful year that a twelve year old spends away from his family, the adolescent loves of a teenager, the insipid courtships of an indifferent young schoolteacher, the brief disappearance of a gold chain). One critic has complained that the reader is moved to ask after reading an Anthony novel: "So what?" or "Was the story worth telling?" (Review of *Green Days by the River* in the Jamaica *Gleaner*, cited in Paul Edwards and Kenneth Ramchand, introduction to *The Year in San Fernando*, p. viii). The genius of Anthony, however, is that despite the apparent simplicity of his plot, his stories are narrated with such power that not only does the reader never doubt the significance of whatever seemingly trite experience the protagonist is undergoing, but he is also irresistibly caught up in it.

One of the reasons that Anthony is able to involve the reader so intensely is that he frequently evokes in his fiction actual events and individuals that were significant in his own life and experiences with a captivating and familiar reality and a poignant sense of immediacy. *The Year in San Fernando*, for example, is a touching account of the year that a twelve-year-old boy from the village of Mayaro spends living and working as a servant in the home of a well-to-do family in San Fernando. Young Francis's sense of pain, fear, rejection, despair, and loneliness, as well as his fascination and excitement at being in a larger city, were all experienced by the author himself, who felt compelled to write about that year "because I remembered it so well and because it meant so much to me." The writing of the novel helped him to deal with the trauma of the event more objectively and to understand his mother's motivation for sending him to San Fernando, but he even now maintains: "*I* wouldn't let my children go to live with *anybody*, you know." Anthony's portrayal in that novel of the Chandles family with whom Francis lived, their cruel treatment, their scandalous affairs, and their sordid behavior, was so accurate that, fearing their reactions to the book when he returned to Trinidad from Brazil, he deliberately avoided any possibilities of contact with them. He was relieved to discover later, however, that, on the contrary, they were "very pleased about it, . . . and happy to see me." While the events in *The Games Were Coming* do not draw directly from his own experiences, the novel does focus upon the Southern Games that were held in Guaracara Park during the time that the author lived in Marabella and make use of superficially fictionalized personages whom he knew there. The protagonist, Leon, was based, he notes, "on a particular person called Lyons who lived at Marabella just by the Red Bridge [whom] I knew very well, a young fellow who used to work in the refinery." Leon's fiancée, Sylvia, and several other characters were likewise based on people whom Anthony knew. Indeed the affair between Sylvia and the Indian storekeeper was so well known that Naipaul's sister called it to the attention of Deutsch, who held up publication of the novel until some changes could be made to disguise the actual occurrence. Furthermore, the relationship between father and son in *The Games Were Coming* and in *Green Days by the River* reflects the author's previously noted obsession with the loss of his own father. Gidharee, the kindly neighbor but fiercely protective father of the "wronged" daughter, was patterned after Anthony's next-door neighbor, the same person who inspired the protagonist in "Drunkard of the River" (*Cricket*). Similarly, the plot of *Streets of Conflict* builds up to a climax with the student riots of 1969, which occurred when Anthony was living in Rio de Janeiro, and it fictionalizes individuals whom he knew and was fascinated by there. Finally, Anthony's pictures in *All That Glitters* and "Sandra Street" of the young schoolboy writing compositions, learning to observe and appreciate the beauty of his surroundings, to capture details in descriptions, and to express and discover himself in his writing are also obviously autobiographical.

One of the paradoxes of Anthony's work is that on one level each work is a model of unity—a compact, orderly, well-organized whole, as Ramchand and Edwards have illustrated with *The Year in San Fernando* (introduction Heinemann ed.); but on the other hand, Anthony always manages to develop the reader's interest in a whole series of other issues that sometimes seem more important than the ones that are resolved in the story and thereby to leave him with a certain sense of frustration. For example, in *The Games Were Coming*, the games come and the protagonist wins the bicycle race and the novel ends, *but* the reader is left wondering if Leon will keep his promise and marry his complacent sweetheart Sylvia, who has suffered so much neglect as he prepared for the games; if so, will he discover that she is pregnant by someone else; can so dedicated (and selfish) an athlete really give up the races and commit himself to marriage, etc., etc. In *Green Days by the River* the fifteen-year-old Shellie knows his "green days" are over when he is forced by his incensed Indian neighbor Gidharee to marry his daughter Rosalie, and thus the novel ends; but despite Shellie's apparent capitulation, the reader is not satisfied by what *must* be viewed as a temporary acceptance of such an awkard resolution, and he remains inquisitive about the outcome of so inauspicious a marriage as well as about the future relationship between Shellie and his pertinacious father-in-law. In *The Year in San Fernando* the year is over and the novel ends, but the reader wishes to know more about the impending death of Mrs. Chandles, the outcome of the affairs of the various members of the Chandles family, and the impact of this year on Francis's return to home and family.

It is interesting to observe that in Anthony's works some of the major concerns in West Indian literature generally (such as the quest for identity, the problems of the exile, the conflicts between the older traditional society and the modernized industrialized one) are not central issues. His major concerns seem rather to be with simple human relationships: family relationships and male/female relationships. Within this cycle of relationships between very ordinary people with whom the reader can easily relate, one is always shocked at the unexpected, uncharacteristic, and inhumane cruelty of which at times these people are capable. In *The Year in San Fernando* we are appalled at the cruelty of the educated and cultured Samuels to Francis's mother, their employee. One is likewise nonplussed by the refined, well-to-do Chandleses' ruthless exploitation of the twelve-year-old Francis as well as their barbarous treatment of one another. Despite an awareness of the demands of athletic training, the reader is stunned at Leon's cold insensitivity to his loving family and sweetheart as he prepares for the races in *The Games Were Coming*. Mr. Gidharee, who has been portrayed in *Green Days by the River* as a loving father and a kindly neighbor, arouses the reader's (though not Shellie's) outrage when he forces Shellie to marry his daughter (who, because of Shellie's rejection, has accused him of having "fooled around" with her [p. 169]) by sicking vicious dogs to attack him brutally and torturing him with all manners of threats. Finally, in *Streets of Conflict* we are shocked when Merisa's ardent suitor Craig suddenly becomes violent and threatens to kill his friend Mac and Merisa; just as shocking is Mac's brutal beating of his wife, whom he leaves unconscious and seriously injured, if not dead, without even ever checking to see how seriously he had beaten her.

Also notable in Anthony's fiction is his treatment of women. There are several of the strong, enduring mother figures so familiar in West Indian literature (notably in "Drunkard of the River" [*Cricket*], "The Distant One" [*Cricket*], *The Year in San Fernando, Green Days by the River*, and *All That Glitters*); but there are also some beautiful young Black women, whom Anthony develops with uncharacteristic sensitivity and empathy. Though some might accuse Anthony of characterizing Sylvia, of *The Games Were Coming*, Merisa, of *Streets of Conflict*, and Mona and Roomeen, of *All That Glitters*, as being on one level vapid and lacking in any strong social consciousness (a criticism that could be leveled against his male characters as well), all would have to concede that Anthony does reveal an extraordinary understanding of their needs and desires and an uncommon ability to portray *black* Black women as sensuous and strikingly attractive. Further, though one might argue that Anthony's male characters are the ones with whom he is most concerned, even when, as in *Streets of Conflict* and *All That Glitters*, the female is ostensibly the protagonist, there is no denying that he has created some memorable and unusual portraits of attractive, often passionate, sometimes surprisingly resilient and resourceful Black women.

CRITICAL RECEPTION

Because of Anthony's apparent lack of concern with the major racial, sociological, political, and economic issues that engage many Caribbean writers, several critics have tended to dismiss his work as insignificant. Typical is the previously cited reviewer's query, "Was the story worth telling?" and Arthur Kevyn's charge in his review of *The Year in San Fernando* (*Bim* 41 [June-December 1965], 70–71) that the work is "an apparently meaningless chronicle with no foundation in any strong or profound philosophy. It moves along unrelieved and in the end signifies little." Less caustic, but no less condescending, is Edward Baugh's description: "If one says that [Anthony's] best work has the clarity and luminosity of a shallow stream, this is not to disparage it but only to define its limitations and the nature of its appeal. Anthony attempts nothing grand, and is hardly concerned with 'messages' " ("Since 1960: Some Highlights," in *West Indian Literature*, ed. Bruce King, 1979, p. 80).

Despite such objections to Anthony, even his detractors generally concede his success in evoking place, developing characters, and presenting a story through the mind of a child. Baugh observes, "His memory-sharpened evocations of particular place and time verify some basic, universal truths of the human condition. At the same time, by being so true to time and place, he naturally captures some of the realities and nuances of West Indian social relationships" (ibid.). In *An Introduction to the Study of West Indian Literature* (1976), Kenneth

Ramchand praises Anthony's masterful evocation of place, his narrative form, and his character development in *The Games Were Coming*. (The same essay, with minor modifications, introduces the 1977 Heinemann edition of the novel). Harold Barratt (''Michael Anthony and Earl Lovelace: The Search for Selfhood,'' *ACLALS Bulletin [1980])* argues that the significant strength of Anthony's work (as well as Earl Lovelace's) is the ability to capture ''the physical reality of the West Indies'' (p. 62) and to portray the ''stolid'' West Indian personality. Barratt's praise of the admirable strong characters in *Green Days by the River, Cricket in the Road and Other Stories*, *The Year in San Fernando*, and *The Games Were Coming* does not, however, carry over to *Streets of Conflict*, for in this later novel Barratt deplores Anthony's change of milieu: ''In *Streets of Conflict*, . . . Anthony makes his first excursion outside the territory he knows intimately. . . . It is not a successful excursion. The novel is not particularly substantial, and it must be said that it leaves a sour taste in the mouth'' (p. 62). Dexter Noel (''The Muses Inhabit Mayaro: Michael Anthony's *Cricket in the Road*,'' *International Fiction Review* 5 [1978], 61) treats Anthony's focus on ''the need to appreciate one's surroundings'' in *Cricket*. He observes that ''Sandra Street'' and ''Habiscus,'' in particular, illustrate Anthony's love for and appreciation of Trinidad. In his introduction to *Green Days* Gareth Griffiths reflects on Anthony's ability to restrict his point of view to the limits of consciousness of his child narrators. He notes that, while Anthony's refusal to intrude as narrator may confuse some readers, the results compensate: ''But in compensation [the reader] is engaged with [the world of the child] more intensely and more immediately than he could hope to be in a novel where his judgments are more consciously controlled and where his exposure to the actual confused process of experience is less total and less open'' (p. viii).

In their introduction to the Heinemann edition of *The Year in San Fernando*, Paul Edwards and Kenneth Ramchand argue the technical sophistication and brilliance of the novel, which represents for them ''art of a subtle and powerful kind'' (p. viii). Much of this argument also appears with minor modifications in Ramchand's treatment of ''Novels of Childhood'' in *The West Indian Novel and its Background*. Anthony Luengo (*Ariel* [April 1975]) illustrates how Anthony sets Francis's physical and psychological development against ''a background of change and growth in nature'' (p. 94). His extended treatment of the manner in which Anthony incorporates birth, growth, death, and regeneration in nature with the events of the year covered in the novel is clearly an expansion of aspects of Ramchand's thesis, which Luengo charges ''does not recognize sufficiently the process of growth'' (p. 87).

BIBLIOGRAPHY

Works by Michael Anthony

The Games Were Coming. London: André Deutsch, 1963; Boston: Houghton Mifflin, 1968; London: Heinemann, 1977.

The Year in San Fernando. London: André Deutsch, 1965; London: Heinemann, 1970.
Green Days by the River. London: André Deutsch, 1967; London: Heinemann, 1973.
Cricket in the Road. London: André Deutsch, 1973.
Sandra Street and Other Stories. London: Heinemann, 1973.
Glimpses of Trinidad and Tobago: With a Glance at the West Indies. Port of Spain: Columbus, 1974.
King of the Masquerade. London: Nelson, 1974.
Profile Trinidad: A Historical Survey from the Discovery to 1900. London: Macmillan Caribbean, 1975.
Folk Tales and Fantasies. Port of Spain: Columbus, 1976.
Streets of Conflict. London: André Deutsch, 1976.
All That Glitters. London: André Deutsch, 1981; London: Heinemann, 1983.
Bright Road to El Dorado. Walton-on-Thames, Surrey, England: Nelson Caribbean, 1982.
The Making of Port of Spain. Port of Spain: Key Caribbean, 1978.

Studies of Michael Anthony

Barratt, Harold. "Michael Anthony and Earl Lovelace: The Search for Selfhood." *ACLALS* [Association for Commonwealth Literature] *Bulletin* 5 (1980), 62–73.
Edwards, Paul, and Kenneth Ramchand. "The Art of Memory: Michael Anthony's *The Year in San Fernando*." *Journal of Commonwealth Literature* 6 (July 1969), 59–72.
———. Introduction to *The Year in San Fernando*. London: Heinemann, 1970.
Griffiths, Gareth. Introduction to *Green Days by the River*. London: Heinemann, 1973.
Luengo, Anthony. "Growing up in San Fernando: Change and Growth in Michael Anthony's *The Year in San Fernando*." *Ariel: A Review of International English Literature* 6 (April 1975), 81–95.
Munro, Ian, and Reinhard Sander. "The Return of a West Indian Writer: An Interview by Ian Munro & Reinhard Sander." *Bim* 14 (January-June 1973), 212–18.
Niven, Alastair. " 'My Sympathies Enlarged': The Novels of Michael Anthony." *Commonwealth Essays and Studies* 2 (1976), 45–62.
Noel, Dexter. "The Muses Inhabit Mayaro: Michael Anthony's *Cricket in the Road*." *International Fiction Review* 5 (January 1978), 61–62.
Ramchand, Kenneth. Introduction to *The Games Were Coming*. London: Heinemann, 1977.
Sander, Reinhard. "The Homesickness of Michael Anthony: The Predicament of a West Indian Exile." *Literary Half-Yearly* 16 (January 1975), 95–124.
Smyer, Richard I. "Enchantment and Violence in the Fiction of Michael Anthony." *World Literature Written in English* 21 (Spring 1982), 148–59.
See also General Bibliography: Allis, Griffiths, Hughes, King, James, and Ramchand (1970, 1976).

NORVAL "NADI" EDWARDS

Lindsay Barrett (1941–)

BIOGRAPHY

Lindsay Barrett was born in Jamaica in 1941, in the town of Lucea, capital of the western parish of Hanover. After graduating from high school, he worked with the island's only major newspaper, the *Daily Gleaner*, and its sister publication, the afternoon tabloid the *Star*, as an apprentice journalist. In early 1961 he began working for the Jamaica Broadcasting Corporation as a news editor, a post that he relinquished later in the year when he left the island for England, where he free-lanced with the British Broadcasting Corporation Overseas Department for a year. He left England for France, and for the next four years he was based in Paris. From there he traveled throughout Europe and North Africa. His travels eventually took him to Dakar in 1966 for the Arts Festival, and he remained in West Africa, working as a lecturer at Fourah Bay College in Sierra Leone and as a teacher in Ghana; finally he settled in Nigeria. He has taught at the University of Ibadan and has worked in radio and television in Nigeria.

Lindsay Barrett, or Esoghene as he is now known, is one of that small group of Afro-Caribbean persons who have made the Atlantic crossing in reverse, and his creative work reflects a preoccupation with the themes of Black identity, dispossession, and survival in the Diaspora. In his well-traveled and varied life, Barrett has worked in every literary genre, with a prolific output of short stories, poetry, plays, and several unpublished novels. His first published work was *The State of Black Desire* (1966), a privately published collection of three poems and three essays. This was followed by his first and only published novel, *Song for Mumu* (1967), a work which introduced Barrett as a distinctively new and worthwhile voice to Caribbean fiction. *Song for Mumu* was followed by a collection of poems, *The Conflicting Eye* (1973). Barrett has also had his short stories, essays, and articles published in a variety of journals. He has written radio plays for Nigerian National Radio, and five plays have been staged: *Sighs of a Slave Dream*, *Home Again*, *Blackblast*, *Jump Kookoo Makka*, and *After This We Heard of Fire*.

Lindsay Barrett, who is married to a Nigerian actress, remains committed to upholding Caribbean and African culture. His readiness to advance the cause of African, Caribbean, and Third World interests is evidenced in his continuing jounalistic activity as a contributing editor to the magazines *Frontline* and *West Indian World* in Britain.

MAJOR WORKS AND THEMES

Lindsay Barrett's major work, to date, is his first and only published novel, *Song for Mumu*. Its importance lies partially in the themes evoked but mainly in the significance attributed to these themes by Barrett's fictive techniques: his transformation of the lives, loves, and deaths of his characters into poetic myth and fable, lyrical encounters, and intense evocations of human emotions.

The novel is set in an unnamed yet recognizably Caribbean island, and its action occurs within two starkly opposed settings: the green countryside and the harsh, stony, and metallic city. The mythical undertone of the narrative is enhanced by the anonymous setting, which is, however, vividly realized in the intensely sensed descriptions of scenery. It is within this sensuously felt yet distant world that Barrett tells the story of Mumu, a fable of black desire, of the search for identity, of love, separation, madness, and death. These plangent themes are coupled with a subtle atavistic resonance of Africa. Mumu's individual quest, her loves and losses, become allegorical markers for the psychic condition of the uprooted children of the Black Diaspora. This historical groundswell of alienation and exile adds gravity to the novel and colors setting, action, and character.

Song for Mumu has a relatively simple episodic plot. Scully, a boy from the green countryside, is drawn to the city by a desire to find its "harsh and mysterious soul" and is seduced into its life style, the language of the street and the waterfront, the fascination with vehicles and machines at the garage where he works, and the nightlife with the whores on Prudent Street. He breaks with this life style after contracting a venereal disease from one of the whores and travels into the green peace of the countrysides, where he encounters Papa Peda, a farmer who, after initially treating Scully in a hostile manner because of the latter's careless tossing of a cigarette butt into a river, takes pity on the tired hungry youth and takes him home to meet Papa Peda's wife, Olida, and his daughter, the beautiful Meela, with whom Scully falls in love. Papa Peda adopts Scully as his son, and the two of them farm Papa Peda's plot of land. In the meantime Scully and Meela have become secret lovers, a fact which Papa Peda discovers after Scully blurts it out to him while drunk from a visit to the village bar. Papa Peda whips Scully severely, thus alienating his daughter's affection, and she promptly leaves her home to go to live with Scully as soon as the latter's wounds have healed. They build a hut in the hills, intending to farm and pass their time in idyllic loving. This happy state of affairs is interrupted by the exigencies of economic survival. Scully's plot is unable to compete with the plantation of the Rich Man, who is symbolic of the White plantocracy and business interests that have the countryside under their strangling economic monopoly. Scully has to descend from his hillside perch to seek employment from the Rich Man, who hires him as a stable boy. While carrying out his duties, Scully is kicked on the head by the Rich Man's demonic white horse, and as a result he loses his mind.

As a result of Scully's accident, Papa Peda relents and takes the lovers back under his roof, where Scully spends his days carving birds and his nights making love with Meela, who eventually gives birth to twins. This birth is accompanied by tragedy, however, as the deranged Scully kills the youngest twin at the moment of birth, because it had caused so much pain for his beloved Meela, and he also blinds Papa Peda with Papa Peda's own whip. Scully is carted off to the asylum, and Meela continues to live with the surviving child, a girl, Mumu, who grows into a startling bird-like beauty. From here on, the narrative is the story of Mumu's life and subsequent death, but her story is intertwined with that of her mother Meela, an intertwining which establishes important structural and thematic relationships within the novel.

Mumu's childhood is presented in idyllic terms. She is loved by her mother Meela, by Papa Peda, Olida, and the River Women, the village women in the novel who function as a choric utterance of the links of ancestral memory, who give voice to the themes of desire, and who also represent the avenging collective nemesis of the Rich Man, who is dismembered by them in a surreal scene that blends play, allegorical action, confession, and judgment into a ritual of moral vengeance. An early childhood experience of Mumu is that of being taken to the asylum in the city, where she meets her father Scully without being aware of his identity. Meela later learns via a telegram that Scully has hanged himself from the bars of his cell window with Papa Peda's whip. The news of Scully's death is juxtaposed against the Rich Man's wild gallop on the mad horse which was responsible for Scully's insanity. The Rich Man falls off his horse into the river, where he is ritually dismembered at the hands of the River Women, who thus avenge Scully's death and enable the farmers to regain their land, which had been appropriated by the Rich Man. Meela and Mumu's loss is symbolically avenged, but a certain psychic vacancy lingers within their lives with its hints of foreboding tragedy and recurring loss.

Mumu grows into a beautiful adolescent who is loved by Joker, the son of her mother's lover, Junji the sailor. The pastoral romance of both women is again interrupted by separation. Junji and Joker go off to sea, where both are drowned, and the sorrowing women burn their hut and leave the countryside for the hard stone city, where they lodge at the house of a crippled woman, Megmaria. Meela finds a job in a canteen and takes as her lover Oboe, the cartman who had carried their luggage and directed them to Megmaria's house on their first day in the city. Mumu also finds a lover, Chino, the gambling man who places Megmaria's bets and whose attention she tolerates rather indifferently.

Meela is befriended by a one-eyed woman, Caressy, at her workplaces. Caressy takes Meela to a religious meeting, where she comes under the influence of Preacher, the spiritual shepherd of the cult. Preacher becomes Meela's lover, and she leaves with him to return to the green peace of the countryside, where he builds a house of worship, the Stone House. Mumu ridicules her mother's newfound faith, refuses to go back with her to the country, and remains behind at Megmaria's house. Oboe becomes her lover, but their liaison is tragically ended when Oboe loses his life in a road accident. Mumu, shocked by her misfortune and loss, finds a job as a maid to a wealthy White woman, who promptly fires her after her refusal to sleep with her employer's brother-in-law.

Megmaria and Mumu grow closer during this period, and the older woman reveals certain secrets to the younger. Megmaria had been Scully's lover in his youthful days in the city, but her refusal to go with him to the countryside had broken his heart and driven him into a life of debauchery on Prudent Street. Megmaria's revelation serves to fasten Mumu's ties to the city, but the kind-hearted crippled woman dies shortly thereafter, leaving Mumu to cope with her various losses and to search for a form of self-knowledge in her own limited, groping, and questioning fashion.

She is not left alone for long however. Her rare bird-like beauty attracts Sidnisweet, a trick cyclist and unsuccessful petty thief, whose love for her leads him to attempt burglary and jail. While Sidnisweet is serving time, Mumu meets a strange, intense young man, a dreamer and semi-mystic, known only as Poet, who provides a link between her present and her ancestral past, and whose almost sadomasochistic lovemaking offers her a painful insight into self. Sidnisweet's release provides a complication resolved in a strange surreal duel between Poet and Sidnisweet in a forest of birds. Both men exhibit their talents: the poet his songs; the cyclist, his stunts, but the birds, who are Poet's friends, pass their judgment in his favor and peck Sidnisweet to death. Poet, on his return to the city, is accused of the cyclist's murder, and because he refuses to plead rationally, he is committed to the asylum, where, in a gesture reminiscent of Scully's, he hangs himself.

Mumu breaks down under all this terrible strain. The loss of her men and the futility of her love drive her into madness, but she refuses to go back to the country with Meela and Preacher. Preacher leaves his Book of Jaja, his sacred text, with her. She reads the Book of Jaja, fasts, and rereads it, until finally she comes to an acceptance of self which prepares her for the renunciation of her brief, grief-laden life with its recurring losses and the acceptance of death as the final resolution of broken dreams and tragic lives. She returns to the countryside, where Preacher ritually stabs her to death in the Stone House. Mumu's sacrifice is complete.

The novel is structured by recurring deaths, recurring losses, thus its mode is primarily elegiac, a cyclic structure of recall, divided into two sections, book 1, "The Beginning," and book 2, "Links." It opens with a prologue of Mumu's funeral in an evening of rain and thunder. The pathetic fallacy pervades this prologue; nature itself is weeping at Mumu's death; the rain mingles with the mourners' tears, "mourning, moaning, and tears storming the evening,"(p. 2). Barrett utilizes religious ritual, prayer, hymn, and a crudely rigorous elliptical discourse to evoke the atmosphere of grief, loss, sacrifice, and simultaneously the sense of hope and possibility. The brief prologue has its moment of climactic intensity when Meela, distraught with grief, tries to jump into her daughter's grave and is put out of her misery by Papa Peda's long knife. Her death with its sacrificial overtones recalls Mumu's own at the hands of Preacher. Both mother and daughter are buried together.

The prologue thus prepares us for the series of deaths that dramatically punctuate the narrative and provide its various peaks, its points of transition, and its relentless revelation of loss as a recurring factor in human existence. Despite its heavy tragic overtones, *Song for Mumu* does not, however, articulate the triumph of despair; rather it presents a world view based on transcendence through harsh suffering, stoic endurance, and acceptance of life with its contingencies, contradictions, reversals, and losses. This world view is evoked through Barrett's use of myth, symbols, metaphor, ritual, and the implacable fatalism of the narrative.

Within the world of *Song for Mumu*, death is seen as a resolution of loss and suffering. The meanings of the deaths in the novel are as varied as the characters, but the recurring deaths which echo each other point to a guiding principle. Thus Scully's death is echoed by Poet's and Mumu's by Meela's. There are other echoes. The men in the lives of Meela and Mumu all die violent deaths except Chino and Preacher. Junji and Joker are drowned together; Oboe the cartman is killed while chasing after his runaway cart, and Sidnisweet's rivalry with Poet for Mumu's love results in his strange death by mutilation. Mumu and Meela are destined to suffer the loss of their loves, and such loss compels them to seek for a sense of selfhood or some form of belief that can fill the psychic vacancy and abolish the traumas created by loss. The theme of loss underscores the theme of identity, since in order to compensate for her losses, Mumu seeks knowledge of her origins. Her outward quest takes the form of a search to discover who her father was. The impetus of the narrative is, however, directed toward larger mythic and archetypal resonances. Hence Mumu's quest becomes symbolically a quest for lost racial origins. In book 1 Mumu as quester is aided by the keeper of ancestral memories, the oldest of the River Women, Mother River, who functions as a guide initiating Mumu into the secret, submerged history of her race. Mother River is a symbol of the tenacious link with the past, and she imparts to Mumu and Joker a sense of racial identity, informed by the knowledge of exile, slavery, and suffering: "Yes yes Mumu we are the descendants of great hours and time will uncover the bones of all lives even thin existence grows thinner in time. . . . But there is more weight to a loss unknown and recovered than there is to a thing owned and then disowned" (p. 65).

Mother River's teachings take the form of fable, a lyrical, poetic, and mythical history that recounts in allegorical fashion the encounter between Africans and Europeans and the sea. The ocean is personified as evil, it is "the evil river" dividing two worlds. The river on the other hand is a metaphor for the continuity of the past and, by implication, for psychic and spiritual bonds with Africa. This view of the river as a link between past and present is echoed in the River Women's song to the river, where she asserts the need to go to the river "the ancient blood to see" (p. 18).

The ocean is the Blacks' enemy, but the river is their friend: "Only the rivers in the land have we mastered / The ocean is not our friend" (p. 67). The destruction of the Rich Man by the River Women occurs allegorically in the river, and this scene is a vivid example of Barrett's penchant for merging the realistic and the surreal into an allegory evoked via different stylistic registers arranged in a climactic order and drawn from children's games, trial scenes with elements of interrogation and confession, as well as stark ritual morality drama. The river is both medium and witness to the destruction of the oppressor. It is a metaphor of ancestral resilience, and it links past, present, and future into the timeless world of fable, where the individual quest assumes mythic proportions and selfhood becomes a sacred trust.

If Mother River is Mumu's guide to racial identity, Poet and Preacher function in varying degrees as her guides toward a sense of individual identity forged from catastrophe and marked by renunciation of a life seared by losses, madness, and suffering. Poet's emotional relationship with Mumu becomes for her a merging of sexual need and racial identity. Their sexual coupling provides some kind of continuity from the teachings of Mother River: "He became the bone, that bone, that tiny bone hung all these years around her neck, the bone Mother River had given her, the toe-bone of a leopard" (p. 130). Poet introduces Mumu to a strange visionary existence. She blooms in this relationship, and because throughout the novel both she and Meela have been imaged as birds, her appearance is described in terms of the brilliant colors of birds: "Mumu hovers like the brilliant bird she is in his sight, the many colours glow in her feathers so she lives . . . they live the colours . . . she hovers around, above, beneath him and sometimes she takes to the wing and disappears from his vision and leaves him there being still" (p. 131).

Poet despite stillness and long silences possesses nevertheless an active and intense inner life. This intensity borders on madness, in fact it escalates into madness, but he possesses a strange hold on Mumu's affections. Through the painfulness of his lovemaking she begins to understand how pain can be a gateway to transcendence.

Preacher's spirituality is grounded in the African based syncretic cults of the

Diaspora. Preacher administers to the spiritual needs of the urban dispossessed, loveless women like Caressy, "survivors of the crossing," and Meela recovering from loss. Preacher's message is from his sacred text, the Book of Jaja, and it is an oracular, riddling, yet rooted message. He speaks to his flock of their desires, their need for love, for a balm to soothe the hardships of their living. It is this message which fascinates and attracts Meela:

> It is a shallow river this life . . . it ain't all it should be but the soul cries out for love and we gotta dream the dreams of green waters . . . do you hear me . . . how must a life be more than a shallow thing, deepen the river, deepen the soul. Is there a new one here tonight? Follow this love. Meela's heart leaps. From rib to gut. Yes yes, she thought, love, a kind of love it is. (p. 95)

"Jaja is self," Preacher proclaims, hence "salvation is self-knowledge," and it is the message he leaves for Mumu to decipher within his Book of Dreams. Mumu's reading of the Book of Jaja opens her mind finally to an understanding of self. She learns that loss and despair are all conditions of the mind; that she should not shun pain; that to be alive is to desire, and desire brings a train of events. Memory, she learns is important: "Do not discard ancient noises . . . do not forget things known and forms seen" (p. 147). She accepts the promise of death as the ultimate of desire, not as an ending but as part and parcel of the eternal process of being and becoming in the animistic universe postulated by the Book of Jaja. Her death is thus a voluntary sacrifice, a transcendence of her tragic, limited existence, and Barrett's finale remains true in his oracular depiction of Mumu's death, with her last vision being one of red birds flying, as a poetic image of the soul's transcendence. The antiphonal epilogue sung by the chorus of River Women as they prepare Mumu's body for burial links beginning and ending, restates the theme of death, and throughout it all the river functions as metaphor, as an agent of purgation and the continuity of living.

Lindsay Barrett's *State of Black Desire*, a collection of three prose essays (meditations on the themes of Black art, alienation, and exile) and three poems, was published in Paris in 1966, one year before the publication of his major work, *Song for Mumu*, and some of its themes, such as Black desire and alienation, prefigure their imaginative variants in the novel. *The State of Black Desire*, however, offers no major insights. It is largely informed by an awareness of the Black Aesthetic movement of the 1960s and as such is self-consciously "Black" and topical. It possesses however a raw driving intelligence, and Barrett's facility for couching his arguments in a cliché-free, sometimes lyrical, and cogently worded prose prevents *The State of Black Desire* from being dated or banal. His stance in this book is that Black art, specifically jazz and other forms of Black music, contains positions of strength capable of shaping as well as articulating an aesthetic of survival for the Black man in the West. Music is thus the form, the shape of Black desire; it is a weapon as well as an art.

The collection of poems *The Conflicting Eye* (1973) has had no major critical impact. It explores a cluster of themes (racial conflict, emotional conflict, the landscape of exile), but these poems rarely impress, except for now and again a brief flash of elliptical, startling imagery. Barrett's poetry is highly metaphorical and impressionistic, with a feel for the vivid instant and nuances of shade and colors. It is very often like the text of the "Book of Jaja" in his novel *Song for Mumu*, compressed, oracular, and riddling.

CRITICAL RECEPTION

The publication of *Song for Mumu* was received for the most part with mild approval by critics. There is in fact very little in the way of critical reviews or articles on *Song for Mumu* by Caribbean critics. Edward Baugh in an extremely insightful review alerts us to the novel's concern with "the souls of black folk" and its polyphonic texture of prose, verse, and dramatic dialogue as well as its "blending of different worlds into one anonymous allegorical world" (*Caribbean Quarterly* [1967], 53). The novel's mode is seen as primarily lyrical, and its subject matter one of "primal passions." Baugh emphasizes the atavistic elements within the novel and also its unconventional narrative method and form: "This unusual treatment is appropriate to the whole unusual conception of the work, to the way in which it moves in worlds of magic and madness, myth and primitive ritual, not so as to exploit their strangeness, but to make them familiar, to emphasise their immediate reality, no less real than the reality of the natural and everyday. In his own distinctive way, Barrett is doing something not dissimilar to what, in their separate ways, Wilson Harris and the Cuban Alejo Carpentier have done" (p. 54).

George Panton in a rather cursory review of the novel in the *Sunday Gleaner* (August 18, 1968), is concerned with the novel's readability or lack of it. "The Jamaican Lindsay Barrett, in his first novel has written what he wants to say in his own way, his own poetic way without any thought as to whether or not anyone will read what he has to say" (p. 4). For Edward Kamau Brathwaite, Barrett's novel, despite its metaphorical richness and its orchestrated polyphony grounded in Black music, religious ritual, hymn, chant, worksong, and dance, falls short. The narrative line cannot convey the vision. It sinks too easily into sentimentality and a naive eroticism: "It becomes a private, wilful and erotic indulgence, an aesthetic escape out of a hopeless landscape" (*Black World*, 1971).

HONORS AND AWARDS

Lindsay Barrett received the Conrad Kent Rivers Memorial Award in 1970.

BIBLIOGRAPHY

Works by Lindsay Barrett

The State of Black Desire. Paris: Alemeon, Imp. Corbiere et Jugain, 1966.

Song for Mumu. London: Longmans, Green, 1967; Washington, D.C.: Howard University Press, 1974.

The Conflicting Eye. Amsterdam: Paul Bremen, 1973.

Studies of Lindsay Barrett

Baugh, Edward. Review of *Song for Mumu*. *Caribbean Quarterly* 13 (December 1967), 53–54.

Brathwaite, Edward. "West Indian Prose Fiction in the Sixties." *Black World* 20 (September, 1971), 15–29.

Maxwell, Marina. "Towards a Revaluation of the Arts in the Caribbean." *Savacou* (September 1970), 19–32.

See also General Bibliography: Allis, Herdeck, and Hughes.

MERVYN MORRIS

Louise Bennett (1919–)

Louise Bennett is now generally acknowledged as a distinguished writer who has captured in print the language and attitudes of Jamaican oral folk culture. She was, for decades, underestimated by readers who did not see beyond the comedy and were not yet ready to reflect on poems written in Creole. Her work lends itself to performance, at which she is adept. Some critics argue that only in performance are the poems truly realized.

BIOGRAPHY

Louise Bennett, an only child, was born in Kingston, Jamaica, on September 7, 1919. Her mother often talked to her of life in the rural parish of St. Mary, but Louise herself did not go farther afield than Spanish Town (the capital of St. Catherine, a parish adjacent to Kingston) until she was ten. Much of her knowledge of Jamaican folklore and oral history was acquired in her adult years, by travel and research.

Her father, who had owned a bakery in Spanish Town, died when she was only seven. Her mother was a dressmaker, sewing "for every type of Jamaican" (Bennett, interviewed by Don Buckner, JBC TV, October 1, 1976). Louise Bennett had early opportunities to observe and listen to a cross-section of Jamaican people, whom her mother taught her to treat with respect: "Everybody was a lady—the fish lady, the yam lady, the store lady, the teacher lady." She was, from early on, critical of Black self-contempt, fruit of the colonial experience: "When I was a child nearly everything about us was bad, yuh know;

they would tell yuh seh yuh have bad hair, that black people bad . . . and that the language yuh talk was bad. And I know that a lot of people I knew were not bad at all, they were nice people and they talked this language'' (Buckner interview).

Jamaican Creole, Jamaican dialect, ''nation language,'' patois, Jamaica talk: ''this language'' spoken by the majority of Jamaica has been called by various names. The terms most often employed by Louise Bennett herself are ''dialect'' and ''our Jamaican language''—the one acknowledging a connection with Standard English, the other insisting on the developed status of Jamaican Creole. As a colonial schoolgirl (St. Simon's College, 1933–36; Excelsior High School, 1936–38) Louise Bennett tried at first to write poems in Standard English, the usual language of the literature she encountered and loved in school. Then one day on a Kingston tramcar her imagination was fired by a vivid remark in Creole which she happened to overhear, and she began to write poems in Creole.

Her schoolmates liked them; and soon her audience widened, with many invitations to perform. Her first professional fee was for appearing in the 1938 edition of the popular Christmas morning concerts organized by Eric ''Chalk Talk'' Coverley. The first collection of poems by Louise Bennett was published in 1942. In May, 1943, the *Gleaner* newspaper began to publish each Sunday a column of her verse.

Contemplating a career in writing, she resisted the advice of those who urged practical alternatives, such as nursing. She was supported and encouraged by her mother, whom she reports as having said: ''If you can write as well as I can make a frock, I'll be satisfied'' (Buckner interview).

She continued with formal education beyond high school. She did a correspondence course in journalism in the late 1930s and a course in social work at Friends' College in Highgate, St. Mary, beginning in 1943. On the basis of her talent as a performer, she was awarded in 1945 a British Council scholarship to the Royal Academy of Dramatic Art (RADA), the famous drama school in London, England. Within months of her arrival in London, she had a BBC program of her own; she wrote and broadcast many poems there. She did well at RADA, and she rejected opportunities to remain in Britain as a professional actress. She returned to Jamaica in 1947. In 1950 she went back to England, to work for the BBC again, in charge of ''West Indian Guest Night.'' She performed with repertory companies in England: in Coventry, Huddersfield, and Amersham. At the urging of an aunt in America, she moved to New York in 1953. She performed in New York, New Jersey, and Connecticut and did some radio work. She also sang folk songs at the Village Vanguard in Greenwich Village. In May 1954 she married Eric Coverley in New York; they returned home to Jamaica in 1955.

In Jamaica again, Louise Bennett worked for the Jamaica Social Welfare Commission as drama officer until 1959, when she was made a director. In her JSWC job she traveled a great deal throughout Jamaica and was able to continue the serious study of Jamaican folklore and oral history which she had begun in the early 1940s. She lectured on drama and Jamaican folklore for the Extra Mural Department of the University College of the West Indies.

Since the appearance in 1966 of *Jamaica Labrish*, her most substantial collection of poems, her work has been consistently available and widely bought. Her *Selected Poems* came out in 1982, designed to encourage detailed literary study of the work.

Although abroad from time to time to lecture or perform, Louise Bennett has been based in Jamaica since 1955. She has continued to build her reputation as a writer, a folklore scholar, and a professional performer. She has been of particular importance to the development of the Jamaican pantomime, now only distantly related to its English antecedents of the 1940s; it is an annual, very popular folk musical in which Louise Bennett last performed in 1976. For several years, 1965–82, she wrote and delivered four-minute prose monologues on radio, often three times a week. From 1970 until 1982 she hosted "Ring Ding," a weekly television show for children, in which children performed and were reminded of various elements of Jamaican folk culture. As she puts it on *Yes M'Dear: Miss Lou Live*, the record of a London performance in April, 1983, she has always thought it important that "de pickney-dem learn de sinting dat belong to dem" (that the children should learn about things that belong to them—their own culture, that is). It is her vocation: to share her pride in Jamaican culture. This pride is at the center of her work.

MAJOR WORKS AND THEMES

Interviewed by Dennis Scott ("Bennett on Bennett," 1968), Louise Bennett was asked how she would explain the fact that it took long for people to regard her art as "respectable." She replied: "Because for too long, it was considered not respectable to use the dialect. Because there was a social stigma attached to the kind of person who used dialect habitually. Many people still do not accept the fact that for us there are many things which are best said in the language of the 'common man' " (p. 101). She is clearly not uncomfortable in Standard English. She is a folk poet in the sense that the main materials of her art are the language and culture of the Jamaican folk—those little affected by the standards of formal education she herself received. At the beginning of her career she studied "the English poets" and was "influenced by their techniques" (p. 99). But she "began to wonder why more of our poets and writers were not taking more of an interest in the kind of language usage and the kind of experiences of living which were all around us, and writing in this medium of dialect instead of writing in the same old English way about Autumn and things like that" (p. 99). She recognized herself as "interested in people and what the people were doing and the 'now' of their lives" (p. 99).

Characteristically, the Louise Bennett poem is a comment in Creole on "the now" of Jamaican lives, often on something topical. It offers insight into, and corroborative evidence of, people's responses to particular events. To make sense of the poem, we sometimes need to know of the occasion that provoked it; and the topicality was often an important factor in the initial impact. Lloyd Brown (*West Indian Poetry*, 1978, p. 111) makes the important point, however, that many of the poems survive their original contexts because "by virtue of their style their focus is less on the specific topics of the 1940's (food shortages, high prices, the war itself) and more on the continuing modes of perception they dramatize."

The modes of perception being dramatized are often themselves subjected to critical irony. The form most often employed by Louise Bennett is the dramatic monologue; and what Philip Drew wrote of Browning's also applies to Louise Bennett's: "In poem after poem the vital point to observe is . . . that the speaker understands himself and his own situation less thoroughly than the reader, who nevertheless derived all his understanding from the poem" (*The Poetry of Robert Browning*, 1970, p. 32). Poems by Louise Bennett often provoke in us that "combination of sympathy and judgment" which Robert Langbaum has identified as a common response to dramatic monologue (*The Poetry of Experience*, 1957, p. 96).

In "Uriah Preach," for example, the persona is boasting about her son who substitutes as preacher "when rain fall or parson sick." She describes one such recent occasion, proud that Uriah seized the opportunity to castigate family enemies:

> Him tell dem off, dem know is dem,
> Dem heart full to de brim;
> But as Uriah eena pulpit
> Dem cyaan back-answer him.
>
> (*Selected Poems*, p. 61; hereafter cited as *SP*)

The vitality of the monologue draws us into sharing her wicked delight; but we know, all the same, that her behavior and her son's behavior are un-Christian, not (really) to be approved. Similarly, in "Proverbs" a hypocritical tale-bearing snob is exposed and criticized by implications in the Jamaican proverbs and Bible verses she cites, ostensibly in her own defense.

Sometimes the irony—a pervasive quality in Louise Bennett's work—is directed outward. "Jamaica Oman," for example, is a poem in praise of Jamaican women who discreetly manipulate their men:

> Jamaica oman cunny, sah!
> Is how dem jinnal so?
> Look how long dem liberated
> An de man dem never know!
>
> (*SP*, p. 21)

In "Independence" the persona reports on Mattie, who believes that everything, including Jamaica's size and location, should change with Independence:

She hope dem caution worl-map
Fi stop draw Jamaica small,
For de lickle speck cyaan show
We independentness at all!

Moresomever we must tell map dat
We don't like we position -
Please kindly teck we out a sea
An draw we in de ocean.

(*SP*, p. 118)

Louise Bennett poems go well in performance, and many are performed. It is a mistake, however, to believe that "publication has really been an afterthought of sorts in terms of her function and achievement as an artist in an oral medium" (Lloyd Brown, *West Indian Poetry*, p. 108). She was always interested in getting published; and her first book appeared in 1942. In speaking to Dennis Scott ("Bennett on Bennett," p. 98), although she agreed that people tended to think of her "as a performing artist primarily," she added: "I did start to write before I started to perform," and "I felt I wanted to put on paper some of the wonderful things that people say in dialect" (pp. 98–99).

Presentation varies from book to book, and this can be a problem. The equivalent of Standard English "can't," for example, may appear as "kean" or "cyaan." In *Selected Poems* the spelling "assumes that the *reader* is accustomed to English and anyone familiar with Jamaican Creole will 'hear' the Creole sounds even when the spelling looks like Standard" (p. xx). Printed texts that are unconventionally punctuated and difficult to read encourage the notion that Louise Bennett is essentially for performance and is inadequate on the page.

The *London Times Literary Supplement* (December 15, 1966), reviewing *Jamaica Labrish*, remarked: "In print these ballads are like a phonetic libretto for performance, but they cannot recreate for us the performance itself. Not merely something, but too much, is lost." That is unlikely to be true for any reader to whom the words on the page suggest recognizable noises and nuances of meaning. The reviewer argues that the poem on the page "must offer its riches to the reader through a verbal, even at times a typographical wit, rather than a vocal one." Typographical wit is rare in Bennett's verse, but verbal wit is plentiful. In "Po Muffeena," for example, the persona sees "May straighten out har head" (that is, get her Negro hair straightened), and the poem implies that May needs to straighten out her thinking. In "Pass fi White" the poem's central meaning is focused in the rhymes and in puns. There are repeated rhymes on "white" and repeated rhymes on "pass"; and in the two stanzas which vary from those the rhymes again suggest the opposing values: education versus color ("education"/"complexion"; "D.R."/"colour bar," recalling "pass exams"/ "pass fi white"). Some of the art involved is unavailable to even the most alert of listeners; it is when we can linger over the page that the tightness of the organization becomes more fully apparent:

Miss Jane jus hear from Merica—
Her daughter proudly write
Fi seh she fail her exam, but
She passin dere fi white!

(*SP*, p. 101)

In stanza 8 there is a superbly functional pun:

De gal puppa dah laugh an seh
It serve Merica right—
Five year back dem Jim-Crow him, now
Dem pass him pickney white.

(*SP*, p. 102)

The pun turns on a Jamaican proverb, "Ebery John Crow tink him pickney white," which asserts that parents tend to overestimate the potential of their own children. At birth the John Crow—a Jamaican vulture—looks white; its feathers grow jet black. The poem is commenting on the relationship between color and status not only in the United States but in Jamaica also. The pun on John Crow/Jim Crow criticizes, inter alia, the father's pride in his daughter having passed for White.

Allusions in Louise Bennett's poems, when pondered, often turn out to be of more complex significance than we are likely to perceive in performance time. In "Independence Dignity," for example, the third stanza parodies a British poem familiar to many a colonial schoolchild. Charles Wolfe's "The Burial of Sir John Moore at Corunna" begins:

Not a drum was heard, not a funeral note
  As his corse to the rampart we hurried;
Not a soldier discharged his farewell shot
  Oe'r the grave where our hero we buried.

In the Louise Bennett poem, at Independence time:

Not a stone was fling, not a samfie sting,
Not a soul gwan bad an lowrated;
Not a fight bruck out, not a bad-wud shout
As Independence was celebrated.

(*SP*, p. 116)

(A samfie is a confidence man.) It is as though the colonizer is being buried as a new nation is born. Reflection reveals other ironies. In the poem by Wolfe there is further battle ahead. The Bennett poem, aware of battles to be fought and of the need for leadership, mentions areas of inadequacy and unpreparedness: some Jamaicans have been dishonest, unruly, ill-mannered, lazy, disunited, feeble, and (in spite of Independence) may well be so again.

The parody of Wolfe is smoothly integrated into the overall rhythms of the poem. Some admirers of Bennett have remarked on what they consider the constriction of the ballad quatrain, which they contend is astonishingly transformed in performance. They assume that Louise Bennett is working with or against the iambic stress patterns of the English/Scottish ballad norm, although she seems to me to measure in syllables rather than iambic feet. The norm is eight syllables followed by six, then eight, then six, with the rhyme scheme *abcb*. There is an extra syllable or two sometimes, or one or two syllables short; but, fairly regularly, each pair of lines has fourteen syllables (or their equivalent in time). The regularity gives Louise Bennett's most characteristic verse an underlying structure she herself usually suggests in performance. Yet, unconcerned about iambic stress patterns, she is free to follow the contours of Jamaican speech and to point each line for meaning and for dramatic effect. Occasionally, for one reason or another, she sets herself the task of relating to a tighter rhythmic pattern (as in the example from "Independence Dignity," or in "Pedestrian Crosses," "Cousin Joe," or "Mout-Amassi Liza").

Whether in print or in performance, many of the poems are remarkable as social commentary and as works of art. They deal with a variety of topics, including problems of colonial education, the vagaries of politics, economic hardship, bureaucratic humbug, strategies of survival. The poems in general promote acceptance of Jamaican culture; they draw on the customs, beliefs, language of ordinary Jamaicans, the living tissue of Jamaican life. They are critical of gossip. They expose people ashamed of being Jamaican or ashamed of being Black. They ridicule class and color prejudice, but are more concerned to tackle Black self-contempt or to express pride in being Black. They undermine pretension of various kinds.

Her other work is similar. In her topical prose monologues, which sometimes quote from the verse, the persona frequently cites her "Aunty Roachy," an evidently wise and forthright woman of the people. In Louise Bennett Anancy stories the telling is infused with her subtle wit and humor, with the particular flavor of her personality.

CRITICAL RECEPTION

Louise Bennett's poems have long been popular, but critical acknowledgment of their literary worth was slow in coming. The first comment of more than a very few words was my "On Reading Louise Bennett, Seriously" (1964; reprinted in *Jamaica Journal* [December 1967]). The article tilts at people said to regard Louise Bennett "more or less as a local joke" (*Jamaica Journal*, p. 69). It considers Louise Bennett "a poet, and, in her best work, a better poet than most other Jamaican writers" (p. 70). Most often employing the dramatic monologue, "[s]he writes for the voice and the ear, and when her poems are expertly performed something more, movement, is added" (p. 70). Although there is warm appreciation, approval is qualified: "I do not believe that Louise Bennett is a considerable poet. . . . She does not offer her readers any great insight into the nature of life or human experience, but she recreates human experience delightfully and intelligently'' (p. 70). Suggesting that certain poems and passages are less successful than others, the article recommends that Louise Bennett ''present a Collected Poems, dropping all the ephemera and choosing the best of the others'' (p. 73).

Jamaica Labrish (1966)—notes and introduction by Rex Nettleford—does more than that. It is ''designed to give an overview of her art and artistry''; it seeks to ''reveal Miss Bennett in her multiple roles as entertainer, as a valid literary figure and as a documenter of aspects of Jamaican life, thought and feeling'' (p. 10). Nettleford emphasizes the context of oral performance. ''If on the printed pages her poems appear to be dated frozen jingles, in the renditions she gives of them they take on vitality and meaning'' (p. 16). Louise Bennett ''stands firmly in a tradition of the spoken word, living as she does in a society in which anything worth knowing by a great many people has for a long time been told and not written'' (p. 12). Nettleford stresses the need for serious readers of Bennett to undertake the closest study of Jamaican dialect, and he recommends particular works of scholarship toward that end. He remarks that Bennett, with ''her developed sense of irony,'' ''allows certain devastating facts to speak for themselves, and like her Jamaican compatriots she can 'tek bad tings mek laugh' '' (p. 15). He relates the ''tragi-comic expression'' (p. 15) to a similar quality in Black American blues and jazz and in Trinidad calypsos. ''Humour becomes, as it were, the expression of a people's will to live'' (p. 24). On Bennett as a social commentator, Nettleford, identifying some of the topical stimuli, shows that many of the poems ''bear testimony to her keen sense of observation through eyes and ears of the way people felt, lived and thought about issues that affected them from day to day'' (p. 17).

In ''The Folk in Caribbean Literature'' (1972) Gordon Rohlehr examines Louise Bennett's ''people and their milieu, and . . . the way she handles her masks'' (p. 8). He finds her people ''are largely semi-illiterates, caught in various stages of the transition from village to city'' (p. 8). ''Bewilderment and survival are two of the poles between which her people oscillate. Part of the technique of survival lies in the scuffler's use of language as mask'' (p. 9). He notes certain similarities between calypsos and Louise Bennett poems: in similes of abuse, for example, and the skill at caricature which often defines people by their deformities. Like Nettleford, he finds the poems are transformed in performance: on the page they ''assume a hymn-book monotony,'' in performance there are ''sudden changes in pitch and tone and speed, a complete departure from the stress patterns which the ballad form would seem to be imposing'' (p. 15). He sees problems of critical approach: ''Louise Bennett's poetry . . . depends so much on tones of voice, on the fluidity of the voice as it breaks out of the strict metrical limitations of the quatrain, that one ought to comment on the words in audible motion, rather than in their comparatively frozen form on the page'' (p. 8).

In "Noh Lickle Twang: An Introduction to the Poetry of Louise Bennett" (1978), Carolyn Cooper, to "clarify the complex indigenous context within which Bennett writes" (p. 317), surveys 20th century Caribbean poetry in English and notes "the progressive respectability of Creole" (p. 322). Evaluating the scope of Bennett's poetry and identifying significant themes, Cooper affirms that the strength of Bennett's poetry "is the accuracy with which it depicts and attempts to correct through laughter the absurdities of Jamaican society" (p. 325).

In the judgment of Lloyd Brown in *West Indian Poetry* (1978), Louise Bennett "clearly surpasses any of the [other West Indian] poets who attempt to transfer the dialect mode of the oral folk tradition to the written page, largely because she chooses to work within, rather than merely with, the oral tradition of folk poetry as a vital art form in its own right" (p. 106). In proverbs, for example, Louise Bennett "discovers the precise, built-in antitheses through which the folk verbalize their sense of conflict and social contradictions, and which the poet adopts as a ready-made mode of ironic statement" (p. 107). As performer in the oral tradition "she is immersed in the modes of rhetoric and perception that are enclosed by that tradition" (p. 108). As a highly disciplined artist, "she subordinates the authorial voice completely to the cultural personality and values described by her art" (p. 115): "ambiguities or inconsistencies may be traced not so much to Bennett herself as to the world whose viewpoints she reproduces with a ruthless eye, and ear, for authenticity" (pp. 115–16). "Her poetic voice fascinates and challenges her audience precisely because her characters seem to be so irrefutably independent of a controlling artistic vision or authorial judgment" (p. 116). What women experience clearly dominates her work, but generally "Bennett eschews characters who make direct statements about the woman's situation, and instead allows her women to offer indirectly revealing, sometimes contradictory, levels of awareness about their sociosexual condition" (p. 116). "In effect Bennett is concentrating on the presentation of a succession of various viewpoints" (p. 117).

Similarly alert to the variousness of Bennett's personae, Rhonda Cobham-Sander (*The Creative Writer and West Indian Society: Jamaica 1900–1950*, 1983) remarks: "Though Bennett often works through apolitical female figures who are more likely to react to the cut of a politician's clothes than what he says, she often expresses a feminist perspective on topical issues" (p. 241). But Cobham-Sander finds a hint of "self-depreciation" in some of the monologues which "is a sign of one of the weaknesses inherent in Bennett's techniques of speaking through a 'naive' persona whose point of view was often more circumscribed than that of the author herself" (p. 167).

In "Louise Bennett in Print" (1982), an article based on editorial work for the Louise Bennett *Selected Poems*, I note that a characteristic effect of dramatic monologue is the apparently unintentional self-exposure of the speaker and argue that "the author is always there, an ironic guide; the characters only *seem* to be independent of her" (p. 53). The piece recognizes that Jamaican folk culture is central to the poetry but points out that Louise Bennett "does not restrict herself to either the knowledge or the perceptions we tend to associate with the Jamaican folk (in the sense of a comparatively unlettered community)'' (p. 52). It argues that ''although some aspects of her verse are clarified and/or enhanced in performance, there are others more fully appreciated by a reader savouring a text'' (p. 44). The introduction and other editorial material in *Selected Poems*, poems ''chosen primarily for their literary merit'' (p. x), make reference to performance but focus mainly on text. ''The poem in print is, however, fully available only when readers are in touch with the oral and other cultural contexts the words imply'' (p. xi). Attention is directed to literary detail, including ''the many allusions in her work—sometimes to English literature, more often to hymns or the Bible (which are deeply embedded in our Jamaican culture), or to Jamaican folksongs, Jamaican proverbs'' (p. xv).

In ''Proverb as Metaphor in the Poetry of Louise Bennett'' (1984) Carolyn Cooper writes: ''Thematically, the proverb provides conclusive evidence of the socially recognized truth of the argument that a particular Bennett *persona* articulates; structurally, the metaphorical proverb employs graphic imagery derived from everyday Jamaican life as the vehicle for social commentary. In both subject and structure the metaphorical proverb affirms Bennett's umbilical connection to [the] matrix of oral Jamaican folklore'' (p. 21). Cooper considers Louise Bennett ''the quintessential Jamaican example of the sensitive and competent Caribbean artist consciously incorporating features of traditional oral art into written literature'' (p. 22).

HONORS AND AWARDS

Louise Bennett has received several honors, including an M.B.E. (1960), a Silver Musgrave Medal (1965), the Norman Manley Award for Excellence in the Arts (1972), the Order of Jamaica (1974), a Gold Musgrave Medal (1978), an Institute of Jamaica Centenary Medal (1979), and an honorary D.Litt. from the University of the West Indies (1983).

BIBLIOGRAPHY

Works by Louise Bennett

(Jamaica) Dialect Verses. Kingston: Herald, 1942.
Jamaican Humour in Dialect. Kingston: Jamaica Press Association, 1943.
Anancy Stories and Poems in Dialect. Kingston: Gleaner, 1944.
Miss Lulu Sez. Kingston: Gleaner, 1949.
Anancy Stories and Dialect Verses (New Series). Kingston: Pioneer Press, 1957.
Laugh with Louise. Kingston: City Printery, 1961.
Jamaica Labrish. Kingston: Sangster's Book Stores, 1966.
Anancy and Miss Lou. Kingston: Sangster's Book Stores, 1979.
Selected Poems. Kingston: Sangster's Book Stores, 1982.

Discography: Louise Bennett Recordings

Jamaican Folk Songs. New York: Folkways, 1954.
Jamaican Singing Games. New York: Folkways, 1954.
The Honourable Miss Lou. Kingston: Premiere Productions, 1981.
Anancy Stories. Kingston: Federal Records: FRM–129, n.d.
Carifesta Ring Ding. Kingston: Record Specialists, n.d.
Listen to Louise. Kingston: Federal 212, n.d.
Miss Lou's Views. Kingston: Federal 204, n.d.
Yes M'Dear: Miss Lou Live. Kingston: Imani Music, n.d.

Studies of Louise Bennett

Baker, Peta-Anne. "Louise Bennett-Coverley: A Poet of Utterance." *Caribbean Contact* 1 (August 1973), 6.

Brathwaite, Edward Kamau. *History of the Voice: The Development of Nation Language in Anglophone Caribbean Poetry*. London: New Beacon Books, 1984, pp. 26–30.

Brown, Lloyd. "The Oral Tradition: Sparrow and Louise Bennett." In *West Indian Poetry*. Boston: Twayne, 1978. Second Edition, London: Heinemann, 1984, pp. 100–17.

Cobham-Sander, Rhonda. *The Creative Writer and West Indian Society: Jamaica 1900–1950*. Ann Arbor, Mich.: University Microfilms International, 1983, pp. 158–68, 241–42.

Cooper, Carolyn. "Noh Lickle Twang: An Introduction to the Poetry of Louise Bennett." *World Literature Written in English* (April 1978), 317–27.

———. "Proverb as Metaphor in the Poetry of Louise Bennett." *Jamaica Journal* 17 (May 1984), 21–24.

James, Louis. *The Islands in Between*. London: Oxford University Press, 1968, pp. 15–21.

Morris, Mervyn. Introduction, notes and teaching questions. *Selected Poems*. By Louise Bennett. Kingston: Sangster's Book Stores, 1982.

———. "Louise Bennett in Print." *Caribbean Quarterly* 28 (March-June 1982), 44–56.

———. "On Reading Louise Bennett, Seriously." *Jamaica Journal* 1 (December 1967), 69–74; reprinted from *Sunday Gleaner*, June, 1964.

Nettleford, Rex. Introduction and Notes for *Jamaica Labrish*. By Louise Bennett. Kingston: Sangster's Book Stores, 1966.

Panton, George. "Our Well-Known Well-Loved Poet." *Sunday Gleaner*. August 11, 1974, p. 23.

Rohlehr, Gordon. "The Folk in Caribbean Literature." *Tapia* 2 (December 24, 1972), 8, 9, 15.

Scott, Dennis. "Bennett on Bennett" (interview). *Caribbean Quarterly* 14 (March-June 1968), 97–101.

See also General Bibliography: Allis, Baugh (1971, 1978), Herdeck, and Hughes.

HIMANI BANNERJI

Dionne Brand
(1953–)

BIOGRAPHY

Dionne Brand was born on January 7, 1953, in Guayguayare, Trinidad. After graduating from Naparima Girls' High School in Trinidad in 1970, she moved to Toronto. She graduated in 1975 from the University of Toronto with a degree in English and philosophy. She is currently doing her M.A. in philosophy of education at the Ontario Institute for Studies in Education, University of Toronto.

Since coming to Canada, Ms. Brand has worked with many facets of the Black community, including the students' movement and the Black Education Project, an advocacy agency with the educational system. She is also involved in the women's community, having worked in women's health with the Immigrant Women's Centre as a Caribbean counsellor. In 1983 she worked with the Agency for Rural Transformation in Grenada.

She has read her works across Canada in Winnipeg, Edmonton, Regina, Ottawa, Montreal, Toronto, and Vancouver. Ms. Brand has also worked with *Contrast Newspaper* and *Spear Magazine*.

MAJOR WORKS AND THEMES

I am not a refugee
I have my papers,
I was born in the Caribbean,
practically in the sea,

fifteen degrees above the equator,
I have a canadian passport,
I have lived here all my adult life,
I am stateless anyway.
(*Chronicles of the Hostile Sun*, p. 70)

Historical novels have been much in vogue, much written about, but historical poems have a lesser visibility and are perhaps more difficult to write. In spite of the slogan that "the personal is the political," the two get written about in separate pieces, though sometimes joined by an "and." The sense of history that could lead to the fusion of both, that would lead to the writing of historical poetry, shows itself rarely. The ability to make history concrete by capturing the small, ordinary things of life along with a sense of broader historical actions is not to be found too frequently in English poetry, particularly on the land mass of North America. But of course it does happen that some poets do come along—dragging behind them the long chain of history, poets from groups who have been hidden in history such as women or Black people, who institute themselves, their people, their history, centrally in the poetic universe. Dionne Brand, born in Trinidad, immigrant to Canada, woman and Black, is such a poet. To read her poetry is to read not only about her but also about her people, her identification with their struggles both in the metropole of Canada and in the hinterland of the Caribbean.

It is this sense of history that makes the reading of Dionne Brand's poetry a dynamic experience. The reader is continuously struck by a set of complex movements that range from the past to the future, swiftly building connections between places, peoples, feelings, and times. The reader just as much as the writer is required to be in many spaces all at once. But when one really thinks about it to "be" actually does amount to being in that state of simultaneity. Both the content and the rhythm of her poetry suggest that she is always ahead of and trying to catch up with herself all at once. This amounts to catching up with the past to sense out the present mainly in order to seize the future. Her book of poems *Primitive Offensive* (1982) is just such an enterprise, where delving deep into the ancestral past of slavery—"I will take any evidence of me even that carved in the sky"—she releases herself into the future:

. . . to be a bright and violent thing
to tear up that miserable sound
in my ear
I run
my legs can keep going
my belly is wind.
(p. 59)

And the future is neither for Dionne Brand nor for any colonized, enslaved people one of a linear development to a genuine freedom, a happy place in the sun. The forces that once pillaged the world, structured the system of slavery, of colonialism, that now thrive on racism and neocolonialism can push back the victory of the people into new dark ages, new slaveries. Then once more the struggle begins, to emerge as a free people, through a populated time filled with cumulative experiences of victories and defeats. In her most recent book of poems, *Chronicles of the Hostile Sun* (1984), she remarks about the frustrations involved in describing such a process:

> I'm sick of writing history
> I'm sick of scribbling dates
> of particular tortures
> I'm sick of feeling the boot
> of the world on my breast
> my stomach is caving in and
> I'm sick of hearing chuckles
> at my discomfort
> I am sick of doing literacy work
> with north americans.
>
> (p. 65)

It is here that she deals most extensively with the contemporary Caribbean history, particularly in relation to the destruction of the Grenadian revolution by the U.S. military invasion in October, 1983, following the collapse of the government headed by Maurice Bishop.

Chronicles of the Hostile Sun synthesizes many experiences, many kinds of knowledge—an intimate knowledge of Trinidad, where she grew up, her travels through the other islands and Nicaragua, and finally her work for the Agency for Rural Transformation in Grenada during the year 1983 until the very moment of the U.S. invasion. The poems in this volume show her understanding of the need for change in Third World countries as much as her profound sadness and anger at the world's wealthiest and most militarily equipped nation smashing the work and the hopes of 110,000 people inhabiting a 133-square-mile island. The memories and legacies of underdevelopment and slavery that the New Jewel Movement sought to eradicate returned in full force dressed in U.S. military uniform:

> america came to restore democracy,
> what was restored was faith
> in the fact that you cannot fight bombers
> battleships, aircraft carriers, helicopter gunships
> surveillance planes, five thousand american soldiers
> . . . .
> You cannot fight this with a machete
> you cannot fight it with a handful of dirt

you cannot fight it with a hectare of land free from
bosses.

(p. 42)

The bottom line of history is after all the lives of people, and by people is meant the poor, the oppressed of any society. The poem "Amelia" (written on her grandmother) is born out of the knowledge of their lives. Brought up by this woman as her child, as her "co-conspirator," the writer reproduces the daily grind, the reality of their world:

I know that lying there in that bed
in that room
smelling of wet coconut fibres
and children's urine
bundled up in a mound
under the pink chenille and cold
sweating sheets
you wanted to escape,
run from that room.

(*Chronicles*, p. 24)

It becomes apparent as one reads through the volume that in this cramped, poor reality there is only room for one thing—change for the better—but a change will not be given, it must be taken through popular action.

The need for change takes in the whole of the Caribbean as well as Central America. Dionne Brand's poetry sweeps through the panorama of El Salvador, Guatemala, Nicaragua, Honduras—all private estates of landowning gunmen who put their guns at the service of the United States and fatten from the leavings at their master's table. The country that she lingers over the longest is Nicaragua, once the estate of Anastasio Somoza, struggling to survive a U.S. siege carried out by the old ruling class and its military beneficiaries. In the poem "Mount Pamby Beach" the life under such a constant siege is depicted forcefully. It points out the fact that the people of Nicaragua are not gun-happy, that they would rather be doing literacy or health care work or developing people's arts. But this opportunity has been denied to them; instead what overhangs their life is

this contra of a night
[which] spilled criminals and machismo
on our mountains
fouling the air again
eagle insignaed somocistas
bared talons on the mountains of Matagalpa.

(*Chronicles*, p. 9)

Not only this "night of the contras" initiated by external agents but also the allies of U.S. imperialism receive their fair share of criticism from Dionne Brand. Prime Ministers Edward Seaga of Jamaica, Eugenia Charles of Dominica, and Tom Adams of Barbados are rewarded for their "internal initiatives":

> The OECS riding like birds on a cow
> led america to the green hills of St' George's
> and waited at Point Salines
> while it fed on the young of the land,
> eating their flesh with bombs,
> breaking their bellies with grenade launchers.
>
> (*Chronicles*, p. 42)

Chronicles of the Hostile Sun is not sure of what is to become of Grenada. It can only depict what is in the present, and it seems that much has been destroyed. The specter of communism has been raised again and plugged into the cold war channel, which has all North America in its mind-numbing grip. But for the destruction of Grenada or the assassination of Walter Rodney the same lines can be applied:

> and never, never for walter
> no words for walter, no forgiveness,
> every bit of silence is full of walter.
>
> (*Chronicles*, p. 18)

The historical character of the *Chronicles* cannot be sufficiently understood without an exploration of an earlier volume of poems, *Primitive Offensive* (1982). Here the project is explicitly one of writing a historical poem, divided into several long cantos. But it is writing history with a difference since it involves locating herself at the heart of the history of the Caribbean, and indeed within the history of all colonized peoples. Her own subjectivity is the starting point of her query, from which she branches back into the past exploring the construction of her own identity. To begin with, then, she is alone:

> when you decide
> you are alone
> when you dance
> its on your own
> broken face
> when you eat
> your own plate of stones
> for blasted sure
> you are alone.
>
> (p. 8)

But this aloneness is not an individualist, solipsistic enclosure: it is accompanied, filled with voices from the past, her ancestors, their experience of slavery. She has consented to inherit, to taste, no matter how painful and unsavory, all that her ancestors have left her. It is a legacy of blood, bitterness, death, rage, shit, and tears as well as militant love that rouses her to defend her people. But she does something special with her inheritance. She picks up as weapons two adjectives with which her oppressors have labeled her and her people—*primitive* and *offensive*. She lifts these from the ongoing imperialist discourse and hurls them back to her oppressors as a call to war. Through an act of reinterpretation she has rid the word *primitive*, for example, of its pejorative connotations and returned it to its meaning: the original, the essential, and the basic. By reworking the word *offensive* back to its military sense she is now on the "offensive." No more a strategy of retreat, the days of Black defensiveness are certainly over.

Primitive Offensive is a book about war strategies and tactics, as much as about survival itself as a form of war against the oppressors. It is a book about countering the violence of domination in order to set right the violent world order created by colonization, slavery, and imperialism. It is a poem borrowing from Franz Fanon, about decolonization, which cannot be waged without declaring and waging a war—a war of liberation. Dionne Brand also declares her intention when she says:

> I went to Paris
> to where shortarsed Napoleon said,
> "get that nigger Toussaint,"
> Toussaint, who was too gentle,
> He should have met Dessalines,
> I went there to start a war
> for the wars we never started
> to burn the Code Noir
> on the Champs Elysees
>
> (p. 32)

The world as it stands, produced by the long history of domination, is an inverted one. Both with sword and pen the people of the colonized nations have been reduced to the status of objects, their subjectivity distorted or simply negated. And it is this inverted world that must be set back on its own base; the negation must be negated. It must be fought against—at all levels: social, economic, and cultural. A struggle with the destructive Other is inevitable—but also there must be a project of retrieving or salvaging from the past whatever is relevant for now. Nothing that can be used will be thrown away. The task of some of the cantos in *Primitive Offensive* is to reassemble first, piece by piece, this lost world as one would the shards of the ancient African pottery:

> I pored over these
> like a palaeontologist

I dusted them
like an
archaeologist

(p. 12)

The way to accomplish this task is to go back in time, to seek out the lost steps back to the first moment of encounter with the Whites, the moment of the Fall, as it were. The records of time are not to be found in the official textbooks of history or the archives. Rather, an appeal must be made to memory, to the oral tradition persistent among all people who are denied access to many tools of culture. So, an invocation is in order to an ancient spirit, who must speak in the sibylline tongue—to an ancient medicine woman. It is with this ancient woman that the young rebellious woman, the poet, must merge to know what really happened in history. This knowledge and acknowledgment of the past gives strength—"only when I remember I find myself."

The long nightmare of the past is then joined with the horrors of the present. A road runs straight through the old plantations into the present-day South Africa. The horrors of apartheid are laid bare in canto 12, and yet the tone of the poems, their messages or messages to their readers, is not one of defeat but of courage, defiance, and struggle. Even though the poet acknowledges her loneliness of an evening in an empty apartment in cities of the metropole, she also persistently congratulates herself and others like her, because just to survive is an act of heroism. For this ability to survive, no matter on what—"I can eat stone / and oil / I can eat barbed wire . . . I can grow fat on split atoms" (p. 27)—she projects courage and optimism. The Cuban revolution becomes the herald of a bigger revolution:

havana twinkles
defiant, frightening
all the lights are on

(p. 36)

Any discussion of *Chronicles of the Hostile Sun* and *Primitive Offensive* is incomplete without an assessment of their formal qualities. It is safe to begin by saying that they are a rare breed of poems: they are not short lyrics but mostly long poems; *Primitive Offensive* in fact is an attempt at an epic. The tradition of long poems, in the English language at least, seems to be on the wane. Epics are rarely attempted and even more rarely successful. The difficulty of writing long poems or narrative, epic-like poems, is obvious. They require much more than powerful feelings or an ability to catalyze these feelings into strong, moving images. They require a coherent, well-articulated world view and an ability to create a sustained narrative since one cannot possibly attend to a hundred pages or so of climactic moments. Both the books are successful in this blending of the imagistic, symbolic moments with narrative ones. In *Primitive Offensive* this entails an ability to create a general movement as well as an eye for details. The reader can almost taste, smell, see the gold and the blood of primitive accumulation in the pages of that book. Structuring the poem on different types of contradictions and inversions, the poet has kept a historical narrative in balance and located herself as a conscious subject within that frame. She has guided her reader through these turmoil-filled times with her sense of history. And finally she has created and sustained the reader's interest with her strong sense of drama, through the use of historical details, vignettes, names and dates, of rituals and constellations of images, by frequently returning to the same image, as a signpost or an echo.

The *Chronicles of the Hostile Sun* does not depend on the epic and the mythic qualities that characterize *Primitive Offensive*. In this set of poems, which must also be read as parts of a whole developing sequence (and can be read individually as well), the narrative and the historicism take on some characteristics of reporting, recording, witnessing, and commenting. The contemporariness of the poems demands this form above the chanting, incantating tone predominant in the earlier book. The poems fuse ordinary everyday images that convey, not a photographic naturalism, but a well-selected sense of the environment, or a conjunction of meanings worked up through the poet's own perception of the world, her own philosophy and politics. The long poem "P.P.S. Grenada" is perhaps the best example of this. Describing the humble details of her everyday life in Grenada, this poem manages to convey the simplicity and the peacefulness of Grenada before the invasion. It is as though the writer was looking at photographs of a lost landscape. It is a recounting, a piece of history which is also a lamentation.

While *Chronicles of the Hostile Sun* is about the contemporary Caribbean and *Primitive Offensive* mainly about its historical past, *Winter Epigrams* (combined in a volume with *Epigrams to Ernesto Cardenal in Defense of Claudia* [1983]) directly addresses Dionne Brand's experiences in Canada as struggles for survival in a frozen landscape. Seen through the eyes of an immigrant from the tropics, Toronto or Montreal come to life, shivering in the cold, a concrete desert, a social space constructed through racism:

> Snow is raping the landscape
> Cote de Neige is screaming
> writhing under
> winters heavy body
> any poem about Montreal in the winter is pornography.
> (*Winter Epigrams*, p. 6)

A small taut piece on racism is captured in a few quick strokes and the helplessness of the victim:

> I had planned the answers all my life
> rehearsed my "fuck offs"

practiced my knee to the groin
decided to use violence;
now, leaving the train at Montreal,
gone!
all my rebuttals,
all my "racist pig"
nothing,
dried up!
iron teeth of the escalator
snickering like all of "them,"
my legs stiff as the cold outside,
my eyes seeing everything in blood,
a piece of cloth
a white mound of flesh atop
like a cow's slaughtered head,
emitting,
"whore, nigger whore."

(*Winter Epigrams*, p. 17)

Alienation and long months of winter (and there seems to be no other season in the cities of the metropole) are negotiated by an underground life, surrounded by fetish objects from the past life and wry humor. The *Winter Epigrams* are quick parries and thrusts at the enemy. They are, if such an expression can be permitted, a sort of guerrilla poems—a set of quick attacks and rapid withdrawals.

The second section of the *Winter Epigrams*, entitled *Epigrams to Ernesto Cardenal in Defense of Claudia*, assumes an ideal communicant in the Nicaraguan revolutionary poet and priest Ernesto Cardenal. Taking the Nicaraguan poet to task for his censoriousness about the average woman—the Claudias of this world—Dionne Brand proceeds to tell him a thing or two about the situation of women, about men, living, and loving. But this is done humorously, whimsically, even lovingly, and sometimes with downright craftiness. In "Epigram 27," for example, she points out the loving though polemical nature of her poems to him—with humor:

Dear Ernesto,
I have terrible problems convincing
people that these are love poems.
Apparently I am not allowed to love
more than a single person at a time.
Can I not love anyone but you?
signed,
"Desperate."

(p. 27)

About Claudia, whom Cardenal reprimands for her lack of rectitude, for selling herself to the foreigner, she has this to say:

Some Claudias are sold to companies,
some Claudias sell to street corners
even debasement has its uptown,
even debasement has its hierarchy.
(p. 25)

The formal aspects of *The Winter Epigrams* and *Epigrams to Ernesto Cardenal* are wholly of a different nature than that of the books earlier discussed. Unlike the long and the medium-length poems where ideas are discussed in their full ramifications, where images are grouped together in clusters and political viewpoints extensively developed, these poems are amused or serious experimentations with short, inconclusive, but suggestive quick sketches. It is here that we see some of the more so-called personal poems of Dionne Brand—except that in each of these there is embedded a politics, an awareness of the dynamics of power. Patriarchy, or sexism, to be more precise, as a mode of social organization is penetratingly discussed in these short pieces. What appear from one point of view to be aspects of her own relationship with men, is also a window into male–female relations in general; personal accounts such as, ''You're lucky I have a bad memory/ . . . or I'd remember that I loved you / then'' (p. 28), acquire a social meaning, available to all members of patriarchically organized societies, when joined with the insights of the following kind:

Have you ever noticed
that when men write love poems
they're always about virgins or whores
or earth mothers?
How feint-hearted. (p. 29)

It is in this little book, through a small poem, that Dionne Brand writes about a new and a feminist aesthetic. And again the personal, the political, and the aesthetic work together, simultaneoulsy and inseparably. A thought on feminist aesthetics deserves to be fully quoted:

Since you've left me no descriptions
having used them all to describe me
or someone else I hardly recognize
I have no way of telling you
how long and wonderful your legs were;
Since you've covetously hoarded all the words
such as ''slender'' and ''sensuous'' and ''like a
young gazelle''
I have no way of letting you know
that I loved how you stood and how you walked,
and forgive my indelicacy,
your copulatory symmetry, your pensile beauty,
since you've massacred every intimate phrase

in a bloodletting of paternal epithets
like "fuck" and "rape," "cock" and "cunt,"
I cannot write you this epigram.

(pp. 28–29)

For centuries men have written love poems to women, coining words or phrases or appropriating the language in a way that leaves very little room for women's subjectivity. It seems in the end writing anti-poems to this tradition or making use of consistent irony has to become the feminist mode to undercut the tradition of a male-dominated aesthetic.

Dionne Brand is a poet who gives a great deal of thought to her own poetic projects as well as to poetry in general. Totally deploring "artiness," she aspires to write a kind of poetry that is "usable" in the business of everyday life, not one that is transcendant over it. It is not set apart as a special activity, but rather it is one of the many things that people do to struggle through life, against forces that make ordinary everyday life impossible. Poets are not prophets in her eyes; poets are not even the revolutionary ones, the vanguards of revolutions. But wherever there is a struggle, she would accept that poets, like others in society, have a role to play—in their own particular way. She is reluctant to write poetry that is divorced from struggles and confusions or detached from the texture of daily life. In the last analysis her writing of poetry is a form of struggle, and her poems a witness to the struggles of others. It is this that joins profound compassion with militancy in her poetic work.

CRITICAL RECEPTION

Although, as a recently published poet, Dionne Brand has not received much critical attention, her works are being noted by reviewers. In a lengthy review tracing the themes of *Winter Epigrams*, Edward Brathwaite asserts that with this collection of poetry by "our first major exile female poet . . . we can at last begin, with some confidence, to see and overstand [*sic*] what the voice of the Caribbean woman poet is telling us, doing for us" ("Quick Radicle of Green: To See and Overstand the Voice," 1983, p. 179). Linda Hale ("Brand Draws Poetry from Her Anger," 1984, p. 18) compares *Primitive Offensive* and *Winter Epigrams*, noting that both books are "heavy stuff," and are "characterized by an impassioned and revealing honesty." Alexa DeWiel also reviews *Primitive Offensive* and *Winter Epigrams* together, suggesting that "Brand's strength is in her crashing imagery" ("No Odes to Fried Eggs," 1984, p. 12). In his introduction to *Winter Epigrams*, Roger McTair traces the history of the epigram to illustrate how Brand makes use of it and concludes, "These epigrams are fun: sarcastic, lyrical and keen in their observations."

HONORS AND AWARDS

Dionne Brand received a Publisher's Grant and an Artist in the Schools Award from the Ontario Arts Council in 1978. She received a Canada Council Arts Grant in 1980 and another grant from the Ontario Arts Council in 1982.

BIBLIOGRAPHY

Works by Dionne Brand

'Fore Day Morning. Toronto: Khoisan Artists, 1978.
Earth Magic. Toronto: Kids Can Press, 1980.
Primitive Offensive. Toronto: Williams-Wallace, 1982.
Winter Epigrams & Epigrams to Ernesto Cardenal in Defense of Claudia. Toronto: Williams-Wallace, 1983.
Chronicles of the Hostile Sun. Toronto: Williams-Wallace, 1984.

Studies of Dionne Brand

Brathwaite, Edward. "Quick Radicle of Green: To See and Overstand the Voice." *Fuse* (November-December 1983), 179–83.
DeWiel, Alexa. "No Odes to Fried Eggs." *Broadside* (February 1984), 12.
Hale, Linda. "Brand Draws Poetry from Her Anger." *Kinesis* (June 1984), 18.
McTair, Roger. Introduction to *Winter Epigrams & Epigrams to Ernesto Cardenal in Defense of Claudia*. Toronto: Williams-Wallace, 1983.

MARK A. McWATT

Edward Kamau Brathwaite (1930–)

BIOGRAPHY

Lawson Edward Brathwaite was born in Bridgetown, Barbados, on May 11, 1930—the same year in which was born that other great West Indian poet, Derek Walcott. Brathwaite was educated at Harrison College and won an island scholarship to Cambridge University. Like so many other West Indian writers, he arrived in England in 1950; he read history at Pembroke College, Cambridge, graduating in 1953. He spent a further year at Cambridge doing a certificate in education, after which his wanderlust and the need for a job took him to Ghana, where he worked in the Ministry of Education for seven years (1955–62). As anyone familiar with his poems will appreciate, Brathwaite's years in West Africa constituted a crucial experience out of which many of the major themes and concerns of his poetry grew. He himself has told us something of what that experience meant to him: "Slowly, ever so slowly . . . I was coming to an awareness . . . of cultural wholeness, of the place of the individual within the tribe. Slowly, ever so slowly, I came to a sense of identification of myself with these people, my living diviners. I came to connect my history with theirs, the bridge of my mind was linking Atlantic and ancestor, homeland and heartland" ("Timehri," 1970, p. 38). In fact, the historical and geographical resonances at the end of this quotation are so pervasive in Brathwaite's work as to have become, almost, a feature of craft or technique itself: his very use of word and image constantly figures forth that transatlantic arc of concern, linking every Diasporic branch of the New World Black man with its African roots, every present dilemma with past hurts.

During his time of discovery and self-discovery in Ghana, Brathwaite organized a theater for children and wrote a number of plays, which were later published as *Four Plays for Primary Schools* (1964) and *Odale's Choice* (1967). The period from 1950 to 1962 was also that of Brathwaite's poetic apprenticeship, as Gordon Rohlehr points out, in that he published poems fairly regularly in Cambridge University journals and in West Indian periodicals such as *Bim* and *Kyk-Over-Al* (*Pathfinder*, 1981, p. 4). By the time he returned to the West Indies in 1962 to take up an appointment as a University of the West Indies extra-mural tutor in St. Lucia, he had also begun that now considerable and remarkable body of work consisting of his cultural and critical essays. These have appeared in a wide variety of periodicals over the years and have become some of the most authoritative and consistently positive commentaries on West Indian society and letters.

In 1963 Brathwaite was appointed lecturer in history at the Mona, Jamaica, campus of the University of the West Indies. During his first year there he completed his first book of poetry, *Rights of Passage*, which was published in 1967 as the first volume of a trilogy. *Masks* and *Islands* followed swiftly (1968, 1969), and the three were later published in a single volume as *The Arrivants: A New World Trilogy* in 1973. This remarkably rich and complex work firmly established Brathwaite's reputation, both in the West Indies—as one of a few major West Indian poets—and internationally—as "one of the finest living poets of the Western hemisphere" (*Sunday Times* review of *Islands*).

Brathwaite has since published four other major collections of poetry: *Other Exiles* (1975), *Black and Blues* (1976), *Mother Poem* (1977), and *Sun Poem* (1982). Apart from writing poetry, Brathwaite has sustained a distinguished academic career as a historian at Mona; one of the high points of this career came in 1983, when he was appointed professor of social and cultural history. His scholarly publications have included such important works as *The Folk Culture of Jamaican Slaves* (1969) and *The Development of Creole Society in Jamaica 1770–1820* (1971). In pursuit of his two careers—which he would certainly regard as complementary halves of a single career—Brathwaite has traveled widely in Europe, Africa, North America, and the Far East, reading his poetry and lecturing to university and other audiences. He is a superb reader of his own poetry, and his readings emphasize the social context of his poems as well as his understanding of and concern for the way language works. His experiments with Barbadian and other West Indian dialects ("Nation Language") in his writings have become another important facet of his career.

Another interesting biographical detail that is of importance in understanding Brathwaite's poetry is his interest in music, especially jazz. Rohlehr informs us (*Pathfinder*, pp. 4–5) that this interest stems from the poet's schoolboy days at Harrison's College and was probably strengthened by the disapproval expressed by the Barbadian cultural elite of the period toward music that seemed chaotic and iconoclastic. In any case, several commentators on Brathwaite's poetry have pointed out the way in which jazz and other musical forms of the Black communities of the Americas underlie and emphasize the rhythm, meaning, and mood of the poetry. "It is such music," Rohlehr tells us, "that provides Brathwaite with the basis for an aesthetic in *The Arrivants*" ("Metaphors of Making," in *Critical Approaches to West Indian Poetry*, ed. Erika Smilowitz and Roberta Knowles [Charlotte Amalie, St. Thomas: College of the Virgin Islands, 1981], p. 71). Brathwaite himself has published an article called "Jazz and the West Indian Novel" (*Bim* [1967]) in which he sets forth his theory concerning the relationship between jazz and the literature. It is necessary only to read *Rights of Passage* to discover the importance and the omnipresence of Black musical forms in Brathwaite's poetry, and indeed Rohlehr has provided an appendix to *Pathfinder* (pp. 333–40) detailing some of the background music to *Rights*.

It is probably important to note, in terms of appreciating the quality and importance of Brathwaite's influence in the field of West Indian letters, that he is a founding member of the Caribbean Artists movement and the main editor of its Savacou publications; he has also been, for a number of years, an editor of *Bim* magazine.

MAJOR WORKS AND THEMES

The three volumes of poetry that constitute *The Arrivants* remain Brathwaite's major achievement as a poet. In these works the reader encounters most of the author's major poetic themes and obsessions and many of the facets of his complex imagination and craft. Perhaps the foremost of these themes is that of history itself. Brathwaite's academic discipline is made to serve very well his interests and preoccupations as a poet; the reality one confronts in the poems, however clear or "raw," is always colored, as it were, by a sense of historical time, an overlay of reverberations from past events and personalities which cause in the reader a kind of mental or imaginative shift toward a historical perspective. From the first words of *Rights of Passage*, "Drum skin whip / lash" we are introduced to the history of the New World Black man: the African drum, of which the resounding skin is also the Black man's skin that feels the slave's lash, that is subjected to the cruel sun (*Arrivants*, p. 4). In fact, the first two poems of *Rights* trace, in a rapid, powerfully evocative way, the large historical movements of the Black man—across the continental desert to the western coast of Africa and then, after the fiery advent of the White slavers, the journey in chains across the sea to the New World.

These journeys are seen as part of the series of repetitive cycles of which the Black man's history is composed. Each journey echoes a past or an original journey, and each new suffering echoes the hardship and suffering of the past. Brathwaite returns to the transcontinental journey of the Black man in *Masks*, where it is treated in great detail: each way station carefully mentioned and gathered incrementally into the collective memory of the people. This original journey is the original cycle, to be echoed in the middle passage, in the journey from Southern plantation to Northern metropolis, in the return journey to the islands, in the journey back to Africa. In the end the journey almost becomes a strategy of survival, suggesting both homelessness and weariness on the one hand and, on the other, the constant need for a new beginning.

If *Rights* presents us with a kind of rhythmic circular dance through the historical journeys of the Black man, then *Masks* concentrates on the imaginative reenactment of the primordial journey across Africa—on the establishment of the civilization from which the New World Black man's slave ancestors were looted and transported. The volume demonstrates Brathwaite's keen sense of the spiritual profit of historical knowledge; the careful descriptions of ritual and of domestic arrangements, of living landscape and of human corruption, help achieve the paradoxically simultaneous sense of both spiritual amputation and spiritual consolation or healing. Brathwaite is seeking to develop the full, complex, and paradoxical awareness of the cultural privation and the cultural roots of the Black man through these cyclic processes of historical memory—which are themselves echoes in the cyclic processes of the poet's art.

Indeed, the notion of the cycle is itself of vital importance for Brathwaite, not merely as a structural ploy, but in terms of emphasizing the continuous possibility of a new beginning, a new hope. Of all other West Indian writers, only Wilson Harris presents as persistently positive a vision of the possibility of spiritual and social regeneration for West Indian man and society—in spite of their painful history. At the end of each volume of the trilogy there is the sense of a new beginning conveyed in an image of dawn: in *Rights* there is mention of "rain," "bird calls," a "green" opening, and a "walk in the morning" (p. 85); at the end of *Masks* there is the picture of "akoko the cock," crying in the morning (p. 157); and the final poem of *Islands* is "J'ouvert," which ends with the "walking" and "making" of "some- / thing torn / and new" (p. 270).

Although *Islands* seems to suggest a return to the West Indies, the island landscape is suffused with the presence of African deities and folk memories, as the very names of some of the individual poems suggest: "Legba," "Ogun," "Negus," "Vèvè," "Ancestors." The atmosphere of the poem is a kind of imaginative double-exposure, where the rich and haunting historical suggestiveness is superimposed upon the barren landscape and people; it is a creative juxtaposition of themes and perspectives that infinitely enriches the reader's sensitivity to, and awareness of, the total "myth" of West Indian man.

In keeping with the wide historical focus on journeys and civilizations, there is, in Brathwaite's poetry, no private, individual voice (agonized or otherwise) as tends to be found in brooding domination in the poems of, say, Derek Walcott. Brathwaite speaks with a communal voice—the voice of the tribe or of a public representative of some aspect of the Black man's consciousness or struggle. For this reason the main human figures in the trilogy tend to be archetypal ones. The first archetype we meet is Uncle Tom: hat in hand, he is, Brathwaite says, the ''father / founder / flounderer'' (p. 15), the last repository of African memory in the New World, worn into subservience by his cruel history and floundering, incapable of communicating his spiritual heritage to his sons, who are impatient with his attitude of submission to the White man. Brathwaite treats Tom very sympathetically precisely because he intends the reader to see the whole historical picture—that Tom's submission is a strategem of survival, not just personal survival, but survival of Black consciousness in a larger cultural sense. Tom's sons do not survive as a people, only as individuals, fragments. Their last chance for unity and community is discarded with Tom.

We see Tom's sons wandering away from the land toward the cities, where they are transformed into that other archetype, the ''spades.'' Harsh and selfish, the ''spade'' defines himself and governs his actions in accordance with the White man's racial anxieties and in complete ignorance of the African past. Ostentatious and sexually aggressive, the zoot-suited ''spade'' shuffles through an urban demimonde of cheap hotels, seedy nightclubs, and petty crime—his mind fixed desperately on the glamor of his urban ''freedom'' rather than on the spiritual emptiness of his life. Brathwaite paints all this—figure and ground—with a few swift, vigorous strokes (pp. 37–41); he does not dwell on the ''spade'' as individual, merely as another archetypal mask of the Black man.

Other, lesser, representative figures in *The Arrivants*—hardly meriting the term *archetypes*, perhaps, but emphasizing nevertheless the essential features and purpose of Brathwaite's characterization—would include the cold, clear-eyed White slaver (p. 11), the tourist ''from the frozen nawth'' (p. 45) who invades the Caribbean islands, ''Brother Man the Rasta / man'' (p. 42), the emigrants ''with their cardboard grips'' (p. 51), crowding the wharfs and train stations of Northern cities, the West Indian politician ''with dirty hands'' (p. 60). All of these conspire, as it were, to present the total picture of the Black man of the Diaspora—the self-serving or lost fragments of what was once a whole community. They emphasize Brathwaite's concern with large, impersonal movements and forces rather than with an examination of the individual mind and motivation.

Other figures in the trilogy represent a folk presence, the ordinary man or woman of the village who has a personal name but who functions nevertheless as a voice—or part of a chorus of voices—representing the features of a folk culture or exemplifying a prominent attitude or institution in the community. The poem ''The Dust'' in *Rights* presents us with such a group: the women, Miss Evvy, Miss Maisie, Miss Olive, and Miss Maud (p. 62), who, in lively choric fashion, discuss the rhythms that govern their lives, their achievements, struggles, and anxieties. The poem is a splendid vignette of fairly narrowly focused concern in a work that treats for the most part of large historical movements and entire civilizations. These characters therefore provide a sense of balance and comic relief, as they speak their concerns in Barbadian dialect. Other such folk figures would include Tizzic and Francina from *Islands*.

Another important theme or motif in *The Arrivants* is that of music. Music, especially jazz, is a structural as well as a thematic device in the trilogy. We find there the music of the Black man from North America and the West Indies, sometimes mentioned in the titles of individual poems: "Work Song and Blues," "The Twist," "Limbo," "Calypso"—and there are titles that suggest popular songs, like "Wings of a Dove." Again, the very breadth of Brathwaite's musical references is intended to evoke the total experience of the Diaspora, to surround a people with the sound and the sense of themselves.

In 1975, when *Other Exiles* appeared, it was something of an anticlimax. It is not a structurally and thematically unified work like the trilogy, but more of a traditional "collection" of poems. It appears to contain Brathwaite's "other" poems that had accumulated over time and that were not part of *The Arrivants.* Although some of these poems are interesting and important in terms of demonstrating different emphases and concerns on Brathwaite's part, the volume on the whole has received less critical attention than most of his other work. The subsequent volume, *Black and Blues*, was Brathwaite's prize-winning entry in the Cuban Casa de las Americas poetry competition in 1975. Most of the poems seem to be grounded in Brathwaite's Jamaican experience, more specifically his experience of the Rastafarian subculture ("we burnin babylone," p. 20) and of the restlessness and violence of the urban slum areas. There is lots of violent and demonic imagery, skulls and rats, fire, corruption, and suffering. Rohlehr says of this volume that it "intensified Brathwaite's focus on the contemporary diasporan person in the Caribbean and America. . . . One perceives an emerging secular eschatology in which historical process increasingly creates the possibility of apocalypse" ("Megalleons of Light," 1983, p. 81).

When *Mother Poem* appeared in 1977, it became apparent that it was a major poetic achievement. Brathwaite had turned away from the concerns of *Black and Blues*, or rather had sought to balance those concerns with the historical/autobiographical evocation of his homeland. As he says in his preface to the volume: "This poem is about porus limestone, my mother, Barbados." The figure of the mother, which dominates the poem, is a considerable imaginative achievement: she is a protean figure, a fusion of geographic/geologic as well as human reality—a highly functional thematic and unifying device in the poem. Her geographic imagery with its emphasis on dry, barren land, stone and boulder, shrunken watercourses, sea and canefield, powerfully identifies her with the physical landscape of Barbados; but at the same time she is a mother of flesh and tears as well. She struggles to survive, to raise and nourish her children, to comfort and "contain" her history-crippled man.

Echoing some of the concerns of the poem "The Cracked Mother" from *Islands*, the mother here is seen in several guises: at times she is more than mother, she becomes the embodiment of "woman" as Brathwaite portrays her several strategies for keeping "body and soul seam together" (p. 35), abandoned by her men, whether husband, lover, or children. These guises of the woman include the shop or store worker (a function which allows Brathwaite to castigate the soulless and predatory mercantilism of Barbadian commercial institutions), seamstress, street-vendor, commercial typist, mistress, and childbearer to some casually interested man (pp. 34–44).

Mother Poem also returns to several of Brathwaite's themes from *The Arrivants*: there is the ironic view of religion as part of the apparatus of oppression and materialist exploitations—there is a fine parody of the Twenty-third Psalm ("Sam Lord," p. 8); there is the sense of a historical time superimposed on the events and setting of the poem—the mother's husband had slaved for the merchant for 300 years ("Bell," p. 14); and we find that familiar concern, at the end of the poem, with the renewal or rebirth of the historical cycle and of the mother herself, as fresh water once again begins to flow like a benediction in her worn watercourses to the sea.

Sun Poem, published in 1982, is Brathwaite's most recent volume of poetry. It is a kind of companion volume to *Mother Poem*, and like *Mother Poem* it is largely autobiographical. In *Sun Poem* Brathwaite's Barbadian world is examined from a male perspective, and the poet explores the cycle of masculine existence from the games and dreams of boyhood through the rites of adolescence, sexual initiation, manhood, marriage, fatherhood, and death. In all this the thematic focal point is the external son-ship of man, who is son of the mother, the motherland, the mother-history, performing and embodying in his rise, zenith, decline, and disappearance, an enactment of the fortunes and misfortunes of his people, the private and public hurts, the privilege and folly of all manhood. As we have seen, Brathwaite's poetry very seldom remains on the personal or individual level. Here, by identifying the man's cycle of existence with the heavenly cycle of the sun, Brathwaite universalizes the autobiographical details and avails himself of a cosmic imagery of light and color which transfigures character, event, and situation and shifts the authority and effect of the poem from the autobiographical to the archetypal.

In this regard it is significant that the central character of the poem is given the name Adam and is thus meant to represent the first and the universal man, as well as the individual autobiographical subject. If character and event always manage to suggest the archetypal, the poem's setting is almost always easily identifiable as Barbados. In fact, the poem owes much of the richness of its texture to the hauntingly precise evocation of scenes and situations that are specifically Barbadian. The beach, for example, where the boys play and fight and rehearse the postures of manhood is identified as Brown's Beach. Brown's Beach turns out to be a microcosm of the society, with its social distinctions between beach-boys and land-boys and with Mr. Queen, the "big-able Pilot," who is lord of the beach and sends his man to chase the boys off his boat. Brathwaite even distinguishes between the expert dives of the fleeing beach-boys, who make the water go "chow," and the frantic belly-flops of the land-boys, who make the water go "wham" (p. 12). Such distinctions and hierarchies are to be found everywhere and are simultaneous with, and equally as important as, the sensual power of the language that makes the reader actually feel the contact of flesh and water in these beach scenes.

The poet is obviously reliving experiences that were powerfully felt, and this density of experience and sensation is often better served by the several passages of poetic prose in the volume, passages that are governed by a rich associative rhythm appropriate to the processes of memory.

The idyllic nature of boyhood experience is clearly communicated in these sections of the poem. Adam is "trailing clouds of glory" like the archetypal innocent child that we find in the poetry of Vaughan, Traherne, Blake (in the "Songs of Innocence"), and Wordsworth. Brathwaite achieves this suggestion largely through effects of light. There is a supernatural quality in the repeatedly mentioned "shower of green light" around the gooseberry tree where Adam plays with his sister in the yard, and, early in the poem, the young Adam has just moved into town from the country and awakens to light in a very special sense as it invades his bedroom from the street outside. Adam and the poet play with and meditate upon this light for more than sixty lines (p. 7). The beach scenes are also bathed in an almost excessive brilliance, as Adam explores the subaqueous light as he dives toward the white sand (p. 13).

But this light has its sinister aspect as well, as it is also associated with Batto, the beach bully and a type of the Biblical Lucifer, who also trails light behind him as he plummets toward darkness (we're told that Batto has already spent time in Dodds—a juvenile correctional institution—for assaulting another child and is even looking forward to going to "a proper prison" when he becomes a man). It is Batto who ambushes Adam as he rises from his dive, and the underwater struggle that ensues is a struggle to belong, a rite of adolescence (p. 18). Childhood is also evoked in these sections of the poem through references to childhood games and rhymes; we find lines from "Twinkle, twinkle little star" and "Humpty Dumpty" woven into the poem, and the whole of the jingle that begins: "Mosquito one, mosquito two, mosquito jump on the ole man shoe." The fragile, ephemeral nature of boyhood is perhaps best symbolized by the "bubble." There are several references to bubbles in the poem: the bubbles of breath underwater; the soap bubbles that are perfect little worlds of light and color, until they burst; the bubble that Adam foolishly tries to blow in the sea as a source of air for his long dives (pp. 25–29). The suggestiveness of the bubble is taken up again later in the poem when the bubble becomes that other childhood toy, the balloon: Brathwaite speaks of Adam's expectation "blown up like a balloon" as he waits for the bank holiday Sunday School excursion to Cattle Wash (pp. 39–40).

At this point Brathwaite lets us know that Adam is traveling to the island's wilder shore, its untamed shore of origins, where, as we discover later, the link with Africa and the slave past is closer to the surface. Adam, then, travels backward in time simultaneously as he travels forward in time in terms of knowledge, experience, and discovery—a dual movement that is perhaps suggested in Adam's wild panic that the bus which is groaning steadily upward will slip back down "Hearse Hill" into the dark terrors of death and the past (p. 44).

It is only after the trip to the east coast that we get—in "Noom"—the history of the landing of slaves, and, just as the "beach boys" were the source of Adam's acquisition of the physical strength and courage to face his world, so the "Cattlewash boys" are the suggested source of a more spiritual knowledge connected with his African origin; they tell him about the Loa, Legba, coming out of the sea (p. 51). It is a wonderful breathless story of the past and of the spiritual legacy of Africa, and it is at the central turning point of the poem, of Adam's life and (Noom) of the sun's journey across the inverted bowl of the heavens. Adam is an innocent boy no longer—his bubble/balloon has burst. The story of Bussa's slave rebellion is superimposed upon the autobiographical details of the poem, importing the aspects of suffering, violence, and pain, confirming for the reader the shift to the world of adult experience. Scatological references proliferate toward the end of "Noom," as the persona is wrapped around with suggestions of wars and rebellions, of dust and decay, and he is literally mired in his own excrement as he contemplates a pool of his own urine "hot / by me toe" (p. 59). This emphasizes the sense of fear connected with the first positive act after a life of submission and shelter; Adam, inhabiting the persona of Bussa, undergoes a rude awakening into the terrors of his Barbadian "manscape."

The poem returns to the domestic sphere with several versions of fatherhood in "Clips." The portraits are all unflattering, negative, and symptomatic of this phase of the son/sun's decline. The fathers, whether materialistic, religious, or Rasta, are all portrayed as irresponsible toward their wives/women and toward their children, who do not fail to disappoint them, who supplant them in their mothers' hearts, and who swim casually and bewilderingly beyond their control and even beyond their recognition (pp. 67–68).

This portrait of fatherhood casts its gloom over the subsequent scene of courtship and seduction between Adam and Esse. It is a scene that takes place in and around a dunks tree, nicely echoing and balancing the earlier childhood scene with Adam and his sister under the gooseberry tree. The green light of innocence is conspicuously missing in the later scene—indeed, the dunks tree has thorns that threaten the girl, and there is rather the suggestion of ripeness in the dunks they eat. There are overtones of the Fall in Eden, complete with the woman proffering fruit, the man eating, and the subsequent emphasis upon a shameful sexuality—a sexuality which is rendered, significantly, in an extended mechanical image about starting and driving a lorry. The serious potential consequences of their sexual playfulness overshadow the occasion—"when a accident come and the lorry dey pun de dump heap" (p. 79)—and firmly emphasizes the atmosphere of adult experience rather than childhood innocence in this section of the poem. The lightness of tone and language in this scene (including Esse's lisp) tugs against the serious, even lugubrious import of the actions and the symbolism, maintaining that creative duality that we have seen operating throughout the poem—the simultaneously upward/downward, forward/backward movement of the sun/son.

Sun Poem ends with the funeral of Adam's grandfather in the house in the country that is peopled with Adam's earliest memories; birth and death conjoin in his mind, and he glimpses the serial masks or mirrors of his manhood in his father and grandfather. He sees that his father too is made aware of this decline toward death, and the endless cycle of sun-ship and fatherhood is exposed (p. 93). Typical of Brathwaite, this ending (of the grandfather's life and of the poem) is also a beginning, as he insists once more upon that circle or cycle that is such a familiar structural ploy in his poetry. The poem retrieves the upbeat by reference to the recreation of light, to the new (renewed) *son* in a section that bears that name, in which a new sun and new "thrilldren" are rising at the very end (p. 97).

CRITICAL RECEPTION

Probably the most important feature of the critical reception of Brathwaite's poetry has been a long literary controversy concerning the nature and purpose of his art and its relationship to West Indian man and society. The initial uneasiness, felt by some West Indian commentators, about Brathwaite's poetry, had to do with their perception of a sinister aspect to the motive and meaning behind its rhythm and power. Given the very historical processes that Brathwaite examines so thoroughly in *The Arrivants*, it was perhaps inevitable that he should be criticized, on ethnic and ideological grounds, for what these critics considered to be an "exclusive" emphasis upon African origin and culture. This was of course not new, but never had it been presented in poetry of such sweep and hypnotic power—in a sense their objections are a tribute to the poet's consummate craftsmanship.

It was also inevitable that the other major West Indian poet, Derek Walcott, should be dragged into the controversy as a countervailing force or influence. By 1971, when Patricia Ismond published her seminal article "Walcott versus Brathwaite," the two camps had already been formed and the battle lines drawn. Ismond is to be applauded for defining the controversy with courage, candor, and incisiveness, and in fact her polemic (favoring Walcott over Brathwaite) turned out to be a lot more fruitful than it was mischievous. There is a sense, from the perspective of the 1980s, in which both the controversy and Ismond's article are creatures of the anxieties of a particular era, a specific phase of the intellectual life of the community. After recent events in Jamaica and Grenada, these particular aspects of the debate, even in strictly literary circles, loom a lot less large.

Nevertheless, a survey of the critical response to Brathwaite's poetry does show how many firmly opposing positions were held at the time. Ismond herself saw Brathwaite's efforts to rehabilitate the spiritual life of the Black man as entirely worthwhile, but she objected to such things as the gratuitous (as she saw it) replacement of familiar Western literary symbols with obscure African ones; she speaks of Brathwaite's preoccupation with "an African Twilight of the gods" (p. 61) and bristles at the suggestions of some critics—unmentioned, but probably including Anne Walmsley ("Dimensions of Song," *Bim* 13 [July-

December 1970], 152–67)—that Brathwaite was championing the causes of the West Indian, while Walcott was indulging his private visions and clinging slavishly to the trappings of a Western literary tradition. Edward Baugh (Review of *Masks*, in *Bim* 12 [July-December 1968], 209–11) and Kenneth Ramchand (*Introduction to the Study of West Indian Literature*, 1976) seem to favor Walcott over Brathwaite in the sum of their critical remarks, while on the other hand Samuel Asein (''The Concept of Form: A Study of Some Ancestral Elements in Brathwaite's Trilogy,'' 1971), Rohlehr, in his reviews of the individual volumes of the trilogy, and Maureen Warner-Lewis (''Odomankoma Kyarema Se,'' 1973) sought not so much to champion the ''cause'' of Brathwaite as to place his work within a certain social and philosophical perspective, to elucidate the less familiar aspects and references of the poems, and to present the total vision of Black consciousness and awakening that the poet strove to create.

One aspect of the debate, and one that persists, is in terms of form and poetics. Rohlehr's remarks about the influence of jazz and many other forms of music upon the ''shape'' of Brathwaite's poetry (*Pathfinder*) is a counterpoint to Kenneth Ramchand's humorous/mischievous salvoes against what he considers the fortuity of form and rhythm in certain passages of the poetry and their tenuous relationship to the poem's meaning (Ramchand, 1976, pp. 134–35). The debate itself, according to Lloyd Brown, is ''understandable since there has been a tendency to describe [the two poets] in exclusive terms—Walcott as the Western-oriented craftsman and individualist and Brathwaite as the epic poet and master seer of the black diaspora'' (*West Indian Poetry*, 1978, p. 139). Brown himself sees the two poets as largely similar in concern and in social and ethnic consciousness, and indeed several other critics treat each of the two poets on his own terms and appreciate the contribution of each toward an understanding of West Indian realities.

Maureen Warner-Lewis's careful work on *Masks* (*Notes to Masks*, 1977) is of great value and importance as an aid to understanding one of the less readily ''available'' areas of Brathwaite's poetry, but by far the most important critical commentary on Brathwaite's poetry is Gordon Rohlehr's *Pathfinder*. It is at once a close reading, a meticulous exegesis of the poems in *The Arrivants*, as well as an impressively informed commentary on the social and cultural context of the poems and on the influences and echoes embodied in them. As the other sections of this article demonstrate, Rohlehr's is an indispensable analysis of Brathwaite's poetic consciousness and craftsmanship.

HONORS AND AWARDS

Among Brathwaite's many honors and awards are the following: Poetry Book Society Recommend for *Rights of Passage*, 1967; Hampstead Arts Festival Poetry Prize, United Kingdom, 1967; Arts Council of Great Britain Bursary, 1971; Cholmondeley Award, 1970; Guggenheim Foundation Fellowship, 1971; Bussa Award, 1973; and the Casa de las Americas poetry prize for *Black and Blues*, 1976.

BIBLIOGRAPHY

Works by Edward Brathwaite

"The Controversial Tree of Time." *Bim* 8 (January-June 1960), 104–14.

"Roots." *Bim* 10 (July-December 1963), 10–21.

Four Plays for Primary Schools. London: Longman, 1964.

Odale's Choice. London: Evans, 1967.

"*Kyk-over-al* and the Radicals." *New World Quarterly* [Guyana Independence Issue] (1966), 55–57.

"Jazz and the West Indian Novel." *Bim* 11 (January-June 1967), 275–84; pt. 2: *Bim* 12 (July-December 1967), 39–51; pt. 3: *Bim* 12 (January-June 1968), 115–26.

Rights of Passage. London: Oxford University Press, 1967.

Masks. London: Oxford University Press, 1968.

Islands. London: Oxford University Press, 1969.

"Caribbean Critics." *Critical Quarterly* 11 (Autumn 1969), 268–76.

"Timehri." *Savacou* 2 (September 1970), 35–44.

Folk Culture of the Slaves in Jamaica. London: New Beacon Books, 1970.

The Development of Creole Society in Jamaica 1770–1820. London: Oxford University Press, 1971.

The Arrivants: A New World Trilogy. London: Oxford University Press, 1973.

"The African Presence in Caribbean Literature." *Daedalus* 103 (Spring 1974), 73–109.

Contradictory Omens: Cultural Diversity and Integration in the Caribbean. Mona, Kingston, Jamaica: Savacou, 1974.

Other Exiles. London: Oxford University Press, 1975.

Black and Blues. Cuba: Casa de las Americas, 1976.

Mother Poem. London: Oxford University Press, 1977.

"The Love Axe/1: Developing a Caribbean Aesthetic, 1962–1974." *Bim* 16 (June 1977), 53–65; pt. 2: *Bim* 17 (December 1977) 100–06; pt. 3: *Bim* 17 (June 1978), 181–92.

Sun Poem. London: Oxford University Press, 1982.

Third World Poems. London: Longman, 1983.

"Kumina—The Spirit of African Survival." *Jamaica Journal*, no. 42, pp. 45–63.

Studies of Edward Brathwaite

Asein, Samuel. "The Concept of Form: A Study of Some Ancestral Elements in Brathwaite's Trilogy." *ASAWI Bulletin* (December 1971), 9–34.

Brown, Lloyd. "The Cyclical Vision of Edward Brathwaite." In *West Indian Poetry*. Boston: Twayne, 1978, pp. 139–58.

D'Costa, Jean. "The Poetry of Edward Brathwaite." *Jamaica Journal* 2 (September 1968), 24–28.

Grant, Damian. "Emerging Image: The Poetry of Edward Brathwaite." *Critical Quarterly* 12 (Summer 1970), 186–92.

Ismond, Pat. "Walcott Versus Brathwaite." *Caribbean Quarterly* 17 (September-December 1971), 54–71.

Mackey, N. "Edward Brathwaite's New World Trilogy." *Caliban* 3 (Spring-Summer 1979), 58–88.

Maxwell, Marina. "The Awakening of the Drum: A Review of Masks." *New World Quarterly* (Guyana) 5 (1971), 39–45.

Morris, Mervyn. "This Broken Ground: Edward Brathwaite's Trilogy of Poems." *New World Quarterly* 23 (June-September 1977), 91–103.

Pollard, Velma. "The Dust—A Tribute to the Folk." *Caribbean Quarterly* 26 (March-June 1980), 41–48.

Ramchand, Kenneth. "Edward Brathwaite." In *An Introduction to the Study of West Indian Literature*. Kingston: Nelson Caribbean, 1976, pp. 127–42.

Risden, Winnifred. "Masks: Edward Brathwaite." *Caribbean Quarterly* 14 (March-June 1968), 145–47.

Rohlehr, Gordon. "The Historian as Poet." *The Literary Half-Yearly* 11 (July 1970), 171–78. Reprinted as "Islands: A Review." *Caribbean Quarterly* 16 (December 1970), 29–35.

———. "Islands." *Caribbean Studies* 10 (January 1971), 173–202.

———. "Megalleons of Light: Edward Brathwaite's *Sun Poem*." *Jamaica Journal* 16 (1983), 81–87.

———. *Pathfinder*. Port of Spain: Author, 1981.

Senenu, K. E. "Brathwaite's Song of Dispossession." *Universitas* 1 (March 1969), 59–63.

Walcott, Derek. "Tribal-Flutes: Review of *Rights of Passage*."*Sunday Guardian Magazine* (Trinidad), March 19, 1967.

Warner-Lewis, Maureen. *Notes to Masks*. Benin City: Ethiope, 1977.

———. "Odomankoma Kyerema Se." *Caribbean Quarterly* 19 (June 1973), 51–99.

See also General Bibliography: Allis, Baugh (1971, 1976), Griffiths, Herdeck, Hughes, King, and Moore.

EVELYN O'CALLAGHAN

Erna Brodber (1940–)

BIOGRAPHY

On April 20, 1940, Erna May Brodber was born in the village of Woodside, St. Mary, Jamaica, to Ernest Brodber, a farmer, and his wife Lucy, a teacher at Woodside Elementary School, which Erna subsequently attended. Both parents were very involved in the local community—her father believed in "socialism" in the truest sense of the word and was president of various societies as well as being instrumental in the founding of a community center. Brodber's sense of affiliation with a particular community was strengthened by the obvious love of the countryside which comes across in her fiction. She remembers sitting for hours in a natural grotto near the school simply watching the ferns and insects and listening to the birds (interview with Evelyn O'Callaghan, Kingston, Jamaica, December 29, 1983). Another early influence was the active cultural life at home. Her parents read together, and her father told stories, organized plays, and recited poetry whenever the mood took him. Their home was a place of books and music and constant activity.

Brodber attended Excelsior High School in Kingston, living with relatives and returning to the country at every opportunity. She graduated in 1958 and worked for a time in the civil service and then as a teacher in Montego Bay. She subsequently won a government exhibition to University College of the West Indies (now University of the West Indies, but at the time affiliated to the University of London). She graduated in 1963 with an honors B.A. in history and was awarded a UWI postgraduate scholarship but first worked for a year in Trinidad as head of history, St. Augustine High School for Girls.

In 1964, Brodber returned to Jamaica and served as a children's officer with the Ministry of Youth and Community Development before registering for her master's degree in sociology. Her first choice had been the field of social work, but this was not possible according to the terms of the scholarship, and so she settled for sociology, sitting in on social work classes whenever possible. The project for her master's thesis on the socialization of Jamaican children entailed training in social psychology, which she obtained as a partial student at McGill University in Canada. She later won a Ford Foundation pre-doctoral scholarship and set off for the University of Washington in 1967. There she was able to study child psychology and found the practical experience in clinics and therapy sessions invaluable for both her own growing process and the illuminating "awareness of the insides of peoples' heads." In addition, the Black Power struggle and the emerging Women's Liberation movement made America in the late 1960s an exciting place to be.

But Brodber was determined to come home, and in the fall of 1968 she joined the Department of Sociology, UWI, as a research assistant, receiving her M.Sc. in sociology the same year. The homecoming was not an easy one. Ill-health, financial constraints, and above all an adjustment to the Kingston life she had never really been a part of made for a depressing time. The social and political climate seemed years behind the United States—only the stirrings of the Black Power movement were beginning to be felt on the Jamaican campus. "Also, I had an afro, and it was too early for afro in Jamaica," she observes; "coming back to settle in Jamaica, it hadn't struck me that everybody *wasn't* black, or everybody wasn't *conscious* of what that meant. So when I came home I had to deal with it [the awareness of Black consciousness] for the first time, as I hadn't been forced to in America."

Nevertheless, she persevered and continued at UWI as a lecturer in sociology, taking a year off for research as a supernumary fellow in the Institute of Social and Economic Research (ISER) from 1972 to 1973. She also took part in radio and theater drama and in 1972 joined the cast of the popular revue *8 O'Clock Jamaica Time*, which ran for six weeks, five nights a week. In the summer of 1973 she traveled to the University of Michigan (Ann Arbor) as visiting scholar to the Summer School of Social Research.

It was during the early 1970s that Brodber began to write. One catalyst was the Barbadian poet and historian Edward Brathwaite, and especially his poem *Rights of Passage* (1967). Another was Lloyd Best, Trinidadian economist and founder of the Tapia House movement. And, of course, there were her students. She explains that she was then trying to clarify her thoughts on issues such as Black Power, Women's Liberation, and male/female relations, as part of her teaching: "Where I was, teaching students Human Growth and Development, I had to grapple with all these things—and I had to write them out—and that's how I started writing *Jane and Louisa*" (1980).

In 1974 Brodber joined the staff of ISER and began work on a massive project, now being prepared for publication as *A History of the Second Generation of Freemen in Jamaica, 1907–1944*. Research involved many hours of conversation with older people throughout Jamaica, whose valuable history she felt she owed it to them to document. She was awarded an Association of Commonwealth Universities staff fellowship in 1980, and 1981 found her a visiting fellow at the School of African and Asian Studies, University of Sussex, investigating through archival sources the attitude of the British administration to the Black population of Jamaica in the early 20th century. She left ISER in 1983 and is at present a free-lance writer and researcher, completing her Ph.D. thesis in history at UWI and preparing other projects for publication.

Brodber has been a member of Twelve Tribes of Israel, a Rastafarian sect, since 1976. She has traveled widely within the Caribbean, the United States, Canada, Britain, and Africa and presently lives in Kingston.

MAJOR WORKS AND THEMES

Erna Brodber has, in a sense, *always* been a creative writer. Before starting secondary school, she had already earned the grand total of seventeen shillings and sixpence in prize money for three short stories, published in the children's section of the Jamaican paper, *The Weekly Times*. Since then, she has been involved with theater, had poetry and short stories published in Caribbean journals, and written one acclaimed novel.

But until recently she was perhaps better known as a budding historian and a respected sociologist, with extensive publications in these fields. Brodber's intellectual research exerts a vital influence on her fictional work. She explains that her sociology and her fiction are inextricably linked; though formerly the fiction helped to refine and clarify concepts for her sociohistorical research, she now feels it is important in its own right.

Because of this link, it is useful to examine her creative writing from the point of view of themes also explored in some of her academic publications. One such is her concern with oral history and the importance of traditional wisdom. In "Oral Sources and the Creation of a Social History of the Caribbean" (1983), Brodber suggests that though there may be little written history of the cultural life of the subordinate (Black) sector of the West Indian population during the slavery/emancipation period, this history exists—in the work patterns, dances, dreams, songs, stories, and memories of Jamaicans who lived through those times and passed the history on. Analysis of these cultural phenomena of the "underclass" can be useful in the field of social history.

The creative writer in the West Indies also turns to social history, imaginatively reconstructing the perceptions of *people* to historically documented events, as in V. S. Reid's *New Day* (1949), Orlando Patterson's *Die the Long Day* (1972), and Edward Brathwaite's *Rights of Passage* (1971). The social historian, like the writer, must extend research boundaries to include oral history, thus tapping a long neglected source. This Brodber herself has done, and the result makes fascinating reading. ''Life in Jamaica in the Early Twentieth Century: 90 Oral Accounts'' (1980) uses the technique of the ''life-history interview'' to compile a sociohistorical profile of the devices traditionally used by Jamaicans for coping with life situations. Brodber maintains that an understanding of these survival patterns is necessary for successful design and implementation of developmental projects.

The motive for such research is a concern with the community and communal wisdom, and this interest also informs her award-winning short story ''Rosa'' (1975). Set in a tiny Jamaican district ''where everybody is related by blood and share more or less the same surname'' (p. 2), it tells simply of Zackie Menzie's decision to remain committed to communal peasant ways rather than choose the path of modernization and upward social mobility. The catalyst for his decision is Rosa, who comes to stay after Zackie's deceased grandfather has instructed her in a dream to ''tek care of Zackie'' (p. 4).

Under her tutelage Zackie learns the value of peasant ways. Committed to the land as his ancestors were, rearing the child of another as he and Rosa had been reared, worshipping in the Creolized Baptist faith of his community, Zackie is at peace with himself and respected by his neighbors. There is a pride and dignity in his life that makes it ''different-but-equal'' to that of his cousins, who ''had become big fellows talking with Ministry officers and going to farmer's meetings'' (p. 2). The sense of a strong, continuing peasant way of life, connected with and sanctioned by those who have gone before, is the dominant impression left by the story.

The opening of *Jane and Louisa Will Soon Come Home* situates the reader in the same type of close-knit rural community, isolated but secure. ''Mountains ring us round and cover us, banana leaves shelter us and sustain us'' (p. 9). Here also is the extended family of small farmers, and here also ''everybody is related,'' with the life of one impinging upon the lives of others. The community is an entity in itself and, much like the ''chorus of people in the lane'' in Roger Mais's *Brother Man* (1954), it speaks with one tongue: ''the voice belongs to the family group dead and alive'' (p. 12). That the dead ancestors are as vital a part of the community as the living is made clear early in the novel by the comparison of the White plantocracy's dead, safely ''tombed and harmless'' with the Black peasant dead, imaged in terms of continual growth and influence on the living: ''Our dead and living are shrouded together under zinc, sweet potato slips and thatch. Step warily—one body raises itself into a mountain of bodies which overtop to form a pit or a shelter for you'' (p. 12). Community and communal ancestors, then, have power that can be positive (''a shelter'') or negative (''a pit'') for the individual.

The central character, Nellie, whose sense of self has been fragmented by a combination of societal pressures, learns to tap the community's power for psychic healing—but only through communication with and reconstruction of the communal ancestry. It is significant that it is Miss Elsada's grandson Baba, a figure from Nellie's past, who helps to initiate the process. She learns that to know and value the self it is necessary to know and value *all* her communal "roots": "I saw that if I knew all my kin . . . I could no longer roam as a stranger; that I had to know them to know what I was about . . . the black and squat, the thin and wizened, all of them" (p. 80).

Brodber makes it clear that reconnection with the past through the community is as necessary for the society as it is for the individual: "I'm making the same claim for the history of the nation—that you have to go back and look at it, no matter how distressing, no matter how dirty, no matter how your myths have to be destroyed, you still have to go back and look at it. And when you finish, you have to decide whether you're going to live with it, whether you're going to forget it, or—hopefully—you say, well it's so it go and let me do my piece and claim it" (Interview with Evelyn O'Callaghan, Kingston, Jamaica, April 7, 1982).

Brodber's sociological writings are also concerned with Caribbean women and their relationships with men. In "Afro-Jamaican Women and their Men" (in press), oral history is again used as the research method for surveying male–female relations as they affected Black, working-class women in all areas of their lives from the late 1800s to the 1950s. These women emerge as strong, independent, and often economically self-sufficient after acquiring initial capital or land. In striking contrast to this reality are the stereotyped images of women appearing in the media during the same period, documented in Brodber's *Perceptions of Caribbean Women: Towards a Documentation of Stereotypes*. For the working-class woman, stereotypes such as "Excellent Ellen" and "Household Pearl"—the accomplished middle-class wife and mother, the decorative yet resourceful lady—are too remote to inspire behavior modification. But as Merle Hodge points out in her introduction to the document, such images can and do become internalized as "right," negatively affecting the Caribbean woman's assessment of her own worth (p. xiii).

Jane and Louisa also tackles the problem of real and ideal images of Caribbean womanhood as contradictory role models available to the central character. The conflict for Nellie begins with puberty, the approach of "it," which Brodber explains as referring to "the whole thing of womanhood, the whole frightening magic of woman-ness" (interview, 1982). Sexual maturation involves a change in the way Nellie is perceived by others, a change to be ashamed of: "Have you ever seen a new sucker trying to grow out of a rotten banana root? My whole chest was that rotten banana root and there were two suckers" (p. 119). Sexuality is not "bounty" but something to be hidden "under a bushel or else it will shame you" (p. 24).

This shame is due to the negative image of the womb as scrap heap, personified in the mysterious Cousins B., Letitia and Teena, fallen women who had simply "dropped" their unplanned, unwanted, "nameless pointless children" and "vanished into the crowd" (pp. 142–43). Brodber explains that "the womb has the capacity that people can just fling something up there that they don't intend to retrieve . . . which is what you do with a scrap-heap'' (interview, 1982). These women and their men abused the source of female creativity (the womb), thus sullying their sexuality and creating a negative image of woman for Nellie.

Feeling the ''need to be cleansed'' of this shameful sexuality, she is entrusted to the care of Aunt Becca, another model of womanhood—educated, brown, and superior—who has achieved middle-class respectability only at the terrible price of aborting her illegitimate child. Her advice is to avoid men altogether: ''These people will drag you down child . . . save yourself lest you turn woman before your time'' (pp. 16–17). Against this ideal of repression is set the pressure toward sexual liberation at the university Nellie attends: ''But when you live on a compound with eight hundred men and women, they press you, Auntie. Everywhere; trying to spoil your life. What can you do?'' (p. 18)

Caught between the two extremes of woman as slut and woman as virgin, extremes that are internalized and described in terms of conflicting voices impinging on her consciousness, Nellie is psychologically traumatized. Her own sexual initiation, bowing to the pressure to be normal—''now you have a man, you'll be like everybody else'' (p. 28)—is clouded by shame (her mother's face ''pained with disgust'') and dominated by revolting phallic imagery: ''One long nasty snail, curling up, straightening out to show its white underside that the sun never touches. Popped it out of its roots, stripped off its clothes and jammed my teeth into it sucking'' (p. 28). The effect on Nellie is to drive her toward yet another female type, the ''cracked doll.''

She becomes the dry, cerebral, intellectual woman, involved in idealistic programs to ''improve'' the masses, taking minutes and listening to the carefully rehearsed arguments of her ''progressive'' group. The mocking tone used to describe the death of her ''young man,'' who had simply burnt/dried up in an excess of zeal, indicates that Nellie is only going through the motions of emotional involvement and remains essentially sterile: ''I went on as before. I took the minutes with a stiff upper lip'' (p. 52). Like all stereotypes, this one represses aspects of Nellie's femininity and, thus, of her very identity.

There are other models of woman in the novel: Aunt Alice, who never married and, as Brodber explains, ''cannot cope with the whole business of existing as a woman so she just withdraws into dumbness'' (interview, 1982); and Nellie's great-grandmother Tia Maria, who chooses for her children, as Aunt Becca chose for herself, affiliation with the lighter-skinned, more socially mobile side of the family but, again like Aunt Becca, at a terrible cost—repression, then annihilation, of her own identity. Nellie's growing understanding of these women and their reasons for assuming self-destructive roles leads through the twin catalysts of Aunt Alice and Baba to an understanding of the self she herself must rebuild.

She learns that one cannot be a ''one-sided drum,'' neither womb alone nor brain alone, neither self-sacrifice alone nor ambition alone, without severe psychic damage. Sympathetic examination of the images of Caribbean woman is a necessary step toward this knowledge. The only way toward an authentic male–

female relationship is first of all a restructuring of self as a real fusion of aspects of womanhood, rather than ideal stereotype.

Brodber's academic and fictional writing has always been primarily concerned with Black consciousness, its developing and changing perceptions in the West Indies. Her awareness of the need for Black solidarity came early, influenced to an extent by the growth of Rastafarian in the 1960s and the Black Power movement in America in the early 1970s. It was on her return to Jamaica from America, however, that "I was forced to stand up, as it were, and be counted—or forced to be *aware* that I had to stand up and be counted" (Interview, 1983).

In *Jane and Louisa* this choice is central to Nellie's psychic healing and is developed through the complex image of the kumbla. A kumbla, as outlined in the Anancy story within the novel, is a self-created protective camouflage assumed by an individual to cope with societal pressures. In Nellie's case, the assumed role consists partly of sexual repression but also involves social exclusivity—a total identification with "Papa's grandfather and Mama's mother," members of the clan who were "brown, intellectual, better and apart" (p. 7). Tia Maria had earlier chosen for her kumbla the protection of her common-law husband's white skin, for she, like Nellie realizes that it is people of this class and color who prosper. And Aunt Becca warns Nellie to identify with this side of her ancestry, rather than the Black, working-class members of the community who will "drag you down child," who are "so different—different from us" (p. 73).

Thus Nellie initially makes "a distinction between them and us. Those people throw dice, slam dominoes and give laugh for peasoup all day long. They have no culture, no sense of identity, no shame or respect for themselves" (p. 51). But she learns that reclamation of herself and her history must also be a reclamation of "those people" as part of her Black ancestry, her Black community (p. 73). It is not an easy task. Her lapse into Creole, the language of the people rather than that of the intellectual, shocks her: "Is that me? with such expressions. Am I a fishwife?" (p. 71). In time, with Baba's help, she finds her way out of the kumbla and is, in a sense, reborn: "Morning had broken. I was no longer alone. Baba had settled me in with my people" (p. 77).

The novel creates a wonderful family dynasty, an ancestry composed of many races and classes. The message that emerges is that acknowledgment of *all* one's ancestors is essential for complete liberation of the individual and the group. This is particularly the case for Creole societies, which are the product of racial and cultural mixing and often produce individuals who are, in the words of the poet Derek Walcott, "divided to the vein" ("A Far Cry from Africa," *In a Green Night*, 1962, p. 18).

Brodber's training in psychological disorders and ways of ameliorating such disorders has informed much of *Jane and Louisa*. As she explains, the novel was originally intended as a case study of the dissociative personality for her social work students (interview, 1982). The dissociative personality has been fragmented through a series of traumatic experiences and is thus unable to connect and integrate aspects of the self and the past—hence the disjointed nature of "Voices," the first section of the novel, which consists of snippets of experiences and conversations from her past that impinge at random on Nellie's consciousness. Through a reexperiencing and reanalysis of this fragmented past, Nellie is able to achieve a sense of wholeness—self-integration and historical reconstruction. As she sifts meanings from past traumas, the narrative structure becomes more comprehensibly ordered, and the initially scattered "bits and pieces" (imaged by her "therapist," Aunt Alice, as still-life slides) form into a chronologically accurate "moving picture" of her life and the family history that shaped her in a particular way.

Brodber is at present researching "folk psychiatry" or, more accurately, non-European alternatives to medical psychiatry, and has discovered that "a lot of our notions concerning 'healing'—besides those from the African tradition—in religion as well as medicine, come from America" (Interview, 1983). Accordingly, she is at present working on this "American Connection," analyzing the transmission of religious and medical ideas from the United States to the Caribbean. As can be expected, these ideas on alternative healing methods as well as her research into the effect of colonialism on the Jamaican psyche in the 1920s are being worked out in the novel she is writing concurrently, where again one can observe the cross-fertilization at work between psychological and historical conceptualization on the one hand and fictive exploration on the other.

It can be posited then, that Brodber's creative writing draws on many sources of knowledge and research for the exploration of certain themes. Her stylistic achievement is also a fusion of some of the rich resources of the Jamaican linguistic continuum, carefully selected to fit the tone and mood of each section.

On the very first page of *Jane and Louisa*, one can observe the juxtaposition of a cool, analytical, and faintly ironic narrative voice using standard Jamaican English ("It is hard work that gets a Baptist Amen through lips pursed for the *Te Deum*" [p. 7]), and a credible representation of Granny Tucker's mesolectal Creole syntax and intonation ("Cock-fighting on a Sunday! Lord take the case" [p. 7]). This is not simply a juxtaposition of voices but also of the cultural orientations embodied in these various language registers. As the novel continues, more voices are heard, building up a specifically Jamaican linguistic/cultural spectrum, with echoes from the Bible ("Paul may sow and Apollos may water" [p. 8]), from literature ("Vivian Virtue called our part of the universe 'mossy coverts, dim and cool' " [p. 9]), from popular song ("Two Gun Rhygin" [p. 10]), and from folk tale ("Brer Anancy begged his son Tacuma" [p. 15]).

The appropriate and expert style shifting is achievement enough but it is not only the accretion of voices and tones of voices that creates the multilayered meanings in the work. Imagery is also used as a series of silken webs that bind episodes together; the reading process untangles echoes and references, so that by the chapter entitled "The Spying Glass" all the strands of story and theme have been drawn together into a smoothly flowing, comprehensible whole.

Space does not permit even a merely adequate analysis of Brodber's stylistic fusion of language registers, images, and echoes into a novel that combines autobiographical, narrative, lyrical, and dream-vision modes—among others. Suffice it to say that *Jane and Louisa* is itself a finely crafted kumbla, elusive at first, but yielding rich insights on closer examination.

CRITICAL RECEPTION

Since *Jane and Louisa Will Soon Come Home* was only published in 1980, the number of critics who have responded to it is still fairly small. The anonymous reviewer of the work in the *Sunday Gleaner* (1981, p. 7) introduces Brodber to the reading public, and notes the fusion of her talents as poet, sociologist, dramatist, and writer in the creation of a fascinating "prose-poem." Dorothy Parker's review in *Black Books Bulletin* (1981–82, p. 57) also observes in the novel "a creative mix of poetry and prose."

Indeed, most critics are primarily struck by the extraordinary style of the work and its ability to draw on several genres in the production of a complex whole. Jean Pierre Durix (*Afram*, 1982) claims that the novel transcends distinctions of genres and draws its inspiration from several sources. Rhonda Cobham elaborates on this trans-genre style in her review, noting the interweaving of folk tales, proverbs, nursery rhymes, motifs from *Alice in Wonderland*, and refrains from old-time calypsos ("Getting out of the Kumbla," 1981–82).

Evelyn O'Callaghan's article on *Jane and Louisa* ("Rediscovering the Natives of My Person," 1983) calls attention to other stylistic techniques characteristic of the novel, notably "its shifting impressions, detailed treatment of certain experiences, lack of regard for chronological time in the narrative, and the use of different stylistic registers to indicate the different stages in the individual's development" (p. 61). Parker perceives Brodber's style as similar to that used by Gayl Jones in *Corregidora*, particularly the "skillful use of flashback and . . . emphasis on the bloodline" (p. 57). Both the *Gleaner* reviewer and Durix comment on the haunting, incantatory qualities in the musical texture of the prose. But this stylistic range and flexibility leads to confusion for some critics, especially since the earlier sections of the work are structurally disjointed. Parker has problems connecting time and place of certain events and finds "a sense of incompleteness at the end of the novel" (p. 57), while the *Gleaner* reviewer warns that the book "will not be everyone's choice nor will everyone understand it" (p. 7).

Durix, however, points out that the stylistic and structural multiplicity is deliberate and an accurate medium for the depiction of characters groping toward meaning among contradictory and often unexplainable facts. O'Callaghan interprets the novel as a therapeutic process of psychic reconstruction, which concurs with Cobham, who notes that by the work's final section, "the reader, who until now has probably been as confused as the central character by the jumble of sensations and experiences recorded in the novel, is able to share

Nellie's sense of discovery, and the feeling that, after all, a coherent pattern of forces have contributed to Nellie's alienation'' (p. 34).

Obviously, since critical response is divided on the formal variations, there are similarly varied interpretations of content. Durix is fairly general in his précis of the novel: ''In the process of growing up, the girl faces the reality of a tumultuous past in which the problems of race and identity are amplified by the institution of slavery and its consequences on human relationships in the present'' (n.p.). Parker also sees the work as concerned with the maturing adolescent, but in an attempt to discover a specific plot, becomes vague and sometimes misleading: ''She knows that a lot of women on the island have experienced what will soon happen to her and that her friends Janie and Louisa will experience it too, but she can only guess what it is'' (p. 57).

Cobham traces Nellie's career from childhood to maturity via ''total psychic collapse'' and a process of piecing together her own and her family's history. O'Callaghan takes the same approach with a more detailed analysis and uses the linguistic device of ''code-switching'' as a metaphor for Nellie's assumption of various identities to suit the roles she ''tries on'' in an attempt to find herself. Cobham also comments on the female perspective, praising Brodber's achievement as ''a fictional resolution of the contradictions inherent in the figure of the all-powerful West Indian matriarch that does not negate the heroism of such women or the potential destructiveness of their strength'' (p. 34).

Most of the critics identify the theme of ''growing up'' in *Jane and Louisa*; Durix, Cobham, and O'Callaghan recognize the themes of alienation and historical trauma and the necessity of reexamination of the claims of the ancestral past in order to achieve full consciousness of self. Cobham suggests the achievement goes beyond personal wisdom, and O'Callaghan develops on this, claiming that the novel shows ''that the need to repossess the past is the way toward psychic reintegration for the community, the society, as well as the individual'' (p. 64). In an unpublished paper (presented to the English Department's Annual Conference on West Indian Literature, UWI, Jamaica, May, 1982), O'Callaghan notes that one of the ways of achieving the strong sense of community essential to the novel is ''the shared usage of several registers of Jamaican Creole, primarily in dialogue'' (p. 4) and goes on to analyze the main features used by Brodber to approximate Creole speech.

The novel's central image is that of the ''kumbla,'' explained by Durix as a word introduced by the narrator to refer to ''a safe, imaginary place where one's integrity is not threatened by the encroachments of other people.'' O'Callaghan explains the device with reference to the Anancy story in the text, as a deceptive facade erected through linguistic double meanings and social role playing, and traces the societal pressures which force Nellie to assume the protective camouflage. Cobham comments on the danger of this ''disfiguring/protective'' disguise.

Despite the differing interpretations of a work that, by its very nature, invites complex and various readings, critical evaluation of *Jane and Louisa* has tended toward unanimous eulogy, particularly in its formal status as a new milestone in Caribbean creative writing. Cobham hails the novel as "probably the most exciting piece of prose fiction by a West Indian author to appear in recent years" (p. 33), and Durix makes the significant claim that "probably no one else in the West Indies, apart from Wilson Harris, has revolutionized the art of fiction as much as Erna Brodber in *Jane and Louise.*"

HONORS AND AWARDS

Erna Brodber has won several scholarships, including a Jamaica Government Exhibition (1960), a UWI postgraduate award (1964), a Ford Foundation fellowship for pre-doctoral research (1967), and an Association of Commonwealth Universities staff fellowship (1980). She was a prize-winner in the short story competition of the 1975 Jamaica Festival Commission.

BIBLIOGRAPHY

Works by Erna Brodber

With Nathaniel Wagner. "The Black Family, Poverty and Family Planning: Anthropological Impressions." *The Family Co-ordinator, Journal of Education Counselling and Services* 19 (April 1970), 168–72.

Abandonment of Children in Jamaica. Mona, Kingston, Jamaica: UWI, ISER, 1974.

"Social Psychology in the English-Speaking Caribbean: A Bibliography and Some Comments." *Social and Economic Studies* 23 (September 1974), 398–417.

A Study of Yards in the City of Kingston. Working Paper no. 9. Mona, Kingston, Jamaica: UWI, ISER, 1975.

"Rosa." *Festival Commission* (Kingston) (1975), 1–7.

"Sociological Research and Personal Involvement." In *Methodology and Change*, ed. Louis Lindsay. Mona, Kingston, Jamaica: UWI, ISER, 1978, pp. 227–33.

"Trends in Social Work Practice and Research in the Caribbean." *Journal of Ethnic Studies* 3 (Spring 1980), 16–29.

Jane and Louisa Will Soon Come Home. London: New Beacon Press, 1980.

Perceptions of Caribbean Women: Towards a Documentation of Stereotypes. Women in the Caribbean Project no. 4. Cave Hill, Barbados: UWI, ISER, 1982.

"Oral Sources and the Creation of a Social History of the Caribbean." *Jamaica Journal* 16 (1983), 2–11.

Reviews

"Michael Rutter: Maternal Deprivation Reassessed, Penguin, 1972." *Social and Economic Studies* 24 (March 1975), 160–61.

"Lee Rainwater: *Behind Ghetto Walls*, Pelican, 1974," *Social and Economic Studies* 24 (June 1975), 257–62.

In Press

A Short History of St. Mary, commissioned by the Ministry of Education, Jamaica.

Interview with Eddie Burke, *Jamaica Journal*.

Afro-Jamaican Women and Their Men in the Late Nineteenth Century and First Half of the Twentieth Century. ISER, Eastern Caribbean.

"Programme Planning in a Multi-Cultural Milieu." *Social and Economic Studies* 28.

Tapes

"Jamaica 1907–1944: The Old People Speak: Life-histories of 90 Jamaicans Born in the Early Twentieth Century." Mona: UWI, ISER, 1980, 120 hours.

Studies of Erna Brodber

Anonymous. "Review of *Jane and Louisa Will Soon Come Home* by Erna Brodber." *Sunday Gleaner*, June 28, 1981, p. 7.

Cobham, Rhonda. "Getting out of the Kumbla: Review of *Jane and Louisa Will Soon Come Home*." *Race Today* 14 (December 1981-January 1982), 33–34.

Durix, Jean Pierre. "Review of *Jane and Louisa Will Soon Come Home*." *Afram* 14 (1982).

O'Callaghan, Evelyn. "Rediscovering the Natives of My Person: Review Article on *Jane and Louisa Will Soon Come Home*." *Jamaica Journal* 16 (August 1983), 61–64. (This is a shortened version of an unpublished paper presented to the English Department's Annual Conference on West Indian Literature, UWI, Mona, May, 1982).

Parker, Dorothy. "Review of *Jane and Louisa Will Soon Come Home*." *Black Books Bulletin* 7 (1981–82), 57–58.

KENNETH RAMCHAND

Wayne Vincent Brown (1944–)

It is customary to link the name of Wayne Brown with those of Anthony McNeill, Mervyn Morris, and Dennis Scott, the group being seen as the new wave of West Indian poets following Derek Walcott and Edward Brathwaite. What, apart from chronology, the "newness" consists of has not been looked into; nor has there been any attempt, paying due respect to the life of our language and the evolution of poetic forms, to define or describe the tradition which, by implication at least, contains the work of Walcott and Brathwaite and the contributions of the poets who have come after them. Part of the problem is that Walcott and Brathwaite are still active, their work just as capable of exhibiting "newness" as that of their younger contemporaries. Walcott and Brathwaite, moreover, are so emphatically the established West Indian poets that the younger writers are less read and less written about; and, such are the hard facts of the business, the younger writers are less likely to be taken up by a publisher capable of affording them exposure to a wide readership including their fellow poets from other countries.

In this entry it is not possible to go much further in the right direction. But there are necessary preliminaries. The younger poets here and in other countries may still have to testify to the necessity for poetry, but the recognition of Walcott and Brathwaite has freed their younger countrymen from the kinds of discouragement all too often handed down to the would-be artist in these islands by "solemn Professor Eunuch" and the "Suppressor of His Majesty's Conscience in the Colonies" (Walcott's titles in *Epitaph for the Young* [1949] for those who have given up): "I was a blind bat, my boy," seeking alternates and rejecting tradition.

The younger poets, released from spurious pressures, and with no apologias to submit, have responded independently to the strict and intimate demands of their calling, though in each case there is the strictest concern with craft. Each may be assailed by the doubt of feeling "the star in his reared wrist wink out," but each is excited as in the last three stanzas of Brown's "Light and Shade" by the thought of another breakthrough, another successful raid upon the inarticulate:

> This poem is a wall.
> Or maybe a string
>
> Of mountains, out of whose blue haze
> may yet come (if I am patiently dumb)
>
> Hannibal, swaying widely as his elephant sways.
> (*On the Coast*, p. 28)

Wayne Brown was an undergraduate in Jamaica at the Mona campus of the University of the West Indies from 1965 to 1968 and lived there more or less continuously until 1973, returning as a resident again during 1982 and 1983. The three Jamaicans (McNeill, Scott, and Morris) and the Trinidadian have known one another personally for nearly twenty years. They have read one another's work and work-in-progress. Brown, whose sense of an artistic community of the living and the dead makes him a voracious reader, has remained in touch with his contemporaries when he is not in Jamaica. These poets, however, do not constitute a school, nor do they subscribe to a common aesthetic or political program.

But they share a peculiarity. Though born too late to have been inspired by the Federal feeling that the writers of the late 1950s responded to, they are still not like those ten years their junior whose lives took shape during the period when each island had been granted independence as a little nation. Brown, McNeill, Morris, and Scott retain a West Indian outlook and a tough optimism about the future which makes them healthily distrustful of the political kingdoms and economic castles created ever since the death of Federation, raged at by Walcott: "One morning the Caribbean was cut up / by seven prime ministers who bought the sea in bolts—," who then "sold it at a markup to the conglomerates" who "retailed it in turn to the ministers," after all of which "the dogfights / began in the cabinets as to who had first sold / the archipelago for this chain store of islands" (*The Star-Apple Kingdom*, 1979, p. 53). The concern with the deeper reaches of the self foregrounded in the work of the younger poets, gets density and representative quality from being related to their anxiousness about the shape and drift of culture and society in the West Indies.

But these four poets are quite different from one another, and it indicates a change in attitudes to poetry partly brought about by the quality of what has been written by the younger group, as well as by Walcott and Brathwaite themselves after all the fuss, that nobody now encourages us to choose on the ground of content or message between this one and that other. The differences in temperament between Brown, McNeill, Scott, and Morris have made themselves felt as differences between poems not as differences between the men to be traced, in Brathwaite's inglorious phrase, to "the bedroom of their assumptions." Between Brown, the subject of this sketch, and the other three, the first difference has to do with geography: it is worth pointing out that Jamaican poets (including McNeill and Scott, and Morris, who seems to omit landscape deliberately) hardly respond to the sea with the intensity and obsessiveness of southern Caribbean writers like Walcott, Eric Roach, and Wayne Brown.

BIOGRAPHY

Brown was born on July 18, 1944, an only child whose mother died giving birth. From the age of nine months he lived with an uncle and aunt, but when he was nine years old a decision was taken to send him to boarding school at Mt. St. Benedict (The Abbey School, Tunapuna, Trinidad), about ten miles out of Port of Spain. From this time till he was sixteen, home was the boarding school during term, with visits from the family on weekends. Aunt Helena died when the boy was nine, and at age eleven he was transferred to another set of aunts, until at age sixteen the by now uncontrollable young man was taken in by his father, a distinguished and aloof Trinidadian judge who treated him like an adult and sometimes like a boarder. There were no questions and no protectiveness. But there was freedom at last and his own key. This "orphaned islander," the only young person in a family of middle-aged people, early looked out on the world with eyes searching the distance ("the dark boats slip by me as by a lantern, / darkness devours the voices," p. 40).

In this early period a number of crucial influences are to be located. At his Uncle Willie's holiday home on the wild and windy coast, Wayne Brown spent many of the holidays between his eighth and thirteenth year alone and free, climbing rocks, taking in the sea, absorbing how wind and water were eroding the rocks and the lowest of the steps that led up the cliff to the house. Those rocks that stood fast were even more food for wonder:

> That boulder
>
> How many seasons had it passed
> resisting metamorphosis?
> I stared at it as into deep space.
>
> (p. 26)

Brown's sensuous awareness of place and of the inner life in things developed in this period, and to this time we can attribute the recurrence of sea and sea creatures in Brown's poetry and the animism in the whole *On the Coast* volume.

The sea is as good a cue as any for introducing a discussion of the place of Walcott in Brown's development. *On the Coast* is dedicated to Derek Walcott. Brown began reading Walcott in 1963, saw him frequently during 1963–65, and showed his early efforts to the published author of *In a Green Night* (1962). For the first time, a young West Indian poet was able to find a master from his region, the kind of predecessor who could be seen to be involved in the making of a distinctive West Indian tradition. It is in this light that the particulars of the Walcott influence on Brown have to be considered.

The person fretting about his alienation; the use of an extended conceit (dropping an anchor, ''rusted candelabra of roots'' [p. 10], is successively a reaching for foothold, a prayer with the chain a rosary, ''metal beads,'' and a ''contrived navel string'' trembling toward contact); and the quotation from Walcott's ''Laventille,'' a virtual epigraph in the middle of the poem ''Monos,'' might all be adduced as influence. Yet the Brown impress makes its appearance in the last two lines in an image of disconnection and voiceless calling that encapsulates the poem, the image of the one (*Mono*/s?) ''beached quiet fish / opening and closing useless jaws'' (p. 11). The image is also crucial in ''Crab,'' one of the poems in ''Aquarium,'' where a series of pictures are brought into relation by the suggestion of sexual initiation, release, and metamorphosis in this picture as the crab

> crouched on the jetty's last blind step, flayed
> by drenching tide, grips
> rock and stiffens,
> drowning vaguely like the slow surge of dreams.
>
> For him the oceanbed bares her breast, him
> her tresses brush against,
> who, squatting drunk beneath darkening surges, finally
> breathes water.
>
> (p. 13)

The idea of writing a series of poems about sea creatures in ''Aquarium'' obviously connects with Walcott's ''Tropical Bestiary,'' yet to compare the two sets of poems even in a foreshortened way is to notice some crucial differences in outlook and method between Walcott and Brown. Many Walcott poems show a dialectical progression, with image and felt thought acting upon one another and the syntax of the poem sometimes becoming too convoluted as it seeks to enact the windings of the thought. In ''Tropical Bestiary'' there is also the sense of a *moralitas* lurking in each item. With Brown, there is no attempt to convey either the process of thinking or the result of thought in a direct or didactic way, and nowhere does the poem depart from a prose-like lucidity on account of thought. In ''Devilfish'' we can say that Brown is writing about modern man, including ''the fisherman riding a storybook calm'' (p. 13), being swallowed up by totalitarian forces, but we say this only as one of the poem's possible applications. ''Ballad of the Electric Eel'' is a fast-moving narrative unlike anything in Walcott, though the example of Ted Hughes's ''crow'' poems is in the background; and in ''Mackerel'' the moralizing person (''Men will have their truths, their tidy legends, / Their ends'' [p. 15]), aware of his games, is made to ironize himself in his confession that he imagines every end for the mackerel except ''That somewhere, hanging in streams / Of light, some ice-blue Purpose / Keeps in quiet its / Unfathomable self'' (p. 15).

The Walcott influence upon Brown's poems changes from early to later as Brown's distinctive vision and expressive modes establish themselves. The more secure a poet, the more he will feel free to draw upon what exists in the language he serves.

At the Abbey School, Brown's fourth-form essays began to be full of descriptions of horses and illustrated with drawings of horses galloping. From earliest childhood Brown was exposed to the horse-racing enthusiasms of the family. He was taken to the races at the Queen's Park Savannah and taken by Uncle Willie to study the horses at their early morning exercises. In addition, there was the year-round talk about horses coming to a climax at the Christmas Day lunch made richer by a savoring in advance of the Boxing Day meeting and followed up by a last look at the horses on Christmas afternoon. Brown was to work from 1963 as a sports columnist with the *Trinidad Guardian*, covering horse racing. But the Abbey School English teacher had commented that the Fourth-Form essays were written with love. If we take the full significance of this it can be claimed that it was the horses that gave Brown his start as a writer. There is an early poem about a racehorse in the St. Mary's College Annual for 1961, but on the whole the horses have been absorbed in Brown's pervasive sense of power and beauty in Nature, the destructive/creative subterranean force, the risk that the poet takes:

> You may turn on all lights, you may turn to TV,
> You may pray in your pillow, ''Shall it be war?''
> You may ask of the woman, ''How shall I plead?''
> You may cry, ''Lift me, mother!''
>
> You may cry, ''Bury me, stars!''
>
> I am the horse that has killed its owner.
>
> I am the flesh in the dark.
>
> (p. 7)

As a sixth former at St. Mary's College, Port of Spain, in the early 1960s, Brown was part of a remarkable flourishing of drama and poetry, as the College Annuals for the period record. In Fr. Quesnel the boys had an English teacher to whom literature was alive, and important, and quite everyday. He was also a strict taskmaster, making his pupils write poems in different stanzaic forms and modes and using specified metrical patterns. It was Quesnel, unhappy with

"A Country Club Romance" but impressed by the writing, who first mentioned the name of Derek Walcott to Wayne Brown ("Obviously he has talent but he has a chip on his shoulder"), and it was Quesnel who presented Brown with a copy of T. S. Eliot's *Selected Poems*. Brown was not the only promising member of the company writing in the College Annual at this time, but he persisted after Sixth Form was over. Again and again, the historian of West Indian culture comes upon talent needing encouragement, needing to be worked but losing heart and impetus for want of nourishment in a society that can no longer blame others for its failure to become a civilization. Like Walcott before him, Brown saw the wreckage, "flotsam of other purposes" as well as his own, and made the decision to move toward a possibility.

Between 1963 and 1964 Brown worked as a journalist with the *Trinidad Guardian*, reading Wordsworth, Eliot, and Walcott, talking with Walcott, and reading at his instigation poems by Robert Lowell and Ted Hughes. But in these same years Brown was living the life of a free young man with his own house key, a job, a car, and therefore everything else in Port of Spain. On a beach in Barbados at Christmas 1964, Brown turned against the free life and against journalism. The unpublished free verse poem "Twilight," which was written here, was followed by a spate of poems on his return to Trinidad, including "Famine," a poem in five parts. The decision was taken to seek entry to the University of the West Indies in Jamaica. Walcott was supportive of the decision and on reading "Twilight" and "Famine" had said, "Good; you have to start working hard."

After graduating from the University of the West Indies, Brown lived in Jamaica for a time; returned to Trinidad to teach in 1970–71; saw the publication of *On the Coast* (1972); and went back to Jamaica during 1972–73 to do research on a biography of Edna Manley; then he lived in England for two years, writing the biography and holding in 1975–76 the Gregory Fellowship in Poetry at the University of Leeds. In 1977 Brown, an excellent pedagogue and an inspiring presence, returned to Trinidad, where he taught at Fatima College for two years. There then followed seventeen months as information officer at the U.S. Embassy in Port of Spain, till Jamaica called again, this time holding him for three years. At the end of 1983 Brown moved again, once more to Trinidad, where he now writes an outstanding column, "In Our Time," for the *Trinidad Guardian*, and teaches part time at the University of the West Indies, St. Augustine Campus.

Brown's poems always seem to come out of the life at the time, and those written since *On the Coast* reflect a richly turbulent period. There seems little point in discussing the moving and accomplished poems of *Voyages* in this short sketch since the collection is still seeking a publisher.

MAJOR WORKS AND THEMES

In Wayne Brown's poems we find a mind feeding on the metrical experiments of other poets and an imagination attracted by poets whose work moves toward the archetype. Out of this contemplative bank strange birds, fish, and beasts flow. But Brown is also above all a lyric poet, a poet of isolation, nostalgia for happiness lost or about to be lost, a poet of love, as can be seen in the title poem "On the Coast":

> The warehouse on the waterfront
> is empty tonight. The ocean shines.
> Moon, it is a winter moon,
> a moth's wing netted in cloud.
>
> Why do I sit up these late nights
> barefooted on a broken pier?
> I never saw the galleons enter the moon,
> nor the great house that burned on the hill,
>
> And the unpunctual fisherman
> who came out of nowhere suddenly
> rounding the point on long oars,
> had nothing to say to me.
>
> Night, I am getting nowhere.
> Island girl, I am scared, don't leave me.
>
> (pp. 39–40)

But it is probably better to begin with the easily recognizable.

Brown's social awareness can be seen more or less directly in poems like "Wide Sargasso Sea," "Red Hills," and "The Tourists," which together cover a wide range of West Indian issues. In "Wide Sargasso Sea" the immediate social reference is to the complex relationship between European, White West Indian, and Black and between the landscapes of Europe and the Caribbean. (The treatment of this subject is extended in "Snow," "Trafalgar Square," perhaps "Soul on Ice," and in a number of poems in the unpublished *Voyages*.) "Red Hills" (the title comes from the name of a middle-class hill retreat in Jamaica) points to class and color division, racial self-hatred, and middle-class embarrassment and nervousness at the underprivileged and unwashed. And in "The Tourists" Brown takes into account the exploitation and prostitution that tourism means in the so-called independent Caribbean islands. But to put it like this is to touch neither the experience nor the meaning. The Englishman in "Wide Sargasso Sea" (a figure consistent with the nameless husband in Jean Rhys's novel with the same title), safe in his "steel age" (the echo of "cage" is obvious but not therefore to be discounted) is, however, haunted by a sense of loss and diminution now that he has left his life on the island. The seventh stanza, a three-liner, ends "Yet at times, on a ship, or fleeing train" (p. 46); and the eighth picks up the rhyme across the double space to continue lyrically, "The watermill whirrs within me again, / the sea gleams, the Negroes erupt, / the woman waits by the improbable stile, / And I am the lover between hill and sky / with one other, going away, caught / at the picture-frame of escape" (pp. 46–47). Loss is also the emotional focus in "Red Hills" as the line "bloom towards us with red eyes" (p. 44) zooms in upon the maimed and representative speaker ("us with red eyes"). The theme is treated more explicitly and more sinisterly in "The Witness," but here the poem is satisfied to bring us closer to the fumbling suburbanite fighting off kinship with the dreaded figure in the garden ("we keep love in / and find no use for memory" ["Red Hills," p. 44]). The studiously casual tone of "The Tourists" guides us through familiar scenes on a beach in the tourist belt, where "nothing unusual" is to be found:

But for one parrot fish which turns
grave somersaults on the stainless steel
spear that's just usurped its dim
purpose; which was to swim
as usual through the blue air, in silence, like the sun.
(p. 8)

Brown's poems work more often through expressive image and symbol than reducible statement, as much by lyric tone as by theme or idea. Here the harsh "f" alliteration, followed by that on the "s" sound in lines 2 and 3 suggesting the piercing of the fish, the medial rhyme "spear"/"air," and the simultaneous pointing to and deemphasizing of "dim"/"swim" by enjambement all contribute to the sense of disturbance, the rupturing of an instinctive order out of the blue, the emphasis shifting to a pervasive menace of which tourism happens to be only one manifestation.

Many of Brown's poems deal with subterranean forces, not with the perceptible cracks and faults on the social surface. This makes it possible to "interpret" or "translate" a Brown poem into terms consistent with the ideology of our time and place—which we cannot help doing—but we do so with an awareness that the fit is not exact, the humility being neither prudential nor strategic. We can notice, for example, that "Vampire" combines the folkloric *soucouyant* (blood-sucking old woman in the shape of a ball of fire), a science fiction creature ("clammy, from its bed of hairs / And thirsty" [p. 24]), the moon again (Brown's poems are obsessed by the moon); and we can see in it a possible reference to the Black Power riots in Trinidad in 1970, yet we have no ready thematic equivalent, feeling only the aweful challenge to the human spirit, the terrible beauty of apocalypse and the desolation of the landscape emerging after the flood:

The bat's abroad.
The thick earth, drenched in darkness, sucks
At the valves of night like a wild child.
The dark drains visibly.

Now what strains through the thinned
Air is the hallucination of its fear:
Fields, a few trees, by morning mist dimmed—

How strange and bright and terrible is
The uninhabitable landscape that swims clear!
(pp. 24–25)

Brown's awareness of man in face of the grandeur or just the baffling quality of what is more than man and other than man (its laws are not moral laws, its nature not defined by our "anthropomorphic graffiti") can be seen in a large number of poems including "Insomnia," "Trip," "Boulder," "Passing Out," "Soul on Ice," "Cat Poem," and "Remu." In "Insomnia" there is the quiet assertion of a human construct involving love and the family against the sense of the meaningless. The insomniac figure, like the ocean "working in the dark without wages" (p. 17), and like the cliffs and mad uncles "standing fast at wars standing fast / Over the nothing," paces his room at a loss "Like a just-dead man trying / To haul himself back along a memory / He cannot quite remember," till his eyes fall, savingly, upon a reminder of sleeping woman and child:

The muddy footprints on the stone floor
Lead to *their* rooms and back out through the door, that's
still ajar.
(p. 17)

In "Cat Poem" Brown's familiar has the knack of turning up enigmatically as cause, omen, innocent bystander, furtive agent, never just cat again; and in "Remu," another poem in numbered stanzas, the poet celebrates pure amoral energy, following its trail through time and place, in aptly varied linguistic registers and tone to this identification of poetic sources and another human assertion—the poet's ordering task:

8
I would write poems like mainsails drawn
up the bent masts of motor schooners
floundering in the remu's flow:
held clear of that chaos but quivering,
holding the strain below.
(p. 22)

The difficulties and the consolation of writing poems, a metaphor for conducting one's life, is a recurrent subject in *On the Coast*. The poet hopes in "Light and Shade" that if he is "patiently dumb," the poem may yet break through and he will exult like "Hannibal, swaying widely as his elephant sways" (p. 28), not be forced to withdraw like the poet in "Boulder" who feels "the star in his . . . wrist wink / out" (p. 26) as he faces an intractable immensity. The layout of lines on the page is used in "Conquistador" to suggest both the landscape of the Andean poet and the rugged spiritual territory the poet must cross and recross to gain the poem. The heroic and defeated conquistador poet's struggle is paralleled in the makings of his counterpart in the contemporary Caribbean, who scans the same ruins and relics and is threatened by the same despair. The sea seems to collapse on the coast

> but always there is more . . .
> Therefore, like poor
> fishermen, when the tide goes
> we scour the shoreline for its news:
> black driftwood, a starfish, the eyeless corpse
> of one whose hope, like ours, dipped
> strangely; like moon, poem, bird;
> and wait for the bottle
> to bring the Word.
>
> (p. 9)

(The medial rhymes and assonance; the suggestive collocation "moon, poem, bird"; the double reference to "bottle"—alcoholic escape or message in the bottle from afar; the ambiguous "Word" which can be deluding Christianity or the creating word; the symbolic suggestiveness of "black driftwood," "starfish," "eyeless corpse" especially if we pronounce them liberally and freshly: all of these make the lines a useful illustration of Brown's textural complexity.)

As a New World poet making new out of the castaway condition, Brown recognizes his kith in Latin American poets and his kinship with poets from other times and places. In "Rilke," written in 1968, Brown like Auden before him admires Rilke's "drought and silence" before the coming of the Duino Elegies. Brown uses the fullness of the four-stress line and the reach of the lengthened stanza to suggest the artist's prolonged torture and self-scrutiny and the fury of the creative process:

> But one night
> Exhausted, slept on his chest, coals
> Tiny as stars, and the animal entered.
>
> All night in nightmare he dreamt of the wail
> Of the wind, taking new shapes within him
> Like flames; and the next day was sure he'd glimpsed
> (Too briefly for charting, it left no trail)
> The shadow of a great unkempt beast,
> Bounding through billowing veils of mist,
> The poem swung like a kite at its tail,
>
> Crying in the teeth of the wind
>
> (p. 34)

Lawrence Durrell's "Fang Brand" lies behind the baldness of the language and the Noah figure in "Noah," where Brown searches for the meaning of life, death, and rebirth, carrying out an inquisition into the dream of change, a new start, a new world, by implication an examining of the point of the creative effort.

The absence of the West Indian landscape in "Rilke," "Noah," and other poems by Brown points to his essential concern with the archetypal. Even when the landscape is sensuously present, it is not there as decoration or for nationalist identification but as the vehicle for discovering and revealing symbolic meanings. One of the finest poems in *On the Coast* is able to suggest the tension between rural and urban, the polluting spread of industrialization ("the city, / crawling south like an oil-slick" [p. 20]) through an island, the soul's thirst, a desolate woman's longing for a redemptive love, and all of this is done in "Drought" without sacrifice of the sense of a specific endangered Caribbean place:

> The woman is barren. And the blackbirds
> have had a hard time this year with the drought
> and fallen like moths to the field's floor.
>
> The woman is barren. And the city,
> crawling south like an oil-slick,
> will soon be around her ankles.
>
> So she sings: "Will you marry me?
> I will go searching under many flat stones
> for moisture of the departed rains."
>
> Sings, "O World, will you marry me?"
>
> (p. 20)

In another major poem, "Song for a Ship's Figurehead," the figurehead shaped out of wood from the Amazon forest is made to tell of the decimation of the Amerindians, the desecration of their gods, and still the survival of the spirit in the piece of wood at the bow of the alien vessel. In the fourth stanza "Now she scythes as the bowsprit scythes" (p. 18) she is the despoiled and abused but still furiously kicking native woman rejected by the "fire-haired sailors" in favor of their ideal "long-limbed Miss Americas." But between stanzas 6 and 9 she comes to life, having learned in the furious brine "a pitiless virginity," becoming a finally impenetrable presence. She is too a vengeful force, hauling her somehow bewitched tormentors to destruction, or to uncharted areas of being:

> For her breasts' black milk
> has been salted and dried,
>
> her nipples are only
> weapons now, shearing, hurling the ocean
>
> over her shoulder she strains she
> hauls

at last her tormentors' quivering hulk
clean off the map's page

(pp. 18–19)

The poem is steeped in the geography and in the schisms of Caribbean history, but it drives into the timeless realm of eternal conflict between implacable forces in balance:

untethered from time she shall not die,
but over the crew's foolishly lolling

heads, her silhouette's risen claw
plunges and rears in the space between stars,
and finds the moon's face, and savages it.

unceasingly: but neither will give in.

(p. 19)

Brown's voice is distinctive; and the struggle between form and energy in his work is an epic one. The publication of *Voyages* will show an even more mature talent setting itself further technical trials.

CRITICAL RECEPTION

Wayne Brown is generally regarded as one of the most promising of the poets whose work began appearing in the 1960s, that group of "a new generation of poets whose work is of a high standard and who are still young enough and prolific enough for us to expect even bigger things of them," as Edward Baugh put it (*West Indian Poetry 1900–1970: A Study in Cultural Decolonisation*, 1971, p. 18). Lloyd Brown places Brown among the "four poets who have emerged to be the most distinguished of [their] generation" (the other three are Anthony McNeill, Dennis Scott, and Mervyn Morris; [*West Indian Poetry*, 1978, p. 161]). Indeed, Baugh insists that Brown's "Noah" "is one of the very finest poems to have come out of the West Indies" ("Since 1960: Some Highlights," in *West Indian Literature*, ed. Bruce King, 1979, p. 87).

In one of the most extended treatments of Brown's poetry, Lloyd Brown considers the influence of Derek Walcott on the younger poet's work, an influence that he regards as positive insofar as it reflects Brown's sense of a tradition of West Indian poetry, but one which at times becomes "embarrassingly obtrusive" (*West Indian Poetry*, p. 161). The critic goes on to consider the poet's complex view of the world in his poetry, observing especially his "anticolonial temper" (p. 163). He suggests also that "Brown's perception of his contemporary West Indies allows for the possibility of genuinely new beginnings, in the usual tradition of rebirth and re-creation in West Indian poetry" (p. 164).

BIBLIOGRAPHY

Works by Wayne Brown

On the Coast. London: André Deutsch, 1972.
Edna Manley: The Private Years. London: André Deutsch, 1976.
Derek Walcott: Selected Poems. Selected, annotated and introduced by Wayne Brown. London: Heinemann, 1981.

Studies of Wayne Brown

Brown, Lloyd. "West Indian Poetry Since 1960: Wayne Brown." In *West Indian Poetry*. Boston: Twayne, 1978, pp. 161–65.
McFarlane, Basil. " 'The Century of Exile': Basil McFarlane Speaks to Wayne Brown." *Jamaica Journal* 7 (September 1975), 38–44.
See also General Bibliography: Allis, Baugh (1971), Herdeck, Hughes, and King.

KWAME DAWES

Jan Carew (1925–)

I have searched
I have searched
I have searched
But the faces of the cities
The old cities
And the new cities
Across the Atlantic seas
were the same.

(Jan Carew, from "The Cities,"
in *A Treasury of Guyanese Poetry*,
A.J. Seymour, ed., 1980)

The memory of home is like the bread of life
to those who roam.

(Jan Carew, from "Requiem for My Sister,"
in *A Treasury of Guyanese Poetry*)

BIOGRAPHY

Jan Carew was born on September 24, 1925, in Agricola, Guyana (then British Guiana). He was educated at Berbice High School, after which he pursued tertiary studies at several universities in Europe and the United States. His educational background reflects the trend of many of the significant writers of his time, and these similarities become even more apparent in the thematic focus of his work.

His travels, starting at age nineteen, began what was to become a life of "endless journeyings" and searching for Jan Carew. He has visited five continents: North and South America, Europe, Asia, and Africa. While in Africa he lived for a few years in Ghana, where he did some writing and a spot of editing. In 1962 he moved to Jamaica with his wife, novelist Sylvia Wynter, and lived there for a few years. In 1966 he traveled to Toronto, Canada, where he lived until 1969. He then returned to the West Indies and lived in Jamaica and Guyana for a few years with his wife and their son Christopher, who received his secondary education in Jamaica.

Currently, Jan Carew is professor of African American Studies at Northwestern University. He is also a senior lecturer in the Department of Afro-American Studies at Princeton University. He and his present wife, Dr. Joy Carew, live in Evanston, Illinois, with their young daughter.

Carew's journeys have enhanced his work significantly. His perceptions of the communities that he writes about are usually authentic and his appreciation of the people compassionate. His two early novels, *Black Midas* (1958) and *The Wild Coast* (1958), capture vividly the rhythms of the Guyanese landscape to the extent that the reader is drawn into the density of the natural environment of forest, savannahs, rivers, and swamplands. For Carew, universal literature emerges when the writer writes about his people in a "tense and heightened way that . . . reflects the problems of the peoples all over the world" (Jan Carew, "Caribbean Writing," *W. I. Gazette* [Christmas 1960 (Supplement)]).

In 1960 *The Last Barbarian*, set in Harlem, New York, was published. In 1964 he published *Moscow Is Not My Mecca*, which is set in Soviet Russia. A collection of short stories entitled *Save the Last Dance for Me* (1976) is set in Britain. In each of these works there is a strong sense of the environment and the people, especially the West Indian exile within these societies.

While better known as a novelist and perhaps as an editor, Jan Carew has written a good deal of poetry and a few plays, and he has done a tremendous amount of work in broadcasting on radio and television in Canada, the United States, and Britain. Jan Carew is also an author of juvenile literature, and he has published several beautifully illustrated books for children.

It would not be difficult to tag onto Carew the name "political writer," though it would prove rather difficult to decide what label to place on the tag. Certainly he is a "revolutionary-minded" type who has been aware of the political realities that face the Black people of the world. But his role may be best described as an iconoclast of political systems and a propagator of unity and singleness of purpose among peoples. Carew encourages his people to identify their own answer to their political problems rather than to look outside for help. Jan Carew is an extremely talented individual who is able to explore his artistic skills without losing sight of the realities around him. His perceptivity and humor are commendable traits. I met Jan Carew in the mid–1970s while he was in Jamaica.

My recollections of the man, though sparse, seem to correspond with the voice in his work. I remember a tall, lanky individual with a vibrant sense of humor and a searching stare. He enjoyed recounting the stories of his childhood days in the Guyanese savannah and interior with a contagious excitement and was noticeably amused at my childish fascination.* An excellent storyteller!

Hena Maes-Jelinek, in an article entitled "The Myth of El Dorado in the Caribbean Novel" (1971), observes, "For Carew, the richness of Guyana does not lie in its lodes of gold but in its people: he perceives close links between them and the landscapes in which they have been toiling and suffering for several centuries, and he thereby contributes, albeit tentatively, to the shaping of a Guyanese consciousness" (p. 121). Maes-Jalinek was writing only about his first two novels in this review, but this analysis speaks to all of his works that have contributed to the shaping of a Black consciousness among the exiled "landless, harbourless spade" of the New World (Edward Brathwaite's description, *The Arrivants*, p. 34).

MAJOR WORKS AND THEMES

Carew's first novel, *Black Midas*, gives early indication of his skill as a storyteller. Like most of his contemporaries, he attempts in the work to use the language of his own people and to capture the rhythms of his landscape. The work is written in the picaresque mode, and it is a novel filled with adventure, intrigue, a great deal of color, and relatively explicit sexual overtones. In this novel Carew begins his development in the difficult art of characterization, and while this work is filled with a large number of type figures, there are hints of psychological realism and authenticity that will blossom out into whole characters in his later works.

The novel is a "fictional biography" of the legendary Guyanese "pork-knocker" Ocean Shark, whose development and search for identity serves as an archetype of the West Indian Black man. Aron Smart ("Shark") knows neither his mother nor his father and is brought up by his grandparents. Their deaths, which occur early in the novel, mark the beginning of a life of dependence for this young man. Aron becomes the recipient of financial assistance and an education through the kindness of a mystery benefactor who happens to be a White man. We later discover that this benefactor was a close partner of Aron's father, a legendary "pork-knocker," and his kindness stems from his desire to appease his own conscience since he was responsible for the tragic death of Aron's father.

Aron's education has a deep effect on him, and he becomes the divided individual of West Indian literature who is caught between the world of books and distant lands and the rhythms of his environment. After returning from his examination in the city, Aron declares: "I suddenly realized that I hated . . . the

*Jan Carew was a close friend of the late Jamaican novelist Neville Dawes, father of Kwame Dawes. [Ed.]

village, and the black faces with their white eyes and white teeth shining in the sun. Mahaica was a womb out of which I had been wrenched and I did not want to return to it. Books had made me divided in myself and I knew I would remain that way as long as I lived. On one hand the language of books had chalked itself on the slate of my mind, and on the other the sun was in my blood, the swamp and river, my mother, the amber sea, the savannahs, the memory of self and wind closer to me than the smell of my sweat'' (p. 42). Aron is sent away to be an apprentice to an Indian, Dr. Ram, and then after a time of frustration under the control of this Indian doctor and his daughter Indra, who becomes Aron's first love, he escapes to the forest and joins the mad quest for gold and diamonds among the ''pork-knockers.'' The story tells of Shark's success as a diamond miner who eventually returns to the city—Georgetown—and in an attempt at establishing his own selfhood he squanders all his money, destroys his relationships, and is left destitute. He eventually returns to the forest and there he drowns himself in the search for gold and wild inexplicable sexual exploits. Finally he loses a leg and decides to return to his village as a wiser, more sober individual. He learns that the way to self is not through materialistic gain.

In this novel, Carew explores several themes that will recur in his other novels. Aron represents the West Indian exile who is an exile within his own homeland. In ''The Caribbean Writer and Exile,'' (*Komparatistische Hefte* 9/10 [1984], 23–39) Carew describes the ethos of this individual: ''The colonizing zeal of the European made indigenous peoples exiles in their own countries—Prospero made Caliban an exile in his. The West Indian writer by going abroad is in fact, searching for an end to exile.'' Carew's explanation of this almost paradoxical statement gives us further insight into the development of Aron's character: ''The West Indian person is subjected to successive waves of cultural alienation from birth—a process that has its origins embedded in a mosaic of cultural fragments. . . . The European fragment is brought into sharper focus than the others'' (p. 1).

Aron seeks to find his identity in a number of ways, and none of them seems to be successful as his own ''divided self'' renders him an outcast in his own society. Aron is never fully comfortable among the people he relates to; he is either too educated or too uncultured. He tries to establish respectability by using his wealth as a tool. This creates a superficial sense of superiority that crashes as soon as the money is finished.

The sexual relationships of this character, if examined carefully, give us some idea of the different ways in which he chooses to discover his identity. There is no question in the reader's mind that Aron's alienation creates in him a selfishness that forces him to use people and at the same time to depend upon them for his sense of worth.

Aron's days with Dr. Ram teach him in no uncertain way the reality of being Black and subservient. His relationship with Indra, the doctor's young daughter, is filled with childish passion, but he slowly realizes that he is being used by this Indian girl. This revelation sickens him and begins what becomes a trend in his other relationships. He promises to make Indra pay for her rejection of him because he is Black and poor, and this vengeance is meted out to his other lovers. Belle, the prostitute, becomes his exploration into people of his own color and class. He can't leave her because of the intensity of her physical prowess. She is described as possessing the rhythms of Africa in her being. His communion with her lasts only as long as he does not need to establish himself socially with anybody. Eventually he tires of her as he tires of the Africa in himself.

He then looks for social status in his relationship with a brown girl called Beryl. This relationship is also a part of the vengeance he decides to hand to Indra, and he uses Beryl as a status symbol. There is apparently no genuine fondness for this girl, who is manipulated by her mother to draw from Aron as much of his wealth as possible. Aron does not marry the girl, and she is pulled away from him when he becomes poor. Eventually she dies after her mother tries to abort Aron's child. The demented lament of her mother at the death of her daughter points to the essence of Aron's relationship with her: "Beryl! Beryl! How often me tell you that you musn't play with them nigger yard children gal! Come inside at once Beryl yuh hear me. The sun going to make you too black girl!" (p. 254).

Aron's final haphazard and quite maddening search for identity is reflected in the wild escapade of sexual relationships that characterize this section of the novel. He digs for gold, finds some, and spends the money on liquor and women. His close companions, who realize that he is obviously searching for something, have to steal him away in a drunken stupor to save him from the madness of his actions. This is the time of self-revelation for Aron. He says in retrospect after his wild days in Ikowan: "During my two years at Ikowan my life lost all purpose. Perhaps it was that my life had to lose all purpose so that I could really come to terms with myself—who I was and what I was" (p. 26). He describes the advice of his fellow "pork-knockers" as "voices trying to save me from myself." In essence they reveal to him the helplessness of all his attempts at finding his identity.

Carew does not seem to answer Aron's question as to who he is or where he belongs. The closest thing to such a revelation is at least a clear statement of the things that will not lead him to the answer. Aron does state that he has found where he belongs. We are forced to wonder whether this is merely another "pork-knocker" dream. But Carew may have meant it to be a real hope. Aron says to Pancho during the last moments in the novel: "I am going to buy land in Mahaica, a piece of land that will stretch from the sea to the forest and I'm going to grow coconuts and rice and ground provisions. I am a village boy and I know the land just like my grandpa knew it and wrestled with it all his life" (p. 275).

In this work, the search for selfhood is symbolized by the quest for diamonds or "El Dorado." It is an illusive quest but one that becomes a purpose for existence that is almost addictive in nature. Joyce Sparer ("Attitudes Towards

Race in Guyanese Literature,'' 1968–69) states what may be a central theme in this novel: ''Carew's novel explores false answers—illusions of happiness, illusions of freedom'' (p. 32).

Perhaps the most positive aspect of this novel is Carew's ability to describe vividly an environment. Anyone who reads *Black Midas* receives a sound introduction to the geographical features of the varied Guyanese landscape. Aron's journeys carry him from the cramped claustrophobia of the dark swamplands along the coast to the cities that are dry and marked by human relationships. He then enters the green density of the forests and riverlands with the wild life and the almost otherworldly mentality of the ''pork-knockers.''

Carew's characterization is generally lacking, though Aron's character is relatively well explored. It is as hard for us as it is for Aron to understand himself because he has traveled so far and so quickly. He never settles down long enough to explore his psychological makeup. The other characters are shadows that act as foils to Aron's personality. Carew is unable to develop subplots to build his other characters because the narrative is in the first person. Hence all the action develops around Aron, and the characters, especially the women, turn out to be types. Our introduction to Carew's understanding of women is an accurate one in *Black Midas*, in which his women are either manipulated prostitute types whose entire sense of purpose lies in their relationships (sexual) to men and who become weighty appendages to the main protagonist after a while or they are old women, too old to be sexual tools, with a wisdom about life and a hint of individual personality. This trend continues in his other novels, where the women continue to be less developed than the male characters.

Carew's second novel, *The Wild Coast*, reflects the development of a new writer who is trying to explore in greater detail the motives and thoughts of human beings. He utilizes the third person omniscient narrative voice to this end and spends a great deal of the novel describing the thoughts of different characters.

The novel tells the story of the Guyanese middle-class youth Hector, whose sickly disposition forces his father to send him into Tarlogie, the village of his ancestors, where he seeks to survive under the guardianship of Sister, an old house maid who has been elevated to a position of authority in the great house of the village since the death of its original owners. In Tarlogie, this swampland village, Hector is brought up as a landowner's son would be, and he holds a position of superiority over the peasants in the community. His education is guided by a young frustrated peasant, whose attempts to achieve educational status are hampered by his poverty. Hector's education creates a division in his being, a division similar to that experienced by Aron in *Black Midas*. Hector's growth into manhood becomes one of the numerous subplots in this novel.

Hector is thrown into a conflict of cultures in an environment that is essentially characterized by an ambiguous cultural and religious ethos. In this world, Hector has to decide who he is, and he is faced with the problem of unraveling the mystery of his own background. This sense of mystery and intrigue is perhaps the single thread that maintains the interest of the reader from beginning to end.

Like Hector, we want to know who his mother was and why no one seems to want to tell him, or us for that matter. Carew disappoints us in the end because the build-up is so carefully and tediously prolonged that we expect something climactic and significant. All we learn is that Hector's real mother was the sister of the woman who is thought to be his mother and that she had seduced Hector's father. This reality has no notable effect on Hector or any of the characters, so we wonder why it was kept a secret so long. It does not make Hector's father's promiscuity any more shocking, nor does it change Hector's social standing.

Eventually Hector's father goes completely mad (for no apparent reason); Sister, Hector's guardian, dies suddenly; the people in the village take out their frustrations on Hector's father's Amerindian concubine and his driver Taljee. These events further alienate Hector from this environment, and the novel ends with an assurance that Hector will be going off to England to study, and perhaps to join the searching exile in pursuit of his identity.

Carew succeeds in painting a vivid picture of the village people of Guyana in *The Wild Coast*. He explores their attitude toward race and religion and their reactions to natural disasters and social conflicts. Carew describes their attitude toward religion through the mouth of Tojo, a young companion of Hector. He says of the people: "Them same folks who does warm up the Church pews on Sunday does dance Shango 'til the moon tumble down and the sun jump up" (p. 152). Then Carew himself describes their attitude to religion as the narrative voice: "But they wore their Christianity like the clothes they put on to go to church on Sunday only, for the rest of the week the Shango gods Dunballa, Legba, Moko were theirs" (p. 155). His description of the Shango celebration is mysterious and thumps with the vitality of the celebration. We are never certain what to think of Hector's reaction to it since for some unknown reason it drives him to Elsa's hut, where he demands that she submit her body to his. He does this in a trance-like state, and we wonder whether Carew identifies that moment at the Shango celebration as a time of growth into manhood for Hector.

As in that instance we are often left wondering why people do a lot of things in *The Wild Coast*. This is perhaps the greatest weakness in the work. The characters are often not convincing because we are given too little to work with in understanding them. Carew's women do not improve in this work, and the types occur again. The Tengar/Elsa relationship is very much a repetition of the Aron/Belle relationship, which is hampered by her "whore-like" disposition (described as her religion) and her resultant promiscuity and unfaithfulness. Sister is the parallel of Tanta Moore and Aron's grandmother all over again, though she is a little more intensely developed and her actions and experiences are given a significant psychological realism.

Yet that which Carew loses in his characterization is made up for by his ability to describe his environment. We learn a great deal about swamp and forest life in an interesting way. His description of the flood is filled with the darkness and stagnation of poor people suffering, and the moods of the people seem very authentic. The characters may be types, but once thrown together, they form a beautifully painted canvas of a community in which Carew can explore the themes of alienation and selfhood effectively.

Hector in response to his sense of exile chooses to travel, and this theme of the West Indian exile abroad is central to Carew's third novel, *The Last Barbarian* (1961), which is set in the Black community of Harlem, New York.

In this novel, the artist is in exile. The novel focuses upon the life of Tiberio, a Brazilian painter who has traveled through Europe and now finds himself in an old building in the middle of poverty-stricken Harlem. His conditioning is one of exile. His father is a Barbadian living in exile in Brazil. Tiberio himself ends his university career prematurely in search of himself. He joins the army and travels to Europe. In Italy he deserts the army and spends several years developing as an artist, trying to find himself, having several sexual explorations and coming to grips with his Blackness. Europe helps him to cope with the latter, and he points out to Don in the novel: "I remember when I used to wish I were white . . . the damned funny thing was that European women made me lose my self-hatred, they made me feel really assured for the first time in my life" (pp. 80–81).

By way of flashbacks, Carew gives us greater insight into his characters, and he improves noticeably in his use of the omniscient narrator in this work. We get some insight not only into Tiberio's life but also into the lives of those who live in close proximity to him in this ghetto landscape. He shares a small attic with Don, a Guyanese student, who very often seems to become the central figure in the novel. In the buildings on the street we find Black West Indian students, White people, Chinese exiles, and Americans exiled within their own environment. There is a strong sense of community among these alienated individuals.

While Tiberio's development is central to the work, the novel does not hinge entirely on this figure. The work portrays what Brathwaite would describe as "jazz in the West Indian novel." The entire work becomes a composite whole made up of a series of solo pieces that rise above the steady beat of existence and fall away softly into the rhythms, while another soloist fills up the gap. The soloists in this work include Don, the Guyanese student; Laura, a young lady sold into marriage by her enterprising Jamaican mother; Ho, Laura's Chinese husband, whose alienation and exile drive him to kill his wife; Joe and Alice and their son Bob, who is a drug addict and a trumpet player; the Baron, who is the benevolent landlord and guardian of many of the students; and Mary, a wealthy White woman whose sense of purposelessness in life drives her into seducing and trying to control Don and several others.

The chapters are not numbered but are each given a title, thus making them appear very much like a chain of short stories written in an episodic manner for a periodical. This technique allows Carew to develop several subplots simultaneously, and he does so with greater success than he does in his earlier works.

In this work, the themes of hopelessness and the crashing of false dreams are explored. Ultimately pain overrides any sense of joy, and life is essentially a short period of frustrations, conflicts, and then death. There are several searches for the "El Dorado" of selfhood in materialism that all fall through. Don uses Mary, his wealthy White lover to live in comfort, spending weekends in her country home on an island outside New York. There is in him a sense of personhood being discovered in his ability to exploit sexually the White woman, but he eventually has to return to Harlem and then further exile abroad because he does not belong to Mary's environment. That route to the "El Dorado" of selfhood therefore fails. When Joe wins the numbers, a lottery competition, he buys a car, but this car has to be hidden away in order that he might remain accepted in his environment. Alice, his wife, fears that the money will change him, and she embarks on a campaign to have him spend it quickly and recklessly. Here financial stability is again a failure in leading a man to security in himself since it actually alienates the individual from those within his community.

Carew's characters are commendably developed in this work, and he spends a great deal of time exploring their growth and psychosocial background. Laura's disintegration from a coy, though slightly frustrated wife who submits to her mother's authority and her husband's will, to an angry and aggressive lover who begins to drink heavily and is blatant about her unfaithfulness, is carefully and convincingly portrayed. Her apparent calmness at her own death is not strange as Carew shows her almost catatonic and hopeless state created by her frustrating love affair with Don.

Carew's treatment of color and race in this novel is reflective of his poem "Aimon Kondi":

> White sun raping black rivers
> White sun arched and indolent like an ocelot
> White sun dying
> like a comet
> burning out itself
> to light the earth.
>
> (*A Treasury of Guyanese Poetry*, p. 189)

Mary represents the "white sun" who slowly burns out herself in an attempt to take full control of Don. Mary dies away slowly when she becomes more and more aware of the fact that the inferior Don is slowly becoming a superior user and the stronger character in their relationship. She soon becomes Don's tool as the "tables are eventually turned." The relationship has to die, and this time it is the Negro who gets fed up.

Tiberio becomes Carew's propaganda piece as he expounds upon issues of race and politics. Long sequences are devoted to his speeches, which essentially decry the imperialist influence of the White man on Black society and call the Black man to unite in his stance against racial injustice. His statements are also those of the artist ranting against the world of people who use the artist for their own ends. Tiberio also propagates a type of cynicism and self-assuredness that allows him to live a life of poverty that is at least free from the clutches of the White man. He shows a confidence in himself that allows him to look down upon Mary, the rich White woman, and insult her with great joy. It is a trait that startles the White woman, but a characteristic that Carew seems to uphold as positive.

Tiberio is betayed by Franco, his Iago-type friend, and he is eventually interrogated by the FBI and has to leave the United States. Don leaves Harlem for Europe, while Ho runs away to Chinatown after killing Laura. Snowball, a West Indian student, dies of tuberculosis. Bob, Alice's son, is shot dead by a (White) policeman for no justified reason, and then the novel ends.

This novel by Carew is perhaps his best in that his characterization and skill in storytelling make an excellent partnership. His political and social commentary merges into the plot and characterization comfortably, and the vision, though dark and gloomy, is vividly presented. His characters will endure among the memorable characters to be found in West Indian literature.

In his fourth novel, *Moscow Is Not My Mecca* (1964), Carew sets out to shatter some of the myths about Soviet Russia. The main protagonist, Tojo Robertson, after a harsh awakening in Russia—that comes about when a Black West Indian student is beaten by racialist Russians who call him "black monkey" mainly because he is walking with a White girl—declares candidly that "there is no paradise on earth" neither in the East nor the West. The political statement is explicit, and though the work loses its artistic strengths in character portrayal and development, some important statements are made which reflect Carew's political stance. His suggestion of Marxism as an alternative for the African and West Indian nations emerges in this work. Malcolm speaks boldly on this issue in the novel: "We have been colonials long enough to be suspicious of all great powers who would save us from ourselves, and who would offer gifts of beads and baubles in exchange for this privilege" (p. 85).

By creating two victims of racial violence and discrimination in "imperialist" countries in *The Last Barbarian* and *Moscow Is Not My Mecca*, Carew emphasizes his political statement. Tiberio is a victim of political harassment because he is Black and rumored to be a Communist. Bob is shot by the police because he is Black. Tojo is almost murdered by racialist Russians who were thought by this young man to be part of the only nonracialist White society in the world. Ultimately Carew is suggesting that imperialism is the same regardless of the banner it bears.

CRITICAL RECEPTION

Reviewers of the novels of Jan Carew have commended his ability as a storyteller but questioned his characterization, especially the depth of his insight into the psychological reality of his characters. Carew started writing at a time when several new West Indian novels were appearing every year and each writer was challenged to produce something fresh and authentic. The early reviewers did not see Carew as succeeding in this effort. George Panton in his review of *Black Midas* in the *Sunday Gleaner* of May 4, 1958, states: "His book has been long awaited. Now that it has arrived one feels that the long wait has not been worth it" (p. 11). Panton identifies the book as the usual "run of the mill" adventure story that goes on and on. However, out of this "run of the mill" novel Hena Maes-Jelinek in her essay, "The Myth of El Dorado in the Caribbean Novel" (1971), is able to identify some significant ideas that reflect the Guyanese people: "Aron Smart's adventures, his restlessness, his response to the magnetism of the jungle, are distinctly those of a Guyanese sensitive to the atmosphere and moods of the landscapes of his country" (p. 120). She concludes that Carew's contribution to the Guyanese consciousness is a positive one in this novel, though she does admit that the characters are romanticized and the plot moralistic.

Carew's second novel, *The Wild Coast*, came under greater censuring from the critics, especially from Oliver Jackman in a review published in *Bim* in 1959. While grudgingly praising Carew's ability to describe violence effectively, he declares, "Mr. Carew seems to know next to nothing about people" (p. 65). He finds most of Carew's characters unbelievable and stereotypical. Ivan Van Sertima (*Caribbean Writers: Critical Essays*, 1968) identifies in this novel an adequate handling of the theme of "flight from origins and the quest for roots" (p. 31), but he also agrees that Carew's handling of his characters is generally shallow.

Colin Rickards in his review of *The Last Barbarian* ("Carew's Latest Not His Best," *Sunday Gleaner*, 1961, p. 8) finds Carew's third novel to be "unfortunately his poorest book" and regards Tiberio's rantings as an act of the writer to ram "the reader too full of negro-white propaganda." He asserts that Carew's portrayal of Black Americans is not authentic and is overly influenced by his preoccupation with race and color. Frank Collymore in his review of this work in *Bim* (1962) is far more positive: "In spite of a few recognizable 'types' the main characters are subtly and convincingly drawn, and the author has shown considerable skill in presenting their development" (p. 149).

Alex Gradussov, in a review of *Moscow Is Not My Mecca* (*Bim*, 1966) suggests that Carew "gives a penetrating picture of the problems of human relationships in a communist society" (p. 224).

HONORS AND AWARDS

Jan Carew has received several awards including the Burton Annual Fellowship, awarded by the Howard University's Graduate School of Education for the years 1974 and 1975. Princeton University honored him in 1975 by establishing the Jan Carew Annual Lectureship Award. In 1964 his television play, "The Big Pride," was selected by the London *Daily Mirror* as the best play of the year. In 1969 he was the recipient of the Canada Arts Council Fellowship. In 1974 he won the Illinois Arts Council Award for Fiction, as well as the American

Institute of Graphic Arts Certificate of Excellence for Children's Books for *The Third Gift*. He received the Casa de las Americas Award for Poetry in 1977.

BIBLIOGRAPHY

Works by Jan Carew

Black Midas. London: Secker & Warburg, 1958; New York: Coward McCann, 1958 (as *A Touch of Midas*); London: Longman, 1969.

The Wild Coast. London: Secker & Warburg, 1958, 1963; Liechtenstein: Kraus Reprint, 1972.

The Last Barbarian. London: Secker & Warburg, 1961, 1964.

Moscow Is Not My Mecca. London: Secker & Warburg, 1964; New York: Stein & Day, 1965 (as *A Green Winter*); New York: Avon Books, 1967 (as *Winter in Moscow*, a special edition for nonnative speakers of English).

Cry Black Power. Toronto: McClelland & Stewart, 1970.

Sons of the Flying Wing. Toronto: McClelland & Stewart, 1970.

The Third Gift. Boston: Little, Brown, 1972.

Rape the Sun. New York: Third Press, 1973.

Children of the Sun. Boston: Little, Brown, 1976, 1980.

Save the Last Dance for Me. London: Longman, 1976.

The Twins of Llora. Boston: Little, Brown, 1977.

Grenada: The Hour Will Strike Again. Prague: The International Organization of Journalists, 1985.

Studies of Jan Carew

Cartey, Wilfred. "The Rhythm of Society and Landscape: Mittelholzer, Carew, Williams, Dathorne." *New World* (Guyana Independence Issue) (1966), 96–104.

Collymore, Frank. Review of *The Last Barbarian*. *Bim* 9 (January-June 1962), 149–50.

Gradussov, Alex. Review of *Moscow Is Not My Mecca*. *Bim* 11 (July-December 1966), 224–25.

Jackman, Oliver. Review of *The Whole Coast*. *Bim* 8 (June-December 1959), 64–67.

Maes-Jelinek, Hena. "The Myth of El Dorado in the Caribbean Novel." *The Journal of Commonwealth Literature* 6 (June 1971), 113–27.

Seymour, A. J. Review of *Black Midas*. *Kyk-Over-Al* 8 (December 1958), 86–87.

Sparer, Joyce. "Attitudes Towards Race in Guyanese Literature." *Caribbean Studies* 8 (July 1968), 23–63.

———. "Carew—an Unfinished Search for Identity." *Sunday Chronicle* (Guyana), April 30, 1967.

See also General Bibliography: Allis, Brown, Herdeck, Hughes, King, McDowell, Ramchand (1970), and Van Sertima.

LLOYD W. BROWN

Martin Wylde Carter (1927–)

Martin Carter's earliest poetry was shaped by the turbulent days of anti-colonial radicalism and protest in Guyana (British Guiana) during the 1950s. During the thirty years since then, especially since the publication of his hallmark *Poems of Resistance* (1954), his has been *the* voice of radicalism in Anglophone Caribbean poetry. This preeminence as the poet of revolution has generally tended to be emphasized by the fact that revolutionary rhetoric in general, and revolutionary literature in particular, has been a rarity in the English-language Caribbean (with all due respect to the ethnic intensities that have become de rigueur in the literature during the last twenty years). Indeed, this very uniqueness probably accounts for the fact that Martin Carter's preeminence as the poet of revolution has not been seriously eroded by the muting of his revolutionary voice over the twenty years since Guyanese independence.

This silence, or near silence, may be linked to the profound disillusionment which has engulfed so much of the Third World intelligentsia, including that of the Caribbean, since the achievement of (nominal) independence. In Guyana that disillusionment has been especially intense in the wake of racial violence between Blacks and East Indians, political stagnation and repression, and the economic as well as social malaise which has undermined the experiment in cooperative republicanism. In this period the Guyanese government has been accused of seizing and maintaining its power by means of a fraudulent electoral system gerrymandered in cooperation with the British and the Americans; and more recently, the government has been accused of complicity in the violent death of one of its most vocal and popular critics, historian/activist Walter Rodney

(1980). Against such a background Carter's relative silence as revolutionary poet may be interpreted either as prudence or complete disillusionment—or both. But that silence *is* relative: Carter's days of overt revolutionism and rebellion may be past, as have been the days of active political involvement and direct participation in government; but he has continued to write and publish his poetry—poetry which sometimes manages to convey a special intensity of feeling and purpose by the very manner in which it studiously avoids a certain directness of statement. The voice itself may have been muted, but the fiery sense of *engagement* which has made that voice all but unique in Anglophone Caribbean poetry still burns.

BIOGRAPHY

Carter was born in 1927 and received his secondary school education at Queen's College. During his early twenties he joined the turbulent political movement for national independence, quickly becoming a leading spokesman for the more radical forces of the movement. This prominence inevitably led to his arrest and imprisonment by the British colonial administration in 1953. At the time of his detention Carter had already launched his career as a poet, having contributed works to A. J. Seymour's literary magazine, *Kyk-over-al*, and to Seymour's "Miniature Poet" series of poetry pamphlets (*Hill of Fire Glows Red*). But it was during his imprisonment that he composed his most important collection, *Poems of Resistance*, which was eventually published in London, in 1954.

After his release from prison Carter remained active in the independence movement and in 1965 was a member of the colony's delegation to the Guyana Constitutional Conference in London, the final hurdle before the formal achievement of nationhood. Thereafter he served for two years (1966–67) as a member of Guyana's delegation to the United Nations. He has also served in the Guyanese government at home, most notably as minister of information and culture, finally leaving the government in 1971. Throughout this entire period he has maintained the dual roles of poet and activist, an appropriate choice in one whose most important writings have passionately advocated involvement and commitment. Consequently the years of political activity and government service also saw the appearance of the first half of his published output, followed by works ranging from the last of his outspoken collections, *Poems of Shape and Motion* (1955), to the cryptic reticence of *Poems of Affinity: 1978–1980* (1980).

MAJOR WORKS AND THEMES

From as early as his first significant publications Martin Carter's distinctive voice of protest and rebellion is unmistakably clear. Unlike so many early collections, especially in the Caribbean, *The Hill of Fire Glows Red* avoids the neo-Romantic idealization of landscape. Instead of the familiar pastoral clichés, the young Carter's landscape vibrates with historical memories, which, in turn, inspire an urgent demand for change. In "Listening to the Land" the poet hears a "tongueless whispering," the possible voice of a buried slave who embodies the past. The response to the landscape is activist rather than escapist, and when the young poet dreams, his are dreams of social change ("Looking at Your Hands"). In earlier works like these it is fairly easy to grasp the dominant features of Carter's poetic personality. It is a personality in which the imagination of activist and artist is indivisible, and in some respects these poems are *about* the imagination and its transforming powers—it transforms the land itself into an insistent voice of history and, simultaneously, responds to the voices of history by envisioning change, including revolutionary change, as the desirable and inevitable consequences of that history. And, finally, the poet's own persona as the embodiment of the transforming imagination incarnates the vision of change. Accordingly, the revolutionary idealist envisions change as a creative process which produces vital forms (social and political structures) out of the chaos of colonial inequities, in much the same way that the poetic imagination creates living forms in art ("The Kind Eagle").

In a sense the poems of *The Kind Eagle* (1952) suggest an interesting paradox: chaos and repression are reprehensible on the one hand; but on the other hand, they emerge as indispensable factors. In political terms the liabilities of history have inspired the kind of intellectual and political ferment which fuel an (apparently) inevitable process of fundamental change. Prison, both as literal experience and as colonial symbol, therefore inspires a fierce ecstacy in the title poem of the collection: "I Dance on the Wall of Prison!" (*Poems of Succession*, 1977, p. 19; hereafter cited as *POS*). And by a similar token, the *poetic* imagination thrives on political adversity and on the reminders of historical injustices: it carves monuments out of the poet's "time," from the "jagged block of convict years" (*POS*, p. 19). Moreover, the consistent integration of imagination and historical memory imparts a powerfully suggestive sense of *inevitability* to Carter's ethics of change. The envisioned changes, even if unrealized, are as much a part of a distinctive historical pattern, as is the past which made the present itself inevitable. And this pervasive sense of inevitability inspires recurrent images and themes of *movement* to the poems of *The Kind Eagle*—movement as history, history as change, change as the collective, irresistible pilgrimage undertaken by a special breed of visionaries: the universe of history moves, "revolves / like a circling star," and "Only men of fire will survive" ("The Discovery of Companion," *POS*, p. 24).

Altogether, these early collections reflect a tightly knit dialectic, with its closely integrated poetic forms, which are to define a good part of Carter's poetry for much of the next fifteen years. The ethos of change is both political ideal and the creative principle of imagination. The patterns of history are mirrored in the imaginative patterns of the poet's art, and since both patterns have been shaped by the same social forces, then the poetic imagination must, perforce, be politically involved. Or in the words of the poet himself, "Like a web / is spun the pattern / all are involved" (*Poems of Resistance*, p. 18).

That assertion is the climactic statement of "You Are Involved," a work which is one of the most typical, in tone and feeling, of the celebrated collection, *Poems of Resistance*. This is the collection in which the twenty-seven-year-old Carter fuses the characteristic themes and forms of the preceding works into the compact designs of his best, and most famous works—"Till I Collect," "Cartman of Dayclean," "I Come from the Nigger Yard," and "University of Hunger." It is characteristic of Carter's writings at this stage of his development that these successful poems owe much to the turbulent times and frankly repressive circumstances in which they were written. They were composed, for the most part, while he was in political detention—in "the dark time," in "the season of oppression," the "carnival of misery" ("This Is the Dark Time My Love," *POS*, p. 42). While it is less celebrated than its companion pieces, few poems in the collection surpass "I Clench My Fist" in this regard. The very intensity of feeling and statement owes its very essence to the forces of repression and exploitation against which the poet rebels. British colonialism represents social chaos in the immediate, Guyanese context, and in the broader, global context, the fragmentation of humanity between the oppressor and the powerless, the haves and the have-nots. The confrontation between colonizer and colonial rebel is therefore an allegory of a divided universe, the microcosm of historical patterns of chaos and conflict. Conversely, the poet's reaction, as artist-activist,to this chaos amounts to a harmonizing, creative power, the transforming power of the imagination. The defiant act of clenching the fist in the face of British weapons and political power suggests a compact wholeness as well as creative energy which contrasts with the prevailing chaos, and it is synonymous with the harmonizing patterns of poetic art itself ("I sing my song of FREEDOM!" ["I Clench My Fist," *Poems of Resistance*, p. 41]). Finally, the thematic progression within the poem itself, from images of fragmentation and conflict to the vision of a powerful, harmonizing energy, is in itself a structural or formal emphasis on that sense of movement—*historical* progression or inevitability—which is always so integral to Carter's revolutionist vision.

On the whole, works like "I Clench My Fist" exemplify Carter's protest poetry at its best. The underlying dialectic is compact, limpid, and consistent. The dialectic statement is tightly controlled through a disciplined, highly economic use of language and sense of form; and as a result, the poetic form itself becomes the imaginative microcosm of that moral wholeness and social unity which the poetry envisions. Given this tightly integrated schema, it becomes clear that "poems of resistance" are not simply poems *about* political resistance: they *are* acts of resistance. This implies an aesthetic that has been rather rare in the generally conservative context of Anglophone Caribbean literature. It was not to be aired in any significant sense, in *any* Caribbean language area, until the successful Cuban revolution began to define its own revolutionary aesthetics during the 1960s: the only valid revolutionary art is that which is committed to, and a part of, the revolution; writing about the revolution is not enough, the writer must be an active participant in the revolution. Or to phrase this ideal in Carter's poetic language, the poet must not simply write about resistance, he himself and his poetry must be directly involved in resistance.

However, notwithstanding this kind of analogy, and notwithstanding the power of Carter's own rhetoric of change, it is important to recognize the substantial limitations of his revolutionism. These limitations are both external and internal. Externally, Carter has lived and written in a political and social context in which the idea of change has always been sharply delineated in nonrevolutionist terms. The rhetoric of rebellion or "revolution" in the English-language Caribbean of the 1950s and 1960s seldom encompassed fundamental (i.e., genuinely revolutionary) changes in the social fabric. "Resistance" as such was conceived and fashioned in relation to the British colonial order and its associated bureaucracy. In other words, resistance was the movement of a bourgeois nationalism, which would replace the colonial overlord with nationalist leaders and political structures, which would leave the social and economic order relatively unchanged. Neither has radical revolutionism demonstrated significant grass-roots appeal in the English Caribbean—a fact which needs to be borne in mind when one is tempted to blame the failures of the Guyanese promise on the demonstrable *and* alleged sins of the Forbes Burnham regime. The electoral rejection of "democratic socialism" in Jamaica during the early 1980s is another example of this limitation, especially when one remembers the definite, built-in limitations of Michael Manley's democratic socialism as a revolutionist principle. And in retrospect, the recent collapse of the New Jewel Movement in Grenada, even before the inevitable U.S. intervention, suggests that beyond the personal popularity of Maurice Bishop the New Jewel Movement, as *revolutionary* ideology, was less deeply rooted than its most ardent supporters seemed to have imagined.

It is necessary to emphasize this historical and social context because these are the broader circumstances which go beyond Guyana's immediate boundaries and which explain, in part, the long-term sense of futility that now envelops Carter's revolutionist poetry, especially in retrospect. The limited impact and relevance of his revolutionary themes reflect the limited capacities of his society for the idea of fundamental change. This, in turn, leads to the internal limits of Carter's revolutionism itself. Poems like "University of Hunger," "Cartman of Dayclean," and "I Come from the Nigger Yard" reverberate with the passions, even violent potential, of the dispossessed. But there is really no substantial evidence, even in these works, of a revolutionary vision that goes beyond the immediate anti-colonial nationalism of "I Clench My Fist." The ferocity with which the poet assaults an entrenched (colonial) status quo undoubtedly continues to exert a powerful appeal to present readers who dream of "resistance" to the *neocolonial* establishment which succeeded the British colonizers. But this ought not to obscure the clearly limited implications of Carter's original vision.

While the scope of the revolutionary vision is circumscribed, so is the poet's realism. The poet's passionate commitment to change of sorts is not really counterbalanced by a realistic awareness of the substantial barriers to significant change. In these earlier poems of "resistance," from the first collection to *Poems of Shape and Motion* (1955), technical polish and thematic coherence go hand in hand with what, on the whole, is a relatively limited emotional range or appeal—limited, that is, by an absence of complex self-awareness vis-a-vis the limits of his own vision and of his society's capacity for change. It is not surprising that, when those social limitations were made painfully manifest in subsequent years, Carter's poetry seems to have retreated into a state of shock from which it has never really recovered.

On the whole, the assessment of Carter's overtly "revolutionary" or "committed" poems leads to a historically significant, albeit unintended, irony: his real achievement as a poet of resistance is, in the final analysis, an exclusively *aesthetic* one, rather than the effective political-aesthetic synthesis that is envisaged and structurally symbolized by his poetry. That is, we can always admire the consistent coherence of thematic statement, the telling integration of formal structure and theme, the striking tension between intense feeling and the spare, tightly disciplined language; and throughout all of this we can admire the skill with which the poet weaves his complex patterns of imagistic and structural variations on the fundamental theme of change-as-creation. But that theme is often less profound or far-reaching than it may sometimes sound.

The poems since Guyana's independence are, collectively, an implicit admission of the earlier limitations. A somber silence broods over the post-independence poems first published in *Poems of Succession*. Silence as speechlessness and paralysis is the dominant motif here, in contrast to the defiant energies and perpetual *movement* in the earlier works. Here silence and inactivity suggest that history moves, not toward inevitable change and creation, but in repetitive, predictable cycles. Indeed, this kind of silence is the main topic of poems like "A Mouth Is Always Muzzled," "Even As the Ants Are," "In the When Time," and "Fragment of Memory." These works also demonstrate that despite the changes in mood and historical circumstances, the older Carter still commands the talents for striking, arresting poetry. The brooding silence of these poems is not the silence of a lost idealism, or of a crippled imagination. Far from it, he manages to develop his themes of silence and futility through "confessional" modes of private experience, or even through abstract statements, communicating a powerful sense of repression and stasis in his society while avoiding explicit political protest. Both the explicit theme of silence and the suggestive absence of overt protest in themselves become rhetorical symptoms of his real, but implied, subject. As in his earlier works, the better poems in this later collection demonstrate his characteristic ability to develop form *as* statement.

This highly suggestive silence continues in his most recent collection, *Poems of Affinity: 1978–1980*. The disillusionment with "history" is more pronounced, and we are left with only a quiet despair in the face of history's relentless repetitiveness. It is the image of death, not creation, that dominates "Playing

Militia'' where the uniform sleeves droop ''like the wet feathers of a crow's wing / over secret carrion'' [*Poems of Affinity*, p. 17]). And in ''For Cesar Vallejo ii'' the decay is everywhere. Clearly, he still remains the poet of passionate commitment. Where that commitment will lead his future poetry depends as much upon Carter's world as it does on himself.

CRITICAL RECEPTION

Edward Brathwaite's ''Resistance Poems: The Voice of Martin Carter'' (1977) is one of the more comprehensive studies of Martin Carter's poetry thus far. The critic examines all the major publications up to the mid–1970s, with special emphasis on Carter as the voice of revolutionary change. Briefer, more general comments also appear in Brown, *West Indian Poetry* (1977), and Herdeck, *Caribbean Writers* (1979).

BIBLIOGRAPHY

Works by Martin Carter

Hill of Fire Glows Red. Miniature Poet Series. Georgetown: Mater Printer, 1951.
To a Dead Slave. Georgetown: Author, 1951.
The Hidden Man. Georgetown: Author, 1952.
The Kind Eagle. Georgetown: Author, 1952.
Returning. Georgetown: Author, 1953.
Poems of Resistance. London: Lawrence, Wishart, 1954; Georgetown: Guyana Release, 1979.
Poems of Shape and Motion. Georgetown: Author, 1955.
Conversations. Georgetown: Author, 1961.
Jail Me Quickly. Georgetown: Author, 1963.
Poems of Succession. London: New Beacon Books, 1977.
Poems of Affinity: 1978–1980. Georgetown: Release, 1980.

Studies of Martin Carter

Brathwaite, Edward. ''Resistance Poems: The Voice of Martin Carter.'' *Caribbean Quarterly* 23 (June-September 1977), 7–23.
See also General Bibliography: Allis, Brown, Herdeck, Hughes, and McDowell.

DARYL CUMBER DANCE

Austin Clarke (1934–)

BIOGRAPHY

Austin Chesterfield Clarke was born in Barbados on July 26, 1934, and raised by his mother and stepfather. The very strict rules of class divisions in Barbados ("Barbados is perhaps the most socially *proper* or *improper* country in the world" [interview with Daryl Cumber Dance, Toronto, Canada, December 6, 1979; unless otherwise indicated, all quotations of Clarke are from this interview]) had made it impossible for his mother, Gladys Clarke, to marry his father, Kenneth Trothan, who was "a bit of an artist (he used to paint and write poetry)" and who was "two or three social levels below her." The family had ordered that there be no communication between their daughter and the father of her child; thus, "In my home my mother never *once* mentioned my father's name." Numerous Clarke stories deal with the theme of young men growing up in fatherless homes and with their attempts to relate to their fathers later in life. Yet Clarke insists that their dilemma did not reflect his own situation, but rather a common situation in Barbados. In his own case, "I didn't miss my father. My mother was my mother and my father, and my stepfather was my father."

Following his education at Combermere and Harrison College, the most prestigious schools in Barbados, Clarke taught for three years in Barbados. He went to Canada in 1955 to study economics at the University of Toronto. He has taught at several American universities, including Yale, Indiana University, Williams College, the University of Texas, and Duke University. He has done several special documentaries and literary programs on the Canadian Broadcasting Corporation. In 1974 he served as cultural attaché to the Barbadian Embassy in Washington, D.C., and from 1975 to 1976 he was cultural officer and advisor to the prime minister in Barbados, an experience which motivated *The Prime Minister* (1978), where he acknowledges, "John Moore may be regarded as Austin Clarke . . . the *essence* of John Moore . . . but not the *details* of John Moore."

Outspoken, provocative, witty, and at times outrageous, Austin Clarke is himself an unforgettable character. Everyone who knows him has at least one hilarious Austin Clarke memorate to relate. Aside from brief visits to the United States, Europe, and the Caribbean, Austin Clarke has spent all of his adult life in Toronto, where he lives with his wife, the former Betty Joyce Reynolds. They are the parents of three children: Janice Elizabeth, Loretta Anne, and Mphahlele Soyinka.

MAJOR WORKS AND THEMES

Austin Clarke is the author of five novels, a collection of short stories, and an autobiography. While his first two novels, some of his short stories, and his autobiography focus upon the problems of, as he phrases it in the title of his autobiography, "growing up stupid under the Union Jack," his major theme is the exile. Indeed, even those works which are set in Barbados, before exile begins, lay the foundations for this exploration. His first novel, *Survivors of the Crossing* (1964), relates the attempts of Rufus, a Black peasant worker on a sugarcane plantation, to revolt against the White-controlled establishment, a revolt at least partially inspired by rumors about the outside world—Canada and the United States. Clarke's second novel, *Among Thistles and Thorns* (1965), focuses on a young Barbadian schoolboy, Milton Sobers, who runs away. His efforts at flight are obviously a desire for exile, inspired by the stories of his real father, who had migrated to the United States and brought back tales of Harlem, which inspired Milton's persistent dreams of Harlem. He longs for "new worlds and countries and happiness like Columbus; and perhaps, if the day was long enough, I could even reach as far away from this village and from Nathan [his mother's lover] and my mother, as Harlem New York, America" (p. 179).

Growing up Stupid Under the Union Jack (1980) is a hilarious account of the details of the Barbadian society that created and shaped Clarke and his generation, one which furnishes a basis for a clearer understanding of his exiles whose values and mores, goals and desires, actions and behaviors may impress us as warped, extreme, ridiculous, irrational, self-defeating, and unrealistic. Clarke illustrates how upwardly mobile Barbadians are led to a blind, unquestioning acceptance of the superiority of the British in all things and are motivated to make a desperate effort to emulate English culture in every conceivable manner. Through a system of cruel intimidation, brutal floggings, and constant drills, Barbadian children are trained to accept blindly British propaganda, culture, standards, and values and to repress all natural inclinations and intellectual curiosity, and most importantly to reject any and all aspects of their own culture (including their religion, their speech, even their own families) in an "educational process" whereby progress is in effect a move toward greater ignorance. Quite appropriately, the boys who were most highly accomplished in any particular subject area were designated as that specific kind of fool. Thus when Clarke was promoted to a higher form, he had to determine what kind of fool he wanted to become. He considered being "an English fool, a French fool or a Geography fool. But there were already enough bright-bright-bright boys, foolish boys, in my class. It remained for me to be a running fool" (McClelland and Stewart ed., p. 80). Later, as his family's economic situation improved, new opportunities opened up to him: "The future looked good. I could become a barrister: a legal fool" (p. 172). Given the experience of the Barbadian youth, it is no wonder that when one completed his education he was already an exile in his own land: Clarke notes, "We lived in Barbados, but we studied English society and manners. . . . I was more at ease in England, the Mother Country, than in Barbados" (p. 72).

Several of Clarke's short stories and his trilogy (*The Meeting Point*, 1967; *Storm of Fortune*, 1973, and *The Bigger Light*, 1975) treat the theme of the Barbadian in exile, usually in Canada, occasionally in the United States. Most of his male characters suffer a real or a symbolic death in their alien home as they destroy themselves through their rejection of their background, their culture, and their identity, in the effort to emulate, assimilate, and adopt a foreign culture. Though the conditions of exile are no less bitter for the female Barbadians, they tend to be stronger in their sense of themselves and in their retention of their cultural roots and their humanity.

Most of Clarke's male exiles in their quest for goals motivated by Canadian (or Western) society's materialistic symbols of success (a big bank account, a big car, a house in Rosedale) continue that process of repudiation and denial of self begun in their childhood education in Barbados. Boysie, of *The Bigger Light*, throws out his West Indian records, changes his speech, avoids association with other West Indians, and will not return to Barbados, not even for a visit. Throughout this novel, as well as in *The Meeting Point*, he lusts after White women and becomes increasingly alienated from his Black Barbadian wife. He buys a big luxury car, which he keeps hidden from Dots. Jefferson Theophillis Belle of "Four Stations in His Circle" (in *When He Was Free and Young and He Used to Wear Silks*, 1971; hereafter cited as *F & Y*) is so embarrassed by his Black friends after he acquires his big house in Rosedale that he determines never to speak to Black people again. Belle, whose neighbors assume he is the gardener rather than the owner of the house, spends his time sitting in his big empty house looking at his bank book or dressing in formal attire and walking in and out of the thirteen rooms in his house pretending he is talking to sophisticated and aristocratic ladies and gentlemen visiting him. Even before he completely lost touch with reality, this wealthy miser ignored a plea from his sick mother to send her money for an operation. Similarly Calvin of "The Motor

Car'' repudiates all human ties to achieve his goal: *''I am here working for a living and a motor car and if my mother herself come in my way and be an obstacle against me getting them two things. . . . I would kill her by Christ''* (*F & Y*, p. 57).

Destroyed by their denial of self, their loss of humanity, their futile efforts at assimilation, and their obsessions, most of Clarke's males either lose their lives or their sanity. The idea of death—symbolic and real—permeates these works. Throughout *The Bigger Light* Boysie listens to ''*dead* music'' (p. 25), he lives in a ''coffin-bedroom'' (214), he frequently thinks about his dead friend Henry, and ''he wondered if he was dying too; or if he was already dead'' (p. 223); Clarke observes, ''It was dead inside the apartment.'' This sense of death is reinforced by the fact that by and large West Indians in Canada seem infertile—they do not procreate (the only one who conceives in Canada is the unmarried Estelle in *The Meeting Point*, who is impregnated by a White man, and she aborts). Despite the numerous Barbadian exile couples we see in Clarke's trilogy, no one else ever seems to conceive. The situation reaches its most ludicrous apogee with Dots and Boysie: when Boysie talks to her about having a child, she misunderstands him and brings home a cat. Later she becomes obsessed with adopting a child, but the child she desires is a hopelessly crippled child, one with brittle bones who can never walk. Clarke implies that his exiles have substituted their unnatural obsessions with wealth for their natural ability to reproduce—thus ''the bank account was mounting and climbing like a woman belly when she in the family-way'' (''The Motor Car,'' *F & Y*, p. 58). Clearly there is not much promise of continued life for Clarke's Barbadian exile community in cold Canada.

Despite their unhappiness in Canada, a return home also seems impossible. John Moore of *The Prime Minister* goes back to Barbados to accept a high-level government position, but though he returns physically, he cannot really return. Upon his arrival, he suffers more difficulties than the other travelers (mostly tourists) getting through immigration. He knows he is ''not really at home'' (p. 16). His efforts at return are exacerbated by the fact that he has forgotten the language; he simply can't reacclimate himself; his sinuses, which had not bothered him for twenty years, start acting up again. Symbolically Moore keeps recalling *Paradise Lost*, but he can't remember anything about *Paradise Regained*. Obviously the paradise that was Barbados *is* lost—to the tourists and the corrupt, inept government. The prostitution or rape of the island is suggested in the fact that both men and women prostitute themselves to the hoards of tourists who overrun the island and that the government protects these tourists at any cost. Ultimately, John Moore, unable to regain his Paradise, has to flee the island to save his life.

Here and elsewhere Clarke characters reminisce about the days BT (before tourists). This is most memorably treated in one of Clarke's most masterfully executed stories, ''Bonanza 1972 in Toronto.'' This story is narrated as a telephone call, where we hear a Barbadian domestic's part of her telephone conversation with a friend, whom she has called to tell about a promotional affair at the Holiday Inn in Canada to which her Canadian mistress had been invited but which she attended in her stead. The Barbadian Tourist Board royally entertained. The whole show, with the drinks, the refreshments, the motion picture showing a White woman on a Barbadian beach sifting sand through her hands, is a kind of symbol of the surrender of the island to the tourists. She is suddenly angered that any foreigner can go to Barbados and live like royalty and sift "*my* sand in her hands" (p. 132). Recognizing that her land is being lost to the tourists, she notes, "I feel that I did lose a baby" (p. 132).

The technical brilliance of "Bonanza" is not always realized in Clarke's works. He is a competent novelist and storyteller, but he is sometimes careless and impatient about some of the finer details of characterization and plot development. When I complained about some of the unanswered and inadequately treated loose ends of the plot of *Storm of Fortune*, such as the mystery about who wrote the letter to Agatha warning her against marrying Henry, whether or not anyone was following Henry just before his death, and the nature of Henry's death, Clarke noted, "I became very tired and fed up with Henry. Henry became a bore when I was writing the book, and my frustration came to such a head that I *had* to get rid of him and that's how I got rid of him. If I was writing the book now with, what I presume, more skills about writing, I would not have gotten rid of Henry that way." He also confided that it was Dots who wrote the letter to Agatha—but the novel itself does not provide clues to lead the reader to this conclusion. Similarly the episode regarding Mrs. Macmillan and Estelle in the same novel seems contrived and unrealistic and unrelated to the rest of the novel. At other times Clarke creates considerable suspense about a situation and then drops it—such as Boysie's continual reading about rape and his obsession with the woman whom he watches get off the subway each day in *The Bigger Light*; or the nature of the pictures that Weekesie keeps saying he wants to show to John Moore and about which he is presumably killed (*The Prime Minister*). Despite these occasional lapses, Clarke's prose is usually lucid, clear, simple, and direct. He convincingly captures the essence of the Barbadian communities which he portrays, creates memorable characters, and explores the sociological and psychological realities of their lives and relationships. His tone ranges from bitter and tragic to comic and satirical, but his forte is the humorous or satirical account.

CRITICAL RECEPTION

Austin Clarke has received very little critical attention. Edward Baugh ("Since 1960: Some Highlights," in *West Indian Literature*, ed. Bruce King, 1979) gives a general review of his works through the Toronto trilogy. He rejects *Survivors of the Crossing* as "a failure, crudely propagandising, overambitious and rather hysterical in its angry, implausible narrative of a latter-day uprising on a Barbadian sugar plantation" (p. 81); *Among Thistles and Thorns* he judges "a worthy contribution to the West Indian literature of childhood'' (p. 81). But he claims that it is with the trilogy and the short story collection ''that Clarke lays claim to his own territory'' and makes a ''substantial'' and ''valuable contribution to the literary presentation of the Black man in the white world'' (pp. 82–83). In ''Friday in Crusoe's City: The Question of Language in the West Indian Novels of Exile'' (1981), Baugh compares the treatment of the theme of exile in *The Bigger Light* and in Samuel Selvon's *Moses Ascending*.

Among the most extensive studies of Clarke's fiction are Keith S. Henry's overview ''An Assessment of Austin Clarke'' (1985) and Lloyd Brown's ''The West Indian Novel in North America: A Study of Austin Clarke'' (1970), Lloyd W. Brown explores the major themes in Clarke's fiction from *Survivors of the Crossing* through the trilogy, especially the theme of Black awareness and identity and the impact of the North American experience on the development of these themes. In another essay, ''Austin Clarke in Canadian Reviews'' (1968), Brown responds to White responses to Clarke's work, which he asserts suffer from an ignorance of the Black experience and the psychological realities growing out of that experience.

HONORS AND AWARDS

Clarke has received the President's Medal, University of Western Ontario (1966), the Belmont Short Story Award (1965), the Canada Council Senior Arts Fellowship (1967 and 1970), and the Casa de Las Americas Literary Prize (1980).

BIBLIOGRAPHY

Works by Austin Clarke

The Survivors of the Crossing. London: Heinemann, 1964; Toronto: McClelland and Stewart, 1964.

Amongst Thistles and Thorns. London: Heinemann, 1965; Toronto: McClelland and Stewart, 1965.

The Meeting Point. London: Heinemann, 1967; Toronto: Macmillan, 1967; Boston: Little, Brown, 1972.

When He Was Free and Young and He Used to Wear Silks. Toronto: Anansi, 1971; Boston: Little, Brown, 1973.

Storm of Fortune. Boston: Little, Brown, 1973.

The Bigger Light. Boston: Little, Brown, 1975.

The Prime Minister. Ontario: Ontario General, 1977; London: Routledge & Kegan Paul, 1977, 1978.

Growing Up Stupid Under the Union Jack. Havana: Casa de las Americas, 1980; Toronto: McClelland and Stewart, 1980.

Studies of Austin Clarke

Baugh, Edward. "Friday in Crusoe's City: The Question of Language in the West Indian Novel of Exile." *ACLALS Bulletin* (Mysore) 5 (1980), 1–12.

———. "Since 1960: Some Highlights." In *West Indian Literature*, Bruce King, ed. 1979, pp. 78–94.

Boxill, Anthony. "The Novels of Austin Clarke." *The Fiddlehead* 75 (Spring 1968).

Brown, Lloyd. "Austin Clarke in Canadian Reviews." *Canadian Literature* (Autumn 1968), 101–04.

———. "The West Indian Novel in North America: A Study of Austin Clarke." *The Journal of Commonwealth Literature* (July 1970), 89–103.

Henry, Keith S. "An Assessment of Austin Clarke." *CLAJ* 29 (September 1985), 9–32.

MacCulloch, Clare. "Look Homeward, Bajan: A Look at the Work of Austin Clarke, a Barbadian Expatriate as Seen by an Outsider." *Bim* 55 (July-December 1972), 179–82.

See also General Bibliography: Allis, Herdeck, Hughes, and Ramchand (1970).

EDWARD BAUGH

Frank Collymore (1893–1980)

BIOGRAPHY

Frank Appleton Collymore, teacher, actor, artist, poet, short story writer, lexicographer, and editor, was born in the parish of St. Michael, Barbados, on January 7, 1893. An only child, born to parents relatively late in their lives, he was nurtured in love and affection in a secure little world of parents, grandmother, aunts, uncles, nursemaid, cook, and garden-boy. John Wickham, his friend and colleague, recalls that once, in his later years, Colly, as he was affectionately known, said to him, "I don't think that there has ever been anyone who has been as loved as I have been" (*The Nation Carifesta Bulletin*, July 20, 1981, p. 4). No wonder, then, that when Collymore came to publish a brief memoir of his childhood, he should have entitled it "Non Immemor" (*Bim* [March 1974 and June 1975]), taking the title from the motto on the crest of an ancestor, Captain Robert Cullimore—*non immemor beneficii* (not unmindful of kindness).

Frank Collymore came of middle-class stock of modest means. His father was a government customs officer. The Captain Robert Cullimore from whom he traced his descent had arrived in "the Barbadoes" from Britain in the mid–17th century. A dash of color eventually darkened one branch of the family tree, as a result of a liaison with a slave girl. Collymore himself has conjectured that this color may have been what delayed the marriage of his parents, Joseph Appleton Collymore (1857–1932) and Rebecca Wilhelmina, née Clarke (1850–1934), although the cause may well have been the smallness of Joseph's salary. "My parents had married late in life . . . their engagement being a protracted one of some ten years, and I suspect that this was because my mother's father did not wholly approve of his daughter's marrying into a family that was not impeccably Aryan'' (*Bim* [March 1974], 3–4).

Collymore attended Combermere School, a grammar school for boys, between 1903 and 1910, and the happiness of early childhood gave way to the happiness of schooldays. His close association with Combermere was to last for sixty years. No sooner had he left school than the headmaster asked him to join the staff. When he retired in 1958 he was deputy headmaster, but he continued to teach at the school, in an acting capacity, until 1963. He taught mainly English and French and was well liked by the boys. Through his artistic talent, his understanding and approachability, he exerted a lasting influence, from their formative years, on a few who were to become outstanding West Indian writers, most notably George Lamming. The friendship which developed between the two opened to the youth the marvellous world of Collymore's library at his home, ''Woodville.'' In an interview (*Kas-Kas: Interview with Three Caribbean Writers*, ed. Ian Munro and Reinhard Sander [Austin, Texas: Afro and Afro-American Research Institute, 1972], pp. 5–20), Lamming said: ''I was fascinated by Collymore. He used to write a great deal in private. I always remember the very first time I went to his house. He had these volumes of poems in a sort of exercise book. . . . For me, the whole school curriculum became absolute nonsense. When I was supposed to be studying school material, I was reading books from Collymore's library'' (p. 6).

Collymore's flowering as a poet was sudden, late, and short-lived. In July, 1942, while confined to his house on account of illness, he began to fill an exercise book with poems and drawings. The drawings existed in their own right and were not always illustrations of the poems. Other exercise books were similarly filled in quick succession. His first published book of poetry, *Thirty Poems*, appeared in 1944. Then followed *Beneath the Casuarinas* (1945) and *Flotsam: Poems 1942–1948* (1948), the three books comprising 103 poems in all. Then his muse deserted him and he wrote only a handful of poems after the 1940s. He also wrote short stories, eighteen of which appeared in *Bim* between 1942 and 1971. Some of these were also broadcast on the BBC ''Caribbean Voices'' program.

But it was through his editing and publishing of the little magazine *Bim*, even more than through his own writing, that Collymore earned his reputation as a doyen and godfather of West Indian literature. The significance of the magazine was summed up by Lamming in a special introduction to the June 1955 issue: ''There are not many West Indian writers today who did not use *Bim* as a kind of platform, the surest, if not the only avenue, by which they might reach a literate and sensitive reading public, and almost all of the West Indians who are now writers in a more professional sense and whose work has compelled the attention of readers and writers in other countries, were introduced, so to speak, by *Bim*.''

Through *Bim*, Collymore came to be at the center of the West Indian literary awakening of the 1940s and 1950s. The contacts with writers which he made through the magazine enabled his encouragement to work at a very direct and personal level and gave scope to the generosity of spirit and capacity for friendship which were among his chief virtues. Edgar Mittelholzer, Lamming, Derek Walcott, Edward Brathwaite—these are a few of the notable cases in point.

Collymore died on July 17, 1980. He is survived by his second wife, Ellice (née Honychurch), whom he married in 1947, and four daughters, the eldest by his first wife, who had died in 1943.

MAJOR WORKS AND THEMES

Short Stories

One of *Bim*'s achievements is that it encouraged the development of the short story form as a significant medium for the West Indian literary imagination. Collymore was himself no mean practitioner, adept at inventing and telling a story.

Most of his stories deal with solitaries, eccentrics, psychotics even, and involve something of the morbid. They are usually structured toward the climactic revelation of some dark secret or grotesque-ironic resolution. The earliest published story of this kind, "Shadows" (published under the pseudonym Francis Appleton in *Bim* [December 1942]), expresses a general thematic interest that runs through these stories. The narrator asks: "The mind. What do you and I know of the mind, and of the vast forces which lie around us, in us and yet not wholly of us, secret, prowling, mysterious, fraught with such power as is beyond our knowledge, watching and waiting to encompass us, to overthrow what we call the seat of the reason—the mind whose powers and weaknesses we can never hope to comprehend?" (p. 27).

"Shadows" takes the form of a letter written by the narrator-protagonist, from a mental asylum as is eventually made clear, to a friend of his youth, apparently the only friend he ever had, with whom he has not been in touch for many years. The letter is a cry for help, and it naturally becomes an account of how the writer came to be in the asylum. He establishes early in the story that he "was always reticent and retiring, a dreamer" (p. 27). His circumstances encourage that disposition. After his one friend goes away, his father dies and leaves him "alone in the old house by the woods" (p. 27). He is physically frail and sickly, unfit for outdoor life or for the rigors of a commercial or professional life. However, his father has left him well provided for, so he is able to lead the life to which he is temperamentally drawn, "to be alone and to dream" (p. 27).

The house, and in particular his own room, exerts a strange, seemingly unhealthy fascination for him. The house is a sort of alter ego: "I was aware of the strangeness of that particular room, its strangeness and its sinister beauty: they entranced me. In its gloomy recesses lay thick shadows which invaded me day by day, but at night, when all was silent and dark, the shadows thronged triumphant, whispering to me strange secrets obscene and fleeting as my troubled dreams'' (p. 28). The room and its shadows become symbolic of the dark, secret places of his own mind, as well, perhaps, as of inherited personality traits.

His only companion, his dog, dies, and in his sorrow he becomes so ill that the doctor advises a change of surroundings. So the house is closed and he moves into town, where, as his health revives, he becomes caught up in a social bustle which overexcites his precariously balanced nerves: ''I was excited, tremendously excited, borne on by a nervous energy that was totally foreign to me'' (p. 29). But even as he is excited by this new, alien life, so he misses the house of shadows. He is to learn, in effect, that the old house will not let him go, that he cannot escape from his true self.

He takes a wife, mainly out of a ''desire to acquire one of these products of the [new] artificial society in which [he] moved'' and ''to establish power over another human being'' (p. 29). His bride is beautiful but strange, and he is drawn by her ''dark and wayward aloofness which seemed to scorn everyone, a passionate pride of spirit that lurked and peered, untamed and unafraid from those half-veiled eyes'' (p. 29). He takes her back to the old house, and under its malevolent influence the two are locked in a morbid attraction of mutual hatred. One night he attempts to strangle her while she is apparently asleep. But as he moves toward her she ''awakens,'' mockingly aware of his intention. Mysteriously, she dies, hurling a curse at him, saying that she will return to claim him.

After her death he feels a great sense of relief, and in a sort of euphoria he ''actually [takes] pleasure in mixing with others'' (p. 27). He takes a second wife, Elaine, open, outgoing, cheerful, who seems to strengthen his new state of psychic health. Inevitably, he takes her back to the old house, feeling now that it holds no more terrors for him. He awakens in the night to a frightening sense of the presence of some malevolent force in the room: ''Something mephitic and obscene, something too awful for the human mind to contemplate had taken place'' (p. 81). It is that the evil spirit of the first wife has taken possession of Elaine, who is transformed into a physical likeness of the evil one. In his horror he strangles the creature, only to find, to his greater horror, that she turns again into Elaine. Driven by the ''shadows,'' he has killed his beloved Elaine. He has killed whatever is healthy and normal in him, and the story may be read as a fable about the ways of evil and the terrors which the mind holds for itself.

Other stories by Collymore which explore the mind's dark places include ''Miss Edison'' (*Bim* [June 1943]), ''Some People are Meant to Live Alone'' (*Bim* [April 1944]), ''There's Always the Angels'' (*Bim* [February 1945]), and ''The Man Who Loved Attending Funerals'' (*Bim* [June 1955]). (See Sander, *An Index to Bim*, 1973.)

In ''The Snag'' and ''Mark Learns Another Lesson'' Collymore depicts, with his usual sensitivity and precision, the world and mind of childhood and shows himself no less adept at handling what may be called domestic realism than he is at handling the psychological bizarre. In ''The Snag'' (*Bim*,no. 2), seven-year-old Mark goes to spend a week with his spinster aunts. It is his first experience of sleeping away from home, and we share his excitement at his new freedom to enjoy the delights of Graham Lodge. But this freedom, like his imaginativeness, has, alas, to recognize restraint and reality in the shape of imperious Aunt Jane: "When Mark visited Graham Lodge Aunt Jane was a perpetual reminder that one could not escape authority. Nothing was ever quite perfect; there was always a snag somewhere" (p. 15). And there are other snags, such as having your face and hands soaped and scrubbed by Aunt Jane after you have made a mess of them with the "greasy crumbs" from the "crackly thickly buttered toast" at "early morning tea" (p. 77).

Mark's amusingly precocious awareness of life's snags is put in ironic perspective and given a new, serious dimension with the "true" snag with which the story ends. The aunts take in a lodger, an old lady of eighty-nine, who had been a friend of their parents and whose sisters have now died. Mark cannot imagine anyone as old as that and asks, with unintended humor, when he first hears about her, if she is alive. But nothing which he can imagine can prepare him for the actuality of the old lady. He sees her for the first time "in the early January dusk," with "the drawing room lamp . . . shining wanly. In the far corner of the room beside the chiffonier a figure was seated, a figure that seemed too fantastic to be real. He came to an involuntary halt and had to be pushed on by Aunt Jane" (p. 83). We expect a Dickensian character, perhaps, and indeed, for a moment we might recall not only Miss Havisham but also Wemmick's Aged P (*Great Expectations*).

However, any suggestion of the comic is quickly dispelled by the harrowingly pathetic. Mark is so disturbed by his encounter with the old lady that he awakens in the middle of the night from a nightmare in which she is "chasing him round and round the house" (p. 87). Tearfully he asks Aunt Jane if everybody has to get old. She tries to "get round" his question in the way of adults with the awkward questions that children ask. But we sense that her evasive answer and her desire to change the subject are an indication of her own secret disturbance at the question. This gives the author the opportunity to convey the full significance of the old lady's presence by shifting from the point of view of the child to that of Aunt Jane. Through her consciousness, we see all three, the child, middle-aged "solid" Aunt Jane, and the decrepit Miss Martha, held in the baleful light of a quiet, Joycean epiphany: "She came back to Mark's bed and looked down at him. He was so young, so full of life. And downstairs, Miss Martha! And poised between the two slipping dangerously fast over to the wrong side, herself. . . . Ah, well, there was always a snag somewhere. She took up the lamp, gave Mark another glance, closed the door behind her and went downstairs" (p. 89).

In "Mark Learns Another Lesson" (*Bim*, no. 14), we see another instance of the child getting a rude awakening from an encounter with the adult world; however, this time the point is not so much tragic as grimly satirical. The criticism of values which Collymore undertakes in this story is widened in "R.S.V.P. to

Mrs Bush-Hall'' (*Bim* [July-December 1962]), the only one of the stories in which society becomes the center of focus. It is also the most obviously West Indian of Collymore's stories, one in which class, color, and colonial values are central issues.

Poetry

Virtually all of Collymore's poetry was written within the space of six or seven years, and it is difficult to speak of stages of development. Little or nothing is lost by not discussing each of his first three collections individually; so for the sake of convenience this commentary is based on the *Collected Poems* (1959), which contains almost all of the pieces in the three earlier books, including all of the better pieces.

Collymore's poems were written mostly during or just after World War II, but in the few poems which treat of war there is none of the patriotic fervor which might have been expected from a loyal son of ''little England,'' as Barbadians are said to have called their island. Rather, there is horror at the human suffering and degradation, and cynicism at the national vanity which wars express. The horror, revulsion, and sense of human degradation inspire ''Newsreel from Buchenwald'':

> . . . they cry out, these dread
> Grey dead: the harvest
> Of the barbed-wire heaped,
> The heaped sheaves garnered.
>
> (p. 87)

''De Angelis'' and ''E Pluribus Unum'' look at war as an expression of questionable national pride. In the former, nationalism is the new religion, and the unholy angels of this religion are war planes. In ''E Pluribus Unum'' we see people reduced to mere statistics to glorify national pride (e.g., the impressive numbers of troops mentioned in war dispatches).

To see the individual in the mass rather than to see the many (individuals) reduced to one mass of conformity and impersonality is a theme of a few other poems Audenesque in style and content. ''Portrait of Mr X'' describes the average nonentity of a citizen, a creature ''of appropriate catchwords / (Sing yo-ho for the status quo), / And tinted with the sober shades of respectability'' (p. 96). A similar sort of portrait is painted in ''Voici la plume de mon Oncle,'' where the educational system is seen as playing a large part in producing Mr. X.

But although Collymore satirizes a socially comfortable conformity and the social factors that make for a self-satisfied anonymity, and although he can ''Thank God for rebels'' (''Rebels,'' p. 88), he is no radical and takes a conservative view of West Indian history in the few poems which treat that subject, e.g., ''Triptych'' and ''Homage to Planters.'' In the latter he says of the old

West Indian plantocracy: " 'Tis said they are a grasping lot / Who grudge the peasant all; / Who chiefly live to fill their guts" (p. 34). His picture of them may be somewhat of a caricature, but he evasively and naively concludes:

Perhaps they do. I do not know
    Much about sugar-kings;
But I salute with gratitude
    The loving care which wrings
    Such beauty from the soil.

That it is *loving* care which wrings "such beauty from the soil" is taken for granted; and the role of the peasant/laborer in that enterprise is not acknowledged.

But if Collymore's broad view of West Indian history, as expressed in such poems (see also "Old Windmill," p. 33), is perhaps disconcertingly acquiescent, he holds a sharper focus on the lot of the individual poor and Black, in poems such as "Day's End," "Amanda," and "Ballad of an Old Woman." "Day's End," which makes a striking parallel with A. L. Hendriks' "Road to Lacovia," describes "an old peasant woman" whom the poet sees "one evening" in the

. . . neglected fringe of a fishing-village,
Bare with the sea-blast, where only
Cactus flaunt their flagpoles in the sun
And the scorched grass seeks precarious tenure
Of the sharp-toothed cliffs of clay.

(p. 101)

The landscape is a metaphor for the hard, meager existence of the woman, and like the landscape, her life is marked by a stark resilience. The poet sees into the depth and strength of her humanity and praises the indomitable spirit with which, "regal and proud," she faces death as she had faced life, going "Down to her marriage-bed within the earth / Where bone shall bloom to everlastingness."

"Amanda" and "Ballad of an Old Woman" are also sympathetic poems about poor Black women. The latter uses a bitingly ironic blend of the nursery rhyme about the old woman who lived in a shoe and the folk tradition of narrative protest songs to record the tragic life and death of the woman who is the poem's subject. The poem economically traces her "progress" from being the unwed mother of twenty-one children to her lonely death in the almshouse, with the refrain "Singing Glory to God" acting as an ironic comment on the religion which surrounded her, and to which she no doubt subscribed, but which seems to have done nothing for her.

The bare, rocky, wind-swept coastal landscape which Collymore describes so accurately, and uses so appropriately as metaphor for the "manscape" (Edward Brathwaite's word) of "Day's End," recurs in a few other poems and helps to distinguish his treatment of Nature, another of his main themes. In the Barbadian landscape, one that is not generally dramatic or colorful, not marked by lush vegetation or richly endowed with grand effects, one that can seem generally bland, Collymore's sensitive eye picks up, and turns to symbolic use, the low-key drama of scrub and wind-swept, barren, rocky terrain. This landscape, too, provides an appropriate theater for the quiet, easily overlooked triumph of survival which is the "Blue Agave" (p. 36), as well as an appropriate symbol for the life, as it is an appropriate resting-place for the remains of the persona who is the subject of the elegiac "Requiescat" (p. 113).

But Collymore also has his more conventionally poetic genuflections to the beauty of Nature (see "Homage to Beauty," p. 15), in some of which fancy heightens the colors of Nature and arranges them into aesthetically pleasing compositions, guided by the painter's sense of color and form. The sea is a particular passion of his, and his sea poems extend his fidelity to Barbadian landscape. Poems like "Return," "Hymn to the Sea," "Schooner," and "Sea-plunge" are a tribute to the place and power of the sea in the small-islander's consciousness, a tribute which goes beyond the merely local to suggest a deep universal symbolism.

Some of the better Nature poems, like "Beneath the Casuarinas," "That Day," "Newhaven," and "Treasure Trove," are quiet, carefully recorded epiphanies which capture the fleeting moment when the commonplace is transfigured and the isolated, reflecting mind suddenly is at one with the world and sees "into the life of things" ("Newhaven," p. 38). Love and mortality, and the painful link between the two, are also among Collymore's main themes. Love itself makes its poignant, eloquent, paradoxical appeal to man in "Solicitation":

> Will you take me, the lightning flame
> Entwined with roses, the sword
> Stained with wine, the unbroken silence
> Of the reverberating word?
>
> (p. 114)

The poet also evokes the bittersweet of sexual love with sometimes a wry, playful detachment, sometimes an epigrammatic terseness, sometimes a slow, plangent music. He achieves a remarkable variety of tone and movement within the compass of a few short poems.

In his treatment of the themes of loss and death, Collymore shows the same versatility and good sense which typify his work as a whole. There is, for example, the gravity and classical restraint of "V.C. Invictus," in memory of a friend killed in World War I:

> We part here, Publius, my friend;
> You to the swift, heroic end
> Where dreams and action soon will meet
> In the fated moment.
>
> (p. 104)

That contrasts with the satirical vivacity of the dramatic monologue ''Roman Holiday'':

> O, it was a lovely funeral!
> One hundred and thirty-two cars,
> And three of them packed high with flowers
> And the streets thronged with people—
> It reminded me of the Coronation.
>
> (p. 90)

Collymore's playfulness and ironic wit make way at times for pure levity, knowingly, unapologetically offered, an essential part of a poetic persona that refuses to take itself or the world too seriously. It is to this side of Collymore that we owe the delightful diversion of his ''collybeasts,'' a zany bestiary of fantastic creatures which enlivened the early pages of *Bim*, as well as his Ogden Nash-like *Rhymed Ruminations on the Fauna of Barbados* (1968).

CRITICAL RECEPTION

Because it has had such limited exposure, Collymore's writing has enjoyed very little critical notice, and that has so far been confined to the poetry, since the short stories have not been collected.

Henry Swanzy, reviewing *Flotsam* (1948), says that the ''predominant note'' is ''visual'' (p. 77). He finds that in their philosophical content the poems are a ''conventional assertion of human values'' (p. 78), marked by ''a certain lack of vigour, of spiritual energy, perhaps of the desire to shock and hurt'' (p. 78), but that the collection ''asserts, in its own way, quite as triumphantly as anything more vigorous, the self-justification of the imagination regarded as a way of life'' (p. 79).

Generally speaking, Swanzy's estimate of Collymore's poetry is echoed by Bruce Hamilton, who, in his introduction to the *Collected Poems*, categorizes it as ''minor,'' and finds that its ''peculiar distinction and charm lies in what Wordsworth called 'a wise passiveness' '' (p. 9). He also claims that ''the most telling'' of the poems ''are not organized. Words, phrases, pictures, images, have come unbidden, almost one suspects from the obscurely drawn frontiers of sleep'' (p. 9).

On the other hand, M. H. Combe-Martin, in his review of *Collected Poems* (1960), feels that the poet ''disciplines . . . decisively'' even those poems that come from ''a half dream world'' (p. 139). He praises Collymore for his qualities of humility, sensitivity, felicity, variety, and youthfulness and concludes that Collymore's poetry deserves to be remembered ''because he has found for the bodiless mood a body which comes with colour and melody which please eye and ear, because he loves this island land, the people of it, the sea around it, because he is happy loving it, and because he refuses to take himself too seriously'' (p. 139).

The point about not taking himself too seriously is echoed by Lloyd Brown when, referring to "Roman Holiday" and *Rhymed Ruminations*, he says that such works offer "a diversion from the solemnity with which pastoralist and cultural nationalist alike have treated the West Indian landscape" (*West Indian Poetry*, 1978, p. 91). Collymore, he says, "is the only comic talent of any significance, in standard English, in West Indian poetry" (p. 91).

Brown finds that Collymore's landscape poems are "a throwback to the neo-romantic imitativeness of the Caribbean pastoral" (p. 89), but he commends Collymore's "talent for narrative structure" (p. 89) and for "an incisive, yet subtle irony" (p. 89). He singles out "Words Are the Poem," "Triptych," "Voici la Plume de Mon Oncle," and "Roman Holiday" as exemplifying Collymore's strengths.

Like Brown, Edward Brathwaite and Edward Baugh address themselves to the question of Collymore's place in the history of West Indian poetry. Baugh sees his poetry as having marked "something of an advance in West Indian poetry," his influences having been "more twentieth-century than those of his coevals" (*West Indian Poetry 1900–1970*, 1971, p. 8). Brathwaite calls him "the great poet of the West Indian transition," but says that he "is not yet concerned with social reality" ("Frank Collymore," 1975, p. 278). Brathwaite makes special mention of the poem "Blue Agave," saying, "No other West Indian poet . . . has captured the desolation of the windward Caribbean coasts as precisely and as symbolically as Collymore in this poem" (p. 277).

HONORS AND AWARDS

For his work in the arts, Collymore was awarded a British Council fellowship to visit the United Kingdom in 1947. In 1958 he was made an Officer of the Order of the British Empire (OBE). In 1968 the University of the West Indies conferred on him an honorary master of arts degree.

BIBLIOGRAPHY

Works by Frank Collymore

Thirty Poems. Bridgetown, Barbados: Advocate, 1944.

Beneath the Casuarinas. Bridgetown, Barbados: Advocate, 1945.

Flotsam: Poems 1942–1948. Bridgetown, Barbados: Advocate, 1948.

Notes for a Glossary of Words and Phrases of Barbadian Dialect. 1955; 4th ed. Barbados: n.p., 1970.

Collected Poems. Bridgetown, Barbados: Advocate, 1959.

Rhymed Ruminations on the Fauna of Barbados. Bridgetown, Barbados: Advocate, 1968.

Selected Poems. Bridgetown, Barbados: Coles Printery, 1971.

For a checklist of Collymore's short stories, see *An Index to Bim*, ed. Reinhard W. Sander. Trinidad and Tobago: UWI Extra-Mural Studies Unit, 1973.

Studies of Frank Collymore

Baugh, Edward. "Frank Collymore: A Biographical Portrait." *Savacou* 7/8 (January-June 1973), 139–48.

———. Review of *Selected Poems*. *Bim* (July-December 1971), 58–60.

———. "Frank Collymore and the Miracle of *Bim*." In *New World Quarterly* (Barbados Independence Issue) 3 (Dead Season 1966/Crop time 1967), 129–33.

Brathwaite, Edward. "Frank Collymore." In *Contemporary Poets*, ed. James Vinson. 2nd ed. London: St. James; New York: St. Martin's, 1975, pp. 275–78.

Combe-Martin, M. H. Review of *Collected Poems*. *Bim* 8 (January-June 1960), 137–39.

Hamilton, Bruce. Introduction to *Collected Poems*. Bridgetown, Barbados: Advocate, 1959.

Swanzy, Henry. Review of *Flotsam*. *Bim* 3 (December 1948), 77–79.

Wickham, John. "Colly—a Profile." *The Bajan and South Caribbean*, (January 1973), 12, 14, 16–19, 31. First published in *Opus* (Port-of-Spain) (1960).

Wickham, John. "None More Loved nor More Loving: A Personal Note on Frank Collymore." *The Nation Carifesta Bulletin* (Barbados), July 20, 1981, p. 4.

See also General Bibliography: Allis, Baugh (1971), Brown, Herdeck, and Hughes.

LEOTA S. LAWRENCE

O. R. Dathorne (1934–   )

BIOGRAPHY

Oscar Ronald Dathorne was born on November 19, 1934, in Georgetown, Guyana, to Oscar Robinson Dathorne, a machine mechanic, and his wife, Rosalie Piezer Dathorne. He was the oldest of seven children. Young Dathorne's involvement with reading and writing began at an early age. The author claims that even as a child writing was important to him: it was the only medium he knew through which he could capture and contain any and all experiences. He also states that he viewed himself as a "comic," "a funny person," who was able to see humor in the behavior of the people around him. The young author hoped to capture this humorous side of life in his early stories and poems (telephone interview, December 21, 1983; the following quotations of Dathorne are from this interview).

In 1946 the young Dathorne was awarded one of the few highly competitive government county scholarships, which would enable him to attend the prestigious boys' school, Queen's College, in Guyana. At Queen's College, where he was a student for the next seven years, Dathorne first completed successfully the Cambridge School certificate and two years later wrote the advanced general certificate of education. According to the author, his one overriding ambition was to be the head teacher of a country school. While awaiting the results of his examinations, Dathorne, in preparation for his career as a rural head teacher, applied to a university in London for enrollment as an external student. He hoped to earn his bachelor of arts degree through private study and tutoring.

An unforeseen incident at this time, however, irrevocably altered the plans and the entire future of the author. The older Dathorne lost his job. His efforts to start his own business were unsuccessful. In the words of the author, "Those were dark days for us . . . in those days when you lost your job, you lost it for all time." As a final resort, the Dathorne family emigrated to England and a new life. In London, the father, the oldest son, and the oldest daughter became the breadwinners. After two years Dathorne left the family home and entered the University of Sheffield to study English. In 1957 he received his bachelor's degree in English and enrolled in the master's degree program. The author received a certificate in education from the University of London in 1959. This was also the year he married Hilde Ostermaier and traveled to northern Nigeria to take a position as lecturer in English at the University of Ahmadu Bello.

While in Africa, in addition to teaching, Dathorne became involved in the production of the Radio Nigeria Educational Series. In 1960 he received his master's degree from the University of Sheffield and began work on his doctorate. In 1964, the year in which the Dathornes became parents of a daughter, Shade Cecily, the author accepted a position as lecturer in the English Department at the University of Ibadan. Two years later, Dathorne formally received his Ph.D. degree from the University of Sheffield. It was at this time also that there was a second political coup in Nigeria, and the Dathornes left.

Dathorne obtained a position with the United Nations and embarked on a lecture tour of Europe. In 1967, while on tour, the author obtained a diploma in education from the University of London. In 1967, too, a son, Alexander Franz Keith, was born to the Dathornes. Dathorne's sojourn in the United States began in 1970 with an invitation to lecture at Yale University. Following a year at Yale, he taught at Howard University, Washington, D.C., in the Center for African Studies from 1970 to 1971. His next position was at the Ohio State University as professor of English from 1971 to 1974. The year 1974–75 he spent at the University of Miami (Florida) as a visiting professor of English. Then he returned to Ohio for two more years. In 1977 Dathorne returned to the University of Miami as director of American studies. His current position at the University of Miami is director of Caribbean, African and Afro-American studies. In 1979 Dathorne founded the Association of Caribbean Studies and the *Journal of Caribbean Studies*, which he has edited ever since.

MAJOR WORKS AND THEMES

As stated above, Dathorne has commented that his first intention in writing was to depict humor. He wanted in his stories to evoke laughter at the foibles of all people. This is what he attempted to do in his first novel, *Dumplings in the Soup* (1963). Dathorne himself has quoted Andrew Salkey, the Jamaican writer, as saying that West Indian writers "wear the comic mask with more assurance than the tragic" (*Caribbean Narrative*, p. 13). But he also pointed out the paradox that the West Indies has produced only two comic writers, noting that "perhaps one of the reasons why West Indian novelists have steered clear of humour in general is that they see it as their business to interpret and classify their world—one in which politics seems to play a leading role" (*Caribbean Narrative*, pp. 13–14). However, Dathorne in *Dumplings in the Soup* is certainly following in the tradition of Samuel Selvon, who makes use of explicit humor in his *Lonely Londoners* (1956), for example, and V. S. Naipaul's more subtle humor in his tragicomedies *The Mystic Masseur* (1957) and *The Suffrage of Elvira* (1958), to name two of his works.

Dumplings in the Soup, set in London, brings together a motley crowd of neo-Londoners, thrown together in an alien environment. These characters, West Indians, Africans, an English landlord, and even a dubious Pole, display a curious need for and resentment of each other. Most of these unlikely characters call the rooming house at Number 30 their home. Bofo, the arrogant and penniless African, in pursuit of some vague career, manages to occupy a room at Number 30 and to eat rather regularly without making any monetary contributions. Then there is Hazel, under whose strident laughter one detects a hint of pain and lost dreams. Hazel, who shares a room with Bigphil, is generous with her food as well as her love. Hazel maintains that she is "decent," was a nurse "back home," and insists repeatedly that "all men is dogs." Then, there is the bus conductress, fondly referred to as Pouncy by her rather timid lover Lilphil, with whom she shares a room. Pouncy is so proud of her career as a bus conductress that she wears her uniform night and day. There is also the newcomer, Jiffy Jacket, the only authentic student at Number 30. Jiffy is welcomed at Number 30 by the big-hearted Hazel, who has secret visions of being able to escape Number 30 with Jiffy. When her scheme to make Jiffy her permanent lover fails, Hazel is not angry. She moves quietly back into the room with Bigphil, and Jiffy remains her friend and confidant. It is in an exchange with Jiffy that another side of the boisterous Hazel is revealed:

> "Jiffy, I don't know what you think of me. But I can say I had a damn good try. But it ain't easy."
>
> "There ain't no standards to go by Hazel. That is the trouble, yes. Home, you belong to a Church and a family and a circle. They got certain things you can't do."
>
> She agreed with him, saying, "Yes, but here you black. Anything goes. We is all the same tarbrush and everybody walk 'pon we." (p. 74)

The novel concludes on a note of despondency; things have changed for no one but Jiffy, who is on his way to take up residence in the university to conclude his studies in architecture. Even as Jiffy is on his way out, Bofo is up to his old ways, trying to swindle Jiffy out of his money. And when Hazel informs Bill, the landlord, that everybody is looking for employment and soon there will be no tenants left at Number 30, he laughs and retorts: "Oh! It's just a phase! They all come back to Number 30 when there is nowhere to go. Number 30 is like a rest house, hotel, hostel and brothel all rolled into one" (p. 188).

In reading this novel, one assumes that the author, himself a West Indian student in England in the 1950s, is drawing on his own observations and experiences of the way life was for non-English students in England at the time. On this level, the work succeeds. An overall assessment of the structure of the novel, though, reveals that it is rather episodic with minimal character development.

By 1964 Dathorne had been living and teaching in West Africa for five years. Not surprising, then, is the fact that in his second work of fiction, *The Scholar Man* (1964), his scene shifts from London to Nigeria, and his protagonist, Adam Questus, becomes a Black West Indian ostensibly in search of his African heritage. Dathorne has said that he decided in the 1960s to research Caribbean literature because for him this literature was "an important way of discovering self." He was also aware that a great literary gap needed to be filled because in the discussion of world literature no one mentioned the literature of the West Indies.

Asked about his reasons for migrating to Africa, he answered simply, "Oh, that was to get a job!" The author explained that being Black in England in the 1950s and 1960s rendered it almost impossible for him to get the kind of teaching position for which he was qualified. One University of London professor informed him that the comprehensive and grammar schools as well as the universities in England had "a certain kind of tradition," implying, no doubt, that this "tradition" would be alien to a Black West Indian.

When Dathorne published *The Scholar Man* in 1964, he was perhaps unknowingly pioneering what was to become a persistent thematic concern among Afro-Caribbean writers, that is, the search for identity through an involvement with Africa. Just one year before, Denis Williams had explored in *Other Leopards* (1963) the dilemma of the schizophrenic West Indian in Africa. This theme was picked up in 1974 by Oliver Jackman in *Saw the House in Half*, and most recently it was viewed from the woman's perspective by the Guadeloupean Maryse Conde in *Heremakhonon* (1982). In poetry, this same theme was powerfully explored by Edward Brathwaite in *Masks* (1968). On the most basic level, then, Adam Questus, an English university graduate, originally from the West Indies, leaves England to teach English in a West African university. On another level, however, the protagonist is in Africa in quest of his African self.

Dathorne has said that as a teacher in West Africa he was struck by the ironies and absurdities of the education system, including the courses as well as the administrative process. The incongruity of teaching only English literature courses to the total exclusion of anything African struck him as being especially self-defeating. In 1963, at the University of Ibadan, Professor Dathorne was to introduce the first course in African literature to be taught in a West African university. Hence on another level his novel is a satire on the "new Africa" and what it stands for. The author highlights the absurdities of the education system which sanctions the study of nursery rhymes in an introduction to literature course and an administrative system that requires one to face the investigating committee of the university to account for a hole in a bed sheet. He also reveals the patronizing attitude of the Europeans. The chairman of the English Department says of his students, ''This country is not yet ready for the truth. . . . You have to tell them they're right every so often'' (p. 74).

Meanwhile, Adam Questus is determined to get to know the ''true Africa.'' He frequently leaves his European quarters and friends to fraternize with the villagers in an effort to understand their rites and customs. Once during a ceremony when Adam is struck by a whip he feels excruciating pain. The witch doctor disdainfully tells him, ''For a true African [the whiplash] is only a light touch. Nothing'' (p. 56). Later, the same witch doctor has reason to inform him, ''[Africa] is in your skin but not in your bowels'' (p. 62). On the symbolic level, Adam is the typical West Indian torn between his European heritage and his African. Like Lionel Froad, the protagonist in *Other Leopards*, Adam falls in love with an Englishwoman in Africa. It is to her that he confides: ''As a person who has grown up away from my past, I don't know anything about myself. I know all I'm not. I'm not English. I suppose I'm not even really West Indian. . . . But . . . I do want to know what's what—where I belong'' (p. 48).

Finally, it is with an outcast African woman that Adam seeks his salvation. It is with their union in the mud and the rain that the book ends. Thus, the suggestion is that Adam's quest in Africa has been fulfilled. But the reader is left uncertain. Perhaps the union of Adam, the ''outcast'' African, and the outcast African woman anticipates the coming together of the New World Black man and the new Africa which Dathorne suggests will have to replace the old. Or perhaps the union of the Europeanized Adam with the true African woman suggests that the new Africa will be a harmonious coming together of two worlds—Africa and Europe.

The reader is left with a vague sense of dissatisfaction. Why, for instance, does a work set in Africa in the 1960s offer no realistic portrayal of the African woman? Significantly, the only two African women who appear in the work remain nameless: the servant Henry's wife and the outcast African woman. The novel also raises the troubling question of the relationship between the Black man and the Black woman. When Adam first sees Henry's wife, he grudgingly concedes that she has a ''certain amount of beauty in her dark features.'' Whatever charms she has, however, are immediately canceled because she is ''half-naked and sweating, with a large box on her head'' (p. 63). As he looks at her, he sees her submissiveness and obvious devotion to her husband as the reason that the African male can survive the day-to-day humiliation which is his lot. ''[For] when he got home . . . there was this woman . . . who sat at his feet and told him that he was her master'' (p. 63). The implications here are less than positive; the book on the whole raises more questions than it satisfactorily answers.

Dathorne's interest in fiction writing is still alive. He has just recently completed his third novel, *Dele's Child*.

Dathorne's efforts as a nonfiction writer have been quite prolific. In 1966 he edited *Caribbean Prose*, his first of many anthologies. *Caribbean Verse* followed in 1967. Both of these works are useful introductory reference sources, each with an informative introduction by the editor. In 1969, Dathorne coedited an anthology of African prose writings with Wilfried Feuser, entitled *Africa in Prose*. While a visiting professor of English at the University of Miami in 1974, Dathorne brought out his most ambitious scholarly work to date: *The Black Mind: A History of African Literature*, a culmination of ten years of research, is an invaluable source of African literary history. An abridged form of this work was published in 1975, titled *African Literature in the Twentieth Century*. Professor Dathorne's most recent scholarly book is *Dark Ancestor: The Literature of the Black Man in the Caribbean* (1981). In this work, the author, in addition to making the connection between African and Caribbean cultures, has included African America to form a concentric cultural circle. This work proves to be Dathorne's most sustained attempt at literary criticism.

CRITICAL RECEPTION

Terms usually used by critics to refer to the nonfiction works of O. R. Dathorne are "uniquely comprehensive," "monumental work of scholarship," "timely and necessary," and "all-inclusive." The author himself is often called a "pioneer," and by one critic, "a happy combination of poet, novelist, and scholar" (Lester Goran, "Review of *Dark Ancestor*," 1981, p. 45). An examination of Professor Dathorne's writings does indeed reveal his penchant for inclusiveness and detail, a trait for which some critics fault him, though most students approaching the literature for the first time will find it useful.

Dathorne has received much greater critical attention for his two most recent works than he received for his early fiction and nonfiction works combined. The novels and early anthologies were reviewed briefly in Caribbean periodicals and critical works. Of *Dumplings in the Soup*, Harold Marshall wonders whether the author was "too liberal with the spices and too skimpy with the salt of characterization as [the characters] eat, fight, drink and turn to religion in the short chapters" (*Bim*, 1964, p. 227). L. E. Brathwaite states that *The Scholar Man* is more than the author's reactions to his job in Nigeria. It is a work whose central theme "is the eternal one of the West Indian's search for identity" (*Bim*, 1965, p. 68). However, his assessment is that "the search is unconvincing and finally meaningless" (p. 68). But Brathwaite does give Dathorne credit for a surrealistic scene in which Adam Questus attempts to be initiated into the African tribal rites. He calls this scene "a delightful moment—truly, truly African and a gem in its own right" (p. 69). Kenneth Ramchand, on the other hand, does not think that the novel succeeds on any level and asserts that Dathorne fails to convince his readers that "his hero has returned to the rejected earth rhythms of the pre-expatriate African" (*The West Indian Novel and its Background*,1970, pp. 159–60).

The Black Mind: A History of African Literature is by far Dathorne's most comprehensive work, for which he obviously did a great deal of research. Paul Edwards in his review of the book acknowledges that clearly Dathorne has done a great deal of reading and as a result has offered much more than the usual "uncritical praise-songs" of mediocre work coming from Africa in the past fifteen years (*Modern Language Review: The Yearbook of English Studies*, 1978, p. 176). He charges, though, that on the whole the author's "critical sense emerges as blurred" (p. 176). His final assessment is that "the volume . . . offers a wide, though not altogether complete survey of the literature of Africa; its weakness is that it attempts comprehensiveness and pays for this with superficiality of critical comment" (p. 177).

In reviewing *African Literature in the Twentieth Century*, Francis E. Ngwaba cites Dathorne's insistence that "modern African writing has its roots in Africa's oral literary culture" as being of particular interest (*The International Fiction Review* 5 [1978], 73). He concludes that the book is "timely and necessary" for the student who is interested in the "origin, development, and regional characteristics of African literature," as well as the foreign student of African literature "who will require much background information in order to explore with confidence the world of modern creative writing in Africa" (p. 73).

Dathorne's most recent publication, *Dark Ancestor: The Literature of the Black Man in the Caribbean*, has been his most widely reviewed work. Some of the critics have charged that the author has attempted too much and, as a result, has defeated the purpose of the book. For example, Peter Sabor refers to the book as "[an] ambitious but sometimes unreliable study . . . which provides illuminating comparisons, but little sustained analysis of any one work or body of literature" (*Library Journal* [1981], 883). Evelyn O'Callaghan places the work in the tradition of Janheinz Jahn's *Bibliography of Neo-African Literature* (1965). She asserts, however, that "the wideness of scope sometimes leads to disorganized presentation and repetition" ("African Adaptations," 1982, p. 391). Perhaps the most gratifying compliment that Dathorne has received from any of his critics was paid him by Funso Aiyejina. This critic places Dathorne's book among those of such pioneering West Indian scholars as Eric Williams in *Capitalism and Slavery* (1964), Franz Fanon in *Wretched of the Earth* (1965), and Walter Rodney in *How Europe Underdeveloped Africa* (1972). Aiyejina concludes, "Now Dathorne . . . has added another title to this growing body of serious books on the plight of the African people" ("Ancestral Africa: Surviving the Modern Age," 1981, p. 20).

HONORS AND AWARDS

Professor O. R. Dathorne has received several honors, including a gold OAK medal. He was twice nominated Professor of the Year—in 1973, at the Ohio State University, and in 1983, at the University of Miami. He was also among "The Men and Women of Distinction" honored by the International Biographical Center of Cambridge, England, in 1972. He also received a Certificate of Appreciation for contributions to Black History Month by the Veterans Administration in 1982. He was twice honored, in 1980 and 1982, by the United Black

Students Organization of the University of Miami for "Outstanding Services and Contributions to Black Culture Week."

BIBLIOGRAPHY

Works by O. R. Dathorne

Dumplings in the Soup. London: Cassell, 1963.

The Scholar Man. London: Cassell, 1964.

Caribbean Narrative, ed. London: Heinemann, 1966.

Caribbean Verse, ed. London: Heinemann, 1967.

Africa in Prose, co-ed. London: Penguin, 1969.

The Black Mind: A History of African Literature. Minneapolis: University of Minnesota Press, 1974.

African Literature in the Twentieth Century. Minneapolis: University of Minnesota Press, 1975.

Dark Ancestor: The Literature of the Black Man in the Caribbean. Baton Rouge: Louisiana State University Press, 1981.

Dele's Child. Washington, D.C.: Three Continents Press, forthcoming.

Studies of O. R. Dathorne

Aiyejina, Funso. "Ancestral Africa: Surviving the Modern Age." *West Africa*, November 2, 1981, pp. 2–3.

Brathwaite, L. E. Review of *The Scholar Man*. *Bim* 10 (June 1965), 68–69.

Cartey, Wilfred. "The Rhythm of Society and Landscape: Mittelholzer, Carew, Williams, Dathorne." *New World*, ed. George Lamming and Martin Carter. Georgetown, Guyana: New World Group Associates, 1966, pp. 97–104.

Edwards, Paul. Review of *The Black Mind: A History of African Literature*. *Modern Language Review: The Yearbook of English Studies* (January 1978), 176–77.

Goran, Lester. Review of *Dark Ancestor: The Literature of the Black Man in the Caribbean*. *Miami Magazine* (October 1981), 45, 114.

Marshall, Harold. Review of *Dumplings in the Soup*. *Bim* 10 (June 1964), 226–27.

Morris, Mervyn. "West Indian Literature: Some Cheap Anthologies." *Caribbean Quarterly* 13 (June 1967), 37–38.

Ngugi, James. *Homecoming: Essays on African and Caribbean Literature, Culture and Politics*. London: Heinemann, 1972.

O'Callaghan, Evelyn. "African Adaptations." *Times Literary Supplement*, April 2, 1982, p. 391.

Paul, Angus. "New World Blacks and Nation Language." *The Chronicle of Higher Education* 23 (September 1981), 23.

Sabor, Peter. Review of *Dark Ancestor: The Literature of the Black Man in the Caribbean*. *Library Journal* 106 (April 15, 1981), 883.

See also General Bibliography: Allis, Hughes, James, McDowell, Moore, and Ramchand.

EDWARD BAUGH

Neville Dawes (1926–1984)

BIOGRAPHY

Neville Augustus Dawes was born in Warri, Nigeria, on June 16, 1926. His parents were Jamaican, Augustus Dawes, a Baptist missionary and teacher, from Sturge Town in the parish of St. Ann, and his wife Laura. When Neville was three years old the family returned to Jamaica, to Sturge Town. The boy grew up in the hill country lovingly remembered in his two novels.

In 1938 he won a scholarship to Jamaica College in Kingston, at that time an elitist high school for boys. On leaving Jamaica College, he taught at Calabar High School, before entering Oriel College, Oxford, in 1948, to read for a degree in English. After completing his university studies in 1951, he returned to teach at Calabar and to conduct classes in English literature and the teaching of poetry for the Department of Extra-Mural Studies of the University College of the West Indies.

In 1955 he took up a teaching post at the Kumasi Institute of Technology, Ghana. He later moved to the College of Administration, Achimota, and from 1960 to 1970 he was lecturer and later senior lecturer in English at the University of Ghana, Legon. In an unpublished interview with Daryl Cumber Dance (Kingston, Jamaica, March 10, 1979) he gave his political consciousness as a factor in his decision to migrate to Ghana. He said that he felt that he "ought to go and see what was happening" in "a country that was *determined*to be independent of British colonialism." He became a leading figure in the cultural wing of the African Liberation Movement and was one of the editors of *Okyeame*, a journal of the Ghana Society of Writers. In a tribute delivered at Dawes's funeral service, the Ghanaian poet Kofi Awoonor recalled with appreciation the encouragement and critical advice which he and other young Ghanaian writers had received from Dawes.

In the academic year 1963–64, Dawes returned temporarily to the Caribbean region as visiting professor of English and dean of the Faculty of Arts in the University of Guyana. Then in 1970 he settled once more in Jamaica, having accepted an invitation to take the post of deputy director of the Institute of Jamaica, an "umbrella" organization which administers many of the cultural programs of the government. In 1973 he was appointed executive director, a post which he held until 1981. In the "Remembrance" delivered at Dawes's funeral service, Rex Nettleford, who was chairman of the Council of the Institute for much of the time that Dawes was executive director, said: "He was crucial to the restructuring of the Institute of Jamaica during the Seventies and contributed not a little in winning the international respect Jamaica enjoys for its efforts in the fields of cultural administration and cultural development" (*Jamaica Journal* 17 [August-October 1984], 64).

On a visit to Ghana in 1975, Dawes delivered a series of lectures on Caribbean literature to the Institute of African Studies, University of Ghana. These lectures, published as a monograph entitled *Prolegomena to Caribbean Literature* (see Bibliography), are significant in any consideration of the development of literary criticism in the West Indies.

After leaving the Institute, Dawes wrote book reviews and feature articles for the *Sunday Gleaner*. He died on May 13, 1984, in Mandeville, Jamaica, as a result of an accidental fall. He had only recently assumed duties as a teacher at a high school in Mandeville. At the time of his death he was considering an invitation to return to Ghana as professor of English at the University of Ghana. Three Ghanaian ambassadors, to Brazil, Cuba, and the United Nations, took part in his funeral service, held at the University Chapel, Mona, on May 20, 1984. Twice married, he left six children, the eldest by his first wife, a Jamaican, and the others by his second wife, a Ghanaian, who also survives him.

MAJOR WORKS AND THEMES

Dawes's first published book was a collection of poems, *In Sepia* (1958), but this has virtually disappeared. In the interview with Daryl Cumber Dance mentioned above, he himself admitted to not having a copy. It may be that some clue to the subject matter of that volume is contained in his statement that he "used to write a lot of political poetry working in Africa" (Dance interview). However, between 1948 and 1958 nineteen of his poems were broadcast on the BBC "Caribbean Voices" program (in addition to seven short stories), and a few have appeared in periodicals and anthologies. He seems to have been chiefly a poet at first but gradually turned more and more to prose. In this regard it may be significant that in one of his early poems, "Advice to Myself About to Write a Lyric,'' in the process of praising lyric verse and defining its virtues, he says, ''Leave thought for prose'' (Broadcast, March 23, 1952, *Caribbean Voices* transcript, UWI Library, Mona, box 9, item 695).

In terms of subject matter, Dawes's poems fall roughly into three main groups: those which describe the impressions of the young West Indian intellectual in England; those which celebrate Jamaican rural life and landscape; and those which celebrate Africa. The first group includes poems such as ''In Oxford,'' ''I cup the city's two-dimensioned secret. . . '' (both read by Dawes on ''Caribbean Voices,'' June 15, 1952), ''You England,'' ''Intellectual Soiree: London, 1951,'' and ''City Blues, 1952'' (unpublished?). Some of these poems are crowded with allusions to English literature, showing the young colonial under the spell of the English cultural tradition and at the same time anxious to assert a cool detachment from it.

The second group includes poems such as ''Acceptance,'' ''Definition,'' ''Perspective,'' and ''Dedication,'' all broadcast on ''Caribbean Voices,'' November 15, 1953, and the well-known ''Fugue'' (''Caribbean Voices,'' November 11, 1952). The first four were intended to form part of a sequence entitled ''Portrait of a Village.'' They are a counterpart in verse to those sections of Dawes's novels which affirm the sense of rootedness in the Jamaican hill country of his childhood. These roots are traced further back, to Africa, in the third group of poems, which includes ''To an African Girl'' and ''Origin'' (*Jamaica Journal* 6 [March 1972], 51), the latter of which sings a Black muse, ''composite negress.''

A gap of eighteen years separates Dawes's two published novels, *The Last Enchantment* (1960) and *Interim* (1978), but there is much similarity in their concerns, as well as appreciable parallels in tone and point of view. Both look critically at the politics of a newly self-governing or independent excolony, Jamaica. Both see the situation in terms of a conflict of class interests, complicated or deepened by conflicts of color. Both explore, rather despairingly, the likelihood of a revolutionary solution. In both, the protagonist is a boy of peasant stock who, exposed to the privileges of the higher reaches of a colonial education, finds himself naturally sympathetic to the idea of socialism at a time of burgeoning nationalist fervor. However, in both, an ingrained skepticism and socially conditioned cynical detachment retard the gradually earned impulse toward socialist commitment.

Ramsay Tull, protagonist of *The Last Enchantment*, is very much the Outsider after the fashion of the late 1950s and early 1960s. (Colin Wilson's trend-setting *The Outsider* had appeared in 1956.) The novel is of a predominantly picaresque and satirical mode. In the first of its three parts we meet nineteen-year-old Ramsay, bright, precociously world-weary, unable to muster the expected grief at his father's death, unable to participate comfortably in the routine post-interment small talk and socializing of family and friends.

By way of Ramsay's drifting through typical scenes in the social and political life of the Kingston bourgeoisie, we are given a portrait of a superficial, social-climbing group, still deeply infected with the Anglophile values of a colonial society waving its new-found flag of nationalism. Dawes paints an iconoclastic picture of Jamaica in the mid–1940s, a period usually remembered with reverence as a landmark in the island's progress toward independence from Britain, the period of post-war exhilaration, when the spontaneous labor movement of the 1930s, and the new spirit of nationalism which it helped to foster, found a kind of fulfillment in the limited self-government conceded by Britain through the New Constitution of 1944.

In Dawes's fictive recreation of the politics of the period, there are three main parties. The Merchant's Party, as its name suggests, upholds the interests of "big business," but buys itself working-class support and so wins handsomely the first election after the adoption of the new constitution. Then there is the People's Democratic Party, "a middle-class party with a vaguely socialist leadership and no programme" (p. 26). These two correspond roughly to the two major political parties of the time. The third, the People's Progressive League, has no formal counterpart in the period, but represents a development on an embryonic, radically socialist nucleus that did exist within or on the fringes of one of the two major parties.

Dawes and his protagonist pay scant attention to the Merchant's Party, regarding it perhaps as too obvious a target for attack, beneath serious imaginative notice. The novel's satirical energy is reserved largely for the leaders of the PDP and their sympathizers, middle-class opportunists and pretenders to "culture" and enlightenment, although the leader, Dr. Raymond Westlake Phillips, is acknowledged to be a well-intentioned man who sincerely believes in "the inevitability of gradualness" (p. 82). On the other hand, the author's sympathy is clearly with the PPL, whose leaders are seen as genuinely, if in some respects idealistically, committed to the cause of the working class. And they are the underdogs, not easily able to challenge the combined advantages of the Merchant's Party and the PDP.

In Part 2, Ramsay, following the traditional colonial pattern of privilege, drifts up to Oxford University to read English, with little conviction concerning this "progress." The Oxford experience marks a refinement on his chronic sense of alienation and highlights his quest for himself. His uncertainty and self-questioning are brought into sharp relief by the contrast drawn between him and a compatriot at Oxford, Cyril Hanson, his friend from schooldays. Cyril, *angst*-free and opportunistic, becomes more English than the English, a caricature of the Black Englishman from the colonies. With his "rolled umbrella, bowler, black coat, clean white collar, B.N.C. tie, briefcase and a copy of *The Times* under his arm" (p. 210), he "was so wonderfully integrated that he even developed a stutter" (p. 164).

There are also satirical set-piece character sketches of various other West Indian types at Oxford, but Ramsay's closest friend, appropriately for his career as the Outsider, is "a classless Englishman, a product of the war and statistics and evacuated schools and levelling up" (p. 161). Together "they drifted about and got bad reports from their tutors at the end of term" (p. 171). Ramsay's education also includes the mandatory affair with a White woman. She is herself somewhat socially marginal, half-Irish and thirty. Ramsay writes an autobiographical short story which ends with his strangling her, an exorcism which anticipates Makak's beheading of the White Goddess/apparition in Walcott's *Dream on Monkey Mountain* (1970).

In Part 3, Ramsay returns to Jamaica, as disaffected as ever, just after the PDP has turned the tables on the Merchants' Party and won the second election. But this reversal makes no real change in the lot of the people, in spite of the protestation of Ramsay's brother, Bobsie, an erstwhile hanger-on of the PDP, who has now come into his own: "You don't understand what happening in this country today. I tell you black man is really ruling!" (p. 229). However, this signifies only that the means of corruption have passed from one set of hands to another. Bobsie is himself the arch-opportunist and manipulator, ready to "arrange" a headmastership for his Oxford-educated brother by displacing a powerless and needy incumbent.

Fifty pages from the end of the novel, Ramsay is "still waiting for something to happen to him" (p. 234). He clutches at a chance to act purposefully when Edgar Bailey, heir-apparent to the leadership of the PPL, is arrested for having Communist literature in his possession, and a protest march is staged. Ramsay's not-altogether-pure motive is further sullied by the fact that Bailey is his sexual competitor, having just proposed marriage to Ramsay's mistress. Ramsay, as insecure in these matters as in others, has broken with her over this development. His attempt at political action comes to a pathetic end, confirming an absurdist element in the novel, when a policeman's baton "quite accidently" (p. 273) inflicts a blow on the back of his head and he becomes, "absurdly" (p. 273), the only casualty of the march.

He spends the next three days in bed with a delirious fever and then, his nerves and will broken, retires to the country to recuperate, but it is not clear that he will ever be well again. The sense of failure is paralleled in the public sphere with the death, from cancer, of the PPL's founder and leader and the apparent decline, at least temporarily, of the party. The disease symbolizes the cancer consuming the body politic.

But the book ends on a note of affirmation when, in a sort of coda, an unidentified first person narrator, who hails from the same hill country as Ramsay, takes us back to those rural, pastoral roots. This closing celebration of the folkways asserts a sense of belonging, of security and community, which is in sharp contrast to the urban world of alienation and social divisions. It is as if there is no possible bridge between the two, and the return to the idealized world of rustic simplicities and certainties must itself be a kind of withdrawal, the mark of failure to cope with the challenge of disillusion presented by the wider outside world.

The contrast between these two worlds is continued, but modified and subtlized, in *Interim*. In that novel we follow the career of a protagonist who is of the same origins and mold as Ramsay Tull and who finds himself challenged by much the same kind of sociopolitical situation as that which had defeated Ramsay. But the protagonist of *Interim*, although being essentially a detached, indecisive observer, is hardly afflicted by Ramsay's datedly existential *angst*.

In *Interim*, Dawes takes up the challenge of Edgar Bailey's prediction, made towards the end of *The Last Enchantment*, that "there'll be a real revolution right here in Jamaica" (p. 264). Dawes again recreates the Jamaican sociopolitical scene of the 1940s, but this time he imagines a revolution taking place. It succeeds briefly but is put down by a combination of betrayal from within and U.S. military intervention. (Published more than a decade before the Grenada invasion, the novel reads prophetically now.) Through this scenario, Dawes is able to explore seriously the idea of the possibility of revolution in the kind of political milieu whose conflicting and complex forces he evokes. Now he is more concerned, than in the earlier novel, to imagine himself into the revolutionary situation, into the revolutionary action and mind, than to satirize the bourgeoisie. Which is not to say that satire is not used, and more subtly than in *The Last Enchantment*. One of the main achievements of *Interim* is its incisive portrayal of the brown bourgeoisie. It brings into sharper focus than did the earlier novel the idea of the political situation as being ultimately determined by a conflict of class interests.

For his purposes in *Interim*, Dawes has to devote a good deal of attention to the figure of the revolutionary, which James Duncan, the protagonist, does not really become until the end of the story. So he creates, as a co-protagonist and the one who looms larger and is more easily the center of the reader's attention for most of the book, Lucien Taylor, friend and companion of James from childhood. By making them products of the same environment and educational system, Dawes cleverly establishes that there is no simple, predetermined cause–effect relationship between environment and character. Where Lucien is the protagonist as hero, James is, for the most part, the protagonist as anti-hero. And engaging problems of interpretation are posed for the reader as a consequence of the fact that Lucien is presented through the eyes of James, even if James tries hard to present himself only as a self-effacing, objective pair of eyes.

In Part 1, "A Village in Pimento," Dawes depicts the rural beginnings of the two boys in the same hill country as that from which Ramsay Tull has come. These chapters commemorate a way of life, a sense of community ("the interrelations of near and far blood relatives and in-laws that bound the little village together like a single will" [p. 16]), values which were to be lost in the outside world, but which represented something of what the protagonists were to fight to preserve when they became men. Dawes evokes vividly the sights, smells, sounds, taste of life in the hill country, the seasonal changes, the feeling of human life and communal activity being in tune with the rhythms of Nature. The people live "in a simple and firm relationship to the land, impoverished but unalienated" (p. 55).

But what might otherwise have seemed a too idyllic picture is tempered and subtlized by the fact that Dawes makes us aware of the class tensions, the half-concealed power struggle which is basic to the politics of the village, a politics which has been historically determined and which in turn helps to shape the political consciousness of the future revolutionaries. This politics is dramatized in the uneasy or tense relationships that exist between the three figures of authority. On the one hand, there is Busha Burton, the crude, bullying relic of the slave-owning class, who virtually rules the village from Nesfield Great House. Over againt him are two Black men, Teacher Sampson and the proudly independent Ebenezer Taylor, Lucien's father, who are without Burton's material resources but who constitute a moral authority.

The story of the making of the revolution is developed in Part 2, when Lucien and James win scholarships to Victoria College, a high school in the city modeled on the Jamaica College which Dawes had attended. Through James's satirical sketch of the school, we see how he and Lucien develop a deepening awareness of the nexus of class, color, and colonialism which grips the society. In a typical gesture of revolt, Lucien, now a sixth-former, leaves school prematurely when he refuses to compromise on his principles by apologizing to a master for what the school authorities see simply as an act of insubordination. He goes off to join the Royal Air Force (World War II is in progress), but really to continue his quest for himself.

We are not made to share his experiences of the war, but when he returns home after the war he is dedicated to the idea of revolution, and the time seems ripe. The polarities in the social structure are widening under the government of a charismatic, demagogic prime minister whose party is really on the side of "big business" and who is a neocolonial stooge and samfie man (trickster).

The revolution takes place but soon runs into difficulty, partly because Lucien is apparently unable to resist the insidious force of the bourgeois establishment and too quickly makes accommodating gestures toward them. In any event, that establishment will undermine the revolution from within, in the person of Donald Burton, Busha Burton's son, who had been Lucien's playmate and schoolmate and who has insinuated himself into the leadership of the revolutionary government. Donald acts in collusion with the U.S. government, which sends in its troops to put down the revolution. Lucien, a beaten man, suffers his final betayal when, having discovered Donald's treachery, he allows Mercedes, Donald's sister, who had become his (Lucien's) mistress, to persuade him to let her carry out his order to have Donald shot. Blood proves thicker than love or politics, and Mercedes lets Donald escape. Lucien shoots himself, but at the end of the novel the revolutionary remnant is regrouping in the hills, and one assumes that when their opportunity comes they will not repeat Lucien's mistakes.

Lucien's problematic relationship with the children of the Great Houses dramatizes one of the many interesting issues raised by the novel, that of the dilemma of mediating or choosing between emotion and sentiment on the one hand and political expediency or necessity on the other, in the revolutionary situation. Also striking is the subtheme of sex as arena and metaphor for political conflict, as shown in the love affair between James and the "off-white" Marjorie Reynolds. Other issues raised thought-provokingly by *Interim*, and in some instances carried over from *The Last Enchantment*, include the question of reconciling Black nationalism and Marxism (Capleton, in *Enchantment*, "had seen a red dream get mixed up with a black dream in the States" [p. 222]), the question of the possibility or viability of a specifically Negro art, and the question of the role of the writer in relation to politics.

CRITICAL RECEPTION

Critical notice of Dawes's work has been confined to his novels and more particularly to *The Last Enchantment* (if we exclude unpublished papers). Comment on this book has in general been concerned with identifying the sources of what the critics see as its shortcomings. The most complimentary of the critics is Basil McFarlane ("Jamaican Novel," 1975), who sees the novel as being in more ways than one a refreshing development in the West Indian novel, although he too betrays much uneasiness, sometimes tending toward self-contradiction, about various aspects of the work. For instance, he commends Dawes for engaging more rigorously than any previous Jamaican novelist with "the Jamaican, twentieth-century political scene" and for affording the "enjoyment" of identifying well-known Jamaicans among the characters (p. 51). At the same time, he remarks that the Jamaican scenes and characters are generally "thinly observed . . . verging on caricature" (p. 51). Other critics, paying even less attention than McFarlane to the novel's engagement with politics, are even more disconcerted by the allegedly thin disguise of the satirical portraits. Gerald Moore complains of the "too-overt political satire; the original targets of Dawes's wrath glare at us through the thinnest of disguises" (*The Chosen Tongue*, 1969, p. 48). W. I. Carr speaks of "portraits of recognisable contemporaries of quite astonishing malice" ("Reflections on the Novel in the British Caribbean," 1964, p. 589). The feeling that the characters are not sufficiently realized, for one reason or another, is also voiced by Edward Brathwaite, who considers that the "cause and [political] theory [of the novel] prevail too much upon its people" (Review of *The Last Enchantment*, 1961, p. 75), while George Panton says that Dawes is too inclined to settle for mere reporting, rather than for imaginative recreation of incident and character. Curiously, in contrast to Brathwaite, McFarlane feels that "it is to Dawes's credit as an artist that the political theory, such as it is, is given no appreciable ascendancy throughout the book" (p. 52). Carr, McFarlane, and Panton feel that Dawes idealizes certain categories of Black people in the novel, and Panton says that the author is "obsessed with the colour question" ("Have We Really Solved the Race Problem?" 1961, p. 14).

There are other sharp differences of response to certain features of the work. For example, whereas Moore finds "the most sustained piece of writing" (p. 46) marked by "the quality of the detail" (p. 48) in the sequence which evokes the village life at the time of Ramsay's return to the island, McFarlane finds "the best sustained writing" (p. 51) to be in the middle section depicting Ramsay's rootless life in England. And whereas McFarlane consequently regards the novel as being "essentially . . . a song of exile and alienation" (p. 51), Brathwaite is saddened because, identifying Dawes with his protagonist, he sees the novel as yet another representation of a flaw in the character of the West Indian artist, a flaw "which sends [him] seeking exile" and which derives not from society, but from "his own basic rootlessness" ("Roots," 1963, p. 15).

Moore is the only critic who pays any appreciable attention to the novel's narrative technique. He argues that it "constantly suffers from uncertainty of focus" (p. 46) because of the way in which the shifts in point of view and narrative voice are handled. But, he argues, while these shifts "create a sense of restlessness and uncertainty in the reader," they may also constitute a virtue, in representing the protagonist's restless search for identity.

In a paper on "The Artist as Revolutionary: Political Commitment in *The Dragon Can't Dance* and *Interim*," (*West Indian Literature and its Social Context*, ed. McWatt [1985]) David Williams finds remarkable similarities between Dawes's novel and Earl Lovelace's in terms of the treatment of the development of a relatively alienated but myth-hungry artistic consciousness towards a position of political commitment. Williams sees this development as representing "a statement of guarded hope about our collective psyche." (p. 147).

BIBLIOGRAPHY

Works by Neville Dawes

In Sepia. [Ghana], [1958].

The Last Enchantment. London: MacGibbon and Kee, 1960; Kraus Reprint, 1975.

Prolegomena to Caribbean Literature. [Kingston]: Institute of Jamaica, 1977.

Interim. Kingston: Institute of Jamaica, 1978.

Studies of Neville Dawes

Brathwaite, Edward. Review of *The Last Enchantment*. *Bim* 9 (July-December 1961), 74–75.

———. "Roots." *Bim* 10 (July-December 1963), 10–21.

Carr, W. I. "Reflections on the Novel in the British Caribbean." *Queen's Quarterly* 70 (Winter 1964), 585–87, 589.

Lamming, George. Review of *The Last Enchantment*. *Race* 2 (May 1961), 92.

MacFarlane, Basil. "Jamaican Novel." *Jamaica Journal* 9 (1975), 51–52.

Panton, George [pseud. C. G. Lindo and Hugh P. Morrison]. "Have We Really Solved the Race Problem?" Review of *The Last Enchantment*. *Sunday Gleaner*, March 19, 1961, p. 14.

Walcott, Derek. "New Novel by Dawes Sticks to Formula" (Review of *The Last Enchantment*). *Sunday Guardian*, September 11, 1960, p. 5.

Williams, David. ''The Artist as Revolutionary: Political Commitment in *The Dragon Can't Dance* and *Interim*,'' in *West Indian Literature and its Social Context*, ed. Mark McWatt. Barbados: Department of English, Cave Hill, 1985, pp. 141–47.
See also General Bibliography: Allis, Hughes, Moore, and Van Sertima.

REINHARD W. SANDER

Ralph de Boissière (1907–   )

BIOGRAPHY

Ralph de Boissière was born in Trinidad on October 6, 1907. His father, a solicitor, was a descendant of the unofficial colored line of a well-known French Creole family. De Boissière's mother died of yellow fever three weeks after his birth, and the author recalls a lonely, unhappy childhood in Trinidad, enlivened by occasional visits to Grenada, where his stepmother's parents lived. In the course of his education, at Tranquillity Boys Intermediate School and Queen's Royal College, de Boissière encountered the typical colonial syllabus: "We learned English history, which seemed to consist mostly of England's military and naval conquests. In geography you had to know what was made in Sheffield and Birmingham. You were required to draw maps of England showing its principal towns and seaports" (unpublished autobiography; the following quotations from de Boissière are from this same source). Music was de Boissière's first passion, especially the piano, and he dreamed of a career as a performer. When this failed to materialize, he turned to creative writing. To secure a livelihood, however, he underwent training as a typist/bookkeeper and worked in this capacity for various English and American firms until he left the island in 1947.

In the mid–1920s de Boissière was introduced to a group of young Trinidadian intellectuals and expatriates, who were to spearhead the island's literary awakening. Among them were the editors of the literary magazine *Trinidad*(1929–30), Alfred H. Mendes and C. L. R. James, as well as Albert Gomes, who upon his return from the United States launched the first monthly cultural magazine, *The Beacon* (1931–33, 1939). Within the group de Boissière was encouraged to write, and in their magazines were published his first short stories, exploring the island's pervasive race and class prejudices. At around this time he became an ardent admirer of the work of such 19th century Russian writers as Turgenev and Tolstoy. He felt an immediate affinity with the social situations which they described and came to the conclusion that "life in colonial Trinidad was not at all unlike life in the towns and countryside of tsarist Russia." He was to emulate the Russians' realistic style and social vision in his Caribbean novels, *Crown Jewel* (1952) and *Rum and Coca-Cola* (1956), but it was his firsthand experience of everyday life at all levels of Trinidad society that provided him with his raw material. For several years one of his jobs entailed the delivery of bakers' supplies all over Trinidad: "Every day found me in little shops and hovels and stinking alleys among Chinese, Indians, Blacks, Portuguese and mixtures of all the races." When Trinidad's oilfield workers went on strike in 1937 and the island was engulfed in major social upheavals, de Boissière was not only a keen observer but subsequently became involved in radical trade unionism. He was especially attracted to the Marxist-oriented Negro Welfare Cultural and Social Association, whose leaders included Bertie Percival, Clem Payne, Jim Barrette, and Elma François.

De Boissière's political sympathies were anathema to his employers and led to a nine-month period of unemployment for him in 1939. During the commercial boom that followed the establishment of a U.S. military base on the island he was again able to find a job, but by now it had become evident that a secure existence for himself, his wife Ivy, whom he had married in 1935, and their two daughters would not be possible in Trinidad, given the social conditions and his political views. In 1947 he took a six-month course in motor mechanics in Chicago and then migrated to Australia, where his family joined him. His first job was on the assembly line at General Motors in Melbourne, an experience which deepened his understanding of the working-class issues he was exploring in writing *Crown Jewel* and which provided the subject matter for his third novel, *No Saddles for Kangaroos* (1964). In Australia de Boissière moved more and more to the left. He began to study Marxist literature and literary criticism, became a member of the Realist Writers Group, and finally joined the Communist Party in 1951, remaining a member until 1967. It was a left-wing publishing house, the Australasian Book Society, that published his novels (in fact, *Crown Jewel* was its very first title), and both *Crown Jewel* and *Rum and Coca-Cola* appeared in translation in several Eastern-bloc countries. In 1955 he rewrote a section of *Rum and Coca-Cola* as a musical, which he called *Calypso Isle*. He himself composed the songs and calypsos and played the part of Charlie the shoemaker in several successful performances of the show at the Melbourne New Theatre. In 1957/58 de Boissière went on a seven-month tour of China, with a brief visit to the Soviet Union. On his return to Australia he remembers feeling that he "had stepped, it seemed, from the future back into the present, which ought to be the past.'' He nevertheless applied for Australian citizenship some years later and became an Australian citizen in 1969.

De Boissière is the type of writer who continuously rewrites his work: Both the 1981 republication of *Crown Jewel* and the 1984 edition of *Rum and Coca-Cola* differ significantly from the original 1950s editions, which themselves were developed in a long process of rewriting. In the case of *Crown Jewel* this process goes back as far as 1935. De Boissière has rationalized this procedure with the remark, ''My life was my novel, and the novel my life.'' He is still working on a novel he began in the early 1970s entitled *Homeless in Paradise*, which is set in Australia and Trinidad. To refresh his memory of the Caribbean he visited Trinidad in 1976—assisted by a travel and research grant from the Australian Literature Board—and spent several months there. At present he is writing a voluminous autobiography, from which his remarks cited in this section have been culled. At seventy-seven he looks like fifty and is full of plans for the future.

MAJOR WORKS AND THEMES

Crown Jewel (1952) and its sequel *Rum and Coca-Cola* (1956) are a dramatization of ten crucial years in Trinidad's history, 1935 to 1945. The two central events during this decade were the uprising in Trinidad's oilfields in 1937 and the U.S. military presence on the island during World War II. Other West Indian novelists, including H. G. de Lisser, V. S. Reid, and George Lamming, have also written novels set in the turbulent 1930s and 1940s, and the Trinidadian novelists Samuel Selvon and V. S. Naipaul have both dealt with the American impact on Trinidad society during and after the war. What makes de Boissière's treatment of this period unique is his radical social perspective and his commitment to militant working-class politics. In order to achieve a vast social and historical canvas and to suggest the continuous sweep of political events, de Boissière builds up a series of interlocking life histories which develop and repeat a given motif that he considers central to his ideological perspective. Thus the patterns of exploitation during the war, for example, are given a personal dimension within the patterns of experiences which the major and minor characters undergo, and each personal choice provides a further permutation of the types of alternatives open to the individual within the society portrayed. Our attention is constantly being shifted from one character to another, from one aspect of the political crisis to an aspect of an individual's crisis.

André de Coudray, a semi-autobiographical figure, is one of the major characters in *Crown Jewel*. The plot follows his development from an insecure, guilt-ridden member of the colored middle class to an observer of and ultimately a participant in the working-class struggle. Following a parallel path but moving away from committed participation is the character Joe Elias, while Cassie, an initially timid domestic servant who lives in a barrack yard, is portrayed as she develops into a courageous and self-assertive member of the working-class political movement. In *Rum and Coca-Cola* we continue to follow the development of André and Cassie, but two new major characters, Mopsy and Indra Goodman, are introduced. Their life histories demonstrate the consequences of the new forms of corruption and social disintegration that the author associates with the American presence in Trinidad. In spite of their symbolic functions within the novels, none of the major characters become flat stereotypes. Their decisions to love, hate, assist, or betray are taken within the context of personal weaknesses and loyalties common to all forms of characterization in fiction. De Boissière varies from the norm in that he continuously holds before the reader the direct and indirect political bases for such decisions as well as their ultimate political consequences in the society as a whole.

André de Coudray's social and political dilemma is dramatized in *Crown Jewel* by his attraction to two women: Elena Henriques, the colored daughter of a seamstress of Venezuelan descent; and Gwenneth Osborne, the daughter of an influential English judge. André's relationship with Gwenneth at first alienates him completely from Elena and the racially mixed group with which he has become involved in his attempts to break out of his narrow near-White social clique. He is uneasy about Gwenneth's evident dislike for Blacks but is human enough to become totally disillusioned with her only after he realizes that her family's racial prejudices also exclude him as a potential marriage partner for her. The movement back toward Elena and his lower-class friends is a slow, painful process, and he must overcome many social reservations that his higher social status raises in the minds of these associates, but eventually he marries Elena and is privileged to assist from the sidelines as the working-class movement gains in members and self-confidence.

One of the most human, moving sequences in *Crown Jewel* concerns the development of Cassie. In the beginning she is portrayed as an ordinary servant and barrack-yard dweller partially supported by a "keeper" and inclined to accept her position as inevitable. Her keeper's brutal death at the hands of the police as well as a growing sense of her self-worth draw her into the political movement, and she develops a relationship with one of the movement's leaders, Ben Le Maître. Le Maître in turn is influenced by Cassie. At the start of the book he is depicted as an inflexible, almost puritanical leader. The growing intimacy with Cassie, which is fostered by their shared involvement in the historical workers' march from San Fernando to Port of Spain, allows him to let down his emotional defenses, and for the first time he is able to admit to someone else his fears and uncertainties about the movement's success.

De Boissière's wide range of characters drawn from all social levels provides him with a challenging task as far as the reproduction of dialogue is concerned. Not only does he succeed in capturing a variety of nuances in his reproduction of direct speech, but also, in the case of his lower-class characters, he is able through language to suggest those qualities of courage and optimism which, when diverted to political ends, were capable of keeping mass movements like that of the 1930s alive. A good example of this technique occurs in his description of the workers' march already mentioned:

> They left Claxton Bay at eight. Le Maître headed the column. French walked in its rear. On either side staunch comrades hemmed in the womenfolk, and the men who limped morally or physically, and halted the column for the stragglers.
>
> "Hold up, Frederick!"
>
> "Frank, ohi! Hold that, boy."
>
> "What happen, flat tyre?"
>
> "No, we stop for passengers."
>
> "Right-o. All-you in front! Conductor say hold up."
>
> "Well! B'Christ! This is the longest free ride I ever get. Quite from Fyzabad and I ehn't pay a cent."
>
> "Who the hell legs so long in front there?"
>
> Cheerful voices called to one another, halting the column; and then called out still more cheerfully, urging it forward.
>
> "Walk like tourists! Watch the scenery. All-you ever see this part-a you' country yet?"
>
> "In trut', i's no difference. Tourists look at scenery t'rough dark glasses, we look at it t'rough dark night."
>
> "All-you start off bold to walk to town, as if you expect to take taxi back home," a thin wag of a fellow said. (1952 ed. pp. 301–2)

In *Rum and Coca-Cola* de Boissière is able to sustain the linguistic diversity and broad social spectrum of the first novel. A full range of new minor characters is introduced to suggest the altered interplay of social forces after the 1937 upheavals and during the war years. Old characters like André and Le Maître find themselves in increasingly difficult social situations. André loses his job because of his political involvement, while Le Maître for most of the book is imprisoned under wartime emergency regulations, leaving it to new, less-experienced members of the political movement to carry on the work. Among the more memorable of these is Charlie the shoemaker, a veteran of World War I, who is literally bulldozed into political awareness after the abandoned car in which he lives and works is demolished to clear a site for the Americans. There is also a host of deftly satirized politicians who have used the nationalist ferment spun off by the workers' movement as the basis for an opportunistic bid for political power. Above all, we are presented with "The Invaders," the American soldiers and civilians whose presence in the island places its inhabitants in a state of moral and economic siege. Although their presence helps lessen the significance of money and a white skin as status symbols in the society, the author portrays them ultimately as a socially disintegrative force that almost destroys the working-class initiative of the preceding years.

De Boissière focuses on the love affairs of two Trinidadian women with Americans to symbolize what he considers destructive about the American presence in the island. In the 1956 edition of *Rum and Coca-Cola*, both Indra

Goodman, a middle-class sympathizer of the workers' movement, and Mopsy, a prostitute, fall in love with and marry the same man—Wal Brown, an American civilian employed at the base, who in addition has a wife back home in America. In the 1984 edition there are two Americans involved: Wal Brown and a handsome womanizer called Wilbur Kemp. However, the methods used to depict these relationships and their consequences remain similar in the two editions of the novel. De Boissière again uses the strategy of a love triangle employed in his portrayal of André in *Crown Jewel* to illustrate Indra's political vacillation. Here the alternatives are represented by the social possibilities offered through her American lover and the political commitment of her fiancé Fred, who is one of the new young leaders in the workers' movement. After her eventual disillusionment with the American and an abortion, Indra herself draws closer to the workers' movement. Mopsy is not as fortunate. Her initial economic success as a prostitute provides the novel's most striking image of the general prostitution of Trinidad society to the Americans. When her American husband is sent back to the United States, she gives him all her savings to invest in a business. But Mopsy never hears from him again, and faced with the necessity of returning to prostitution, she goes out of her mind.

De Boissière's third novel, *No Saddles for Kangaroos* (1964), is set in Australia, and though it continues the novelist's concern with political issues, there is nothing Caribbean about its themes or subject matter. It is set in the early 1950s, when the Australian labor movement was seriously debilitated by widespread anti-Communist hysteria, and tells the story of an Australian working-class family who become involved in a series of industrial actions in an American-owned automobile factory and in the peace movement to end Australian involvement in the Korean War.

CRITICAL RECEPTION

Until the republication of *Crown Jewel* in 1981, Ralph de Boissière and his work were virtually unknown in the Caribbean, England, and the United States, although a few stray copies of his novels had found their way into Trinidadian, American, and British libraries. De Boissière recalls, for example, that twenty-five copies of the East German English-language edition of *Crown Jewel* were sent on his request to a bookshop in South Trinidad, and during his 1976 trip to the island he discovered a long extract from the novel in some old Oilfield Workers' Trade Union paper. Kenneth Ramchand may have stumbled across a copy of *Crown Jewel* when writing *The West Indian Novel and its Background* (1970), as he refers to it in passing in a footnote (see p. 128). In the same year Frank Birbalsingh published a first brief assessment of the author and his work in the *Journal of Commonwealth Literature*—a singularly insensitive and hostile piece of criticism in which he raised objections to the novelist's ideological commitment and claimed that "superficial portraits and generalized social sketches are de Boissière's stock in trade" and that the writing is "undramatic and pedestrian'' (pp. 105–6). Even in conservative Australia the reception had been warmer when the novels were first published there in the 1950s and 1960s, although the Australian *No Saddles for Kangaroos*, in the words of the reviewer in the *Bundaberg News-Mail* (September 12, 1964), ''could almost be described as subversive.'' The Caribbean novels were generally praised. The *Tribune* (September 1957) declared, ''De Boissière has created an art work valid not only for the West Indies but for all oppressed humanity,'' while the arts reviewer of Radio Australia's Overseas Service considered *Crown Jewel* ''one of the most talented *first* novels I have ever read'' (broadcast on November 7 and 8, 1952).

Unfortunately, reviews which must have appeared in the various Eastern-bloc countries where translations were published have not been available in writing this essay. The journal *Soviet Literature*, however, featured a perceptive study of ''Ralph de Boissière's Novels in Russian'' in May, 1966, in which Alla Petrikovskaya drew attention to the novels' use of the ''spacious epic form which provides the scope for a comprehensive analysis of the relationship between individual human fates and the historic process'' (p. 181). In the Caribbean in the mid–1970s it was the lone voice of Clifford Sealy in his little magazine that insisted that *Crown Jewel* was Trinidad's ''most important political novel... the fundamental work of fiction in our society'' (*Voices*, 1973, p. 3). My own publications, *From Trinidad* (1978), an anthology of material from *The Beacon* and *Trinidad* magazines, my article on writers of the 1930s and 1940s in Bruce King's *West Indian Literature* (1979), and my longer study, *The Trinidad Awakening* (forthcoming), have helped awaken interest in de Boissière's work, and through a series of fortunate accidents the publishers Allison and Busby became interested in bringing out the two Caribbean novels by de Boissière in England, in association with a paperback edition from Picador.

Allison and Busby announced *Crown Jewel* as ''one of the lost masterpieces of world literature,'' while Picador advertised it as ''a Caribbean classic and a major work of realist fiction which in the urgency of its narrative drive and the depth of its moral concerns can prompt parallels with Turgenev and Tolstoy.'' While publishers may be suspected of exaggeration, almost unanimously reviewers on both sides of the Atlantic seemed to agree with the publishers' claims. *The Observer* (June 14, 1981) set the tone: ''Once in a blue moon a lost gem is unearthed from the general rubble of period fiction. *Crown Jewel*... is one such find.'' Everybody was intrigued by the novel's curious publishing history, and there was much speculation as to why an English edition of it had not appeared in the 1950s when almost every West Indian writer capable of putting pen to paper had been snapped up by British publishing houses. ''One can only guess that its profoundly anti-British slant has prevented until now its publication in this country,'' surmised the reviewer in *Head and Hand* (July 1981). De Boissière's handling of political themes also excited a great deal of interest. Louis James, in a review article in the *Journal of Commonwealth Literature* (1982), described it as ''political writing without political postures'' (p. 13), and the Indian novelist Salman Rushdie, writing for the *Times Literary Supple-*

ment (1981), felt that "the enormous appeal of this book lies not so much in its committed socialism as in its ability to integrate politics with the lives of its characters." Especially interesting was the attempt of some reviewers to contrast de Boissière with his fellow Trinidadian V. S. Naipaul. *The New York Review of Books* (May 27, 1982) commented: "The book seems written from the point of view of a participant. This sense of participation may account for the difference between de Boissière's idea of Trinidad and that of V. S. Naipaul, the supreme, and supremely critical, observer"; and Salman Rushdie in his *TLS* review rejoiced: "*Crown Jewel* remains a salutary corrective to the feckless, irresponsible image that Trinidadians have been given by V. S. Naipaul." Nobody in the long line of reviewers doubted that "at last de Boissière takes his rightful place beside such as Reid, Lamming, Selvon and Salkey" (Michael Thorpe in *British Book News* [October 1981]). The most interesting speculation, at least for the literary historian of West Indian writing, was put forward in Louis James's *JCL* review: "If this novel had been published [earlier in Britain], what other writing would it have made possible? Would it have changed the direction of young writers in the way *In the Castle of My Skin* influenced a whole generation? We will never know" (p. 15).

BIBLIOGRAPHY

Works by Ralph de Boissière

Early short fiction was published in *Trinidad* (1929–30); *The Beacon* (1931–33, 1939; Millwood, N.Y.: Kraus Reprint, 1977); and in Albert Gomes, ed., *From Trinidad: A Selection from the Fiction and Verse of the Island of Trinidad, British West Indies* (Port of Spain: Author, 1937). Two short stories, "The Woman on the Pavement" and "Booze and the Goberdaw," were republished in Reinhard W. Sander, ed. *From Trinidad: An Anthology of Early West Indian Writing* (London: Hodder & Stoughton, 1978; New York: Holmes & Meier, 1978).

Crown Jewel. Melbourne: Australasian Book Society, 1952; Leipzig: Paul List, 1956; London: Allison & Busby, and Picador, 1981. Translations appeared in Poland, East Germany, Romania, Czechoslovakia, Bulgaria, Yugoslavia, China, and the Soviet Union.

Rum and Coca-Cola. Melbourne: Australasian Book Society, 1956; London: Allison & Busby, 1984. Translations appeared in Poland, East Germany, Czechoslovakia, China, and the Soviet Union.

No Saddles for Kangaroos. Sydney: Australasian Book Society, 1964. "On Writing a Novel." *Journal of Commonwealth Literature* 17 (August 1982), 1–12.

Studies of Ralph de Boissière

Birbalsingh, F. M. "The Novels of Ralph de Boissière." *Journal of Commonwealth Literature* 9 (July 1970), 104–08.

Hart, Richard. Review of *Crown Jewel*. *Caribbean Contact* (August 1981), 3.

James, Louis. Review of *Crown Jewel*. *Journal of Commonwealth Literature* 17 (August 1982), 13–15.

Petrikovskaya, Alla. "Ralph de Boissière's Novels in Russian." *Soviet Literature* (May 1966), 180–82.

Rushdie, Salman. "Exemplary Lives" (Review of *Crown Jewel*). *Times Literary Supplement*, August 7, 1981.

Sander, Reinhard W., ed. "A Caribbean Writer in Australia: An Interview with Ralph de Boissière." *Komparatistische Hefte* 5/6 (1982), 195–208.

———. "The Thirties and Forties." In *West Indian Literature*, ed. Bruce King, 1979, pp. 45–62.

———. *The Trinidad Awakening: West Indian Literature of the Nineteen-Thirties*. Westport, Conn.: Greenwood Press, forthcoming.

Sealy, Clifford. "A Backward Glance: *Crown Jewel*." *Voices* 2 (April 1977), 8–11.

———. "*Crown Jewel*: A Note on Ralph de Boissière." *Voices* 2 (March 1973), 1–3.

Thieme, John. "Socialist Classic" (Review of *Crown Jewel*). *The Literary Review* (September 1981).

See also General Bibliography: Allis and Herdeck.

JOYCE JOHNSON

Jean D'Costa (1937–   )

BIOGRAPHY

Jean Constance D'Costa (née Creary) was born on January 13, 1937, in St. Andrew, Jamaica. Her parents were both elementary school teachers who worked for a time in rural Jamaica. Jean D'Costa recalls: "My first memories are of the Jamaican countryside: village life, estate life, hills, empty Crown Lands and small coastal towns. We moved often, but finally settled in Kingston though I was sent to high school in the country. The experience of those years has had a very strong effect on my outlook and temperament" (personal communication with Joyce Johnson, undated). She attended St. Hilda's High School in Brown's Town, St. Ann, and in 1955 won a University College of the West Indies open scholarship. At the University College, which was then in special relation to the University of London, Jean D'Costa read for an honors degree in English literature and language (with a minor in French literature). Graduating with first class honors in June, 1958, she was awarded an overseas scholarship and went on to read for a B.Litt. in Jacobean drama at Oxford University.

On her return to Jamaica in September, 1962, D'Costa joined the Department of English at the University of the West Indies, where for the next fifteen years she taught courses in English literature and linguistics, one of her special areas being Anglo-Saxon. Both by natural inclination and as a consequence of her academic position, D'Costa became involved in activities related to the teaching of English in schools. She became a resource person and consultant for the Ministry of Education and the Joint Board of Teacher Education, served on many committees, frequently lectured at high schools and training colleges, and gave readings and talks at primary schools. D'Costa has participated in many conferences in Jamaica, other Caribbean islands, Britain, and North America on topics related to her professional and creative activities and has published articles on Caribbean literature and Caribbean dialectology. Some of her poetry (which she started writing as an undergraduate) has also been published (see especially Mervyn Morris and Pamela Mordecai, eds., *Jamaica Woman: An Anthology of Poems* [London: Heinemann, 1980]).

Jean D'Costa is now an associate professor of English at Hamilton College, New York. She is at present working on a historical novel set in Jamaica in the 1770s and a historical study of the origins of Jamaican Creole, in collaboration with Dr. Barbara Lalla of the UWI, Trinidad. She shares many interests with her husband, David, a graduate in English from Harvard and a journalist and writer to whom she has been married since 1967.

MAJOR WORKS AND THEMES

Jean D'Costa's interest as a professional in the field of education and her talents as a creative writer are effectively brought together in her novels written for children. She writes for the eleven-to-thirteen age group. *Sprat Morrison* (1972), her first novel, will appeal to the younger ones in this group, while *Escape to Last Man Peak* (1975) and *Voice in the Wind* (1978) will appeal to the older ones. So too will the book of children's stories *Over Our Way* (1981), which she edited with Velma Pollard and to which she contributed two stories.

In writing for the eleven-to-thirteen age group, D'Costa has kept two of their basic needs in view: on the one hand, their need to relate to actuality; and, on the other hand, their need to retain some of the comforting illusions of childhood. In the modern context, however, the effective writer of children's fiction cannot be overly didactic, and D'Costa, despite her concern with the expansion of the child's emotional and social experience, creates stories which entertain, excite wonder, and provoke mystery. Her novels show a clear line of development in narrative technique, and it is important to examine them in the order in which they were written.

Sprat Morrison, which was accepted by the Ministry of Education Publications Department in 1968 and published by Collins-Sangster in 1972, is widely used in Caribbean schools and was reprinted in 1973, 1976, and 1979. The hero of the novel, Sprat Morrison, is an eleven-year-old primary school boy who is coping with certain family and peer group matters and with the prospect of his "eleven-plus" examination, success in which will ensure him a place in a high school. In the course of the story, Sprat gains a realistic idea of his own capabilities and is started on the road to self-discovery.

Sprat Morrison is a third person narrative set in Papine, a village approximately six miles from downtown Kingston, Jamaica. It is a place D'Costa knows well, situated as it is less than a mile from the University of the West Indies. Papine draws attention to itself with the steep hillsides in the background alternating wooded areas, grassy patches with protruding rocks, and little pockets of settlement, which D'Costa has effectively conjured up in the novel. The novel is episodic and allows for the introduction of a variety of persons who are important to Sprat's well-being at a crucial stage in his life. The episodes described recall topics on which children are often required to write, at that age when composition and creative writing classes emphasize the experientially based account. Thus Chapter 1, "Fire," describes an exciting, grueling, and unexpected adventure on Sprat's way to school; Chapter 2, "The Artist," is about a rainy day which Sprat spends at home by himself. Then there is the chapter devoted to the trip to Duppy Bay, showing sophisticated narrative skills being applied to two of the Jamaican primary school teacher's favorite topics for children, "A Day by the Seaside" and "The Picnic." Very fittingly, the story ends with Sprat and his friends writing their "eleven-plus" examination (perhaps writing compositions on some of the topics mentioned above) and gaining their places in high school. For them, there has been a process of maturation: they have completed, in effect, a rite of passage.

Escape to Last Man Peak, which appeared in 1976, is a more complex story than *Sprat Morrison* and combines both childhood and adult perspectives. The narrator Nellie recounts her experiences as a twelve year old when along with nine other children she made an extraordinary journey across the island of Jamaica. D'Costa uses both the example of science fiction and the pattern of the classical novel with the journey motif. Ten orphans living in a home near Spanish Town, Jamaica, find themselves on their own when a devastating epidemic, mutant viral pneumonia, strikes in the eastern section of the island. Children are immune to this disease. When the adults who run the home die, the children, afraid of having their group split up, flee the orphanage, setting out for Last Man Peak in western Jamaica, where one of them once lived with his grandfather. The children have several significant encounters with adults as they move from the restricted environment of the orphanage through the wider society on their journey across the island.

The novel focuses on the children's attempt to reconstruct a way of life together, when their world is disrupted by an unexpected event. To do this, they must undertake the roles of adults on whom they formerly depended. Throughout the story, D'Costa places emphasis on the practical rather than the conventional—good sense coupled with generosity of spirit.

Like *Sprat Morrison*, *Escape to Last Man Peak* is useful in the classroom. It can be discussed very satisfactorily in terms of plot, narrative structure, characterization, and style. Thus it provides a useful introduction to the novel for juniors. D'Costa's use of language is particularly important. In *Escape to Last Man Peak*, one recognizes a successful attempt to normalize a situation in language long seen as problematic for the Jamaican child and to put it into perspective. D'Costa's style moves easily between the prose of the narrative passages—a relaxed and flexible rendering of educated local usage—and the dialogue ranging from broad vernacular to English showing only slight Creole interference. As the entry in *Caribbean Writers* notes: "Her children's books have caught the particular Jamaican atmosphere beautifully and use the Jamaican speech rhythms with great accuracy and insight" (Donald Herdeck, ed., 1979, p. 62).

Voice in the Wind, D'Costa's third novel, was published in 1978. It is in some ways a more ambitious undertaking than *Escape to Last Man Peak*. In *Voice in the Wind*, D'Costa deals with children's ideas about death and the supernatural. The novel is a successful attempt to reconcile the claims of fantasy and reality on the life of the child. The children's make-believe world, in which an eleven-year-old boy may imagine himself to be a secret agent in the war and a ten-year-old girl going upstairs becomes a queen going to her secret temple, is juxtaposed to a reality which requires responsiveness to familial and social duties and to the world of the adult. In the particular local environment in which the children live, the world of the imagination extends into the realm of the supernatural. Thus it becomes possible for the children depicted in *Voice in the Wind* to accept mysterious and strange happenings as part of their total world.

The setting of *Voice in the Wind* is Jamaica in the early 1940s, and the story recounts the experiences of three children whose great-uncle by marriage is a Norwegian sea captain who loses his ship in a submarine attack during World War II. D'Costa conveys how World War II impinged on the consciousness of Jamaican children in a country village. In shifting her setting yet again, she has given a realistic account of a small mixed farming community in St. James, the village of Somerton where her family lived from 1942 to 1945. In *Voice in the Wind*, as in her other novels and stories, the reader is aware of the carryover from D'Costa's work in historical linguistics. Before writing this novel she did intensive research into contemporary newspapers' accounts of World War II. In this, as in the other works, the quest is for authenticity. There is a feeling for time and place; memory is buttressed by research.

Jean D'Costa's novels show her to be an imaginative, versatile, and meticulous writer. She demonstrates a capacity to penetrate the inner world of the child between the ages of ten and thirteen as sensitive but unsentimental, drawing attention to the ironies which children recognize in the world of the adult. In her novels, Standard English and Jamaican Creole are used to complement each other effectively, and she is clearly aware of the extent to which the written word may become a model for the child's own writing. A major aim in her work has been to give her Jamaican readers an idea of the complexity and variety of the society and the culture to which they have become heirs and of the wider experience open to them. As she observes in a prefatory note to *Over Our Way*:

> Our way stretches far, so far-all the way to Detroit and Birmingham and to Toronto, and all the way through to Dahomey, India, Scotland and China. Our way splits like a spider-road leading all over the face of the earth.
>
> Our voices echo down our way, throwing out words from Yoruba and English, Hindi

and Gaelic, French and Arawak, and singing the music of the dozen languages living and dead. (p. ix)

Jean D'Costa has also established herself as one of the major critics of Caribbean literature, particularly as a Roger Mais scholar. In addition to a number of essays on Mais, including the introduction to the Heinemann edition of *Black Lightning* (1983), she is the author of the only full-length study of Mais (*Roger Mais*, 1978).

CRITICAL RECEPTION

Jean D'Costa has enjoyed a favorable reception from Jamaican critics, who applaud her novels for providing exciting, well-written stories about Jamaican people with a distinctively Jamaican locale, flavor, accent, and rhythm, stories to which the Jamaican child can immediately relate. Francis M. Shim ("Jean D'Costa, *Escape to Last Man Peak*," 1975) asserts that "this positive affirmation of a Jamaican identity in literature is important to the development of our children and is something of which they have for too long been deprived" (p. 36). Several critics note as well that the stories may well prove interesting and appealing to adult readers. Shim observes, "*Escape to Last Man Peak* is not simply and exclusively a novel for children. There is a depth of emotion here that any adult can relate to" (p. 37), and Myrna Daley ("Well-written Kiddies Book," 1978) concurs, noting that *Voice in the Wind* "could prove good reading for adults."

D'Costa's language has been widely commented on by various critics. *Sprat Morrison*, in which D' Costa "deliberately experimented with Jamaican standard and literary Standard [English]" (letter to Daryl Cumber Dance, February 9, 1985) because of the widespread sentiment against vernacular fiction in the schools, still employs, according to Gwladys Junor (Review of *Sprat Morrison*, 1973) "a large number of local expressions accepted in Jamaican usage but not in English" (p. 40). Junor suggests that D'Costa's use of Standard English "is perfectly legitimate, even wise (in view of examination requirements)" (p. 40) and concludes that "although [D'Costa's] 'typical Jamaicans' have been made to speak reasonably standard English, they do not at any time sound strained or unnatural; . . . I should have thought this an almost impossible achievement, but Mrs. D'Costa has brought it off splendidly" (p. 40). In the later novels D'Costa made full use of the Jamaican dialect, and critics considered them all the better for it. Shim applauds the fact that in *Escape to Last Man Peak* "the language . . . is boldly and unash[a]medly Jamaican with all the dialogue passages being in the dialect." (p. 36).

D'Costa's work has been enthusiastically received by the audience for which it was intended—Jamaican schoolchildren. *Sprat* has been standard required reading in the first grade of high schools in Jamaica since 1972. Many schools use *Escape* and *Voice in the Wind* as well, the latter having been acclaimed by the *Sunday Gleaner Magazine* reviewer ("A Very Good Children's Story,"

1978) "a must for schools." Student letters to the author attest to their ardent responses to her stories. D'Costa is frequently invited to visit the schools and speak about the books.

HONORS AND AWARDS

Jean D'Costa was awarded a University College of the West Indies Open Scholarship in 1955; an Allen Lane Essay Prize, UCWI, in 1957; and a University Overseas Scholarship in 1958. She won the Children's Writers Award for the Jamaica Reading Association in 1976 and the Gertrude Flesh Bristol Award from Hamilton College in 1984.

BIBLIOGRAPHY

Works by Jean D'Costa

Sprat Morrison. Kingston: Collins-Sangster, 1972, 1974, 1977, 1979.

Escape to Last Man Peak. London: Longman, 1975, 1976, 1980.

Voice in the Wind. London: Longman, 1978, 1980.

Roger Mais: The Hills Were Joyful Together and Brother Man [critical study]. London: Longman, 1978.

Over Our Way [short stories edited jointly with Velma Pollard]. London: Longman, 1980.

Studies of Jean D'Costa

Daley, Myrna. "Well-written Kiddies Book." *Jamaica Daily News*, October 22, 1978.

Junor, Gwladys. Review of *Sprat Morrison*. *Orch* (Journal of the Ministry of Education, Jamaica) 22 (Christmas 1973), 39–40.

Shim, Frances M. "Jean D'Costa, *Escape to Last Man Peak*." *Arts Review* 1 (April 1975), 36–37.

"A Very Good Children's Story" (Review of *Voice in the Wind*). *Sunday Gleaner Magazine*, October 22, 1978.

See also General Bibliography: Allis, Herdeck, and Hughes.

RHONDA COBHAM

Herbert George de Lisser (1878–1944)

BIOGRAPHY

H. G. de Lisser was born in Falmouth, Jamaica, in 1878. His parents were of Afro-Jewish descent, and his father was the editor of a small newspaper in Trelawney that ran into difficulties after championing the wrong side in the debate over the importation of East Indian indentured labor at the close of the 19th century. The de Lissers eventually moved to Kingston, where the elder de Lisser found work as the editor of the *Gleaner* newspaper, at that time a fairly modest local publication. When de Lisser was fourteen years old his father died, leaving the family practically destitute. The young de Lisser was forced to leave school and find a job. In later years de Lisser seldom spoke directly about this period of his life, during which he worked at an ironmonger's and in various lowly clerical positions, but in his novel *Triumphant Squalitone* (1917) he allows his protagonist John Squalitone to describe with heavy irony the struggle for survival and respectability that must have characterized these early years:

> The average respectable youth of poor parentage is usually one of six or eight brothers and sisters, and so begins life upon short allowance as it were. During all the days of his life his parents maintain a desperate struggle with circumstances, and Johnny—we will call my illustration Johnny, my name being John—grows up in an atmosphere of compulsory fasting. (p. 24)

Squalitone goes on to describe how Johnny's parents scrimp and save to be able to send their son to a private school where he will not be obliged to mix with the lower classes but how his attendance there is often interrupted on account of his having no shoes. At fourteen or fifteen Johnny leaves school:

> About this time Johnny's father dies. I have noticed that it is the custom of most poor but respectable fathers to die before their children are properly grown up. His mother is a weak, over-driven, devoted woman, so Johnny at once becomes liberated from all parental control. . . . Yielding to the solicitations of the boy's mother, someone employs him in a store or office, and this employer kindly agrees to give him five shillings a week to start on, and thinks he is a philanthropist. Thus Johnny is launched upon the waters of commercial life, to sink beneath its waves at a later date. (pp. 24–28, *passim*)

Johnny's progress, from cigars and smart clothes bought on credit to precipitate marriage to the sister of a friend, is charted, but ultimately the wheel comes full circle. Burdened with mortgages, unable to rise in his job or support his growing family, Johnny dies from overwork before his own children are properly grown up.

In the novel, Squalitone fights desperately to avoid the fate he predicts for Johnny, even to the point of "selling out" to a corrupt politician. In real life de Lisser fought even harder and more ruthlessly to avoid his father's fate. After several ill-paid clerical positions, he went to work at the Institute of Jamaica. Here he read voraciously, teaching himself French and Spanish as well as becoming something of an expert on Caribbean history and politics. After three years at the institute he moved to the *Gleaner* as a proofreader. In 1889 he obtained his first job as a journalist at the *Jamaica Times*, and it was in this weekly that his first extended articles on Jamaican society appeared. In 1903, at the age of twenty-five, de Lisser was offered the position of associate editor at the *Gleaner*. Twelve months later he became the newspaper's youngest ever editor-in-chief, a position he was to hold unchallenged for the next forty years.

Under de Lisser's editorship the *Gleaner* established itself as the most important newspaper in the island. Its tremendous influence on public opinion, which has been maintained to this day, was mainly the result of de Lisser's forthright and controversial editorials and his satiric column, "Random Jottings," in which he poked fun at all aspects of Jamaican life. De Lisser married Ellen Gunther, the daughter of a well-established White Jamaican family in 1909—the same year in which his first book, a collection of essays on Cuba and Jamaica, was published. His second documentary *Twentieth Century Jamaica*, appeared in 1912, and at about the same time his first novel, *Jane, a Story of Jamaica*, began to be serialized in the *Gleaner*. Thereafter de Lisser published a new novel practically every other year, some in book form, others as extended magazine stories in *Planters' Punch*, an annual magazine which de Lisser established in 1920 as the unofficial publicity organ of the Jamaica Imperial Association.

Two Englishmen seemed to have influenced de Lisser most profoundly during his formative years: J. H. Froude and Sir Sydney Olivier. Froude was a well-known historian and travel writer of the conservative Victorian school. In 1888, around the time that de Lisser went to work at the *Jamaica Times*, Froude's travel documentary, *The English in the West Indies or the Bow of Ulysses*, appeared. In it Froude argued that the Whites in the West Indies had become so debased as a result of isolation from the benign intellectual traditions of the mother country that they were incapable of drawing the bow of Ulysses—that is, of self-rule. Froude's book caused a furor among Black and White West Indians alike and drew a famous rejoinder from the Black Trinidadian schoolmaster, J. J. Thomas, called *Froudacity* (1889). De Lisser, by contrast, was attracted to Froude's ideas, as they reinforced his own instinctive impatience with the pettiness and imitativeness of colonial society. Froude blamed the culture of the slaves rather than the depravity of the system of slavery for these shortcomings, a rationalization which exonerated "cultured" individuals like de Lisser from the general morass. De Lisser often cited Froude directly, and in an article called "Marriage" in the *Jamaica Times* (August 25, 1900) we can see him consciously applying Froude's standards of civilization to the Black man and finding him wanting:

> Good humoured and impulsive, an admirable imitator when well taught but with no inventive faculty whatever. His political and social organisation is of the most primitive type, his cities are collections of huts which cannot withstand a season's rains. He has no literature, and no art. His music is of the rudest. He is sometimes brave to recklessness and sometimes a deplorable coward.

De Lisser was to hold this view of the Black man with only minor adjustments in tone for all his life, and he consistently portrays even the most sympathetically drawn Negro characters in his novels as having some or all of the above-mentioned traits. In addition de Lisser, like Froude, had scant respect for the White and colored classes in Jamaica and enjoyed shocking and satirizing them in his work. In the article on "Marriage," for instance, he argues that it was ridiculous for respectable well-meaning Jamaicans to try to urge the Black masses into formal marriage as the latter were incapable of the higher sentiments which made marriage important to the civilized races. It was this sort of perversely radical conservatism that was to become a hallmark of de Lisser's style as a novelist and journalist. On the one hand he was adept at undermining the stuffy and hypocritical tenets of public morality. On the other hand his cynicism and elitism propelled him into increasingly racist attitudes toward his fellow Jamaicans.

Sydney Olivier's influence on de Lisser is perhaps more widely recognized. Olivier was colonial secretary in Jamaica from 1900 to 1904 and governor of the island from 1907 to 1913. In England Olivier had been one of the founding members of the Fabian Socialist movement, and as colonial secretary he confounded the Jamaican establishment by holding public lectures critical of the colonial system of government of which he was a representative. Olivier's unorthodox style attracted a circle of admiring young colonials for whom public debate at this level was a heady new experience. De Lisser belonged to this group, and under the liberal Englishman's influence he tempered some of the least agreeable aspects of his social snobbery. In his documentary, *Jamaica, the Blessed Isle* (1936), Olivier claims that it was he who instigated de Lisser to write *Jane's Career*, and perhaps this may account for de Lisser's relatively sympathetic treatment of the novel's Black protagonist. Friendship with Olivier also brought de Lisser into contact with several prominent English literary personalities connected with the Fabian Socialist movement, such as George Bernard Shaw, who visited Jamaica as Olivier's guest during the latter's term of office there. In his novels de Lisser developed an arch satiric style reminiscent of Shaw, which he was able, however, to make uniquely his own.

There can be no doubt that Olivier's patronage of de Lisser enhanced the latter's reputation as both a journalist and a creative writer. De Lisser's prestige reached its greatest heights, however, after Olivier's departure, during the interwar years, when public opinion was more conservative than it had been before World War I or was to become after 1938. His influence only began to wane as a new generation of nationalist politicians began to make their presence felt on the cultural scene. In 1938 he resigned from the board of governors of the Institute of Jamaica and withdrew from most of the cultural institutions with which he had been previously connected. As editor of the *Gleaner* he continued to campaign relentlessly against internal self-government until his death, which, with an irony he himself would have considered fitting, occurred in 1944, the year in which Jamaica received its new constitution.

MAJOR THEMES AND WORKS

Despite his racial biases and political conservatism, de Lisser was in many respects an astute and accurate observer of his society and a pioneer in the field of literature. He ranks among the first West Indian writers to offer a realistic treatment of contemporaneous society in his novels and was also one of the first Jamaican journalists to try to attract a popular readership for locally produced fiction in the pages of his annual, *Planters' Punch*. Of his twenty-odd full-length works of fiction, about half are historical romances. Most of the rest may be classed either as social realism or as political satire.

De Lisser's best-known early novels, *Jane's Career* (1914) and *Susan Proudleigh* (1915), fall into the category of social realism, but it would be inaccurate to claim that de Lisser's interest in this type of writing waned as his conservatism gradually isolated him from the mainstream of his society. *Myrtle and Money* (1942), conceived as a sequel to *Jane's Career*, is one of de Lisser's best-written works, and *Under the Sun* (1936) and *The Rivals* (1921) are both entertaining comic pieces on the near-White Jamaican middle class to which de Lisser himself belonged. *The Jamaica Bandits* (1930) is built around a series of robberies that took place in Kingston in the year preceding the story's publication, while *The*

Sins of the Children (1928) and *The Crocodiles* (1933) explore a recurrent theme in all de Lisser's novels—the problem of miscegenation.

Jane's Career follows the story of a young girl from the country who comes to Kingston to work as a domestic for a mulatto lady called Mrs. Mason. After several years of exploitation and harassment in the Mason household (including seduction by her employer's nephew), Jane goes to live with a friend, Sathyra, in a Kingston tenement yard and finds a job pasting labels in a factory. She is rescued from further debauchery at the hands of the factory supervisor and near homelessness when she contracts an alliance with a promising young typesetter. The birth of their first child is followed by an ostentatious white wedding, and we leave the couple at the end of the book well on the road to middle-class respectability.

In spite of the ironical tone de Lisser uses to describe the way in which Jane takes over many of the trappings of respectability of her former employer, the author engages our sympathies convincingly in the novel for a class of person who would hardly have been considered human by the upper strata of Jamaican society of his day. At the same time de Lisser resists the social protest writer's temptation to portray exploited individuals merely as passive victims. After her initial misery in Kingston and sense of having been betrayed by her family, Jane quickly learns how to make the most of her situation. Even her seduction in the Mason household is made to work for her as she leaves her predatory suitor considerably out of pocket. In the frequent confrontations that take place between Mrs. Mason and her various domestic servants, the employees often win out on the level of words, even though ultimately they may lose their positions. De Lisser had a fine ear for the rhetorical niceties of Creole "tracing" matches and is able to reproduce these with all the dramatic flair of the real life situation:

> Sarah felt that the term of her service with Mrs Mason was speedily drawing to an abrupt termination, and at once made up her mind to give word for word, and so leave, at the least, with all the honours of war.
>
> "Who you callin' liard?" she insolently asked. "Y'u better call you' two brown niece liard, or your mamparla nephew. You is a liard you'self if y'u say y'u did see me last night. What sort of hie you must be 'ave to see t'rough board and brick! . . . I don't know what kind o' lady you can be when you always counting how much piece of yam come into de table, an' always followin' up you' sarvant. . . . I know I am black, an' I know that God meck two colour, black an' white, but it must be de devil meck brown people, for dem is neider black nor white! In fact y'u better pay me at once an' let me go. I not stayin' here any longer. Pay me me wages, an' meck me leave you' yard." (*Jane's Career*, pp. 55–56)

Indeed, whatever his reservations about their race may have been, de Lisser invariably portrays working-class women as pragmatic and resourceful, shrewd at business and adept at manipulating their lovers and employers in the struggle for survival.

Not so de Lisser's men. While constantly harping on the resourcefulness and physical attractions of the Black woman, he depicts her male partner as lazy, intellectually confused, and unnecessarily aggressive. In terms of plot he also uses the women's desire for social security at a personal level to thwart the attempts of the men to organize politically. In *Jane's Career*, Jane's lover, Vincent Broglie, is faced with the choice of losing Jane to the factory supervisor or breaking the strike at the newspaper printery where he works in order to offer Jane protection and financial security. Broglie's decision to betray his striking colleagues wins him favor with Jane and advancement at his place of work. In *Susan Proudleigh*, the pattern is repeated and elaborated as we follow the heroine through two marriages and three affairs, against the background of the struggle for better working conditions among Jamaicans involved in building the Panama Canal. In each case the prize of Susan's affections goes to the man who shows the least inclination to challenge the system.

In addition, de Lisser is able to denigrate the aspirations of his male characters by distorting the Creole language which they use. Sentiments which, in a different context, the reader may have been inclined to give serious consideration are deflated by association with a particularly bombastic form of Creole, close enough to the actual language spoken to seem authentic. Even before Samuel Josiah Jones, one of the most politically active of Susan's admirers, migrates to Panama, we are prepared to see him as blustering and illogical because of the way he speaks. On one occasion, for example, he dismisses reports of racial discrimination in the Canal Zone out of hand:

> Most Jamaican people is foolish; they have no cranium whatsoever. I bet you those men never told they were British subjects. Now, if it was me, I would have made everybody to understand that I was an Anglo-Saxon, an' that if they touch a hair of me head, war would be declared. That's the way to talk in a foreign country. I wouldn't make a man bluff me out. No sir! (*SP*, p. 102)

Jones's linguistic confusion of racial and legal status, his bravado and false understanding of conditions in Panama are communicated through his use of malapropisms and a form of syntax which sounds clumsy when contrasted with the free-flowing Creole speech of Mrs Mason's servant already quoted. As a result the reader is encouraged to interpret his later bitterness about conditions in the Canal Zone as the predictable overreaction of an ill-informed and self-opinionated malcontent.

In de Lisser's more explicitly political satires, *Triumphant Squalitone* (1917), *Revenge* (1919), and *The Jamaica Nobility* (1926), language manipulation is heavily relied upon to differentiate between "good" and "evil" characters. *Revenge* is a fictional representation of the events and motives which caused the Morant Bay Rebellion of 1865. De Lisser predictably sides with the government against Bogle and Gordon and ascribes much of the blame for the troubles to the war-mongering tone of the newspapers of the day. When the fighting breaks out, a particularly fiery journalist is challenged by his associates to take up arms in the struggle. De Lisser uses his confusion of language registers to imply cowardice and hypocrisy:

> "No," replied Mr Mace. "My duty keeps me pinned to the point of action. From here I address the people and bring to their keen understanding a sense of the existing conditions that exist. That is purely constitutional." As usual with the editor, after he had balanced himself for some time on the dizzy heights of the Queen's English, he immediately dropped to the colloquial. "Not me, me brother." He added, "I don't want policeman to put hand 'pon me. Coward man keep sound bones, an' my bones don't too strong already. (*Revenge*, p. 45)

Many of de Lisser's historical romances are potboilers of little literary merit. Their pattern of intrigue woven around a well-known historical event tends to be predictable; however, de Lisser had the uncanny knack of picking historical events which occurred at crucial points in Jamaican history on which to hinge his stories, and a reading of these lesser works reveals the extent to which he used fiction as a polemical weapon in his antinational campaign. In addition, the historical romances throw light on de Lisser's attitudes toward a number of issues, including obeah, miscegenation, and the capabilities of the African race.

Almost all de Lisser's heroines in the historical romances are colored women involved in love affairs with White men. *Morgan's Daughter* (1931) is the story of pirate-governor Morgan's mulatto bastard, whose love for an English renegade leads her into complicity in his crimes. *The Cup and the Lip* (1932) explores the relationship between a female East Indian indentured laborer and a White overseer in the late 19th century. *Anacanoa* (1937) takes its name from an Arawak princess, in love with one of Christopher Columbus's officers shipwrecked on Jamaica's north coast in the 16th century. In *Haunted* (1940), a visiting English beau is bewitched by the mother of an attractive mulatto girl so as to lure him into marriage. The offspring of this liaison, which predictably ends in tragedy, becomes a pivotal figure in the 1938 riots, depicted in the novel's sequel, *The Return* (1944). Indeed, few of de Lisser's mixed liaisons end happily. The initiative in starting the affair is invariably taken by the colored woman, and often, as in *Haunted*, the girl or her relatives resort to witchcraft to attract or bind the desired lover.

De Lisser's preoccupation with the theme of miscegenation must have been due to social realities as well as personal history. He himself was a man of color: brown enough to be recognized as such in shade-conscious Jamaica, but "respectable" enough, due to his Portuguese Jewish name and ancestry and his excellent connections in England, to call himself White in a social situation not renowned for its logic or consistency on the question of race. Indeed, there could have been few Creole White families in Jamaica in which, somewhere along the line, intermarriage with persons of mixed blood had not taken place. What de Lisser seems to be exploring in many of his novels is the fear of exposure that must have been a source of constant worry for "respectable" Jamaicans not far removed from the historical point of mixing on the one hand, and the trauma of self-hatred experienced by those Jamaicans who, for financial or physical reasons, were just below the color bar. In *The Sins of the Children* (1928), one of the few novels in which a mixed couple is actually allowed to marry (albeit after migration to Nicaragua), we are given this description of the heroine, a well-educated young woman with good financial prospects, as she examines her reflection in the mirror:

> She looked long and earnestly at her face in the mirror: she saw that it was pretty; saw her large black eyes gleaming with excitement and something else besides; and her smooth, healthy skin, her carefully combed, carefully arranged hair, the arch of her nose and the self-willed, small mouth of which she was so proud. Yes, she knew that she had her full share of attractiveness, need envy no girl of her complexion and class. ''But I am so dark,'' she murmured, ''so dark . . . too dark,'' and the burning eyes became misty. (*Sins*, p. 30)

Clearly de Lisser understood only too well the racial tensions within his society. Had he been a writer of greater integrity he could have made through his novels an important contribution to his society's self-awareness in this respect. As it is, he shies away ultimately from examining the deeper social issues behind the miscegenation taboo, relying instead on clever coincidences to divert the reader's attention and round off his plots.

In de Lisser's best-known historical novel, *The White Witch of Rosehall* (1929), the theme of miscegenation is relegated to subplot. However, its position remains pivotal as it is the rivalry between Rose Hall's mistress and a Black girl for the attentions of a visiting Englishman that makes the White woman turn to the voodoo arts she had learned from her slave nanny in Haiti before the revolution there and her family's flight to Jamaica. One of de Lisser's abiding concerns was the ''civilizing'' of the Jamaican upper class. His magazine *Planters' Punch* is full of journalistic pieces comparing the new gentility of the Jamaican elite with the raucous decadence of their forebears during slavery. In *The White Witch of Rosehall* this issue becomes the central theme. Each of the leading European characters is portrayed as having been contaminated on account of his or her close association with slave culture and isolation from the civilizing influences of the mother country. As Rider, the drunken clergyman, explains in commenting on his own debauchery and warning against prolonged residence in the tropics:

> The life here, for a man like me, was infinitely easier than it could be in England. My duties were light, my pay was sufficient to keep me, and I could do what I pleased to a great extent without being called to account for it. I liked the life, at first; I didn't realize what it was leading me to. I liked the drink; I didn't grasp that it was making me a drunkard. When I did, I was down. (*WWR*, p. 193)

But condemnation of the planter class during slavery should not be mistaken for commendation of the slaves. De Lisser remains true to his mentor Froude, and in his historical romances he goes out of his way to ascribe any notable acts of bravery, leadership, or even ruthlessness historically ascribed to Black Jamaicans, to White, or almost-White characters. Thus, the White witch's voodoo is shown to be more potent than that of the Black obeahman; the Sam Sharpe rebellion in *Psyche* (1943) turns out to have been an act of personal revenge organized and carried out by the mulatto Psyche after she is rejected by her White lover: The Maroons are given a near-White leader of Arawak-Spanish descent in *The White Maroon* (1939). Even Three-fingered Jack, the legendary Black runaway slave whose deeds struck such terror in the hearts of British soldiers that they refused to hunt him, turns out to have been the White lover of Morgan's daughter in disguise. When one takes into account the fact that the majority of de Lisser's novels were written at a time when nationalism was on the increase and the role of the Black man in Jamaica's history was being reassessed, it becomes clear that de Lisser's choice of historical events and characters in his fiction is anything but arbitrary. His historical romances must rather be seen as a polemical extension of his argument as a journalist that Jamaicans, especially Black Jamaicans, were incapable of leadership, innovation, and, therefore self-government.

The only novel by de Lisser which seems to suggest a movement away from racial and political polemic on the writer's part is *Myrtle and Money* (1942), the sequel to *Jane's Career*. The book must have been written in the aftermath of the 1938 riots and after the outbreak of World War II. It examines the consciousness of a completely new class within the Black middle class, a class which no longer necessarily strives after "whiteness," as it is better educated and often better off financially than the White middle class. Myrtle, Jane's youngest daughter, has been born into a life of comparative luxury and takes for granted the education, servants, and social freedom which her parents have spent a lifetime struggling to acquire. The contrast between Myrtle's generation and that of her mother is striking. The heroine of the earlier novel, whose ostentatious white wedding after the birth of her first child had been considered the last thing socially by her lower-class neighbors, is presented now as a shadow of her former self. The spoiled and pampered Myrtle does not know that her mother was once a domestic servant or that her elder sister was born out of wedlock in a tenement yard. The strain of living this permanent lie about the past has reduced the once pragmatic and resourceful Jane to a timid, socially insecure middle-aged lady, tyrannized by a complacent and unfeeling husband and held in mild contempt by her own children. And yet, as de Lisser points out, it is Jane's soul-destroying suppression of the past which allows Myrtle to operate with such comparatively liberal moral attitudes and social ease. Jane's only friend is Miss Mason, the niece of her former employer, who in spite of her mulatto respectability has been ruined socially because of a long-forgotten fling with a visiting Cuban, after which she had given birth to a still-born child. Jane knows Miss Mason's secret and protects her through her friendship. In turn Miss Mason contributes to the myth that Jane had lived as an equal in the Mason household when she first came to Kingston. The subtle ironies of contrast between mother and daughter, friend and former employer, and the comment which the novel makes on the burgeoning materialism of the new Black middle class make this novel one of the finest de Lisser ever produced.

CRITICAL RECEPTION

Although one of the veiled polemical points of *Myrtle and Money* is that the new Black middle class was unfit to assume the political leadership of Jamaica, one is forced to wonder aloud, as did H. P. Jacobs in his review of *Myrtle and Money* for *Public Opinion*, how the novel's publication in *Planters' Punch* excited so little attention from the society it so faithfully portrayed.

The answer is not far to seek. De Lisser was a journalist first and a novelist second, and though his novels were popular and almost universally read, they were read as extensions of his journalism rather than works of literature in their own right. By 1942, when *Myrtle and Money* appeared, de Lisser was completely identified as a journalist with a brand of political conservatism that was slowly becoming untenable both at home and abroad, and as de Lisser fell out of favor politically, his creative work was also dismissed. In addition, his well-known racial attitudes have made it difficult for critics to reconcile themselves to the apparently sympathetic treatment of Black characters in his novel. The earliest review of his life and literary achievement, W. Adolphe Roberts' essay on him in *Six Great Jamaicans* (1952), tries to deal with this seeming contradiction by suggesting that de Lisser was a typical case of a young revolutionary turned old reactionary. In this way early novels like *Jane's Career* and *Susan Proudleigh* were put into a different category from the later historical romances, a solution which fails to account for the rabid racism of early works like *Revenge* or the sympathetic treatment of Black characters in the later *Myrtle and Money*. Roberts' theory is reiterated by Kenneth Ramchand in his discussion of de Lisser in *The West Indian Novel and its Background* as well as in his introduction to the Heinemann reprint of *Jane's Career*. Ramchand adds a qualitative perspective as he sees the historical romances as ephemeral fantasy, the production of an imagination that had lost touch with the social reality of Jamaica. Such an interpretation misses the very direct thematic parallels between the historical romances and the nationalist debate in Jamaica during the 1930s. Ramchand, however, concedes the contradiction between the view of de Lisser as young radical and the blatant ironies in the portrayal of Jane at the end of *Jane's Career* and concludes:

> De Lisser's loss of sympathy with his black heroine at this stage can be related to his real-life attitudes. But there is more to be said. The imitative dead-end to which de Lisser ironically drives Jane is the same dead-end now being explored by writers like V. S. Naipaul . . . Garth St. Omer . . . and Orlando Patterson. . . . De Lisser can hardly be blamed for failing to initiate the search for an alternative tradition that is to be found in the differing works of Wilson Harris and L. Edward Brathwaite. (*Jane's Career*, p. xvi)

Responding to the newly available novel and Ramchand's introduction to it, both John Thieme ("Careering Uphill," 1973) and John Figueroa ("*Jane's Career* by H. G. de Lisser," 1973) take issue with Ramchand. Figueroa fails to find the ironic distancing from the heroine to which Ramchand attaches such significance, while Thieme takes a much less uncritical view of de Lisser's basic intention in creating such a character in the first place.

Apart from Ramchand, only H. P. Jacobs and Mervyn Morris have given serious critical attention to works by de Lisser other than *Jane's Career*. Jacobs' long review article of *Myrtle and Money* has already been mentioned. In his article on de Lisser in *Carib* ("H. G. de Lisser: The First Competent Caribbean Novelist in English," 1979), Morris examines the language and style of de Lisser's first two novels. He comments particularly on de Lisser's skill in reproducing dialogue and using landscape to suggest inner conflict in his characters. Unlike Ramchand, he sees de Lisser's conservatism as predating the publication of *Jane's Career*, but since he does not go on to discuss further works by de Lisser, he does not offer any alternative theories about the contradiction between de Lisser's well-known racial and political ideas and his portrayal of Jamaican characters in his novels. My own doctoral thesis, "The Creative Writer and West Indian Society: Jamaica 1900–1950" (1982), begins to develop a coherent picture of the man and his work, but a definitive study of de Lisser as writer, journalist, and public figure is still to be written.

HONORS AND AWARDS

H. G. de Lisser received the Musgrave Silver Medal for Literary Work in 1919 and the C.M.G. of the British Empire for Journalistic and Literary Achievement in 1920. He served as Chairman of the Board of Governors of the Institute of Jamaica from 1922 to 1937.

BIBLIOGRAPHY

Major Fictional Works by H. G. de Lisser

Jane: A Story of Jamaica. Serialized in the *Gleaner* (November 1912); republished in book form in Jamaica under the same title (Kingston: Gleaner, 1913); English edition appeared as *Jane's Career* (London: Methuen, 1914; New York: Africana, 1971; London: Colonial Novel Library, 1971; London: Heinemann, 1972).

Susan Proudleigh. London: Methuen, 1915.

Triumphant Squalitone. Kingston: Gleaner, 1917.

Revenge: A Tale of Old Jamaica. Kingston: Gleaner, 1919.

The Rivals. In *Planters' Punch* (*PP*) 1, no. 2 (1921).

The Devil's Mountain. In *PP* 1, no. 3 (1922–23).

The Jamaica Nobility. In *PP* 1, no. 6 (1925–26).

The Sins of the Children. In *PP* 2, no. 2 (1928).

The White Witch of Rosehall. In *PP* 2, no. 3 (1929); London: Ernest Benn, 1929; Kingston: Macmillan Caribbean, 1984.

The Jamaica Bandits. In *PP* 2, no. 4 (1929–30).

Morgan's Daughter. In *PP* 2, no. 5 (1930–31); London: Ernest Benn, 1953; Kingston: Macmillan Caribbean, 1984.

The Cup and the Lip. In *PP* 2, no. 6 (1931–32); London: Ernest Benn, 1956.

The Crocodiles. In *PP* 3, no. 1 (1932–33).

The Poltergeist. In *PP* 3, no. 2 (1933–34), and 3, no. 3 (1943–45).

Under the Sun. In *PP* 3, no. 4 (1935–36); London: Ernest Benn, 1937.

Anacanoa. In *PP* 3, no. 5 (1936–37); in book form as *The Arawak Girl* (Kingston: Pioneer Press, 1958).

Conquest. In *PP* 3, no. 6 (1937–38). [Sequel to *Anacanoa*.]

The White Maroon. In *PP* 4, no. 1 (1938–39). [Sequel to *Conquest*.]

Haunted. In *PP* 4, no. 2 (1939–40).

Myrtle and Money. In *PP* 4, no. 4 (1941–42). [Sequel to *Jane's Career*.]

Psyche. In *PP* 4, no. 5 (1942–43); London: Ernest Benn, 1952; Kingston: Macmillan Caribbean, 1984.

The Return. In *PP* 4, no. 6 (1943–44). [Sequel to *Haunted*.]

Studies of H. G. de Lisser

Cobham-Sander, C. Rhonda. "The Creative Writer and West Indian Society: Jamaica 1900–1950." Diss., University of St. Andrews, Scotland; Ann Arbor, Mich.: University Microfilms International, 1982.

Cooke, Michael G. "West Indian Picaresque" (Review of *Jane's Career*). *Novel* 7 (Fall 1973), 93–96.

Figueroa, J. J. "*Jane's Career* by H. G. de Lisser." *World Literature Written in English* 12 (April 1973), 97–105.

Hughes, Michael. *A Companion to West Indian Literature*. London: Collins, 1979.

Jacobs, H. P. "*Myrtle and Money*: A Brief Review." *Public Opinion*, January 3, 1942, p. 8.

Morris, Mervyn. "H. G. de Lisser: The First Competent Caribbean Novelist in English." *Carib* 1 (1979), 18–26.

Panton, George (pseud. for Cedric Lindo). "The Arch Conservative Who Was Also a Pioneer." *Sunday Gleaner*, July 4, 1974.

Ramchand, Kenneth. Introduction to *Jane's Career*. London: Heinemann, 1972.

Roberts, Walter Adolphe. "Herbert George de Lisser." In *Six Great Jamaicans*. Kingston: Pioneer Press, 1952.

Thieme, John. "Careering Uphill" (Review of H. G. de Lisser's *Jane's Career*). *Sunday Chronicle* (Guyana), February 18 and 25, 1973.

See also General Bibliography: Allis, Gilkes, Herdeck, Hughes, King, and Ramchand (1970, 1976).

PAMELA C. MORDECAI

John Joseph Maria Figueroa (1920–   )

BIOGRAPHY

John Figueroa was born on August 4, 1920, in Kingston, Jamaica. His antecedents on his father's side hailed from Panama; on his mother's, from Cuba. His great great grandfather "came from Panama when Panama was a part of Colombia . . . I suspect . . . because of some involvement in evolutions and governments there" (interview with Pamela Mordecai, Guelph, Canada, August 12, 1983; hereafter, all quotes refer to this interview unless otherwise cited). Involvement in radical politics was also what led the family of his maternal grandfather, Palomino de Castro, to flee Cuba. This Latin connection on his mother's side Figueroa refers to as "the real Spanish connection that we know of"; as the poet tells it, at the age of fourteen Lorenzo Palomino de Castro "rowed a boat with his family from Santiago de Cuba to Bowden in Jamaica . . . becausehis family [were supporters] of José Martí and when José Martí was defeated they decided to leave."

Figueroa remembers his Cuban grandfather clearly. Lorenzo Palomino spoke English and Spanish and taught the young poet to drink black coffee. Figueroa was not taught Spanish at home but grew up hearing his aunts speak it so that when it was time for him to learn it at school it seemed quite natural that he should do so.

The poet grew up in Kingston. He went to St. George's College early—he remembers being ten when his peers were twelve—and, a slight frame among heftier athletes earned him the nickname "Broomstick." He read and enjoyed

Thackeray quite young and benefited from the worm-eaten books of his father's sister Lilian, whose library included Keats and Tennyson. These were possible early influences on the poet's developing sensibility; but clearly an important formative experience was the opportunity of studying Horace at St. George's College—a Jesuit-run Catholic Boys High School. In this the poet considers himself "extremely lucky," construing it as one of two or three things which led to his "knowing what writing meant."

Figueroa's father was a traveling insurance salesman. Although the family lived in Kingston, the poet grew up knowing something of Jamaica's country parts because after the age of twelve he would sometimes travel to the country with his father. In addition there were relatives and family friends who lived in the country and whom the family would visit. His grandfather Palomino de Castro had planted tobacco at Colbeck Castle, so there were friends in Spanish Town and Old Harbour, and there was also a German family at Ulster Spring in Trelawny, where summer holidays were sometimes spent. His youngest aunt, Ellorine Marie, a nun, was attached at one stage to a convent in Montego Bay, so there were visits there as well. And also, the poet was given to "doing a lot of walking in the Blue Mountains." It is perhaps this familiarity with Jamaica's country parts that would later contribute to his poetry the strong awareness of shape, color, and landscape upon which Frank Getlein would comment with approval in his introduction to *Ignoring Hurts* (1976).

At eighteen years of age John Figueroa left Jamaica to go to college in Worcester, Massachusetts. At Holy Cross College he did a liberal arts degree, studied creative writing under John Julian Ryan, whom he remembers as a gentle but exacting taskmaster, and was exposed to the poetry of Ezra Pound, E. A. Robinson, and Gerard Manley Hopkins. He developed a reputation for writing vital, sensuous poetry because, as he explains, so many of the other young men who were trying their pens were taken up with achieving the economy fashionable in the poetry of that time.

Figueroa has been an educator all of his working life. He began as a secondary school teacher in Jamaica, having returned after leaving Holy Cross. In 1946 he went to the United Kingdom to do post-graduate work at London University. He taught at the Institute of Education, London University, from 1948 to 1953, returning to Jamaica in 1953 to be senior lecturer in education at the University College of the West Indies. In 1958 he became professor of education. He left UWI in 1971, first on secondment to the University of Puerto Rico and then to join Centro Caribeño de Estudios (also in Puerto Rico) in 1973. He has subsequently worked at the University of Jos in Nigeria and, most recently, at the Open University in the United Kingdom.

He reads his own and other poetry well. He read for the BBC's *Caribbean Voices* for a long time and has given readings in many parts of the English-speaking world. He is also responsible for one of the early recordings of West Indian verse—Caedmon TC1379, "West Indian Poets Reading Their Own Work."

The poet has traveled widely in Europe, North America, Latin America, the

Caribbean, Africa, and the Soviet Union. He has lived in North America, the United Kingdom, Puerto Rico, and Nigeria as well as in Jamaica.

He is modest about his work, avowing a little sadly that the exigencies of his having to earn a living never permitted him time to concentrate on his poetry as he would have liked. He presently lives in England with his wife, Dorothy, and works at the Manchester Educational Authority. The Figueroas have six children; a seventh, Thomas Theodore, is deceased.

John Figueroa continues to travel widely, pursuing strong interest in Creole linguistics, cricket (he has been a commentator and is a respectable spin bowler), and Caribbean studies generally. He keeps in touch with West Indian writers and critics, many of whom have been his colleagues and friends of long standing.

MAJOR WORKS AND THEMES

John Figueroa's first collection (of poetry and prose), *Blue Mountain Peak*, appeared in 1946. It was published by the author and contained five prose pieces and twenty-four poems. His second collection, *Love Leaps Here*, appeared in 1962 and was also privately published. *Ignoring Hurts* was published by Three Continents Press in 1976 and contains work from the previous two as well as poems published or recorded elsewhere. Although Figueroa's total oeuvre is limited—a limitation which he feels is also a constraint on the quality of his achievement—he does deserve a place in the account of the development of poetry in the Caribbean.

Of the poets of his vintage with a sufficiently large body of work to warrant consideration, there are only George Campbell, A. J. Seymour, M. G. Smith, Louise Bennett, Gloria Escoffery, and himself (Frank Collymore was twenty-seven years older). Of these, Figueroa's work most readily betrays the influence of other cultures and other literatures. He would see readiness to acknowledge a wide literary tradition as something necessary for all literary persons. He has often expressed impatience with those in the literary audience who assume that a writer's exposure is necessarily limited if he is from a small island; indeed, he is aggressive about the right of any artist to the tradition of all literatures. As he puts it in "Cosmopolitan Pig":

> No sharp stroke shaping stone
> No bend of metal or curve
> Of well-kept hill
> No plotted field of cane
> Or wheat or rice;
> No garden by the railroad
> Or formal as the French
> No Ife bronze
> Or illuminate script
> Is alien to me
>
> (*Ignoring Hurts*, p. 105)

It is natural that his growing up in a Creole society, in a family which united Anglo-Saxon and Latin traditions, would have heightened his awareness of cultural variety. His contact with the language and culture of Rome in the poetry of Horace and the rites of the Roman Catholic Church were also important influences, as were his subsequent encounters with a broader set of cultural experiences: he has read and traveled widely; studied Spanish literature and translated Lorca; sustained a scholarly interest in philosophy; examined educational systems across cultures; contributed to the development of Creole linguistics in the Caribbean; remained a committed Catholic.

Many of these preoccupations manifest themselves in his work. "For Thomas Aquinas," "Pastores," "Psalm 120: A Song for Pilgrims," "Too Late," "Hymns at Evening," "Tenebrae, Holy Week 1945," "Christmas," and "Christmas 1948" are some of the poems in which the poet explores his faith experience, distills his life experience in terms of his beliefs, or celebrates the objects of his faith—Christ, the Trinity—and the community of the faithful—St. Thomas Aquinas, St. John of the Cross. In "The Grave Digger," what begins as an exploration of a physical and emotional circumstance (the Mediterranean landscape in Cette, where Paul Valery is buried, as it impinges on the poet after he hears a reading of Valery's verse) turns into a recognition of the inevitability of death and an assertion of resurrection life:

> Yet for you, too, Christ
> A grave-maker swung his spade
> And then the resurrection
>
> (*Ignoring Hurts*, p. 75)

Sometimes his faith offers Figueroa the subject matter for his poetry in more material ways: in "Chartres Window," "On Seeing the Reflection of Notre Dame in the Seine," and the two fine prose poems entitled "Brou, Philbert Le Beau I & II," actual physical structures of churches prompt the poet's reflections. "Chartres Window" is interesting for its spare, sensual aspect, a quality not unrelated to his religious awareness. His ruminative poems—on love, birth, death, the nature of existence, and so forth—are rarely conceived of in other than Christian terms, and frequently, as in "On Hearing Dvorak's 'New World' Symphony," the counters for his metaphors in ostensibly secular verse derive from his religious experience.

Wide reading and extensive travel mark his verse strongly, sometimes in ways that seem a little too deliberate. There is everywhere evidence of his broad acquaintance with literature: in his translations of Horace's odes, his poems "after" Sappho, St. John of the Cross, Lorca, Horace again; in the quotations subscribed to his poems and the references to classical mythology, the Bible, other literatures. James Livingston has called Figueroa "the most classical of West Indian poets," perhaps because the poetry taps the classics by frequent allusions. The poet may also earn the distinction, however, because quite early on the poetry laid uninhibited claim to the "body" of art and literature and determined to use it at will.

The use is not always successful. There are times when the erudition calls attention to itself by appearing too calculated, or overdone. "Love Leaps Here," the title poem of his second collection, tries to accommodate Eros, Aphrodite, and Venus in a celebration of landscape and sexual vitality. They do not fit comfortably. "Other Spheres" is so busy with Oistrackh, Beethoven, Milton, crescendoes, octaves, triplets that it does not explore convincingly the deeper significances of a delightful bit of serendipity: the poet, listening to classical music, finds himself in the company of a lizard who is eating with his hands!

As for the poet's extensive travel, different environmental circumstances are repeated sources of inspiration, whether dimensions of his island landscape, landscapes abroad, noteworthy architecture, a statue, a season, a foreign circumstance, or an incident. I have already referred to two of the "Brou" poems, "Chartres Window," "On Seeing the Reflection of Notre Dame," and "The Grave Digger"; his strong sense of place, of existential circumstance, if you want, is also manifest in poems like "The Ladies of Spain," "The Moon Awakes in Coral Isles," "Spring Has Come," "Tender Is the Night," "Spanish Dancer in New York," and "The Winged Victory of Samothrace." The poet's response to this broad range of geographies as he encounters them is formidable, in a way, but one is sometimes left with the feeling that the poems have come too easily, that they have not had the chance to ripen and settle into themselves the way the Brou poems (I and II, certainly), and some of the overtly religious pieces ("Psalm 120: A Song for Pilgrims" or "Too Late . . . ") manage to. On occasion the poet himself seems overwhelmed by the weighty stuff of his life experience. Traveling in Europe he hears news of the death of his grandmother, who was obviously very much a part of his growing up in Jamaica. But the self-conscious subscript to "Epiphanies III" ("On his grandmother's death, news of which he received in Lans-en-Vercours"), the extravagant metaphors, and the rather high-flown turns of phrase ("I read the note from occidental hills," "the sapling I beneath the shade," "the rose you were and are ever will be") do not serve his purpose of simple praise and decent sorrow very well.

Closely related to his sense of landscape is the unabashed sensuality of the verse, its readiness to respond to the color and shape of things and to the physicalness of man, his vitality and sexuality. Louis James has suggested that a characteristic of West Indian writing is its "peculiarly acute awareness of the relationship between man and setting" (*The Islands in Between*, 1968, pp. 31–32). If this is so then Figueroa certainly helped to articulate that tradition.

There is a kind of awe in the poet's voice as he grapples with this fulsome materiality, and frequently his faith must enter to inform his response and soothe his tremulous senses. I find this an appealing quality, part of the impulse to be open and to share that represents itself less successfully elsewhere (in poems like "You Cannot Hear Silence" and "Birthday Poem").

The poet is generous with his use of languages: Latin and Spanish frequently appear and, sometimes, Jamaica's English-based Creole. When he uses the Creole it is usually in counterpoint to the standard language, and on occasion the contrasting codes do not compose an entirely satisfactory whole—"I Have a Dream . . . " suffers in this way. On the other hand "Portrait of a Woman (and a Man)" uses a Creole voice to present the dilemma of its young heroine poignantly; and, used as a refrain, the vernacular adds a strong quality to "Epitaph" (1983).

Although aesthetic and religious concerns do predominate in Figueroa's work, there are poems that address issues of a social and political nature, that question fashionable and easy attitudes and alignments. Among them are "I Have a Dream Columbus Lost or All o'wi a Search," "Portrait of a Woman (and a Man)," "Spanish Dancer in New York," "From the Caribbean with Love," and a recent poem, "For Nelson Mandela" (1983).

Other recent poems like "Hartlands/Heartlands" (1983), "Christmas Breeze" (1982), and "Stone Hills, on Nearing Jos, Nigeria" (1983) continue to recount his involvement with setting, with "Hartlands/Heartlands" using place names in a kind of train conductor's litany. His preoccupations with love and death persist in "The Chase" (1977) and "Epitaph."

It is not possible to regard John Figueroa's contribution to West Indian poetry as major. But if George Campbell's work broke ground by its celebration of all the aspects of the island circumstance, its innovative forms, and its concern for the common man, Figueroa's contribution was to make way for those poets in the Caribbean who, like Derek Walcott, would regard all literature and every civilized experience as appropriate grist for their poetic mills. His work is also special in its strong religious aspect and its celebration of both the sensuous and spiritual in man.

CRITICAL RECEPTION

In a generally negative response to *Focus 1956* (edited by Edna Manley, Kingston), Orford St. John gave John Figueroa about the most acerbic critical comment he was to receive: "It is no discourtesy to the work of T. S. Eliot to say that he gave birth to a generation of vipers. John Figueroa is unfortunately among the offenders" ("Perspective on *Focus*," p. 83).

Figueroa's first collection, *Blue Mountain Peak*, received no comment of which there is current record. His second collection, *Love Leaps Here*, had careful notice from three fellow poets—Mervyn Morris, A. N. Forde, and Derek Walcott. Morris's is the lengthiest and most rigorous critique (*Caribbean Quarterly*, 1963). In the book he says he finds "things to admire and . . . a few poems I shall refer to lovingly from time to time" (p. 91). He recommends "Epiphanies III," but he finds that the book's "great weakness [is] that not many of the poems persuade us they are about experiences that pressed on the poet and forced him to cry out" (p. 92). Some of the poems, he says, are "palpable frauds" (p. 92), overly-literary, self-advertising, and pretentious. Still, he finds Figueroa capable of lines which are "suggestive simplicities" (p. 94), and he commends his descriptive abilities and telling use of imagery in several poems.

A. N. Forde identifies Figueroa's mold as "classical and conservative" (*Bim* 10, [1963], 63–65). Like Morris he sees Figueroa's literariness, his propensity for the decorative classical allusion, as a weakness and prefers it when the poet "lets his own voice speak" (p. 64). He commends the "Epiphanies" but complains that the translations of Horace's Odes do not quite come off. Finally he points to the humble note in "A Prayer" that, he says, "exemplifies the spirit that informed this slender but rewarding volume of poems" (p. 65).

It is Derek Walcott who points most clearly to the virtues of the collection ("Lazy at Times but Honest," 1963). Walcott speaks of the book as "more than Roman Catholic in themes, positively Roman in manner." He finds "the tone of the verse . . . civilized and much travelled" and comments on "the freshness of its feeling" and "its restrained exuberance." In Walcott's estimation, *Love Leaps Here* "is a volume whose chief merit is self-respect and whose demerits are a naive sentimentality that is mistaken for compassion and an occasional gaucherie that is nothing less than laziness." Interestingly enough he considers Figueroa's adaptations of Horace and Virgil—though "by no means remarkable"—to have "an affecting sincerity." He concludes, "in this small book, better than a score of West Indian novels if only for its struggle with self rather than style, [the] struggle somehow seems more important than its resolution. Perhaps because it is honest?" (p. 5).

Lloyd Brown sees Figueroa as sustaining, along with Ken Ingram and Carl Rattray, the old-fashioned Caribbean pastoral, "albeit as a minor tradition": "Notwithstanding an erudite hearing of sorts . . . John Figueroa fails to rise above this kind of mere word-painting in either of his two collections, *Blue Mountain Peak* and *Love Leaps Here*" (*West Indian Poetry*, 1978, pp. 65–66). Gerald Guinness, in reviewing Brown's book (*Review/Revista Interamericana* 10 [Spring 1980], 125), takes issue with his evaluation of Figueroa, using it as an example of "unjust deprecation of work which doesn't measure up to the degree of 'ethnicity' required." In Guinness's estimation, "Figueroa proves himself as quintessentially Jamaican in his imitations of Horace (say) as several of his more grittily 'ethnic' colleagues."

Ignoring Hurts, Figueroa's third collection, received fairly wide critical comment. Writing in the introduction to the book, Frank Getlein, a classmate of Figueroa's at Holy Cross, recalls that his poetry, even in those days, "throbbed with the primary colours and plenty of them" (Introduction to *Ignoring Hurts*, p. vii). He notes that Figueroa persists in writing about the erotic, which, in his college years, he "wrote about . . . constantly" (p. viii). Getlein makes one "new" critical observation: he says "Figueroa has based much of his poetry . . . on the bed-rock foundation of 'the folk' . . . has drawn upon this basic source of strength in his poetic diction and more fruitfully, in his view of the way life works." He observes also that "there is a touch of intellectual playfulness in this poetry of John Figueroa, as . . . there is in the man himself'' (p. x). He sees this frivolity in several poems in the collection, but most notably in ''Other Spheres.''

Stuart Hall, writing in *Melanthika* (''Review,'' 1977), asserts that this collection reveals that the poet ''has grown in stature . . . considerably matured in his command, and thus the flexibility, the suppleness of his poetic idiom'' (p. 39). Hall agrees that on occasion Figueroa's ''genuinely lyrical imagination'' is ''too disciplined'' (p. 39)—something he finds especially surprising in a West Indian poet writing out of a ''very extraordinary and tumultuous period of history'' (p. 40). He is singular in that he feels that Figueroa manages satisfactorily to integrate his references into the poetry. (A significant portion of *Ignoring Hurts* appeared in the previous collections, *Love Leaps Here*, and *Blue Mountain Peak*: It is not unfair, therefore, to compare critical comments across the collections.)

Elaine Fido, commenting in *Bim* (1978), notes in Figueroa's poetry ''a widespread emphasis on the general . . . especially noticeable in the poems which deal with intimacy'' (p. 282). She considers most successful those poems ''which more deeply plumb the poet's individual self and only after . . . relate him to our larger world'' (p. 283). She finds Figueroa ''often amusing, often very serious'' (p. 285) and concludes that he is a very public poet, but a rather private person. She feels it necessary to acknowledge his contribution to the development of Caribbean literature ''in his work for others who write'' (p. 285).

St. George Tucker Arnold, writing in *Caribbean Review* (''A Celebration of Caribbean Color,'' 1978), notes the exuberance of Figueroa's verse, his preoccupation with the island folk, his depiction of the ''primal themes'' of sex and desire, his profound faith, his wit and whimsy. His review is clearly indebted to Frank Getlein's introduction to the collection. He refers to Getlein frequently and largely addresses those aspects of the work which Getlein highlights. Arnold quotes the poems generously; he comments on Figueroa's ''expressionist's touch for projecting the mood of the external as a function of the observer's inner landscape'' (p. 56). He also points to the poet's ''characteristic tendency to see universal human patterns in historical specifics'' and feels the religious poems present the poet ''at his most humane and candid'' (p. 59).

Figueroa's work is not mentioned in Baugh's study, *West Indian Poetry 1900–1970* (1971). There is a brief note on *Ignoring Hurts* in *Cross Currents* (27 [Summer 1977], 210). The collection also receives comment in *Review* (23 [1979], 83–84) and *The Sunday Gleaner*, (April 17, 1977). Bio-bibliographical entries in Michael Hughes, *West Indian Literature* (1979) and Donald E. Herdeck, ed., *Caribbean Writers* (1979) set some store by James Livingston's comment in a bibliographical note in *Caribbean Rhythms* that Figueroa is ''perhaps the most classical of West Indian poets.'' In one of the few commentaries on Figueroa's short stories, Hughes obseves that those stories ''which deal with the West Indies are typically ironic and witty observations [are] made at the expense of the region's intellectual and often expatriate literary coteries'' (p. 45).

HONORS AND AWARDS

John Figueroa has received various scholarships and fellowships, most notably a Carnegie Fellowship (1960) and a Guggenheim Fellowship (1964). In 1960 he also received the Doctorate in Humane Letters from Holy Cross College, his alma mater.

BIBLIOGRAPHY

Poetry by John Figueroa

Blue Mountain Peak. Kingston: Author, 1944.
Love Leaps Here. Kingston: Author, 1962.
Ignoring Hurts. Washington: Three Continents Press, 1976.

Studies of John Figueroa

Arnold, St. George Tucker. "A Celebration of Caribbean Color." *Caribbean Review* 7 (July/August/September 1978), 54–59.
Fido, Elaine. Review of *Ignoring Hurts*. *Bim* 16 (December 1978), 282–85.
Getlein, Frank. Introduction to *Ignoring Hurts*. Washington, D.C.: Three Continents Press, 1976, pp. vii-x.
Hall, Stuart. "Review." *Melanthika: An Anthology of Pan-Caribbean Writers*. Birmingham: LMW, 1977.
Hughes, Michael. *A Companion to West Indian Literature*. London: Collins, 1979.
Marzan, Julio. Review of *Ignoring Hurts*. *Review* 23 (1979), 83–84.
Morris, Mervyn. "Love Leaps Here" (Review of *Love Leaps Here*). *Caribbean Quarterly* 9 (March-June 1963), 91–95.
Review of *Ignoring Hurts*. *The Sunday Gleaner*, April 17, 1977.
St. John, Orford. "Perspective on *Focus*." *West Indian Review* 1 (December 1956), 83.
True, Michael. "Contemporary Idioms" (Review of *Ignoring Hurts*). *Cross Currents* 27 (Summer 1977), 210.
Walcott, Derek. "Lazy Sometimes but Honest." *Sunday Guardian*, January 27, 1963.
See also General Bibliography: Allis, Brown, Herdeck, and Hughes.

ANTHONY BOXILL

Wilson Harris (1921–   )

BIOGRAPHY

Wilson Harris was born into a middle-class family on March 24, 1921, in the town of New Amsterdam, in what was then the colony of British Guiana and is now the independent country of Guyana. Similar in its history of slavery and colonialism to the islands in the West Indies, Guyana differs from them in size and in the fact that it is of the mainland of South America. A country of seemingly impenetrable forests, mighty rivers, treacherous rapids, imposing waterfalls, and vast savannahs, its landscape has had an overpowering effect on its writers. Harris in his fiction has made remarkable descriptive and symbolic use of its rivers and jungles.

Furthermore, the variety of the population of Guyana and the coexistence there of people of Asian, African, European, and Amerindian cultures must have had a great influence on the development of his concept of the cross-cultural imagination, a concept that is intrinsic to all his work. Harris, himself of mixed racial origin, attended Queen's College in Georgetown, the capital of Guyana, from 1934 to 1939. This school was one of the finest in the Caribbean for boys and was run like an English grammar school, many of its masters at that time being English. There he studied the standard classics of English literature and encountered some works of classical literature. Such reading was to have a major effect on his own work.

After leaving school, Harris studied land surveying, qualifying to practice in 1942. Starting as an assistant government surveyor, he was promoted to government surveyor in 1944 and to senior surveyor in 1955. He made several expeditions to the coastal areas and to the interior of the country, becoming intimate with the forests and rivers and with the Amerindians, the people of the interior. These close experiences with nature and landscape, and with the men of different races and classes who were his surveying crews and who were isolated with him in jungle or on riverbank for considerable periods of time, were later to be used in an integral way in his fiction. The surveyor is a recurring character in his work.

During the years he was a surveyor, Harris became associated with a literary journal, *Kyk-over-al*, which was published and edited by the Guyanese poet Arthur Seymour from 1945 to 1961. In that period, Harris published numerous poems, stories, critical essays, and reviews in this journal. These were the years of his apprenticeship as a writer, and the reader who examines his efforts in chronological order can observe his ideas taking shape and developing and the technique growing more confident. In 1951 he published a small book of poems, *Fetish*, under the pseudonym Kona Waruk, and followed this with another, *Eternity to Season*, in 1954.

In 1954 Harris married Cecily Carew. The marriage ended in divorce, and, in 1959, he left Guyana for Britain. He married Margaret Burns, a writer from Scotland, and settled down in London to try to become a professional writer. At the same time that he abandoned Guyana for England, and surveying for writing, Harris gave up poetry for the novel.

Palace of the Peacock, his first novel, appeared in 1969, bewildering and intriguing many a reader. Few who read him remained indifferent to the quality of his language and to the power of his imagination. Harris has followed this book, for a time at the rate of a novel a year, with a series of equally remarkable and unconventional works of fiction.

So unusual and perplexing are his ideas and his technique that Harris has frequently been called upon to lecture on them and their relationship to other West Indian writing. His lectures and essays have been collected in two books, *Tradition the Writer & Society* (1967) and *Explorations* (1981), which are invaluable companions to his fiction, as is his most recent work of criticism, *The Womb of Space* (1983).

Harris's career as lecturer and writer-in-residence, which he has carried on simultaneously with his career as novelist, has taken him to universities in many different parts of the world. In 1970, he was writer-in-residence at the University of the West Indies and at the University of Toronto in Canada. He has been visiting professor at the University of Texas at Austin on three occasions: in 1972, in 1980, and in 1981–82. He was guest lecturer at Aarhus University in Denmark in 1973 and at Mysore University in India in 1978. He managed in 1979 to fit in both a visiting lectureship at Yale University in the United States and a stint as writer-in-residence at Newcastle University in Australia.

Although Harris travels a great deal—and the growing interest in his work will put him more and more in demand as a lecturer—his base remains London, from which, no doubt, will continue to come new and challenging works of fiction and criticism.

MAJOR WORKS AND THEMES

Wilson Harris is a prolific and versatile writer. While he was still in Guyana he published two small books of poetry, and after his arrival in England in 1959 he produced thirteen novels, a volume containing two novellas, two books of short stories, and three works of criticism. Even though he has given up writing poetry, when a new edition of his early volume of poetry *Eternity to Season* was to be brought out in 1978, he took the trouble to make several adjustments to the text. All of his work is strongly interconnected, and although his reputation undoubtedly rests on his novels, his poetry is a good introduction to his fiction, and his criticism frequently provides a useful commentary on what he is trying to achieve as a novelist.

Lloyd Brown in *West Indian Poetry* (1978) criticizes Harris's first book of poems as pretentious, turgid, and unreadable (see p. 93). In *Eternity to Season*, which Brown admits is better written, the juxtapositions and relationships which are an important part of Harris's style are made with greater confidence and subtlety and, consequently, come to seem more inevitable. In the opening poem, "Troy," the death of Hector is speculated on and compared to the cycle of death and rebirth of a tree. Hector "must die first to be free" (p. 11) and, in so doing, become part of the tree of man. Some of Harris's main themes occur in embryo in this poem: the unity of man and nature; and the unity of all men throughout the ages. The interest in classical mythology in this book and the identification of heroes such as Achilles and Heracles with poor peasants in remote Guyanese villages not only anticipate a similar device by Derek Walcott in *Another Life* (1973) but also prepare the reader for a character such as Poseidon in Harris's fourth novel, *The Secret Ladder* (1963). Many years later in 1967, in a lecture to the English Society at the University of Edinburgh, Harris continued to speculate on the applicability of classical mythology to modern life. Using the story of Ulysses and Circe to illustrate the theme of life-in-death death-in-life, he went on to say: "A reconstruction of this myth in poem or novel would be, I feel, a major achievement" (*Tradition the Writer & Society*, p. 52). Such a reconstruction he was himself attempting in *The Waiting Room* (1967). This continued interest in Greek mythology illustrates an important aspect of Harris's work; his ideas do not change so much as they grow in depth and sophistication. They become fuller and more complex, and they embrace more of the paradoxes of life with each new work. He himself has said in the prefatory note to his *Tradition the Writer & Society* that he is "groping toward something . . . within a deepening cycle of exploration."

This groping has led Harris to become skeptical of the conventional realistic novel, which he refers to as the novel of persuasion in which "the author *persuades* you to ally yourself with situation and character" (*Tradition the Writer*

& Society, p. 30). Instead of this conventional, chronological relationship with his reader, Harris strives to immerse him in fluid, perpetually altering situations in which he will have to shed his preconceptions and learn to see in a new way: "Within the art of fiction we are attempting to explore . . . it is a 'vacancy' in nature within which agents appear who are translated one by the other and who . . . reappear through each other, inhabit each other, reflect a burden of necessity, push each other to plunge into the unknown, into the translatable, transmutable legacies of history" (*Explorations*, pp. 17–18). That he is doing something difficult and challenging, Harris is aware. But he is not daunted by the difficulty of his task. His persistence with his kind of fiction derives, in large measure, from his respect for his reader, to whom he refuses to talk down:

> Had I realized I was less isolated than I thought I was—I may have been able to insert more explicit facade to my novels, to lean upon certain terminologies, etc. Perhaps it was just as well since the reality of the experience—however half-cloaked and difficult for the impatient reader—may have been diminished in narrative substance or authentic imagery that belongs to the exploring consciousness as it makes contact with genuinely new terrain and with a self or selves far deeper than historical or conventional ego. (*Explorations*, p. 103)

In reading Harris, the reader is challenged to allow his imagination to be as active as that of the writer, to grope much as Harris does himself, and to explore new terrain.

In his most recent book, *The Womb of Space* (1983), significantly subtitled *The Cross-Cultural Imagination*, Harris again emphasizes the important function of the imagination to move beyond convention to new discoveries and creations: "The paradox of cultural heterogeneity, or cross-cultural capacity, lies in the evolutionary thrust it restores to orders of the imagination, the ceaseless dialogue it inserts between hardened conventions and eclipsed or half-eclipsed otherness, within an intuitive self that moves endlessly into flexible patterns, areas or bridges of community" (p. xviii). The literature that Harris chooses to discuss in this book—works such as Ellison's *Invisible Man*, Rhys's *Wide Sargasso Sea*, White's *Voss*, Rao's *The Serpent and the Rope*—is a good indication of his attitude to conventional realistic fiction and of the standards he has set for his own work. In making his choice of what to discuss, he avoids the purely nihilistic and totalitarian and includes instead works which, while not denying the difficult lead of experience, have the alchemical quality of being able to suggest the possibility of creating gold out of it.

Alchemy is an important theme in Wilson Harris's own fiction. Even though he does not turn a blind eye to the potential for evil in man, the novels usually move toward some kind of redemption, some kind of transcendence. In his first novel, *Palace of the Peacock* (1960), a work of remarkable maturity, produced, one should recall, when Harris was already thirty-nine years old and after he had put in a long apprenticeship, he exposes the inadequacy of his central character's obsession with power but allows him, after he has made a journey by river inland and into his own soul, to achieve a clearer vision of himself and of his relationship to life and eternity.

Many of the themes Harris is to go on exploring are introduced in this novel. The interrelationship of various races of mankind, the preoccupation with history and mythology, the paradox of life-in-death death-in-life, the arbitrariness of chronological time, the assault on the reader's preconceptions—these are themes that are interwoven to create the complexity of the novel. Its specific history may refer to Guyana in particular, but it is made to suggest the history of mankind. The use of mythology, especially Christian in this first book, encourages the reader to make connections with other mythologies and with the search of other people for self-awareness.

The technical devices of this first novel, with its frequent allusions to other works of literature, its symbolic journey of self-discovery, its paradoxical juxtaposition of images, its use of the jungles of Guyana as a symbol of the eternal present and of the rivers as reminders of the passage of time, are used by Harris in his later fiction to attempt to do justice in his art to the complexity of life as he sees it.

Harris's first four novels, *Palace of the Peacock* (1960), *Far Journey of Oudin* (1961), *The Whole Armour* (1962), and *The Secret Ladder* (1963), are frequently referred to by critics, and by Harris himself, as the Guiana Quartet. However, *Heartland* (1964), his fifth, seems to be more closely related to the first in image, atmosphere, and theme than are the other three. Perhaps Harris has produced a quintet without meaning to. These novels explore various aspects of Guyana's people, history, and landscape, introducing at the same time mythologies of other cultures: in *The Whole Armour* the references are Biblical, while in *The Secret Ladder* many are classical.

Hena Maes-Jelinek identifies Harris's next four novels, *Eye of the Scarecrow* (1965), *The Waiting Room* (1967), *Tumatumari* (1968), and *Ascent to Omai* (1970), as constituting the second phase of his work. They are all set in Guyana, and, as Harris himself puts it, they are connected to his first four and "are related to a symbolic landscape-in-depth—the shock of great rapids, vast forests and savannahs—playing through memory to involve perspectives of imperilled community and creativity reaching back into the Pre-Columbian mists of time" (*Contemporary Novelists*, ed. James Vinson [Chicago: St. James Press, 1972], p. 563). Maes-Jelinek is right when she suggests that what distinguishes these novels is "an increasing interiorization of experiences" (Preface to *Wilson Harris*, 1982) and that "the condition explored in each novel is one of void or loss" (in *West Indian Literature*, ed. Bruce King, 1979, p. 188). These novels complement each other in other ways. Memory is important in each, and the first two of them are in the form of diary or journal. The balance between male and female is explored; in two, *The Eye of the Scarecrow* and *Ascent to Omai*, the central consciousness is male, Idiot Nameless and Victor, respectively; while in the other two, *The Waiting Room* and *Tumatumari*, it is female, Susan Forrestal and Prudence, respectively. In his deepening cycle of exploration into human psychology, Harris challenges his reader more profoundly in these novels than in any others.

Harris's next two books, *The Sleepers of Roraima* (1970) and *The Age of the Rainmakers* (1971), differ from the rest of his fiction in that they are collections of short stories or fables and they concentrate on the lives of the aboriginal people of South America. In them the reader is made to see the Caribs as victims of conquest, but he is not allowed to forget that the Caribs themselves victimized others by conquest. The myths and legends of these remote people coincide remarkably with those of better-known cultures, and they help underline Harris's belief in the cross-cultural imagination and in the unity of man.

Black Marsden (1972) begins a new phase in Harris's work. The novels that continue it, *Companions of the Day and Night* (1975), *Da Silva da Silva's Cultivated Wilderness* and *Genesis of the Clowns* (1977), *The Tree of the Sun* (1978), and *The Angel at the Gate* (1982), are connected by the metaphor of painting, which permeates them, and by the recurrence, as Maes-Jelinek points out, of the theme of resurrection. Characters recur in different novels, *Companions of the Day and Night* and *The Angel at the Gate* being sequels to *Black Marsden*, and *The Tree of the Sun* to *Da Silva da Silva's Cultivated Wilderness*. In this group of novels, Harris for the first time makes extensive use of settings and landscapes other than Guyana: Edinburgh, London, Mexico, and India. This reflects a willingness by Harris to use the experience of his travels. That he should begin to choose diverse settings for his fiction was indeed to be expected, given his belief in the community of man. That he does so also indicates his concern about the disintegration of modern society and his desire to suggest ways in which it might be renewed.

Harris's fiction has always contained autobiographical elements. Fenwick of *The Secret Ladder* and Wellington of *Genesis of the Clowns* are both Guyanese surveyors; and Da Silva of *Da Silva da Silva's Cultivated Wilderness* is, like Harris, a South American artist of mixed racial background living in London. In a couple of his novels, by means of prefatory notes, Harris inserts himself into the world of his fiction, thus bridging the physical world and the world of the imagination, the world of art and the world of everyday life.

As one considers Harris's body of work, one cannot help but be impressed with the unity of his vision and by the power of his imagination. But this is not a willful, self-indulgent imagination. Rather it is one tempered by respect for life and compassion for mankind, one that exerts itself to help restore respect for creativity and community. Just as praiseworthy is Harris's integrity as an artist who refuses to simplify his perception of the world or to condescend to his readers to try to earn a larger readership.

CRITICAL RECEPTION

Wilson Harris has been quite fortunate in his critics. That this is so has, no doubt, much to do with Harris's work itself. Difficult and demanding, it does not encourage the dilettante or the superficial reader. Consequently, those critics who persist in reading his work do so out of a sense of fascination and commitment. His detractors and those who have no time for the effort that reading him requires quickly abandon him. Not many are as vehement as David Ormerod, who insists: "I utterly decline to take seriously any work which is prepared to indulge in any serious discussion of Mr. Harris, his friends and their semantic collywobbles." He maintains that Harris's novels "float, like brightly coloured dirigibles, in an inane vacuum where we find no experiential context, no discernible yardstick for meaning—just a simple bland identification, where X is symbolic of something, perhaps Y or Z, because the author has just this minute decided that such will be the case" ("Bad Talk and Sweet Speaking," *CRNLE Reviews Journal* [May 1979], 45). A significant number of insightful, diligent, and serious critics, among them C. L. R. James, who has written a pamphlet on certain philosophical aspects of *Palace of the Peacock*, and Michael Gilkes and Hena Maes-Jalinek, who have both written book-length studies of his fiction, do not agree that Harris's symbols are as arbitrary as Ormerod suggests. Their criticism, while acknowledging the difficulty Harris poses, seeks to point out the logic of the extraordinary juxtaposition of images that is so typical of Harris. Far from arbitary, they find such juxtaposition consistent with Harris's concept of the relationship of time and eternity, of the interconnection of the myths of different cultures, and of the essential unity of man. Hena Maes-Jelinek begins her book by stating categorically, "Wilson Harris is one of the most original and significant writers of the second half of thc twentieth century" (*Wilson Harris*, 1982, Preface). She goes on to suggest that some of the difficulty certain people have in reading Harris is the result of their "own incapacity to relinquish conventional expectations in art" (Preface).

Since Harris is not a conventional artist, critics have exerted themselves in different ways in attempting to abandon the old ways of seeing and to embrace the new. Some, such as Fleming Brahms and Jean-Pierre Durix, have tried to come to terms with his meaning by engaging in detailed, almost page-by-page explications of his work. Others approach him by attempting to compare his work with that of other difficult, unconventional writers. John Moss and Michael Hench have seen similarities between Harris and Blake; Eva Searl compares Eliot's *Four Quarters* with Harris's *The Waiting Room*; and *Palace of the Peacock* has been compared to Conrad's *Heart of Darkness* and Rimbaud's *Drunken Boat*. There has been considerable interest in the criticism in the allusions in Harris both to literature and to mythology. Critics such as Gary Crew have examined the theme of time in some of the novels, while Kenneth Ramchand has talked about the significance of the Amerindian in the fiction. Another approach used by some critics has been to try to see him in a particular context. Hearne and Gilkes see his work in the context of West Indian literature; Louis James relates the Guiana Quartet to the new Black literature; and Joyce Adler sees Harris as a twentieth-century man responding to his age.

There is already a substantial body of criticism of Harris's work, and it will no doubt continue to grow. Harris was a poet before he became a novelist and critic. The relationship between his poetry, fiction, and criticism has yet to be addressed in detail by a critic. Some articles have considered Harris's poetry, but much has yet to be done. Rhonda Cobham [Sander] has suggested a vast new area in her examination of one of Harris's texts. Some of the novels, *Palace of the Peacock* especially, have received considerable critical attention, while others such as *Heartland* and *Far Journey of Oudin* have been neglected.

Wilson Harris goes on producing works of fiction and criticism which continue to fascinate a select body of readers. This exclusive readership is a matter of some concern to some such as A. J. Seymour, who seems to have reservations about the fact that Harris's novels are becoming "more and more attractive to international academics, and more and more difficult to the normal reader" (*The Making of Guyanese Literature*, 1980, p. 60). On the other hand, Michael Gilkes asserts, "The work of Wilson Harris deserves serious attention for this reason above all: it suggests the possibility of a response to the West Indian cultural and historical reality which is neither a revolt against, nor a passive acceptance of, a divisive situation" (*Wilson Harris and the Caribbean Novel*, 1975, p. 152). The value Gilkes finds for West Indians in Harris's work, of course, applies equally to people of all cultures and ages. C. L. R. James makes the point that "Harris, grappling with a West Indian problem, had arrived at conclusions which dealt with the problem of language as a whole in the world at large" (Introduction to "Tradition and the West Indian Novel," in *Tradition the Writer & Society*, pp. 71–72). It is not accidental that this should have happened because Harris, one should not forget, insists upon the fundamental unity of all mankind.

HONORS AND AWARDS

Wilson Harris's work has earned him several awards and fellowships. He received the Arts Council Award twice (1968 and 1970) and has served as a Commonwealth Fellow at Leeds University (1971) and as a Henfield Fellow at the University of East Anglia (1974). In 1973 he was awarded a Guggenheim Fellowship, and in 1976 a Southern Arts Fellowship at Salisbury in England.

BIBLIOGRAPHY

Poetry by Wilson Harris

Fetish. Guyana: Miniature Poets Series, 1951.
Eternity to Season. Georgetown: published privately, 1954; London: New Beacon Books, 1978.

Fiction by Wilson Harris

Palace of the Peacock. London: Faber and Faber, 1960.
Far Journey of Oudin. London: Faber and Faber, 1961.

The Whole Armour. London: Faber and Faber, 1962.
The Secret Ladder. London: Faber and Faber, 1963.
Heartland. London: Faber and Faber, 1964.
The Eye of the Scarecrow. London: Faber and Faber, 1965.
The Waiting Room. London: Faber and Faber, 1967.
Tumatumari. London: Faber and Faber, 1968.
Ascent to Omai. London: Faber and Faber, 1970.
The Sleepers of Roraima. London: Faber and Faber, 1970.
The Age of the Rainmakers. London: Faber and Faber, 1971.
Black Marsden. London: Faber and Faber, 1972.
Companions of the Day and Night. London: Faber and Faber, 1975.
Da Silva da Silva's Cultivated Wilderness and Genesis of the Clowns. London: Faber and Faber, 1977.
The Tree of the Sun. London: Faber and Faber, 1978.
The Angel at the Gate. London: Faber and Faber, 1982.

Criticism by Wilson Harris

Tradition the Writer & Society. London: New Beacon Books, 1967.
History, Fable and Myth in the Caribbean and Guyana. Georgetown: National History and Arts Council, 1970.
Fossil and Psyche. Austin: African and African American Studies and Research Center, University of Texas, 1974.
Explorations. Edited by Hena Maes-Jelinek. Aarhus: Dangeroo Press, 1981.
The Womb of Space: The Cross-Cultural Imagination. Westport, Conn.: Greenwood Press, 1983.

Studies of Wilson Harris

Adams, Rolstan. "Wilson Harris: The Pre-novel Poet." *Journal of Commonwealth Literature* 13 (April 1979), 71–85.
Adler, Joyce [Sparer]. "The Art of Wilson Harris." *New Beacon Reviews: Collection One* (1968), 22–30.
———. "*Tumatumari* and the Imagination of Wilson Harris." *Journal of Commonwealth Literature* (July 1969), 20–31.
———. "Wilson Harris and Twentieth-Century Man." *New Letters* 40 (October 1973), 49–61.
Boxill, Anthony. "Wilson Harris's *Palace of the Peacock*: A New Dimension in West Indian Fiction." *College Language Association Journal* 14 (June 1971), 380–86.
Brahms, Flemming. "A Reading of Wilson Harris's *Palace of the Peacock*." *Commonwealth Newsletter* 3 (January 1973), 30–44.
Cobham [Sander], Rhonda. "The Texts of Wilson Harris' *Eternity to Season*." *World Literature Written in English* 22 (Spring 1983), 27–38.
Crew, Gary. "The Eternal Present in Wilson Harris' *The Sleepers of Roraima* and *The Age of the Rainmakers*." *World Literature Written in English* 19 (Autumn 1980), 218–27.
———. "Wilson Harris's Da Silva Quartet." *New Literature Review* 7 (1979), 43–52.

Durix, Jean-Pierre. "Along Jigsaw Trail: An Interpretation of *Heartland*." *The Commonwealth Novel in English* 1 (July 1982), 127–46.

———. "Crossing the Arawak Horizon." *Literary Half-Yearly* 20 (January 1979), 83–92.

———. "A Reading of 'Paling of Ancestors.' " *Commonwealth Newsletter* 9 (January 1976), 32–41.

———. "Ripples in the Water: An Examination of *The Eye of the Scarecrow*." *World Literature Written in English* 22 (Spring 1983), 55–72.

Fabre, Michel. "The Reception of *Palace of the Peacock* in Paris." *Kunapipi* 2 (1980), 106–09.

Gilkes, Michael. "The Art of Extremity, A Reading of Wilson Harris's *Ascent to Omai*." *Caribbean Quarterly* 17 (September-December 1971), 83–90.

———. "*Da Silva da Silva's Cultivated Wilderness* and *Genesis of the Clowns*." *World Literature Written in English* 16 (November 1977), 462–70.

———. "An Infinite Canvas: Wilson Harris' *Companions of the Day and Night*." *World Literature Written in English* 15 (April 1976), 161–73.

———. *Wilson Harris and the Caribbean Novel*. London: Longman, 1975.

Gowda, H. H. "Wilson Harris' *Tumatumari*." *Literary Half-Yearly* 11 (January 1970), 31–38.

Hench, Michael M. "The Fearful Symmetry of *The Whole Armour*."*Revista Interamericana* 4 (Fall 1974), 446–61.

Howard, W. J. "Shaping a New Voice: The Poetry of Wilson Harris." *Commonwealth Newsletter* 9 (January 1976), 26–31.

———. "Wilson Harris and the 'Alchemical Imagination.' " *Literary Half-Yearly* 11 (July 1970), 17–26.

———. "Wilson Harris's Guiana Quartet: From Personal Myth to National Identity." *Ariel* 1 (January 1970), 46–60.

James, C. L. R. *Wilson Harris—A Philosophical Approach*. Trinidad and Tobago: University of the West Indies, 1965.

James, Louis. "Structure and Vision in the Novels of Wilson Harris." *World Literature Written in English* 22 (Spring 1983), 39–46.

———. "Wilson Harris and the 'Guyanese Quartet.' " In *A Celebration of Black and African Writing*, ed. Bruce King and Kolawole Ogungbesan. London: Oxford University Press, 1975, pp. 164–74.

King, Bruce. "Naipaul, Harris and History." In *The New English Literatures: Cultural Nationalism in a Changing World*. London: Macmillan, 1980, pp. 98–117.

Kulkarni, Madhav. "*The Far Journey of Oudin*: In the Light of Biblical Epigrams." *Commonwealth Quarterly* 1 (1976), 47–53.

Mackay, Nathaniel. "The Imagination of Justice: *Ascent to Omai*." *World Literature Written in English* 22 (Spring 1983), 72–87.

———. "Limbo, Dislocation, Phantom Limb: Wilson Harris and the Caribbean Occasion." *Criticism* 22 (Winter 1980), 57–86.

———. "The Unruly Pivot: Wilson Harris' *The Eye of the Scarecrow*." *Texas Studies in Literature and Language* 20 (Winter 1978), 633–59.

Maes-Jelinek, Hena. "Altering Boundaries: The Art of Translation in *Angel at the Gate* and *The Twyborn Affair*." *World Literature Written in English* 23 (Winter 1984), 165–74.

———. "*Ascent to Omai*." *Literary Half-Yearly* 13 (January 1972), 1–8.

———. "Faces on the Canvas: The Resurrection Theme in *The Tree of the Sun*." *World Literature Written in English* 22 (Spring 1983), 88–98.

———. " 'Inimitable Painting': New Developments in Wilson Harris's Latest Fiction." *Ariel* 8 (July 1977), 63–80.

———. *The Naked Design, A Reading of Palace of the Peacock*. Aarhus: Dangaroo Press, 1976.

———. "The True Substance of Life: Wilson Harris's *Palace of the Peacock*." In *Common Wealth*, ed. Anna Rutherford. Aarhus: Akademisk Boghandel, 1971, pp. 151–59.

———. *Wilson Harris*. Boston: Twayne, 1982.

———. "The Writer as Alchemist: The Unifying Role of Imagination in the Novels of Wilson Harris." *Language and Literature* 1 (Autumn 1971), 25–34.

Moss, John. "William Blake and Wilson Harris: The Objective Vision." *Journal of Commonwealth Literature* 9 (April 1975), 29–40.

Petersen, Kirsten H. and Anna Rutherford, eds. Introduction to *Enigma of Values*. Aarhus: Dangaroo Press, 1975, pp. 9–41.

Ramchand, Kenneth. "The Dislocated Image." *New World Quarterly* (Guyana Independence Issue) (1966), 107–10.

Ramraj, Victor. "*Palace of the Peacock*: A Portrait of the Artist." *World Literature Written in English* 22 (Spring 1983), 47–55.

Russell, D. W. "The Dislocating Art of Memory: An Analysis of Wilson Harris's *Tumatumari*." *World Literature Written in English* 22 (Spring 1983), 17–27.

Searl, Eva. "The Dynamic Concept of Community: Wilson Harris' *The Whole Armour* and *The Secret Ladder*." *Commonwealth Newsletter* 4 (July 1973), 32–35.

Seymour, A. J. *The Making of Guyanese Literature*. Georgetown: Author, 1980.

———. "The Novels of Wilson Harris." *Bim* 10 (January-June 1964), 139–41.

Sharrad, Paul. "*Palace of the Peacock* and the Tragic Muse." *The Literary Criterion* 16 (1981), 44–58.

Urs, S. N. Vickram Raj. "Wilson Harris: A Major Voice from the Caribbean." *Commonwealth Quarterly* 4 (1980), 87–109.

Van Sertima, Ivan. "Into the Black Hole: A Study of Wilson Harris's *Companions of the Day and Night*." *ACLALS Bulletin* 4 (1976), 65–77.

———. "The Sleeping Rocks: Wilson Harris's *Tumatumari*." In *Enigma of Values*, ed. Kirsten H. Petersen and Anna Rutherford. Aarhus: Dangaroo Press, 1975, pp. 109–24.

Walkley, Jane. "*Ascent to Omai* or the Ascent of Man." *Commonwealth Newsletter* 9 (January 1976), 42–45.

See also General Bibliography: Allis, Baugh (1978), Brown, Cudjoe, Gilkes, Griffiths, Herdeck, Hughes, James, King, Maes-Jelinek, McDowell, Moore, Niven, Ramchand (1970, 1976), and Van Sertima.

DAVID INGLEDEW

John Hearne (1926–)

BIOGRAPHY

John Hearne was born in Montreal, Canada, in 1926, to Jamaican parents who had migrated to Montreal from "a sense of adventure" (unless otherwise indicated, this and following quotations from Hearne are from an interview with Mervyn Morris, Creative Arts Centre, Kingston, Jamaica, July 12, 1984). Suffering from some of the early economic difficulties preceding the Depression, the family returned to Jamaica in 1928, where Hearne lived until leaving at the age of seventeen for service in World War II.

Hearne's account of his early personal history in Jamaica reveals his sense of being part of a continuous past, part of a particular branch of Jamaican history. His mother's family, for example, consisted mostly of gentlewomen, including his "Aunt" Norah, who was born in 1833 and died when Hearne was nine; she was a "source of so much oral history of the time—of course, seen from a certain perspective." The "certain perspective" is that of one of the more privileged sections of Jamaican society, a section that has provided Hearne with his personal sense of rootedness in the society.

Hearne's educational experience in Jamaica was varied. His preparatory education consisted, at different times, of a "small dames' school," a "crammer's school," and private tutoring; he was accepted into Jamaica College in 1937, following an entrance exam that consisted of the headmaster recounting for him a "long and fascinating" story of himself rounding the Horn in a clipper and then quizzing Hearne about characters in Dickens' novels. Jamaica College, staffed mainly by Englishmen, afforded him ''astounding freedom'' and encouraged the keenness for reading which had been for him ''a constant.'' At times he was sent to the library for no other purpose than to read as he willed.

The war broke out while Hearne was still in school, and although it seemed to be a ''remote happening,'' he volunteered for service overseas; his main reason for doing so was that he ''just wanted to get out of the island.'' His own involvement in the war, where he served as an air gunner in the RAF, was, he recalls, ''nothing extraordinary,'' though on the whole he is reticent about his wartime experiences.

With the war over, Hearne entered Edinburgh University to study history. He feels that the degree he took at that university gave him ''the most thorough preparation for the life of the mind afterwards.'' While at university, Hearne worked for the university newspaper, which ''maintained a very professional standard''; it was suitable training for the newspaper job he took after leaving university, as well as for subsequent journalism.

In 1950 Hearne returned to Jamaica, where he took up a teaching post at Jamaica College, his old school. He found that he had ''come back too soon''; the Jamaica of 1950–52, although ''cosy and enjoyable,'' was, for Hearne, culturally ''boring.'' The as-yet ''undiscovered culture of continental Europe'' was, on the other hand, ''hypnotic.'' He left Jamaica in 1952 to return to England, where he was a supply teacher for the London County Council.

In 1955 Hearne returned to Jamaica for another two years, during which he taught at Calabar High School. He left again in 1957 to teach again in England where he stayed until 1962. But metropolitan life became ''dull'' for Hearne, and after a brief stop in Jamaica in 1961 he decided to return to Jamaica to work in the Public Relations Office of the government. What should have been a year's assignment turned out to be more permanent; Hearne became resident tutor in the Extra-Mural Department of the University of the West Indies from 1962 until 1967.

Between 1967 and 1974 Hearne was secretary of the Creative Arts Centre, the performing theater of the University of the West Indies at Mona. He briefly moved back to working for the government, first as executive chairman in the Agency for Public Information and then as special assistant to the then prime minister, Michael Manley, where he was responsible for research into history, political theory, foreign and economic affairs and for the preparation of position papers on these subjects. In 1976 Hearne returned to the Creative Arts Centre, where he is presently director. He is also the current chairman of the Council of the Institute of Jamaica as well as a regularly featured columnist for the *Daily Gleaner*.

Between 1955 and 1961 Hearne published five novels. Then after a long silence he published his latest novel in 1981. The twenty-year break in the novels is related to an ''increasingly intense involvement in the brute facts of a newly-assembling society'' which ''called on a lot of creative energy.'' The ''protean nature of Jamaican society, its unpredictability of development, the toil of creating institutions'' lay in part behind his literary silence and his growing involvement in journalism. After *The Land of the Living* (1961) Hearne felt he had ''come to an end of a certain phase of writing,'' and he was ''seeking a new direction.'' Now he sees that period of intense political involvement as over, and he is hard at work on the second novel of his second phase of productivity, a novel which he told Daryl Cumber Dance (Interview, Creative Arts Centre, March 10, 1980) ''has *nothing* to do with Jamaican or West Indian politics.''

MAJOR WORKS AND THEMES

Hearne's novels are concerned primarily with the individual, more specifically the middle-class West Indian individual. It is precisely this concern that gives importance to his work. In a literature chiefly concerned with the ''peasant,'' as George Lamming terms it in *The Pleasures of Exile* (1960), it is vital to have the representation of a part of society that is as much West Indian as any other: a part that, while often of mixed racial heritage, frequently nurtures and values European connections over those of Africa. Hearne's works provide insights into the concerns, preoccupations, and choices of this smaller but important section of West Indian society. Although Hearne's work allows for critical approaches from several fronts, this overview intends to examine the ways in which his characters seek to find their place within a society that is itself chiefly ''peasant.''

Hearne's first novel, *Voices Under the Window* (1955), portrays a young mulatto lawyer, Mark Lattimer, who, in facing imminent death, reviews his life in a series of flashbacks. Lattimer's thoughts fall mostly on his failures to live up to a code of decency and faithfulness in personal relationships—an important code in reference to Hearne's work, since it remains throughout his novels and short stories as an accepted ideal—but never far away are Lattimer's own difficulties in relating to his society. As a child, Lattimer lives in the unquestioned assumption that he is White, until he is disillusioned in what is for him a traumatic realization that he is of mixed blood (pp. 34–38). It is a loss of un-self-questioning innocence: hereafter Lattimer tries restlessly to adjust himself in new ways to his Jamaican society.

Lattimer's attempt at a deeper involvement takes two forms. First, there is the conscious political commitment to a party that is concerned with ''the people,'' but up to his death Lattimer is unable to overcome innate barriers and give himself entirely to it. ''The people out there aren't part of me. . . . They knew it, the people out there; the people I've tried to love. They smelt out the failure, and the fear; that's why they chopped me'' (pp. 113–14). Lattimer's mortal wound is the result of the gap between ''the people'' and himself, a gap he is unable to fill. The second attempt at integration, less conscious, is his relationship with Brysie, a Black woman who is unacceptable to those of Lattimer's class; but death prevents the working out and proving of the relationship. *Voices* shows, broadly speaking, politics and love as two avenues through which integration is sought by its middle-class protagonist.

Although Lattimer's problems are clearly connected to his personal upbringing and are in many ways individual to him, the novel does present the basic dilemmas facing the sensitive middle-class West Indian attempting to relate to a society that is, in these five pre-Independence novels, beginning to see serious social changes. The concerns are carried on in Hearne's second novel, *Stranger at the Gate* (1956), which has as its main character Roy McKenzie, another middle-class lawyer who is politically both less vague and more romantic than Lattimer: he is a Communist who is trying to start a party in Cayuna, the fictional West Indian setting for the next four novels. In this novel, McKenzie's politics ultimately call for a greater act of commitment than Lattimer faced: his life is given, in a moment of choice, for the party's cause. Equally important to the novel, however, is the nonpolitically involved Carl Brandt, McKenzie's closest friend and equal, who significantly lives on and reappears in later novels. Brandt embodies other values: those of a benign but segregated social order, and of the code of decency, integrity, and respect for self and others that was Lattimer's ideal. *Stranger at the Gate* contains the last of politically active middle-class West Indians in Hearne's novels and shows the search for integration through radical political action unrealized. Hereafter the attempt at integration takes a different turn.

The Faces of Love (1957) concentrates on romantic love, a subject already presented as of considerable importance in the first two novels. The social problems of Cayuna (which as a society contains, we are told, "the reasons for revolution" [*Stranger*, p. 44]), slip well into the background. In the quest for self-fulfillment and rootedness, Hearne's characters pursue more fully the acceptance of a lover. The movement toward finding one's place in the larger community through an active attempt to answer its ills has been replaced by the search for a smaller world of two. The impulse behind each of the several couples in *Faces* is summarized in the narrator's assessment of Lovelace, an expatriate who makes the issue of "home" more obvious: "I was glad that he had found a place where he wanted to make his home. Everyone needed such a place . . . he had . . . found the woman who made it real for him" (*Faces*, p. 218). The movement is toward a belief in one's positive relationships as forming the basis for one's acceptance and belonging in the society, and in the immediacy of such relationships the larger question of social structures is left unanswered.

The Autumn Equinox (1959) continues to stress the importance of relationships and to devalue the worth of political involvement. Political commitment is represented by Jim Diver, who is in Cayuna to aid, at a distance, the anti-Batista revolutionary movement in Cuba. Over the novel, however, presides the detached voice of wisdom, that of Nicholas Stacey, an old Cayunan planter whose life experiences have brought him to the conclusions that political change by revolution brings a "change of governors . . . no change of government" (*Autumn Equinox*, p. 100) and that politics are the manifestation of a personality disorder:

"The sickness of governors is not in the abuse of power, but in the desire to govern. Power merely serves to make the disease obvious" (p. 101). Jim Diver does not in the space of the novel disprove Stacey's opinions of politics or of his view that Diver's commitment is only the blind response to "an unbearable itch" of rootlessness (p. 104). Diver's departure removes whatever challenge he may have brought to the comfortable world of the Staceys of Cayuna and leaves the strong interpersonal relationships intact.

A more serious confrontation between the world of the middle-class and the broader, poorer segment of Cayunan society (the world Lattimer and McKenzie had tried to reach) is presented in *Land of the Living* (1961). The theme of rootlessness is again evident: Marcus Heneky, an Old Testament-type figure, feels divinely called upon to lead his brethren of African descent out of the wilderness that is Cayuna and back to Africa. The narrator is Stefan Mahler, a displaced Jew who, given the history of his own race, feels sympathy for the impulse behind the movement. Mahler recognizes that both he and Heneky are wounded by the "same . . . hurt of the psyche" (p. 152) and are on personal odysseys, seeking "a territory the heart can occupy" (p. 110). Once again the function of love as a stabilizing influence that provides one with roots is evident: first through the maternal Bernice and later through Joan, Mahler finds his territory in a relationship that pushes the rest of the society into oblivion: "The world outside ourselves was so irrelevant that we did not even find it trespassed" (p. 236). Heneky's quest leads to a less happy outcome, since his uncompromising stance, coupled with his manipulation by unscrupulous opportunists, leads to his death. Integration has been possible for Mahler, but it is only seen in the short term; the fictional device of death or departure enables Hearne to avoid trying to resolve the issues at hand in any more long-term way.

Hearne's first five novels end with the affirmation that integration is possible for his educated, middle-class characters, and this integration is based upon the strength of one's immediate relationships with others; the uneasy guilt of Mark Lattimer has been replaced with the intimate world of Stefan and Joan. Yet the peace seems an uneasy one, since basic questions, such as whether the social structure of Cayuna will survive the disparities within it, are left unanswered. Moreover, the underlying tension that exists is presented by Hearne himself: the texture of his novels allows for the darker sides of his West Indian society to be presented by such characters as Johnson in *Stranger at the Gate*, by Heneky in *Land of the Living*, and by the riot in *Voices Under the Window*, for example. Overall, however, the vision is positive: after *Voices*, the resolution of the novels is consistently toward the comic, in Frye's sense of the term.

It is with this in mind that one turns to examine the world of *The Sure Salvation* (1981), published twenty years after *Land of the Living*. There are several departures from the patterns established in Hearne's earlier novels: the context is no longer contemporary West Indian society; the setting carries symbolic and allegorical overtones; and Hearne has altered the narrative style to allow himself to wander through an unprecedented number of intimately presented characters.

In viewing the work from the aspect of integration, one is struck by the reversal of the positive note established by the earlier works. Isolation and fragmentation are paramount; each character, as Edward Baugh writes, revolves on his own "particular, obsessive, flawed centre of self" ("Men Acting as Men: John Hearne's *The Sure Salvation*," 1983, p. 61). This point is more importantly illustrated by the relationship between the two most powerful men on board, Hogarth and Alex, since a personal betrayal is the result of five years of working together in what Hogarth thought was mutual trust. Yet it is not only the individual failures of each that work against the type of friendship Hearne has described in positive terms in earlier works. At the central point of betrayal, Hogarth launches into a denunciation that goes beyond the immediate and personal to a racial and social statement with a hint that the breakdown is predestined, a fact of their difference in race:

> I was coming to an understanding of . . . brotherhood with all men . . . because of you. I was beginning to realize that men like you and I, despite our differences in appearance, truly belonged to a greater purpose than we could prove in an argument. . . . In your betrayal, Alex, I discern an inevitability, a fixity of future if you like, against which I had begun to hope, foolishly, for equality and fraternity. . . . You could no more help your betrayal than an ape can help stealing fruit from the house in which it has been taken as a privileged pet. (pp. 201–2)

This speech sounds the note on which the book ends: Hogarth and Alex both exit unreconciled and separate, Hogarth to trial and prison, Alex very much alive on the very mainland on which he has planned to establish his kingdom. There are no real heroes in this novel, though it is Hogarth who comes closest to the protagonists of earlier novels. It is a significant break in the pattern that this time it is the protagonist who is left on the outside with nothing achieved: the darker side has finally triumphed.

Further, love between man and woman as a means to integration offers no consolation here. The principal relationship between Elizabeth and Hogarth is one of estrangement and isolation, the result of faithlessness on Hogarth's part. It stands in sorry contrast to the love Hogarth's parents had shared—a love that is not found on the *Sure Salvation*. The final reconciliation between Eliza and Hogarth is unsatisfactory since it occurs after Eliza becomes insane. In this novel sexuality is further devalued, portrayed as an expression of lust and power, as the relationship between Reynolds and Mtishta reveals. The positive effects of love as a uniting force are not realized in *The Sure Salvation*.

An overview of Hearne's serious work, then, reveals an emerging pattern in the earlier novels of the characters' ability to become rooted in their society mostly through their attachment to others of similar outlook. Friends and lovers form a small but solid environment. *The Sure Salvation*, Hearne's latest novel, seems to reverse many of the earlier conclusions: friendship is either nonexistent or found to be false; men are deeply divided by race and class; and love has become the barren wasteland of Eliza and Hogarth. The gap of twenty years has wrought changes not only of form and style but of content, indicative perhaps of changes in Hearne's outlook over that period. The canon is divided not only by years but by sensibility, a dark divide that reveals a movement from optimism to pessimism.

CRITICAL RECEPTION

Critical assessments of Hearne's novels as a whole are few. There has not been, to date, a published critique of all six of Hearne's serious novels. Significant reviews of the early body of novels include work by Barrie Davies (''The Seekers: The Novels of John Hearne,'' in *The Islands in Between*, 1968), Wilfred Cartey (''The Novels of John Hearne,'' 1969, pp. 109–20), Sylvia Wynter, (''We Must Learn to Sit Down Together and Talk About a Little Culture: Reflections on West Indian Writing and Criticism, Part 2,'' 1969, pp. 27–42), and Frank Birbalsingh (''Escapism in the Novels of John Hearne,'' 1970, pp. 28–38).

Both Davies and Cartey are basically complimentary to the early novels and similar in their insights. Davies holds that ''human commitment in unselfish love is of more importance to Hearne than political commitment'' (p. 117), which is echoed by Cartey: ''Hearne's preoccupation is the inter-relationships among people'' (p. 45). Both feel that the political aspect plays a less significant and convincing role; both acknowledge and accept Hearne's concern with the middle-class and praise his consistent contribution to awakening the imaginative sense to West Indian phenomena. On Hearne's style, Davies feels that at times the detail is overdone: occasionally ''the seeing eye does not know when to limit, to select, to stop'' (p. 114); for Cartey, Hearne's use of superlatives lends a ''monumental, grand dimension to Hearne's work'' (p. 54).

The presentation of a West Indian island through the fictional Cayuna does not pose a problem to either Davies or Cartey. They do recognize, however, that the works do not offer a synthesis of the elements of a society obviously divided by race and class. Davies asks, of the typical resolution of the early novels, ''Is a cosy adjustment into the middle-class domestic life any answer to the challenge posed by the life and death of Heneky?'' (p. 120) He immediately answers his own question: ''Any clear solution in the present state of the Caribbean communities would of course be suspect'' (p. 120). Cartey states that Hearne sees the inequities of West Indian society, but ''is not deeply preoccupied with them, nor does he posit a solution for them'' (p. 49). The author's ability to provide an ''answer'' to the West Indian situation is not insisted upon by these critics.

Less forgiving are Sylvia Wynter and Frank Birbalsingh, who take Hearne to task for what they see as his political and social position. Wynter sees the idealization of ''Carl Brandt and his like'' as necessary to ''evade the reality of injustice that would otherwise, press in too closely on them'' (p. 35). She sees

Hearne's presentation of the middle class and its values, which he makes appear "timeless and static," as indicative of a deep commitment to a status quo that is socially unjust: Hearne "wants to keep the system, making a change here and a change there; but making sure that the 'human values' which are important to them are not thrown overboard. Yet because these values are reserved only for the few, the more than equal, they partake of the sickness of all privilege, of all injustice" (p. 37). What Wynter calls "the failure of the later novels of John Hearne" is caused for her by the movement away from political concerns that could have led to involvement with the lower strata of society toward the narrower framework of love. It is an unworthy framework in Wynter's opinion: "Hearne's characters have become trapped in trivia" (p. 39). Wynter's closing recommendation to Hearne is that he "exile" himself "into a new way of seeing, of feeling." This "seeing" and "feeling" belongs to a different class from the one Hearne belongs to; Wynter's appeal is for Hearne to become "peasant," in Lamming's sense of the term.

Frank Birbalsingh has similar views to Wynter but his criticism is far less sensitive. It is based on the (to me, erroneous) statement that "the main theme of Mr. Hearne's five novels is race and colour consciousness" (p. 29), and with equal reductiveness he asserts that in choosing this Hearne "isolates the single factor that animates and regulates" West Indian society. There are also serious misreadings, such as believing Roy McKenzie is Black. Birbalsingh's general thrust is given in the title: Hearne's novels are "escapist." The term is not well defined in the essay, but the overall judgment is that Hearne's work, in not concerning itself with trying to overthrow "apartheid" in the West Indian context, is "exceedingly trivial" (p. 39). The use of Cayuna rather than Jamaica is also an escapist feature of Hearne's work; all in all, only *Voices* (set in Jamaica) is worthy of praise: describing a positive attempt to overthrow apartheid, "the one 'non-escapist' novel, *Voices Under the Window*, is the only thoroughly satisfactory feature of Mr. Hearne's entire work" (p. 37).

There are a number of useful reviews on the individual novels. Of special note are Mervyn Morris's "Pattern and Meaning in *Voices Under the Window*" (1971), which throws added light on the novel through a careful examination of the novel's structure and answers through attention to detail several aspects of Wynter's critique of the novel. Ramchand (*The West Indian Novel and its Background*, 1970) gives an in-depth account of the character of Rachel Ascom in *The Faces of Love*, focusing on her as an example of a sensitively and convincingly portrayed mulatto. More recently, Edward Baugh's "Men Acting as Men: John Hearne's *The Sure Salvation*" (1983), comments on characters and their preoccupation with each "particular, obsessive, flawed centre of self" (p. 61).

General reference to Hearne's work can be found in W. I. Carr's "Reflections on the Novel in the British Caribbean" (*Queen's Quarterly* 70 [1963–64], 585–97), and O. R. Dathorne's "The Theme of Africa in West Indian Literature" (*Phylon* 26 [Fall 1965], 255–76).

HONORS AND AWARDS

John Hearne was granted a John Llewellyn Rhys Memorial Prize in 1956; the Institute of Jamaica Silver Musgrave Medal for Literature in 1965; and the Institute of Jamaica Centenary Medal for Literature in 1979.

BIBLIOGRAPHY

Works by John Hearne

Voices Under the Window. London: Faber and Faber, 1955.
Stranger at the Gate. London: Faber and Faber, 1956.
The Faces of Love. London: Faber and Faber, 1957.
The Autumn Equinox. London: Faber and Faber, 1959.
Land of the Living. London: Faber and Faber, 1961.
The Sure Salvation. London: Faber and Faber, 1981.

Studies of John Hearne

Baugh, Edward. "Men Acting as Men: John Hearne's *The Sure Salvation*." *Jamaica Journal* 16 (February 1983), 61–63.

Binder, Wolfgang. " 'Subtleties of Enslavement': An Interview with the Jamaican Writer John Hearne." *Komparatistische Hefte* 9/10 (1984), 101–113.

Birbalsingh, Frank M. "Escapism in the Novels of John Hearne." *Caribbean Quarterly* 16 (March 1970), 28–38.

Cartey, Wilfred. "The Novels of John Hearne." *The Journal of Commonwealth Literature* 7 (July 1969), 45–58.

Davies, Barrie. "The Seekers: The Novels of John Hearne." In *The Islands in Between*, ed. Louis James. London: Oxford University Press, 1968, pp. 109–20.

King, Bruce. Review of *The Sure Salvation*. *World Literature Written in English* 21 (Autumn 1982), 656–58.

Morris, Mervyn. "Pattern and Meaning in *Voices Under the Window*." *Jamaica Journal* 5 (March 1971), 53–56.

Wynter, Sylvia. "We Must Learn to Sit Down Together and Talk About a Little Culture: Reflections on West Indian Writing and Criticism, Part 2." *Jamaica Journal* 3 (March 1969), 27–42.

See also General Bibliography: Allis, Griffiths, Hughes, James, King, Lamming, Moore, Ramchand (1970), and Van Sertima.

MARK A. McWATT

Roy A. K. Heath (1926–)

BIOGRAPHY

Roy Aubrey Kelvin Heath was born in Georgetown, Guyana, in 1926. He attended the Central High School and Queen's College in that city, and at the age of twenty-four he left Guyana for London. He arrived in England around the same time that hundreds of West Indian workers were making the same trip in quest of employment; at the same time, too, that West Indian writers like Mittelholzer, Selvon, and Lamming were beginning the London "exile" that was to become so prominent a feature in the lives and works of many West Indian artists. Unlike these fellow West Indians, however, Heath was making the trip in order to enter the University of London. Heath read modern languages, and upon graduation he began his long career as a high school teacher of French.

Although he subsequently studied law and was called to the English bar in 1964—and to the Guyana bar in 1973—he does not practice law, but has remained a schoolmaster in a London Comprehensive School. This is perhaps because his job as a teacher nicely complements his career as a writer and also enables him to visit his native Guyana during school holidays. Guyana is always the setting for his fiction, and its capital and rural villages are evoked in the kind of powerful and minute detail that would seem to require the author's frequent visits.

By the early 1970s Heath had written a number of poems and short stories, a few of which had been published. As he himself tells us, he began to write his first novel at around the time of Guyana's independence (1966)—an event which he describes as being somehow "formative" in his quest to be a writer

(''Art and Experience,'' Eighth Series, The Edgar Mittelholzer Memorial Lectures, Georgetown, 1983, p. 29). This novel was initially rejected by publishers as too long; it was eventually extended and published as the Armstrong Family Trilogy: *From the Heat of the Day* (1979), *One Generation* (1981), and *Genetha* (1981).

The publishers' initial rejection prompted Heath to write a shorter, entirely new work, and this was accepted and became his first published novel, *A Man Come Home* (1974). Heath tells us how he reacted to this important event: ''My excitement was indescribable; so much so that by the time the book appeared, I had completed two other novels'' (''Art and Experience,'' p. 26). Next to be published was *The Murderer* in 1978, and then the individual novels of the trilogy appeared in quick succession (1979–81). To date Roy Heath has published seven novels and has had a play, *Inez Combray*, performed at the Theatre Guild Playhouse in Georgetown (1981). During a vacation to Guyana in 1983 Heath was asked to present the eighth series of the Edgar Mittelholzer Memorial Lectures.

Heath speaks of the way in which aspects of his work were shaped and influenced by his Georgetown childhood. His love for stories and storytelling stems from his listening, as a child, to Guyanese folk tales and stories about pork-knockers, told by barbershop storytellers in the city; he also ''devoured'' what little published material there was that included accounts of Hindu ceremonies and beliefs and stories about the creatures of local superstition such as ''Old Higue'' and ''Bakoo'' (''Art and Experience,'' pp. 27–28). These stories and folklore figures have found their way into the novels.

Some of the novels' vivid scenes are recollections from the author's childhood: ''There are scenes from my childhood about which I have written consciously: A Queenstown pillar box overflowing with letters in December; a man with a metal cylinder on his back spraying the alleyway gutters with a solution of oil; The Sunday Argosy and Chronicle being exchanged by neighbours; front doors left open, shadows of leaves glistening with points of light after the rain; roofs painted olive green; branches of lightning playing interminably in the southern sky; traders unfolding bales of cloth in Stabroek market, scenes for all to see, but looming in retrospect like the contents of a vivid dream'' (''Art and Experience,'' p. 29). It is clear that for storyline and setting, for the brilliant, often incongruous detail, for the haunting evocation of the supernatural, for the peculiar turn of phrase, Heath, in novel after novel, continues to mine that rich store of memory and experience collected during his childhood and adolescence in Guyana.

In the end, however, Roy Heath remains a very private person; little has been made public about his family, his life in London, his habits of work. This is perhaps because, as his own remarks on the subject confirm, he carefully guards his privacy: ''The price the artist pays for his egotism is a high one. On one level egotism obliges him to create, while the same egotism threatens to destroy him. Success not only goes to his head, it remains there, creating demands he cannot hope to satisfy. I am acutely aware of all this and therefore try to shun gratuitous publicity'' (''Art and Experience,'' p. 28).

MAJOR WORKS AND THEMES

Roy Heath's first published novel, *A Man Come Home*, is an unusual work of West Indian fiction in that it does not have any large historical or sociological view or argument to present; rather, it encloses the reader within a very powerfully evoked world of the range yards and poorer housing areas of Georgetown, Guyana, and it concentrates on the actual processes of life and experience within this context.

The "man" referred to in the book's title is Bird Foster, but neither he nor any other character in the novel achieves the status of hero or even main protagonist. Heath presents instead members of the Foster family—and their yard-dwelling friends and neighbors—and concentrates upon portraying their relationships and experiences in a thoroughly convincing way. As one critic has remarked, the novel "projects a sharp sense of time lived, giving the texture of experience so subtly that the reader is enchanted into accepting the world of the novel as his own" (Jean D'Costa, review article in *Jamaica Journal*, 1975, p. 54).

Foster, Bird's father, is a middle-aged, semi-retired craftsman who is proud of his life's modest achievements; these include a small house of his own in the same neighborhood as the slum yards, a measure of respectability among his neighbors, a wife and a mistress—who had served concurrently and in the same house, although the wife dies before the novel begins—and a total of nine children. One of the Foster boys, Benjy, lives in Canada, and his distant action of purchasing a house is what interrupts life's calm routine for the novel's characters: Foster's financial security is threatened when the monthly money orders from Canada stop coming, and Bird's amiable pose as a perfect lover and the god of idleness is disturbed by his older brother's wealth, and he is determined to become rich himself. Bird mysteriously disappears for a few weeks and returns a rich man; he buys a house into which he moves with his mistress Stephanie. The rest of the narrative circles around Bird's sudden, inexplicable wealth and its effect upon his own household, his family, and his friends. This storyline itself, however, is subordinated in the novel to the concern with the characters and their interaction with one another: their gestures, their language, their imperfectly concealed desires and motivations as they maneuver toward their goals, their hurts and bewilderments. These aspects are all flawlessly rendered by Heath and create that palpable texture of life itself that claims the reader's attention and admiration.

It is perhaps appropriate that *A Man Come Home* should be the first novel published, for in this book Heath displays most of the major themes and concerns that dominate the later works. Already in this novel one has the sense of the family or household and its domestic concerns as somehow central to the work's design and the locus of curiously powerful emotions and conflicts. It is the context of actions that are frequently tragic in their consequences. Heath exposes the accumulated animosities and frustrations within the domestic situation as well as the sudden explosions of violence that they ultimately precipitate. In this novel, for example, we see the gathering mistrust and animosity between Foster's mistress Christine and their daughter Melda as the girl (the last child) grows older and more independent. When Melda announces that she is pregnant and refuses to discuss it with Christine, Heath portrays, in his powerful, understated technique, how the mother's anger and anxiety overflow into violence: "Christine could hear her daughter brushing her hair. Somehow the thought of Melda sitting in front of the mirror in her slip, pulling the brush down on her hair as if nothing has happened, infuriated her. . . . Snatching the brush from Melda's hand she brought it down on her head and back several times. Melda's arms were raised above her head one moment and covering her face the next, until she fell to the floor at her mother's feet. Only then did Christine stop" (*A Man Come Home*, p. 36).

In a way that exemplifies Heath's psychological acuity, this violent action becomes tragic as both women, as well as Foster, become trapped by its consequences. Melda miscarries, becomes deranged and ineligible for marriage; she is a burden on her parents, who, out of guilt and pity, are forced to stand by while Melda is shamelessly seduced and repeatedly subjected to the sexual predations of Bird's friend Gee.

There is the sense in the novel of people trapped or threatened by forces that they do not understand. There is Stephanie's strange reluctance and sense of foreboding about moving into the new house with Bird and living a life of wealth. And their relationship deteriorates from the moment they do go to live in the new house; it is subjected to that hopeless failure of communication, symbolizing the failure of love between characters that becomes such a dominant feature in later novels, especially in the relationship between Armstrong and Gladys in *From the Heat of the Day*. The characters long to say things or perform a simple gesture that might heal the relationship, but somehow they cannot: "Stephanie wished he would say something pleasant to her, so as to give her an excuse for taking his hand. Should she do so now he would only brush her aside. She knew that whatever she said would make him angry, yet she persisted in talking to him" (p. 53).

Also typical of Heath is the treatment in *A Man Come Home* of the supernatural. Much of the effect of the supernatural in the novel is achieved through "atmospherics": repeated references to the dark water of the rivers and canals of the city and to churchyards and graveyards with their "endless rows of grave stones which stretched as far as the eye could see" (p. 30). Bird's unexplained riches are attributed to his dealings with a "fairmaid" who furnishes him with money in return for the exclusive right to his love. Heath provides no other explanation of Bird's wealth, and yet the novel does not become far-fetched. There remains a great psychological plausibility in Bird's actions and preoccupations, in his strange dreams, and in the manner of his death. The "fairmaid" business, rumors of which estrange Bird's family and friends, is handled by

Heath with economy and sophistication and seems to intensify the sense of mystery in life itself and in human motivations and obsessions.

One of the foremost achievements of the novel is a nice balance and creative tension between the ordinary, often degrading, and overwhelmingly physical reality of the slum yards on the one hand and the mysterious world of the human mind on the other. When Gee is forced to abandon his dream of tricking Foster out of the money Bird gives him and is thrown back, in physical and spiritual defeat, into his room in the range yard, these two worlds invade each other as he contemplates the future in a passage that seems to sum up both the concerns of the characters in the novel and the consummate techniques by the author:

> His mind began to cloud over with images of shadows and puddles as sleep overcame him. He would, after all, finish his days in the range yard, where he was born, where he learned his childhood games and the games older people played as well. Here he had made his kites in April, fashioned his spinning tops from okari seeds and competed with his round glazed marbles in the games of his district. Henceforth, the course of his manhood was clear: when he was not baking bread at night he would, naked from the waist up, be looking through his window at the goings-on on the door-steps or round the standpipe, where the women gathered to wash and gossip. . . .
>
> The ghosts of white houses receded with the images of tenements, long, into the long days and nights that break like spring tide over the wall. (p. 146)

In *The Murderer* the novelist's focus is somewhat narrower, the psychological portrait of Galton Flood more intense and relentless. There is no doubt here that Galton is the central figure of the work, and while the reader still finds himself firmly in touch with the urban landscape of Georgetown, he also finds himself inside the mind of Galton. Heath probes far more insistently into the shaping influences and motivation of his main character than he did in *A Man Come Home*. What we find, as this relentless exploration proceeds in the novel, is something that we would have suspected from the earlier work: that the domestic household and the interweave of relationships therein can be sinister and frightening and their effects destructive in the extreme.

Galton Flood is the murderer of the title, but he is also the novel's principal victim. Heath allows the reader to see the way in which Galton's personality and actions were shaped from childhood by the powerful influence of his mother. The mother hated Galton's father—as mysterious and unexplained a hatred as was Bird's sudden wealth in the previous novel, although we sense that the mother's problem has something to do with notions of class, status, and propriety. This hatred however is visited upon the son—and surrogate husband—in the fiercest way, so that Galton, from the beginning, is described as being incapable of normal relationships, derided by his own timidity, and severely disturbed: "The sustained humiliation at his mother's hands, the inability to match his father and brother at any skill, imbued Galton with a distaste for competition of all kinds and often led him to indulge in fantasies of self-abasement" (p. 11).

His parents both die before Galton leaves home, but the mother's influence remains with him. He spends some time in the mining town of Linden, where he meets and falls in love with Gemma, his landlord's daughter. They eventually get married when he returns to Georgetown, but Galton's severe sexual repression is immediately an obstacle to their relationship: "He insisted she wear underclothes in bed, even during their acts of intimacy" (p. 78); "not once had he fondled Gemma's breast, in the belief that he would be engaging in an abnormal practice" (p. 95). These anxieties are directly traceable to the influence of his mother, whom Galton remembers as having punished him on one occasion for reporting that he had seen some "East Indian women . . . suckle their infants on the stairs in full view of everyone" (p. 173).

Galton's marriage to Gemma is therefore foredoomed. When he discovers that his wife had had an earlier sexual experience with an older man, he cruelly drags her away from the fairly comfortable suburban house they were living in and installs her in a bleak and filthy room in a tenement building in the slum area of Albouystown. Later, when he discovers that she is unfaithful to him, the reader recognizes that he is incapable of any other solution but to kill her. His psychological motivation might be unclear to Galton himself—another Heath character who is trapped and flailing in a web of forces beyond his comprehension—but these motivations are clearly legible to the reader, who, through Heath's remarkable techniques, discerns every shifting tide within the mind of the protagonist.

In Galton's fantasies and dreams after the murder is committed, it is his mother whom he sees as the murderer and his father as the victim—he himself is forced to be a powerless observer within a cage of glass: "From behind the glass, which he began to pound furiously with his fists, he could only remain a powerless observer of his father's distress; and when the latter fell forward into the river, his mother pursued him, hacking away with the stick" (p. 186). This vision clarifies the events of his life for Galton and, together with his helplessness within the glass enclosure, causes his terrible rage and anxiety to subside; he becomes a harmless lunatic roaming the streets of Georgetown, constantly crying out, "Don't cork the bottle." He has become a creature in a bottle, hopelessly exposed and humiliated beyond any recall to sanity.

The figure of Galton's mother in *The Murderer* extends a concern of Heath—evident in the earlier novel—with the problems and preoccupations of women in the Georgetown society he writes about. One discerns, in the figures of Christine, Stephanie, and Muriel in *A Man Come Home*, a sense of frustration and bewilderment that has to do with their dependence on their men. Their actions, and even their thoughts, seemed always to take into consideration their dependent status, and therefore the need to satisfy and placate their men. In Galton's mother Heath takes this preoccupation a step further; she is not merely passively overwhelmed and bewildered by her condition but actively rebels against it. She frequently castigated the real and imagined faults of her husband,

and we have seen the extent to which Galton is *her* creation, sprung from her discontent.

It is typical of Heath that he never moralizes or even comments on his characters' actions, but the reader must still consider the motives behind these. Galton's mother is obviously a product of her society. In the end her actions can probably be read as a terrible longing or quest for dignity—a dignity denied her by birth and social station, by the marriage which has trapped her in the awful role and function of a physical and spiritual dependent who must experience the world only through her husband. It is the very condition of her womanhood in that society that is the root of her anxiety. The rape of spirit that she performs upon Galton is an entirely plausible act, both of revenge and of compensation for the hurt life inflicted on her.

Perhaps the most thorough exploration of the role and fate of the woman in Georgetown society is conducted in the trilogy of novels dealing with the Armstrong family, especially *From the Heat of the Day* and *Genetha*. Gladys Armstrong, in the first novel, marries to escape the trap of spinsterhood into which her two sisters appear to have sunk. She discovers that marriage is equally a trap, and one for which she had been very poorly prepared in her father's home, with its emphasis on the genteel passivity of middle-class domestic accomplishments. Unlike Galton's mother, Gladys suffers passively the insults and abuses of Armstrong, his unfaithfulness, and his smoldering inexplicable hostility; but she does brood on her fate as a woman. Concerning the different personalities of her two servants she wonders: "Why was Marion not as ambitious as Esther? . . . Her only goal appeared to be to get married and to bring children into the world. Was that really all there was to life for a woman?" (*From the Heat of the Day*, 1979, p. 45)

We find here the kind of specific concern with the role of women that was only hinted at in the earlier novels. This kind of passage is repeated at various points throughout *From the Heat of the Day* and becomes a sort of background commentary on the fate of Gladys, who comes to represent all women: "It was a man's world. Women were not in a position to change it and were therefore obliged to accept it" (p. 94). Gladys accepted her condition, but the reader is nevertheless allowed to enter her bewildered thoughts on the subject. Toward the end of her life Gladys is still wondering: "She searched for a reason for this terrible liaison, but could not find one. Things were just so. There was a sky and an earth; there was the wind and the sun; and there was marriage" (p. 140).

Genetha's entire life is a commentary on the condition of woman. Unlike her mother, to whom she serves as a lively contrast, Genetha is active in seeking her freedom. Her desire for love and for the fullest experience of life leads her into precisely the kind of reckless relationships that her mother only dreamt about. She loses all her property and in desperation turns to prostitution—as did Esther, her mother's servant, who was fired when Armstrong could no longer afford to pay her. Prostitution is another of the traps for women that Heath is examining. Genetha comes to the sad conclusion that the quick fix of sexual pleasure is all the good that she can expect from life, although she feels the desperate need to escape from it all. The two stories she tells Michael toward the end of the novel—about her uncle who escapes into Guyana's interior with "a gun and a dog," and about the foreign woman who would wait all day in a cab outside her husband's office (*Genetha*, pp. 146–47)—illustrate Genetha's perception of the freedom of the man and the unfreedom of the woman. Her heart is with those who escape to the interior and refuse to return, the pork-knockers and adventurers. She declares to Michael, "One day I'll discover my hinterland . . . and all the wild demons rushing by in their phantom carts wouldn't stop me from travelling there" (p. 149).

Yet by the end of the novel Genetha is further away than ever from that kind of physical escape. Instead, she fully explores the dark hinterland of her own mind, of what it means to be a woman—in terms of pleasure and suffering. Her spirit is subdued, but perhaps not broken by the harshness of experience. At the end of the novel we find her still residing in Esther's brothel, grown accustomed to the place, seeing the meaning of her life with a terrible clarity while calmly awaiting death.

The trilogy as a whole is an impressive artistic achievement, and *Genetha* especially so. Heath depicts with great resourcefulness and in significant detail the haunting mental landscape of the woman Genetha. There is at the same time the sense that the whole of reality, so wide and varied in the first two novels of the trilogy, has shrunken into the person and mind of Genetha, the only surviving member of the Armstrong family. She is the only member of that family, and the first of Heath's characters, to have a sense of the past. Present experiences are always linked in her mind with the past, and she attempts to reforge links with her maternal grandparents and aunts as well as her one surviving paternal aunt; she is attempting to make a large sense out of lived experience, to negate the notion that her parents' and brother's lives were in vain. At the very end of the novel, she has nothing to show for these efforts except a sense of "the mystery of time, and insights into the unexplored countries of the heart" (p. 186).

If there is something of the picaresque in Genetha's varied wanderings and experience in Georgetown, then Heath's next novel, *Kwaku*, takes over and amplifies this particular fictional mode. It is a departure for Heath in that the hero's adventures are more far-fetched. In a sense the hero is familiar, conventional: he is the trickster or the fool, the hero of African folk tales, and the scapegoat about whom funny and uncomplimentary stories are told. Heath tells us of his own late enchantment with African folk tales and his method of making use of this and other folk material: "My way of tackling the problem is to incorporate similar material in my books. Thus the last, *Kwaku* has two riddles of my own invention" ("Art and Experience," p. 28).

These concerns and techniques of the author make *Kwaku* lighter in tone than the previous novels; parts of it are very funny, and its simplicity of narrative and characterization—its very conventional quality—somehow places its events and characters at the center of our experience of literature.

Roy Heath's seventh novel, *Orealla*, returns to the familiar physical and mental landscapes of Georgetown and its people.

CRITICAL RECEPTION

When *A Man Come Home* first appeared in 1974, it received enthusiastic acclaim from reviewers in British newspapers and weeklies. These reviewers tended to concentrate upon the novel's evocation of what they saw as an ''exotic'' setting and local color. West Indian reviewers were also struck by Heath's powerful creation of his Georgetown world. Jean D'Costa says, ''Everything seems solid and as credible as the light of common day'' (*Jamaica Journal*, p. 54). Mark McWatt speaks of ''Heath's extremely realistic portrayal of his fictional world'' (''Tragic Irony—The Hero as Victim: Three Novels of Roy A. K. Heath,'' 1984).

The other point to which reviewers were immediately attracted was Heath's style. D'Costa describes this as being ''spare and economical to an extraordinary degree'' (p. 54), and Wilson Harris, in a review of *The Murderer*, describes it as ''a style that truncates emotion'' (*World Literature Written in English* 17 (November 1978), p. 656). McWatt sees this spareness of style, along with the author's complete ''detachment from the action in the novels,'' as ''the deliberate stratagem of the ironist'' (''Tragic Irony,'' p. 55). D'Costa also dwells upon Heath's language, especially in dialogue: ''balancing this spare language is Heath's masterly handling of dialogue'' (p. 54). And Heath's British reviewers have tended to spice their reviews with samples of dialogue from the novels.

D'Costa's review article is concerned exclusively with Heath's first novel and is a highly complimentary study. She sees the novel on the whole as a triumph of language and style and notes ''the incredible rightness of every phrase and sentence'' (p. 58). McWatt's article deals mainly with *The Murderer* and the first two novels of the Armstrong trilogy, *From the Heat of the Day* and *One Generation*. It is concerned in part with Heath's exploration of the minds of his characters and the psychological plausibility of their actions.

HONORS AND AWARDS

In 1978 Roy Heath's novel *The Murderer* won the *Guardian*Fiction Prize. In 1983 Heath was invited by the Guyana Department of Culture to present the eighth series of the prestigious Edgar Mittelholzer Memorial Lecturers in Georgetown.

BIBLIOGRAPHY

Works by Roy A. K. Heath

A Man Come Home. London: Longman Caribbean, 1974.
The Murderer. London: Allison and Busby, 1978.
From the Heat of the Day. London: Allison and Busby, 1979.
Genetha. London: Allison and Busby, 1981.
One Generation. London: Allison and Busby, 1981.
Kwaku. London: Allison and Busby, 1982.
Orealla. London: Allison and Busby, 1984.

Studies of Roy A. K. Heath

D'Costa, Jean. Review Article of *A Man Come Home*. *Jamaica Journal* 9 (1975), 53–58.

McWatt, Mark. "Tragic Irony, the Hero as Victim: Three Novels of Roy A. K. Heath." In *Critical Issues in West Indian Literature*, ed. Erika Smilowitz and Roberta Knowles. Parkersburg, Ia.: Caribbean Books, 1984, pp. 54–64.

See also General Bibliography: Allis, Hughes, and McDowell.

CAROL P. MARSH

Frank E. M. Hercules (1917–)

BIOGRAPHY

Born on February 12, 1917, to Felix Eugene Michael and Millicent Hercules, Frank E. M. Hercules lived in Port of Spain and San Fernando, Trinidad. There he was largely under the influence of family members, who would help shape the intellect that would later find expression through his carefully crafted prose. Hercules remembers and describes his father as a brilliant, principled, moral, outspoken man who was ultimately penalized by the society in spite of his belief in the humanitarian potential of British colonialism. The elder Hercules had made fine contributions to Trinidad as both a civil servant and an educator. Nevertheless, when he voiced his insights during a period of turmoil, he was charged with inciting "disorder." He was subsequently permanently deported on the grounds that he had been born in Venezuela in spite of his having resided in Trinidad for most of his life and his parents' having themselves been British subjects.

Even though his father's treatment did not prove damaging to the younger Hercules, it was significant in its later impact on his world view. It would become a part of the objective process through which he would recognize the ills of colonialism and subsequently reject the notion of its viability as a benign political and economic system. Moreover, through direct teaching and example, Hercules' father encouraged in him intellectual curiosity and independence which would later manifest itself in the clarity of vision and erudition which typifies his writing. Hercules also speaks of his mother and aunt, who were influential in his deep respect for womanhood. Thus armed, Hercules left Trinidad for the intellectual stimulation of London, where he read law at the Honourable Society of the Middle Temple of the Inns of Court from 1935 to 1939 and from 1950 to 1951. However, Hercules' awareness of the sociopolitical implications of being a colonial lawyer motivated him to abandon his pursuit of a career in law. In the 1940s, then, he immigrated to New York City. In 1946 he married the former Dellora Howard, and he became a U.S. citizen in 1959. At this point it is especially interesting to note that Hercules met W. E. B. Du Bois when he initially arrived in the United States. Du Bois invited Hercules to join with him in his work. Hercules, however, pursued his own orientation but later wrote in *American Society and Black Revolution*, "I have at length done so in my own way and on my own terms" (1972, p. 10).

In the United States, Hercules was first a businessman, but later, on the counsel of his wife, Dellora, he abandoned that career for writing. In addition to the support of his wife, he acknowledges other influences on his writing. Outstanding among these was C. L. R. James, who, he asserts, had a great impact on many, if not most West Indian writers. Yet another was his extensive reading in English literature from the Old English through the Romantic periods and his reading in the Bible, which influenced his style and his perception of the prophetic mission of the novelist.

As an artist, Hercules has insisted on pursuing his craft on his own terms and has thus avoided pandering to the tastes of and the demands of critics and criticism. Being published and recognized as a writer and scholar has posed virtually no problem for him. As early as 1942 he was approached by the editor of *Opportunity* to submit an article on the Harlem Renaissance. All of his major works have been immediately accepted for publication. His article "To Live in Harlem" (1977) was read into the *Congressional Record* and subsequently translated and distributed abroad. He has also written for such European publications as *Die Zeit* and *Geo* (Hamburg). In addition he has lectured and been interviewed widely, and he has been a member of the final review panel for the National Endowment for the Humanities as well as a visiting scholar and writer-in-residence at Loyola and Xavier universities in New Orleans, Louisiana. Hercules currently lives in New York with his wife Dellora.

MAJOR WORKS AND THEMES

While Hercules has produced both fiction and nonfiction, the strength of his contribution lies in his fiction. There is, nonetheless, an obvious link between the polemic of his nonfiction and the ideological issues which inform the subject matter of his novels. At the foundation of all Hercules' writing is an essential concern for the individual's definition of himself and his place in the environment, be that environment the Caribbean or points beyond.

Perhaps the most finite expression of Hercules' assessment of the human condition lies in an essay he contributed to *Voices for Life*, an anthology of essays (1975) that considers the quality of contemporary life. In his essay Hercules postulates that mankind has made no social or moral progress over the past two thousand years. He holds that, if man is to achieve true civilization and a meaningful quality of life, he must replace technological progress and material success with more positive spiritual pursuits. The need for such a hierarchy of values is the thread which links all of Hercules' writings.

We find an implicit statement of this theme in Hercules' major works which treat Afro-American concerns. In the sociohistorical work *American Society and Black Revolution,* Hercules brings the West Indian immigrant's perspective to bear on his assessment of the position of Black Americans in the larger American society. The West Indian, he holds, experiences culture shock upon his arrival in America. Nothing, he asserts, in the "varying degrees of blatancy and subtlety" of the racial practices in the West Indies prepares him for "the monolithic institution of white supremacy he must confront on his entry to the United States" (p. 216).

In his observations of the race issue in the United States, Hercules contends that the treatment of Blacks at the hands of Whites has always been indicative of the moral condition of American society at any given moment. In the context of his discussion of American history, he goes further to suggest a certain myopia on the part of White America, whose dogged adherence to racism coupled with the exclusion of Blacks from industry has undermined the national interest. Hercules' vision of the Black American condition, however, is not bleak. He sees cooperation between Blacks and Whites as an avenue to the improvement of the Black condition and submits, further, that the success of Black people lies in their ability to process psychologically the past and the present with a view to conquering the future.

The extended metaphor for Hercules' views on American society preceded *American Society and Black Revolution* with the publication of *I Want a Black Doll* (1967–68). Through the central and peripheral actions of the novel, we see the destructive nature of racism and the devastating effects it has on both the racist and the victim. Therefore, while racism takes its toll on the physical and psychological existence of its victims, the Black underclass, the practice of racism does nothing to advance the moral growth of the dominant White culture.

Hercules' ethic finds its finest expression, however, in his two Caribbean works, *Where the Hummingbird Flies* (1961) and *On Leaving Paradise* (1980), in both of which he portrays the individual's relationship to a colonial society and simultaneously furnishes the reader with a portrait of aspects of the Trinidadian experience. Nevertheless, when the reader considers these two novels, he cannot evade the realization that approximately twenty years separate their publications. As a result, Hercules brings vastly different experiences to each work.

The political reality underlying the fictive world of *Where the Hummingbird Flies* no longer exists. For the time of the novel, however, Hercules' theme and tone were appropriate. He conveys to the reader the foibles of a colonial society and the insidious effect it has on the psyche of the colonized. Thus, while we see a ruling class morally and intellectually unfit for rule, we see an even more pathetic portrayal of the ruled, who accept the legitimacy of the status quo. Just as Trinidad's island geography imposes physical boundaries and limits on the mobility of its people, so the colonial system imposes social and psychic limitations on the colonized. All of this is demonstrated through the omniscient narrator's kaleidoscopic portrayal of the social dynamics of Trinidad during the reign of King George. On the one hand, the reader sees a Mrs. Napoleon Walker and a Carlo Da Silva, both enamored of vacuous values, forever seeking to justify themselves as a social elite with no real understanding of the true nature of their relationship to the ruling class. On the other hand, the reader has to consider Mary Redeson, Francis Herbert, and Dulcina, the laundress, who do not accept the legitimacy of the social order. When Francis, out of intellect and morality, and Mary, out of naiveté, do not subscribe to the notion of limits prescribed by the nature of colonialism, they cannot exist within the shores of Trinidad and are driven to emigrate to the United States. Dulcina, regal and self-possessed, pehaps the most admirable character in the novel, stands in sharp relief to Francis and Mary. She cannot be beaten and forced into physical and psychological exile. She, too, however, is a victim of the limitations imposed by colonialism and by virtue of the inequities of the color-caste considerations inherent in colonialism and her membership in the grass-roots element of society will never be able to transpose her own psychological health to the larger environment. Yet another effect of the psychological limitations imposed by the colonial system is seen in the portrayal of Robert Herrick, Ivor Griffiths, and Henry Redeson, all moral men who possess a clear-sightedness which enables them to perceive the ills of the system under which they live. Their acumen and inherent honesty allow them to acknowledge the need for change, but they lack the fiber to effect it. Hence they resign themselves to accommodation. That this caliber of human being understands the vicious essence of colonialism is graphically conveyed in the reported musings of Robert Herrick: "He considered the legend of the lake, of how the Carib gods, incensed at the wanton killing of a hummingbird, had transformed a beautiful silver reach of water into this ghastly, bubbling lake of pitch. In a sense, was not that a parable of the historic guilt of mankind? The murder of the beautiful that inseminates the birth of ugliness? What greater expiation, what more agonizing atonement would wipe away this sordid stain from the brow of the beautiful earth?" (p. 206). In this explication of the symbolism of the title of the novel lies an indictment of the destructive nature of colonialism which ravages the innocent, the unsuspecting, the beautiful. The result, of course, as we see from the world of *Where the Hummingbird Flies*, ranges from silliness and psychological waste to petty, insensitive demonstrations of human baseness.

If the reader is aware of authorial anger with the colonial system, he is nevertheless heartened by the potential for change. Indeed, Hercules' vision is not nihilistic. And he incorporates the inevitability of change in the fictive world that is borne out in the history of the West Indies and most, if not all, places that have experienced colonialism. This we see in his effective use of counterpoint. The novel begins and ends with the central character, the foolish and pretentious Mrs. Napoleon Walker, preparing a guest list for a party. As a result of the passage of time and events in the world of the novel, however, we find that Mrs. Walker is forced to amend the list for her next party in the light of social and political changes in her world. The list, then, becomes the metaphor for the evolution of a new social order in Trinidad and, by implication, all of the West Indies.

The need for a new social order which *Where the Hummingbird Flies* argues is no longer an underlying assumption in *On Leaving Paradise*. Indeed, the mirth in the authorial tone so readily apparent in the hilarious depictions of the adventures of the protagonist, Johnny de Paria, the total celebration of life and the West Indian experience, and the affirmation achieved in the novel are indicative of how the history of Trinidad since the publication of *Where the Hummingbird Flies* had to have an impact on the creative imagination and reader expectations.

In the novel, Hercules makes use of the picaresque tradition in portraying Johnny's existence in Trinidad and the circumstances which force him abroad. Like the picaro, Johnny is an outsider who in the process of recounting his existence presents and judges life. In spite of his naiveté, his narrative point of view is prejudiced even though the total perspective of the work is reflective and morally judgmental. Also like the picaro, Johnny addresses the material level of existence, comments on society's institutions, and moves horizontally through space and vertically through society throughout the fictive world.

Through Hercules' use of the picaresque tradition, we see a cultural failure—that is, the disintegration of the larger colonial system—and the rise of the healthy West Indian identity. Through the consciousness of the truly emancipated West Indian, we see society stripped of its social masks, its naked folly exposed. In the larger sense, the use of the first person narrator suggests the polarization of the West Indian consciousness from the colonial value system. Hence we see Johnny juxtaposed to the superstructure; but psychologically beyond the need to be at hostile odds with it, he sits in benign judgment on it. Such judgment is illustrated in the shipboard scenes which begin and end the novel. Initially, in the Marquis of Padbury's patronizing attitude toward Johnny, we see Johnny as would-be colonial underdog; but we recognize in Johnny's final observation that "these people have good manners" (p. 312), a complete psychological reversal and dismissal of received colonial values. Johnny, then, becomes the symbol of the indomitable West Indian spirit, which can transform its position outside the colonial system into a personal freedom.

As we survey the writings of Frank Hercules, we can regard him as a scholar/artist/social critic who often expresses his penetrating insights into the larger human condition in tones which upon occasion threaten to be Juvenalian. In so doing, however, he is without rancor. He confronts the reader with his larger humanistic mission, which is to force the reader into the same dialectic Hercules himself has entered with society. This Hercules achieves through the use of his creative imagination, which results from a successful fusion of analytic intellect and cultural sensibility.

CRITICAL RECEPTION

While Hercules' works have not been treated by West Indian scholars, they have, in spite of his indifference to critics, captured the attention of popular reviewers in the United States and Great Britain. *Where the Hummingbird Flies* was an immediate success and was heralded by *Newsweek* as one of the five best first novels of 1961. The *Newsweek* reviewers saw a parallel between Hercules and Evelyn Waugh and stated that the novel "manages to be vigorously wrathful at British colonialism without losing its sense of laughter" (February 27, 1961, p. 95). *I Want a Black Doll* achieved similar success in Great Britain, where it was reviewed favorably in the *Times Literary Supplement*(April 13, 1967, p. 301) on the basis of its exposure of the precarious existence of Blacks in a race-conscious society. The work was not favorably received in the United States, however.

Of all the responses to Hercules' work, perhaps the most rewarding came from the National Association for the Advancement of Colored People, which in 1976 featured *American Society and Black Revolution* at their annual convention. In addition, they reviewed it in *The Crisis*, (May 1976), where they judged Hercules' insights as important to the future of Black survival.

HONORS AND AWARDS

Frank Hercules has received several honors and awards, two of the most notable being the Fletcher Pratt Memorial Fellowship in Prose by the Breadloaf Writers Conference of Middlebury College, Vermont (1961), and a Rockefeller Fellowship presented by the Aspen Institute for "distinguished scholarship in the humanities" (1977).

BIBLIOGRAPHY

Works by Frank Hercules

"An Aspect of the Negro Renaissance." *Opportunity* 20 (1942), 305–6, 317–19.

Where the Hummingbird Flies. New York: Harcourt Brace, 1961; Dusseldorf Hamberg: Econoclasser, 1969.

I Want a Black Doll. New York: Simon and Schuster, 1967/68; Zurich: Neue Schwiezer Bibliothek, 1968; Stockholm: P. A. Norstedt Söners Födag, 1971; Den Haag: Zuid Hollandsche Uitgevers Maatschapu, 1971.

American Society and Black Revolution. New York: Harcourt Brace, 1972.

Untitled essay. In *Voices for Life: Reflections on the Human Condition*, ed. Dom Morales. New York: Praeger, 1975, pp. 226–40.

On Leaving Paradise. New York: Harcourt Brace, 1980.

Studies of Frank Hercules

Hunter, Charlayne. "Living in New York: Writer Finds World in Harlem." *The New York Times*, July 14, 1975.

Marsh, Carol P. "Frank E. M. Hercules." In *Dictionary of Literary Biography*, vol. 33: *Afro-American Fiction Writers after 1955*, ed. Thadius M. Davis and Trudier Harris. Detroit: Gale, 1984, pp. 115–19.

See also General Bibliography: Allis, Herdeck, and Hughes.

LEOTA S. LAWRENCE

Merle Hodge (1944–   )

BIOGRAPHY

Merle Hodge was born in 1944, in Curepe, Trinidad, to Ray Hodge, an immigration officer, and his wife. She was one of four daughters born to the Hodges. Hodge received her early education in Trinidad. After elementary school, she attended Bishop Anstey's High School, where in 1962 she was awarded the Trinidad and Tobago Girls' Island Scholarship. This scholarship enabled her to travel to England to pursue her studies in French. In England, she attended University College, London, where she earned her B.A. Hons. in 1965 and her M.Phil. in 1967. Her master's thesis dealt with the poetry of the French Guianese Negritude writer Leon Damas.

After completing her education in England, Hodge traveled widely in Eastern and Western Europe, paying her way by working as a typist and babysitter. Returning to Trinidad in the early 1970s, she taught French briefly there at the junior secondary level. Her next appointment was that of lecturer in French at the University of the West Indies in Jamaica at the Mona campus. While lecturing at UWI, Hodge began work on her Ph.D. degree in French Caribbean literature. She also completed a translation of *Pigments*, a collection of poetry by Leon Damas.

When in March 1979 the late Maurice Bishop became prime minister of Grenada after leading the socialist revolution that ousted his predecessor, Eric Gairy, Hodge traveled to Grenada to work with the Bishop regime. In Grenada, Hodge was appointed director of the development of curriculum, in which position her mandate was to focus on implementing a type of socialist education program. She also worked with the Adult Education and the People's Education programs in Grenada. Hodge was forced to leave Grenada in 1983, after the assassination of Bishop and the subsequent U.S. invasion. She is at present back in her native Trinidad, where she is engaged in free-lance writing and lecturing.

MAJOR WORKS AND THEMES

Among West Indian writers, very few women are represented. Interestingly, when women do write, they tend to be poets rather than novelists. And with the exception of Jean Rhys, those who do write novels rarely create more than one work. In this tradition, Merle Hodge has published one major work of fiction, *Crick Crack, Monkey* (1970), which is a signal literary achievement in many ways. This work, using the first person point of view, is narrated through the unbiased eyes of the child protagonist, Tee, as she matures from childhood to young womanhood. The themes examined here—cultural ambivalence, alienation and isolation, the search for identity, the ramifications of the matriarchal household, and the conflict between the rural folk culture and urban middle-class society—have been dealt with time and again by West Indian writers. However, Hodge allows for a startlingly fresh interpretation of these themes, when, for the first time, they revolve around a female protagonist rather than a male.

The novel opens with the death of Elizabeth, the mother of Tee and Toddan, Aunt Beatrice's sister. We learn that Tee's mother had committed a social faux pas when she married the dark-skinned, lower-class Selwyn, Tantie's brother. Both Tantie and Aunt Beatrice become contestants for guardianship of the children, thus setting the stage for the conflicts and tensions of the novel. Tee will eventually become irretrievably entangled between the different worlds Tantie and Aunt Beatrice represent. In the beginning, though, the conflict is limited to the adults. Tee's preference for the world that Tantie creates for her is clearly evident. Aunt Beatrice is the outsider, with "a voice like high-heels and stockings" (1970, Deutsch ed., p. 8). Aunt Beatrice soon "[grows] horns and a djablesse face and a thousand attributes of female terrifyingness" (p. 20). On the other hand, "Tantie's company [is] loud and hilarious and the intermittent squawk and flurry of mirth [makes Tee] think of the fowl-run when something fell into the midst of the fat hens" (p. 11). Tantie's household also includes Mikey, her godson, whom the children idolize. They readily discard the scooter which one of Tantie's male friends gives them for Christmas for one that Mikey makes for them with board and motorcar parts.

Then there is Ma, Tee's paternal grandmother. Ma completes Tee's secure world. The close relationship between grandmother and grandchild is a West Indian phenomenon that has been documented in the literature. Nowhere, however, has this relationship been more sensitively portrayed than in Hodge's work. Ma, the traditional African matriarch, is a marketwoman. She has "adopted" several children. When Tee and her brother join this group during their August vacation, we see the loving bond between Ma and Tee. We read:

> Sometimes when the others were not about [Ma] would accost me suddenly: "An who is Ma sugar-cake?"
> "Tee!"
> "An who is Ma dumplin'?"
> "Tee!"
> And all at once she put on an expression of mock-displeasure and snapped at me gruffly "Who tell yu that?"
> "Ma tell mih!"
> "Well Ma is a liard ol'-fool"; and she thrust a hunk of guava-cheese at me. (pp. 31–32)

Thus, during the early years of Tee's life, she is totally in harmony with and a part of the rural folk culture which she and her brother share with Tantie, Mikey, Ma, and all the neighbors. It is, therefore, all the more ironic that Tee will become confused about her identity. Tee's ambivalence begins when she wins a scholarship which enables her to attend one of the better girls' schools in Trinidad. Tantie now has to make a concession, whereby Tee will live at Aunt Beatrice's during the school term. It is at this point that Tee becomes as it were a member of two worlds: two worlds that she is never able to reconcile.

Tee's entry into Aunt Beatrice's world is forced and painful. She soon discovers that this new world is diametrically opposed to the one from which she has come. Aunt Beatrice does not suffer nicknames; therefore, Tee becomes Cynthia. Her feelings of isolation and loss of identity are heightened when her cousins, Aunt Beatrice's daughters, insist on treating her as an intruder and refuse to acknowledge and accept her presence. They continue to refer to Tee as "she." And when their friends ask about Tee's identity, the disdainful response of the oldest is, "Oh, that's some lil relative Mommer found up in the country" (p. 117). Tee soon learns also that, in the middle-class society in which she finds heself, Whiteness or being as close to Whiteness as possible is the ideal in appearance as well as in behavior. In this desperate imitation of an alien culture one rejects all that is native or local. Thus Aunt Beatrice's preference for imported foods over local dishes.

In this new environment, Tee is forced to look at herself. In so doing, she sees herself to be a total misfit. All the feelings of well-being and self-confidence that she had acquired in the world that Tantie had created for her begin to dissipate. She is on her way to ambivalence, alienation, and total self-hatred. This startling transformation is poignantly recorded by Tee, the narrator. In the new school she now attends, her dark complexion stands out, setting her apart. On the first day of classes, she instinctively sits at the back of the class. "I had a feeling," she states, "that it would be somehow presumptuous for me to sit anywhere but in the back row (pp. 106–7). Tee realizes and accepts the fact that because of her dark skin and lower-class background she will never be fully accepted in this society in which she finds herself. Girls like herself can never hope to penetrate the inner circles of the activities of the various school clubs. And she passively accepts her teacher's unprovoked verdict on her: "You are one of those who will never get very far" (p. 142).

Actually, two things are taking place in Tee's life simultaneously. Even as she is being rejected by the inhabitants of this "cultured" environment, she begins taking on their system of values and their standards of judgment. In doing so, she sees Tantie and all that she stands for through their eyes, and what she sees she rejects. She therefore loses her inner core, the centeredness that had kept her whole. Her thoughts now turn to self-destruction. At the beach with her aunt and cousins, she thinks fleetingly of drowning herself. She admits that the death wish is the only "agreeable thought" she has had that day. Next, she enters into a world of fantasy: one in which she had never lived with Tantie, one in which she had been brought up by Aunt Beatrice and had acquired all the social graces of her cousins. In her fantasy, she is not an outsider, not an outcast; she belongs to this upper middle-class world. Thus, we read: "I wanted to shrink, to disappear. . . . I felt that the very sight of me was an affront to common decency. I wished that my body would shrivel up and fall away, that I could step out new and acceptable" (p. 140).

Finally, it is Tantie who rescues Tee, so to speak. She writes Aunt Beatrice (not Tee) that the children's father has sent for them to join him in England. (Tee surmises correctly that Tantie has more to do with this timely request than she admits.) At this point, too, the superficiality of the middle class is laid bare. For immediately, as if by magic, all those who have so far treated Tee as an outsider are now drawn to her in awed envy. Why? Because she is going to live in England—England, the epitome of Whiteness, and culture, and goodness. Paradoxically, therefore, Tee gains acceptance in her departure. In leaving, too, she is following in the tradition of many West Indian protagonists who are forced to resolve their conflicts through escape from their environment.

Finally, one sees that Hodge raises several basic issues to which no solution has really been offered—issues dealing with identity and culture, issues that have been raised and left unresolved by other Caribbean writers. One obvious question the book raises is whether the West Indian person is actually forced to choose between the two worlds portrayed by Hodge or whether there is some middle ground between the two. The Barbadian writer Edward Brathwaite, in *Masks*, seems to think that a compromise is possible. On the other hand, Derek Walcott in "A Far Cry From Africa" and Claude McKay in "Outcast" seem to suggest that the West Indian is doomed to cultural schizophrenia. One wonders too about Tee. Will her displacement be permanent? Or will she be able eventually to reconcile her two disparate worlds and emerge as a whole person? These are real and burning questions that remain unresolved in the literature but continue to plague the West Indian psyche.

In 1982 *Crick Crack, Monkey* was translated into French by Alice Asselos Cherdieu. Unfortunately, Hodge's study of the poetry of Leon Damas remains unpublished. In the meantime, Hodge has become an outspoken literary voice on behalf of the Caribbean woman, whom she sees as the victim of a society which has historically been male-dominated. In keeping with this concern, she has written some scathing prose essays. Two of these are "The Shadow of the Whip: A Comment on Male-Female Relations in the Caribbean" (1974) and "Young Women and the Development of Stable Family Life in the Caribbean" (1977).

CRITICAL RECEPTION

Crick Crack, Monkey was reviewed in the *Trinidad Guardian* on June 28, 1970, in an essay titled "Growing up in Colonial Trinidad." It was later reviewed in *World Literature Written in English* by Elizabeth Harvey in 1971. Harvey asserts that the novel "sparkles with humor" as well as "poignant reality." She also recognizes the unique character of Ma, whom she sees as being determined to give the children "a sense of family tradition and history" as well as "a true sense of security." She concludes by stating that since the novel deals with universal experience, it makes worthwhile reading.

BIBLIOGRAPHY

Works by Merle Hodge

Crick Crack, Monkey. London: André Deutsch, 1970; London: Heinemann, 1981; Paris: Karthala, 1982 (trans. Alice Asselos-Cherdieu).

"The Shadow of the Whip: A Comment on Male-Female Relations in the Caribbean." In *Is Massa Day Dead? Black Moods in the Caribbean*, ed. Orde Coombs. New York: Anchor Books, 1974, pp. 111–18.

"Young Women and the Development of Stable Family Life in the Caribbean." *Savacou* 13 (Gemini 1977), 39–44.

Studies of Merle Hodge

Brown, Wayne. "Growing up in Colonial Trinidad." *Sunday Guardian* (Trinidad), June 28, 1970, pp. 6, 17.

Harvey, Elizabeth. Review of *Crick Crack Monkey*. *World Literature Written in English* (April 1971), 87.

Lawrence, Leota S. "Three West Indian Heroines: An Analysis." *CLA Journal* 21 (December 1977), 238–50.

———. "Women in Caribbean Literature: The African Presence." *Phylon* 44 (March 1983), 1–11.

Thorpe, Marjorie. "The problem of Cultural Identification in *Crick Crack Monkey*." *Savacou* 13 (Gemini 1977), 31–38.

See also General Bibliography: Allis, Herdeck, and Hughes.

EUGENIA COLLIER

C. L. R. James (1901–)

BIOGRAPHY

Cyril Lionel Robert James was born on January 4, 1901, the son of a schoolteacher in Tunapuna, a little town eight miles out of Port of Spain, Trinidad. As a child James would stand on a chair at a window in his aunt's home, where he spent half of every year, and watch the men and youths play cricket. From the same chair he could reach the books on top of the wardrobe. Thus converged three vital influences on his formative years: cricket, books, and the fierce middle-class Puritanism of his family. James remembers his childhood self as "a British intellectual long before I was ten, already an alien in my own environment among my own people, even my own family" (See chapter 1, "A Window to the World," in *Beyond a Boundary*).

At ten he received a scholarship to the Queen's Royal College, the government secondary school, where he had wider opportunities to play cricket and read books. When he was fifteen he published an essay in the school magazine. "Cobden's Match" was the retelling of a cricket match of a half-century earlier. The next term his English teacher published in the same magazine a theme which James had written for a class, "The Novel as an Instrument of Reform." These first two publications contained the seeds of his subsequent thought: cricket as many-sided metaphor; literature as an instrument for change.

For about a dozen years, James taught at the Queen's Royal College. He continued to play cricket and began writing fiction. Meanwhile, James and a Portuguese Creole named Alfred Mendes became central figures among the young intellectuals of the island, thinkers and artists who played a vital role in accelerating the intellectual development not only of Trinidad but of the entire West Indies. Trinidad had become a nexus where a number of gifted individuals were concentrated. At the core of the group were James and Mendes.

James was writing fiction. In 1927 he published a story, "La Divina Pastora," which was reprinted in the *Saturday Review of Literature* (October 15, 1927) and gained an audience abroad. Edward J. O'Brien published it in his annual series *The Best British Short Stories* in 1928. This recognition had tremendous impact in bringing West Indian writing to the attention of metropolitan countries. The following year a story by Mendes was published in O'Brien's collection for that year, and other publications by Mendes and others followed. In August, 1929, James wrote a novel, *Minty Alley*.

At Christmas, 1929, and Easter, 1930, James and Mendes published a small magazine, *Trinidad*, which was to have profound influence upon West Indian literature. The first issue included James's stories "Triumph" and "Turner's Prosperity." The two issues contained stories, poems, and essays by the gifted young intellectuals who came to be known as the Beacon Group. In 1931 the group began publication of a new magazine, *The Beacon*, edited by Albert Gomes. This publication continued for two years. These two magazines fostered the emerging West Indian literature and were, in a sense, models for the Caribbean literary magazines which were to follow. In 1932 both James and Mendes left Trinidad, Mendes for the United States, James for England, where he helped his friend and cricket opponent Learie Constantine to write an autobiography. James brought with him the manuscript of his first political book, *The Life of Captain Cipriani*, about a mayor of Port of Spain who had spoken out against colonialism. The book was published later that year. Three chapters were published in 1933 as a pamphlet, *The Case for West-Indian Self-Government*. With this pamphlet James became a founding father of West Indian independence. The novel *Minty Alley* was published in 1936.

Supporting himself by working as cricket correspondent for the *Manchester Guardian*, then the *Glascow Herald*, James became politically active. As a member of the Independent Labour Party he contributed articles to the party newspapers *Controversy* and *The New Leader*. Leaving that organization, he helped form the Revolutionary Socialist League and edited their journal *Flight*, as well as *International African Opinion*, the organ of the International African Service Bureau. James was by now active in the international arena, taking key roles in the movement of the unemployed, the founding of the Trotskyite movement in France, protesting the Italian invasion of Ethiopia, and other issues. His writing was prolific: much of it was written under assumed names. In addition to articles in various journals, he published *World Revolution 1917–1936* (1937), a history of the Communist Third International, and *A History of Negro Revolt* (1938). Both books were unprecedented in presenting material and views never before assembled. All the while, James was working on what is regarded as his most important work. He had long been interested in Toussaint L'Ouverture. In

1936 he wrote a play, *Toussaint L'Ouverture*, and acted in it along with Paul Robeson. In 1938 he published his now-famous work, *The Black Jacobins: Toussaint L'Ouverture and the San Domingo Revolt.*

James's vision was constantly expanding. In England he renewed his relationship with his childhood friend George Padmore and became friendly with a number of young Africans who were to become political forces—people such as Jomo Kenyatta and Kwame Nkrumah. Now he formulated principles for an autonomous Black Marxism, which he discussed with Trotsky. At the end of 1938 he took a lecture tour to the United States. He stayed for fifteen years.

He was in the United States when his translation of Boris Souvarine's *Stalin* was published in 1939, the first major work exposing the underside of that era. Now James participated in the various labor movements, especially the strikes of Black sharecroppers in the South. He became even more convinced of the autonomy of the Black movement and of its key position in the labor movement internationally. Ten years after his discussion with Trotsky, James published his program in an essay, "The Revolutionary Answer to the Negro Problem in the United States of America" (See *Documents on the Negro Struggle*, 1948, a report on a conference of the Socialist Workers' Party). James's thought on Marxism had by now outgrown Trotskyism, and he was exploring an independent Marxism. In addition to numerous articles, James elaborated his views in *Notes on the Dialectic* (1948) and *State Capitalism and World Revolution* (1950). But the 1950s were not conducive to exploration of Marxist thought in the United States. In 1952 James was interned on Ellis Island. Irrepressible, he wrote a study of the classic American writer Herman Melville, *Mariners, Renegades and Castaways* (1953). In 1953 James was expelled from the United States.

He went to England for five years, where he worked with the Pan-Africanist movement and visited Africa. He also continued his interest in U.S. politics through various articles. In 1958 he published the fruit of his political ideas in *Facing Reality*. But James was drawn to the West Indies, where the independence he had so long advocated was now becoming reality. That year he returned to Trinidad, where he became secretary of the Federal Labour Party. Here James edited the journal of the People's National Movement, *The Nation*. In addition to writing and lecturing, James published *Modern Politics* (1960), reissued as *A History of Pan-African Revolt: Party Politics in the West Indies* (1961). James differed with Trinidad's political leader, Dr. Eric Williams, on vital issues, especially on the breakup of the West Indian Federation, and in 1962 James returned to England, where he published *Marxism and the Intellectuals*. A year later he published *Beyond a Boundary*, an autobiographical account of cricket. When he returned to Trinidad in 1965 as a cricket correspondent, he was placed under house arrest for vague reasons, but he was released as a result of public outcry. During the next several months he founded the Workers' and Peasants' Party and started a newspaper, *We the People*. That year he published a critical study, *Wilson Harris: A Philosophical Approach*. He returned to England, then to the United States, where he has taught and continued to write. He has been back and forth to London and Trinidad many times. Among his important works since then have been *Notes on Dialectics* (1971) and *Nkrumah and the Ghana Revolution* (1971). His selected writings have been published in *The Future in the Present* (1971) and *Spheres of Existence* (1980). He is working on an autobiography.

MAJOR WORKS AND THEMES

C. L. R. James's work has been too copious and diverse for exhaustive treatment here. His importance lies not merely in *saying* but in *being*: for all his life he has been an innovator, an activist, a moving force. He has written on everything from world revolution to a peasant woman's lonely despair. This essay will focus on James's fiction, emphasizing three levels of importance: James's works as literature in their own right; as a vital step toward the development of a West Indian aesthetic; and as a stage in the development of James's own sensibilities.

James wrote his fiction well before he was thirty. He had always been a voracious reader, feeding his insatiable curiosity with a wide variety of material. In his twenties, he was intellectually stimulated by the young artists and thinkers who were changing the direction of West Indian culture. "La Divina Pastora," brief and complete as a miniature portrait, was his first success. Then came "Triumph," which he still considers one of his finest works, and finally the novel *Minty Alley*. All concern the grass-roots people, whom James considered the lifeblood of the culture.

"La Divina Pastora" is the story of Anita Perez, whose shy but affluent lover Sebastian Montagnio visits nightly but cannot break through his inhibitions. He smokes while Anita knits or sews and her mother sits on the ground just outside chatting away in patois. Marriage to Sebastian (or somebody) is Anita's only chance to escape her daily labor in the cocoa fields, and that hope is fading with Anita's fading beauty. The routine is broken when Anita visits her aunt in Siparia and presents her case at the altar of the renown saint La Divina Pastora. Anita leaves as a sacrifice her only ornament, a little gold chain. Upon her return, Sebastian, jarred by her unprecedented absence, becomes more demonstrative and even asks to take Anita to the cocoa-house dance. Discounting the influence of La Divina Pastora, Anita wishes she had her gold chain back to wear to the dance. By the end of the dance, a coolness has arisen between the lovers. Later, undressing for bed and telling her mother about the dance, Anita suddenly falls silent, then faints—for on her table, in its accustomed place, is the little chain.

Brief though it is, the story is perfectly crafted. It is an interesting balance of realism and mysticism. The objective narrator neither denies nor affirms the powers of La Divina Pastora but merely tells concisely what happens. The ending leaves many questions unanswered—which is, of course, the way of our lives and of good fiction. The basic *fact* of the story, the dominant thought with which the reader is left, is the impact of generations-long poverty.

"Triumph" portrays life in the urban barrack yards. Again the story focuses on the plight of impoverished women, whose only resource ultimately is their sexuality. In "Triumph" Mamitz has lost her lover and is therefore destitute since, like the other women in the yard, her survival depends upon her ability to maintain a relationship with a man. Her friend Celestine, suspecting that their enemy Irene has put a curse on Mamitz, performs Obeah rites, after which Mamitz attracts not one but two lovers. Popo is a flashy playboy who soon moves on. Nicholas the butcher is a steady type who pays Mamitz's rent and supports her well. When Popo returns for a brief but impressive fling, Irene hastens to tell Nicholas, who rushes to the scene. Fortunately, Popo has left. The ensuing quarrel is classic, but Mamitz convinces Nicholas of her fidelity. Her triumph is the dramatic display of the money Nicholas has given her, nailed in small denominations to the double doors of her house, proclaiming to the yard-world the defeat of the enemy Irene.

These two stories, still reproduced in anthologies, were groundwork for the novel *Minty Alley*. In the novel several important themes converge. Again the work portrays life in the barrack yard. Mainly the novel is about the women—Mrs. Rouse, the landlady, betrayed by Benoit, her common-law husband; Nurse Jackson, the other side of the triangle; Mrs. Rouse's niece Maisie, young and high-spirited but with no healthy outlet and no viable future in the barrack yard.

More important, the novel is about the fragmentation of West Indian society—a direct result of colonization. The story is told through the perceptions of Haynes, a middle-class youth of twenty, who moves into the yard through economic necessity. Haynes, who works in a bookstore, has little experience with life beyond home and books, has had no sexual experience, and has, in fact, no friends at all. Yet at Number 2 Minty Alley he is respected for his class and education, and despite his inexperience he is consulted in matters involving the most basic of human emotions. Everyone calls him *Mr.* Haynes, including his bed-partner Maisie. Haynes is thus basically an outsider. Even his affair with Maisie never cracks his middle-classness. He retains his faithful servant Ella, who manages his domestic affairs, from doing his shopping to polishing his shoes. He is, in fact, lost without a servant.

Haynes is never quite a complete person, certainly not in the sense of his yard neighbors. He experiences life vicariously through books and through peering surreptitiously into the yard through a hole in his wall. He expresses little real emotion about anything and is reluctant to become involved. Maisie is his friend as well as his lover, but he never considers her life material. Haynes does change to an extent during the course of the novel—he becomes a little more confident, more assertive. But when the household breaks up and Maisie leaves for good, Haynes returns to middle-class lodgings and the Minty Alley experience becomes a remote memory.

Haynes's detachment is not snobbishness: it is something far more profound and disturbing. It is a feature of West Indian life which Edward Brathwaite in his essay "Timehri" (*Savacou* 2 [September 1970, pp. 35–48]) describes as "its sense of rootlessness, of not belonging to the landscape: dissociation, in fact, from the act of living.'' This sharp distinction between classes is made clear by James's use of Haynes as the focus of the point of view. The dramatization of this fragmentation, this rootlessness of the middle class, wrought by a history of colonialism, is a major achievement of the novel.

It is the yard people who live life to the fullest. Their struggles are not pretty: they sometimes prey upon each other, and their victories are often pyrrhic. But they confront their lives in a way that Haynes cannot do.

Mrs. Rouse exemplifies this toughness of spirit. She is a hardworking woman in her forties whose life has been hard from the start. Now Benoit has been making love to one of the lodgers, a nurse whom Mrs. Rouse long ago befriended. (It is said that if you put a skirt on a stick, Benoit will chase it. And this apparently is true.) The affair is helped along by Maisie, whose raison d'être seems to be to pester Mrs. Rouse. Discovering the mass betrayal, Mrs. Rouse is outraged. But when Benoit subsequently marries the nurse, Mrs. Rouse descends to the depths of despair. Yet she gathers a certain strength and dignity when, learning that Benoit has had a stroke and has been deserted by his wife, she decides to bring him home. He dies before she is able to see him; instead, she arranges his funeral. Benoit, in spite of everything, is finally hers. She wins, though the victory is bitter. But she wins.

In all of his fiction, James attains authenticity in his portrayal of the folk through several means. One such means is the use of realistic details in descriptions of setting. His description of the barrack yards in ''Triumph,'' for example, provides an extremely realistic backdrop for the action to follow. Another means of achieving authenticity in folk portrayal is the inclusion of folk customs and beliefs. Obeah, for example, is used in both ''Triumph'' and *Minty Alley*.

Perhaps the most effective way of making his portrayal real is his skill in using language. James reproduces the sound of the speaking voice, utilizing rhythm, idiom, and vocal intensity. Nicholas, for example, rushes into the yard, his white coat bloody from butchered animals, and grabs the unfaithful Mamitz by the throat:

> ''I will stick my knife into you as I will stick it in a cow. You had Popo des Vignes in that room for the whole day. Speak the truth, you dog.''
>
> ''You' mother, you' sister, you' aunt, you' wife was the dog,'' shrieked Mamitz. (*The Future in the Present*, p. 20)

Another example of James's skill with language is in Miss Atwell's description of Benoit's wedding to the nurse:

> ''She didn't look well. And one foolish little hat on 'er head, and as for he, in the old grey suit. I look to see what kind o' shoes 'e had on, if was new ones in truth, but where I was sittin' I couldn't see. Then they ring the bell little bit when they was goin' away, but the whole thing was tame, tame, tame. You could see was a pick-up wedding. The

man did look too shame. . . . Man ties the marriage rope, but only God can unloose it." (*Minty Alley*, 1971, New Beacon ed., pp. 107–8)

These three works—"La Divina Pastora," "Triumph," and *Minty Alley*—are fine pieces in their own right. They also are important to the development of a West Indian aesthetic. One legacy of colonialism is that the colonized looks to the metropolitan country for cultural standards. James saw the common West Indian people as artistic material—the people furthest from the British Puritanism that marked the articulate middle class. In turning attention inward to the indigenous folk rather than outward to imposed cultural concepts, James helped to lay the foundation for a literature based upon West Indian truths, a West Indian vision of the world. He initiated a change of direction for his own generation and broke new ground for writers yet to come. His fiction facilitated the development of a West Indian aesthetic and, through its early publication abroad, announced this aesthetic to the world.

Another dimension of James's fiction is its significance in the development of its creator, James himself. His successful fiction was all written within a four-year period, when he was teaching at Queen's Royal College, editing *Trinidad*, and functioning as a prime mover in the Beacon Group. But he was not entirely satisfied. Despite his involvement with cricket and despite his great interest in literature, something was missing. Later he recalled, "Intellectually I lived abroad, chiefly in England. What ultimately vitiated all this was that it involved me with the people around me only in the most abstract way. . . . I taught at schools, but there were no controversies on education. I taught the curriculum. I didn't think it was any good, but I didn't bother about it" (*Beyond a Boundary*, p. 71). Something was missing.

James knew that the grass-roots people—the folk, the yard people—were the essence of West Indian folk culture. As a middle-class intellectual he had been reared *among* but not *of* the folk. His cricket activities had taken him close, but there were still unexplored dimensions. A fiction writer must put himself into the world, into the people of whom he writes. The early stories were a coalescence of James's love of literature, his study of the art of fiction, and his growing political convictions. But something more was needed.

In the middle-class world, James explained many years later in an interview with Daryl Cumber Dance (San Fernando, Trinidad, March 18, 1980), nothing was happening. They went to work and to church and that was about all. Life teemed in the yards, among the people from whom the middle class kept away. James did a thing which would have been considered strange indeed: He went to live in a yard. He rented rooms and lived in a place very similar to Number 2 Minty Alley, where he observed some of the same people and situations which he later transformed into art in his novel. The character Haynes resembled James himself, although James was older and not nearly so naive, and James did not have some of Haynes's experiences (no love affair with a Maisie, for instance). Returning to his usual life, James wrote furiously, a chapter a day, for a full month—on red paper—until he had told the story of a bourgeois lad living among the proletariat. When he finished, he showed the work to his friend Mendes. Then he put it away.

The fiction of C. L. R. James, culminating in *Minty Alley*, may be viewed as a rite of passage. These pieces were his life's journeywork, his way of gaining intimate knowledge of the people who were to be the basic element in his political convictions. When an author creates a character, he must know that character's history, that culture's history, and its potential for the future. To create a novel is to explore a world. James did that in *Minty Alley*. The fact that he did not, apparently, push for immediate publication indicates that for him the writing of the novel had another significance. James planned another novel that would be his master-work. But he never wrote a word of it. In England he was caught up in politics and, having learned what fiction taught him, put those lessons to practical use.

Literature, however, has remained an important concern for James. "A supreme artist," he once told an audience of young West Indians, "exercises an influence on the national consciousness which is incalculable. He is created by it but he himself illuminates and amplifies it, bringing the past up to date and charting the future" ("The Artist in the Caribbean," *The Future in the Present*, p. 85). He has contributed a number of critical commentaries, which are based on politics and philosophy as well as traditional aesthetic principles.

It is by no means far-fetched to see a link between James's fiction and his political and historical works, including the influential *The Black Jacobins*, still widely read and used as a text in university courses, and the unique *Beyond a Boundary*, which is infinitely more than a history of cricket.

CRITICAL RECEPTION

James's fiction is considered important both for its intrinsic value and for its influence on the development of West Indian literature. All discussions of West Indian literary history include *Minty Alley*; most also include "Triumph." Kenneth Ramchand gives an incisive discussion of James's fiction in his introduction to the 1971 edition of *Minty Alley* and in his *The West Indian Novel and its Background* (1970). He emphasizes particularly the effect of point of view in *Minty Alley*. By limiting the narration to Haynes's perspective, Ramchand says, James achieves several important effects: vividness in the portrayal of the yard people, expressing "life's triumph over narrow surroundings" (p. 70); and depth in the presentation of characters, since Haynes cannot observe them in all their activities and is too inexperienced even to guess the full range of possibilities. Most important, the use of Haynes's point of view focuses upon a central concern of subsequent literature: "the mutually impoverishing alienation of the educated West Indian from the people" (p. 70). Moreover, Ramchand sees Haynes as a vehicle through which James is able to come to grips with his own alienation from the grass-roots people.

The effect of Haynes's point of view is also a focus in Michael Gilkes' discussion of *Minty Alley* (*The West Indian Novel*, 1981). He sees Haynes as an extension of James's voice and sympathies, obviously valuing "lower-class vitality as opposed to the dullness and snobbery of middle-class life" (p. 29). Yet, Gilkes says, Haynes himself is given an extravagant middle-class pomposity, which results in his being one-dimensional. Gilkes also finds some of James's authorial devices rather obvious, such as the peephole through which Haynes for a brief while observes life in the yard. However, Gilkes acknowledges the novel's "occasional insights into the 'yard' ethos" (p. 34). He concludes that, despite shortcomings, the novel is interesting and important, its strong points being the author's "inwardness" with folk language and character and his commitment to the folk themselves.

Other assessments provide additional dimensions to the understanding of James's fiction. Leota Lawrence's article "Three West Indian Heroines: An Analysis" (1977) considers Maisie as an effective and realistic portrayal. Edward Brathwaite in "Timehri" (*Savacou* 2 [September 1970], 35–48), sees *Minty Alley* as exemplifying the "unconscious concern of many of the most articulate West Indian intellectuals and artists in the post-colonial period"—that is, the problem of having been born and educated into a fragmented culture and thus lacking a sense of wholeness, and often being plagued by a sense of rootlessness. James's novel, Braithwaite says, portrays this dissociation.

Regardless of approach, critics agree on James's centrality to the shaping of West Indian culture.

HONORS AND AWARDS

James is widely honored as the grand old man of West Indian culture. In 1972 he was awarded an honorary Doctor of Literature degree from the University of the West Indies.

BIBLIOGRAPHY

Selected Works by C. L. R. James

"La Divina Pastora." *Saturday Review*, October 15, 1927. Widely reprinted, including in E. J. O'Brien, *Best British Short Stories of 1928* (New York: Dodd, Mead, 1928); C. L. R. James, *Spheres of Influence* (Westport, Conn.: Lawrence Hill, 1980).

"Triumph." *Trinidad* I (Christmas 1929). Widely reprinted, including in C. L. R. James, *The Future in the Present* (Westport, Conn.: Lawrence Hill, 1980).

"Turner's Prosperity." *Trinidad* 1 (Christmas 1929). Reprinted in C. L. R. James, *Spheres of Influence* (Westport, Conn.: Lawrence Hill, 1980), pp. 9–13.

The Life of Captain Cipriani: An Account of British Government in the West Indies. Nelson, England: Coulton, 1932.

The Case for West-Indian Self-Government. London: Hogarth Press, 1933; New York: University Place Book Shop, 1967.

Minty Alley. London: Secker and Warburg, 1936. London: New Beacon Books, 1971.

World Revolution 1917–1936: The Rise and Fall of the Communist International. London: Secker and Warburg, 1937.

The Black Jacobins: Toussaint L'Ouverture and the San Domingo Revolution. New York: Dial, 1938; New York: Vintage Books, 1963.

Mariners, Renegades and Castaways: The Study of Melville and the World We Live in. New York: Author, 1953.

Modern Politics. Trinidad: P.N.M., 1960.

Party Politics in the West Indies. San Juan, Trinidad: Vedic, 1962.

Beyond a Boundary. London: Hutchinson, 1963.

"From Toussaint L'Ouverture to Fidel Castro." In *The Black Jacobins*, 1963 ed., pp. 391–418; also in Richard Frucht, *Black Society in the New World* (New York: Random House, 1971), pp. 324–44.

Wilson Harris: A Philosophical Approach. St. Augustine, Trinidad: Busby's Printerie, 1965.

"The Atlantic Slave Trade and Slavery: Some Interpretations of Their Significance to the Development of the United States and the Western World." In *Amistad I*, ed. John A. Williams and Charles Harris. New York: Random House, 1970, pp. 119–64.

Nkrumah and the Ghana Revolution. Westport, Conn.: Lawrence Hill, 1977.

The Future in the Present: Selected Writings. London: Allison and Busby, 1977; Westport, Conn.: Lawrence Hill, 1980.

Spheres of Influence: Selected Writings. London: Allison and Busby, 1980. Westport, Conn.: Lawrence Hill, 1980.

Studies of C. L. R. James

"*Afras Review* Talks to C. L. R. James." *Afras Review* 2 (1976), 4–8.

Glaberman, Martin. "C. L. R. James—the Man and His Works." *Flambeau* 6 (November 1966), 22–23.

Griffith, Patrick. "C. L. R. James and Pan-Africanism: An Interview." *Black World* 21 (November 1971), 4–13.

Lawrence, Leota S. "Three West Indian Heroines: An Analysis." *CLA Journal* 21 (December 1977), 238–50.

———. "Women in Caribbean Literature: The African Presence." *Phylon* 44 (Spring 1983), 1–11.

Martin, Tony. "C. L. R. James and the Race/Class Question." *Race* 14 (October 1972), 183–93.

Munro, Ian, and Reinhard Sander. "Interview with C. L. R. James." In *Interviews with Three Caribbean Writers in Texas. Kas-Kas*. Austin: University of Texas, African and Afro-American Research Institute, pp. 22–41.

Oxaal, Ivor. *Black Intellectuals Come to Power: The Rise of Creole Nationalism in Trinidad and Tobago*. Cambridge: Schenkman, 1968.

Radical America. Special Issue 4 (May 1970).

Wickham, John. Review of *Minty Alley*. *Bim* 14 (January–June 1972), 111–13.

See also General Bibliography: Allis, Baugh (1978), Cudjoe, Gilkes, Harris, Herdeck, Hughes, King, Lamming, and Ramchand (1970).

HAROLD BARRATT

Marion Patrick Jones (1934–)

BIOGRAPHY

Born in Trinidad during the traumatic 1930s, Marion Patrick Jones has had a varied and intellectually rewarding career. After attending the all-girls St. Joseph's Convent in Port of Spain, certainly the most respected and regimented of the secondary schools in the 1940s and 1950s, and the female counterpart of the equally prestigious St. Mary's College, she was admitted to the Imperial College of Tropical Agriculture (now the St. Augustine campus of the University of the West Indies). This was followed by a year's sojourn in Brooklyn, where she worked in a ceramics factory. Work at the Carnegie Free Library in Trinidad and a diploma in library science followed her American stint. In 1959 she enrolled in graduate studies in social anthropology at London University, becoming during her time in London one of the founders of CARD (Campaign Against Racial Discrimination). She is currently living in Paris and is active in race relations.

The variety of her experiences and wide traveling notwithstanding, Marion Patrick Jones is authentically Trinidadian. This Trinidadianness—and by extension, West Indianness—is the hub around which almost everything in her two novels turns. *Pan Beat* (1973) and *J'Ouvert Morning* (1976) accordingly are palpably West Indian. This can be seen, for instance, in the sensibilities of her characters, her facile handling of West Indian dialect, her use of West Indian ethos for dramatic purposes, her disconcertingly realistic settings. Her schooldays at the fiercely Catholic St. Joseph's Convent are particularly important. The regimen of St. Joseph's, the nuns' asceticism, the profound influences upon the developing consciousness of the young girls—all of these are effectively transmuted into her fiction and provide much of the dramatic tension in several sections of her novels.

MAJOR WORKS AND THEMES

In a 1964 essay V. S. Naipaul observed, "Until they have been written about, societies appear to be without shape and *embarrassing*." It required courage, he added, "to give a quality of myth to what was agreed to be petty and ridiculous-Frederick Street in Port of Spain, Marine Square, the districts of Laventille and Barataria" (*The Overcrowded Barracoon and Other Articles* [New York: Penguin, 1976], p. 26). In her two novels, *Pan Beat* and *J'Ouvert Morning*, Marion Patrick Jones has written rather courageously about the "petty and ridiculous" of Port of Spain. Far from being embarrassed by the derelict locations and fetid slums of Trinidad's capital city, she examines with detailed and sometimes brutal candor the harried lives of the men and women who live there, drawing one's attention as she does so to "the dirtiness of the streets, the life overflowing on to the street corners, rats rummaging by the side of the road, the overpowering scent of lavatories and dead animals" (*Pan Beat*, p. 84).

Both novels are set in the lower middle-class worlds of Belmont, Woodbrook, and Behind the Bridge—a somewhat felicitous euphemism for Port of Spain's congested slums. In *Pan Beat* one meets the youthful Flamingoes steelband in the early, turbulent days of the steelband's growth from middle-class ostracism to acceptance as an indigenous art. Earline Hill, one of the band's female satellites, is the novel's central intelligence. She has returned to Trinidad emotionally scarred from years of promiscuity in London and New York and nursing the wounds of a disintegrating marriage to a homosexual intellectual. Earline's need to rediscover her West Indian roots is matched by her efforts to connect her traumatic years abroad to the lives of Alan, Louis, Leslie, and the other members of the steelband, many of whom are now leading lives of tense desperation in a stagnant, superficial society. *J'Ouvert Morning* explores the lives of the tormented Grant family in Woodbrook, a fusty suburb of Port of Spain. It is an unpleasant, disgruntled, and abrasive family bound together, paradoxically, by alienation rather than affection. Darkness seems to be the novel's dominant metaphor, and this is matched by a pervasive claustrophobia, which is suggested from time to time in the mountains enclosing Ellerslie Park, the ritzy suburb to which John and Elaine Grant aspire. Each member of the family, from Mervyn, the ineffectual, placid head, to the embittered, obnoxious adolescent Junior is unwilling or unable to come to terms with a neurotic sense of failure. All of them, including Helen, the priggish matriarch, seek refuge in ultimately unrewarding shelters—drink and maudlin, unfulfilling religion for one, womanizing for another, a fashionable house in Ellerslie Park for a third, an ill-conceived, abortive revolution for yet another.

Pan Beat is undoubtedly the better of the two novels. The writing is facile and coherent, and the major characters are drawn in depth and with insight and sensitivity. *J'Ouvert Morning* shows signs of careless composition and, alas, little revision. The tautness of *Pan Beat* is missing; the writing is often desultory, the syntax uncommonly clumsy, and Jones's attempts at stream of consciousness, which works rather effectively in the first novel, peter out into a disconcerting incoherence. Even so, *J'Ouvert Morning* should not be dismissed out of hand; it is full of penetrating insights into Trinidadian and, by extension, West Indian society; and some of the characters, the pathetic Elizabeth, for instance, are potentially fascinating and deserve, indeed, a better-crafted novel.

Marion Patrick Jones concentrates largely on the unique flavor of Trinidad society, which she uses to illuminate the frustrated, often unrewarding lives of her men and women. She is interested, one feels, in the obsessive, driven personality, and Earline Hill is the most fully embodied example of the type. The feisty Earline is a sort of Flying Dutchman figure, forever doomed to chase the phantom of Dave Chow, whose suicide turns her into a vengeful London whore forever handicapped by Dave's betrayal. But underneath Earline's brash, cynical exterior there is a fragile, vulnerable woman subconsciously seeking redemption and living continually just this side of hysteria. Cool on the surface, she is tormented by primal drives she does not fully understand. Repelled early in life by the smallness and claustrophobia of Trinidad—and there is an implication here of intellectual and artistic smallness—Earline leaves for London and New York only to discover, with Monday morning hindsight, as it were, that she too must suffer the typical West Indian *angst*—dread and love of her small, insular roots: "There just came a time," she says, "when Central Park couldn't be stretched into looking like Trinidad for a single second longer. I believe that it is the hills that put me right. They center my soul" (*Pan Beat*, pp. 10–11). In New York she straightens her hair and passes for Brazilian. This denial of her West Indianness is only temporary, however; eventually she comes to recognize in herself another typical West Indian schizophrenia—denial of, but deep and lasting attraction for, one's irreversible West Indianness. But Earline's experiences abroad also help to exacerbate her island's insularity: her family seems Puritanical and shallow, and she is repelled by the tightness of a somewhat moribund Woodbrook. Only the lambent beauty of the foothills around Port of Spain's famous Savannah brings her fleeting moments of inner peace. Other furies also plague her. Earline, for all her jaunty sensuality, nurses a cleverly disguised hatred for men that surfaces in her relationship with Alan Hastings, another disaffected Trinidadian, estranged from an embittered and shrewish wife, and bitter about having been born in Trinidad. His relationship with his ex-prostitute mother, moreover, is latently incestuous. Meanwhile, his tenuous association with the well-heeled men and women of oil-rich Southern Trinidad urges him to seek an identity in his Mercedes Benz, an ephemeral but nonetheless important security blanket for him.

In *J'Ouvert Morning* Marion Jones probes the fragile psyche of Mervyn Grant, "a second-class clerk in a second-class government office" (p. 79). As a youngster, he had been infected with all the viruses of youth—falling in love at first sight, for instance. Instead, he has to settle for a more prosaic relationship with Helen, whose pregnancy forces him to marry her. The honeymoon, we notice, is ruined by the unromantic sound of the bride's continual vomiting. One thinks here of Elaine Grant, Mervyn's harassed daughter-in-law, who planned her whole world at nineteen and whose triumph of owning a house in Ellerslie Park is soured by her husband's blatant and unrepentant philandering. The happiness she set out to achieve turns into "a giant lie with none of us getting anywhere, with nothing behind us and nothing before us" (p. 193). Frustrated by a society where there is neither recompense nor retribution, Mervyn, for his part, prefers to escape in fantasy and self-pity, dreaming about fighting "like hell in a blitz over London" (p. 79) and marrying a fair English rose.

Two other types of severely disturbed human beings interest Marion Patrick Jones: the emotionally immobilized man and the disillusioned woman. Of these Father Leslie Oliver, Denise Jenkins, and Elizabeth Grant are perhaps the most engaging. Alienated at St. Mary's among his Irish colleagues, Leslie is uncertain of his vocation and, moreover, cannot cope with the loneliness and celibacy of the religious life. His usefulness as a priest is also hobbled by chronic anxiety about a seemingly unintelligible world. He is also an ambivalent, deeply insecure man, hounded by sex and terrified of using up his weekly quota of cigarettes. Much of Leslie's character is summed up in the following: "He was just an old sexless priest, getting older. . . . At sixty he would get a rest from the continual battle against his desire for a woman, but then he would be . . . too old for anyone to care for" (*Pan Beat*, p. 104). This sort of character might easily have become an uninteresting stereotype; instead, Marion Jones turns him into a vulnerable, sympathetic human being. We notice this, for instance, in his anxiety-ridden relationship with Denise, whose fetching sexuality and emotional vulnerability force him to become increasingly introspective and a more tolerant person. Denise, indeed, is a fully realized person, and some of the best sections of *Pan Beat* are her brooding interior monologues. She is an unfulfilled artist who carries around with her—like a recurring toothache—the ego-destroying experience of failure and the familiar claustrophobia. Her husband's dream of creating a new and perfect society is shattered when he is murdered in a steelband war. She reminds us of Elizabeth, the "failed nun, the failed heroine" of *J'Ouvert Morning*. She, too, had put her faith in a false messiah—the effervescent but vulnerable Ray Burnett, who believes that his mission is to bring salvation to the wretched of the earth. She also makes the fatal mistake of believing "in all of the things we were taught to believe in" (p. 127). Insanity is the price she pays for this; but Denise, who is spared madness, eventually comes to worship all of the gods of middle-class respectability. There is also Tony Joseph, Earline's torpid, rather inept friend. Emotionally crippled by the premature death of his adolescent sweetheart, he seems to have become a fossil, unwilling to leave Trinidad and sharing an obviously submerged incestuous relationship with his sister, who is herself abused by her brutish husband.

Pan Beat and *J'Ouvert Morning* are in many ways pungent and disquieting explorations of Trinidad society in both the pre- and post-independence periods. The island's preoccupation with things American is an implicit criticism in both novels. The men of Alan's Staff Club, for instance, are without identity and are obsessed with New York, seeing that city as the measure of all things good and true. V. S. Naipaul has written candidly of this fixation in his notorious *The Middle Passage*. Modernity in Trinidad, Naipaul wrote in 1962, means "a constant alertness, a willingness to change, a readiness to accept anything which films, magazines, and comic strips appear to indicate as American" (1962; [New York: Penguin, 1969], p. 45). Twenty-two years later Naipaul's criticism, alas, is still valid. Meanwhile, Trinidadians have not lost all of their scorn for things Trinidadian. The steelband is now accepted as a unique contribution to the world of music, but this was not always so. In *Pan Beat* Louis Jenkins, who sees the seed of a West Indian identity in the creation of the remarkable steelband, is regarded as a crazy fanatic. His mother is typically contemptuous of the steelband and would prefer to see her son studying the violin instead. Albert Gomes has commented on this middle-class contempt in his autobiography, and it is worth quoting: "It was the illiterate and semi-illiterate Negroes who kept the ancestral fires burning . . . who filled the Calypso tents with song and music in the early days before this Aristophanic art form became a tourist attraction . . . who invented the steelband and fought and died to keep it alive so that it would become eventually a status symbol . . . of the same middle-class, who during its embryonic period joined forces with British officialdom . . . to stamp it out as another culturally retrogressive influence" (*Through a Maze of Color* [Port of Spain: Key Caribbean, 1974], p. 82).

Those who read the high-voltage novels of, say, Naipaul and Lamming may be inclined to give *Pan Beat* and *J'Ouvert Morning* short shrift. The second novel is severely flawed, to be sure; but together with *Pan Beat* it does explore areas sometimes considered too banal and insignificant for serious literary treatment. But the slums and lower middle-class areas of Port of Spain are indeed worth exploring, as Earl Lovelace, another Trinidadian novelist, recognizes and has effectively done in *While Gods Are Falling* (1965) and *The Dragon Can't Dance* (1979). The squalor of Lovelace's Port of Spain, where "life has no significance beyond the primary struggles for a bed to sleep in, something to quiet the intestines, and moments of sexual gratification" (*While Gods Are Falling*, p. 8), reminds us of Marion Jones's *Behind the Bridge*. Human beings do live in the slums and semi-slums of Port of Spain, and their lives, cabined, cribbed, and confined by "scrunting"—to use Marion Jones's word—are as important as those in the fashionable suburbs.

The world of *Pan Beat* and *J'Ouvert Morning* is often "a lengthening darkness" (*J'Ouvert Morning*, p. 1); but it is not irreversibly murky. Nor is the nihilism altogether pervasive. The despair and failure are counteracted by two disarmingly simple but evocative images: the beautiful flamingo, which is set against the squalor of shantytown in *J'Ouvert Morning* and the uncommon presence of grass growing in a scarred Laventille playground in *Pan Beat*.

CRITICAL RECEPTION

Marion Patrick Jones's fiction has, unfortunately, been neglected. *Pan Beat* and *J'Ouvert Morning* are listed in the second edition of Kenneth Ramchand's *The West Indian Novel and its Background* (1983), but her work is not discussed. In Donald Herdeck's *Caribbean Writers* (1979), *Pan Beat* is said to capture ''the growing crisis of racial and national identity of [Trinidad] and particularly of the failure of the middle-class of the 1940s in the crisis of under-development'' (p. 109). *J'Ouvert Morning* is described as ''a warm study of the passionate, often defeated people spanning three generations in a place much like Trinidad'' (p. 109). Andrew Salkey's perceptive introduction to *Pan Beat* emphasizes the novel's ''poetic prose which accurately matches the mood and tone of the narrative content.'' This poetic prose, he adds, ''is deeply rooted in the meaning and momentum of the story.''

Salkey also praises the unique structure of *Pan Beat*, in which ''the leading characters are actually those on the periphery of the narrative, an ironical reflection of the position of their real-life human counterparts on the outermost rim of the society.'' He is equally impressed by Jones's ''depiction of the strength, courage, and gritty integrity of Trinidadian women,'' and he mentions Jones's treatment of the symbolic steelband ''in the historical formation and thrust of Trinidad and Tobago.'' The central meaning of *Pan Beat*, Salkey argues, is ''that both middle-class aspirations and those of the dispossessed usually come to nothing, if only because the inherited political, economic, and social systems are so rigidly opposed to their breakthrough.''

Harold Barratt emphasizes the social realism of Jones's novels and her candid portrait of Port of Spain's slums (''A Shuttered Cleavage,'' 1980, p. 58). He discusses Jones's treatment of the neurotic Trinidadian circumscribed by the insularity and claustrophobia of a small island. He also examines Jones's use of stream of consciousness and shows that, while it is largely effective in *Pan Beat*, it degenerates into ''desultory writing'' and ''clumsy syntax'' in *J'Ouvert Morning* (p. 58). The article also draws tenuous parallels between Jones's work and that of Sam Selvon, V. S. Naipaul, and Earl Lovelace.

HONORS AND AWARDS

In 1950 Marion Patrick Jones won the prestigious Girls Open Island Scholarship, the equivalent of the all-male scholarship, which was won, incidentally, by V. S. Naipaul, her distinguished compatriot. She also has the distinction of being the first of two women ever accepted by the Imperial College of Tropical Agriculture.

BIBLIOGRAPHY

Works by Marion Patrick Jones

Pan Beat. Port of Spain: Columbus, 1973.
J'Ouvert Morning. Port of Spain: Columbus, 1976.

Studies of Marion Patrick Jones

Barratt, Harold. "A Shuttered Cleavage: Marion Jones' Tormented People." *World Literature Written in English* 19 (Spring 1980), pp. 57–62.

———. "Marion Patrick Jones Weaves a Rich Fabric of Life in Trinidad and Tobago with the Novels of Steelband and Mas'." *People* (Port of Spain) (February 1980), 54–55.

Salkey, Andrew. Introduction to *Pan Beat*. Port of Spain: Columbus, 1973.

See also General Bibliography: Allis and Herdeck.

ARTHUR DRAYTON

Ismith Khan (1925–   )

BIOGRAPHY

Ismith Khan, the only son among five children, was born on March 16, 1925, in Port of Spain, Trinidad, opposite the very Woodford Square that features so prominently in his first novel, *The Jumbie Bird* (1961). His parents, Faiez and Zinab Khan, were both Pathans, as was his paternal grandfather, Kale Khan, the original of the grandfather of the same name in the *The Jumbie Bird*. Like his fictional namesake, his grandfather was fiercely proud of his military past and Pathan origins in India. Ismith Khan observes with a tinge of ancestral pride that the Pathans are "this group of people who are in the hills of Afghanistan right now fighting with the Russians, and they are a very colorful people." (interview with Daryl Cumber Dance, Anaheim, California, August 14, 1981).

The young Ismith was the center of his grandfather's attention and grew up in a home and an ethnic community in which Kale Khan was something of a legend. At a time when almost to a man Indians in Trinidad not locally born had been brought to the island as indentured laborers, including Ismith Khan's maternal relations, Kale Khan was proud of the distinction of having migrated a free man. He had taken his family first to then British Guiana and some fifteen years later to Trinidad. There they took up residence at Princess Town, a southern township with a large Indian population in the vicinity of sugar plantations and later to be the scene of one of Trinidad's important Hosein riots. Kale Khan owned two revolvers, being called upon as a jeweler to travel regularly with valuables and cash. The riot scene in *The Jumbie Bird* faithfully records how the use of those revolvers elevated him to the status of hero in his community. Back in India "during one of the uprisings, when Indians were called upon to shoot Indians, he fired at the British, chucked the military, and took off with his family. . . . My grandfather was ever involved in all things anti-British . . . his was a rebelliousness, his life was one of dissent, he ridiculed the Raj, [and] chastised fellow Indians for being run over roughshod by the Sahibs" (private correspondence, Ismith Khan to Arthur Drayton, October 29, 1983).

It is clear from his novels that Ismith Khan was influenced by two not unrelated Kale Khans, the Indian nationalist and the anti-colonialist. In Trinidad the one would express itself mainly through agitation for the return of Indians to a resurgent India and the other in a perception of poverty and oppression as a direct result of British colonialism. It would appear that the latter was the more influential in shaping the novelist-to-be. Other early experiences no doubt catalyzed this. Hailing from a Muslim family, Ismith the boy was educated first at an Anglican church school in the city and then at the prestigious nondenominational Queen's Royal College, at the time only barely accessible to the poor of the colony. It is not inconceivable that like Jamini, the young protagonist in *The Jumbie Bird*, he experienced there, or knew others who did, the uncomfortable sense of not belonging socially and economically. Then, too, living at the heart of the city close to both the colonial legislature and the City Council, he was aware of and witnessed the political commotion of the 1940s, heady and theatrical, sometimes spilling over into the streets, always making the national headlines as the twin-island colony struggled through its birth pains of democracy. Not much later he would become a reporter on the staff of the Trinidad *Guardian*; and if this led him to appreciate the power of the word and pointed him ultimately in the direction of creative literature, it also, in his own words, "did sharpen my interests, not only in the Indian community, but the island as a whole, all of its peoples, its direction" (private correspondence, Khan to Drayton, October 29, 1983). The grandson of Kale Khan had begun to bring to bear on his vision of the new natal land the political instincts of his illustrious grandfather.

It is in keeping with this development that his chosen path on leaving Trinidad would lead him to a B.A. in sociology at the New School for Social Research in New York (after a brief spell at Michigan State University) and an M.A. in creative writing at Johns Hopkins University, Baltimore, Maryland, where his thesis submission was a still unpublished short novel, "The Crucifixion."

Looking back at this period and beyond, he thinks it would have been impossible to become a writer if he had remained at home, a view shared by most English-speaking Caribbean writers who chose in the 1950s to live abroad. In the Dance interview Khan amplifies:

> Apart from the community as an audience, I think that for myself I really needed a community of writers and artists when I wished to become a writer, and it was most helpful to me. I think that at the point in time when I wished to be a writer, there wasn't

> that kind of ambiance in the Caribbean . . . I found it in New York [at] the New School for Social Research. . . . And while I came from the kind of background that I did and was trying to do something with that, it was nonetheless very important to me to be in the company of these people and exchange ideas with them and have some sort of picture of where is literature headed, where is painting headed, where is sculpture headed, how are all these arts related to one another. And I don't think that it would have been possible to find an ambiance like that in the Caribbean.

He lived in Manhattan for eighteen years and between 1955 and 1970 held various jobs in the East, including that of research assistant at Cornell University in the Department of Far Eastern Studies (1955–56), instructor in creative writing at the New School for Social Research (1956–69), and teaching assistant in writing at Johns Hopkins University (1969–70). In 1970 he moved to California, where he was first a visiting professor in the Department of English at Berkeley (1970–71) and then taught Caribbean and comparative literature at the University of California, San Diego (1971–74), the University of Southern California (1977), and California State College, Long Beach (1978–81).

Twice married and the father of one daughter and an adopted son, Ismith Khan moved back to New York in 1982, where he now writes full time. Although none of his published work so far has been set in the United States, he has been gradually extending his interests to include the impact of social changes on human relationships in his country of adoption. Work recently completed or in progress includes two short stories set in Trinidad, but also three novellas and a full-length novel set in New York and in California.

MAJOR WORKS AND THEMES

Ismith Khan was preempted by colleagues in the fictional treatment of East Indians in the Caribbean. But it was left to him in his first novel, *The Jumbie Bird*, to treat of the historically antecedent traumatic experience of indenture, and in this respect he remains unique. Indenture is but a trace element in Edgar Mittelholzer's first two novels, as it also was in Seepersad Naipaul's work, later published as *The Adventures of Gurudeva and Other Stories* (London: André Deutsch, 1976); and no others come as close to the subject as do these.

The Jumbie Bird presents the tragic story of East Indians stranded in Trinidad, betrayed by the authorities who had lured them into indenture with promises now largely unfulfilled, and forgotten and discarded by Mother India. We get an early glimpse of "old and decrepit Indians [who] . . . had left the sugar plantations long ago and come to the city" (p. 27). How close to the historical reality this depiction is can be gauged by comparing the detail presented in chapter 2 with nonfictional accounts, such as Albert Gomes, *Through a Maze of Colour* (Port of Spain: Key Caribbean, 1974).

But not all East Indians were the broken remains of the indenture system. Ismith Khan's paternal grandparents take their historical place in this novel as free migrants, and the enduring pride of the real life and the fictional Kale Khan derives from this. The novel also presents successful professionals and businessmen, like Samuel Salwan, obsequious in the presence of colonial officials, distant and arrogant in his relationship with his less fortunate countrymen, East Indians who "could no longer cross their legs and eat on level ground like their parents did" but who know how to "turn Indian overnight" when there is a situation inviting ethnic exploitation (pp. 183, 185). By assembling a variety of East Indian responses to the historical situation, the novel avoids the more emotional but perhaps also less momentous theme of the Indian in a hostile plural society and examines instead the enveloping colonial miasma that is ultimately responsible for their condition and to which they must respond creatively. Thus the tragic undertow of the story depends less on the depiction of those derelict lives in Woodford Square and more on the perception of certain ironies. Kale Khan flees the inequities of British colonialism in India only to encounter them again within the narrower compass of Trinidad. Or again, the Indians are brought to Trinidad in conditions that encourage and facilitate the retention of religious customs and traditions; yet once they are stranded in Trinidad it is necessary to modify their way of life if they are to survive in these new circumstances—only they are to surrender parts of their traditional culture to enter and become part of a host society that is as yet unlicked and unformed.

The novel's most recurrent motif is death, and it speaks to several issues, most obviously the death of the Indian dream of repatriation. But alongside this there is also the symbolic death that renews, that is to say, the death of an old way of life and the birth of a new, pointed in Kale Khan's Christ-like sacrificial death. Above all it speaks to the decay of the colonial condition. On the very first page of the prologue the jumbie bird's call, "a message of death," is hurled as a "fearful reminder" to people and institutions: lovers in nocturnal embrace (a symbol of hope and the future), the Town Hall and the Red House (seats of municipal and national government), Trinity Church (actually the Anglican cathedral), and Woodford Square (the *enduring* symbol of the past living on into the present). The almost verbatim repetition of the prologue as the beginning of the penultimate chapter of the novel and the reappearance of the bird in between emphasize the structural significance which Ismith Khan is feeling for. Within this frame we are treated to several glimpses of the realities of colonial life, instance after instance of its spiritual, social, economic, and physical impoverishment.

The bird reappears once more at the beginning of the final chapter, in which Kale Khan dies, as if the bird's call were for him. But the hour of his death is also the hour of liberation for Jamini, the grandson who had increasingly fallen under the old man's repatriation spell, the third generation in whom the promise of adjustment to the new land ought to be found. And so it comes to pass that Ismith Khan places the last reference to the bird (but not an actual reappearance) in a significantly different context and outside the frame that encloses all but the last few pages of the novel:

> When the sun came up in the morning, the old woman was the first to rise. From his room behind the coal shop, the boy could hear the sounds to which he was becoming accustomed. *They were no longer bird calls* nor wind in the trees. He heard the old woman place her feet in her slippers, then, as if she were stretching her body, he heard her sigh, and then she was moving about. Later on, he could hear her at the pipe in the yard gurgling water in her throat, then spitting it out. Then it was time for him to get out of bed and help her in the coal shop. (p. 217; emphasis added)

This complete identification with the industrious, resourceful, adaptive grandmother, Binti, comes after Kale's death, beyond the reach of the bird's message, outside the symbolic frame of death and its messenger, where the motifs are of renewal, of the possibility of growth.

The story of *The Jumbie Bird* is about three generations of East Indians in Trinidad, represented by Kale Khan, his son Rahim, and his grandson Jamini; and the underlying trichotomy is important for the novel's theme of death and renewal. Kale Khan's nationalistic urge to return to India and the desperation with which his less fortunate countrymen share that sentiment are understandable. In the end, however, as we listen to the frigid rationality of the Indian commissioner, which is in reality Mother India's, and try to relate Kale's death to this, we take stock of the true nature of his failure. This unrelenting nationalist also had interesting and reliable insights into the nature of colonialism and knew how crucial it is for the individual in a colonial society to find and fulfill himself through self-respect as well as through commitment to others, to community. But these fine qualities do not appear to come together in him to produce a whole person. His deep love for his son and his grandson in reality masks a deeper-seated desire for his reincarnation in his male offspring, and his sense of the importance of continuity and indeed community is tainted by an enormous egoism.

Just how incomplete he is as a person is well brought out in his relationship with his wife. Deserted by Kale, Binti remains kind, gentle, and loving and is on hand to restore him to some semblance of health when she finds him lying alone in his room ominously ill, a scene in which the author points the latent symbolism of the restorative act (p. 173). But it is only to the old self, not to a new personhood, that he is restored. Still a loner and feeble as he is, he rouses himself to a final display of his erstwhile prowess as a stickfighter and in the process brings about his death.

Kale Khan's fatal weakness as heroic leader is brought out in the death scene. So egotistically consumed by the cause is he that he seeks to assume it and the glory of the group within his own person. But it is a dead cause, and this reality which he had tried to suppress now rises to destroy him. The rich symbolism of the episode invites us to interpret Kale's death as due to a self-serving rigidity reminiscent of Achebe's Okonkwo in *Things Fall Apart* (London: Heinemann, 1958), an unyielding but vain attempt to epitomize in himself a way of life for which there was no longer a future. The torch is passed on to a younger generation, represented in the youthful stickfighter and the rejuvenated Rahim.

Rahim is the second generation of Khans in Trinidad and the first to be born there. Ismith Khan portrays this generation as transitional, and for this purpose he departs from the autobiographical facts. Whereas his father was a strong person, in the novel Rahim is weak. As a transplanted Indian he is also lost: ''We ain't belong to Hindustan, we ain't belong to England, we ain't belong to Trinidad'' (p. 68). We witness his decline as the novel progresses and begin to feel, as Okonkwo did in *Things Fall Apart*, that the father's fire has brought forth ash. In him we see that it is one thing to be freed from the enfeebling, futile imprisonment within a memory of the motherland but another to develop the resourcefulness necessary to cope with the new circumstances. Ismith Khan presents the emptiness of colonial life in terms of the characters' perception of eventlessness and their acceptance of mere diurnality and identifies Rahim with this condition. But later, restored to his manhood by his mother and his wife and no longer emasculated by the colonial system or corrupted by it as are Gopal the doctor and Salwan the lawyer, Rahim is now able to give to his son a new sense of direction. Ismith Khan provides just the merest of hints that in Binti and Meena and the rejuvenated Rahim we have East Indians conscious of their origin and nourished by those roots but oriented to the climate and demands of their new environment.

Jamini, as is true of first or second natal generations in the new land, is a more integral part of the new society but also grows up under the spell of his grandfather and of Mother India. The logic of the novel requires that he be liberated from the sentimental embrace of the past, and Kale Khan's death is accordingly presented in sacrificial terms. But the future which he faces will be fraught with all the dangers of a colonialism now at high noon. So the new Rahim delivers the crucial lecture, denying the reification and nihilism of colonialism through individual fulfillment and a conviction of the uniqueness and the adequacy of the self: ''A man have to find work in this world, he have to do something that great—I don't mean big—I mean something that only he could give to the world. . . . because if a man can't find that something then he life finish!'' (p. 223)

It is appropriate that Rahim should pass on to his son these sentiments (which look forward to the second novel), acquired in his turn from his father, and that he should couch them in terms of creativity, for the ever present filigree motif deriving from their jeweler's craft on another level represents the creative response required of the individual for fulfillment and survival. Throughout the novel it is a countervailing image to that of death, and through the repetition of the motif in Rahim's lecture to Jamini we are reminded for the last time that Kale Khan's death was not in vain.

Khan's second novel, *The Obeah Man* (1964), confirms his primary interest in the colonial rather than the ethnic experience. The major characters are emblematic of Trinidad's ethnic potpourri. Of Zampi the Obeah man: ''he was the end of masses of assimilations and mixtures, having the eyes of the East Indian, the build of the Negro, the skin of the Chinese, and some of the colour of all''

(p. 11); of him and Massahood the stickman: ''Their chocolate-brown faces bore the same question mark of lost races and cultures'' (p. 32); and of Zolda, the woman for whose affection they compete: ''All the races that had lingered lost in these island blossomed in her face'' (p. 164). It projects a sense of the unifying if also the divisive aspects of the colonial experience. In the Dance interview Khan draws attention to the strength and resilience which both Africans and Indians needed as transplanted peoples in order to survive. Certainly his presentation in *The Jumbie Bird* of the back-to-India movement brings to mind similarities with Garveyism and Rastafarianism; and the arrival of the Indian commissioner in that novel is an uncanny foreshadowing of Haile Selassie's historic visit to Jamaica in the late 1960s. To be aware of these things is to be prepared for *The Obeah Man* as a novel of the colonial condition.

Emptiness and lack of direction are portrayed as characteristic features of that condition. This view of the society is emphasized over and over again in the novel and made all the more emphatic by the immersion of the action in the hedonism of the annual Carnival—itself presented as a microcosm of the year-long meaningless colonial life. The voluptuous Zolda and the self-indulgent, pleasure-seeking Massahood are standouts in a mass of rum-drinking, night-clubbing escapists. But Zampi the Obeah man and Hop-and-Drop the cripple are even more important. Hop-and-Drop is intended to be symbolic of the colonial condition. A cripple and a mendicant, at Carnival he is dressed in an absurd back-to-front costume. His makeshift home, like his life, is made up of ''discarded ends of other people's lives'' (p. 184).

Set over and against all these characters is Zampi. Called to the office of Obeah man, he renounces his former hedonism and strains every nerve to make his life whole and wholesome and in humbly rendering service to try to help others to do the same with theirs. In the end he even persuades Zolda to abandon the hollow city and return to his love and caring in the hills above Blue Basin. Khan intends Zampi to be the representation of possibilities. Others together represent acceptance of the colonial condition and destiny or frustrated attempts to alter it. But Zampi, himself frustrated in realizing his boyhood dreams of being a doctor, snaps out of the colonial syndrome that attends such frustrations, dredges deeply within his being, and learns to be himself, to care for others, to serve with humility, and to help others find a center and meaning in their lives. As Obeah man he is diviner, spiritual guide, physical healer (herbalist), and magical transformer, all of these functions being symbolic of the internal resources which the colonial society must mobilize for its restoration.

Ismith Khan's greatest triumph in this novel is his serious treatment of Obeah. By presenting the story largely from Zampi's point of view, Khan is committed to an exploration of Obeah culture from the inside. Earnest but humble and unassuming, Zampi sets out responsibly to learn the mysteries of that calling and to respect its limitations, to sort out which of his achievements are due to his herbal skills, which to psychology, and which to mystic power. But to whatever these phenomenal manifestations are to be ascribed, to him they are real, as indeed they are also to everybody else. To be sure, there are skeptics, but skepticism is never carried to the lengths of reckless disbelief. The result is a rendering of marvelous realism that compares favorably with other instances of the treatment of Obeah in Caribbean and Latin American literature, and even with the portrayal of the *dibia* in the novels of the Nigerian, Elechi Amadi.

CRITICAL RECEPTION

Ismith Khan seems not to have caught the attention of a critic until the appearance of his second novel, and to date no one has done any extended study of his work. *The Obeah Man* is praised in a 1965 review for bringing "a new and exciting voice but also a structure and concentration . . . unusual in a Caribbean novel." His eye for detail is compared favorably with V. S. Naipaul's "but he writes with love . . . [giving to his poverty-ridden characters] a scale and dignity that is missing in Naipaul's street people." His handling of the English language is "exotic and baroque" and the characters' "language of the streets . . . moves with its own poetry" (M. S. Blundell, 1965, pp. 95–97).

The Obeah Man also shares with some nine other novels a brief section on "Obeah and Cult Practices" in Kenneth Ramchand's *The West Indian Novel and its Background* (1970, pp. 123–31). In this company Ismith Khan stands out as the only West Indian novelist to make an Obeah man his central character, though "in the process, a highly personal view of obeah as a spiritual vocation is disclosed" (p. 126). In Ramchand's opinion, the Obeah man sees himself as an artist, and as such must come to "accept alienation as the painful condition of art" (p. 126). Only then does he attain to a kind of peace in a blighted world, where up to now he had been ill at ease. But for Ramchand Zampi's peace is "a naive philosophy of self-control" (p. 127) so central to the theme that though credible enough when presented dramatically within the Obeah man's consciousness, it becomes "a crude externalization" (p. 127) in the Zampi–Zolda relationship and causes the novel to fail.

BIBLIOGRAPHY

Works by Ismith Khan

"In the Subway." *New Voices* 2 (1958), 451–55.

The Jumbie Bird. London: MacGibbon & Kee, 1961; New York: Obolensky, 1962; London: Longman, 1974; London: Longman, 1985.

"A Day in the Country." *Colorado Quarterly* (Autumn 1962), 121–35; *Cornhill Magazine* (Spring 1964), 52–55; in *From the Green Antilles*,ed. B. Howes (New York: Macmillan, 1966), pp. 48–62.

The Obeah Man. London: Hutchinson, 1964.

"The Red Ball." In *New Writing in the Caribbean*, ed. A. J. Seymour (Georgetown, Guyana: Caribbean Festival of the Arts, 1972), pp. 226–33; in *Caribbean Stories*, ed. Michael Marland (London: Longman, 1979); trans. into Tamil in *Manjari*

(Madras, India) (April 1980); in *Short Story International* (Great Neck, N.Y.) 18, (February 1980).

''Dialect in West Indian Literature.'' In *The Black Writer in Africa and the Americas*, ed. Lloyd W. Brown. Los Angeles: Hennessey & Ingalls, 1973, pp. 141–64.

''The Village Shop.'' In *Lambailey*, ed. Ron Heapy and Anne Garside. London: Oxford University Press, 1979.

Studies of Ismith Khan

Blundell, M. S. Review of *The Obeah Man*. *Caribbean Quarterly* 11 (March and June 1965), 95–97.

Brown, Steward, intro. *The Jumbie Bird*, Longman, 1985.

Lacovia, R. M. ''Ismith Khan and the Theory of Rasa.'' *Black Images* (Autumn-Winter 1972), 23–27.

See also General Bibliography: Allis, Herdeck, Hughes, and Ramchand (1970).

BRYANT MANGUM

Jamaica Kincaid (1949–   )

BIOGRAPHY

Jamaica Kincaid was born May 25, 1949, at Holberton Hospital, St. John's, Antigua. In her characteristic style she describes the island as she remembers it: "I grew up on an island in the West Indies which has an area of a hundred and eight square miles. On the island were many sugarcane fields. . . . There were cotton fields, but there were not as many cotton fields as there were sugarcane fields. There were arrowroot fields and tobacco fields, too, but there were not as many arrowroot fields and tobacco fields as there were cotton fields" ("The Talk of the Town," *The New Yorker* 53 [October 17, 1977], 37). She recalls particularly the beauty of early mornings on Antigua and the sound of goats which awakened her family and neighboring families every morning at half past five. Most of the island's inhabitants worked as carpenters, masons, servants in private homes, seamstresses, tailors, shopkeepers, fishermen, or dockworkers. Some grew crops, which they brought to market in St. John's on Saturday mornings. And "a small number—a very small number—of the fifty-four thousand people" on the island worked in offices or banks (ibid.).

Her father was a carpenter and cabinetmaker, whom she described to me as being able simply to look at a piece of furniture and make an exact replica of it (telephone interview with Bryant Mangum, February 9, 1985). She has vivid memories of her father's workshop as a place where everything was "some shade of brown" except the red carpenter's pencil that he always carried behind his ear ("The Talk of the Town," *The New Yorker* 58 [January 3, 1983], 23). Her mother, whose own mother was a Carib Indian, came to Antigua from the island of Dominica; and Kincaid described her to me as a very literate, cultured woman with beautiful pensmanship and a love of books, particularly those dealing with science, health, and nutrition. At the age of seven, Kincaid was given an inscribed copy of *The Concise Oxford Dictionary* by her mother and told that she was to begin apprenticing, a custom of nearly all of Kincaid's friends. During much of the time of her education in the government schools of Antigua—among them the Antigua Girls School—she went on Tuesdays and Thursdays from four until six to the house of Miss Doreen, the seamstress to whom she was apprenticed (interview and "The Apprentice," *The New Yorker* 57 [August 17, 1981], 25).

She recalls getting the idea from her father, who was a "critical and dignified man," that Americans were great; and by the time she was nine Kincaid added to her daily prayers the line, "And please, God, let me go to America" ("The Fourth," *The New Yorker* 52 [July 19, 1976], 23). In 1966 she came to America with the idea of pursuing her education. She submitted articles free-lance to various magazines, two of which were published in 1975 in *Ms*. Already her name had appeared in a "Talk of the Town" piece written by her friend George Trow, and with his encouragement and help she became a contributor to *The New Yorker*. From 1976 to the present she has been a *New Yorker* staff writer, contributing some eighty pieces—a few as letters with her name attached, most unsigned, and all unmistakably Kincaid's—to the "Talk of the Town" section, and fourteen stories. Her first volume of stories, *At the Bottom of the River* (1983), contains ten stories, seven of which originally appeared in *The New Yorker*. A volume of stories about a young Antiguan girl (*Annie John*) was published in 1985. Kincaid lives in New York City with her husband, Allen, and their daughter, Annie Shawn.

MAJOR WORKS AND THEMES

With the exception of some 7,000 who have bought and read Jamaica Kincaid's first volume of stories, *At the Bottom of the River*, and now *Annie John*, readers to date have probably read her fiction irregularly and freshly, which is to say when it has been offered, every few months during the last six years by *The New Yorker*, and with very little knowledge of her life and the intricacies of the body of her work. Indeed, there is much to be said for reading her with precisely this kind of innocence: without a knowledge of the artistic and biographical forces at work beneath the surface; and without a sense of the interrelatedness of images from early and later stories. Reading the stories innocently, one cannot miss the hypnotic effect of her incantations, the mysterious and primitive simplicity of her images, the lyrical phrasings of so many of her passages.

"Girl," her first *New Yorker* story, illustrates particularly well the way Kincaid uses ordinary things to create a kind of litany: "Wash the white clothes on Monday and put them on the stone heap; wash the color clothes on Tuesday and put them on the clothesline to dry; don't walk barehead in the hot sun; cook pumpkin fritters in very hot sweet oil . . . " (*At the Bottom of the River*, p. 3). "Letter from Home" shows her modifying these incantations, intentionally undercutting the comforting rhythm of the litanies with contradictory images: "I milked the cows, I churned butter. . . . Tiny beads of water gathered on my nose, my hair went limp, my waist grew folds, I shed my skin" (p. 37). The creation of these litanies and the juxtaposition of seemingly paradoxical images are, of course, but two of many ways that Kincaid gives especially her early stories a quality that invites the reader to see them first as prose poems whose unity depends at least as much on her use of lyrical devices and the development of central images as on the development of a narrative story line. In "Blackness," for example, that quality is described both as having softness and as possessing deafening silence. It is "like soot from a lamp with an untrimmed wick" (p. 46). The real blackness in the story, though, is the abstract thing standing between the narrator and the light, which when seen helps erase the blackness. On practically every line in *At the Bottom of the River*, Kincaid shows the reader new ways of perceiving old things, involves him at a sensory level in experience that he has probably never encountered, and shows him wonder and magic in the most ordinary.

Kincaid's work, however, is considerably more complicated, more intricately fashioned, than it appears on the surface, and perhaps the best way to make this point is to examine alternate kinds of vision that she presents in the pivotal story of her work to date, "At the Bottom of the River," the title story of her first collection. Here the narrator imagines two men. The first, on waking, remains in bed unaware of all the potential that surrounds him and to which he could have access if only he would get up and go out into the world. In refusing to do so this man is missing altogether such things as the knowledge that there can be joy; that there can be contentment such as that reflected in the image of mother and child; that there can be purpose and beauty in the passing of seasons. He is incomplete, and in Kincaid's words, "He sits in nothing, in nothing, in nothing" (p. 64). To this man she compares another who rises after his wife. He eventually crosses his threshold and is pulled outward by the potential for joy that awaits him outside in the form of such things as the sunrise and the sea. But he is also pulled back inside by the knowledge that all of this potential exists in the context of death, specifically that he is himself mortal and subject at any moment to return to dust, a fact that negates for him the happiness that he is capable of experiencing. Because this man is so torn by living in the presence of the knowledge of death, he exists, though less horribly than the first, also in nothing.

The third alternative, and the one to which the reader will return over and over as he reads through Kincaid's work, is offered by the narrator of the story, who has also come into an awareness of the presence of death. All around her she perceives things of beauty that will die; the things that have lived and now are dead. She goes to the river and at its bottom sees an image which transforms her: in the image there is a house of four sides with two windows on each side. Leading up to the house is green grass bordered by flowers, and leading to the flowers are pebbles. She sees a woman come out of the house and look off into the distance. The narrator gets on her knees and looks at the same thing that this woman sees in the distance, a world in which there is no night, a world in which the sun and moon exist together. It is a world which, like the house itself, has not yet been divided. On sharing the vision of the woman at the bottom of the river, the girl is able to return to the real, concrete world of her own room, seeing the things in it by the lamplight, ''complete, my name filling up my mouth'' (p. 82). Her lesson from this vision is embodied in a metaphorical creature, neither male nor female, who learned the deliciousness of all of life and who, now dead, has left behind a light glowing faintly in the darkness, a light that the narrator has taken into herself.

The reader interested in the philosophical vision that informs all of Kincaid's work must come to terms with the allegory in ''At the Bottom of the River.'' At its most basic level the story affirms the fall of man from innocence into knowledge. Based simply on the fact that the narrator is able to return in her vision to the undivided world, the reader may infer that the knowledge of the prelapsarian world constantly lures the individual who feels its existence back into union with it. In specific terms this accounts for the violently negative reactions of so many of Kincaid's characters when they are forced to endure any kind of separation, perhaps the most excruciatingly painful example of which is the separation of daughter from mother in the story ''My Mother.'' This fear of separation and longing for reunion with the remembered world is also the thing that causes the narrator of ''In the Night'' to create a fantasy of complete happiness as a situation in which she will grow up to marry a woman who will tell her every night a story that begins ''Before you were born'' (p. 12). This desire to go back to a world of wholeness also accounts in part for the appeal of dreaming, where things run together in paradoxical ways, as they might have run together before they were divided by reason. In her dream the narrator of ''In the Night'' can resurrect Mr. Gishard, who has died. She can also reconcile in dreams her love of her father with the fear that he, like Mr. Gishard, will die; and she can reconcile her love for him with what ordinarily might be a loathing for the fact that he is a nightsoil man and that he eats the intestines of animals stuffed with blood and rice.

The reality of the actual world in which people must live, of course, invariably intrudes on the remembered world of harmony as well as the dream world which attempts to recapture it and confronts Kincaid's narrators with truths that they have known and often tried to ignore: that people die; that they hurt each other; that they must be separated from people they love; that one must live in the world with the knowledge that he will die. In short, the narrators in the early stories are most often like the man on the threshold in the ''At the Bottom of the River'' allegory, and for this reason many of the stories offer variations on the mythic story of the fall of man. ''What Have I Been Doing Lately,'' for instance, tells of a little girl who is lying in bed before the doorbell rings and who imagines two versions of a story to be told in response to the imagined question about what she has been doing lately. In both answers the girl tells of intentionally falling into a hole, in effect an acknowledgment, on her part, of the fall of man. In the hole there is writing that she cannot read, an indication that she does not know how to deal with the fall; and so she climbs back out, attempting to deny her knowledge. In one version she thinks of building a bridge or taking a boat across the sea, and she becomes sad. In another she throws a rock at a monkey three times and he throws it back. Both versions of the story underline the point that things are separate from each other: land from land and man from other creatures. The story looks ahead to "At the Bottom of the River," where the androgenous creature learns that if he insists on chasing a bee he will be stung, and through that experience he learns the secret that one must allow each thing in the world to exist exactly as it is.

Story after story in *At the Bottom of the River* shows men and women in varying degrees of alienation from themselves, from each other, and from the wholeness and completeness that characterize the harmonious prelapsarian world. In "Holidays," after debating all of the things that she can do to have fun the narrator finally writes a letter which she will not mail and then chooses the oblivion of a nap over all the other things she might enjoy. The second section of the story shows men who will play cards and be "so pained, so unsettled" (p. 33). Another pictures skunks getting dogs, who will be washed with tomato juice; one of the most disturbing images is of a blind man who has killed a woman he loved and tried to commit suicide, succeeding only in blinding himself. Now he casts only a fat shadow. The irony is that all of this occurs during the holidays, when one is free to celebrate the harmony of creation. In "Wingless" a woman smiles at a man and slays him; she also takes pleasure in frightening her daughter. And aware of all of this the narrator vacillates between being cruel and careless and innocent: "I shall cast a shadow and I shall remain unaware" (p. 27).

Thus far, therefore, the allegory in "At the Bottom of the River" has provided two different kinds of vision. The first is that of the man who simply refuses to accept the burden of consciousness, an alternative that is not really an option for Kincaid's characters. The second is the one that most of them have chosen, or more accurately, inherited: that of living with the knowledge of their mortality and with the understanding that such things as beauty and joy are subject to destruction without warning, a fact which creates frustration and despair. And moreover, memories of wholeness and completeness compound the frustration. In the early stories Kincaid presents the human dilemma inherent in this second alternative in the form of verbal collages which show people existing between the world of harmony and that of lost oneness with nature. A character, for example, becomes frightened to look down at an ash-colored piece of her foot: "And how powerful I then found that moment, so that I was not at one with myself and I felt myself separate, like a brittle substance dashed and shattered, each separate part without knowledge of the other separate parts" ("Blackness," pp. 47–48). Or there is a memory of the patterns that sunlight used to make when it came through the floorboards of the house, and of how at night one had to clean the soot from the lampshade in order to see again. Even in dreams the light is taken away by soldiers who come between the sun and the earth and "blot out daylight" (p. 49), causing night to fall permanently. The tension of these early stories results from the conflict of forces which, on the one hand, pull the characters backward into innocence or, on the other, forward into experience. The happy world is the prenatal world, where "we held hands once and were beautiful" (p. 14). Then the baby is born and is eaten, eyes first, by red ants ("At Last").

In the stories which follow "At the Bottom of the River" Kincaid moves away from the collage form and into the framework of traditional narratives that picture the gradual separation of a young Antiguan girl named Annie John from her family and finally from her island home. Each story recalls images of separation presented in the earlier stories, but now the images mark logical, definite stages of the movement into experience. In "Figures in the Distance," for instance, Annie watches funerals from afar until finally a girl her own age dies and she feels compelled to attend her funeral. In "The Red Girl" she falls in love with a girl of whom her mother disapproves, and Annie is forced to hide gifts that she has gotten to give to this "red girl." Step by step in these stories Annie moves further away from the closeness that she shared with her mother, a closeness that she recalls, often with the defensive bitterness and anger of one who has been rejected. As a part of this she recalls how delighted her mother seemed to be with each phase of their separation from each other. Of her mother's reaction to Annie's first trip alone to the store, according to Annie, "If I had just conquered Persia, she couldn't have been more proud of me" ("A Walk to the Jetty," *The New Yorker* 60 [November 5, 1984], 49). There is a power in each of the episodes that derives principally from the fact that Annie's eye misses nothing, particularly nothing that has to do with the increasing distance that separates her from her mother. She remembers her mother's laughter that has nothing to do with Annie's presence and everything to do with the fact that she enjoys Annie's father's company. She remembers the exact design of the first dress she had that was not made from the same cloth as her mother's. Every detail in her life, it seems, is important because it underlines the inevitability of her separation from her mother.

It is, of course, this inevitability that marks the change in perspective that has occurred between *At the Bottom of the River* and *Annie John*. In the first volume, until the last line of the final story, there remained for the narrator a possibility or a hope that the world "before you were born" could be regained. From the beginning of the *Annie John* collection there is no question that this world is gone forever. The transition into this change in perspective is represented symbolically in the third and final phase of the allegory in "At the Bottom of the River." Before that last phase, as mentioned earlier, the narrator had considered two alternatives: that of the first man who will not leave his bed or his house and even acknowledge the pleasure and pain of existence; and that of the second man who stands on a threshold, pulled nearly in two by the attraction of a safe world of home and family with its image of human contentment, mother and child, and the larger world of exquisite pleasure and pain. Both alternatives are unacceptable to her because the one denies consciousness and potential, while the second offers ambiguity that leads to frustration and ultimately despair. The narrator chooses to confront the vision of perfect harmony represented at the bottom of the river by a house undivided by rooms and a world undivided by night and day—a world where the sun and moon exist together at once. She gains strength from this confrontation, just as the androgenous creature she has referred to earlier has gained strength from learning that everything in the world has a right to exist individually and on its own terms. The narrator internalizes this lesson and refers to it as the glowing light that the creature has left behind to help with the terror of total darkness. This experience obviously has mystical overtones, but it is, in effect, an acknowledgment that the world where opposites are joined exists within the individual, not in the external world. Kincaid's narrator is finally freed from the hope of returning to the prenatal world and can pursue her individuality in the real world. It is this realization that allows her in the last line of "At the Bottom of the River" to "feel herself grow solid and complete, my name filling up my mouth" (p. 82).

Appropriately, the climatic story in the *Annie John* collection, "A Walk to the Jetty," begins with "My name is Annie John" (p. 45), the first words that occur to Annie when she wakes up on the morning that she will leave her mother and father and Antigua, in her mind, forever. The steps that have led her to this point are described in the earlier stories of the volume, and each stage that has led to this final separation has been filled with pain and bitterness. She has attempted usually to hide both of these feelings from her mother and often has succeeded in hiding them from herself. In "A Walk to the Jetty" she reflects in "the half-dark of my room" (p. 45) on her feelings about the process of separation that have consumed her for as long as she can remember. She blames herself for not seeing sooner how hypocritical her mother had been in planning, in the guise of love, separation after separation of mother and child. But she also realizes that she could not then have articulated in that half-light her reason for feeling as she did: "If I had been asked to put into words why I felt this way, if I had been given years to reflect and come up with the words of why I felt this way, I would not have been able to come up with so much as the letter 'A' " (p. 46). She does know, however, that she is ready to leave this house where she feels out of place with her mother and father, where she has outgrown her bed, and where people keep saying, "This happened during the time your mother was carrying you" (p. 46).

Intuitively Annie now understands the point that Kincaid has understood all along and has prepared the reader for in the allegory: she is escaping the pull of the world of prenatal union and harmony, a fact which makes the actual walk to the jetty and the boat that will carry her away from Antigua so painful. All of the sights along the way, some of which have been explored in depth in other stories in the series, mark some memory of a new way that her mother had found of pushing Annie further and further away. As they reach the jetty the most powerful of those images of separation that Kincaid has developed through two volumes of stories come into Annie's mind. She feels herself fall through the cracks of the jetty; she imagines herself held down against her will; she feels a hollow space inside; she sees herself torn into little pieces and drifting out to sea. When her mother at last tells her that she will always be Annie's mother and Antigua will always be her home (symbols of the larger worlds of prenatal harmony and Eden), the words "raked across" Annie's skin. They also sting the reader because these words evoke images of the ritual rake-marks, remembered or feared, at the entrance into individuality and light. As the boat pulls away, Annie lies down on her berth and listens to the sound of the waves lapping around the ship, "as if a vessel filled with liquid had been placed on its side and now was slowly emptying out" (p. 51), the hope of rejoining the perfect world leaving her forever. At last she and the reader can watch from the boat as her mother becomes "a matchbox-size launch swallowed up in the big blue sea" (p. 51).

CRITICAL RECEPTION

Since Jamaica Kincaid has only one book in print (*At the Bottom of the River*) and a second (*Annie John*) in press, she has received very little critical attention. The consensus of the five reviewers who dealt with *At the Bottom of the River* in national magazines is that the stories in the collection are baffling, a fact which bothered some reviewers more than others. Anne Tyler found that the stories "are almost insultingly obscure, and they fail to pull us forward with any semblance of plot" ("Mothers and Mysteries," p. 32). Edith Milton was drawn into the stories' "futuristic sensitivity" and found them to be "a literary equivalent of rock video in which technical adroitness in manipulating an image and sensuous pleasure in what can be done with it rather preclude questions about why" ("*At the Bottom of the River*," 1984, p. 22). Because of the stories' mystery, at least implied by both Tyler and Milton, there is a risk, according to Suzanne Freeman, "that not everyone is willing to decipher the secrets" (Review of *At the Bottom of the River*, 1984, p. 16). Similarly, Janet Wiehe characterized the stories as "abstract and surreal" (Review of *At the Bottom of the River*, 1983, p. 2262), while Gregory Maguire saw the stories as "a bridge and an introduction to more difficult writers like Virginia Woolf" (Review of *At the Bottom of the River*, 1984, p. 91).

In spite of their difficulties with the collection, however, all of the reviewers were quick to point to the beauty of individual parts of it and to recognize that there appears to be something beneath the surface of the stories. Anne Tyler found the stories to have "care for language, joy in the sheer sound of words, and evocative power" (p. 33), qualities that, in one way or another, each reviewer pointed out. Oddly though, none of the reviewers mentioned the title story of the collection, the story that comes closest to providing a key to what Edith Milton calls "the book's difficult vision" (p. 22). The most sensitive reading of the book is Derek Walcott's. In a letter to the publisher of *At the Bottom of the River*, reprinted in part on the dust jacket of the first printing, he points to the subtle feelings in every phrase of the book, and to the "soft succession of 'yeses' that we silently give" its true sentences.

HONORS AND AWARDS

In 1984 Kincaid received the Morton Dauwen Zabel Award for fiction.

BIBLIOGRAPHY

Works by Jamaica Kincaid

At the Bottom of the River. New York: Farrar, Straus & Giroux, 1983.
Annie John. New York: Farrar, Straus & Giroux, 1985.

Studies of Jamaica Kincaid

Freeman, Susanne. Review of *At the Bottom of the River*. *Ms*. 12 (January 1984), 15–16.

Maguire, Gregory. Review of *At the Bottom of the River*. *Horn Book* 60 (Fall 1984), 91.

Milton, Edith. "*At the Bottom of the River*." *New York Times Book Review*, January 15, 1984, p. 22.

Tyler, Anne. "Mothers and Mysteries." *New Republic* 189 (December 31, 1983), 32–33.

Wieche, Janet. Review of *At the Bottom of the River*. *Library Journal* 108 (December 1, 1983), 2262.

IAN H. MUNRO

George Lamming (1927–   )

BIOGRAPHY

Born in Barbados in 1927, George Lamming grew up in Carrington's Village on the outskirts of Bridgetown. He received one of the few scholarships to Combermere High School, but found the school's authoritarian regimen irksome and—perhaps in reaction—began writing poetry encouraged by the example of Frank Collymore, a member of the faculty of Combermere and editor of the newly founded literary magazine *Bim*. In 1946 Lamming left Barbados to take up a teaching job in Trinidad.

The more cosmopolitan society of Port of Spain had a significant effect on Lamming's interest in writing. Acting as an agent for *Bim*, he came into contact with young writers and poets from throughout the West Indies who were articulating a new sense of cultural nationalism and, more important, who took their writing careers seriously. From late 1947, Lamming's own poems and occasional short prose pieces were regularly broadcast over the BBC's new "Caribbean Voices" series. The poems he wrote during this period, if at times derivative of contemporary English poets like Eliot and Auden, were already exploring distinctive themes that would appear later in his fiction, including a frustration with West Indian cultural life and the condition of the artist in a society indifferent to any but imported culture. Trinidad too had fast become confining for Lamming, as it had for many of his peers. "They simply wanted *to get out* of the place where they were born," he recalls in *The Pleasures of Exile* (1960, p. 41). In 1950, on the same ship as Sam Selvon, Lamming sailed for England.

Emigration to England proved a decisive step in shaping Lamming's literary career. It made him sharply aware of the realities of racism and colonialism, as well as of his own distance from a culture in whose language and values he had been nurtured. The last poems he wrote before beginning *In the Castle of My Skin* (1953) return to the West Indies, celebrating the imaginative freedom of childhood and the continuity of West Indian peasant life, two themes important to the novel.

Since 1953, Lamming's small, book-lined flat in London has been his base for travel and a variety of experience unusual even among the peripatetic breed of West Indian writers. After the completion of his second novel, *The Emigrants* (1954), he returned to the Caribbean to gather material for his third novel, *Of Age and Innocence* (1958). Trips to Haiti and West Africa gave him insights into African survivals in the West Indies central to his fourth novel, *Season of Adventure*, published in 1960, the same year his nonfiction work *The Pleasures of Exile* appeared. From 1950 to 1962, Lamming regularly produced programs for the BBC's overseas service.

Lamming has made several return journeys to the Caribbean, including Cuba, and the United States, where he has held visiting lectureships at universities in the East and South. After the publication of his most recent novels, *Water with Berries* (1971) and *Natives of My Person* (1972), he lectured at universities in the United States, Denmark, Tanzania, and Kenya and traveled in India and Australia under the auspices of the Commonwealth Foundation. At present he is once again living in Barbados, where he is working on a novel about the 1930s in the Caribbean and preparing a new collection of essays. He is a regular contributor to the journal *Casa de las Américas*, published in Havana.

MAJOR WORKS AND THEMES

George Lamming's last published poem recalls a custom he must often have witnessed in Trinidad: All Souls' Day, when graves are cleaned and the dead honored with candles. ''The Illumined Graves'' is a sympathetic yet ironic comment on the perpetuation of custom in the absence of faith or understanding: ''a decorous decrepitude is all.'' All Souls' Day is a recurrent symbol in Lamming's fiction of an inert relationship with the past. Its counterpoint is the Haitian ''ceremony of the souls,'' in which the living, in order to make their peace with the dead, must bring to light past misdeeds and accept responsibility for them. For Lamming, both ceremonies have symbolic significance: one is confining and repetitive; the other liberating and redemptive. Lamming's fiction has been an exploration of Caribbean history, attempting to bring that history to light in the manner of the ''ceremony of the souls''; ''Awareness,'' he writes in *The Pleasures of Exile*, ''is a minimum condition for attaining freedom'' (p. 12). Yet, as Lamming points out in the same work, confronting the past is painful: ''colonialism is the very base and structure of the West Indian's cultural awareness'' (p. 35), he writes, since slavery and colonialism founded Caribbean society and conditioned its way of seeing itself and the world. "In order to change this way of seeing," Lamming continues, "the West Indian must change the very structure, the very basis of his values" (p. 36) through some psychic equivalent of the Haitian ceremony of souls. In Lamming's work, exploring the hidden, unacknowledged relation to the past, and synthesizing the fragmented patterns of Caribbean experience is the work of the artist, as the job of actually reshaping social and economic relationships is that of the political leader. Neither can function successfully without the other, or without the yearning of the working and peasant classes toward freedom and Caribbean unity. The existence of such a "peasant consciousness" is an article of faith in Lamming's writing.

The world of the peasants of Creighton's Village in Lamming's best-known novel, *In the Castle of My Skin*, is very much that of "The Illumined Graves": unconscious patterns rooted in slavery continue to dominate village life. "It seemed they were three pieces in a pattern which remained constant," Lamming writes of three village women as they gossip. "The meaning was not clear to them. It was not their concern, and it never would be" (p. 17; quotation and those following from *In the Castle of My Skin*, U.S. ed., 1954). The peasants are rooted in land owned by Mr. Creighton, a descendant of slaveowners, but have no awareness of slavery or of their colonial condition. By adroitly shifting tone and viewpoint throughout the novel, Lamming makes us appreciate the tranquility of the villagers' life—represented particularly by the reflections in Barbadian dialect of Ma and Pa, the oldest villagers—while ironically pointing out how they are confined by their ignorance.

Thus, when change comes to the village in the form of Mr. Slime's land scheme, the villagers are unprepared. Slime is the first of the "leader" figures in Lamming's fiction; his name reflects, perhaps too clearly, Lamming's feelings about him as a betrayer of the villagers' trust, even if in fact he merely represents the rising power of a new, indigenous middle class. In Slime's new economic scheme the land—"priceless, perennial and a symbol of some inexplicable power" (p. 246), from the peasant viewpoint—has become a commodity. Lamming's ambivalence about this change is hardly surprising since what is lost is not only the dignity of Pa, Mr. Foster, and other impoverished villagers dispossessed by those able to afford the land but the world of "G.'s" own childhood.

"G." in the novel is a "portrait of the artist" growing up amid these changes. From the outset he is concerned with the past, but his inquiries about family history are deflected by his mother's singing, "which always happened when I tried to remember" (p. 3). As G. grows older and better educated he moves further from the village and his mother, his increasing objectivity represented in the book's closing chapters by the use of a diary recording his last months in Barbados. Anxious to get away, he is equally regretful at the thought of "seeing things for the last time . . . people, objects, situations" (p. 219). Even the reappearance of his boyhood friend Trumper, preaching a gospel of racial unity learned in the United States, does not overcome G.'s ambivalent, rootless condition; if G. is more aware of freedom, he is also more alone.

Lamming's second novel, *The Emigrants* (1954), can be seen as a continuation of the first, since the emigrants' confrontation with England is, for Lamming, a necessary part of disabusing the West Indian of illusions about colonialism. The crowd of emigrants from throughout the West Indies who ship for England all seek a "better break" in England; almost unconsciously, they are challenging the tradition of colonial passivity and fatalism. While the voyage itself promotes a sort of shipboard nationalism, what really unites the emigrants is their relation to England as colonials: "whatever islan' you bring them from," observes one character, "them want to prove something" (p. 64; quotation and that following from *The Emigrants*, U.S. ed., 1954).

Their reception in the "mother country" is not what they expect: Englishman and West Indian alike are conditioned by stereotypes of one another that colonialism has imposed upon them. Lamming suggests the isolation of the new arrivals from English life through striking descriptions of interior environments: the comfortable middle-class homes of the English, for example; or the steamy flats and subterranean meeting places where the emigrants gather to preserve a vestige of unity. The novel is carefully, almost rigidly plotted to chart the relentless progress of each character, regardless of his background or expectations, toward disillusionment and solitude. In such an environment neither the artist, represented by Collis, an aspiring writer, nor the "leader," in the form of the "Governor," has a useful role to play. Collis is so alienated he cannot synthesize the fragments of experience, while the Governor degenerates into a hustler who denies any responsibility for his fellow West Indians. Emigration proves a phase of discovery which must lead back to the West Indies; its epilogue is Toronado's plaintive dream of "a new land where we can find peace . . . without making up false pictures 'bout other places" (p. 195). Lamming's next two novels, *Of Age and Innocence* (1958) and *Season of Adventure* (1960), concern the struggle for that new community in the Caribbean.

In *Of Age and Innocence* a Black leader, Isaac Shephard, returns to the fictional island of San Cristobal disgruntled by racist experiences in England, organizes a multiracial independence movement with East Indian and Chinese leaders, and wins popular support. As elections draw near, the movement divides along racial lines, violent strikes occur, and Shephard is assassinated. The failure of Shephard's movement lies above all in the inability of its leaders to overcome mutual suspicions rooted in the different relations each group they represent has had to colonialism. The East Indian leader, Singh, is the most vehement in his opposition to British rule; the descendant of indentured laborers, he cannot comprehend the effects of slavery on the African population. Shephard is the most fatally divided, between his desire for freedom and his concern for the approval of the colonizer. Through the towering, tragic figure of Shephard, Lamming offers a penetrating critique of the first generation of West Indian political leaders—men like Cipriani in Trinidad or Bustamante of Jamaica—whose commitment to political independence was undermined by admiration for England and by a demagogic style of leadership.

The "artist" figure, Mark Kennedy, plays only a marginal role in this novel. Searching for his origins on the island where he grew up, Mark briefly attempts to identify with Shephard's movement, but then drifts off into existential brooding, "alone in a world of objects" (p. 312; quotation from *Of Age and Innocence*, 1958 edition). In *Season of Adventure*, Lamming deliberately gives Chiki, a painter, greater significance and substance.

In *Season of Adventure*, the principal obstacle in the newly independent republic of San Cristobal to creating a new community, freed of the conditions of its history, is class division between the ruling elite and the working and peasant classes. The symbols of this division are two African survivals—steelbands and the "ceremony of souls"—which the middle class elite finds shameful and wishes to destroy. In characters like Police Commissioner Piggott, Lamming bitterly satirizes the tendency of the West Indian middle class to imitate the attitudes and habits of the former colonizers even after independence. The novel's central narrative concerns the quest of a middle-class woman, Fola Piggott, for the identity of her father, who could be either African or European. She has inherited the prejudices of her class against the ceremony of souls, but her unwilling baptism into its mysteries makes her aware of her society's African roots and of the prison of respectability which keeps other members of her class from making a similar "backward glance" to the stratum from which it had recently sprung.

Fola's awakening is largely the work of Chiki, an artist who shares the artistic paralysis of Collis and Mark Kennedy but is successful in teaching Fola that her class has been corrupted by money and new power into a refusal of the past and in awakening the drummer Gort to his capacity as a leader. The First Republic is overthrown by Gort and his steelbandsmen, outraged at the government's attempted suppression of the bands; the leader of the Second Republic espouses a more enlightened policy. *Season of Adventure* ends, indeed, on a note of optimism uncharacteristic of Lamming's work, the result perhaps of hopes for a new generation of Caribbean political leaders which seemed to be presaged by Eric Williams of Trinidad. As Lamming was writing *Season of Adventure*, Williams was expounding ideas on Caribbean history and culture not unlike Lamming's, in mass lectures at his "University of Woodford Square."

A long silence followed *Season of Adventure*, ending with the almost simultaneous publication of *Water with Berries* (1971) and *Natives of My Person* (1972). Both novels take up with new energy and determination the "ceremony of the souls" motif, using allegory to explore the half-realized burden of guilt and vulnerability carried by both English and Caribbean characters as a legacy of colonialism.

Water with Berries is an account of two chaotic weeks in the lives of three artists from San Cristobal living in London and pursuing an aesthetic existence with what they assure themselves is "purity of intention." In fact, they have simply shut out their past and sunk into an uncreative routine. Derek, an actor, even makes his living by playing a corpse on stage. In an atmosphere of rising racial tension in Great Britain and uprisings in the Caribbean, their past emerges to haunt them. Teeton, a writer, had betrayed his wife years earlier in San Cristobal, abandoning her there and forgetting the whole matter; her suicide revives his buried guilt. The pregnant wife of the musician, Roger, also kills herself after he has spurned her—again for obscure motives hidden in his past.

In Lamming's work, intently concerned as it is with men unconsciously acting out historical patterns in the manner of "The Illumined Graves," such personal tragedies have roots in the still unexamined, unexorcised history of colonialism, with its legacy of aggression, conquest, and domination. In *Water with Berries*, Lamming draws implicit parallels between the way Teeton and Roger treat their women and the way Shakespeare's Prospero—as an allegorical type of the imperialist—treats Caliban in *The Tempest*. Repeated references in the novel to a "ceremony of souls" point to the need for a meeting with the past, although it is difficult to see the final scenes of the novel in which Roger, Derek, and Teeton commit, variously, rape, arson, and murder, as leading to such a purgation. The three blindly continue a pattern of violence. As race relations in London worsened in the late 1970s, Lamming's concluding vision of a "monstrous shadow . . . spreading through the land" (quotation from *Water with Berries*, English ed., 1971, p. 242), assumed a striking prescience.

Natives of My Person is Lamming's most thorough treatment of the theme of colonial history and a remarkable imaginative achievement. The novel, on one level, describes the secret voyage of the ship *Reconnaissance* from the "Kingdom of Lime Stone" to the Guinea Coast and thence toward San Cristobal. The ship's Commandant embraces in his personal experience the sweep of European colonialism from the rapacious gold-seeking of the conquistadors to the pious "white man's burden" of 19th century imperialists. His purpose for the voyage is noble: to fashion a new society, modeled on that of Lime Stone but purged of its corruption and abuses, "an order as might be the pride and example for excellence to Lime Stone herself" (p. 11; quotation and that following from *Natives of My Person*, U.S. ed., 1972). His dream founders because the Commandant and his officers are unable to break free from egoism and authoritarianism: each is unsure of his power over "the men below," and each, in pursuing his relentless ambitions, has sacrificed the woman who loved him. As in *Water with Berries*, the heart of Lamming's political allegory is corruption in personal relationships caused by unconscious habits of conquest and command rather than mutual commitment.

On another level, the Commandant and his officers represent that generation of Caribbean political leaders whose enthusiasm for independence was compromised by habits of power and status derived from colonialism; their wives, waiting their arrival in San Cristobal, symbolize a new society of mutual commitment they cannot realize: "a future they must learn" (p. 345), says the Lady of the House. Significantly, the quest is continued after the Commandant's murder by "the men below," led by Baptiste, whose fervent anti-authoritarianism is tempered by the visionary capacities of the ship's painter, Ivan. Baptiste's goals are egalitarian, in contrast to the Commandant's, while in Ivan Lamming appears to give a clear picture of an artist whose humanist commitment propels him from passive visionary to ''man of forceful action.'' The conclusion seems a reaffirmation of Lamming's faith, expressed in his earlier work, that the future of Caribbean society lies in the common folk and in a creative union of the visions of artist and political leader.

CRITICAL RECEPTION

George Lamming's work has featured in most discussions of West Indian literature, with *In the Castle of My Skin*, of course, receiving the most extensive critical analysis. In his introduction to the American edition, Richard Wright was among the first to comment on the novel's relevance to social and economic changes in the Third World. As a novelist Wright was also sensitive to ''Lamming's quietly melodious prose'' (*In the Castle of My Skin*, 1954, p. vi). Another novelist, Ngugi wa Thiong'o, ascribes a more overtly political purpose to *Castle* than Wright, seeing it as ''a study of colonial revolt'' and ''one of the great political novels in modern 'colonial' literature'' (''George Lamming's *In the Castle of My Skin*,'' 1972, p. 126). A similar political analysis, focusing on the rise of a new bourgeoisie and its betrayal of hopes for independence, is made by Ambroise Kom in ''*In the Castle of My Skin*: George Lamming and the Colonial Caribbean'' (1979). In *A Double Exile* (1978), Gareth Griffiths argues that the novel is particularly successful in creating ''a world which reflects the general experience of the West Indies, without losing its force of specific experience (p. 136), a point similar to Louis James's, in ''The Sad Initiation of Lamming's 'G' and Other Caribbean Green Tales'' (1972), where he points out that G.'s initiation consistently has wider implications.

More specialized studies of *In the Castle of My Skin* include Edward Baugh's thoughtful treatment of one of the novel's final scenes, the preparation of ''cuckoo'' by G.'s mother (''Cuckoo and Culture: *In the Castle of My Skin*,'' 1977), which Baugh suggests is an integral scene rather than an ''interruption,'' symbolizing love and the creation of an artistic whole out of unpleasant ingredients. In ''Lamming's Poetic Language in *In the Castle of My Skin*'' (1977), David S. West suggests that the novel's language uses sound and rhythm skillfully to sustain a series of symbols, particularly that of the ''castle.'' On the other hand, Elizabeth Nunez-Harell, in ''Lamming and Naipaul: Some Criteria for Evaluating the Third World Novel'' (1978), writes that Lamming's dialect lacks ''authenticity'' because it is ''merely the vehicle of his ideas.'' In her critical study *Black Time: Fiction of Africa, the Caribbean and the United States* (1981), Bonnie Barthold ties *Castle* in to her general consideration of differing views of time in Black literature. In the novel, she feels, there is a ''duality of time'' represented by Pa and Slime; as G. matures he understands time as ''the ultimate antagonist.''

Much of both the praise and the criticism of Lamming's novels after *Castle* revolves around his obvious preoccupation with showing his characters and their actions as a product of historical forces outside their ken. Lamming's works are all symbolic to some degree: his characters frequently embody themes and act out roles appropriate to their place in the symbolic scheme. The importance of ideas in Lamming's work has led to accusations of "tendentiousness" and "lifelessness" by some critics and reviewers, while others have been more willing to accept the donné of the work, that the political goals and issues of the novel ultimately bulk larger than the individual life of its characters. Louis James and Gareth Griffiths, for example, in the essays discussed above, comment with approval on the immersion of character in the larger context. Some studies of Lamming—for example, Sandra Pouchet Paquet's *The Novels of George Lamming* (1982), to date the only full-length study published on Lamming's work—are directed almost entirely to elucidating political motifs underlying the novels, with much less attention to problems of critical evaluation. The same is true of Ngugi wa Thiong'o in his analyses in *Homecoming*.

Lamming's second novel, *The Emigrants*, has received some harsh criticism for its construction. Gerald Moore in *The Chosen Tongue* (1969) refers to it as "the classic document of departure" (p. 49), but otherwise is dissatisfied with its latter half, which he regards as lacking unity of vision and setting. Interestingly, Moore does not regard *The Emigrants* as a "political novel" (just as Gloria Yarde in her essay "George Lamming—The Historical Imagination" (1970) does not regard it as a "historical novel' to the same degree as Lamming's other works). Moore suggests it diverges from "the real experience of England" (p. 41) that Lamming must have known. Sandra Pouchet Paquet does not make the same error of assuming the novel is not "political," though she, too, comments on its relative lack of structure and control compared to Lamming's later novels. In his "Lamming, Selvon and Some Trends in the West Indian Novel" (1955), Stuart Hall points out that Lamming's "shifting perspective" makes evaluation of experience impossible in the absence of a central intelligence or normative perspective. But Hall, while acknowledging that the novel's "central consciousness is a social, not an individual one," remains unwilling to accept the fragmentation of consciousness in the novel's latter half as relevant to its purpose.

The contrast in critical assumptions about what a novel should do is even more apparent in discussions of *Of Age and Innocence*. In a review, V. S. Naipaul objected that "every character, every incident is no more than a constituent idea in Mr. Lamming's thesis; the reader's sympathies are never touched" (*New Statesman* 61 (December 6, 1958), 726–28). Wilson Harris, in *Tradition the Writer and Society* (1967), makes a similar point: that the novel fails to maintain "individuality of character, the distinctions of status and privilege which mark one individual from another" and suggests that Lamming needs to work toward "the continuous development of a main individual character" (p. 38), which in fact Lamming does in *Season of Adventure*. A more thorough but related criticism is made by Kenneth Ramchand in comparing *Of Age and Innocence* to Naipaul's *The Mimic Men* ("The Theatre of Politics," 1973). Ramchand argues that Lamming, lacking a full understanding of the politics of race in the Caribbean, oversimplifies the problem: ''The collapse of the multi-racial ideal is gratuitous,'' he writes, ''and not validated by evidence created in the fiction'' (p. 25).

Gerald Moore, on the other hand, finds that ''nothing that happens there is improbable'' (*The Chosen Tongue*, 1969, p. 55), and Mervyn Morris in his essay ''The Novelist as Poet'' (*Islands in Between*, 1968, pp. 73–85) finds that ''language, theme and symbols are so well managed that the final effect is of a statement rich, complex, and yet in its essentials very clear'' (p. 79). Both Sandra Pouchet Paquet in her book and Gareth Griffiths in *A Double Exile* argue that the success of the novel is in the very way public and private incidents are interrelated and the past is shown to have ''shaped the life of each individual'' (*A Double Exile*, p. 138), to quote Griffiths. Both writers implicitly criticize the notion that Lamming's tendency to associate his characters with ideas is a weakness; on the contrary, they regard it as a strength. Selwyn Cudjoe's criticism of the novel in *Resistance and Caribbean Literature* (1980) is of a different nature: he argues that Lamming fails to perceive the fate of San Cristobal apart from the context of its relation to England. In *Season of Adventure* and later novels, Cudjoe believes, Lamming explores the need for ''an alternative reality'' and ''the necessity of shattering these former ties of dependence'' (p. 206).

Interestingly, Ramchand's and Mervyn Morris's views are reversed on the subject of *Season of Adventure*. Ramchand, in *The West Indian Novel and its Background*, acknowledges that ''society is as important as character in this kind of novel'' and argues that the reader must be willing to respond to both the ''realistic particularity and its symbolic representation'' (p. 140). Ramchand's view is that the ''ceremony of souls'' is not a sentimentalized African remnant but a symptom of social and economic frustration; he refers to *Season of Adventure* as ''the most significant of West Indian novels invoking Africa.'' Morris, in contrast, maintains that the novel fails in attempting to make ''some centrally significant myth out of the music of the steel bands'' (*Islands in Between*, p. 82) and finds characterization and actions unconvincing. His comment ends on a familiar note: ''*Season* fails because of Lamming's preoccupation with themes at the expense of credible life in its characters'' (p. 83).

Water with Berries has been both praised and criticized for much the same reasons. Mike Cook's review (1973) holds that the novel suffers from a ''malaise of tendentiousness'' and that its characters' actions are determined by ''artificial calculations or speculative principles'' rather than ''organic impulses and spontaneous reactions'' (p. 620). Helen Tiffin, comparing the novel to Naipaul's *Guerrillas* (''Freedom after the Fall: Renaissance and Disillusion in *Water with Berries* and *Guerrillas*,'' 1979) finds that in both novels portrayal of character is deliberately subservient to the ''historical equation'' (p. 91) they represent, since they cannot escape from ''the old roles which history has imposed upon them'' (p. 93).

Tiffin makes a similar point about *Natives of My Person* in her article ''The Tyranny of History: George Lamming's *Natives of My Person* and *Water with*

Berries'' (1979), pointing out that the voyage of the *Reconnaissance* is an attempt to escape from history which fails because the revolution is interwoven with the past. A different perspective is offered by Kirsten Holst Petersen in ''Time, Timelessness and the Journey Metaphor in George Lamming's *In the Castle of My Skin* and *Natives of My Person*'' (1976), in which Wilson Harris's concept of a ''fossil awareness'' of the past is applied to Lamming's use of two levels of historical time within the journey motif. The journey, Petersen asserts, is psychological, warning West Indian society that as long as the past is unacknowledged, the quest for a new society is doomed to failure.

General analyses of Lamming's work also appear in Gilkes, *The West Indian Novel* (1981); Baugh, *Critics on Caribbean Literature* (1978); King, *West Indian Literature* (1979); Ramchand, *An Introduction to the Study of West Indian Literature* (1976); Van Sertima, *Caribbean Writers: Critical Essays* (1968) and G. R. Coulthard, *Race and Colour in Caribbean Literature* (London, Oxford University Press, 1962); Griffiths, *A Double Exile* (1978); Moore, *The Chosen Tongue* (1969); Harris, *Tradition the Writer and Society* (1967); Cudjoe, *Resistance and Caribbean Literature* (1980); and Ramchand, *The West Indian Novel and Its Background* (1970).

A descriptive bibliography of criticism (including unpublished theses and dissertations) and reviews of Lamming's work by Arturo Maldonado Díaz was published in *Journal of Commonwealth Literature*, (16 [February 1982], 165–73). A volume *Critical Perspectives on George Lamming*, edited by Anthony Boxill, has been announced by Three Continents Press.

HONORS AND AWARDS

George Lamming received a Guggenheim Fellowship for *In the Castle of My Skin* in 1954 and the Somerset Maugham Award in 1957. In 1962 he was awarded a Canada Council Fellowship and in 1976 a Commonwealth Foundation grant. He recently received an honorary doctorate from the University of the West Indies.

BIBLIOGRAPHY

Works by George Lamming

In the Castle of My Skin. London: Michael Joseph, 1953; New York: McGraw-Hill, 1953, 1954; New York: Collier, African-American Library, 1970; London: Longman Caribbean, 1970.

The Emigrants. London: Michael Joseph, 1954; New York: McGraw-Hill, 1954; London: Allison and Busby, 1980.

Of Age and Innocence. London: Michael Joseph, 1958; London: Allison and Busby, 1981.

The Pleasures of Exile. London: Michael Joseph, 1960.

Season of Adventure. London: Michael Joseph, 1970; London: Allison and Busby, 1979.

Water with Berries. London: Longman Caribbean, 1971; New York: Holt, Rinehart and Winston, 1971.

Natives of My Person. London: Longman Caribbean, 1972; New York: Holt, Rinehart and Winston, 1972; London: Picador Press, 1972.

Studies of George Lamming

Abrahams, Cecil A. "George Lamming and Chinua Achebe: Tradition and the Literary Chroniclers." In *Awakened Conscience: Studies in Commonwealth Literature*, ed. C. D. Narasamiah. New Delhi and Sterling: n.p., n.d., pp. 294–306.

Barthold, Bonnie. *Black Time: Fiction of Africa, the Caribbean and the United States*. New Haven. Yale University Press, 1981.

Baugh, Edward. "Cuckoo and Culture: *In the Castle of My Skin*." *Ariel* 8 (July 1977), 23–33.

Carr, W. I. "The West Indian Novelist." In *Consequences of Class and Color: West Indian Perspectives*, ed. David Lowenthal and Lambros Comitas. New York: Anchor Books, 1973, pp. 281–301.

Cartey, Wilfred. "George Lamming and the Search for Freedom." *New World: Barbados Independence Issue* 3 (Dead Season 1966 and Croptime 1967), 121–28.

Cook, Michael. "A West Indian Novelist." *The Yale Review* (Summer 1973), pp. 616–24.

Cotter, Michael. "Identity and Compulsion: George Lamming's *Natives of My Person*." *New Literature Review* (Canberra) 1 (n.d.), 29–35.

Davies, Joan. "George Lamming: The Novel and Revolution." *Stand* (London) 4 (1960), 52–58.

Figueroa, John. "Introduction to George Lamming." *Revista/Review Interamericana* 5 (Spring 1975), 146–48.

Gunter, Helmut. "George Lamming." In *Introduction to African Literature*, ed. Ulli Beier. London: Longman, 1967, pp. 205–10.

Hall, Stuart. "Lamming, Selvon and Some Trends in the West Indian Novel." *Bim* 6 (December 1955), 172–88.

James, Louis. "The Sad Initiation of Lamming's 'G' and Other Caribbean Green Tales." In *Commonwealth*, ed. Anna Rutherford. Aarhus: Akademisk Boghandel, 1972, pp. 135–43.

Kom, Ambroise. "*In the Castle of My Skin*: George Lamming and the Colonial Caribbean." *World Literature Written in English* 18 (November 1979), 406–20.

———. "Londres des nègres dans *The Emigrants* et dans *Water with Berries* de George Lamming." *Etudes anglaises* 34 (January-March 1981), 44–60.

Maldonado Díaz, Arturo. "Place and Nature in George Lamming's Poetry." *Revista/Review Interamericana* 4 (Fall 1974), 402–10.

Munro, Ian. "The Early Works of George Lamming: Poetry and Short Prose, 1946–1951." In *Neo-African Literature and Culture: Essays in Memory of Janheinz Jahn*, ed. Ulla Schild and Bernth Lindfors. Wiesbaden: Heymann, pp. 327–45.

———. "George Lamming's *Season of Adventure*: The Failure of the Creative Imagination." *Studies in Black Literature* 4 (Spring 1973), 6–13.

———. "The Theme of Exile in George Lamming's *In the Castle of My Skin*." *World Literature Written in English* 20 (November 1971), 51–60.

Naipaul, V. S. Review of *Of Age and Innocence*. *New Statesman* 61 (December 1958), 726–28.

Ngai, Mbatau Kaburu wa. "The Relationship Between Literature and Society and How It Emerges in the Works of C. [*sic*] Lamming, V. S. Naipaul and W. Harris." *Busara* 8 (1976), 53–67.

Ngugi wa Thiong'o. "The Black Experience." *Umma* (Nairobi) 3 (1976), 20.

———. "George Lamming's *In the Castle of My Skin*." In *Homecoming: Essays on African and Caribbean Literature, Culture and Politics*. New York: Lawrence Hill, 1972, pp. 110–26.

Nightingale, Margaret. "George Lamming and V. S. Naipaul: Thesis and Antithesis." *ACLALS Bulletin* (Mysore) 5 (1980), 40–50.

Nunez-Harell, Elizabeth. "Lamming and Naipaul: Some Criteria for Evaluating the Third World Novel." *Contemporary Literature* 19 (Winter 1978), 26–47.

Ojo, Patchechole Poindexter. "Nature in Three Caribbean Novels." *Journal of Commonwealth Studies* 2 (Spring 1981), 85–107.

Paquet, Sandra Pouchet. *The Novels of George Lamming*. London: Heinemann, 1982.

Petersen, Kirsten Holst. "Time, Timelessness, and the Journey Metaphor in George Lamming's *In the Castle of My Skin* and *Natives of My Person*." In *Commonwealth Writers Overseas*, ed. Alastair Niven. Brussels: Didier, 1976, pp. 283–88.

Ramchand, Kenneth. "The Theatre of Politics." *20th Century Studies* 10 (December 1973), 20–36.

Robinson, Jeff. "Mother and Child in Three Novels by George Lamming." *Release* 6 (1979), 75–83.

Rohlehr, Gordon. "Facing the Past: Some Themes in the Writings of Eric Williams, George Lamming, and Derek Walcott." *Pelican* (July–October 1964), 13–16.

Tiffin, Helen. "Freedom after the Fall: Renaissance and Disillusion in *Water with Berries* and *Guerrillas*." In *Individual and Community in Commonwealth Literature*, ed. Daniel Massa. Malta: The University Press, 1979, pp. 90–98.

———. "The Tyranny of History: George Lamming's *Natives of My Person* and *Water with Berries*." *Ariel* 10 (October 1979), 37–52.

West, David S. "Lamming's Poetic Language in *In the Castle of My Skin*." *The Literary Half-Yearly* 18 (July 1977), 71–83.

Wright, Richard. Introduction to *In the Castle of My Skin*. New York: McGraw-Hill, 1954, pp. v–viii.

Yarde, Gloria. "George Lamming-the Historical Imagination." *Literary Half-Yearly* 11 (July 1970), 35–45.

See also General Bibliography: Allis, Baugh (1978), Gilkes, Griffith, Harris, Herdeck, Hughes, James, King, Ramchand (1970, 1976), and Van Sertima.

DARYL CUMBER DANCE

Earl Lovelace (1935–)

BIOGRAPHY

Earl W. Lovelace was born in Toco, Trinidad, on July 13, 1935, and grew up in Tobago and Port of Spain. His first job was as a proofreader for the Trinidad Publishing Company. He later studied agriculture and held jobs as a forest ranger and as an agricultural assistant in the Department of Forestry. He came to the United States to study at Howard University during the 1966–67 school year, and he taught during the summer of 1967 at Virginia Union University in Richmond, Virginia. He then returned to Port of Spain, where he worked as a journalist until he took a position at Federal City College in Washington, D.C., where he taught from 1971 to 1973. The following year he enrolled in Johns Hopkins University's writing program; when a professor in that program left to take a Fulbright Fellowship, Lovelace ended up teaching in his place. During the 1980–81 school year he was in residence in the Writers' Program at the University of Iowa. In 1982 he visited Britain for the first time for the launching of his fourth novel, *The Wine of Astonishment*. Since that time, the novelist's time in Trinidad has been divided between his creative writing, journalism, and lecturing at the University of the West Indies.

Lovelace, who describes himself as "largely a self-educated person" (interview with Daryl Cumber Dance, Port of Spain, Trinidad, March 17, 1980), was a voracious reader as a child, preferring the American writers, such as Hemingway and Faulkner, to the English writers, whom he found boring: "They didn't have as much action for *me* as the American writers" (interview). As an adult he discovered the Black American writers and felt a "certain affinity" with the works of such contemporaries as Don L. Lee and LeRoi Jones.

Presently the writer lives with his wife and three children in the remote village of Matura in an area which Ismith Khan described as "way to hell and gone behind God's back" (interview with Daryl Cumber Dance, Anaheim, California, August 14, 1981) and which others have confirmed is practically inaccessible and completely lacking in modern conveniences. His somewhat anomalous life style seems consistent with his constant focus on the strength, beauty, and stability of pastoral societies untouched and unspoiled by corrupt modern society.

MAJOR WORKS AND THEMES

Lovelace has published four novels—*While Gods Are Falling* (1965), *The School Master* (1968), *The Dragon Can't Dance* (1979), and *The Wine of Astonishment* (1982)—and a collection of plays, *Jestina's Calypso and Other Plays* (1984). A few poems and short stories have appeared in anthologies and journals.

The major theme in Earl Lovelace's work is the quest for personhood, a term which he prefers to *manhood* or *identity* and which he describes as "man's view of himself, the search as it were for his integrity" (interview). Frequently, however, this quest is threatened as his characters encounter the impersonal, dehumanizing urban world.

Lovelace begins the development of this theme in his first novel, *While Gods Are Falling*, where we witness Walter Castle's doomed efforts to assert his manhood in the Port of Spain slum where he lives, which Lovelace describes as "dark, poisonous and stinking, something like a sore in this city" (1966 ed., p. 9). When he moved into the city following the disintegration of his rural family, Castle (whose sense of manhood is thwarted both by his physical shortcomings [he is small and bandy-legged] and his inability to support his wife and children adequately) joined other similarly poor and frustrated remnants of broken families. In poignantly moving and realistic scenes, Lovelace powerfully evokes the many problems that afflict the urban poor and destroy their families, especially their youths; he moves less surely and convincingly to conclude his novel on a positive note with all factions of the community joined together as one family concerned about and assuming responsibility for each other and for the youths in their midst. Walter Castle's role in bringing his community together confirms his sense of personhood.

Such a reinforcing unity naturally characterizes Kumaca, the rural community of *The Schoolmaster*, which, despite its poverty, is unified, orderly, honorable, and secure, bound together by strong traditions and stable family units: "In a place like Kumaca, . . . everybody is one" (1979 ed., p. 95). The dominant tranquility of this pastoral paradise (into which *some* influences of the outside world have already begun to creep at the time of our novel) is fatefully disrupted when a schoolmaster is sent in to establish a school and rumors are heard that a road is to be built to tie the village to the outside world. Both endeavors, designed to benefit the village, serve only to bring the evil and destruction that inevitably accompany the encroachment of urban society into secure rural Edens. The schoolmaster, like many of Lovelace's educated characters, has been educated *away* from self, rejects the basic traditional values of his culture, and embraces the worst elements of the exploiters. Thus Benn rejects the priest's suggestion that "this schoolmaster is your own. Your own people," and retorts, "He is black, yes. But not my own people. Priest, he is closer to your people. I think he is your people. He learned in your schools, and he wears the clothes the way you wear them, and he talks the way you talk, and his thinking is that of your people. He is yours, priest. He is not mine" (p. 66). Many of the tragic problems that result in this novel are shown to be the result of the more sophisticated and educated outsiders' failure to respect the individuality and personhood of the simple country folk whom they encounter. The theme of the quest for personhood here is most effectively emphasized by a minor character, the drunken philosopher Benn, whose reflections on his own life and the drama he witnesses provide an important commentary on the meaning of the events going on around him and reinforce the need of the individual to seek meaning, significance, and dignity in his life.

Though *The Wine of Astonishment* was not published until 1982, it was written before *The Dragon Can't Dance*. It reveals the manner in which laws banning their form of religious worship serve to disrupt and destroy the traditions of the Spiritual Baptists of the village of Bonasse. When they can no longer sing their songs, ring their bells, and speak in tongues, they realize that they have been forced to deny the very essence of their beings. They determine that to save themselves they must assert their manhood, stand up and fight, even if the battle is futile: "We is people. The police have to respect us" (1982 ed., p. 38). Unfortunately, the bright young villager whom they have chosen to educate to become their leader elects to repudiate his people, having become "so civilize [he] forget where [he] come from" (p. 14). His education has led him to advise his people, "We can't be white, but we can act white" (p. 13). His rejection is symbolized by his moving out of the community without taking anything from his family home: "It was as if Ivan Morton was saying to the world that the house his father leave him was nothing, and his father life was nothing" (p. 10). The disappointment and despair of the community is somewhat assuaged by the warrior Bolo, the stickfighter whose dance not only expressed his own beauty but also served to express the beauty and humanity of his people. His fight and his dance were not for himself; "what he really want was for people to see in him a beauty that wasn't his alone, was theirs, ours, to let us know that we in this wilderness country was people too, with drums and song and warriors" (p. 22). Bolo, angry that his people will not join him in his fights against their oppressors, becomes a Bad John, terrorizing his community. His outrageous acts finally provoke his neighbors to determine to kill him, but even as they reach that decision, Bea recognizes the deliberateness and the import of Bolo's actions: "He choose out himself . . . to be the sacrifice. To be the one terrible enough and strong enough and close enough to our heart to drive us to take up our manhood challenge that we turn away from for too long. He push us and push us until we have to stand up against him'' (p. 122). That the possibility of retaining and asserting their personhood remains is reinforced at the close of the novel. The despair the villagers feel when they discover that, though they have regained their freedom to worship, the spirit is gone from their church, is ameliorated when they hear the youngsters playing in their steelband: "I listening to the music; for the music that those boys playing on the steelband have in it that same Spirit that we miss in our church: the same Spirit; and listening to them, my heart swell and it is like resurrection morning'' (p. 146).

Jestina's Calypso, though not published until 1984 (along with two other plays), was first produced in 1976. It treats the poignant efforts of an ugly Black woman to be loved for what she is rather than for her appearance. The play focuses on her preparations to go to the airport and meet a penpal, a Trinidadian immigrant to the United States with whom she has been corresponding. They have fallen in love and plan to marry, but the only problem is that she has sent him a photograph of her attractive, light-complexioned friend rather than of herself. Lamenting, "I should have write and say I is a ugly woman'' (p. 11), she still prays that "you'd come and discover me yourself, that you would see me and care . . . that you would be able to look at me and say: This is my woman. This is my island with the bruises and sagging breasts, with the teeth marks of soucouyants on her thighs, still standing after the rapes'' (pp. 34, 36). Unfortunately, her fiancé is unable to see her for what she really is and to accept her—or by extension, to recognize the realities and the true essence of the Trinidad to which he is returning. Like many others in previous Lovelace works who through their blindness reject some of the basic values of their culture, their past, their source, he compromises something of his own personhood in his inability to appreciate the personhood of Jestina.

Lovelace's most successful treatment of the quest for personhood comes in *The Dragon Can't Dance*, his most recently written novel, though not the most recently published. As in earlier novels, the inhabitants of Calvary Hill have also been repressed, brutalized, dehumanized. Here as elsewhere we see them refusing to accept the condition that society has dictated for them and striving through whatever means are available to force recognition of their personhood. The inhabitants of the Hill have for the most part migrated to the city from a more stable rural family and community. They have left the protective custody of that organized society, which offered them a secure sense of self and a clearly defined role within its confines, to seek their destiny, place, and identity in the larger world. In a world that places its values on wealth, material possessions, political clout, family, etc., these outcasts on Calvary Hill have precious little with which to proclaim their importance. Thus they must ever assert their "right to a humanness unlinked to the possession of any goods or property, arrived at, realized, born to, in consequence of their being'' (1979 ed., p. 151). As Aldrick says to his friend, the Calypsonian Philo, "All we thinking about is to show this city, this island, this world, that we is people, not because we own anything, not because we have things, but because we is. We are because we is'' (p. 111).

Lovelace traces the efforts of a number of characters to assert their personhood through the limited means available to them, including violence, music, rebellion, masquerade, and the attainment of material possessions. The efforts of several of the main characters to achieve such recognition are directly or indirectly related to Carnival, which serves on one hand to link the people with their past and to unite and revitalize them in a symbolic revolution, but which appears, on the other hand, to be a hoax, encouraging the people to dissipate their energies in Carnival revelries rather than to direct them toward any meaningful kind of revolt. Most of the major characters are involved in some pose to effect recognition: Aldrick plays the dragon each year at Carnival, threatening and terrorizing; Cleothilda masquerades as a queen, for these few days showering her ''subjects'' with unwonted friendship and attention; Philo sings his calypsos, calling attention to a persona antithetical to his true self; Fisheye becomes a warrior in the steelband, provoking confrontations with other bands; other young men troop to the steelband tents to produce that ''tune that will sing their person and their pose'' (p. 12).

Those characters who achieve awareness in this novel come to recognize the emptiness of efforts at achieving personhood that are based upon temporary poses, or that rely upon approval from an outside world. After a futile attempt at rebellion against the police, Aldrick recognizes, ''We was saying to them, 'Look at us! We is people!' We wasn't ready to take over nothing for we own self. We put the responsibility on them to act, to do something. . . . We is people. I, you, you, for we own self. . . . We have to act for we'' (pp. 188–89). The enlightened characters recognize that true self-understanding and personhood rest upon an awareness of their responsibility toward those around them, with whom they must join in a loving, caring community. Thus when they acknowledge their obligations to others, they move closer toward the attainment of their own personhood. Aldrick ultimately moves from his self-centered quest for self-comfort, self-recognition, self-satisfaction, self-insulation, to devote himself to Sylvia: ''He wanted to give her life, her self. . . . He had to learn how to live and how to give life'' (p. 127). Similarly the Indian Pariag, who had devoted himself to fighting *his* rejection by his neighbors in the yard, who had bewailed *his* isolation, who had been concerned with *his* image, suddenly looks around him, *sees* his uncomplaining, docile, unassertive wife, and recognizes *her* personhood and *her* needs. He looks at her and asserts:

> ''*We* have to start to live, Dolly, you and me.''
> ''*Me* and you?'' Dolly asked, her voice choking. ''*Me* and You?''
> What did he know of this woman? (p. 212)

Lovelace may not give us in this novel any satisfying political or sociological solution to the problems of the inhabitants of Calvary Hill (as he attempted to do in *While Gods Are Falling*), he may not propose any kind of practical rebellion that can effect recognizable change, but he has powerfully revealed the folk of Calvary Hill and involved us in their lives in such a meaningful and moving manner that we appreciate their traditions, applaud their victories, suffer their defeats, rejoice in their growth, and acknowledge their personhood. Here too, as in all of his previous works, he has successfully captured the sights and sounds and rhythms of Trinidad in a captivating tale, often tragic, but also often relieved by the comic tone, style, language, and interludes that are vintage Lovelace.

CRITICAL RECEPTION

Aside from a few review notices of his first two novels, Earl Lovelace had received little critical treatment until the publication of *The Dragon Can't Dance*. Since the appearance of that work, it has become one of the most highly acclaimed contemporary Caribbean novels and one of the most popular subjects of papers at literary conferences; consequently, one may anticipate that such critical attention will soon find its way into print.

From the beginning Lovelace has frequently been compared to his countryman Michael Anthony. In his review of *The Schoolmaster* (*Bim*, 1969), where he also comments extensively on *While Gods Are Falling*, Edward Brathwaite observes, "Critics might well wish to compare Lovelace's achievement . . . with Michael Anthony's" (p. 273), and goes on to note Anthony's restraint and simplicity and Lovelace's descriptiveness and moving dialogue. In his "Michael Anthony and Earl Lovelace: The Search for Selfhood" (1980), Harold Barratt insists, "The physical reality of the West Indies is at the heart of Anthony's and Lovelace's fiction" (p. 62), and suggests that the "impotent smallness of the West Indies" makes the quest of the West Indian for identity "a matter of chronic anxiety" (p. 63). Unlike V. S. Naipaul, Lovelace and Anthony are not embarrassed by the slums of Port of Spain or the other areas of deprivation in Trinidad, Barratt argues, but rather "they examine the lives of the people there with candour and sympathy" (p. 72).

In his introduction to the 1979 Heinemann edition of *The Schoolmaster*, Kenneth Ramchand praises Lovelace's evocation of the "essence and colour of the region in North-East Trinidad where the real Kumaca and Valencia are to be found" (p. vi), applauds his successful reproduction of dialect, and argues that the novel does not suggest that the villagers should reject the inevitability of change in their lives.

Barratt treats "Metaphor and Symbol in *The Dragon Can't Dance*" in a recent essay (1984), where he observes that Lovelace uses Calvary and the Christian celebration of the Eucharist as his major symbols in the novel, where the Carnival ritual and the rebellion are depicted in the terms of a sacred liturgy. He notes that the rite of Carnival is treated in terms of the Catholic mass, that the "fourteen stations of the cross are telescoped . . . in the experiences of Aldrick, Philo and Pariag" (p. 408), and that Pariag is a Christ figure.

Angelita Reyes (''Carnival: Ritual Dance of the Past and Present in Earl Lovelace's *The Dragon Can't Dance*,'' 1984) presents an extended treatment of Lovelace's use of Carnival in *The Dragon Can't Dance* to convey social change and history in the West Indies. She analyzes the structure of the novel, which she says ''shapes itself around and through seven seasons of carnival'' (p. 109).

In ''Making the Dragon Dance'' (1984), Louis James offers a teaching approach to *The Dragon Can't Dance*, which includes discussions of background information, context, and central issues in the novel. James's frequent allusions to other West Indian works help to place this novel in the broader context of West Indian literature as well as in the more specific context of Trinidadian literature.

In his extended study, *The Trinidad Calypso* (1982), Keith Warner credits Lovelace with ''by far the fullest treatment of the calypsonian in the contemporary Trinidadian novel'' (p. 133). He points to the characteristic traits of the calypsonian and his music that Lovelace employs in his calypsonian Philo, noting similarities to noted calypsonians such as the famed Sparrow, who probably inspired Lovelace's character.

HONORS AND AWARDS

Earl Lovelace received the British Petroleum Independence Literary Award for *While Gods Are Falling* in 1964. He received a Guggenheim Fellowship in 1980.

BIBLIOGRAPHY

Works by Earl Lovelace

While Gods Are Falling. London: Collins, 1965; Chicago: Henry Regnery, 1966; London: Longman, 1984.

The Schoolmaster. London: Collins, 1968; Chicago: Henry Regnery, 1968; London: Heinemann, 1979.

The Dragon Can't Dance. London: André Deutsch, 1979; London: Longman, 1981; (as *Der Drachentanz*) Bornheim-Merten: Lamuv, 1984.

The Wine of Astonishment. London: André Deutsch, 1982; London: Heinemann, 1983; New York: Vintage, 1984.

Jestina's Calypso and Other Plays. London: Heinemann, 1984.

Studies of Earl Lovelace

Barratt, Harold. ''Metaphor and Symbol in *The Dragon Can't Dance*.'' *World Literature Written in English* 23 (Autumn 1984), 405–13.

———. ''Michael Anthony and Earl Lovelace: The Search for Selfhood.'' *ACLALS Bulletin* 5 (1980), 62–73.

Brathwaite, Edward. "Priest and Peasant" (Review of *The Schoolmaster*). *Journal of Commonwealth Literature* 7 (July 1969), 117–22.

———. Review of *The Schoolmaster*. *Bim* 12 (January–June 1969), 273–77.

James, Louis. "Making the Dragon Dance." *WASAFIRI* (London) 1 (Autumn 1984), 13–15.

Pyne-Timothy, Helen. "Earl Lovelace: His View of Trinidad Society." *New World* 4 (Cropover 1968), 60–65.

Ramchand, Kenneth. Introduction to *The Schoolmaster*. London: Heinemann, 1979.

Reyes, Angelita. "Carnival: Ritual Dance of the Past and Present in Earl Lovelace's *The Dragon Can't Dance*." *World Literature Written in English* 24 (Summer 1984), 107–20.

Thorpe, Marjorie. "In Search of the West Indian Hero: A Study of Earl Lovelace's Fiction." In *Critical Issues in West Indian Literature*, ed. Erika Sellish Smilowitz and Roberta Quarles Knowles. Parkersburg, Io.: Caribbean Books, 1984.

———. Introduction to *The Wine of Astonishment*. London: Heinemann, 1983.

Warner, Keith. *The Trinidad Calypso*. Washington, D.C.: Three Continents Press, 1982; London: Heinemann, 1983.

Williams, David. "The Artist as Revolutionary: Political Commitment in *The Dragon Can't Dance* and *Interim*, in *West Indian Literature and its Social Context*, ed. Mark McWatt. Barbados: Department of English, Cave Hill, 1985, pp. 141–47.

See also General Bibliography: Allis, Herdeck, and Hughes.

EUGENIA COLLIER

Claude McKay (1889–1948)

BIOGRAPHY

Born in Sunny Ville, Jamaica, Claude McKay was the youngest of the eleven children of Thomas Francis and Elizabeth Edwards McKay. The father was a successful farmer, and both parents were highly respected members of the community. McKay apparently had a reasonably happy and secure childhood. One important aspect of his formative years was his awareness of the African past. The practice of Obeah, the storytelling sessions (in which his father excelled), the game of making "moonshine babies" out of bits of broken crockery, numerous customs brought by his forefathers from Africa—these influences gave him a sense of ancestry.

At about age six, McKay was sent to live with his schoolteacher brother in a village near Montego Bay. His brother provided books by the great thinkers and writers. By age ten McKay was not only a voracious reader but also a neophyte poet. After about ten years with his brother, McKay moved to Kingston, where he encountered for the first time the social ills of the city—hard-core poverty, oppression, racism. In Kingston he met the English folklorist Edward Jekyll, who made available his extensive library and encouraged McKay's writing, especially the writing of dialect poetry. By now McKay was sending poems to the *Daily Gleaner*. In 1912, with Jekyll's help, McKay published two volumes of poetry, *Songs of Jamaica* and *Constab Ballads*. The latter reflected his brief experience as a (most uncomfortable) member of the constabulary—an experience which deepened his compassion for the downtrodden. Shortly after the publication of these volumes, he left Jamaica to come to the United States. He never again saw his beloved green hills.

He planned to study agriculture and return home. But he was drawn to the American cities. He ended up in New York, where he worked at a number of jobs, had a brief, unsuccessful marriage, and continued to write. In the United States McKay saw for the first time raw, brutal racism. In 1917, working as a waiter on the railroad, McKay published two poems in *Seven Arts* magazine. They gained him entry into the world of White radical intellectuals. Soon he was publishing in the Marxist *The Liberator* as well as in *Pearson's* magazine. In 1919, enraged by the bloody race riots and lynchings, he wrote the poem which became his most famous, "If We Must Die."

A year later he traveled to London, where he worked for a time as a reporter for the Marxist periodical *The Workers' Dreadnought*. That year he published a volume of poems, *Spring in New Hampshire* (1920). Returning to the United States in 1921, he was for a brief time an editor on *The Liberator*. The following year he published his first American volume of poems, *Harlem Shadows* (1922), which marks the beginning of the Harlem Renaissance.

The next eleven years were spent traveling—first to post-revolutionary Russia, where he was highly acclaimed, then to Germany, France, Spain, Morocco. McKay met the great minds and popular writers of Europe, Africa, and expatriate America. Yet, despite his growing reputation as a writer, for most of the time he had to live frugally. For the most part, he lived among the folk. During these years he turned to fiction and published three novels and a collection of stories.

In 1933 McKay returned to a New York far different from the one he had left. These were the years of the Great Depression. McKay now faced a monumental struggle to stay alive. Not only poverty but also illness took its toll. An autobiography, *A Long Way from Home* (1937), and *Harlem: Negro Metropolis* (1940) absorbed these years, as well as poems, fiction, and articles, many of which were never completed or never published. In 1940 McKay became a U.S. citizen. During his last years he turned to Catholicism. He moved to Chicago and taught in a Catholic school. He began work on another autobiography and a collection of poetry. He died in 1948. These last works were published posthumously.

MAJOR WORKS AND THEMES

Songs of Jamaica and *Constab Ballads* pointed a new direction in Black literature. Twenty years later McKay asserted that in these volumes he had "recaptured the spirit of Jamaican peasants in verse, rendering their primitive joys, their loves and hates, their work and play, their dialect" ("A Negro Writer to His Critics," *The New York Herald-Tribune Books*, March 6, 1932). Nobody had done this successfully before McKay. The few previous West Indian writers (most, actually, European expatriates) had pictured the region through a romantic haze as beautiful landscape. In the United States Paul Laurence Dunbar (and later his literary descendants) titillated audiences with dialect poems whose ancestor was the poetry of White Southern supporters of slavery. McKay's works, though not untouched by romanticism, sprang directly from the Black folk. The poems are all the more remarkable because in the Jamaica of his time England was the cultural standard; dialect was considered vulgar. Poetry meant Browning and such. It was McKay who turned to Jamaica's indigenous artistic material—the folk.

Songs of Jamaica primarily concerns the mountain folk among whom McKay grew up; *Constab Ballads* reflects the city. Together they present themes and modes which ever afterward characterized McKay's works. Basic to all is his concern for the Black masses, exploited and oppressed but undefeated. In poems like "Quashie to Buccra," "Two-an'-Six," "Hard Times," and "What Fe Do?" McKay gives essentially realistic pictures of the harsh life of the country folk whose labor supports the money people. "The Apple-Woman's Complaint" exemplifies another face of oppression. Here a street vendor is forbidden by the police to sell her apples. The Black policeman is seen as the henchman of the White oppressors. Deprived of honest labor, the woman is being forced to steal. For the farmer there are compensations—the beauty of the land, the satisfaction of fields which his labor has produced, the joy of an intact family. The city has no such satisfaction. Whereas the soil nourishes, the city corrupts. The "class" Negroes, who feel superior to their darker brothers, are part of the problem. Some of the early works hint at the militancy evident in the later poems.

Nevertheless, the early poems reflect the deep ambivalence of a colonized society. While identifying with the exploited grass-roots people, the poet still extolls the colonizer. One poem especially, "Old England," regards England as the ancestral home, to which the colonial longs to go. Africa appears in one poem, "Cudjoe Fresh from de Lecture," in which the speaker accepts the White lecturer's view that Africa is a "bery low-do-n place," from which Blacks were lucky to have been removed.

The form of the early poems reflects McKay's own dilemma. Upon traditional lyric form McKay grafted the experience and the speech of the Black folk. In sometimes irregular but generally scannable iambics and rhymes, McKay's peasant people speak. Still, the language has the ring of authenticity. Whereas Dunbar's dialect in the United States consists mainly of misspellings of Standard English, McKay's includes idioms, genuine sound variations, and realistic mannerisms. McKay's dialect, despite its aura of romanticism, portrays the folk as real people caught in a political/economic/psychological trap but nevertheless struggling, enduring, and through their own strength prevailing.

In the United States McKay infused Black literature with a new spirit of militant protest. In the bloody year 1919, news of yet another lynching added to the fury boiling in him, and a poem, as he later recalled, "exploded" out of him. "If We Must Die" introduced a new militancy to American literature. In an age when Black American intellectuals were measuring progress by Black people's accceptability to Whites, McKay rallied the oppressed to battle "the mad and hungry dogs'' unmindful even of death. McKay took the rigid form of the sonnet and did things that Shakespeare and the bunch never dreamed possible. He made the sonnet an implement of war.

Among the most prevalent themes in McKay's poems is the theme of exile, a major concern in subsequent Caribbean writing. In cold Northern lands his thoughts turned homeward, and in poem after poem he contrasts the sun and security of Jamaica with the chill and despair of his current environment. In these poems the images are especially vibrant. The toil and eternal poverty of the peasants, so present in the early poems, are missing in the nostalgic poems of home. They reflect the vision of home that haunted the wanderer.

The theme of exile is manifested also in McKay's references to Africa. In the early ''Cudjoe Fresh from de Lecture,'' the speaker sees Africa as a wild, uncivilized place. Years later, in both ''Invocation'' and ''Africa,'' McKay paid homage to Africa's antiquity. In numerous poems Africa is the lost, irretrievable homeland. The Black person suffers a terrible restlessness. ''Something in me is lost, forever lost,'' he mourns in ''Outcast,'' and among men he is ''a ghost . . . a thing apart,'' haunted by racial memories and longing to return ''to darkness and to peace'' but held ''in fee'' by the great Western world. In the Africa poems the theme of exile is broadened and deepened to reach deep into the psyche.

Yet McKay was fascinated by the city. London, Petrograd, Paris, Marseilles, and especially New York appear in his works. The urban poems usually portray the folk meeting the challenge of enduring. In poems like ''Harlem Shadows'' and ''The Harlem Dancer,'' which is probably his finest poem, he paints sympathetic portraits of women who are forced by poverty to exploit their sexuality. In poems like ''The Tired Worker'' he portrays those whose toil enriches the oppressor. ''The White City'' perhaps best conveys McKay's love/hate for the city, which is the metaphor for Western civilization. Here the symbols of the city—the trains, towers, wharves, etc.—''are sweet like wanton lovers because I hate.''

Race is a dominant theme in McKay's poetry. His anger burns in highly disciplined sonnets and other lyric forms. ''The White House'' is among the most eloquent portrayals of the alienated, who through ''superhuman power'' must contain his hate. ''The Lynching'' is a chilling portrayal. ''If We Must Die'' and ''To the White Fiends'' are calls to arms. Certainly there had been nothing in Afro-Caribbean or Afro-American literature to equal the militancy in McKay's poems. Nor would there be for generations to come.

By the mid–1920s McKay had turned to fiction. He continued to write poetry here and there, but his significant output after *Harlem Shadows* was more in fiction than in poetry. McKay became the first internationally known Caribbean novelist.

The first novel, *Home to Harlem* (1928), became a best-seller. Set in Harlem just after World War I, the novel concerns the experiences of Jake Brown, returning to Harlem after deserting the army, which was using him as a laborer rather than a fighting man. The book is a panorama of Harlem folk life. *Banjo*, published the following year, is set in Marseilles, France, and concerns life among the folk who live and work around the docks. By then McKay had lived not only in Marseilles but also in Morocco, where he had been impressed with similarities among African peoples. The major characters in *Banjo*are Black people from Africa and various points in the Diaspora, who come together at a French seaport.

Both novels exploit the theme of cultural dualism. McKay, having experienced Western culture in the United States and Europe as well as in Jamaica, was convinced that the White world was motivated by materialism, greed, and thirst for power. Consequently, White people had lost their ability to respond to life in a natural, spontaneous manner. The Black grass-roots people, on the other hand, had retained these values. Hence, Jake and Banjo are natural men who live the full range of human experience without the hangups imposed by Western culture. Neither character is a simplistic symbol. Both are complex individuals with many-faceted value systems, whose responses to their respective worlds is based upon serious perceptions, not simple knee-jerks.

Contrasted to both Jake and Banjo is Ray, who appears in both novels. Ray is a young Haitian, an intellectual, an aspiring writer. In the worlds of Jake and Banjo, Ray is both insider and outsider, teacher and pupil. Living and working with the folk, he not only gathers material for his novel-to-be but also learns dimensions of Blackness previously unknown to him. Ray resembles McKay himself in many respects; he is often the vehicle conveying McKay's ideas and feelings. Perhaps because of this close identification, Ray never seems as real as the other characters, from whom McKay is able to maintain greater distance.

Setting is vitally important in both novels. With realistic detail McKay has captured the streets of Harlem, the docks of Marseilles, the places where a vibrant Black culture flourishes. The characters are not always lovable. Their world is not easy—but it gives joy as well as pain. And it is the natural world amid the decadence of the West. Thus McKay's first two novels are expressions of racial pride different from the expressions sought by the "uplift" crowd.

Three years after *Banjo* McKay published his short stories. *Gingertown* (1932) consists of twelve stories. The first six are set in Harlem. They present a parade of desperate, laughing people good-timing in cabarets yet economically and psychologically menaced by the White world. The four Jamaica stories, however, show the folk functioning in their traditional home community. Again the influence of White society is destructive; but here there is an intact community, supportive and offering healing. Of the other two stories, one is set in a Mediterranean seaport, one in North Africa. Both continue the theme of cultural dualism.

McKay's last novel, *Banana Bottom* (1933), is his highest achievement in fiction. Bita Plant, removed from her village in Jamaica as a child because of a sexual encounter with Crazy Bow the fiddler, is reared by a White missionary couple, the Craigs. Through an English education and the overwhelming influence of Christianity, they hope not only to cleanse Bita of the so-called rape but also to raise her above her folk beginnings. Returning to Jamaica, Bita lives with the Craigs in Jubilee. Under their influence she becomes engaged to Herald Newton Day, a young preacher who is also their protégé and who has assimilated their value system. The Craigs, as they see it, have done their duty of raising the lowly.

The movement of the novel is Bita's gradually divesting herself of destructive values in Western culture and reintegrating with her community. Her progression can be seen in terms of her acceptance of her sexuality. Bita's sexual initiation by Crazy Bow is a natural act in an idyllic setting. But as a consequence he is imprisoned and she is whisked off to England for purification. The Craigs' own sexual warping is symbolized by their damaged child. The effect of the repression required by their world is seen in the upright Herald Newton Day, who is discovered fornicating with a goat.

Here McKay's theme of cultural dualism is exploited more effectively than in his other works. Kenneth Ramchand points out that in Bita Plant the polarized characters of Jake and Ray or Banjo and Ray are synthesized. With the intellectual development of Ray and the naturalness of Jake/Banjo, Bita is whole (*The West Indian Novel and its Background*, 1970, p. 259). The key to the resolution may be setting. In the earlier novels the characters are basically isolated people far from their origins—like McKay, the eternal outsider. *Banana Bottom* is set in Bita's homeland, the place of wholeness and health.

All the while that McKay was writing poetry and fiction, he was also writing prose nonfiction. These works constitute social commentary not typical of Black writing of his time. During the 1920s his articles and reviews represented the only Black voice in the radical movement both in Europe and in the United States. In his literary criticism McKay urged Black artists to free themselves of the literary conventions which bound them—the protest tradition, imitation of White writing, whatever—and to express to the fullest the spirit of Black culture as they perceived that spirit.

McKay's autobiography, *A Long Way from Home*, comes out of the dreary years of his return to the United States. It is valuable not only because of what it reveals about McKay himself but also because of its vignettes of people and places. The final chapter is an essay, "On Belonging to a Minority Group." His vision here is global. American Negroes, he insists, could take the lead in freeing Black people of the incubus of oppression. But American Negroes, he writes, lack a group soul, without which they will never progress. He points out that Negroes need to recognize that aggregation is not the same as segregation, that there needs to be coalescence of the intelligentsia and the masses, that the key to freedom lies in unity.

At the end of his life McKay was working on a second autobiography. "My Green Hills of Jamaica" was to be a section of a joint work with Cedric Dover. Before the work was finished, McKay was dead. It lacks the vibrancy of the earlier works: McKay knew that he was soon to die. But the work is a distillation of what he had learned in a lifetime of wandering. He remembered Jamaica as an essentially good place, despite the divisive effects of colonization, a place which may indeed hold the key to the future for Black people worldwide. He saw American racism, coupled with parochialism and greed, as a global danger. He saw Black people's salvation in unity and in organization.

McKay cannot be called a great writer because the quality of his work was uneven. He was always somehow the outsider. Mainly he was fiercely independent, a follower of no doctrine but his own thought. He was a man buffeted by many dilemmas. He lived in a transitional time, when directions were unclear. His own direction pointed far beyond his time.

CRITICAL RECEPTION

McKay's work stirred critical controversy during his lifetime. In relatively recent years it has begun to receive the serious study it merits. He was a pathfinder. Only after a West Indian and a Black American criticism took shape—for he is claimed by both—could one look back and see McKay's vital role.

McKay's early volumes, *Songs of Jamaica* and *Constab Ballads*, are undoubtedly landmarks in West Indian literature. Although they were acclaimed in London and Jamaica at the time, there has been little serious study of these early poems. Jean Wagner's *Black Poets of the United States* (1973) analyzes theme and form in these poems and relates them to McKay's subsequent development. Critics generally agree that McKay's best poetry was written from 1917 to 1922. The strict European form and sometimes obsolescent "poetic" diction are seen as limiting their effectiveness. George E. Kent's definitive essay, "The Soulful Way of Claude McKay" (1970), pinpoints these flaws:

> What McKay frequently needs is the single imposing image or the suggestive phrase that will make the poem an extraordinary experience for the mind. In many poems, the images are without the sharply etched visual outlines that would deepen meaning and distinguish them from their use by other poets. Other flaws: the lame last line, excessive labeling of feelings and emotions, over-simple oppositions of the virtues of the country and the evils of the city. (pp. 45–46)

Nevertheless, Kent and most other critics point out that McKay ushered into Black poetry a passionate note of protest and a profound commitment to the folk, who are the lifeblood of Black literature. Kent sums up the essence of McKay's poetry:

> It is the story of a soul whose flight from the village into the machine cultural centers of the West creates a sense of permanent loss. It is conscious now of the disinheritance of all black people, wherever the West has entered with its "wonders," and it can only keep itself together by a sense of its inner rhythms, its occasional glimpses of a warmer world behind, its fleeting loves and fellow-feeling, and its capacity for hatred. (p. 46)

The most noted early assessment of McKay's poetry is to be found in Saunders Redding's *To Make a Poet Black* (1939). Perhaps the most extended analysis of McKay's poetry is in Jean Wagner's *Black Poets of the United States*.

McKay's fiction has had a wide range of assessments. Despite its popularity, *Home to Harlem* horrified several Black American critics with its portrayal of Harlem cabaret life, sex without benefit of clergy, and what they considered the low-nigger stereotype. W.E.B. Du Bois, in a famous putdown, declared that the book was so filthy that after reading it he had the urge to take a bath (*The Crisis* [June 1928], 202). However, subsequent evaluations have seen both *Home to Harlem* and *Banjo* as serious statements on cultural dualism and the search for a Black identity.

Banana Bottom is generally considered a West Indian classic. "Bita Plant," writes Kenneth Ramchand, "is the first achieved West Indian heroine and *Banana Bottom* is the first classic of West Indian prose" (*The West Indian Novel and its Background*, p. 259). The particular significance of *Banana Bottom* to West Indian literature is suggested by critic J. Michael Dash. He recalls that Edward Brathwaite once wrote that West Indian artists and thinkers are born into a fragmented society. Writers must make the society aware of this lack of a sense of wholeness, then seek to heal it (Brathwaite, "Timehri," *Savacou* 2 [September 1970], 36). Dash suggests that *Banana Bottom* is a precursor of this second phase because of Bita Plant's reintegration into the community ("Edward Brathwaite," in King, *West Indian Literature*, 1979, p. 220).

Critics have pointed out flaws in McKay's fiction, which is uneven in quality. Nevertheless, there are many assessments of the value of McKay's contribution to fiction. Wayne F. Cooper sees the thrust of McKay's fiction as vitally important:

> All of McKay's fiction pointed toward the need for a black community identifying itself as such and accepting confidently its own unassailable humanity and cultural values. To participate fully in a larger national or international community, blacks in the United States and the West Indies had first to fulfill their own potentialities as members of identifiable ethnic groups. To be Americans or Jamaicans in any effective sense, they must first be themselves, not rootless imitators of middle-class Anglo-Saxons. (*The Passion of Claude McKay*, 1973, pp. 131–32)

There are now several volumes on McKay. Addision Gayle's *Claude McKay: The Black Poet at War* (1972) considers McKay as a militant protester. James R. Giles's *Claude McKay* (1976) is a thorough analysis of McKay's life and works. In *The Passion of Claude McKay* (1973) Wayne F. Cooper collects samples from McKay's works. The articles and letters are especially helpful, for they are not easily accessible elsewhere.

Certainly Claude McKay has become recognized as an important figure in both Caribbean and Black American literature. St. Clair Drake in his introduction to the 1970 edition of *A Long Way from Home* sees McKay in his ultimate role, a man of the African Diaspora:

McKay's life was a single episode in the 500-year-old drama of the black diaspora, that massive dispersal of millions of men and women out of the great African homeland to the Caribbean islands and onto the American continents. He symbolizes their wanderings backward and forward between Africa and the New World, and from both of these areas to Britain and Europe. They have become detribalized in the process and have developed a pan-African consciousness. (pp. x–xi)

HONORS AND AWARDS

McKay was the first Black man to receive the medal of the Jamaica Institute of Arts and Sciences, 1912. He was posthumously awarded the Order of Jamaica in 1977.

BIBLIOGRAPHY

Works by Claude McKay

Constab Ballads. London: Watts, 1912.

Songs of Jamaica. Kingston: Aston W. Gardner, 1912.

Spring in New Hampshire and Other Poems. London: Grant Richards, 1920.

Harlem Shadows. New York: Harcourt, Brace, 1922.

The Negroes of America. Moscow: Gosizdat, 1923.

Home to Harlem. New York: Harper, 1928; Chatham, N.J.: Chatham Book Seller, 1973.

Banjo: A Story Without a Plot. New York: Harper, 1932; New York: Harcourt Brace Jovanovich, 1970.

Gingertown. New York: Harper, 1932.

Banana Bottom. New York: Harper, 1933; New York: Harcourt Brace Jovanovich, 1961.

A Long Way from Home. New York: Lee Furman, 1937; New York: Harcourt, Brace and World, 1970.

Harlem: Negro Metropolis. New York: Dutton, 1940.

Selected Poems. New York: Bookman, 1953.

"Boyhood in Jamaica." *Phylon* 13 (2nd quarter, 1953), 134–45.

My Green Hills of Jamaica. Washington, D.C.: Howard University Press, 1975; Kingston: Heinemann Educational Books, 1979.

Studies of Claude McKay

Barksdale, Richard K. "Symbolism and Irony in McKay's *Home to Harlem*." *CLA Journal* 15 (March 1972), 338–44.

Bronz, Stephen H. *Roots of Negro Racial Consciousness*. New York: Libra Press, 1964.

Collier, Eugenia W. "The Four-Way Dilemma of Claude McKay." *CLA Journal* 15 (March 1972), 345–53.

Conroy, Sister Mary. "The Vagabond Motif in the Writings of Claude McKay." *Negro American Literature Forum* 5 (Spring 1971), 15–23.

Cooper, Wayne F. "Claude McKay and the New Negro of the 1920s." *Phylon* 25 (Fall 1964), 297–306.

———, ed. *The Passion of Claude McKay: Selected Poetry of Claude McKay, 1912–1948*. New York: Schocken Books, 1973.

Drake, St. Clair. Introduction to *A Long Way from Home*. New York: Harcourt, Brace, 1970.

Gayle, Addison Jr. *Claude McKay: The Black Poet at War*. Detroit: Broadside Press, 1972.

———. *The Way of the New World: The Black Novel in America*. New York: Anchor Press, 1975.

Giles, James R. *Claude McKay*. Boston: Twayne, 1976.

Gloster, Hugh M. *Negro Voices in American Fiction*. Chapel Hill: University of North Carolina Press, 1948.

Huggins, Nathan Irvin. *Harlem Renaissance*. New York: Oxford University Press, 1971.

Kaye, Jacqueline. "Claude McKay's 'Banjo.' " *Présence africaine*, no. 73 (1st Quarterly 1970), 165–69.

Kent, George E. "The Soulful Way of Claude McKay." *Black World* 20 (November 1970), 37–51. Also in Kent, George E. *Blackness and the Adventure of Western Culture*. Chicago: Third World Press, 1972, pp. 36–52.

McLeod, A. L. "Memory and the Edenic Myth: Claude McKay's Green Hills of Jamaica." *World Literature Written in English* 18 (April 1979), 245–54.

Major, Clarence. "Dear Jake and Ray." *American Poetry Review* 4 (1975), 40–42.

Morris, Mervyn. Introduction to *My Green Hills of Jamaica*. Kingston: Heinemann, 1979.

Redding, Saunders. *To Make a Poet Black*. Chapel Hill: University of North Carolina Press, 1939.

Tolson, Melvin B. "Claude McKay's Art." *Poetry* 83 (February 1954), 287–90.

Wagner, Jean. *Black Poets of the United States from Paul Laurence Dunbar to Langston Hughes*. Chicago: University of Illinois Press, 1973.

See also General Bibliography: Allis, Brown, Hughes, King, and Ramchand (1970).

WILFRED D. SAMUELS

Anthony McNeill (1941–)

BIOGRAPHY

In his introduction to *Breaklight: The Poetry of the Caribbean* (London: Hamish Hamilton, 1971), Andrew Salkey wrote that the younger poets were providing a new promise of "spiritual and social definition" (pp. xv–xix); among them he listed Jamaican Anthony McNeill, who was born in Kingston on December 17, 1941, to Mr. Roy McNeill, a former minister of home affairs, and Mrs. Lucille McNeill, now Wint.

A graduate of Excelsior School and St. George's College of Jamaica, McNeill pursued graduate studies in the United States at Nassau Community College, Johns Hopkins University, and the University of Massachusetts (Amherst), where he received the M.A. degree in English in 1976, after having received one from the Writing Seminars at Johns Hopkins, in 1971. Between 1975 and 1981 he was assistant director in charge of publications at the Institute of Jamaica, a post he assumed on returning to Jamaica. He has had a diverse background in the civil service, having worked with Jamaica's Court Office and the Administrator General's Department. He has also worked as a journalist for the *Gleaner*, served as assistant to the editor of *Jamaica Journal*, and written and produced radio programs for the Jamaica Information Service. Between 1982 and 1983 he was a lecturer at Excelsior Community College.

MAJOR WORKS AND THEMES

Although McNeill's early interest was in literature, poetry was not his first choice, in spite of an aunt's claims that Tony was spouting verses at an early age. He wrote his first novel and some stories at the age of twelve and during his high school days was engaged in producing humorous verse to entertain his friends. In 1963, at the age of twenty-one, McNeill wrote what he considers his first serious poem, "Chinaware":

> I do not smoke the more
> Or eat the less,
>
> Nor do I think the world
> a wilderness.
>
> I do not drink in pain
> Each day
> Or in the shadowed night
> Forget to pray.
>
> Yet once my heart,
> A scarlet tear,
> Slid down my cheeks,
> Cracked—
> Like chinaware—
> Upon your marble bier.
>
> (*Jamaica Journal*, 1970, p. 40)

Eight years later, his first collection of poetry, *Hello Ungod* (1971), was published. Two subsequent volumes have appeared: *Reel from "The Life-Movie"* (1972; revised ed. 1975), and *Credences at the Altar of Cloud* (1979). In McNeill's canon, support is found for Salkey's contention that the new Caribbean poets do not speak with a corporate voice but instead with one that, although emergent from "true native concerns," has "broader implications."

To be sure, McNeill's rich Jamaican culture and background provide him with certain themes. Rastafarianism is one example. But even here the focus moves from the specific to the general, and McNeill returns to his overriding concern with the meaning of the human experience in a world that seems ephemeral, one in which inevitable death is the only given. Thus, his central theme is the existentialist's quest for Being in the face of Nothingness.

In "Straight Seeking," for example, the Rastafarian dream of repatriation and ceremonial worship of Haile Selassie are viewed as senselessly optimistic, and even escapist:

> Many believe one day the ship
> will drop anchor at Freeport,
> but now it's enough to praise
> high on the s'liff. The smoke-
> blackened city wounds instant
> divines to enter their pipes
> like dreams. Tonight Jah

rears in a hundred tenements.
Missed by my maps.
Still compassed by reason,
my ship sails coolly between
Africa and heaven.

(*Reel*, 1975 ed., p. 27)

Clearly McNeill's speaker, "still compassed by reason," cannot find in the dreadlocked worshippers' philosophy direction and responses to the meaningful but yet unanswered questions that remain important to his life. We find embedded in the poet's deliberate play on words, "pipes like dreams," a suggestion that the euphoria induced by the locksmen's use of marijuana in their religious ceremonies only leads to "pipe dreams." He remains uninterested if not uncommitted ("coolly") to the fundamental principles of the group.

The failure to view life realistically and even what might be considered the naiveté of the Rastafarian brethren are central to the theme of "Ode to Brother Joe," whose heightened consciousness results primarily from his ritual smoking of the "holy weed," which "opens the door to God," and also by his rhythmic drum praises to "*Hail Selassie I / Jah Rastafari*," after which

. . . the room fills with the power
and beauty of blackness,
a furnace of optimism.

(*Reel*, p. 29)

Oblivious to the fact that Selassie is dead, repatriation is a myth (it is "a million light years / from Freeport"), and smoking marijuana is illegal, Brother Joe is imprisoned when he is caught with the outlawed herb. Although he becomes a martyr to his fellow locksmen, Joe's incarceration and his inability to escape remain concrete: "real"; not even the power of Jah Rastafari can change them:

Meantime, in the musty cell
Joe invokes, almost from habit,
the magic words:
Hail Selassie I
Jah Rastafari,
But the door is real and remains shut.

(*Reel*, p. 30)

It is in "Saint Ras," however, that McNeill's definite statement is made about the liminal experience that Rastafarianism represents. An outsider who marches to the beat of a different drummer, Ras "could never proceed / with the rest." Yet, in his journey toward the ideal "island of Ras," he must come face to face with the realities of his present, absurd world:

But outside his city of dreams
was no right-of-passage, it seemed.
Still-anchored by faith, he idled

inside his hurt harbour and even
his innocent queen posed red
before his poised, inchoate bed.
Now exiled more, or less,

he retracts his turgid divinity,
returns to harsh temporal streets
whose uncertain crossings reflect
his true country. Both doubt and light.

(*Reel*, p. 28)

Life, McNeill suggests through his speaker, must be confronted, not escaped as the Rastafarians choose to do.

In the majority of his earlier works, McNeill further suggests that this confrontation with life is rather painful, for it leads man to a realization of his tenuous or ephemeral existence. In many ways, his speakers come to know the anguish that Sartre claims is known by those who assume the complete and profound responsibility for their lives; it is an anxiety and dread occasioned by the realization that existence opens toward an uncertain future, the emptiness of which must be filled by one's freely chosen actions (see Jean-Paul Sartre, *Being and Nothingness*). McNeill's speakers experience dread in the face of life for they are forced to reach a level of awareness that reveals their aloneness, alienation, and powerlessness; they remain, nevertheless, responsible for the potentiality of their Being, while, like the speaker in ''Blue Sunday,'' acknowledging the absurdity that is their legacy:

I must learn to live with these clowns,
These serious freaks who act out
My own absurdity, these touts
Of fulfilment, these harlequins!

(*Reel*, p. 8)

This is clearly the theme of ''A Dostoevskian Hero or The True Gage,'' in which life (or the world) is metaphorically presented as a circumscribing room whose dimensions must be carefully contemplated. A Camusian alternative is offered:

The actual size of the room
Was, in fact, impressively normal,
But he never quite saw it right;
It was always too large or small.

One day, however, hearing the walls
Like temples about his ears,

He took a gun or a ruler,
Applied it, and got the true gage.

(*Reel*, p. 14)

In taking "a gun or ruler," the speaker faces what for Camus is the "only philosophical problem": deciding whether suicide is the only alternative for a life that is absurd. Given the antinomy that man finds in life/the world, is life worth living, or does suicide offer an escape from hopeless existence? In Camus's words, "Does the absurd dictate death?" (*The Myth of Sisyphus*, London: Hamish Hamilton, 1942). McNeill's speaker must confront this question, and the gun or ruler symbolizes his alternatives. He can attempt to understand it or escape it through suicide.

McNeill's concern with this existential quest for meaning leads him to make death a dominant theme in his work. His approach is Heideggerian, for the very personal tone of his poems in which this theme is found reveals perhaps the poet's effort to come to grips with his own death. At first there is the natural response, fear. In "Who'll See Me Dive?" for example, McNeill's speaker contemplates suicide; he does so from a position of weakness and fear:

Perhaps I should put it off—
but how can I with that fucking note
triggered against a change-of-heart
May as well kill it now, this life

Aimed like a dash so long at death.

(*Reel*, p. 18)

The speaker in "The Crack" ponders the finiteness and meaning of death. He finds it strangely attractive, although oblique and untrammellable:

Today I thought I glimpsed death
in the bougainvilleas;
It had no face,
was oblique as love;
It's what I have been
and would like to be::
a pure chord, a pure stroke
of paint on a canvas,
something without a face,
All poem.

(*Breaklight*, p. 207)

Concomitant to this quest for the meaning of death is often the question of the significance of religion, for man, McNeill's speaker seems to suggest, must come to grips with his own responsibility to create—in fact, to be God. In "First Dark," the speaker declares that it is man's action, not God's, that leads to man's existence. Man must take charge and become; he must move from ''darkness'' (Nothingness) into a state of Being (''were''):

> Lord, your light shone down uncensored
>
> Until we ate darkness and were.
>
> (*Credences*, p. 62)

Exclaiming that ''the light around god is too dark,'' McNeill concludes through one of his speakers that it is in a world devoid of a Christian God or, as he calls it, the world of the ''ungod,'' that man can find meaning:

> un ! god
> you have
>
> touch/d
> me
>
> give
> thanks
>
> (*Credences*, p. 13)

But like Camus, who asks us to imagine the classical Greek mythological hero Sisyphus happy, in spite of his sense of powerlessness in the face of an insensitive world (this is his only way to validate his existence), McNeill, too, resolves that life in all its multifaceted qualities is important: ''I am going to live'' (*Credences*, p. 66), his speaker declares. This resolution is also made by yet another speaker who finds meaning in the flux of life and the renewal of each day:

> [W]rite out the night of death
> the morning will waken
>
> bird on bird   flower on flower
> pebble on pebble   stream
>
> on stream
> ever moving
>
> (*Credences*, p. 8)

A similar determination belongs to the speaker in ''to think i survived being a poet,'' who resolves to ''write it away / the name death'' (*Credences*, p. 34), while yet another speaker shows fortitude and resolve when he asks:

> death when a man so strong
> who could kill him
>
> beside him
> own self
>
> (*Credences*, p. 10)

That life must take precedence over death is echoed in the vociferous declaration of the speaker in ''howling the local'':

I exist I exist I exist
and I

do

(*Credences*, p. 81)

In this adamant declaration is found the speaker's self-affirmation and simultaneous acceptance of the responsibility to piece together the potential, meaningful self that he can become. Assuming an existential stance, he takes reign of his life in spite of its oxymoronic nature—in spite of the fact that ''life is so lovely and dreadful'' (*Credences*, p. 47).

For McNeill, writing becomes the creative act that leads to fulfillment and Being, for ''a poet is someone who lights / words'' (*Credences*,p. 93). He creates and through his creation points the way to meaning and Being. His role is that of ritual leader in a rite of passage to Being.

I give myself bread
and water, water and bread

I will drink no wine
whoever has come for me

tell them I just washed in the steam
whoever has come

tell them
even now

all day
you had wanted poems like these

naked and shoeless
good news

(*Credences*, p. 30)

His poems become sacred gifts like those offered by nature for man's enjoyment and fulfillment. We are told, ''Great poems are radiant flowers / out of the ground'' (*Credences*, p. 27). McNeill admonishes us to find a higher level of consciousness, to find ''light'' by believing in art, i.e., the poem:

the poem

believe in
the poem

believe in
you god

(*Credences*, p. 58)

Poetry becomes the beacon that allows man to affirm himself and transcend his condition to find meaning in the face of his imprisoned state; it allows him to choose the ruler over the gun, in his liminal permeated room. In place of dark death he can in fact find passion and renewal for life in the present.

CRITICAL RECEPTION

In spite of the fact that McNeill's works have not been the subject of any serious critical attention, numerous critics, including Salkey, Bruce King (*West Indian Literature*, 1979), Lloyd Brown (*West Indian Poetry*, 1978), Edward Baugh (*West Indian Poetry 1900–1970*, 1971), and Donald Herdeck (*Caribbean Writers: A Bio-Bibliographical-Critical Encyclopedia*, 1979), have recognized McNeill's promise as an important Caribbean writer and voice. Herdeck acclaims him "one of the most accomplished and promising of the younger group of West Indian poets" (p. 144); and Lloyd Brown notes "the highly polished complexity of McNeill's craftsmanship" (p. 165).

In one of the most extended reviews of McNeill's work, Dennis Scott (*Sunday Gleaner* [January 1980]) fails to note the progression in McNeill's works, one that leads him from anguished seeker to existentialist actor, but concentrates on what he sees as McNeill's "startling development" in his poetic style:

> It employs a number of unusual devices: blurred type, an odd layout, deliberately retained typing errors, photographs, reproductions of favourite painters' work. . . . Much of it is highly personal, referring directly to the poet in a touchingly vulnerable way. And the book is a mixture of miraculously beautiful language and some distressingly self-indulgent experiment. It is conceived as a whole, like some surrealist collage. It celebrates the existence of Tony with a nearly autistic curiosity about himself. It is excessive.

By overlooking McNeill's metamorphosis, in fact, by failing to see McNeill become the existentialist man of action—a god whose prerogative includes creation, i.e., experimentation with language, form, etc.—Scott concludes: "The book needed an editor's hand to remove about one third of the poems."

Also of interest is Scott's introduction to *Reel*, where he describes "the texture of the poems [as] rough and simple like tightly plaited straw" (p. 3) and suggests that "many of McNeill's poems are moving towards a language of myth" (p. 4).

Interestingly enough, McNeill can be said to be victim of the very quality in his work that brought his attention to Salkey, the "broader implications" that can be found in his works. In an interview with Martin Mordecai (*Jamaica Journal* [December 1970]), McNeill suggests as much while discussing the place of a personal voice in Caribbean literature: "I am glad you brought up that point; I think it is precisely this that makes it harder for the man in the West Indies to be an artist, or to be a valuable artist, than possibly anywhere else, because personal poetry is a luxury which we cannot afford. For poetry to have any immediate value in the West Indies, it has got to be concerned with the identity-crisis which exists here."

HONORS AND AWARDS

McNeill is the recipient of several awards and honors, including the Silver Musgrave Medal for Poetry, 1972; First Prize and Gold Medal, Jamaican Festival Literary Competition, 1971; and First Prize and Silver Medal, Jamaican Festival Literary Competition, 1966. His is the only Gold Medal to be awarded in the adult division of poetry since the inception of these awards in 1963.

BIBLIOGRAPHY

Works by Anthony McNeill

Hello Ungod. Baltimore: Peaceweed Press, 1971.

Reel from ''The Life-Movie.'' Kingston: Savacou, 1972, 1975.

The Caribbean Poem [Anthology coedited with Neville Dawes]. Kingston: The Institute of Jamaica, 1976.

Credences at The Altar of Cloud. Kingston: The Institute of Jamaica, 1979.

Studies of Anthony McNeill

Mordecai, Martin. ''Interview with Anthony McNeill.'' *Jamaica Journal* 4 (December 1970), 40–43.

Scott, Dennis. Introduction to *Reel from ''The Life-Movie.''* Kingston: Savacou, 1972, 1975.

———. ''Lightning Words'' (Review of *Credences at The Altar of Cloud*). *Sunday Gleaner* (January 1980).

See also General Bibliography: Allis, Baugh (1971), Brown, Herdeck, Hughes, and King.

DAPHNE MORRIS

Roger Mais (1905–1955)

BIOGRAPHY

As the child of Eustace and Anna Mais, a druggist and college-trained teacher, respectively, Roger Mais belonged to the materially comfortable, educated, colored middle class of colonial Jamaica. He was born in Kingston on August 11, 1905, but his formative years were spent on a remote coffee plantation in the Blue Mountains, where his father decided to take up farming. Here, Mais later wrote, he spent "some of the happiest as well as the most interesting and adventurous years of [his] life" (unpublished manuscript in the Mais Collection, University of the West Indies, Mona). The special significance he attaches to the image of the hills in his writings derives from this early experience. Indeed, throughout his literary career he returned to this source for much of the substance of his creative efforts. The setting of *Black Lightning* (1955), his last published novel, draws on this world.

Anna and Eustace Mais gave their seven surviving children a strict religious upbringing which included daily Bible readings. Thus, from an early age, Mais became intimately acquainted with the Bible, to which he would return throughout his life as much for spiritual insight as for material for his art. Anna taught her children at home until the family moved to a more accessible property, in the same region, where Roger and the younger children attended the local primary school.

At age fourteen he entered Calabar High School in Kingston in order to obtain the all-important Cambridge school certificate. However, although he was successful he made little use of this certificate, which traditionally led either to further study abroad or to a career in the civil service. Between 1922 and 1938 he was, at different times and among other things, a clerk at the West India and Panama Cable Company, an education officer, manager and editor of a short-lived publication called *Jamaica Tit-Bits*, reporter-photographer for the *Daily Gleaner*, garden columnist for the *Jamaica Mail*, insurance salesman, overseer on a banana plantation, and horticulturist.

This restlessness reflected an unwillingness to settle down to middle-class respectability; but more than this, it was indicative of a creative mind in search of its medium. By the early 1930s he had begun writing verse and short stories. But if Mais knew then that he wanted to write, it was not until the social upheavals of 1938, as he told his friend John Hearne many years later while they were in Paris, that he knew why, and for whom, he wanted to write (see Hearne's article, "Roger Mais: A Personal Memoir," *Bim*, no. 6 [December 1955], 146–50).

When workers demanding better wages and living conditions began rioting in downtown Kingston, Mais instinctively felt it his duty to help restore law and order. But on his way to volunteer as a special constable, he changed his mind, pledging his commitment to the people's cause instead. It was the birth of nationalism in the British West Indies, and Mais, like many of his class and education at the time, joined the struggle for universal adult suffrage and self-government.

The National Movement manifested itself as a political, cultural, and artistic awakening, and Roger Mais was actively involved on all three fronts. He was at the launching of the People's National Party (PNP) in 1938, fully supporting the Fabian socialist ideals of its leader, Norman Manley. He began writing for *Public Opinion*, the organ of the PNP, and his was one of the strongest voices calling for an end to colonial rule, wherever it existed—his concern always extended beyond national boundaries. In the events unfolding around him he saw a people fulfilling their destiny, as a nation and as part of common humanity.

No less strong was his call for a national literature and culture, and the zeal of the public voice was matched with a burst of creative energy. Between 1938 and 1944 he wrote numerous short stories and poems and made his first attempts at drama and the novel. Most of the published pieces (stories and verse) appeared in *Public Opinion*, which became the chief outlet for his imaginative writings. He published, at his own expense, two collections of short stories: *Face and Other Stories* (May 1942), and *And Most of All Man* (December 1942). A play, *Hurricane*, was staged in 1943. The unpublished novels, *Another Ghost in Arcady* (dated January 1942), and *The Seed in the Ground* (dated February 1943), are apprenticeship efforts, but the former contains the core of *Black Lightning*. It was also at this time that he began painting, holding his first exhibition in 1943 after painting for less than a year.

Then came his famous piece, "Now We Know" (*Public Opinion*, July 11, 1944, p. 1), roundly denouncing Churchill's warning to the colonies that their participation in the war effort would not affect Britain's intention to preserve the old imperial order. The courts found it seditious and sentenced him to six months in jail. Although he was not badly treated in prison (he served four months), he was deeply affected by the human degradation he witnessed there; this experience is recreated in his first published novel, *The Hills Were Joyful Together* (1953).

After his release he concentrated on his journalism, at first returning to *Public Opinion*. Then in September 1946 he launched his own magazine, *The PEOPLE*. Although declared to be ''Dedicated to the Political, Economic and Cultural Development of the West Indies,'' its chief aim was to expose the failings of the Bustamante government, newly elected in the first general elections of 1944. (Sir Alexander Bustamante founded the Jamaica Labour Party [JLP] in 1943.) To Mais, they betrayed the spirit of 1938; with their victory, he felt, the people's quest to fulfill their destiny was aborted. The magazine, which was irregular and poorly funded, folded after the March, 1947, issue. A bleak period of withdrawal followed during which he wrote little and tried, unsuccessfully,to earn a living by growing rice in the country.

But by 1949 Mais was again writing vigorously, completing a number of plays, many of which derive from either classical mythology or the Bible. One, *Atalanta at Calydon*, was staged in 1950. By December, 1950, he had completed *Blood on the Moon* and *Storm Warning*, the first two parts of an intended trilogy of novels. The third part did not materialize; instead, *The Hills Were Joyful Together* followed. *Brother Man* (1954), his second published novel, was written in 1951. And the definitive version of *Black Lightning*, in the making since 1942, was most probably completed before his departure for England in August, 1952.

It was Cape's acceptance of *The Hills Were Joyful Together* that prompted Mais to join the already growing throng of West Indian writers in Britain. But he was not to savor the pleasures of exile for long. In 1954, while in France, it became clear that he was very ill; yet, the creative imagination of writer and painter was even then giving birth to new ideas. In Paris, with the help of Richard Wright, whom he had met upon his arrival there, he held an exhibition of his paintings. And it was also in France that he began a new novel, *In the Sight of This Sun*. He continued working on it after his return to Jamaica in December, 1954, but was able to complete only about a quarter of what he intended. On June 15, 1955, some weeks before the appearance of *Black Lightning*, cancer, ''that fascist disease,'' as he called it, claimed the life of Roger Mais.

MAJOR WORKS AND THEMES

Mais's three published novels, *The Hills Were Joyful Together*,*Brother Man*, and *Black Lightning*, represent not only his most significant literary achievement but also the natural fruits of his long apprenticeship. The meaning of human existence, which is the dominant concern in all three, is the preoccupation of his entire *oeuvre*. However, it is in these novels that we find the fullest expression of his view of existence and, significantly, his most successful attempt to express this vision in the contemporary reality of the Jamaican common man.

It is significant that his literary career coincided with the formative period of West Indian literature. When he was striving to shape his local raw materials in a form that successfully integrates vision with cultural reality, he had few adequate models on which to draw. In the novels he experiments freely with form and language, exploiting his inherited traditions of Western literature and his indigenous oral tradition, at times fusing elements drawn from both sources. Experimentation is not always successful; indeed, the very fact of experimentation implies that the writer was still in search of his idiom. Yet, with these three novels Roger Mais has made a significant contribution to the literature of the region; in certain important respects he was a pioneer.

As expressed in the novels, his perception of existence is essentially tragic. He recognizes a world in which human suffering prevails but which also embodies hope. This hope lies in man himself, who, through the realization of his innate human dignity and capacity for goodness, can triumph over his suffering, individually and communally. In man's failure to realize his potential to shape his destiny lies his tragedy. The deep faith in man on which this vision of immanent good in manifest evil rests, grew out of Mais's lived experience. It is this faith we find expressed in his best-known poem, "All men come to the hills / Finally . . . ," a short lyric first published in 1940 (see *Year-book of the Poetry League of Jamaica* [Kingston: The New Dawn Press, 1940], p. 55).

But, as we shall see, Mais was still working out his metaphysical concerns. This is implicit in the exploratory approach he takes in the novels. Each approaches the vision from a different perspective; hence, there are shifts of emphasis. However, certain major themes recur: good and evil; fate and free will; chance and choice; human relationships, including sexual relationships; man's relation to God.

In *The Hills Were Joyful Together* (cited hereafter as *Hills*) the emphasis is on the tragic nature of existence. Soon after the novel appeared Mais stated in an interview that his purpose "was to give the world a true picture of the real Jamaica, and the dreadful conditions of the working classes" (*John O'London's Weekly*, May 1, 1953). The novel lives up to the author's declared intention in its unflinchingly realistic portrayal of life in a Kingston tenement yard, a microcosm of the world of the working-class majority. But realism is not an end in itself. For while evoking in vivid detail the dreadful conditions of the yard, Mais gives his yard-world a tragic dimension which transforms it into a metaphor of the human condition.

There is no clear plot. Neither is there a central character in the large cast in which virtually every type common to the slum-world is represented; Mais's concern here is more with the group than with the individual. But, in the main, the focus is on the tenants of the yard, which is the central setting. Episodic in structure, the novel is divided into three books, each composed of several chapters subdivided into short scenes. In a cinematic-like sequence these scenes unfold, interweaving characters and action. The dramatic method of presentation, characteristic of Mais's fiction, is immediately obvious in the author's stage direction ("The scene is a yard in Kingston, Jamaica. Time: Today.") and list of "Characters in the Story" (*Hills*, 1953 ed., pp. 7–8), prefacing the narrative.

The novel opens with a graphic image of the yard:

> The yard counted among its ramshackle structures an old shaking-down concrete nog building with the termite-ridden wood frame eating away until only a crustacean shell under the dirty white cracked and blistering paint remained.
>
> This building stood on the south side. A row of barrack-like shacks at back and another row of barrack-like shacks to the north, with the crazily-leaning fence out front, enclosed what was once a brick-paved courtyard. . . .
>
> Near the cistern in the yard a gnarled ackee tree reached up scraggy, scarred, almost naked-branched to the anaemic-looking sky. . . . A prickly lime tree struggled up from among the earthed-in, seamy, rotting bricks in the yard. (p. 9)

This cramped, physical setting of decay, but also of struggling plant life, reflects the social landscape.

For the yard dwellers life is a daily struggle to maintain their precarious hold on existence. Many live by their wits; Zephyr the prostitute is the most financially secure. Theirs is a violent world, and here we find all the evils that poverty breeds. When Surjue is imprisoned for burglary, Rema, his woman, goes mad and eventually burns herself to death, at the same time that he is killed while trying to escape from prison in an effort to see her. Bedosa, Charlotta's husband and the father of Manny and Tansy, is squashed by a train while fleeing from a vengeful Slocum, who has lost his job because of the other's malicious tongue. Shag brutally murders his woman, Euphemia, when he discovers her infidelity; he is terminally ill with tuberculosis, the result of working long years at the gypsum plant. Another, the no-good Puss Jook, is guilty of incest.

The quality of life remains the same when the focus shifts from the yard to the streets and, later, to the prison, which is the dominant image in the latter half of the novel. Yard and prison eventually merge, as implied in the juxtaposition of scenes of both worlds as the novel draws to a close. Thus, the fatal fire which Rema starts in her cell-like room, and that which Surjue sets off in prison to aid his futile bid to escape, become one and the same. The yard, then, is the world, and for its "inmates" there is no escape. The "crazy front fence" and the gully behind reinforce this image of their entrapment.

The social system is held responsible for the suffering in the yard. Mainly through the prison chaplain, Mais registers explicit social protest. The chaplain tells the superintendent, "we make criminals out of men and women and children in the kind of society we are satisfied to put up with" (p. 238). But, through references to the great earthquake of 1907, which devastated Kingston (including the Mais home), we are reminded that human suffering also originates from a source outside of man's control. However, it is man most of all, each individual, who, Mais suggests, is ultimately responsible for his fate. Again it is the chaplain who states this most clearly: "*we* are all guilty, everyone of us. Myself no less than the other man" (p. 239). The people in the yard, we see, have the capacity to transcend their suffering, but instead of drawing on this innate source they seek various means of escape. The center of interest in the novel, therefore, lies not so much in the circumstances of the yard as in the characters' response to these circumstances; and how they respond not only determines their fate but affects others as well.

Two basic means of escape are shown. One is to trust to luck or chance, and this is explored mainly through Surjue, who emerges as the most central character. To him, life is a game of chance, and neither God ("you wouldn't think a guy like that would hide the joker up his sleeve" [p. 60]) nor "any newfangled system" will make things different. But he is betrayed by the Anancy-like Flitters, who tells him he is "just natural born lucky," and in the end he is killed, it is emphasized, purely by chance. Flitters' horrible demise also illustrates the futility of this path; he too thinks he is luck's favorite.

The other means of escape is religion, and several indigenous forms of religious worship are represented. One of the many who seek solace in religion is Charlotta. She, we are told, "wasn't really cruel and greedy as she appeared, but she suffered from a terrible deep-down insecurity that left a void inside her, and she filled this void with a narrow religion, seeking to cover up her insufficiencies and escape her gnawing fears in that way" (p. 31). The inadequacy of this narrow religion is poignantly revealed through Rema; in her deranged mind Jesus is her tormentor. The failings of organized religion are also exposed in the portrayal of the chaplain, representative of the established church. In spite of his good intentions he is ineffectual; his recognition of his guilt is an indictment of the church. God, like arbitrary chance, is indifferent to the suffering in the yard.

Implicit in such responses is a perception of a meaningless world in which man suffers. This is the perception summed up in Zephyr's repeated observation: "Life has got a stick to beat us with—every last, lonesome, sufferin' mother's son" (p. 123). But alongside this view is another which affirms meaning and hope, and the characters themselves provide evidence of this.

Although representative of types, they manifest all the complexity of humanity, capable of brutality, selfishness, and greed, but also of tenderness, magnanimity, and courage. Suggested in this assertion of their basic humanity is their latent capacity to triumph over their suffering. The compassion and generosity of spirit demonstrated by Zephyr, by Ras, whose life is exemplary of his customary greeting, "peace and love," and by the kindly old cobbler Mass Mose attest to this. These three represent a stable moral force in the yard, but they are peripheral to the main action. However, we glimpse this latent capacity in others: in Surjue's courage and commitment to Rema; in Charlotta's ability to summon up an awesome courage when she learns of Bedosa's death; in Flitters' assertion of his dignity ("Some memory of manhood deep down within him rose in revolt" [p. 232]) in the face of certain death. And it is to their capacity to overcome adversity that the symbolic fish-fry scene, a fine example of Mais's innovative use of the indigenous folk elements, points: "And they all laughed, and bright tears stood in the eyes of some, to witness that they still understood the meaning of miracles" (p. 52). Of course there are some who seem totally devoid of the potential for self-realization, but evidence of this potential in others highlights their loss.

By juxtaposing and contrasting characters, another technique to which Mais is partial, he suggests the possibility of choice; all are free to choose their response to existence. The symbolic pattern of juxtaposed antithetical images (light/darkness, beauty/ugliness) which runs through the work, reflecting the author's perception of the duality of existence, reinforces this. Additional support derives from the fluid structure of the novel, which, despite a surface suggestion of formlessness, reveals a careful pattern linking action and consequence.

But the vision of hope is the author's, not the characters'. Although Surjue ponders on the chaplain's remark, "All are guilty," he never comes to a full awareness of its implications; herein lies his tragedy, and the yard's. It is to this tragic vision that the authorial choruses introducing certain chapters speak. Like the classical Greek chorus they interpret the action and, in so doing, relate it to universal human experience. The fifth chorus best sums up Mais's perception of man's situation:

> This is the story of man's life upon earth that formed him . . . it shudders throughout from cover to cover with terror and pity . . . the demons of light and darkness inform all his days and nights . . . it has been attested that he is of threefold dimensions . . . all his being is encompassed about from birth with dying . . . his separate death matters nothing . . . it matters all, that he has turned his back upon life. (p. 184)

The final portrait of the yard which emerges is one imbued with irony. The novel's title, taken from a revival song based upon a passage from the Psalms, "Let the floods clap their hands: let the hills be joyful together" (Psalm 98:8), points to this. The symbolism of the hills has both Biblical and local connotations, alluding to man's state before the Fall, as well as to a time in the historical past when the yard dwellers revealed their capacity to attain their destiny. And that this power is still latent within them is hinted at in the ironic image of the dead Surjue with which the novel ends: "He fell spread-eagled on his back, and lay still. A scudding, shapeless mass of filmy clouds drew over the face of the moon. The stars put out again. A dog howled in the darkness outside the wall. He lay on his back, his arms flung wide, staring up at the silent unequivocal stars" (p. 288). The implicit allusion to the crucified Christ suggests that only Surjue could have saved himself, not chance, symbolized by the elusive moon, nor indeed any "new-fangled system" or mere faith in a supernatural being. This is the answer to the chaplain's earlier despairing cry: "How many Messiahs must be crucified to save the world?" (p. 242); to this fact "the silent unequivocal stars" bear witness. Moon, stars, night, wind are recurrent images in Mais's work, forming the basis of the symbolic pattern through which the vision is expressed.

Brother Man is a natural sequel to *Hills*. The vision of hope which glimmers in *Hills* is now the focus of Mais's attention. The novel is set in the same tragic world, and essentially the same techniques are employed. But with a greatly reduced cast and a more defined plot, it is tighter in structure. The Chorus of People in the Lane which introduces each of the five major sections of the novel is more obviously integrated into the narrative. Here, too, the vision is not imposed, as in *Hills*, but is expressed in, and developed through, a central character. This is Brother Man (Bra' Man) or John Power, a shoemaker who embodies the life-sustaining qualities noted in Zephyr, Mass Mose, and Ras; he can be seen as a fully developed Ras. But Mais's concern is still with the whole community, for the solution which Brother Man embodies is meant for all.

The other major characters are no different from those in *Hills*. Papacita, like Surjue, plays his luck, but he is basically selfish: "Everyman had to scuffle for himself—that was the law of existence as he knew it" (1954 ed., p. 43). He eventually deserts Girlie, his lover, who proves to be his Nemesis. When the novel opens he is turning his attention to Minette. She is Brother Man's protégée whom he had rescued off the streets, out of compassion rather than lust. Then there are the sisters Jesmina and Cordelia. The latter is suffering a nervous breakdown since her man was jailed for peddling ganja. Left with a sick child to care for, she gets increasingly worse, especially after she rejects Brother Man's help and turns to Bra' Ambo, the Obeah man; he serves as a foil to Brother Man. Cordy ends up murdering her son and committing suicide. Her sister, Jasmina, manages to eke out a living for both of them as a dressmaker. But she is caught between her anxiety for her sister and her love for Shine.

The opening chorus makes us immediately aware that we are still in the world of *Hills*: "The tongues in the lane clack-clack almost continuously, going up and down the full scale of human emotions, human folly, ignorance, suffering, viciousness, magnanimity, weakness, greatness, littleness, insufficiency, fraility, strength" (p. 7). Two interwoven but distinctly different voices make up the chorus. There is the voice of the omniscient narrator, who sets the scene and interprets the action in the light of the authorial vision. Then there is the gossipy voice of the nameless people in the lane. They also comment on the action, but without insight:

—Cordy's man get tek-up fo' ganja . . .
—Bra' Man show de gospel way . . .
—Me-gal still wi' hold wid Bra' Ambo . . .
—Coal-price gone up since todder day . . .
—Lawd Jesus, po' Mis' Brody . . .
—No mind, God is over all . . . (p. 8)

(The chorus illustrates well Mais's attempt to fuse elements drawn from the two major sources of his cultural heritage.) The two voices reflect the two levels of perception suggested in *Hills*, but only Brother Man shares the author's insight.

As the answer to the yard-world Brother Man must be seen to belong to this world and, at the same time, to transcend it. Mais's solution is to present his protagonist as Rasta man and Christ of the yard. The parallel between Brother Man and Christ is closely drawn and reinforced by the use of a heavily Biblical diction. But Mais is always careful to locate Brother Man's experience in the reality of the lane.

After his vision, in which "a voice said: 'Go, and anoint yourself, and fast for three days' " (p. 76), Brother Man goes among the people healing, blessing, and teaching the gospel of peace and love. At the height of his fame he is betrayed. His Judas is Cordelia, who frames him for the possession of "thirty-six pieces of counterfeit money." When a report of a horrible murder committed by a wild, unkempt, bearded Black man triggers off a wave of hostility against bearded men, and Rastafarians in particular, Brother Man is shunned by the very people whom he had helped. Eventually he is "crucified" in the lane by an angry mob: "When they had mauled him to the satisfaction of their lust, they voided on him and fouled him" (p. 188). His faithful "Marys," Minette and Jesmina, fetch him home in Nathaniel's handcart. "They washed his wounds between them, and bound them up, and laid him in his bed . . . and kept watch through the night" (p. 189). On the third day, "coming out of a deep sleep," he rises. The novel ends with Brother Man looking out at the sky "where that great light glowed," and seeing "all things that lay before him in a vision of certitude" (p. 191); his vision is affirmed by Minette.

Mais's choice of a Rastafarian image for his central character, especially at a time when, as the novel reveals, Ras Tafarites were being severely persecuted, is a measure of his conviction that the answer to the yard lies in the yard. However, by presenting Brother Man thus, he is no more espousing the doctrine of the cult than he is that of Christianity. Brother Man is individualistic. In his testament he reveals that he "joined the Ras Tafarites in Nineteen Hundred Thirty-Eight year of our Lord, and shortly after left the Brotherhood because of lacking instruction" (p. 112). Here, too, we learn of his early dissatisfaction with Christianity.

The role he assumes as Christ of the yard is one of his choice, arising out of his personal quest for a solution to the violence and misery he sees around him: "Lord, there was trouble enough in the world. . . . What a man needed above all was a clear vision" (pp. 56–57). His two names reflect his twofold nature. "Brother Man," a form of address used by, and applied to, Rastafarians, defines his role in his world; his given name, John Power, points to his symbolic significance. It combines both his ordinariness, as the common name, John, suggests, and his uniqueness. John also alludes to John the Baptist; Brother Man himself makes this connection. As John the Baptist was the forerunner of Christ the Redeemer, so John Power/Brother Man holds out the hope that others in the yard-world will redeem themselves. His final vision is a reaffirmation of the rightness of his chosen path.

The Christ parallel is also an attempt to universalize character and action.

Mais underscores this when he allows Minette, while reading the Bible, to compare the lane with the ancient world of David: "She could not have put the book down if she wanted to. For these people, and their lusts and their hates, had become real to her. They were as real as the people in the lane" (p. 46); as real as they were to Mais the child, listening to his mother tell these stories.

The self-contained rural setting of *Black Lightning* is far removed from the world of *Hills* and *Brother Man*, but here we find Mais attempting to bring together his tragic vision of misguided man and his vision of wholeness through interdependence, explored in the two earlier published novels. In a synopsis of the novel (typescript in the Mais Collection in the University of the West Indies Library at Mona) he tells us, "It is the story of a strong man's struggle to find self-sufficiency, and how he failed in the least of things and lost all; and of another who grew from weakness to strength, because he found the one thing that the other lacked." There is this story, but, as Mais portrays it, there is an unresolved tension between these two aspects of his view of man's situation.

Jake, blacksmith-sculptor (he is carving a life-size figure of Samson in his spare time) and the central character in the novel, is the strong man whose pride will not allow him to admit his need of others: "He resented, with all a strong, whole man's resentment, any thought of being dependent upon anyone for anything" (1955 ed., p. 69). Yet Jake likes to have others dependent on him. He admits to himself that he encourages Amos, the sullen hunchback and accordion player, "because he wanted to overlay the other's weakness with his own strength" (p. 69). He has a strong sense of social commitment. When Massa Butty and Tata Joe tell him that his vocation as a blacksmith is beneath his education and social status, he replies: "I might have found other things to do that I like better, that would bring in more money, perhaps; but nothing that would have served the needs of a greater number of people" (p. 101). His resentment of his dependence on his wife, Estella, forces her to leave him; her departure takes place soon after the novel begins, but at this point it is suggested that she is deserting him for another man.

After Estella's seeming desertion Jake's struggle for self-sufficiency intensifies. His carving now becomes "the most important thing left to him in life" (p. 82). Alone with it he feels sufficient: "healing went with it" (p. 90). His predicament is imaged in the carving. To Jake, the fascination of Samson's story lies not in the fact of his betrayal but in "what must have secretly lain underneath . . . that the Bible never gave any clue of at all" (p. 60). That Jake identifies with Samson is clear, but the similarity between them is deeper than he suspects. Samson, whose actions were contrary to the purpose for which he was divinely destined, is an archetype of tragic man. (Mais explored this image of Samson in one of his Biblical plays.) In seeking to discover the truth of Samson's situation, which turns on the question of fate and free will, Jake is exploring his, and man's, predicament.

Soon he begins to feel that the carving is "slipping away from him in some intangible manner" (p. 82). The figure of a weak, blind Samson leaning on a little boy that is taking shape beneath his hands is symbolic of Jake, representative of suffering man. Jake is distressed; showing Amos the carving, he asks: "But to what end, Amos? Where will he take that burden. . . . And be restored to himself again, whole?" (p. 110) It is implied that as the carving "takes its own end into its own hands" (p. 112), so Jake/suffering man is responsible for his end; only Jake can relieve his suffering. But to do so means accepting his lack of self-sufficiency, and this he cannot do. His spiritual blindness is made manifest when, at the end of this scene, he is struck blind by lightning, now becoming completely dependent on others.

For a while Jake broods on the question of man's freedom to shape his destiny, trying to understand his situation. Discussing this with Amos he compares the artist's relation to his work with God's to man, then asks: "Does [God] create [man] down to the last atom and pulse of life and intelligence and will that's inside him?" (p. 122). The uncomprehending Amos advises him to "leave all them things alone" (p.123). He withdraws into a deep gloom, eventually chops up his carving, offering it to Bess, his housekeeper, who is in need of firewood, and goes into the woods to shoot himself. Estella (she has returned to the village in secret) and Amos are also in the woods and are aware of Jake's intention, but they can do nothing. That Jake alone is responsible for his fate is affirmed by Estella, who, choric-like, declares: "I believe we shape the circumstances that make us what we are—in the end" (p. 217).

Counterpoised to Jake's tragic decline is Amos's growth. Ironically, he, through Jake's increasing dependence on him, discovers his self-worth and is restored to wholeness with himself and his community. The interwoven subplot of the lovers, Glen and Miriam, also moves from discord to harmony. They are pledging their love in the woods even as Jake is destroying himself. Also contributing to this movement toward wholeness is the depiction of the young boy, George, another of Jake's dependents. His finally realized gallop on Beauty the mare is a celebration of the harmony between man and nature.

Set against this assertion of life, Jake's self-destructive act makes him out to be misguided man at odds with his world. But the overwhelming sense of tragedy that we are left with is evoked by the dilemma, not of misguided man, but of the artist, denied the freedom necessary for his pursuit of truth. It is suggested that Jake's blindness is divine punishment for seeking to understand man's condition. Mother Coby, the village seer, had warned him of making "graven images" "contrary to the word of God." But to deny man self-sufficiency is to contradict the notion of his freedom. Is this the inherent contradiction in the universe Jake recognizes and refuses to accept? The novel does not make this clear. But seen in this light his blindness, then, is symbolic not of the spiritual blindness of misguided man but of the dark vision, the blinding truth he discovers through his art. This is implicit in the novel's paradoxical title. Jake's tragedy, it is implied, lies in the conflict between his public role as socially committed man and his private one as artist. But neither is it clear why these two roles are irreconcilable; that they are is simply given. The questions about man's freedom to shape his destiny and the dilemma of the artist in society, raised through Jake, not only remain unresolved, they modify significantly the vision of wholeness which the novel finally asserts.

Mais's long preoccupation with Jake's story (he also wrote a dramatized version which predates the novel) tells us something of its importance to him. The image of the artist as a tragic figure is also suggested in some of the later plays. One of these, *The First Sacrifice* (see *Focus*, 1956, pp. 186–211), explores the question of fate and free will through Cain, described as "mystic and poet." By departing radically from the Bible story Mais suggests that Cain's sin, like Jake's, is "pride of the intellect"; he, too, is punished by God because he seeks to understand the origin of sin/suffering, "to aspire to the heart and mind of God." Emerging from the portrayal of Cain is an image of the artist as scapegoat, not unlike that intimated in Jake's portrayal; we recall Prometheus when Jake offers his carving as firewood. Like the novel, the play ends celebrating the goodness of life. And it was to the questions raised in *Black Lightning* that Mais was returning in his unfinished novel, *In the Sight of This Sun*. The fragment is a closely reworked version of the David-Bathsheba-Uriah story, but the author's concerns are with his contemporary reality. David, destined to save his nation yet guilty of the gravest sins (like Samson), is the central figure, and he is presented as artist and committed leader. However, as to how Mais would have resolved these questions here one can only conjecture.

Mais's concern with the dilemma of the artist in society, West Indian society in particular—an issue that was first highlighted by him but is now a central concern of others such as Lamming, Brathwaite, and Walcott—grew out of his personal experience. Like Jake, he was an artist estranged from his society. His feelings of estrangement are poignantly expressed in an article he wrote shortly before his departure for England, "Why I Love, and Leave Jamaica" (reproduced in *Public Opinion*, Roger Mais supp., June 10, 1966). Here he speaks of his deep love for "her burnished hills" but also of his contempt for her "loss, or lack of values"; "the Philistines are encamped here," he states. He concludes:

> You think I am angry? Well just listen to this exhortation of another writer in another age:
>
> *Understand, ye brutish among the people; And ye fools, when will ye be wise?*
>
> I am just a small boy among the angry ones making their thunder down the ages; don't kid yourselves about anything, that's all.

CRITICAL RECEPTION

For a number of years after the publication of his three novels Roger Mais's reputation as a writer was seen to rest on his exposure of Jamaican slum life in *Hills* and *Brother Man*. It was not until the late 1960s, when his work began to attract serious critical attention, that the critics began to see Mais as more than a novelist of social protest. But while revealing the wider scope of his achievement, they recognize flaws in the writing. However, as this survey of some of the more noteworthy studies of Mais reveals, opinions vary on the particular strengths and weaknesses of each novel.

Karina Williamson (''Roger Mais: West Indian Novelist,'' 1966) was among the first to draw attention to the tragic quality and ''universal'' dimension of the author's vision. In *Hills* she sees Mais ''aiming at a sort of Jamaican tragedy on Dreiserian lines'' (p. 142) and finds the loose structure and arbitrariness of the choric passages to be the novel's main weaknesses. But, she continues, the two later novels, in which Mais ''moved closer to classical drama,'' though more firmly structured ''lack the prodigious vitality of *The Hills*'' (p. 145). Still, it is *Black Lightning*, most of all, that seems to her ''a landmark in the development of the West Indian novel'' as ''there is nothing exclusively Jamaican about Jake's situation'' (p. 147).

Overthrowing the image of Mais as the angry, political novelist is the prime motive of Bill Carr in his wide-ranging, informative article, ''Roger Mais: Design from a Legend'' (1967). Drawing on his examination of Mais's *oeuvre* (published and unpublished writings), he argues forcefully that ''Mais was a genuinely tragic writer, and his tragic sensibility (which at times expresses mere pessimism) is inadequately represented when it is discussed against Jamaican history and Jamaican economic misery exclusively'' (p. 28). He recognizes in *Hills* ''moments, especially in the choric passages,'' when ''the writing becomes inflated and self-conscious,'' but ''what is truly important is the ways in which the yard, its setting and its people became universal emblems for experience as the novelist perceives it'' (p. 19). The protagonist of *Brother Man* he finds ''incomplete until he can become fully aware of Minette'' (p. 23) and notes that ''apart from [his 'vision of certitude' and Minette's 'little flame'] 'the waste remains' '' (p. 25). To him also *Black Lightning* ''attests most strongly to Mais's talent,'' for here ''his earlier ventures into sentimentality are strongly eschewed, partly by the economy and clarity of the writing, and partly by an insight into human relationships that is not cluttered by assertions as to what relationships should be like'' (p. 27).

Kenneth Ramchand (*The West Indian Novel and its Background*, 1970) also argues that it is upon *Black Lightning* that Mais's reputation must rest. The central weakness in *Hills*, he points out, lies in the author's ''philosophy.'' Noting that the authorial intrusions in the novel advance two main ''philosophies''—''materialistic determinism'' and ''a philosophy of Chance, or the indifference of the Universe''—he states: ''As Mais declares them, however, these philosophies clash, and his art is at its least convincing when he tries to show them working together'' (p. 180). And it is in the presentation of the central character that he locates Mais's failure in *Brother Man*: ''The conflict which ought to have been located in the character registers only as an uncertainty of intention in the author. . . . The shock of Bra' Man's failure is plastered over by an ambiguous 'vision of certitude' '' (p. 184). In *Black Lightning*, on the other hand, ''Mais now invests in the consciousness of his fictional character'' (p. 185). He notes: ''It satisfies our sense of the protagonist's stature that with the tragic discovery of his own and Samson's dependent humanity Jake should move inevitably to an aristocratic suicide'' (p. 186).

But to Edward Brathwaite *Brother Man* ''is Mais's 'best' published work because it brings together in one minor classic, all the aspects of his instincts and talents'' (Introduction to *Brother Man*, 1974 ed., p. x). Claiming that the novel ''could best be studied in aesthetic relation to black urbanized folk music,'' he proceeds to illustrate this in an interesting analysis of the work's formal structure in terms of jazz patterns. (This is more fully developed in his ''Jazz and the West Indian Novel,'' *Bim* 44–46 [1967–68]; the section on *Brother Man* is reprinted in Baugh, *Critics on Caribbean Literature*, 1978, pp. 103–12). But, ''since Bra' Man's 'crucifixion' comes about through the action of the until then structurally passive Chorus/public, rather than through the actions of the personae of the plot, it is in a sense a weakness. . . . Characterization, while not becoming caricature, was becoming, like the Chorus, anonymous'' (p. xviii). However, he considers this failure ''marginal compared to the aesthetic discoveries Mais was beginning to make in the novel'' (p. xviii). *Hills* he describes as ''the English-speaking West Indies' first ghetto novel'' (p. viii), even while recognizing DeLisser, Mendes, and James as Mais's predecessors. But in *Black Lightning* he sees Mais ''moving towards individuation and away from the folk/urban expression of his first two published novels'' (p. xix).

In her study of *Hills* and *Brother Man* (*Roger Mais*, 1978) Jean D'Costa notes, ''The special significance of Mais's achievement is simply its pioneering novelty'' (p. 7). Focusing on Mais's experimentation with form based on a structural pattern she refers to as ''the group-as-hero,'' she illustrates, through a careful and sensitive analysis of the novels, Mais's success with this form. But she also points to the negative side of experiment and innovation. ''Self-indulgent excess and factual inaccuracy'' she identifies as two of Mais's faults as a stylist, especially in *Hills*, where she notes instances of heavy didacticism, unintentional vulgarity and bad taste (p. 68). She concludes, however, that whatever the faults, the ''two novels offer the opportunity to look back into our past and beyond our own history into the illimitable flow of life stretching from the sharp particular moment'' (p. 72). ''*Black Lightning*,'' she writes in her introduction to the Heinemann edition of the novel, ''is the flawed experiment of an artist who takes great risks in order to question the role of the creative man in society. . . . [But] it is worth reading carefully because of the ways in which the exploration succeeds and fails'' (p. 7). (Her essay in James, *The Islands in Between*, 1968, published under the name Creary, is also useful.)

HONORS AND AWARDS

The Order of Jamaica was conferred posthumously on Roger Mais in 1978, ''for his contribution to Jamaica's political development.''

BIBLIOGRAPHY

Works by Roger Mais

The Hills Were Joyful Together. London: Jonathan Cape, 1953; London: Heinemann, 1981.

Brother Man. London: Jonathan Cape, 1954; London: Heinemann, 1974.

Black Lightning. London: Jonathan Cape, 1955; London: Heinemann, 1983.

The Three Novels of Roger Mais. London: Jonathan Cape, 1966, 1970.

Studies of Roger Mais

Brathwaite, Edward. Introduction to *Brother Man*. London: Heinemann, 1974.

Carr, Bill. ''Roger Mais: Design from a Legend.'' *Caribbean Quarterly* 13 (March 1967), 3–28.

Creary (now D'Costa), Jean. ''A Prophet Armed: The Novels of Roger Mais.'' In *The Islands in Between*, ed. Louis James, 1968, pp. 50–63.

Dathorne, Oscar R. ''Roger Mais: The Man on the Cross.'' SIN 1 (Summer 1972), 275–83.

D'Costa, Jean. Introduction to *Black Lightning*. London: Heinemann, 1983.

———. *Roger Mais*. London: Longman, 1978.

Grandison, Winnifred. ''The Prose Style of Roger Mais.'' *Jamaica Journal* 8 (March 1974), 48–54.

Lacovia, R. M. ''Roger Mais: An Approach to Suffering and Freedom.'' *Black Images* 1 (Summer 1972), 7–11.

Morris, Daphne. Introduction to *The Hills Were Joyful Together*.London: Heinemann, 1981.

Ramchand, Kenneth. ''The Achievement of Roger Mais.'' In *The West Indian Novel and its Background*, 1970, pp. 179–88.

Williamson, Karina. ''Roger Mais: West Indian Novelist.'' *Journal of Commonwealth Literature*, no. 2 (December 1966), 138–47.

See also General Bibliography: Allis, Baugh (1978), Cudjoe, Gilkes, Hughes, Moore, and Ramchand (1976).

REINHARD W. SANDER

Alfred H. Mendes (1897–)

BIOGRAPHY

Alfred H. Mendes was born in Trinidad on November 18, 1897. His father was a well-to-do Trinidad merchant of Portuguese descent, and in keeping with this status Mendes was sent to school in England from the age of eight, where he received his secondary education at Hitchin Grammar School. When World War I broke out, Mendes joined the First Rifle Brigade and was posted to Flanders and France. Although he was decorated for bravery during the war, he was appalled by the sordidness of the struggle and began to see the war as a mindless sacrifice of life, engineered by the major European powers in their pursuit of selfish imperialist aims. The 1917 October Revolution in Russia by contrast provided Mendes (and a whole generation of Western intellectuals) with a new framework within which to interpret modern society. Looking back at this phase of his intellectual development, Mendes has commented: "Today, after this long distance from the Russian Revolution, no member of the two generations that followed it can have the faintest idea of how moved, how uplifted and how hopeful those of us were who could sense its implications and its inherent possibilities. World War I with its ghastly disillusionment and its Death, its broken promises and its cynicism had left us eager to clutch at any straw of hope in a drowning sea" (Kenneth Ramchand, "The Alfred Mendes Story," 1977, p. 6). Mendes returned to Trinidad in 1920 fired with socialist ideals. From his new perspective he saw Trinidad as another casualty of British imperialism and the local middle class of which he was a part as subservient imitators of the metropolitan bourgeoisie. He was not a political revolutionary, so his attack was directed mainly at the social and cultural values of the colonial middle class. He challenged the authority of orthodox religion and attacked conservative attitudes to art and literature. In a commentary published in *Trinidad* he maintained: "The *Zeitgeist* is one of revolt against established customs and organic loyalties. Since the War, this revolt has been directed not so much against the Puritanism of the 16th century as against a degenerate form of it popularly known as Victorianism" (Reinhard W. Sander, ed. *From Trinidad: An Anthology of Early West Indian Writing* [London: Hodder and Stroughton, 1978], p. 21).

Soon after his return from Europe, Mendes met C. L. R. James, who was then a junior master at Queen's Royal College. They discovered that they shared a common interest in literature, art, music, and creative writing. Other Trinidadian intellectuals of various ethnic backgrounds and a number of liberal British expatriates were drawn into their discussions, and eventually a group of about twenty people was formed who "met regularly and informally at Mendes' home where they listened to recorded music, argued way into the night, and read excerpts from each other's writings" (Albert Gomes, *Through a Maze of Colour*, 1974, p. 16). Mendes and James remained at the center of this group, and in 1929 they decided to produce a magazine featuring the group's creative writing. The literary magazine *Trinidad* appeared twice: at Christmas, 1929, and at Easter, 1930. At about this time another Portuguese Creole, Albert Gomes, returned from New York to Trinidad and was introduced to the group. Although he shared the general enthusiasm for literature and the arts, Gomes felt that the time had come to launch a magazine with a broader perspective. In March 1931 he published the first issue of *The Beacon*, and over the next three years twenty-eight issues of the magazine appeared. *The Beacon* now became the rallying point of the original literary group, and as its reputation as an anti-establishment journal became known, other Trinidadians made contact with the editor and his friends. The constant supply of new material soon transformed the magazine from being "the mouthpiece of a clique" to what Gomes has described in *Through a Maze of Colour* as "the focus of a movement of enlightenment" (p. 18).

During the 1920s and the 1930s Mendes published about fifty short stories in a variety of local and foreign magazines. Some of his best short stories and a number of poems and essays appeared in *Trinidad* and *The Beacon*. His work attracted the attention of Aldous Huxley, who encouraged him to send the manuscript of his first novel, *Pitch Lake* (1934), to the London publishers Duckworth, where it was recommended for publication by Anthony Powell, one of the firm's readers at the time. Confident of his talent as a writer, Mendes left for New York in 1933 so as to be closer to the metropolitan literary scene. There he made contact with a number of American writers, including Faulkner, Saroyan, Tom Wolfe, Sherwood Anderson, and James T. Farrell. He worked for a time as a reader for Whit Burnett's *Story Magazine*, and in 1938 he was commissioned to write a 150-page brochure for the New York World's Fair as part of the WPA

Federal Writers' Project. His work on the Federal Writers' Project brought him into contact with a number of Black American writers who had participated in the Harlem Renaissance, including Countee Cullen, Zora Neale Hurston, Langston Hughes, and the Jamaican Claude McKay, as well as their younger colleague, Richard Wright. While in America, however, he published only one full-length novel, *Black Fauns* (1935). Mendes recalls that the seven other novels he completed during this time were "destroyed by burning, even before I had offered any one of them to my publishers. That was in New York, in 1940—and now I lament a rash act performed on the edge of a ghastly experience" (Sander, "The Turbulent Thirties," p. 79).

Unable to support his wife and growing family on the earnings from his writing, Mendes returned to Trinidad in 1940, where he took a general interest in the new cultural and political scene. He reviewed art exhibitions for the *Guardian* and wrote articles on calypso, the steelband, and the Little Carib Dance Group led by Beryl McBurnie. A number of short stories he had written in America or published previously appeared in West Indian magazines and in the *Trinidad Guardian Weekly*. On the political side, Mendes became involved in the formation of the United Front, a small socialist party which contested the elections of 1946. However, he soon began to devote all his energies to his demanding new job in the civil service, where he eventually rose to the position of general manager of the Port Services Department. In 1972 the University of the West Indies conferred on Mendes the honorary degree of doctor of letters, in recognition of his pioneering contribution to West Indian writing.

After his retirement Mendes and his wife Ellen moved to Mallorca and the Canaries but finally returned to the West Indies to settle in Barbados. At eighty-seven Mendes is still an avid reader and closely follows new trends in Caribbean writing. He is excited about the republication of his first two novels and hopes that a collection of his short stories, *A Pattern of People*, will also appear shortly.

MAJOR WORKS AND THEMES

Alfred Mendes was the most productive of the writers who contributed work to *Trinidad* and *The Beacon*. In both theory and practice he insisted that West Indian writing should utilize West Indian settings, speech, characters, situations, and conflicts. At first he experimented mainly with poetry, but, like almost all his contemporaries, he failed dismally in indigenizing this genre; consequently he destroyed most copies of a privately published poetry collection, *The Wages of Sin and Other Poems* (1925).

In the short story Mendes found the form and in social realism the narrative techniques to create an authentic West Indian style. The characters in his fifty-odd short stories are drawn from all walks of life. A fair proportion have middle-class settings: two of his stories, "Boodhoo" and "Faux Pas," examine color prejudice within the middle class and its consequences for interracial sexual attraction. In "Colour," which has a Grenadian setting, Mendes describes the tensions which develop between a White American and her near-White West Indian husband, as well as portraying the claustrophobia of middle-class life on a tiny island. Other stories explore themes that would be taken up by later West Indian writers. "Pablo's Fandango" deals with the life of the rural agricultural class, while "News," a humorous story, presents that peculiarly West Indian preoccupation, an enthusiasm for cricket. Like other writers who have since treated the theme, Mendes emphasizes the way in which cricket loyalties in the West Indies have helped to create a sense of communal identity, "uniting the cosmopolitan peoples of the island. What considered legislation so often fails to do, cricket does, for the people become . . . a cricket family" (*Trinidad* 1 [Easter 1930], 119).

Mendes's short stories which deal with Trinidad's lower classes have special significance as, together with those by C. L. R. James, they initiated the tradition of "barrack-yard stories," still very much alive among present-day writers. For Mendes the barrack-yard presented a cultural alternative to the hollowness and conservatism of middle-class life. He was excited by the Creole speech and folk culture of the Trinidadian lower class and set out deliberately to integrate this into his creative work: "What I did in order to get the atmosphere, to get the sort of jargon that they spoke—the vernacular, the idiom—what I did was: I went into the barrack-yard that was then at the bottom of Park Street just before you came into Richmond Street, and I lived in it for about six months. I did not live completely there, but I ingratiated myself. They knew of what I was doing; they knew what I felt about their way of life—that I was sympathetic towards it. So I was *persona* very *grata*. I slept there frequently" (Sander, "The Turbulent Thirties," p. 71). Not all of Mendes's barrack-yard stories are set within the yard. Some take place in dance halls (e.g., "Sweetman"), while others, like "Her Chinaman's Way," take place in lower-class homes. However, with few exceptions all their plots revolve around the struggle of lower-class women to balance the material requirements of everyday life against the desire to satisfy sexual and emotional needs. Mendes attempts to immerse the reader completely in the attitudes and value system of the barrack-yard. He avoids direct moralizing, leaving it to the reader to accept or reject the characters' points of view as expressed in their own words. Through the women's comments on each other and society in general, Mendes is able to extend his attack on the hypocrisy and double values of his own class.

In Mendes's novels, *Pitch Lake* and *Black Fauns*, we encounter the same two thematic interests which dominate his short stories. The first novel is an attack on the Trinidad middle class, especially the Portuguese middle class, while the second is set in a barrack-yard. The central character in *Pitch Lake* is Joe da Costa, a first-generation Portuguese Creole whose father runs a ramshackle rum-shop in San Fernando. When his family decides to migrate to New York, Joe elects to move to Port of Spain and try his luck among the Portuguese elite there. He knows he can be accepted only if he cuts all ties with the lower-class people among whom he has lived and worked as his father's shop assistant. Although

Joe finds a good job in the city, he is haunted by figures from his past. These include his shabby old father, who visits en route to New York; his former mistress, Maria, who is brought to Port of Spain by her belligerent mother to demand money and threaten him with scandal; and an old crony from his San Fernando days, who is constantly trying to draw Joe into what he now considers "low" company. Just as Joe seems to have rid himself of all these embarrassments and looks set to marry a wealthy young socialite, his sister-in-law's Indian maid, Stella, with whom he has been having a clandestine affair, becomes pregnant. Fearing a scandal which could cost him his social position, Joe murders Stella.

Mendes has agreed that the plot of his novel was influenced by Theodore Dreiser's *An American Tragedy* (1925), in which the hero is defeated by a similar combination of environmental factors, but unlike the American novelist he makes no attempt to mitigate Joe's responsibility for his crime. Instead the reader is allowed into Joe's mind and invited to follow the maze of conflicting rationalizations with which the protagonist attempts to camouflage his racial prejudice and social insecurity. He blames his father and the debased social environment of the rumshop, for example, for the relationship with Maria, and as far as Stella's pregnancy is concerned, he is even able to discern cosmic forces at work against him: "If Stella had not been taken on as a maid he would never have come to his present pass. And how had it happened that amongst so many applicants Myra had chosen Stella? Was there not some outside, all-powerful influence at work, an influence against which he was hopelessly inadequate? In that case he was not to blame; he was only a pawn for God to move as He willed, as the fancy took Him" (p. 320). By contrast the author makes it clear from the start that Joe has only contempt for those around him. He has never acknowledged that the people he so despises are the source of his family's income and are therefore worthy of respect: "It hurt him to think that he had wasted so many years of his life in selling rum and cigarettes to common niggers and coolies who were not even fit to tie his shoe-laces" (p. 14). Ironically it is Joe's weakness for lower-class company which wins him a modicum of sympathy from the reader. It is clear that he feels more at home among his old friends than within the exclusive atmosphere of the Portuguese social club. His tragedy is that he cannot reconcile his perfectly normal attraction to pretty girls and comfortable friendships with his idea of what is socially acceptable or likely to contribute to his sense of self-worth.

Joe's personal tragedy becomes a symbol for the sterile, death-bound culture of the group which he aspires to join. Mendes portrays the Portuguese middle class as a clique that would rather die from social suffocation and isolation than risk contamination through contact with their poorer relations or lesser social groups, and he returns again and again to their overt and covert racism. Mendes also accuses the Portuguese community of greed and materialism. In old da Costa this takes the form of miserliness. Conformity to the desired social norms has transformed Henry, Joe's older brother, into a passive nonentity who seems to come alive only during the time he spends gloating over his expensive stamp collection.

Joe's fiancée Cora is one of the few characters in the novel with whom Mendes seems to identify occasionally. Mendes gives her the benefit of a British education rather like his own, which exposes her to more liberal, post-war attitudes to class and the status of women than were current at the time in Trinidad. She is considered the *enfant terrible* of the Portuguese clique but is tolerated because she is pretty, wealthy, and well traveled. Her favorite statement is "I don't care a damn about society," and she enjoys ridiculing the pomposity and narrow-mindedness of her social circle. On several occasions she comments on the oppressed condition of women, especially middle-class women, and on the claustrophobia of colonial life, but ultimately Mendes sees her too as the product of her environment. He portrays her interest in Joe as the instinctive lust for power of a strong-willed individual over someone who is unmistakably weaker.

The writing of *Pitch Lake* preceded that of most of Mendes's barrack-yard stories and *Black Fauns*, and there is a striking contrast between Joe's two mistresses and the barrack-yard dwellers of later works. Both Maria and Stella are portrayed as willing and naive victims of Joe's desires. Only Maria's mother, Miss Martha, with her bold demands and contempt for Joe, has anything like the resilience and pragmatism of the women in *Black Fauns*. It is Miss Martha who stands up for her daughter's rights and refuses to be cowed by considerations of class or race. As she tells Joe in their last encounter: "Not ten like you go put me out of dis yard, you stinking Po'teegee. Not ten like you! I come fo' me rights an, I ain' leavin' till you gie me satisfaction. You hear? I ain' leavin' till you gie me satisfaction! No white man go come an' take dis gerl like a dog take a bitch, you hear? You low dong Po'teegee, you hear?" (p. 215). The women of *Black Fauns* share Miss Martha's independent spirit. Although most of them are wholly or partially dependent on male "keepers" for financial support, the men are peripheral figures. The novel has a loose episodic structure, rather like a series of interlocking short stories, which allows the author to give equal emphasis to each of his female protagonists. Ma Christine is portrayed as the matriarch of the yard. Although she has seen better days as the wife of a schoolmaster, she is versed in the arts of Obeah and provides remedies and advice for the ills of the yard's younger inmates. Two of the latter, Miriam and Ethelrida, are constantly arguing with each other, and their debates allow the author to present a wide range of contrasting views on social issues as divergent as Obeah, sex, marriage, the Catholic Church, and local politics. Both women lament the underrepresentation of Blacks in the City Council, but it is Ethelrida who gives voice to the more militant sentiments of class solidarity and racial pride that were finding currency at the time and would eventually lead to the social upheavals of the late 1930s. Few of the spirited arguments between the two women end in violence, however.

It is Martha, a quiet, withdrawn girl, who provides the most sensational moments in the novel with her two sudden outbursts of violence, one of which leads to murder. She clashes with two other women in the barrack-yard: Mamitz, a mulatto; and Estelle, the mother of a sickly, neglected child. Martha herself has had an unhappy childhood, and in the relationships through which she drifts she seems, unlike some of the more seasoned survivors of barrack-yard life, to be searching for emotional rather than financial security. Estelle exploits Martha's need for love by developing a lesbian relationship with her and forcing her to steal from the other inhabitants of the yard. Martha is able to free herself from Estelle's influence only after she realizes that she is jeopardizing her position of trust in the yard community for someone who does not care for her own child. She reacts by violently attacking her former lover. Her fatal attack on Mamitz occurs when she discovers that Ma Christine's son, Snakey, to whom she has now transferred her affections, has been double-crossing her with Mamitz.

Although *Black Fauns* ends on a note of tragedy and disunity, the author portrays the women for most of the narrative as a closely knit community. The enforced physical proximity of the yard creates for its inhabitants a sense of shared identity. They participate in one another's triumphs and when necessary offer one another advice and material support. Tragedy enters the yard only when its inhabitants break their code of honor and betray a trust. Although Mendes does not minimize the poverty and sordidness of the barrack-yard, he emphasizes the positive human aspects of community life and in so doing makes a case for a life style radically different from the individualism he so abhorred within his own social sphere.

CRITICAL RECEPTION

Within the last decade the significance of the *Beacon* group as pioneers in the field of West Indian fiction has been generally accepted. However, the lion's share of critical attention has tended to go to C. L. R. James, whose short stories, "La Divina Pastora" and "Triumph," had already been anthologized in the mid–1960s. Similarly, the reprint of James's *Minty Alley* (1936) in 1971 preceded the reissue of Mendes's novels in paperback by over a decade. This emphasis on James's work does not reflect the relative quality of the fiction produced by the two erstwhile collaborators, but is rather a reflection of James's deserved stature as one of the foremost Black intellectuals of the 20th century in the fields of political theory and social history. The fact remains, however, that Mendes was by far the more prolific of the two as a creative writer, as is reflected in the greater space Sander deliberately allots in his anthology, *From Trinidad*, to Mendes's short stories, poems, and essays from *The Beacon* days.

Kenneth Ramchand was the first critic to draw attention to the work of Mendes and the rest of the *Beacon* group. In his *The West Indian Novel and its Background* (1970) he points to the published work of James and Mendes as heralding the "decisive establishment of social realism in the West Indian novel" (p. 65). He comments favorably on Mendes's "rendering of the tortured consciousness of his unstable central character" in *Pitch Lake*, but deplores what he sees as a "loss of concentration in the highly exotic *Black Fauns*" (p. 68). Ramchand blames Aldous Huxley's "disastrous" introduction to the 1934 edition of *Pitch Lake* for stimulating Mendes to play "the local colour for more than it is worth" in *Black Fauns* and dismisses the novel as portraying "the lives of a cast of man-hunting, dialect-speaking, slum-dwelling ladies" (pp. 67–68). *Pitch Lake* for him is a better work because of its universal implications. In his introduction to the 1980 New Beacon reprint of the novel, Ramchand comments: "Mendes uses the Portuguese as his raw material but he is not writing specifically for the Portuguese members of the society. The dislocation whose consequences are expressed in *Pitch Lake* is the common experience of all immigrant groups in the islands; increasingly, too, it is being felt as an essential aspect of the experience of the modern" (p. v).

By contrast, Rhonda Cobham in her introduction to the 1984 reprint of *Black Fauns* makes a case for this novel within a completely different context. Drawing attention to the fact that *Pitch Lake* anticipates "the 1950s drift toward a male-dominated perspective" in West Indian writing, she sees *Black Fauns* as belonging to an earlier tradition: "*Black Fauns* is dominated by important female characters—a feature the work shares with most of the novels written by West Indians whose formative years predate the events of 1937–38. This early group includes authors of such widely divergent points of view as Claude McKay, H. G. de Lisser, C. L. R. James, Edgar Mittelholzer, and Ralph de Boissière. Though all the writers listed are men, they all present women as the dominant characters in their novels" (p. vi). She goes on to relate this emphasis to changes in the Caribbean social structure during the period of social mobility that accompanied the movement toward nationalism and sees a connection between early novels like *Black Fauns* and the "new thematic concern with the role of the woman in West Indian society" in the novels of the 1970s and 1980s. Reinhard W. Sander's *The Trinidad Awakening* (forthcoming) puts Alfred H. Mendes's work in the context of his time, contrasts it to that of C. L. R. James and Ralph de Boissière, and offers a close analysis of his short stories, poems, essays, and novels.

BIBLIOGRAPHY

Works by Alfred H. Mendes

The Wages of Sin and Other Poems. Port of Spain: Yuille's Printerie, 1925.

Pitch Lake. London: Duckworth, 1934; Nendeln, Lichtenstein: Kraus Reprint, 1970; London: New Beacon, 1980.

Black Fauns. London: Duckworth, 1935; Nendeln, Lichtenstein: Kraus Reprint, 1970; London: New Beacon, 1984.

"Talking About the Thirties" (Interview with Clifford Sealy). *Voices* 1 (December 1965), 3–7.

Studies of Alfred H. Mendes

Chapman, Esther. Review of *Black Fauns. West Indian Review* 2 (February 1936), 5.

———. Review of *Pitch Lake. West Indian Review* 1 (January 1935), 23.

Cobham, Rhonda. Introduction to *Black Fauns*. London: New Beacon, 1984.

Gomes, Albert H. *Through a Maze of Colour*. Port of Spain: Key Caribbean, 1974.

Gonzales, Anson. *Self-Discovery Through Literature: Creative Writing in Trinidad and Tobago*. Trinidad: The Author, 1972.

———. *Trinidad and Tobago Literature on Air*. Port of Spain: The National Cultural Council, 1974.

Huxley, Aldous. Introduction to *Pitch Lake*. London: Duckworth, 1934.

Ramchand, Kenneth. "The Alfred Mendes Story." *Tapia* 7 (May 29, 1977), 6–7; 7 (June 5, 1977), 6–7, 9; 7 (June 19, 1977), 6–7.

———. Introduction to *Pitch Lake*. London: New Beacon, 1980.

Sander, Reinhard. "The Thirties and Forties." In *West Indian Literature*, ed. Bruce King, 1979, pp. 45–62.

———. *The Trinidad Awakening: West Indian Literature of the Nineteen-Thirties*. Westport, Conn.: Greenwood Press, forthcoming.

———. ed. "The Turbulent Thirties in Trinidad: An Interview with Alfred H. Mendes." *World Literature Written in English* 12 (April 1973), 66–79.

Wills, Leslee and Claire Holder. "The Caribbean Jigsaw: A Portuguese View" (Review of *Pitch Lake*). *The Race Today Review* 14 (December 1981/January 1982), 40–41.

See also General Bibliography: Allis, Herdeck, Hughes, and Ramchand (1970).

VICTOR L. CHANG

Edgar Mittelholzer (1909–1965)

BIOGRAPHY

The general outline of the life of Edgar Austin Mittelholzer, from his birth in New Amsterdam (in then British Guiana) on December 16, 1909, to his sensational and much-publicized suicide near Farnham, Surrey, England, on May 5, 1965, is a pretty clear one. We are fortunate to be able to draw on his autobiography, *A Swarthy Boy* (1963), his book of Travel Essays, *With a Carib Eye* (1958), and the recollections of his second wife recently published in *Bim* (''The Idyll and the Warrior: Recollections of Edgar Mittelholzer,'' 1983), as well as those of A. J. Seymour and Frank Collymore. Together, these give us important information which is missing in the case of most major West Indian novelists. It could also be said that a large portion of Mittelholzer's biography lies in his books and to write about his books is, in a sense, to write about his life for he drew to a remarkable extent on his real life experiences for his fiction, and the places he visited or lived in, the attitudes and beliefs he held, inevitably surfaced in what he wrote. In the end, his fictional world and characters were to prefigure and influence his life in a terrifyingly tragic way.

Mittelholzer was the son of William Austin Mittelholzer and his wife Rosamond Mabel, née Leblanc. He tells us he was the ''offshoot of a Swiss-German plantation manager of the 18th century as well as of a Frenchman from Martinique, an Englishman from Lancashire'' (on his mother's side [Jacqueline Mittelholzer, ''The Idyll and the Warrior,'' 1983, p. 80]) though somewhere along the line, probably through his paternal grandfather—Colin Rickards guesses—

Edgar Mittelholzer's father acquired "a degree of negro parentage" (Colin Rickards, "A Tribute to Edgar Mittelholzer," 1966, p. 98), though he himself was "fair-complexioned, with hair of European texture as were his brothers and sisters" (Edgar Mittelholzer, *A Swarthy Boy*, 1963, p. 17). Always a "confirmed negrophobe" (*A Swarthy Boy*, p. 17), Mittelholzer's father could barely contain his resentment toward, and intense dislike for, this child of his who had "turned out a swarthy baby" (*A Swarthy Boy*, p. 17). It is from this firsthand experience that Mittelholzer undoubtedly derived one of the main thematic concerns in his novels, that of racial admixture and the prejudice, animosity, and hatred engendered by such mixtures.

His restricted and repressed upbringing aroused a rebellious streak in the young Mittelholzer which manifested itself as an urge to violence. As he says, "Any situation that contained the factor of conflict stimulated me" (*A Swarthy Boy*, p. 129), and any disturbance would dissolve the "restless harmony" in him into "roaring chaos" (*A Swarthy Boy*, p. 126). This approach to life was to influence him deeply because he saw everything in terms of a struggle between weak and strong, with the weak being inevitably destroyed. His account of his attempts to get published is cast always in terms of battle and assault, and the last chapter of his autobiography is "Sieg oder Tod" (Victory or Death), an ominously prophetic title.

The autobiography tells us, too, of the sources of inspiration for the young Mittelholzer's literary imagination: the silent film serials, the Buffalo Bill stories, and the detective stories involving Nelson Lee and Sexton Blake. His desire "to create heroes of my own in tales as exciting as those on the screen" led him to decide in January, 1928, having just turned nineteen, that he "had to be a writer" (*A Swarthy Boy*, p. 146). Once he had made the decision, Mittelholzer turned single-mindedly to the task of writing a stream of short stories. He wrote incessantly and quickly, a habit which lasted through his lifetime.

In January, 1929, he began his first novel, *The Terrible Four*, and completed it on the first of March. It was rejected first by Hodder and Stoughton and then by Hutchinson. In this, too, his early life was to prefigure the later struggles to get his work published. In 1937 Mittelholzer published his first book, *Creole Chips*, and Jan Carew recalls that "he published it at his own expense and then walked about the town and country selling it door to door" (Rickards, p. 101).

By 1938 Mittelholzer had had about fifteen rejections of his work, but he persisted. Wilson Harris remembers: "He would never take no for an answer and after each rejection he would try again" (Rickards, p. 101). Receiving a favorable response to the first 30,000 words of *Corentyne Thunder* (1941), Mittelholzer sent the remainder of the novel to a British publishing firm, but before he could get a final reply, war was declared. He volunteered for the army and went into training for six weeks, but the group was soon disbanded for lack of numbers.

In October, 1939, Mittelholzer heard that Thornton Butterworth would publish

Corentyne Thunder in the spring of 1940, but in May the firm went into liquidation. In March of 1941 he moved to Georgetown, where he took a variety of jobs ranging from a tally clerk on a ship, a typist with an American company building military bases on the Demerara, an assistant to an electrical engineer, to a meteorological officer.

In December, 1941, Mittelholzer left Guyana for Trinidad as a recruit in the Trinidad Royal Volunteer Naval Reserve, and *Corentyne Thunder* was published by Eyre and Spottiswoode. He served in the TRVNR, "one of the blackest and most unpleasant interludes" in his life (Letter from Mittelholzer, cited in Seymour, *Edgar Mittelholzer*, 1968, p. 12), until he was discharged on medical grounds in August, 1942, and decided to make Trinidad his home, having married a Trinidadian, Roma Halfhide, in March, 1942. He continued to write and live there for the next five years, during which time he turned his attention to the American market, with the same lack of success. Indeed, he completed a novel, *For Better Things*, which was "intended for the American fiction public" (cited in *Edgar Mittelholzer*, p. 13) and which was to later become *A Morning at the Office* (1950).

In 1947, Mittelholzer decided that he should go to England since he was convinced that only by so doing would he stand a chance of succeeding as a writer. He had been maintaining himself and his family with a variety of odd jobs such as receptionist at the Queen's Park Hotel and clerk at the Planning and Housing Board. He sailed for England with his wife and daughter in 1948, taking the manuscript of *A Morning at the Office* with him. Thus, Mittelholzer was the first of the West Indian writers to journey into exile, recognizing, as Michael Gilkes has suggested, that he needed "a metropolitan audience for his art to grow" (*The West Indian Novel*, 1981, p. 50).

In London, Mittelholzer went to work in the Books Department of the British Council as a copytypist. Through a fellow worker he met Leonard Woolf in June, 1949, and the result was the publication in 1950 by the Hogarth Press of *A Morning at the Office*. Peter Nevill published his third novel, *Shadows Move Among Them*, in April, 1951, and in 1952 brought out the first volume of Mittelholzer's monumental historical epic, *Children of Kaywana*. After its appearance, and despite hostile reviews, Mittelholzer took the crucial decision to give up his job at the British Council and to live entirely by his writing.

In May, 1952, Mittelholzer was granted a Guggenheim Fellowship for Creative Writing. He decided to spend the year in Montreal and to use his time there finishing the second volume of the Kaywana trilogy. The long Canadian winter of 1952–53 made him decide to move to Barbados with his wife and four children, and he spent the next three years in the West Indies. In that time he completed *The Life and Death of Sylvia* (1953), the second volume of the trilogy, *Hubertus* (1954), and his terrifying ghost story, *My Bones and My Flute* (1955). He was also to use this Barbadian setting for four other novels.

In May, 1956, Mittelholzer returned to England. His marriage was deteriorating steadily, and he was granted a divorce in May, 1959, with his wife receiving custody of the two boys and two girls. In August, 1959, he met Jacqueline Pointer at a writers' workshop and married her in April, 1960.

From 1950 to 1965 (with the exception of 1964) Mittelholzer had published at least one novel a year. He had stopped using an agent and handled all his books himself. At first it seemed a wise move, and in 1952 he began an association with Secker and Warburg that was to last over nine years and thirteen books, but in 1961 there was a falling-out over *The Piling of the Clouds*, which they refused to publish because it was "pornographic." The novel was to be rejected by five publishers before Putnam published it in 1961, to be followed by *The Wounded and the Worried* (1962) and his autobiography in 1963. He had promised them a second volume which never materialized after he broke with them as well.

Mittelholzer's problems were steadily growing, and critical reception of his work was increasingly hostile. He had acquired the reputation of being "a problem author," and after 1961, he tells us, he lived "under an ever-darkening cloud-pall of opprobrium" (Jacqueline Mittelholzer, "The Idyll and the Warrior," p. 86). He felt persecuted, convinced that the poor reviews of his books were damaging his literary reputation and interfering with the publication of his work. *The Aloneness of Mrs Chatham* (1965), for example, was refused by fourteen publishers.

The difficulties he encountered in having his books published toward the end of his life affected Mittelholzer seriously. He was badly in need of money to support his first wife and children, as well as his second wife and son. He was putting "a great deal of energy into trying to win a fortune on the football and cricket pools," his second wife tells us ("The Idyll and the Warrior," p. 53).

For Mittelholzer, death had always been a possible solution, as was suggested in that last chapter of his autobiography. If he could not be victorious over the events in his life, then he would rather be dead. He had attempted suicide twice before, once in the 1930s and once after his second marriage. This time he made sure. As "the precarious symbiosis dissolved into roaring chaos" (*A Swarthy Boy*, p. 126), he poured kerosene over himself and set fire to it.

In many ways, it was the logical culmination to the life of one who had always admired the *Gotterdamerung* of Wagner and whose fiction had been so obsessed with disturbed states of being, death, and suicide. Certainly, as Frank Birbalsingh has observed, Mittleholzer's death in circumstances similar to Garvin Jilkington's in his last novel is not perverse coincidence but the "direct result of the unsuccessful sublimation of his own needs and expectations by means of his art" ("Edgar Mittelholzer: Moralist or Pornographer?" 1969, p. 102). The fiction and the reality had tragically and finally merged.

MAJOR WORKS AND THEMES

One immediately striking characteristic of all Mittelholzer's novels is their strongly evoked sense of place. This is as true of his best work, the early novels

Corentyne Thunder, *Shadows Move Among Them*, *A Morning at the Office*, and *The Kaywana Trilogy*, as it is of his later work, including those set in England. He has the ability to conjure up and make vivid any setting, whether it is the tangled Guyanese jungle from which plantations have been newly hacked (as in *Children of Kaywana*) or the dense, insect-infested river forest and moss-covered ruins of Berkelhoost in *Shadows Move Among Them*, or a sleepy English town like Middenshot. This is partly owing to the fact that Mittelholzer drew from his own experience of such places and always used in his fictional world places he had lived in the real world, such as Barbados in *Eltonsbrody*(1960), and Bagshot, Surrey, in *The Weather in Middenshot* (1952).

Throughout his life Mittelholzer was concerned with the weather, and this, too, entered into his fiction. The result is a complex interweaving of setting, atmosphere, and character that is entirely convincing and functions at many levels. In *The Weather in Middenshot*, for example, Mittelholzer has noted that as far as he was concerned, the weather was the chief character, and the atmosphere of that book contributes to its effect because our sense of fear and tension is heightened considerably by the dense fog that envelops the town and under cover of which four gruesome murders take place. Thus, the atmosphere reinforces the plot, the characters, and their actions. Old Herbert Jarrow's obsession with corpses and ways of poisoning people, his taste for newspaper horrors, and his morbid jokes are the psychic equivalent of the physical darkness in the novel.

In *Corentyne Thunder*, on the other hand, we get a depiction of the vast open landscape of the Corentyne coast and a celebration of its physical beauty. Ramgolall and his daughters are seen to be in complete harmony with that landscape, and that identification with the land indicates to the reader that they are whole and sane. But it is not just in his depiction of landscape that Mittelholzer excels. In *A Morning at the Office* he charts for us not only the physical setting of an office in Trinidad but also its psychological dimensions. The barriers and walls erected by color and class prejudice are clearly delineated by Mittelholzer as he shows the shifting emotions of dislike, fear, and envy among the multiracial inhabitants of the office, without scorn or bias.

In addition, then, to his sense of place, Mittelholzer also creates a fascinating array of characters who are sharply individualized and who are three-dimensional, whether it is the ferocious and beautiful Hendrickje van Groenwegal, who dominates the first volume of the Kaywana trilogy with her savage and inhuman treatment of husband, children, and slaves, or the well-meaning and earnest Hubertus, the wretched Sylvia of *The Life and Death of Sylvia*, who cannot survive in the world because she lacks emotional stability, or the delightfully precocious twelve-year-old Olivia in *Shadows Move Among Them*.

Many of Mittelholzer's creations are memorable because they are far from normal. Jacqueline Mittelholzer tells us, "He liked to make the characters in his novels 'a little nutty' for he felt that this would excuse any extraordinary views they express—or any extraordinary incidents he invented" ("The Idyll and the Warrior,'' p. 34). His characters certainly betray a wide range of abnormality, from the eccentric Herbert Jarrow in *The Weather in Middenshot*, who maintains for seventeen years that his wife is dead, though she cooks for him every day, to the deeply disturbed and deranged Charles Pruthick in *The Piling of Clouds*, who first rapes, then murders his neighbor's nine-year-old daughter and then commits suicide, or Mrs. Scaife in *Eltonsbrody*, who delights in cutting people up and stringing their bones together, with the help of a Black assistant.

People with suicidal tendencies exerted a powerful fascination for Mittelholzer, and he has over fifteen characters who at some time or the other either actively contemplate suicide or actually succeed. We can understand Mittelholzer's continuing fascination with this aspect of abnormal psychology in the light of his own three attempts at suicide, the last successful. Indeed, in *The Wounded and the Worried* all the guests at the house party are attempted suicide cases. In one of his last books, *The Aloneness of Mrs Chatham*, he depicts a thirteen-year-old girl who lies down in the road in front of any oncoming motorist she wishes to seduce. Many of these characters are isolated beings who cannot relate to other people because of some deep personality flaw and who seek to invest life with some kind of meaning by doing violence either to themselves or others.

As such, then, we find that Mittelholzer's novels are packed with exciting and frequently violent action, ranging from injecting a murderer and rapist with hydrocyanic acid (*The Weather in Middenshot*) to physical beatings, whippings, castration (*Children of Kaywana*), and murder. This love of action can be traced, in part, to the fact that Mittelholzer's first literary inspiration derived from a love of cheap detective fiction and silent film serials, where frenzied action was the main staple.

But Mittelholzer's work is not just filled with mentally deranged characters or wild and violent action. In the 1950s he wrote to A. J. Seymour that ''sex and religion are my themes as a writer'' (cited in *Edgar Mittelholzer*, p. 14). While the religious part is less clear, he was certainly right that sex and sexuality in its many aspects played an important part in his work, some would say dismayingly so.

Judging from *Shadows Move Among Them*, it would seem that Mittelholzer approved of a free and frank sexuality between consenting adults. This would come about only in a new and truly civilized social system. This he depicts at Berkelhoost, organized and ruled by the benevolent dictatorship of the Rev. Gerald Harmston, one hundred miles upstream the Berbice River. In this mission outpost, all the traditional rules of orthodox religion have been abandoned for a religion of Christ the Man where ''hard work, frank love, wholesome play, spiced with make-believe'' are shown to be ''the life of the kingdom of heaven'' (p. 139). Young Gregory Hawke, who comes to his uncle's jungle mission, is so charmed by his experiences at this hedonistic utopia that he quite forgets his neurosis over his wife's death and is lulled into marriage with the Harmstons' eldest daughter, Mabel. In a sense, this is Mittelholzer's happiest view of the sexual union. In no other book is it so unclouded.

Even in the earliest book, *Corentyne Thunder*, sexual relations are fraught with anxiety and psychic disturbance. Geoffry Weldon, the White hero of that book, suffers a great deal of inner conflict and is unable to reconcile within himself the attraction he feels for Kattree, who is of another race and color, with the responsibility he feels he should have to his family. As Michael Gilkes has pointed out, Geoffry is an embryonic figure in Mittelholzer's fiction for he suffers from a split sensibility that leads to deep inner conflict and a divided psyche which provokes suicidal urges. This is the dominant trait in many of Mittelholzer's leading characters.

It is in the Kaywana trilogy, *Children of Kaywana*, *Hubertus*, and *Kaywana Blood* (1958), that Mittelholzer gives us his most sensational and explicit treatment of the darker side of sexuality. This account of the proud and violent van Groenwegels, starting in 1612 with the half-Indian Kaywana and her Dutch paramour and spanning three centuries down to 1953, gave Mittelholzer unlimited scope to develop variations of sexual attraction and intrigue that were to shock his early readers because of the fusion of sex and violence.

In their settlement of Guyana, the Dutch were undoubtedly vicious and cruel, and their rape of the land was reflected in their interpersonal relationships. Thus, in the novels we get scenes of incest, rape, flagellation, mutilation, castration, adultery, and the further reaches of sado-masochistic behavior. Mittelholzer's reply to the critics, while far from satisfactory, demonstrates what a pioneer he was. He was creating Guyana's early past out of nothing but his own imagination: "*Children of Kaywana* portrayed life as it actually was lived, making no attempt to cater for Sunday School children" (quoted in J. Mittelholzer, "The Idyll and the Warrior," p. 84). He clearly believed, as he makes Dirk say to his daughter in *Kaywana Blood*, that "the sexual urge . . . is the driving force, my child, behind all our actions and all our destinies" (p. 498). In one sense, then it could be argued that for Mittelholzer, sex is a kind of religion.

It is hardly surprising, then, that sexual love appears in no fewer than fifteen of his novels, though it seems always a source of conflict. From Geoffry Weldon down, there is always this sense of the opposing demands of the flesh and the spirit, as voiced by Hubertus, who tries valiantly to tame his "wild blood": "How can one be loyal to God and the flesh at one and the same time?" (*Hubertus*, p. 110). This constant clash between the demands of the spirit and those of the flesh have a direct bearing on two of Mittelholzer's other main concerns. One is his belief that all of life is a constant struggle between strength and weakness and that the strong will inevitably triumph over the weak. It is a philosophy that colored his life and his writing. Characters like Sheila Chatham in *The Aloneness of Mrs Chatham* are shown to be taken advantage of because they are weak and do not assert themselves. In the same way, Sylvia Russell in *The Life and Death of Sylvia* is driven to destitution and death because she is unable to assert her rights and does not have the strength to resist the forces that drag her down.

In Sylvia's case, we find an example of the second of Mittelholzer's pet theories, this time about racial mixing. Sylvia is the product of mixed blood, the daughter of an English architect and a Guyanese woman of Carib extraction. Mittelholzer, both here and elsewhere, suggests that this inevitably leads to genetic imbalance, for the result of such couplings must suffer from bad blood and an attendant weakness that makes the bearer a doomed victim. In fact, what Mittelholzer is suggesting is that heredity determines all. It is a theory that has far-reaching consequences on his conception of character, and he holds it as being true not only for mixtures of Black and White but also—as in the case of Paul Mankay of *Uncle Paul* (1963)—for other mixtures, Jewish in this case. Paul's surname, Mankay, is an obvious play on the French word for "failed," *manqué*. Paul is presented as being "tainted" by his Jewish blood, which gives him a heritage of weakness against which he has to struggle. He is, thus, a schizoid character whose sense of genetic damage—in Michael Gilkes's words—"retards his emotional growth and poisons his relationship with others" (*Memorial Lectures*, p. 32). Dirk, too, in *Kaywana Blood*, obsessed with this sense of tainted blood on his dream of a master family, resists Rose, the mulatto daughter of Hubertus, with tragic results.

Increasingly, as he grew older, Mittelholzer lost that witty, satiric quality, that amusingly ironic view of society which had informed *Shadows*and *A Morning at the Office*. Instead, his writing grew increasingly shrill and ranting. Indeed, he noted in a letter to A. J. Seymour that *The Piling of Clouds* was written to express his "disgust for contemporary society," and that he was "obsessed with the urge to speak . . . of all that I feel about people and the world as I see it . . . I must say what I feel is wrong with society today" (*Memorial Lectures*, pp. 16–17). The tendency to preach had always been in Mittelholzer, for he had seen *A Morning at the Office* as "really a grand tract dressed up" (*Memorial Lectures*, p. 14).

In many ways, it could be seen that Mittelholzer's own rigidly Puritanical upbringing and his sense of his Germanic heritage affected his work deeply. The belief that strength must always win out against weakness, no matter what the cost, caused him to espouse a philosophy that glorified strength of the will and discipline and was nearly fascist in its worse aspects. It would lead him to argue that "the criminal and the mentally unfit ought to be liquidated quietly and without pain—for their own good and for the good of the community" ("The Sibilant and the Lost," *Savacou* [January–June 1973], p. 61). In *The Mad MacMullochs* (1959) he proposed that there should be a eugenics department "to keep our population free of human vermin" (p. 127) and to dispose of the correct percentage of babies at birth. Mittelholzer clearly did not examine too closely the implications of what he was espousing.

That Germanic yearning for order and discipline also manifested itself in Mittelholzer's two versions of experimental communities where enlightened social reform has been effected. In both communities, one in *Shadows Move Among Them* and the other in *The Mad MacMullochs*, Mittelholzer contemplates the concept of a society that offers unlimited individual liberty and yet maintains social order, without recognizing that perhaps the problem is insoluble. In *The Mad MacMullochs*, for instance, divorce is easy but the characters have to seek permission to have children. In *Shadows Move Among Them*, the vision of a hedonistic, rational, enlightened community (where the Indians have been taught to speak French and to appreciate Shakespeare and Beethoven) excludes the Caliban figure of Logan, who is savagely beaten by Rev. Harmston for "disobedience."

Mittelholzer's admiration for his Germanic heritage extended to a hero-worship for Wagner and his music. As a result, he was led to experiment with a *leitmotiv* approach to novel writing in *Thunder Returning* (1961) and in *Latticed Echoes* (1960). With this technique, Mittelholzer hoped to use phrases, much as musical phrases are used, to introduce the appearance of a character. Conventional narration was to be omitted. In a sense, what he devised was a symbol code, with the novel made up entirely of dialogue and these symbolic phrases, for which he provided a key at the start of *Thunder Returning*.

As an experiment in altering the traditional form of the novel, the technique was far from successful because it slowed down the narrative drive and rendered a great deal of the novel unclear. The device was cumbersome because Mittelholzer's choice of word association was entirely arbitrary and inaccessible unless he provided the key. He probably realized it himself since he did not complete what had been projected as a trilogy.

While it must be admitted that Mittelholzer's work is seriously flawed in its excessive detailing of violence, its lapsing into a shrilly denunciatory tone, and its excessive wordiness at times, we cannot deny the extent of his achievement in creating works of fiction that are filled with narrative excitement and memorable characters and which were highly original in their probing of West Indian history and culture.

CRITICAL RECEPTION

When he died in 1965, Mittelholzer left behind him an impressive volume of writing that covered a wide range of styles: twenty-two novels, a collection of humorous pieces (*Creole Chips*, 1937), a travel book (*With a Carib Eye*, 1958), an autobiography, short stories, poems, short plays and sketches, and essays. Since then, most of his work has been allowed to go out of print, with only *Corentyne Thunder* and *A Morning at the Office* still currently on Heinemann's Caribbean Writers Series and *My Bones and My Flute* (1982) available from Longman.

So far there has been no detailed examination of the entire body of his work, and critical attention has tended to focus on the novels, especially the earlier ones, because they won for Mittelholzer his early reputation and have been subsequently confirmed as his finest achievement.

The most important reassessment of Mittelholzer's work has come from A. J. Seymour, Michael Gilkes, Frank Birbalsingh, and Patrick Guckian, while Louis

James and John Figueroa have provided illuminating introductions to the Heinemann editions of the two earliest novels. Seymour was the first to stir a resurgence of interest in Mittelholzer's work with his articles in *Bim* ("The Novel in the British Caribbean," 1967) and in *Kaie* ("The Novel in Guyana," 1967), and especially with the first of a series of Edgar Mittelholzer Memorial Lectures published in 1968, *Edgar Mittelholzer: The Man and His Work.* In this, Seymour not only gave his personal recollections of the man, he also looked at the range of his novels, discussing each one briefly but looking most closely at the earlier work. He also discussed the technique of *leitmotiv*used by Mittelholzer in two novels and found it unsuccessful, however innovative. He also established firmly that the Kaywana trilogy was Mittelholzer's most considerablc achievement, dealing as it did "with the unceasing struggle between heredity and environment" (p. 28). *Corentyne Thunder* is rated highly as "an act of imaginative possession of an important part of Guyana's agricultural area" (p. 21). The later novels are given scant attention because Seymour feels they are merely "a group of morality sermons" (p. 37), filled with "furious preaching" (p. 38).

Michael Gilkes regards Mittelholzer as an important West Indian writer because he was a pioneer, not only in his commitment to his art but also in his treatment of setting and landscape and in his choice of themes. He sees Mittelholzer as a kind of West Indian Hawthorne attempting to exorcize the ghosts of the past. For Gilkes, what "rescues Mittelholzer's work from the category of the merely trivial is the Faustian theme that underscores so much of his writing: the split in consciousness which has to be repaired through associative effort" (*The West Indian Novel*, 1981, p. 84). In this demonstration of the need for psychic integration, and in his treatment of the theme of racial mixture, Mittelholzer's work "embodies and illustrates the dilemma implicit in the whole body of Caribbean literature" (*Racial Identity and Individual Consciousness in the Caribbean Novel*, 1974, p. 110).

Like Seymour, Gilkes regards the Kaywana trilogy as Mittelholzer's most outstanding work, "an epic, imaginative record of the peculiar social and historical reality of Guyana." He finds it filled with a "wealth of detail . . . a sense of mystery and excitement," yet factually and chronologically correct (*The West Indian Novel*, p. 57). More importantly, it is "a prodigious pioneering attempt to examine the cultural and emotional ambivalence which is a heritage of the West Indian past" (*The West Indian Novel*, p. 84). He also credits *Corentyne Thunder* as the "first novel to deal with Guyanese peasant life" ("Edgar Mittelholzer," 1979, p. 97) and *A Morning at the Office* as "unsparingly honest . . . a microcosm of the West Indies" (p. 104). Gilkes does not seem very much interested in the later novels, set in England, and dismisses them as "little more than thinly disguised sermons" ("Edgar Mittelholzer," p. 108), noting their compulsive, dogmatic tone.

He has not overlooked Mittelholzer's serious flaws, noting that the style is occasionally pompous and lacking in depth and that "deeper levels of meaning are often overlaid by self-conscious or prolix writing, and trivial incident and superficial characterization often coincide with real insights'' (*The West Indian Novel*, p. 85). He also notes that Mittelholzer's ''obsession with heredity as a once-and-for-all personality determinant denies his heroes any real, emotional development'' (*Racial Identity*, p. 32). Another aspect of Mittelholzer's work that has upset many readers also worries Gilkes, and this is Mittelholzer's ''delight in vigorous, often violently sensational action'' (*The West Indian Novel*, p. 57) and what he has termed the ''erotic or sadomasochistic titillation'' (p. 65) in the books. Even in the early *Shadows Move Among Them*, Gilkes discerns that ''beneath all the liberalism and naturalness, the idyllic atmosphere of freedom and creative expression lies a disturbingly perverse element of cruelty and sadism'' (*Racial Identity*, p. 27).

Frank Birbalsingh, in his perceptive ''Edgar Mittelholzer: Moralist or Pornographer?'' (1969), examines this aspect of Mittelholzer's work and shows that ''the torrid mixture of fornication, adultery and sado-masochism'' is the result of ''inadequately controlled fantasies'' (p. 92). He sees Mittelholzer's art as ''a means of release to inner tensions and hidden personal conflicts'' and suggests that it derives, as such, from a ''psycho-neurotic temperament which does not quicken sensibility and intelligence but rather gives rein to fantasy and sweet dreams of wish-fulfilment'' (p. 99). Still, he claims, it would be wrong to regard Mittelholzer simply as a pornographer because there is a discrepancy between aim and achievement, and ''because the idealism in his work remains unrealized'' (p. 91).

Like the others, he agrees that the Kaywana trilogy is Mittelholzer's best work, ''a brilliant imaginative reconstruction, . . . a *tour de force* . . . a vivid narrative of extraordinary power'' (p. 99), but he acknowledges that Mittelholzer's work is seriously flawed and attributes his artistic failures to ''the meagre resources of the historical, cultural and literary background against which he wrote'' (p. 98). He concludes that since the majority of Mittelholzer's novels deal with ''psychological themes'' that are of both local and universal significance, Mittelholzer will gradually ''come to be regarded as the true innovator of a literature that is finally free from parochialism'' (p. 103).

Patrick Guckian, in an article in *Jamaica Journal* (''The Balance of Colour: A Re-Assessment of the Work of Edgar Mittelholzer,'' 1970), approaches Mittelholzer's work sympathetically, showing that those who have accused Mittelholzer of racial prejudice are misled and have confused narrator with author in the novels. He has also shown what a careful stylist he was and how important Mittelholzer's knowledge of musical form is to his novels. He also suggests that the later novels ''never engage our deeper sympathies'' (p. 43), whereas those dealing with the West Indies are all ''many-dimensional, multi-voiced and multi-layered'' (p. 45).

One charge occasioned by Mittelholzer's later novels that all the critics have carefully skirted—though Gilkes hints at it in his description of Mittelholzer's later views as ''right-wing''—is that his attitudes and his later novels are ''fascist.'' Geoffrey Wagner states clearly that ''every element of the Fascist state in embryo is represented at Berkelhoost'' (''Edgar Mittelholzer: Symptoms and Shadows,'' 1961, p. 32), but he draws no conclusion about the author's own outlook. It seems very likely—judging from his letter to A. J. Seymour in 1963 in which he admitted that he had become ''a bit preachy'' and that he ''must say . . . what was wrong with society'' (*Edgar Mittelholzer*, p. 17)—that Mittelholzer's novels did reflect a great deal of what he personally felt and that that affected the quality of what he wrote.

HONORS AND AWARDS

Mittelholzer was awarded the Guggenheim Fellowship for Creative Writing in 1952, the first West Indian writer to be so honored. As his project, he submitted the plan for his completion of the Kaywana trilogy.

BIBLIOGRAPHY

Works by Edgar Mittelholzer

Creole Chips. Georgetown: Lutheran Press, 1937.

Corentyne Thunder. London: Eyre and Spottiswoode, 1941; London: Heinemann, 1970; London: Hutchinson, 1970; New York: Humanities Press, 1970.

A Morning at the Office. London: Hogarth Press, 1950; New York: Doubleday, 1950 (as *A Morning in Trinidad*); Toronto: Clark, Irwin, 1950; Harmondsworth: Penguin, 1964; London: Heinemann, 1974; Paris: Gallimard, 1954 (as *Un Matin au bureau*); Milan, 1956 (as *Tempesta a Trinidad*).

Shadows Move Among Them. London: Nevill, 1951; Philadelphia: Lippincott, 1951; New York: Ace Books, 1961; London: Four Square, 1963; Amsterdam: Em. Querido, 1953 (as *En Welke is Onde Zonde*); Paris: La Table Ronde, 1953 (as *L'Ombre des hommes*); Hamburg: Claasen, 1957 (as *Gluhende Schatten*); Milan: Baldini e Castoldi, 1957 (as *La saga delle ombre*).

Children of Kaywana. London: Nevill, 1952; New York: Day, 1952; London: Secker and Warburg, 1952, 1956, 1960, 1969; London: Ace Books, 1959; London: Four Square, 1962; London: New English Library, 1972; New York: Dell Books, 1965 (as *Savage Destiny*); København: Jesperson og Pio, 1953 (as *Kaywanas Børn*); Berlin: Blanvelt, 1954 (as *Kaywana*); Paris: La Table Ronde, 1954 (as *Les Enfants de Kaywana*); Milan: Baldini e Castoldi, 1956 (as *I Figli de Kaywana*); Barcelona: Luis de Caralt, 1956 (as *La Estirpe de Kaywana*); 's-Gravenhage: Zuid Hollandse Uitgevers-Mij, 1957 (as *De Vrouw Kaywana*).

The Weather in Middenshot. London: Secker and Warburg, 1952; New York: Day, 1953; Paris: Plon, 1954 (as *Le Temps qu'il fait a Middenshot*); Turin: Frassinelli, 1955 (as *Strani eventia Middenshot*).

The Life and Death of Sylvia. London: Secker and Warburg, 1953; New York: Day, 1954; London: Ace Books, 1960; London: Four Square, 1963 (as *Sylvia*); New English Library, 1968 (as *Sylvia*); Paris: Plon, 1956 (as *Vie et mort de Sylvia*); Milan: Rizzoli, 1957 (as *Il sole nel sangue*).

The Climate of Eden, by Moss Hart (a dramatization of *Shadows Move Among Them*). New York: Random House, 1953.

The Adding Machine. Kingston: Pioneer House, 1954.

The Harrowing of Hubertus. London: Secker and Warburg, 1954; New York: Day, 1955 (as *Hubertus*); London: Secker and Warburg, 1959 (as *Kaywana Stock*); London: Four Square, 1962 (as *Kaywana Stock*).

My Bones and My Flute. London: Secker and Warburg, 1955; London: Corgi, 1958, 1966; London: New English Library, 1974; London: Longman, 1982.

Of Trees and the Sea. London: Secker and Warburg, 1956.

A Tale of Three Places. London: Secker and Warburg, 1957.

With a Carib Eye. London: Secker and Warburg, 1958.

Kaywana Blood. London: Secker and Warburg, 1958; New York: Doubleday, 1958 (as *The Old Blood*); London: Four Square, 1962; New York: Crest, Fawcett, 1971.

The Weather Family. London: Secker and Warburg, 1958; Bremen: Schünemann, 1959 (as *Hurrikan Janet*).

A Tinkling in the Twilight. London: Secker and Warburg, 1959.

The Mad MacMullochs. London: Owen, 1959 (under pseudonym H. Austin Woodsley); London: Owen, 1961; London: World, 1961.

Eltonsbrody. London: Secker and Warburg, 1960.

Latticed Echoes. London: Secker and Warburg, 1960.

The Piling of Clouds. London: Putnam, 1961; London: Four Square, 1963.

Thunder Returning. London: Secker and Warburg, 1961.

The Wounded and the Worried. London: Putnam, 1962; London: Pan, 1965.

A Swarthy Boy. London: Putnam, 1963.

Uncle Paul. London: Macdonald, 1963; New York: Dell Books, 1965.

The Aloneness of Mrs Chatham. London: Library 33, 1965.

The Jilkington Drama. London: Albelard-Schuman, 1965; London: Corgi, 1966.

Studies of Edgar Mittelholzer

Birbalsingh, Frank M. "Edgar Mittelholzer: Moralist or Pornographer?" *Journal of Commonwealth Literature* 7 (July 1969), 88–103.

Brathwaite, Edward Kamau. "The New West Indian Novelists, Part I." *Bim* 8 (July–December 1960), 199–210.

Carew, Jan. "An Artist in Exile—From the West Indies." *New World Forum* 1 (November 12, 1965), 23–30.

Carr, W. I. "Reflections on the Novel in the British Caribbean." *Queens Quarterly* 70 (Winter 1963), 585–97.

Cartey, Wilfred. "The Rhythm of Society and Landscape." *New World Quarterly* (Guyana Independence Issue) 2 (1966), 97–104.

Collymore, Frank A. "A Biographical Sketch." *Bim* 10 (June–December 1965), 23–26.

Derrick, A. "An Introduction to Caribbean Literature." *Caribbean Quarterly* 15 (June–September 1969), 65–78.

Drayton, Arthur D. "The European Factor in West Indian Literature." *The Literary Half-Yearly* 11 (January 1970), 71–94.

Figueroa, John. Introduction to *A Morning at the Office*. London: Heinemann, 1974, pp. vii–xx.

Gilkes, Michael. "Edgar Mittelholzer." In *West Indian Literature*, ed. Bruce King, 1979, pp. 95–110.

———. "Pioneers." In *The West Indian Novel*, 1981, pp. 41–85.

———. *Racial Identity and Individual Consciousness in the Caribbean Novel*. The Edgar Mittelholzer Memorial Lectures, 5th Series. Georgetown: Ministry of Information and Culture, 1975.

———. "The Spirit in the Bottle: A Reading of Mittelholzer's *A Morning at the Office*." *World Literature Written in English* 14 (April 1975), 237–52.

Guckian, Patrick. "The Balance of Colour: A Re-Assessment of the Work of Edgar Mittelholzer." *Jamaica Journal* 4 (March 1970), 38–45.

Howard, William J. "Edgar Mittelholzer's Tragic Vision." *Caribbean Quarterly* 16 (December 1970), 19–28.

James, Louis. Introduction to *Corentyne Thunder*. London: Heinemann, 1970.

Lacovia, R. M. "English Caribbean Literature: A Brave New World." *Black Images* 1 (January 1972), 15–22.

Mittelholzer, Jacqueline. "The Idyll and the Warrior: Recollections of Edgar Mittelholzer." *Bim* 19 (June 1983), 33–89.

———. "My Husband Edgar Mittelholzer." *Bim* 15 (June 1976), 303–09.

Rickards, Colin. "A Tribute to Edgar Mittelholzer." *Bim* 11 (January–June 1966), 98–105.

Seymour, Arthur J. *Edgar Mittelholzer: The Man and His Work*. 1967 Edgar Mittelholzer Memorial Lectures, 1st series. Georgetown, Guyana, 1968.

———. "An Introduction to the Novels of Edgar Mittelholzer." *Kyk-over-al* 8 (December 1958), 60–74.

———. "The Novel in the British Caribbean." *Bim* 11 (January–June 1967), 238–42.

———. "The Novel in Guyana." *Kaie* 4 (July 1967), 59–63.

Sparer, Joyce L. "Attitudes Towards Race in Guyanese Literature." *Caribbean Studies* 8 (July 1968), 23–63.

Wagner, Geoffrey. "Edgar Mittelholzer: Symptoms and Shadows." *Bim* 9 (July–December 1961), 29–34.

Williams, Denis. *Image and Idea in the Arts of Guyana*. The Edgar Mittelholzer Memorial Lectures, 2nd series. Georgetown: National History and Arts Council, 1969.

Wyndham, Francis. "The New West Indian Writers." *Bim* 7 (January–June 1959), 188–90.

See also General Bibliography: Allis, Gilkes, Herdeck, Hughes, James, McDowell, and Ramchand (1970).

PAMELA C. MORDECAI

Mervyn Morris (1937–)

BIOGRAPHY

Mervyn Morris was born in Kingston, Jamaica, on February 21, 1937, and spent his earliest years there. At "just under eleven, in 1948" (interview with Pamela Mordecai, Kingston, Jamaica, December, 1983; ensuing quotations of Morris are from this source), he went to board at Munro College in the hills of St. Elizabeth. The last of four children, three boys and a girl, he was the only one to be sent to boarding school, an exigency dictated by his father's becoming ill. (His father died later that year.) The poet's family was small but extended by various cousins on his father's side living with the household in order to go to school in Kingston and the presence of another set of cousins, on his mother's side, two houses away. So that, "in the sense of the meaningful experience, I grew up in a very large family."

Morris's father was an accountant at the Island Medical Office and a man of some musical talent. The poet's mother (who died in 1984) was a primary school teacher and eventually a headmistress. After Conversorium the poet went to Half-Way-Tree Elementary School, where his mother was on the staff; author Jean Creary D'Costa was a student there as well. They were both godchildren of Mrs. Edith Dalton-James, a distinguished Jamaican educator and social worker whom Morris recalls as a powerful radical influence "creating really important excitements" in the classroom. One or two dramatic interventions of Mrs. Dalton-James contributed to the poet's discovering early, for instance, that "nationalism meant something."

Mrs. Morris was not a radical; she eschewed the dialect, especially because she felt it had a negative effect on her efforts to induce her pupils to learn Standard English. (Her reservations did not prevent her from successfully producing a play in Creole with her students, however.) Mervyn Morris's mother was, therefore, not a Louise Bennett fan, though his father was: Bennett was read aloud in the Morris household, as was P. G. Wodehouse. The poet assured me that "we didn't feel any embarrassment about the two." (The attitudes to Louise Bennett are worth mentioning since the first important piece of critical writing which Morris would publish was "On Reading Louise Bennett, Seriously" [*Jamaica Journal* 1 (December 1967), 69–74], an essay which also represented the first extended critical appraisal of the folk poet's work.)

Mervyn Morris won a scholarship to Munro College, where he began to write short stories and satirical light verse. He was an avid reader of British magazines like *The Listener*, *The Spectator*, and *The New Statesman*, in which he found a particular kind of journalistic elegance which appealed to him. He also read occasional essays and liked especially J. B. Priestley and George Orwell. In 1953 he sat the higher schools certificate in English, French, and history. As one of the English papers Munro offered "The Age of Johnson." The course content meant a serious contact with certain kinds of values that underlined reason as an ideal. This experience and the exposure to verse in the British magazines he was reading—the Movement poets were then in vogue—supplied some of the influences encouraging his sensibility to value cogency, clarity, force, and tough intelligence.

The poet did quite well in his exams at Munro. He stayed on to do them again in the hope of winning one of the "big" scholarships which would have permitted university study abroad. And then "a crucial thing happened to me which I should probably be eternally grateful for": he sat the UCWI scholarship exams, won an exhibition, and ended up at the young University College of the West Indies.

At the University of the West Indies Morris read English, French, and history. He was determined at the time to be a lawyer. After completing his degree in 1957, he took a job teaching at Munro, liked it, and decided that teaching was probably what he wanted to do. Less than a year later, the poet won a Rhodes scholarship and went off to St. Edmund Hall to read English honors.

The poet has spent most of his professional life in the classroom or lecture room. Barring stints at the university as assistant registrar (1961–62) and warden of Taylor Hall (1966–70), he has worked either at Munro, his alma mater, or at UWI in the Department of English, where he has lectured since 1970. He is currently a senior lecturer there. He has been a broadcaster, an occasional newspaper columnist, and a theater critic for the *Daily Gleaner*. Morris has written many critical articles and edited several books on West Indian literature. He has also taken a continuing interest in the work of aspiring poets and writers. He is married and has two sons and one daughter.

MAJOR WORKS AND THEMES

Mervyn Morris's first collection of poetry, *The Pond*, appeared in 1973; in 1976 *On Holy Week* was published in Kingston by Sangster's Book Stores; and in 1979 New Beacon Books, which had produced *The Pond*, brought out his third collection, *Shadowboxing*.

Commenting on Morris's work in his book, *West Indian Poetry* (1984), Lloyd Brown observes, "The decided individualistic rather than group orientation of Morris's art needs to be viewed in the light of his continuous preoccupation with the private worlds within the individual's private self" (p. 173). I find Morris less self-preoccupied than Brown does. Both in what the poems say and how they say it, the poet repeatedly articulates his reservations about sharing the more intimate, more visceral aspects of his personal response. His craft—and Morris's craft is paramount, his sense of the working of words unerring—continually interposes between the detonating experience and the echoes of it that he sets on the page. Any discussion of his themes will therefore involve close attention to his method.

In the beginning with *The Pond* collection (hereafter cited as *TP*) this was less so than it is now. If one considers the whole *oeuvre*, he observes a progress away from some very personal poems in the first book, like "For a Son," "The Day My Father Died," "Family Pictures," "Little Boy Crying," "To an Expatriate Friend"; through the alterae personae of *On Holy Week*; to the spare poetry of *Shadowboxing* (hereafter cited as *S*), where fewer than half the poems can be seen as the poet "emptying" on us, to borrow a metaphor from Dennis Scott (*Uncle Time*, 1973, p. 37). Along the way the poems have become shorter and the strategy for deploying the symbolic tokens more artful.

The result is that many of the later poems function, in themselves, as signifiers: an experience ostensibly personal and particular is delivered with characteristic economy, irony, and metaphysical wit, in such a way that the whole of what is described becomes a symbol. The power of its resonance is that everyone can claim the experience by recognizing characteristic contours in it. The method is *not* to capture us with the details of what has prompted the poetic insight so we can assent to it by being where the poet was: it is to offer us outlines, a lightly sketched shape, and invite us to fill them in with how-we-know-this-to-be-true in our reality.

So that if our poet is sometimes preoccupied with privacy and the interior life, it is the fact of that preoccupation that is shared, rather than its nature. Poems like "Journey into the Interior," "The Thing Had Wings," "The Pond," "Narcissus," "Dream," "Interior," and "At Every Border" all point, in one way or another, to the complexities involved in the poet-artist achieving self-knowledge, accommodating his darker, shadow side, resolving the dilemma described in "Dream," where the poet, about to "dip some water up / to drink" notices "things floating / in the murk" and wakes up, thirsty (*S*, p. 24). The question is, of course, whether the poet is thirsty for those murky things in the water or because they have prevented him from drinking.

The poem offers no clues to the answer, but the murky things crop up again and again: as the other self Narcissus tries to murder (in "Narcissus," *TP*, p. 43); as the darkness in the brooding pond (in "The Pond," *TP*, p. 42); as the things with wings that "flapped in the dark of the skull" (in "The Thing Had Wings," *TP*, p. 41); as the illegible passage of entrails in which the poet "spends the long day groping" (in "Journey into the Interior," *TP*, p. 40). They are the "thrashing crawling shadows," the "floundering, flapping / slithering" forms which the persona warns his beloved, in "The Reassurance," that she must accept. But we suspect the poet has heeded the message of (the same?) beloved in "An Offering" (*S*, p. 43): he has done the bandages and swaddled the wounds about "the lesions of [his] mind." So we know that there are lesions, but only intermittently do we get inklings of what they are.

This reserve is perhaps part of the strength of the poetry, of a piece with the control that assigns each right word to its proper place; but it is also a weakness. One longs for the poet to share more of the abandon that prompts the passionate declaration of intent in "Valley Prince." One wishes that the powerfully sexual encounters so gently diluted in "Lecture" and "Meeting" had been allowed the chance to become more concentrated brews.

The thing is that Morris leaves us in little doubt about the fact that he knows perfectly well what he is doing, has careful control of how much he is letting on at any one time, and is quite deliberately carving out the poem with this in mind. "Stripper" (*TP*, p. 11) is the most complete statement of that deliberateness. In pursuit of "mirrors," the poet stops for wine and song at a joint and finds that he must "take the stripper too." She forthwith becomes—or rather, her writhing becomes—"an image of his line":

> She put on clothes to take them off, she wore
> performing pieces, such a fuss she made
> of skimpy little veils before
> her parts (*which never were displayed*)!
> Riddling hard to music, she performed
> her *teasing* art.
>
> (*TP*, p. 11; italics added)

There is some doubt as to how completely Morris intends the poet-stripper metaphor to be applied, though it is possible to explicate the whole poem in these terms (with the "ponce" as the publisher!) Nevertheless the stripper's art as predicated on not revealing all is clearly emphasized, and the poem ends with the poet-reluctant-voyeur capitulating to the poet-as-stripper. Thus:

> She took the last piece off the law allowed.
> The poet felt his symbol growing hard.

There are two levels of irony here: the first dictates the wry detachment of the poet as he reports his art in terms of the stripper's performance. That irony is conscious and intended. The further irony is that "the law" (Morris's self-censoring mechanism [in this interpretation]) is still in place; consequently, though he recognizes that response (the hardening symbol) is most powerfully elicited by the prospect of a complete revelation, the exposition, and the poem, stop there. It is possible, though not likely, that in the case of the second irony the poem has taken over from the poet and is making its own statement.

Edward Baugh, writing in Bruce King's *West Indian Literature* (1979), observes that in his love poems Mervyn Morris "makes a valuable, rare contribution, by his explorations of married love and the demands of family life" (p. 92). Some of the early personal poems fall into this category. In "Family Pictures" Morris describes the dilemma of the father-husband-artist, happy and nourished by the family situation, but nonetheless entertaining

> this dream:
> to go alone
> to where
> the fishing boats are empty
> on the beach
> and no one knows
> which man is
> father, husband, victim,
> king, the master of one cage.
>
> (*TP*, p. 36)

"For a Son" and "Little Boy Crying" explore other aspects of fatherhood.

Other poems in *The Pond* allow us into intimacies. "The House Slave" uses a historical metaphor to expose the particular trauma of someone whom experience and circumstance isolate from his "tribe of blood" (*TP*, p. 17); "To a Crippled Schoolmaster" details the poet's reluctance to face a slowly dying teacher (*TP*, p. 24); "The Reassurance" is a lover's complaint.

The poet savaged by a racial-awareness critic leading a side of "censors" in "Catch a Nigger," represents a different aspect of the dilemma of isolation portrayed in "The House Slave." (The problem of this kind of isolation is one which Morris repeatedly considers.) The treatment in "Catch a Nigger" is more immediate for there is no historical setting to remove the incident in time and the poet clearly exists as some version of himself in the poem. The symbolic tokens and the poetic circumstance are heavily charged: the poet is "at home with his creative curse"; he declined to share the public "*strain*" as he "*struggled* with his private pain"; the critic (a "man with an enormous head") "*assaulted*" him, as a result of which he "*bled* outside, in open view" (emphases added). (The burden of all of this must be weighed against the title—"Catch a Nigger" is the recitation children use to select who will be "it" in their games.) In the situation the poet opines that

> Perhaps the pack
> would sniff his blood and classify it black?
>
> (*TP*, p. 13)

To no avail. The poet wins the round only by wit, his victory lurking in the final couplet:

> He stanched the public wound, and bled
> inside again. His blood was red.

The vicious attack has been made light of and the poet's position reiterated; his humanity is what is most common about him; his "race" is human; that is what his poetry explores. (And "red" is also "read.")

The primacy of this commonly shared humanity above solidarities of race, politics, and other "common" interest is an important theme in Morris's work. In poems like "The Early Rebels," "For Consciousness," and "Afro-Saxon," he marshals all the tools of his trade—irony, wit, double entendre, and, on occasion, a deeply sardonic voice—to do battle with those who would promote other alliances above this one.

A few poems in *The Pond* presage the tightly knit offerings of *Shadowboxing*, among them "Mariners," with which the collection ends. Still, there are no poems in the first book that operate like "They," "Notice," or "Storypoem" in *Shadowboxing*. "Storypoem" laconically recites this incident:

> well
> one day at a concert
> with the whole hall full
> he entered to vociferous applause
> he settled at the keyboard
> flexed his fingers
> and didn't play
> just sat there
>
> listening
>
> (*S*, p. 9)

Clearly the whole poem at once, signifies—the title says so. But signifies what? The writer as eccentric? The artist as madman? The artist perverse? The possibilities nag and the poet isn't helping; indeed, he is hard to find—which is, I suppose, what the poem is saying.

Many of the other poems operate in similar ways. Pared down to their essentials, they oblige the reader to scour his imagination to discover the symbolic content. They acquire by this strategy wider resonances and a spare power. But one loses a palpable sense of the poet as guide: of pillion-riding the experience with your arms about his waist.

It is not that there are no private poems in *Shadowboxing*: even in their encapsulated forms, some poems admit us into the private/personal domains. "An Offering" is one of these; "Dreamtime" is another. "One, Two" is a special treat:

I

Lying in the dark together
we
in wordless dialogue
defined community

II

You switch the light on to inspect
an alien remark.
And now your body stutters

No more lying in the dark.

(*S.*, p. 40)

The technique here is the same as for the other "short" poems. The significance moves out from the briefly described incident of interrupted lovemaking in the poem to summon other breakdowns in communication—communal, societal, international. There is something dramatically present about the turning on of the light—something near and real about the stuttering body. It is that nearness and realness that one misses in poems like "Zoo Story," "Theatre," "Womansong," "Terminal," "They."

Morris's propensity for using circumstance as symbol in his poetry could alone give the lie to the suggestion that his concerns are primarily personal/introspective. Nor is it true that his sociopolitical concern is secondary—a peripheral resonance. In poems like "Meeting" and "To the Unknown Non-Combatant" the symbolic circumstance has a clear political definition. The point is that in Morris's perception, social, political, and personal issues are dynamically bound up.

More than this, however, the poetry has from the beginning tussled with that complex of problems characteristic of small excolonial plantation societies, Creolized and liberated but restive in their new syncretic cultures. Some of the poems already mentioned and others, like "Case-History, Jamaica," "I am the man," "To an Expatriate Friend," treat issues of race, physical and cultural dispossession, the sociopolitics of easy postures, the limits, within the society, to alignments of the affections. "Rasta Reggae" responds to the Rastafarian cultural assertion.

Morris's purpose in poems that address sociopolitical issues is to return them to the experiential *locus in quo*: the society is people—people in relation to other persons. If poverty is an issue it is because it informs and defines the lives of real people. In "I am the man" the neglect and dispossession of the poor is explored through a catalogue of the deprivation of an "I" who could be one of many men, in the poem, and who is, symbolically, every destitute person. The poem asserts the uniqueness and manhood of the person by reiterating the phrase, "I am the man" as the stem of each item in this poorman's litany. At the same time, the accumulating "I's" (twelve of them) convey the notion that many share the situation:

I am the man that build his house on shit
I am the man that watch you bulldoze it
I am the man of no fixed address
Follow me now

I am the man that have no job
I am the man that have no vote
I am the man that have no voice
Hear me now

I am the man that have no name
I am the man that have no home
I am the man that have no hope
Nothing is mine.

(*TP*, p. 15)

The "social issue" of violence is defined within the terms of the poem as being, at least in part, the making of this man:

I am the man that file the knife
I am the man that make the bomb
I am the man that grab the gun
Study me now

(*TP*, p. 15)

It is deliberately "oversimplified."

The dig at the scholars supplies part of the irony of the last line of the last verse. (In each verse the last line is heavily ironic.) It is when the man of the poem graduates to violence that he becomes the object of scholarly scrutiny. As robber, murderer, and terrorist, he finally "deserves" serious study. "Study" is also Creole/slang for "look at closely," "scrutinize," with the implicit message that the notice is warranted and the failure to give it may have serious results. And, as street talk, the "study me" phrase is performance rhetoric; some showing off in the "rappin' and stylin' out" tradition is taking place, and attention is being called to it. All these resonances are intended, with the complex of ironies that obtains when they are set against one another. "Study me" serves as a rallying call to the poor, a warning to the society at large, *and* a reprimand to the social scientists.

"Afro-Saxon" tackles race consciousness in a poem in which the poet is very personally present. Reminiscent of "Catch a Nigger," it is an especially sweet revenge, for the poem employs its own doublespeak to deal with the radical members of some kind of Black revolutionary movement. A fine ambiguity in the first six lines of the poem is achieved by qualifiers placed so that they can apply to either of the two personae:

> Another friend arraigns me:
> too detached, he says,
> absurdly free
> of all the ways of feeling
> true blacks, as a rule,
> now share
>
> (*S*, p. 16)

By manipulating the form of the poem, the poet puts the question: Who is the true Black? Who is "absurdly free / of all the ways of feeling / true blacks . . . share"? Him? or the friend?

The poem's resolution is not, it seems, optimistic: this once-upon-a-time Black man who thought his "skin would do" to establish his race

> . . . never made it. Thought-
> inspectors, quivering at the sight
> of an Afro-Saxon on the road
> towards the border, caught
> him sneaking in-
> to Blackness, radioed:
> Don't let that nigger fool you, he is WHITE!
>
> (*S*, p. 16)

A series of related tokens introduces the notion that the "new" Blacks are neofascists: his friend "arraigns" him; true Blacks now share ways of feeling "*as a rule*"; the poet recognizes that he needs a *uniform* to join Blackness; "*Thought-inspectors*" catch him "on the road / *towards the border*" "*sneaking in* / to Blackness" and radio the news that he is "WHITE!" By the end of the poem the cold war/spy scenario is obvious. The careful construction of the situation in the last verse complicates its possible meanings. The thought-inspectors catch the Afro-Saxon on the way to the border "sneaking in- / to Blackness." The line break creates the duplicity. We assume that Blackness is within the border; but it could also be on the other side of the border—in the region toward which the Afro-Saxon is headed, not in the place (controlled by the "new" Blacks) where he is.

What is most ironic of all, and easiest to miss, is that this ambiguity in language, so characteristic of Morris and belonging in our readiest reckoning to "Saxon" styles of language manipulation, is in fact a device that New World Africans have traditionally had to use, in the situation of plantation slavery, as a basic survival strategy.

Finally, it is the ready identification of the Black man as "nigger" in the last line that decides the issue of whether he is or is not Black. The semantic range of ''nigger'' includes—for the purposes of the poem—three possible meanings: first, ''nigger'' may be used perjoratively; second, it may simply describe the person phenotypically; and third, it may refer to membership in the ''niggerhood'' or ''niggerdom'' that the thought-inspectors now purport to police. Whichever of the three is meant (and the possibility is that all three are indeed meant), the man's ready identification as some type of ''nigger''—their word of first choice—allows him into Blackness. Whatever comes after must be glossed in the light of this first definition.

Baugh's remarks on Morris's use of Creole in ''For Consciousness'' are a good point of departure for a consideration of this aspect of the poetry overall. Having noted that the dialect is used to help characterize the persona in ''For Consciousness'' as rural and working-class, he observes further: ''The poem captures the aphoristic power of the grass-roots wisdom of the folk: 'Plenty busha doan ride horse / an' some doan t'ink dem white' . . . A further level of deliciously ironic resonance is in the hint of the Stephen-Foster-Type 'darky' song ('Swanee River')—a hint which comes not only in the reference to 'ol plantation' but also in the rhythm of the piece'' (pp. 91, 92). The level of Creole in ''For Consciousness'' is somewhere around the mesolect—middle-level Creole—which is not inappropriate for the persona in the poem. In ''I am the man,'' a Creolized phonology is required by the statement even though the only syntactic element that is not English is the uninflected verb (''watch'' rather than ''watches''). The poem works no less well, though the level of Creole in this case is much higher up on the continuum.

Perhaps Morris's most powerful statement in Creole is his poem for the musician, Don Drummond, called ''Valley Prince.'' Earthy and full of feeling, completely authentic in dialect register, it is alive with double-entendresand characteristic metaphysical intention. One wonders at the comparative rarity of poems like these in the whole literature of West Indian poetry. Perhaps the Creole is our language of greatest privacy, and only the most urgent situations may induce us to use it.

Elsewhere in Morris—as in ''Give T'anks,'' ''Rasta Reggae,'' ''Pre-Carnival Party''—the Creole informs or contributes obviously to the poetic statement. But it is also a dimension of the language that resonates behind the poetry contributing less evident meanings. In ''A Temperate Love Poem,'' for example, ''real sun / shine for true,'' has an obviously Creole configuration, as well as one in Standard English. ''Real sunshine for true'' is also suggested. The ''for true'' is a Creole idiomatic expression. It invests the anticipated temperate springtime with a robust tropical reality. Similarly ''Lecture,'' the title of the second poem in *The Pond*, becomes in Creole phonology, ''lecha,'' that is, ''letcher.'' Interpreted this way, a level of cynical intention attaches to the poem that is nowhere else evident in it. It is typical of Morris to use the title to add further irony to the poem.

One of the happy inventions of *On Holy Week* is its use of both Creole registers and resonances. This dramatic relationship of the characters in the Holy Week story begins with a "Prologue, by the Maker." He enjoins us "Now hear these people" (p. 5)—English, but Creole as well. The Creole—or some non–Standard English code—resurges in the voices of "Soldiers" and "Simon of Cyrene": "Orders is orders / from a Roman guard" (p. 17). The dialect voice is clear in Mary Magdalene's "A lovely piece of man; real sweet" (p. 26). It is also the channel for the complete statements of both malefactors.

The use of Creole apart, the *On Holy Week* sequence manages to invest the characters in the crucifixion with a vitality that renders them credible—real rather than merely historical persons. We see these persons either ruminating about a situation or in dialogue—their part of the dialogue—with someone. Both states are enlightening. Enigmas, incredulities, protests, taunts, cowardice: a complex of failings presents itself in the utterances of all the characters except Jesus. Holy Week is every week.

Morris's work is unique among his contemporaries. It is not that his concerns are vastly different from theirs, but the spareness of his style—he has said that economy was never his problem (interview)—and the primacy of intellect, of poetic craft, in resolving the creative dilemma, ensure a highly characteristic signature.

It is interesting to speculate on the direction in which his work will develop. The poems in *On Holy Week* are sketches for what could easily be tissued out into a poetic play. (They have in fact been broadcast on Jamaican television in a dramatized version.) Alternatively, he may tussle for a while with the tight, hard-working miniatures which the poems have become in the last collection. Or the almost "dub" voice of "Responses" may require him to follow it. We look forward to the possibilities.

CRITICAL RECEPTION

The critical response to Mervyn Morris's poetry has been largely enthusiastic. This review of critical comment on his work is presented more or less chronologically since in some respects it provides an example of the evolution of criticism of the literature.

It was Louis James who first wrote at length on Morris's work. His comments were made (1968) some years before *The Pond* was published (1973). James says, "At the roots of Morris's poetic technique lies the continuous challenging of all clichés, although his humane values may disguise the sharpness of his wit" (*The Islands in Between*, 1968, p. 32). There are "some technical weaknesses" in these early poems—"a certain slackness," a "failure of emotional control." But "wit and intelligence are [positive] characteristics of his verse" (p. 33). Among the other strengths of the poetry are "the uses of significant ambiguity" and "the witty reassessment of conventional . . . images." James betrays his own biases in his final comment on the poetry: "One could claim that Morris's work shows a fusion of *European verbal and intellectual complexity* with the shrewd commonsense of Caribbean popular culture'' (p. 33; italics added).

William Walsh's appraisal of Morris's work (''West Indies,'' 1973) is enthusiastic, but his critical perspective is also one external to the region. Walsh's point of departure is the poet's reference to two English poets, Larkin and Enright, in a poem entitled ''Literary Evening, Jamaica.'' It is widely anthologized, but Morris did not include it in *The Pond*. Walsh sees Morris's choice of these two poets as indicative of the character of his own verse. Walsh finds in Morris's verse ''a kind of moral steadiness, the gay balance which comes from the play of wit and an appealing honesty directed not only against his enemies but also himself'' (p. 64). The problem is that Walsh's critique does not respond to either the preoccupations or the prosody which infuse the poetry with a West Indian rather than any other sensibility.

It is Bill Carr's review which offers the first extended evaluation of Morris's work within this kind of perspective. Carr, an Englishman who has lived in the Caribbean since the 1960s, regards Morris as ''the most accomplished and sensitive of the younger generation of Jamaican poets'' (''*The Pond: A Book of Poems*,'' 1974, p. 205). He begins his discussion with ''Literary Evening, Jamaica.'' The case the poem makes, in Carr's view, is ''the need for a poetry which will define and express a West Indian sensibility.'' Carr sees Morris as having emotional roots that are ''secure enough'' but also ''the moral sophistication to recognize more than one point of view.'' He applauds Morris's conversational style, ''controlled . . . by a concern for the exact phrases, and a poetic movement that catches the inflections of a *person* talking'' (p. 207).

''The Early Rebels'' is an attempt on the poet's part to exercise irony (which ''comes as naturally to Morris as breathing'') on Caribbean political leaders (p. 207). Carr responds to Morris's ''genuine'' wit and recognizes the breadth of the poet's interests, ''from social and political problems, to the frequently grim struggle with oneself and language that is inescapably imposed upon a serious poet, to the humane privacies that belong in a secure relationship'' (p. 208). He notes the unusual contribution which Morris's poems about home and family life make to West Indian literature. He has one reservation about the poetry: he feels that as one of Morris's admirers he must hope for poems that represent ''a more formidable adventure of the spirit than he has yet attempted,'' though the value of the poetry as it stands is secure (p. 210).

Stewart Brown's comment appeared in 1973 (''West Indian Poetry''). Brown, too, is an Englishman. Reacting to books by Morris, Anthony McNeill, and Dennis Scott, he recognizes the poet's ''very West Indian consciousness'' and his ability to manipulate language. He concludes, ''Though McNeill is more direct, and Scott's command of imagery more striking, Morris makes perhaps the most telling statements with his blend of subtle irony'' (p. 48).

It is the quality of restraint, the traditional aspect of the verse, that is to become Morris's critical nemesis. Trinidadian Ken Ramchand, surveying new West Indian writing in 1973, records the appearance of *The Pond*, thus: ''Morris's *The*

Pond contains poems by a man trying decently to control his life and his craft; sensitive and intelligent enough to be disturbed by what he sees in his society and by his own deeper imaginings, but too committed, perhaps to the fiction of order either to reject compromise or to open himself up to radical questionings'' (*Journal of Commonwealth Literature* 9 [December 1974], 130).

It is interesting to compare this terse notice with Bill Carr's generous salute. There is, nevertheless, some coincidence in the responses: the poet's refusal ''to open himself up to radical questioning,'' of which Ramchand complains, reminds us of Carr's desire that the poet should in the future attempt more formidable adventures of the spirit.

Victor Questel is Morris's least enthusiastic critic. Pity, then, that his attitude is contentious and that his appreciations are less careful than they should be. Despite his sourness (or because of it?) one is persuaded that his response to the poetry is genuine. It is certainly vigorous. His critical framework is difficult to pin down. Ethnic/racial identification seems to be one of his preoccupations; social relevance is another. And he does attend to formal aspects of the verse (though sloppily). His major concern, however, seems to be with discovering a kind of declaration in each poem.

He says *The Pond* ''states an attempt to explore the mulatto's attempt [*sic*] to choose his side'' (''Creole Poet in a Classical Castle,'' 1975, p. 6). Morris in a reply to the review disavowed being mulatto. He was Black, he said, as were his parents. In 1979 Questel, who incidentally was mulatto, or certainly a great deal closer to that ''color'' than Morris, reviewed *Shadowboxing*. In that review (''Monkey Man Makes His Own Zoo,'' 1979) he referred to Morris as a ''cultural mulatto.''

Questel allows that ''*The Pond* is important to us all,'' concerned as it is with the predicament of intelligent informed choice. Nevertheless, he is annoyed that, although Morris ''sees it all, both the fraudulence of the men who preach concern for the poor while being well-off and the fraudulence . . . of walking the middle path . . . yet his poetry never explodes with the kind of pain and complexity that the realization should produce. . . . 'Formal classicism' inhibits him'' (''Creole Poet,'' p. 6).

Questel's response to *Shadowboxing* is much the same as it was to *The Pond*. He contexualizes the creative pursuit in racial/political terms, once more: he feels that in the poems Morris takes issue with Black power leaders from his liberal, middle-of-the-road position. The poems also deal, he says, with ''man on the run from self and society.''

Lloyd Brown is the first West Indian to offer a generous, sensitive, informed elucidation of Morris's work. The poetry waited ten years (counting from Louis James's 1968 comment) for that appreciation. Brown says in his conclusion to the last chapter of *West Indian Poetry* (1978), entitled ''West Indian Poetry Since 1960,'' ''It seems fitting at this point that Morris should be the pivotal figure in an assessment of the present directions of contemporary West Indian poetry'' (p. 176). Morris's relationship with his contemporaries, in Brown's view, is evidence of the extent to which recent West Indian poetry is "an essentially diverse collection of writings that can accommodate the creative eccentric of an individualistic author like Morris" (p. 176). Brown's comments do not include poetry published after *The Pond*.

Brown thinks that Morris's choice of the poems in *The Pond* is "carefully considered"; the poems "reflect a variety of themes ranging from the poet's role in the ethnocultural experience, to the integrity of the private self" (p. 172). The complex of racial/political issues that arises from the poetry and constituted such an irritant for Questel is neatly explicated in Brown's commentary: "Morris does not reject the value of political and social statement as such, but he feels that to define the thematic texture of poetry on the basis of political commitment is to over-simplify the multiple insights and possibilities of poetry itself" (p. 172).

Brown's four pages of commentary mention fifteen of the thirty-seven poems in *The Pond*. He offers an empathetic and discriminating reaction to several of Morris's "political" poems. The lukewarm response of the poet to Black militancy in "Case History, Jamaica" is seen as counterbalancing the poet's eager desire to "look in." Morris's skepticism, in his view, arises from no lack of ethnic pride but from an "uneasiness with the shallow vision and facile rhetoric that are often offered as modes of ethnic identity" (p. 174). The instability characteristic of the responses of the militants is "the more suspect because it seems so repetitive" (p. 174). "The Early Rebels" makes this point. "The House Slave" and "To an Expatriate Friend" condemn both excolonial and neocolonial mentalities, in the case of the first poem and the anger of "a new black intolerance" as well as "the familiar narrowness of the white expatriate" in the case of the second" (pp. 174–75).

In sum, Morris's "skeptical withdrawal from sociopolitical activism, combined with his introspectiveness, has had the effect of marking Morris as the most private, the least activist in orientation of the major contemporary poets" (p. 175). In his reservations about politics and "radical group rhetoric," Morris is not unlike Walcott; in his interest in the private self, he resembles the later A. J. Seymour.

Edward Baugh pays attention to the use of dialect in Morris's poetry: it exemplifies an increasingly subtle "employment of the vernacular in West Indian poetry" ("Since 1960: Some Highlights," 1979, p. 91). "Apparently slight substitutions" of Creolized forms in "I am the man" "affect the pronunciation and intonation of the whole, thereby asserting the dramatic presence of the imagined speaker" (p. 91). In another poem, "For Consciousness," the Creole works differently, acting as a mask "through which Morris makes a sharp satiric comment on the post-colonial situation in the West Indies and on the windier pretensions of the 'consciousness' movement" (p. 91). The Creole also "captures the aphoristic power of the grass-roots wisdom of the folk" (p. 91).

Baugh remarks on the good sense and wit in Morris's verse, its keen irony. He applauds the poet's "refusal to be boxed into positions of monolithic intolerance and unquestioning." He feels that Morris is able to indict validly the self-righteousness of modern-day "thought-manipulators" because of his "vigilance against self-righteousness within himself" (p. 92). The poet is aware of "traps . . . around as well as traps within each single self" (p. 92). "The Pond" and "Narcissus" consider these interior traps.

Baugh describes Morris's method: "The tone of protective but healthy self-mockery in Morris is achieved partly by the deliberate near-parodic use of simple, traditional stanza-patterns, with rhythm and idiom wilfully, playfully skirting the edge of cliché. . . . This manner is part of the poem's meaning" (p. 92).

Pam Mordecai is the only critic to have commented on Morris's three collections. Her review of *On Holy Week* (1976) focuses on the language of the poetry: "Various levels of the language continuum and frequent 'nice' ironies lurk in these poems" (p. 113). The critic is convinced of the authenticity of both the language and the personae in the Holy Week sequence who use it: she compares the poetry in this collection to the poetry of Chaucer and the metaphysicals. Its clarity and availability do not constitute a vice: "I like these poems. The fact that I understand them doesn't bother me" (p. 114).

The appearance of *Shadowboxing* prompted a critique of that collection and *The Pond*. In "A Retrospective Comment on *The Pond* and a Review of Mervyn Morris's *Shadowboxing*" (1979), Mordecai takes issue with Ramchand for requiring a particular position of the poet and with Lloyd Brown for assigning him to the category of private/introspective. She questions the wisdom of Morris's choice of title poem for the first collection: "For fine though this . . . poem is, it lacks that ubiquitous collation of words and images, cohering and contrasting simultaneously, that anchors most of the rest of the work and . . . defines the man's art and particular perception" (p. 63).

The dominant method is *explication de texte*, and the reviewer quotes liberally from the poetry. The review is entirely enthusiastic. The poems in *The Pond* are "hard poems" (p. 61), the craft of those in *Shadowboxing* is "consummate" (p. 70).

Ignacy Eker, a naturalized Jamaican originally from Europe, wrote on *Shadowboxing* for the *Daily Gleaner* in 1979. He recognizes the introspective quality of Morris's poetry, the poet's strategy of confronting mishap and misfortune with "wry amusement," and his "ironic consciousness." This consciousness pushes the poet to believe that "writing poetry is . . . a fascinating game especially when the poems are confessional" ("The Darker Continent," 1979, p. 4). He characterizes the poet's "ability to compromise" as "very Anglo-Saxon."

Eker is an art critic: he does not usually write on literature. Perhaps his comment on the poetry signals the involvement of a wider critical audience in the appreciation of West Indian literature.

HONORS AND AWARDS

Mervyn Morris has received various scholarships, honors, and awards, most notably the Rhodes Scholarship (1958–61) and the Institute of Jamaica's Silver Musgrave Medal for Poetry (1976).

BIBLIOGRAPHY

Works by Mervyn Morris

Seven Jamaican Poets, ed. Jamaica: Bolivar Press, 1971.
The Pond. London: New Beacon Books, 1973.
On Holy Week. Kingston: Sangster's, 1976.
Shadowboxing. London: New Beacon Books, 1979.

Studies of Mervyn Morris

Baugh, Edward. "Since 1960: Some Highlights." In *West Indian Literature*, ed. Bruce King, London: Macmillan, 1979, pp. 90–93.
Brown, Lloyd. *West Indian Poetry*. Boston: Twayne, 1978, pp. 172–77.
Brown, Stewart. "New Poetry from Jamaica." *New Voices* 3 (1973), 48–50.
Carr, Bill. "*The Pond*: A Book of Poems." *Caribbean Studies* 14 (July 1974), 205–10.
Eker, Ignacy. "The Darker Continent." *Daily Gleaner*, July 10, 1979, p. 4.
Hearne, John. "Points of Departure" (Review of *On Holy Week*). *Daily News*, April 18, 1974, p. 14.
James, Louis. Introduction to *The Islands in Between*. London: Oxford University Press, 1968, pp. 32–33.
Mordecai, Pam. "*On Holy Week*" (Review). *Caribbean Quarterly* 22 (December 1976), 113–15.
———. "A Retrospective Comment on *The Pond* and a Review of Mervyn Morris's *Shadowboxing*." *Caribbean Quarterly* 23 (December 1979), 60–71.
Panton, George. "The Tennis-Playing Poet." *Sunday Gleaner*, May 25, 1975, pp. 23, 31.
Questel, Victor. "Creole Poet in a Classical Castle" (Review of *The Pond*). *Tapia*, March 16, 1975, pp. 6–7.
———. "Monkey Man Makes His Own Zoo" (Review of *Shadowboxing*). *Trinidad Guardian*, April 21, 1979.
Vidal-Hall, Judith. "Muse in No Man's Land." *Guardian*, January 8, 1979, p. 13.
Walsh, William. "West Indies." In *Commonwealth Literature*. London: Oxford University Press, 1973, pp. 64–65.
See also General Bibliography: Allis and Hughes.

ROBERT D. HAMNER

V. S. Naipaul (1932–)

BIOGRAPHY

Vidiadhar Surajprasad Naipaul was born in Chaguanas, Trinidad, on August 17, 1932, grandson of a Banaras-trained Brahman who died shortly after Naipaul's father was born. Naipaul's father, Seepersad, left his son a high regard for writing as a career, even though his own journalism and attempts at short stories seem to have entailed great frustration. Naipaul's early childhood was divided between the matriarchal Tiwari clan house in Chaguanas and the bustling streets of Port of Spain. He recalls the circumscribed existence and the Hindu orientation of the East Indian community in Trinidad, a society uprooted and dying on an island that was itself isolated from the "real" world where historical events were taking place.

When he was studying at Queen's Royal College, Naipaul wrote in his *Kennedy's Revised Latin Primer* his pledge to depart from Trinidad within five years. It was six years later that he emigrated to England, in 1950, to take up a Trinidad government scholarship reading English at Oxford University. After Oxford came several years of drifting. It was while he was employed part time by the BBC that he began tentatively to write about his childhood memories of the sights, sounds, and characters in Port of Spain, going back, in print only, to a place to which his fears of anonymity would not let him return physically. *Miguel Street* (1959) was the immediate result, but years passed and two more novels saw print before this first book was published.

Inspiration to become an author came from his father, as did the anxiety and frustration Naipaul admits in his writing practice. It was "fear, a panic about failing to be what I should be, rather than simple ambition, that was with me when I came down from Oxford in 1954 and began trying to write" ("Prologue to an Autobiography," 1983, p. 156). The fiction came, in time—eight novels and two collections of short stories—up to 1984. Along with the fiction, Naipaul also continued his father's journalism. Selections from his reviews and articles which have been published in newspapers and magazines around the world have been collected in *The Overcrowded Barracoon* (1972) and *The Return of Eva Peron with The Killings in Trinidad* (1980). There is the record of his travels in the West Indies in *The Middle Passage* (1962), and his novelist's history of the region entitled *The Loss of El Dorado* (1969). Two trips to his ancestral India resulted in *An Area of Darkness* (1964), and *India: A Wounded Civilization* (1977). Time spent in Africa led to a limited edition of his *A Congo Diary* (1980). Then followed the report of his experiences in the Islamic world of the Near and Far East, *Among the Believers* (1981).

Because he is from a Third World country, Naipaul has faced a problem common to writers from emerging nations. He must choose his audience: either his countrymen in their idiom, or a metropolitan audience in a form that is authentic and at the same time comprehensible to strangers ignorant of his culture. Even though his first novels were set in Trinidad, Naipaul presented his material so that alien readers would find it accessible. Given his comic—at times highly satiric—attitude, the books appeared to be so uncomplimentary that he developed a local reputation as being corrupted by traditional metropolitan tastes. The fact that he began accumulating many of the prestigious literary prizes and received complimentary reviews from the Western press was even used as evidence against his right to be considered a Third World writer. He might have treated his roots with more sympathy, but in later works, he is equally severe dealing with Englishmen and colonizers wherever they are found. Ultimately, Naipaul excoriates most relentlessly within himself that which is his own colonialism.

Naipaul confesses that he felt his background shapeless, uprooted, absurd. Lacking a literary tradition at home, he seemed cut off from generations of writers who could build upon each other. He began, then, writing in a foreign tradition about a location that had to be given its literary voice. It was not until *Mr Stone and the Knights Companion* (1963) that he felt comfortable enough with his London surroundings to attempt writing about a setting other than the West Indian. Naipaul's answer to criticism of his harsh treatment of colonial people and situations is that the artist best serves his country by perfecting his craft. Improvement, he contends, begins with an admission of inequalities, disparities. If he offers no solution, he diagnoses illness deftly and gives vivid form to problems that need critical attention.

Naipaul continues to reside in England. He and his wife Patricia live in a Wiltshire cottage near Stonehenge, where Naipaul likes to walk at times. He travels frequently to other countries to write and teach as artist-in-residence at various universities.

MAJOR WORKS AND THEMES

The early Trinidad novels, *The Mystic Masseur* (1957), *The Suffrqge of Elvira* (1958), and *Miguel Street* (1959), are only slightly exotic accounts of characters in a tropical setting. In spite of their humorous surfaces, they bring to life members of the East Indian and mixed communities of Naipaul's memory. One of their flaws is that characters appear at times to be victims of circumstance. Ganesh Ramsumair, the masseur of the first novel, learns to take things in hand on occasion, but ironically, as he rises in island politics, he loses his claim to personal authenticity. Beginning as an insignificant masseur, he advances to the level of shrewd manipulator and cynic. In the end, he admonishes an admirer to use his new, Anglicized name: " 'G. Ramsay Muir,' he said coldly." The effect of *The Suffrage of Elvira* is to make rural Trinidad villagers seem the self-deluding pawns of acquisitive politicians. The island's first election under universal suffrage arouses all the petty factions in a populace ill prepared for democracy. There is hilarious comedy in the interplay of superstition, family feuds, racial bickering, bribery, and lightning shifts of fortune.

Miguel Street is a series of vignettes of denizens of a back street in Port of Spain during the 1940s. The naive narrator affords a reasonable vehicle for the effortless flow of characters and events: "A stranger could drive through Miguel Street and just say 'Slum!' because he could see no more. But we who lived there saw our street as a world, where everybody was quite different from everybody else. Man-man was mad; George was stupid; Big Foot was a bully; Hat was an adventurer; Popo was a philosopher; and Morgan was our comedian" (p. 79). In the street, men and women strive to assert their personalities in any way they can. Laura, loving children and hating husbands, bears eight children by seven different men. Popo the carpenter undertakes building the "thing without a name," and B. (for Black) Wordsworth pursues the "greatest poem in the world," distilling all his experience into each line, at the rate of one line a month. Disappointment and failure attend most of their schemes, and the youthful narrator's story ends with his boarding a plane for England, never looking back. Naipaul later describes his own departure from Trinidad in exactly the same way. *Miguel Street*, his first novel and the third to be published, was his return glance at the island.

A House for Mr Biswas (1961), Naipaul's fourth book, has been hailed as a masterpiece of modern fiction. Naipaul has described this semi-autobiographical novel as being the closest to him of all his works; yet despite its realistic setting in Trinidad, the novel transcends regional boundaries. The story of Mohun Biswas proceeds on several levels. On the personal plane, Biswas (modeled to some extent after Seepersad Naipaul) is an ambitious but ineffectual "little" man. There is no romance or heroic accomplishment in his life, beyond survival. That may be the key linking his fate to the plight of ordinary man everywhere. His most useful weapon is a gift for making fun of his absurd condition. He faces two equally illusive antagonists. One is the Tulsi family into which he marries, marriage coming simply because he fails to withstand Mrs. Tulsi's intrusion. While the Tulsis are tangible, and can be rebelled against in hundreds of small ways, his second antagonist is a more formidable one. It is his inner fear of being lost, of becoming a nonentity.

Symbolic of Mr. Biswas' desire to establish his own identity and place in the world is the house he wishes to build for his family. Evident on this level of interpretation is the sociological implication for colonial dependency. The Tulsis' Hanuman House is run hierarchically by Mrs. Tulsi and her two sons at the top. Beneath them are the numerous daughters and their spouses. The extended family submits to this central power in even the most personal matters. From on high, favors are dispensed and discipline is administered arbitrarily. Except for the two sons, everyone eats common fare and shares possessions equally. Biswas escapes his mother's shanty by marrying into the powerful family, and he appreciates the maternalistic security provided by the established authority. The problem is that he is allowed no room for personal growth, no independence.

Breaking out on his own is no easier for Biswas than it is for any other insecure individual, or nation for that matter. The Tulsis permit him to "paddle his own canoe" by setting him up in one of their small shops at The Chase. Losing there, he is sent to superintend their laborers' barracks at Green Vale. Trapped into marriage, then burdened by Shama and the children she bears him, he begins writing romances of escape and dreaming up fantastic new releases. He snipes away at the "coal barrel" dark kitchen of Hanuman House, aiming epithets at Shama's relatives: her mother, "the old she-fox"; her brothers, "the gods"; the family pundit, "the constipated holyman." Beneath the jokes is desperation that leads to hysteria. On the one hand he wants independence, but freedom presents its own incapacitating terrors. He needs security, a sense of belonging, which drives him back to the shelter of the Tulsis time after time.

Moving into Port of Spain and becoming a reporter for the *Sentinel*does not alleviate the suffering; it merely gives Biswas more to lose. When he leaves the paper to become a caseworker for the welfare department, he is exposed to more misery than ever before. The one consolation comes when his son, Anand, wins the island's annual scholarship competitions. The triumphant moment is leavened with its own poignancy. Biswas celebrates in a cafe with two friends: "surrounded by flamboyant murals of revelry on tropical beaches, they drank: three men, none over forty, who considered their careers closed and rested their ambitions on the achievements of their children" (p. 439). When near the end of his short life, Biswas does manage to finance a house of his own, it is a flimsy affair thrown together by a charlatan who pays officials to overlook his code violations.

Biswas and his family learn to adjust to the flaws of the house, perhaps the most telling symbol in the novel. On a philosophical level the story becomes a saga of accommodation, the house like the human body, a shell in which the soul assumes its shape. Biswas takes comfort in his property; Anand carries his inherited anxiety abroad to his university studies (sounding remarkably like

Naipaul himself); and Shama learns at last to trust her husband so that she no longer runs to Hanuman House for consolation. His death at the age of forty-six is not the conclusion of the novel. In fact, Naipaul begins with Biswas' death and then relates his history. This device eliminates suspense and focuses attention on the importance of the struggle. If Biswas' reward seems small, the living of his life is its essence, not material gain. On the personal level, Biswas has had a hand in shaping his existence; on the sociopolitical level, he has not allowed the powerful to deprive him of his will; on the spiritual level, he has survived despair and even learned to appreciate the minor blessings that have come his way.

Naipaul's shifting the scene to England for his next novel, *Mr Stone and the Knights Companion* (1963), demonstrates the common thread linking West Indian characters with other men. Naipaul argued in ''The Regional Barrier'' in 1958 that he knew too little of England to write about it (*Times Literary Supplement*, August 15, 1958, p. xxxvii). By limiting himself to the circumscribed world of Mr. Stone, he concealed any damaging ignorance. Mr. Stone, nearing a bachelor's retirement, begins to feel that he has missed something by never marrying. He discovers soon enough after he marries the gay widow Springer that he can be equally lonely with a constant companion. In order to forestall the bleak emptiness of retirement, he dreams up a scheme for involving retirees in his firm's social program. Unfortunately, the public relations officer converts the plan into a crass publicity gimmick. The result is that Mr. Stone, like Mr. Biswas, is thrown back on his innermost resources. He gracefully accepts the unrelenting terms of survival.

Although there are well-wrought stories in the collection entitled *A Flag on the Island* (1967), including the title novella, which was intended as a preliminary screenplay, this book is overshadowed by another that some critics consider to be Naipaul's best (some would prefer most notorious), *The Mimic Men* (1967). The setting, split between England and the Caribbean island of Isabella, makes this work a bridge between the poles of Naipaul's existence. Ralph Singh, an ousted politician in early retirement, begins in the present and works his way backward and forward through the story of his life:

> My career is by no means unusual. It falls into the pattern. The career of the colonial politician is short and ends brutally. We lack order. Above all, we lack power, and we do not understand that we lack power. We mistake words and the acclamation of words for power; as soon as our bluff is called we are lost. . . . Our transitional or makeshift societies do not cushion us. . . . For those we lose, and nearly everyone in the end loses, there is only one course: flight. Flight to the greater disorder, the final emptiness: London and the home countries. (pp. 10–11)

Ralph Singh never considers himself at home in Isabella. He dreams of Aryan ancestors in the Himalayas or the northern winters of metropolitan countries. Therefore, when he leaves the shipwreck existence of the island for London, he has expectations of acclimatizing to his ''element.''

In the great city, he plays roles, the fop, the playboy. Meeting Sandra, a girl just as self-absorbed and lost as he is, gives him temporarily an external point of reference. They return to Isabella, join a leisurely social set, and drift into the political independence movement. Ralph observes the parade of slogans and the ineffectual attempts of his party to wield their nebulous power. It takes no time to recognize the fact that their power had been their protest; in taking the reins themselves, their cause evaporates. Sandra's leaving him comes as no surprise, and he soon takes advantage of a mission to London to separate himself from the new government. As his account closes, he sums up the phases of his life and asserts that the decks are cleared for a new beginning.

The question remains whether he is now any more capable of an authentic statement than he has ever been. Critics have been quick to denounce Singh as a representative of Third World "Mimic Men" politicians. It is even debated whether the novel is political or rather a psychological study. It is both to some extent, with approximately one-third of the length devoted to actual political activity. It is essential to keep in mind the fact that Singh, not Naipaul, makes the claim of his career's being of a pattern for a colonial politician. No matter how reliable his assessments, the revelation of his inner character is a candid gauge of his own personal failings. Insofar as Naipaul once again puts his finger on a sickness, *The Mimic Men* deserves the critical attention it is receiving.

In a Free State (1971) contains several stories and two journal entries depicting more dispossessed people from other countries. Bobby, the expatriate Englishman in the title novella, is trying to prove his love for Africa. Over the period of the story, his homosexual advances are rejected by one African; the wife of a colleague, a reputed "maneater," draws him out and exhausts him emotionally; and he is abused and robbed by undisciplined government soldiers. His only recourse to save face in the end is to fire the Black servant who sees his defeat and is disrespectful enough to laugh. Santosh, in "One out of Many," leaves the streets of Bombay only to discover that the freedom he sought in Washington, D.C., is chaos instead. He is forced to marry a woman he considers his racial inferior in order to keep his "freedom."

Guerrillas (1975) returns the scene to the West Indies. An unnamed independent island is being run through American bauxite interests. The title is ironic in that the guerrillas are members of a dilapidated agricultural commune under the leadership of a hypocritical charlatan, and their farm is supported financially to keep them from making trouble for the country's foreign investors. The main characters—Peter Roche, a washed-out, anti-apartheid Englishman acting as the company liaison; his girlfriend, Jane, so faceless that she is a composite of all the many men she has known; and Jimmy Ahmed, dissident leader without any popular following—exhibit the same desperate futility that has plagued all major figures in Naipaul's fiction. The degree of bleakness is merely turned up.

The fact that the plot is based on a murder case Naipaul reported for the *Sunday Times Magazine* ("The Killings in Trinidad," May 12 and 19, 1974) may lend credence to his vision, for readers who need corroboration in fact, but

Naipaul's strength remains in his ability to discern the inner corruption of men who neither know nor are capable of effecting an authentic existence for themselves. Jimmy Ahmed fantasizes that he could be the humane rapist of a White girl who falls in love with him, an idea remaining with him from a sensational news story of childhood memory. He writes episodes wherein Jane is overpowered by his mixed blood and she sacrifices everything for him. Reality, like the revolution, falls short of his expectations. When trouble comes, no one rallies to his call, and American troops never have to leave the airfield once they have shown their force. Jane comes to Jimmy, but her aggressiveness offends his image, and he reacts violently. In the end, he forcibly sodomizes her and holds her erect while his homosexual partner hacks her to death with a machete. The crowning irony is in Roche's conspiring to conceal her death. Since Jane has entered the country without securing a visa, there is no official record that she exists in the first place. As company scapegoat, Roche must leave; now that Ahmed's impotence is established, the government can dispense with him. In an ending even less hopeful than Ralph Singh's dubious "fresh start," Naipaul leaves no one with a desirable option.

A Bend in the River (1979) involves an East Indian trying to make a living in a new African nation. The river settlement where Salim runs his small shop becomes, first, the site where the "Big Man" (a character inspired by Zaire's Mobutu Sese Seko) in the capital wants to establish a model development. When that effort shows its absurdity and the president then decides to reinstate tribalism, the community becomes his example for bloody retribution. As in Naipaul's fiction from the earliest novels, the plot serves primarily to expose human nature under pressure. Salim does not fit in; his friend Indar and Salim's lover, Yvette, discover their own alienation. The young African boy Salim takes in during his school years is promoted as one of the favored members of the "Big Man's" administration, but by the end, he is driven by fear alone, the fear that is temporarily keeping the country from flying into disorder. Salim luckily escapes down the river at night. The closing scene is vintage Naipaul, the imagery of blind movement, drifting, darkness, and confusion—all in terse, cool precision:

> At the time what we saw was the steamer searchlight, playing on the riverbank, playing on the passenger barge, which had snapped loose and was drifting at an angle through the water hyacinths at the edge of the river. The searchlight lit up the barge passengers, who, behind bars and wire guards, as yet scarcely seemed to understand that they were adrift. Then there were gunshots. The searchlight was turned off; the barge was no longer to be seen. The steamer started up again and moved without lights down the river, away from the area of battle. The air would have been full of moths and flying insects. The searchlight, while it was on, had shown thousands, white in the white light. (p. 278)

The silence, the restraint of describing only detail and obvious appearance, contribute to the irony of that blind whiteness. It is not just what Salim leaves behind; he carries it with him into exile.

CRITICAL RECEPTION

Attitudes toward Naipaul's early novels led him to complain in his 1958 article "The Regional Barrier" that if the size and power of an author's country determine his success, then a writer from Trinidad has little hope. Most critics he felt had been fair up to that time, even generous, but there were those who prejudice the reading public with "political rather than literary judgments" (*Times Literary Supplement*, August 15, 1958, p. xxxvii). Naipaul overcomes his regional barrier, not by the expedient measure of simply broadening his appeal to public taste. He comes to recognize by 1965 in "Images," that "all literatures are local. . . . The problems of Commonwealth writing are really no more than the problems of writing; and the problems of reading and comprehension are no more than the problems of reading literature of any strange society" (*New Statesman*, September 24, 1965, p. 452). Regardless of that discovery, Naipaul continues to find writing to be a painful process. In 1971, he confessed to Israel Shenker his inclination to abandon writing: "In fact writing is just a sort of disease, a sickness. It's a form of incompleteness, it's a form of anguish, it's despair" ("V. S. Naipaul, Man Without a Society," *Words and Their Masters*, 1974, pp. 68, 70). Yet he goes on in spite of the grim picture he draws. His motivation may be discerned in a statement made to Charles Michener in a *Newsweek* interview in 1981: "I am devoted to the idea of the life of the mind. I'm interested in the spread of humane values" ("The Dark Visions of V. S. Naipaul," p. 110).

Reviews and articles on Naipaul's works are too numerous and varied to be summarized conveniently, but perhaps examples of their polarities will suggest the divisiveness of his *oeuvre*. Comments nothing short of vitriolic abuse have flowed from some critics. H. B. Singh in "V. S. Naipaul: A Spokesman for Neo-Colonialism" brands him a "lackey catering to the desires of his imperialist masters" (*Literature and Ideology*, 1969, p. 71). Reviewing Naipaul's latest work of fiction, *A Bend in the River*, Irving Howe joins the company of admirers: "For sheer abundance of talent there can hardly be a writer alive who surpasses V. S. Naipaul" ("A Dark Vision: *A Bend in the River*," 1979, p. 1). He often stands, unfortunately, a litmus test for critical affiliations: friends of emerging societies fault his disparaging depiction of his origins; traditionalists of Western orientation are only too eager to have their own superiority reconfirmed. Such politicized oversimplification is not the whole story. There are well-balanced literary assessments both in the Third World and in metropolitan countries.

The first book-length study of Naipaul was not published until 1972, a treatise on Naipaul's major themes entitled *V. S. Naipaul: An Introduction to His Work*. Paul Theroux examines in fiction and nonfiction the difficulties of creative imagination, the dangers of fantasy, vagaries of the middle class, the weight of history, and the burdens of freedom. Next to appear was Robert Hamner's *V. S. Naipaul* (1973), a general analysis of all Naipaul's works, concluding that the larger considerations of art make his writing a valuable contribution to cross-cultural understanding. Also from 1973, William Walsh's *V. S. Naipaul* considers the consistent growth from the early to the later works. In 1975 two books appeared. Landeg White's *V. S. Naipaul: A Critical Introduction* undertakes the comparison of Naipaul's life with his fictional world, the autobiographical foundation which Naipaul has since corroborated several times. That same year, Robert K. Morris brought into focus the ambivalent interplay of chaos and order in Naipaul's fiction: *Paradoxes of Order: Some Perspectives on the Fiction of V. S. Naipaul.* Michael Thorpe added *V. S. Naipaul* to the Longman's Writers and their Works Series in 1976.

With the obvious increase of critical interest in Naipaul and in light of the controversy which surrounds each book he writes, Robert Hamner edited *Critical Perspectives on V. S. Naipaul* (1977), a collection of articles by and about the author. Since then, at least two full books have appeared: Bruce King's *V. S. Naipaul* (1979); and the most recent, Anthony Boxill's 1983 volume, *V. S. Naipaul's Fiction: In Quest of the Enemy*. Boxill contends that Naipaul's less admirable characters see antagonists as external, while his more complex, more profound characters realize that the enemy is partly within themselves. He finds Naipaul capable of the unrelenting, uninspiring, brutal self-discipline necessary to confront the dark corners of his own soul. Naipaul's unflattering portraits provide a healthy shock to complacency in developed as well as developing nations.

Numerous chapters in books and special issues of journals have been devoted to Naipaul: Michael Gilkes, *The West Indian Novel* (1981); Louis James, *The Islands in Between* (1968); Kenneth Ramchand, *The West Indian Novel and its Background* (1970); Ivan Van Sertima, *Caribbean Writers* (1968), among others. Readers may find of interest the nine essays on Naipaul in *Commonwealth* 6 (Autumn 1983).

HONORS AND AWARDS

Among Naipaul's many awards are the John Llewellyn Rhys Memorial Prize (1958), the Somerset Maugham Award (1961), the Phoenix Trust Award (1962), the Hawthornden Prize (1964), the W. H. Smith Prize (1968), the Booker Prize (1971), the Bennett Award (1980), and the Jerusalem Prize (1983). He is a perennial nominee for the Nobel Prize in Literature.

BIBLIOGRAPHY

Works by V. S. Naipaul

The Mystic Masseur. London: André Deutsch, 1957; New York: Vanguard, 1959; New York: Penguin, 1969; Exeter, N.H.: Heinemann, 1971.

"The Regional Barrier." *Times Literary Supplement*, August 15, 1958, pp. xxxvii–xxxviii.

The Suffrage of Elvira. London: André Deutsch, 1958; New York: Penguin, 1969.

Miguel Street. London: André Deutsch, 1959; New York: Vanguard, 1959; New York: Penguin, 1969; Exeter, N.H.: Heinemann, 1974.

A House for Mr Biswas. London: André Deutsch, 1961; New York: McGraw-Hill, 1961; New York: Penguin, 1969; New York: Knopf, 1983.

The Middle Passage. London: André Deutsch, 1962; New York: Macmillan, 1962; Harmondsworth: Penguin, 1969.

Mr Stone and the Knights Companion. London: André Deutsch, 1963; New York: Macmillan, 1963; New York: Penguin, 1969.

An Area of Darkness. London: André Deutsch, 1964; New York: Macmillan, 1965; Harmondsworth: Penguin, 1968.

"Images." *New Statesman* 70 (September 24, 1965), 452–53.

A Flag on the Island. London: André Deutsch, 1967; New York: Macmillan, 1967; New York: Penguin, 1969.

The Mimic Men. London: André Deutsch, 1967; New York: Macmillan, 1967; Harmondsworth: Penguin, 1969.

The Loss of El Dorado. London: André Deutsch, 1969; New York: Knopf, 1970; Harmondsworth: Penguin, 1973.

In a Free State. London: André Deutsch, 1971; New York: Knopf, 1971; New York: Penguin, 1971.

The Overcrowded Barracoon. London: André Deutsch, 1972; New York: Knopf, 1973.

"The Killings in Trinidad." *Sunday Times Magazine*, May 12 and 19, 1974; reprinted in *The Return of Eva Peron with The Killings in Trinidad*, pp. 1–91.

Guerrillas. London: André Deutsch, 1975; New York: Knopf, 1975; New York: Vintage, 1980.

"A New King for the Congo." *New York Review of Books* 22 (June 26, 1975), 19–25.

India: A Wounded Civilization. London: André Deutsch, 1976; New York: Knopf, 1977; New York: Vintage, 1978; Harmondsworth: Penguin, 1979.

A Bend in the River. London: André Deutsch, 1979; New York: Knopf, 1979; New York: Vintage, 1980.

A Congo Diary. Los Angeles: Sylvester and Orphanos, 1980.

The Return of Eva Peron with The Killings in Trinidad. London: André Deutsch, 1980; New York: Knopf, 1980; Toronto: Collins, 1980; New York: Vintage, 1981.

Among the Believers. London: André Deutsch, 1981; New York: Knopf, 1981; New York: Vintage, 1982.

Three Novels: The Mystic Masseur, the Suffrage of Elvira, Miguel Street. New York: Knopf, 1982.

"Prologue to an Autobiography." *Vanity Fair* (April 1983), 51–59, 138–56.

Studies of V. S. Naipaul

Boxill, Anthony. *V. S. Naipaul's Fiction: In Quest of the Enemy.* Fredericton, Canada: York, 1983.

Durix, Jean-Pierre, ed. *Commonwealth* (Naipaul issue) 6 (Autumn 1983).

Hackett, Winston. "The Writer and Society." *Moko*, December 13, 1968, p. 4.

Hamner, Robert D., ed. *Critical Perspectives on V. S. Naipaul.* Washington, D.C.: Three Continents Press, 1977; London: Heinemann, 1979.

Hamner, Robert D. *V. S. Naipaul.* New York: Twayne, 1973.

Howe, Irving. "A Dark Vision: *A Bend in the River.*" *New York Times Book Review*, May 13, 1979, pp. 1, 37.

King, Bruce. *V. S. Naipaul*. Hamden, Conn.: Archon Books, 1979.

Michener, Charles. "The Dark Visions of V. S. Naipaul." *Newsweek*, November 16, 1981, pp. 104–05, 108–10, 112, 114–15.

Morris, Robert K. *Paradoxes of Order: Some Perspectives on the Fiction of V. S. Naipaul*. Columbia: University of Missouri Press, 1975.

Ramraj, Victor J. "Diminishing Satire: A Study of V. S. Naipaul and Mordecai Richler." In *Awakened Conscience: Studies in Commonwealth Literature*, ed. C. D. Narasimhaiah. New Delhi: Sterling, 1978, pp. 261–74.

Shenker, Israel. "V. S. Naipaul, Man Without a Society." *New York Times Book Review*, October 17, 1971, pp. 4, 22–24; reprinted in his *Words and Their Masters* (Garden City, N.Y.: Doubleday, 1974), pp. 64–70.

Singh, H. B. "V. S. Naipaul: A Spokesman for Neo-Colonialism." *Literature and Ideology* 2 (Summer 1969), 71–85.

Theroux, Paul. *V. S. Naipaul: An Introduction to His Work*. New York: Africana, 1972.

Thorpe, Michael. *V. S. Naipaul*. Writers and Their Works Series, no. 242. London: Longman, 1976.

Walsh, William. *V. S. Naipaul*. Edinburgh: Oliver and Boyd, 1973.

White, Landeg. *V. S. Naipaul: A Critical Introduction*. London: Macmillan, 1975.

See also General Bibliography: Allis, Baugh (1978), Gilkes, Herdeck, Hughes, James, King, Maes-Jelinek, Niven, Ramchand (1970), and Van Sertima.

BRIDGET JONES

Orlando Patterson (1940–   )

BIOGRAPHY

H. Orlando Patterson was born near Frome, in the sugar plantation lands of Westmoreland, Jamaica, on June 5, 1940. His father was a detective in the police, but he grew up much closer to his mother, in the situation of an only child. The six half-brothers and sisters of his father's first marriage were a good deal older.

Moving several times during his early years, he attended infant school at Alley in Vere, and then May Pen Elementary School, where the strict but excellent teaching of Miss Palmer laid the foundations of his career as a scholar. The Jamaica Library Service was at this time extending its work, and the modest May Pen Branch enabled Patterson to acquire a taste for intense and solitary reading, not often a favorite activity of Jamaican small boys. From 1953 to 1958 he attended Kingston College, where Noel White, his history teacher, was an encouraging influence. With excellent results in history, economics, and English, he was directed into the B.Sc. economics course at the University of the West Indies. Thus, rather than going to Britain or the United States for his first degree, he was a student in the Social Sciences Faculty at Mona, during the stimulating years just prior to independence for Jamaica (1962).

Patterson was by now shaping himself quite consciously toward a dual vocation as writer and intellectual and took up a Commonwealth scholarship at the London School of Economics in 1963 to work on a doctoral thesis on slave society in Jamaica. He later taught for a while at LSE and belonged both to the Marxist intellectual milieu around the *New Left Review* and to the group of fellow Jamaican students preparing themselves for a role in socialist politics at home.

However, by the time he returned to a post teaching sociology at UWI in 1967, his taste for activism had abated, and he left Jamaica in 1970 to take up a visiting lectureship at Harvard University. Though he maintains regular links with Jamaica, since that time his academic work has been based at Harvard, where he is now a professor. When Michael Manley was triumphantly elected to power in 1972, Patterson became an active member of the Technical Advisory Committee to the prime minister and shared in that era of hope in a new socialism.

He married Nerys Wyn Thomas in 1965, and they have two daughters, Rhiannon and Barbara.

MAJOR WORKS AND THEMES

It is scarcely an exaggeration to say that all of Orlando Patterson's published writings explore the theme of slavery. His first novel (*The Children of Sisyphus*, 1964) dealt with the modern urban ''sufferers'' most deprived by a plantation economy, their material destitution, and emotional humiliations. His second novel (*An Absence of Ruins*, 1967) had as hero a middle-class character who uneasily reacts against the same tragic heritage. In *Die the Long Day* (1972), the world of the slaves in the late 18th century was directly presented, in a heightened dramatization of the material researched for his doctoral thesis. Many shorter prose writings—fiction, essays, and scholarly articles—amplify the picture, while Patterson's major comparative treatise on *Slavery and Social Death* (1983) can also be seen as deepening and broadening the refletions first aroused by the experience of his own society. It is as if the historical nightmare still possesses this author, who seeks an exorcism by writing it over and over again in diverse modes. Against such a background, a recent unpublished novel set at Harvard should be of particular interest.

Patterson began as a keen and probably rather uncritical reader, early acquiring a sense of the privileged force of the written word. As a schoolboy in Kingston he began to write short stories and enjoyed the satisfaction of seeing his work printed in the *Gleaner* and the *Star* (an evening tabloid) and receiving payment. As well as these short tales, before 1959 he had written a radio play, *The Do-Good Woman*, which was produced by the Jamaica Broadcasting Corporation. Once at university he was an active member of the ''Scribblers'' group and the Literary Society and worked on his novel.

The Children of Sisyphus remains Patterson's best-known and most considerable fictional work. On the recommendation of C. L. R. James, it was taken up with enthusiasm for Hutchinson's New Authors list. It deals with a group of Jamaican characters, linked by the extreme poverty which has reduced them all to dwelling on the Dungle, derelict land near the West Kingston foreshore, used for dumping garbage. The central figure of the book is Dinah, an attractive prostitute who struggles to escape the Dungle through relations with men, especially a special constable and a revival Shepherd, and a short-lived job as a domestic. Quite full treatment is also given to a group of Rastafarian brethren, led by Brother Solomon, and their passionate yearning for repatriation to Africa. A third strand of plot deals with Mary, a mother ambitious for her light brown daughter to "escape" via a high school education. In tracing these main characters, Patterson presents a sequence of episodes of Kingston life, chosen for their dramatic appeal: fights and brawls, a political demonstration, the brothel district by night, a revival meeting, prison, and so on. Much of this material is familiar in the novel or film of low life, especially as it has developed in the Third World to deal with the squatter camps and shantytowns of the new urban dispossessed.

Patterson's distinctiveness arises in part from the barely controlled passion with which he responds to this environment and depicts its horrors. He communicates indelibly his fascinated disgust at the Dungle, built on human excrement and a city's garbage. His vision of human beings cast down to join the filth of the gutter, cast out by their society to rot and perish, carries a powerful poetic charge and is reinforced repeatedly in narrative details. It is difficult to believe that Salkey, for example, in *The Late Emancipation of Jerry Stover*, can be dealing so coolly with the same "Dung'll."

In addition, Patterson situates the tragic failures of his characters, less as socioeconomically determined than as a metaphysical dilemma. Faced with a social reality which posed so strongly questions like Why should human beings live in such abjection? and How can they survive and even continue to hope? Patterson was influenced by existentialist thought in shaping his observed material. The writings of Albert Camus, particularly *The Myth of Sisyphus*, were well known to him. In Camus, and also the early Sartre, we find a radical questioning of accepted human values. Man is seen as living alone against his fate and deriving his only dignity from accepting the absence of any hope. These ideas allow Patterson to invest the sordid struggles of his Dungle dwellers with an aura of cosmic significance. He shows how Brother Solomon tricks his Rastafarian brethren in order to allow them to experience a heightened awareness of themselves and their destiny. Dinah also gains a fuller sense of an ultimate void, despite her baptism into the revival cult. Even minor characters like the garbage men are linked to the notion that, by struggling on, even when the effort is accepted as being in vain, man proves his worth and stature.

Patterson's insistence on shaping his fiction into a fable of the absurd heightens its haunting quality. He rejects values such as solidarity among the deprived (Mabel sets oil-of-fall-back on Dinah), folk religion (the worshipers lynch her), maternal strength (Mary goes mad), which often offer some compensatory warmth and positive force in the yard novel. The Rastafarian faith is frequently shown in Jamaican fiction as a triumph of psychic resistance. In contrast, Patterson puts the stress on the futile unreality of faith in repatriation, though he evokes sensitively their mutual support and fellowship. Brother Solomon may be deranged, a deviant creation, but he remains Patterson's focal Rastafarian character and mouths much of the book's explicit philosophizing. The author developed his views in a 1964 article, reiterating his belief that "the last thing that the cultist, in the depth of his being, would wish is for the ship (i.e., to Ethiopia) to come" ("Ras Tafari: The Cult of Outcasts," *New Society*, November 12, 1964, p. 16). Because Patterson has the unusual courage to face the Dungle with only a stoical nihilism, the tragic dilemma of his characters grips the reader more strongly. Slum clearance, welfare workers, politicians, and priests are all perceived as irrelevant to the heroic struggle of the individual to endure his fate.

Without apparent strain Patterson gives us the view of Kingston society from underneath. The representatives of middle-class power and respectability are all mercilessly reduced to caricature, including recognizable political figures, but his main characters are developed with detailed attention to their thoughts and feelings.

Dinah, a well-rounded figure in every sense, dominates the action of the novel, and her struggles add dramatic momentum. As she packs up to leave the Dungle hut she shares with Cyrus, the Rasta fisherman, and their son, the realistic detail, interwoven with memories and comments in forthright Jamaican folk speech, quickly establishes her as a personality. The reader responds with her to the pleasure of better living conditions with Alphanso, the special constable, and is made to see the dreamlike comfort of Mona middle-class life with her wondering eyes. Having established her with great vigor and warmth, Patterson can carry off implausible details and notes of unduly pompous solemnity. Despite its intrinsic interest, the whole final encounter with Shepherd John and his flock shifts the reader's view of Dinah and brings her story to an overly lurid end.

For many readers, this is a novel "about Rastafarians," which testifies to the impact of the small number of chapters which feature the brethren. Apart from Brother Solomon and, to a lesser extent, Dinah's tenderly faithful Cyrus, these characters are heard as a group, not individualized. As the ironic self-portrait in Chapter 12 makes clear, Patterson had sat around listening very carefully to Rastafarian groups and was thus able to recreate extensive examples of their religious thought, rituals, hymns, even their jokes and curses. He situates the novel at that critical moment in 1959, when belief in imminent repatriation caused many believers to congregate on the Kingston shore. He uses the faith to show that in their fervor, piety, and mutual help the Rastafarians shine superior to "Babylon" and are leaders in the Dungle community. Although Brother Solomon, the unfrocked Anglican, stands apart, manipulated by the author to reinforce the lessons of the absurd, such is the impact of the direct speech which presents the Rastafarian group that even Solomon's suicide does little to attenuate the positive and sympathetic portrait.

Mary is the third major case history, treated with the intense drama Patterson always reserves for the relations between an ambitious mother and her child. Brutalized by the Yankee drunk and by the police, bereaved by the callous social welfare, and finally deranged, Mary is a victim. The author sets up this character, with her pathetic hopes for her daughter to rise in the ladder of class and color, for a savage and punishing series of degradations.

Many other characters are sketched in by Patterson, especially the neat satirical silhouettes of the episode at the Ministry of Unemployment and in the middle-class Mona household. Patterson can write with telling economy and an eye for graphic detail and at his best can recreate various styles of Jamaican speech very skillfully. It is all the more unfortunate that the book has not been revised to eradicate its faults. The whole plot mechanism of the closing chapter, when Dinah returns to die on the Dungle, is contrived, and Solomon's pride in trickery weakens the novel. Whereas much of the text rings true in the vitality of the idiom and rhythms of Jamaican speech, elsewhere Patterson yields to his weakness for overwriting. The reader's sensibility is brutalized by repetition and crude adjectival excess, or a smile may be provoked by the pretentious expression of a philosophical idea. Yet despite its flaws, the text is conceived with a generous indignation and an imaginative power that grips its readers.

Patterson's second novel marked a change. *An Absence of Ruins* is an extremely ambitious short novel, charting with uncompromising rigor the mental dilemmas of an alienated West Indian intellectual. Much of the novel consists of the introspective first person narration of its hero, a young sociologist returned to his native Jamaica after study abroad. An almost pathological detachment from family, friends, and society allows him to reexamine in depth the nature of his existence in the world. He tests out his physical being, thirsting, lusting, almost committing suicide. He tests out his relationships with wife, other women, especially the sensual Carmen, university friends, and most of all, his mother. Indeed, one dimension of the book can be seen as a rite of passage, in which the immature hero accedes to adulthood by liberating himself from sexual taboos and slaying the mother "who fathered him." The climax of the book is certainly the "resurrection" of the son who has caused his mother's death by feigning suicide. In addition, the hero meditates on his society, finding himself unable to share in the political ideals of his radical friends, to return to his folk culture, or to find alibis in history. There is no falsely positive conclusion: the hero does not discover an identity but leaves for the anonymity of London.

The book is an arduous experience for the reader, who must accept the interest of an examination of the nature of the hero's consciousness of himself. His world is seen with an unreal clarity and lack of human feeling, resulting in a telling acuity of perception but a disturbing emotional numbness. The philosophical enterprise can seem pretentious. The author convinces of the pain of his hero's alienated state, but the texture of the experience remains thin. A besetting weakness of Patterson's prose style is the absence of a convincing narrative tone, so that his fiction tends to alternate too unstably between abstract debate and cheap melodrama. This text is more incisively written, but the philosophical project remains more fully achieved than the transmutation of personal experience into fiction.

Patterson's third novel, *Die the Long Day*, abandons the nihilism of the earlier works. It is a historical novel set in late 18th century Jamaica and puts great emphasis on the heroic power of survival of the African slaves. It is less personal and more didactic, balancing a dramatic plot concerning Quasheba and her daughter against a very thorough and informative portrait of plantation life. Patterson had researched this topic for his doctoral dissertation, and it is clear that his historical sources, especially some of the personal documents of the time (letters to the press, diaries, reports of trials) aroused his imagination and inspired various scenes and characters in the novel, for example, the bookkeeper McKenzie.

The plot turns on the efforts of Quasheba, a slave woman of strong personality and great attraction, to save her daughter Polly from the embraces of a syphilitic plantation owner. She fails and dies, slain by the Maroons, but not before we have learned much of the lives of her fellow slaves, especially her partner, the doggedly worthy Cicero, Africanus the wise man, and various others in the fields and in the household. To illustrate his contention concerning the failure of White society to provide any leadership or moral values, Patterson highlights the corruption and weakness of the men employed by the absentee owners to run the plantation. Trapped between the groups are skilled mulattoes like young Benjamin, who seek a freedom which can have little meaning in such a sick society. The action, as so often with Patterson, is lively but episodic, a succession of vivid scenes rather than a close-knit plot which develops in depth and power.

Given the breadth of his canvas, Patterson establishes most of his characters with the bold strokes of popular fiction: wise old Naddy, tough brutal driver Bongo, foolish vain White magistrate, etc. Quasheba is the dominant portrait, established by the vigor of her actions and often seen through the admiring or respectful eyes of other characters. Patterson gives quite full though less heroic treatment to the young bookkeeper McKenzie, who is initiated unwillingly into the "custom of the country," that is, the inhuman treatment of the slaves, sexual license, the brutish self-indulgent life of the masters.

Patterson deploys his material to stress how, in the face of every kind of violence and humiliation, the plantation slaves managed to preserve dignity and self-respect and through their spirit of solidarity were able to establish their social values. Quasheba's funeral is tellingly used to stress the strength of the rites and the collective wisdom of a Black Caribbean community in the making. Africanus affirms a very explicit moral at the close of the novel: "It take courage, it take a great people, to preserve body and mind through all this. Our children will see it this way, and they'll be proud" (1973 ed., p. 287).

In addition to his three novels, Patterson has published some of his short fictional pieces, notably "Into the Dark" (*Jamaica Journal* 11 [March 1968], 62–69), the sad story of a country girl exploited by an overseer, and "The Very Funny Man: A Tale in Two Moods" (in *This Island Place*, ed. H. Fraser [London: Harrap, 1981], pp. 13–19). Both pieces have an existentialist flavor, the second relating closely to *An Absence of Ruins*. It presents the restless self-doubt of a younger Jamaican intellectual, an exam-passing student, who tries to make sense of himself by writing. He creates the ''funny man,'' a richer self who travels to Europe and in the Hall of Mirrors at Versailles is visited by a sudden terrifying awareness of his own meaningless existence. The story ends like the novel, ''eternally going'' nowhere.

Patterson has a good deal more writing in unpublished drafts, but it must be remembered that his main career lies in historical sociology and that academic writing has so far occupied most of his energies. He has published numerous articles and three books: *The Sociology of Slavery* (1967), based closely on his doctoral dissertation; *Ethnic Chauvinism: The Reactionary Impulse* (1977); and a major comparative treatise, *Slavery and Social Death* (1983). It is possible to see the two modes of writing as invigorating each other, as in the case of the European intellectuals Patterson has sought to emulate—the novel, with its focus on specific human reality, enhanced by an awareness of broader realms of philosophical speculation: the academic constructs of theory and hypothesis informed by an artist's insight into individual feeling. What Patterson himself labeled, in discussing the Rastafarians, ''the impossible privilege'' of combining sociological outsider and ''a reckless sense of identity.'' He expects to devote more of his time in the future to fiction, so we can await with interest the next phase in his development as a novelist.

CRITICAL RECEPTION

Patterson's first novel, *The Children of Sisyphus*, by often being prescribed reading for school and college students in the Caribbean, has aroused a broad response. Its poignant scenes have been dramatized and passages recited by young people studying the work, especially in Jamaica. The book has thus to some degree been annexed into a ''folk'' tradition of the spoken word, a process likely to have been promoted by Edward Brathwaite's interest in the novel (see his ''Jazz and the West India Novel,'' *Bim* 11 [January-June 1968], 275–84; 12 [July-December 1967], 39–51; 12 [January-June 1968], 115–26; ''Timehri,'' *Savacou*, no. 2 [September 1970], pp. 35–44; and ''West Indian Prose Fiction in the Sixties: A Survey,'' *Critical Survey* 3 [Winter 1967], 169–74).

On its publication in 1964, the book was much praised for its documentary value. ''Worth a dozen field surveys,'' affirmed the anonymous review in the *Times Literary Supplement* (April 2, 1964, p. 269), while Geoerge Robert Coulthard hailed the language as ''foul, coarse and obscene, but it is true,'' and recommended readers to check the accuracy of Patterson's reporting in the bars of Spanish Town Road (*Caribbean Quarterly* 10 [March 1964], 70). Joseph V. Owens admires the ''astounding verisimilitude'' with which Patterson portrays ''the speech, the reasoning, and the longing'' of the Rastafarian brethren (*Savacou* 11/12 [September 1975], 91).

However, Kenneth Ramchand judges the novel's ''avowedly inherited doctrine'' obtrusive (*The West Indian Novel and its Background*, 1970, p. 131), and Mervyn Morris criticizes the use of an external fatality dooming the characters to the Dungle (*Public Opinion*, April 24, 1964, p. 7). The links with existentialist philosophy are more fully discussed by Bridget Jones ("Some French Influences in the Fiction of Orlando Patterson," 1975, pp. 30–33).

The symbolic vision of poverty is often praised, but this was a first novel by an author of twenty-three, and many critics tried to guide Patterson in the writer's craft, at the level of plot construction and of text. Derek Walcott deplored "phony poeticisms" ("A New Jamaican Novelist," *Sunday Guardian* [Trinidad], May 17, 1964), and Mervyn Morris summed up his detailed notes with a regretful: "Disciplined self-criticism, cutting, re-writing could surely have made this a much finer book" (p. 13).

Reactions to *An Absence of Ruins* were much more varied, ranging from the enthusiasm of Robert Nye ("a very moving book about integrity preserved through an honest appraisal of its apparent loss . . . Mr. Patterson could develop into a worthy heir of Albert Camus" [*Manchester Guardian*, April 13, 1967, p. 10]) to a sarcastic query that Patterson might have intended "a sustained parody of a trendy kind of existential melancholia" (*Times Literary Supplement*, April 13, 1967, p. 301). For most critics the novel's introspection was too nihilistic, though some praised the "pained and telling economy of style" (*Times* [London], April 6, 1967, p. 9). Morris deplored the unconvincing turnabout of plot in Part 3, though analyzing with some sympathy the novel's stance on noninvolvement (*Public Opinion*, May 19, 1967, p. 5). Edward Brathwaite ("West Indian Prose Fiction") relates this work to Naipaul's *Mimic Men* as a novel of frustration and separation, and Gerald Moore (*Bim* 12 [June 1968], 46) usefully develops the comparison.

Die the Long Day was mainly more positively received, especially in the United States. Jan Carew stressed its relevance for the understanding of contemporary West Indian society and praised its psychological exploration of slave society and its "indomitable women" (*New York Times Book Review*, September 10, 1972, p. 46). "Dr. Patterson has performed a most useful service for modern Jamaica," affirmed Cedric Lindo (*Sunday Gleaner*, August 26, 1972, p. 45).

However, the novel sparked off a wholehearted attack by John Hearne, who denies that Patterson has any skill as a writer of fiction for all his "sociological-historical exactitude." He finds no life in the characters and too many examples of careless writing and advises Patterson to stick to writing essays instead ("The Novel as Sociology as Bore," *Caribbean Quarterly* 18 [December 1972], 78–81).

Despite such strictures, *Die the Long Day* has reached a popular audience as a cheap paperback, with a cover designed to emphasize its more sensational aspects.

HONORS AND AWARDS

Orlando Patterson has been awarded several scholarships and fellowships to further his academic work. He has also been granted National Endowment for the Humanities grants (1973, 1978, 1981, and 1983), a Guggenheim Award (1978), and the American Political Service Association's Ralph Bunche Award for best scholarly work on pluralism (1983). He received an honorary degree from Harvard University in 1971. His first novel received a prize at the 1966 Negro Arts Festival in Dakar.

BIBLIOGRAPHY

Works by Orlando Patterson

Fiction

The Children of Sisyphus. London: New Authors, 1964; London: Hutchinson, 1964; New York: Houghton Mifflin, 1965; Kingston: Bolivar, 1968; London: Longman, 1983. Also published as *Dinah*. New York: Pyramid, 1968.

An Absence of Ruins. London: Hutchinson, 1967.

Die the Long Day. New York: Morrow, 1972; New York: Curtis, 1973; London: Mayflower, 1974.

Nonfiction

The Sociology of Slavery. London: MacGibbon & Kee, 1967; Rutherford, N.J.: Fairleigh Dickinson University Press, 1969.

Black in White America: Historical Perspectives. New York: Macmillan, 1975.

Ethnic Chauvinism: The Reactionary Impulse. New York: Stein and Day, 1977.

Slavery and Social Death. Cambridge: Harvard University Press, 1983.

Studies of Orlando Patterson

Jones, Bridget. "Some French Influences in the Fiction of Orlando Patterson." *Savacou* 11/12 (September 1975), 27–38.

See also General Bibliography: Allis, Cudjoe, Hughes, James, and Ramchand (1970).

DARYL CUMBER DANCE

Vic Reid (1911–)

BIOGRAPHY

Victor Stafford Reid was born on May 1, 1911, in Kingston, Jamaica, to Alexander and Margaret Reid. His father, a businessman, worked in shipping, much of the time in the United States. Vic Reid, his two brothers, and one sister grew up in Kingston and attended schools there. He graduated from Kingston Technical High School in 1929.

One of the greatest influences on Vic Reid as he grew up was his exposure to the Anancy stories and other folk tales of Jamaica, which he heard from several storytellers, but particularly from his mother. Originally from the country, she was, he told me, "a woman of almost total recall," a raconteur whom the novelist still at the time of our interview (1980) looked forward to visiting at her home by the sea at Yallahs: "We sometimes go over for weekends and she regales me with stories" (interview with Daryl Cumber Dance, Kingston, Jamaica, March 12, 1980; the writer's mother died in 1981). Inevitably, the novelist came to see his mission as providing Jamaican children, through his stories, the same kind of a sense of history and self that his mother's tales had afforded him.

Through the years Reid was employed in a variety of positions in several countries. He worked as a farm overseer, journalist, editor, and advertising executive and also held several posts in the Jamaican government, most recently serving as chairman of the Jamaica National Trust Commission. Currently he is a trustee of the Historic Foundation Research Centre in Kingston.

The novelist has traveled widely. As a young man he journeyed to Britain in quest of work in publishing but soon found his "passion for Jamaica was too strong for the pallid English area summer" (interview). Surprisingly, it was not until *after* he had written a novel set in Africa (*The Leopard*, 1958) that he visited that continent for the first time—on a government mission in 1960, exploring in East Africa and West Africa the possibilities of the repatriation of Jamaicans (at the behest of the Rastafarians). Reid lived in Canada during 1958 and 1959 and in Manhattan in 1960, the year he received a Guggenheim. It is consistent with Reid's personality and his concerns that he chose that year not to retreat to one of the Ivy League enclaves, such as Harvard or Yale, but rather to immerse himself in the life of the people in Harlem and Greenwich Village. It also seems especially fitting that during his sojourn his good friend Langston Hughes should have been his main companion and his guide through the Harlem that Hughes loved so ardently. Reid's description of Hughes as "a guy who was talking my language" (interview) seems an understatement of the inevitable affinity of these two personalities, both of whom, throughout their lives, seem to have been captivated by their love of the Black folk community and their unmatched ability to capture its colors and rhythms as well as its pain and beauty with sensitivity and intensity. Though their settings vary, their quests and interests are remarkably similar. During our interview Reid told me:

> We keep a flat in town, but I really like living up in the mountains. As I go through the countryside today, I never turn on the radio in my car. You know why? I am *listening* to the countryside. . . . And everywhere I stop I can hear people's voices. . . . I have a *thorough*, unbelievable love for this land. I hear these things and I hear people talking and I pick them up and I must keep them because I just think that the whole rhythm of the country is part of me, and the rhythm of the talk is part of me, and the rhythm of the stories is part of me.

In like manner, Hughes typically asserted that his happiest job was one in an ice cream parlor in a Black neighborhood in Cleveland, where he could listen to the conversations of Black people who had just come up from the South: "I never tired of hearing them talk" (*The Big Sea* [New York: Knopf, 1940], p. 54). He often acclaimed the "wealth of colorful, distinctive material" such folk furnish any artist, and suggested, "Perhaps these common people will give to the world its truly great Negro artist, the one who is not afraid to be himself" ("The Negro Artist and the Racial Mountain," *The Nation* 122 [June 23, 1926], 693). Hughes's supposition seems an apt prophecy of his own later fame in the United States and certainly Vic Reid's in Jamaica as artists who derive their power from the folk.

Considering Reid's fascination with his homeland and his countrymen, it is no surprise that, despite his wide travels, he, unlike many of his fellow writers from the region, has for most of his life remained in Jamaica. Of his voyaging, he says that he was "always heading back home, and recharging my batteries, and going out again with some zest and gusto" (interview).

Vic Reid presently lives in Kingston with his wife Monica, whom he married in 1935. They have four children.

MAJOR WORKS AND THEMES

When Vic Reid's first novel, *New Day*, appeared in 1949, Reid clearly set forth the goal of that work, which, by extension, can be seen as his design throughout his career: "I have not by any means attempted a history of the period from 1865 to 1944. . . . What I have attempted is to transfer to paper some of the beauty, kindliness, and humour of my people, weaving characters into the wider framework of these eighty years and creating a tale that will offer as true an impression as fiction can of the way by which Jamaica and its people came to today" (Author's Note, n.p.; quotation and those following from *New Day*, 1972 ed.). He elaborated on this goal in our interview when I asked what motivated *New Day*:

> Above all, 'twas the need to . . . remind the Jamaicans who they are, where they came from, to show them that the then-self government we were aiming for, the then-change in the Constitution that we were getting, was not entirely a gift. The fact is that historically we had *paid* for it, and we had been paying for over three hundred years, four hundred years counting Spanish times, and therefore they should accept it with *pride* and work at it with the knowledge that it is theirs as a right.

Reid has always been concerned that "Jamaican history was never written. What was written were some works done by English telling the *English*side of the Jamaican history" (interview). He feels strongly that Jamaican children must be taught *their* history in order to help them develop a sense of pride in themselves, and that one of the best ways to do this is to present them with literary works that focus on the strengths and beauty and heroism of Jamaican history through characters to whom they can relate. He shared with me the enthusiastic reaction that he receives when he visits schools where his works are read:

> Their [the students'] faces [light up] and . . . they pelt you with questions because some of them see themselves in the book. They don't see some Little Red Riding Hood. And this is *all*, this is all I want! I mean everybody needs money, but believe me, the money is secondary to see that they are getting what I never got. I had to divorce myself completely from Robin Hood and Sexton Blake and Buffalo Bill and all that stuff. (interview)

Thus it is perhaps not a matter of primary significance to the success of *New Day* and the achievement of Reid's goals that some critics have declared him guilty of occasionally deviating from the historical record or of electing to propagate particular versions of controversial historical figures, especially when we consider the lack of concurrence among historians in judging figures such as Governor Edward Eyre and George William Gordon and the preponderance of partisan historiography that all too often ignores, misrepresents, and maligns the group from whose perspective Reid views the events. Indeed many of us would agree with—and Vic Reid's work is certainly an example of—Ralph Ellison's iconoclastic declaration: ''I don't think that history is Truth. I think it's another form of man trying to find himself, and to come to grips with his own complexity'' (''The Uses of History in Fiction,'' *Southern Literary Journal* 1 [1969], 69). Thus what is a matter of primary significance in the consideration of *New Day* is that the author affords the Jamaican reader an opportunity to experience a series of crucial formative events in the history of his country and his people as seen and experienced and expressed by a Jamaican who lived through them, and Reid has done this with a great deal of fidelity to significant historical incidents and to the experiences and character of his fictionalized Jamaican.

The novel opens as the narrator, John Campbell, now eighty-seven years old, looks forward to the begining of the ''new day,'' when King George will grant to Jamaica self-rule under a new constitution. He is proud that his grandnephew Garth will share the platform with the governor and other notables, that Garth and earlier generations of his family have contributed so much to the attaining of this ''new day,'' and that Garth will assuredly become a leader of the nation. But what is especially gratifying to John at this stage in his life is that ''Garth remembers all the old things I ha' told him'' (p. 4). And hereupon John proceeds to relate those ''old things'' to us so that we, like Garth, can be strengthened by that awareness. Anybody who has ever sat at the foot of a great storyteller realizes at the moment that John Campbell invites him to share in his memories that he is about to experience (not merely hear) a tale of great drama and suspense:

> Memories are a-shake me tonight. Memories o' hot sand and mangrove bush and hunting-Maroons with naked swords. Of the boom of redcoats' muskets, the whistle o' whips, and the crack o' lashes; of a dozen men twitching on Provost Ramsey's gallows.
>
> Memories o' Colonel Judas Hobbs of the Sixth Regiment o' Foot. Memories of Mr. Abram and his forty for forty. Memories of a high wind, and weakness coming to my bro's loins when his woman was no' with him. Memories o' two old men stumbling through dark-night to bring Davie's seed from a plague house.
>
> *Aie*—I must no' be restless longer. Quiet, I will sit quiet, while they sing and make my mind walk back. I will talk o' the years what ha' passed. (pp. 8–9)

And thus we go back with John to 1865, when he was eight years old, and experience through his account the parched land, the hunger of the people, the injustices that they suffer, their frustrations when both the local government and the Crown ignore their pleas for succor, and their anger as all about them they see the wealth and privilege of the White planters. Through John, we are caught up in the crowd in front of the Morant Bay Courthouse, suffering with Deacon Paul Bogle and his followers the insults of the government officials as Bogle futilely demands to see Custos Aldenburg and voice the complaints of his people. We glimpse the women carrying the pots of sumptuous, mouth-watering food past the agitated crowds to the Vestrymen inside, and we hear a voice cry out,

"And Jesus Christ, we hungry!" (p. 120) Then a rock-stone rises in the air, triggering the Morant Bay Rebellion. Custos Aldenburg reads the riot act just before the soldiers open fire, killing several of the protesting villagers. Then the mob, angry for vengeance, sets fire to the courthouse, forcing the government officials out and assassinating many of them. We accompany John and his family as they flee into the mountains to save themselves from the hysterical and vicious revenge of the government's soldiers, hearing with them the periodic reports of the burnings and the executions and the indiscriminate slaughter of the innocent and the guilty alike. Then, after witnessing the callous shooting of most of John's family, we accompany him through the next eighty years as he supports and protects first his brother Davie and his family, as Davie attempts to found an independent community on the Cays, then Davie's son, James Creary, as he establishes himself as a prosperous businessman, and finally Davie's grandson, Garth, as he leads his people toward independence. The excitement and suspense of the final struggle for independence is told no less dramatically than the scene revealing our protagonist's earlier dedication to the protection of his beloved big brother Davie when young John was desperately fighting his way through the Morant Bay mob to get to his shackled brother. Here again there is rioting; this time Davie's grandson, Garth, is a central figure, and the octogenarian John is rushing to aid him, with less speed, perhaps, but no less resolution:

> I am running with breath full in my mouth. Sounds ha' left my ears, and sight only points one way—to where I know Garth must be.
>
> *Come, John Campbell! Run one foot, draw breath, run another foot again. Tiredness can no' drop you now when you know your boy is up there. Sunhot, dust, and scents o' gunpowder. Scents o' gunpowder, and your feet a-stumble? What kind o' old warhorse you?*
>
> The man for the glory was my bro' Davie—he did no' stumble when he took me from Baptism Valley. Will I leave his seed eating dust in Corporation wasteland? Go, John Campbell O! (p. 299)

Frequently during the first part of the novel Reid supplements his dramatization of the events his youthful narrator is experiencing with more mature explications, which aid the reader in interpreting the actions and in envisioning them in the broader perspective of Jamaican history. Often through the speeches of the leaders or the meticulous explanations Davie provides his brother, Reid is able to place the eighty-year span of this novel into the broader context of Jamaican history as well as to introduce the reader to earlier Jamaican (and West Indian) heroes. Thus, on one occasion, Davie strides through thick guinea grease with John on his back "bobbing and listening with all o' my ears" (p. 63) to his brother's accounts of "Tackey's insurrection at Port Maria . . . the great Maroon War o' Ninety-six. . . . He talks of how the English put red coats on the backs of their slaves and took them to fight the Americans in the War o' Independence. He talks o' the war in Haiti, and I hear of Bro' L'Ouverture and his republic" (pp. 62–63).

Such an awareness of history is necessary, Reid demonstrates, in a country where one's history teacher is, according to Davie, paid by the buckra government "to fool poor people's children" (p. 81). John's teacher, Mr. M'Donald, insists, "If the people of the United States of America had obeyed the dictates of His Gracious Majesty, King George III, today they would still be children of the Mother Country, enjoying the wonderful privilege and safety which lies in being a member of the vast British Empire" (p. 82). This same miseducation still continues in later generations, as John sadly observes: "Young ones passing on the streets stop to look at us [him and his old friend Timothy] and wonder what we two must talk of all the time. They do no' know what we have seen, for no place has been found in their English history books for the fire that burnt us in 'Sixty-five. Men ha' forgotten" (p. 262).

It is important to observe that, throughout the novel, Reid suggests that the degree to which a person is receptive to, appreciative of, and able to act upon the history and folk culture of his people is a measure of his worth as an individual, of the "light" (enlightenment) that he possesses. Thus it is that Davie's great knowledge of the history of his people, as well as his enthusiastic sharing of that knowledge with his brother, is one of the marks that he is destined to be "a man for the glory." Conversely, one of the surest indications that despite his economic success Davie's son, James Creary, is not destined to become such a man is presaged in James Creary's lack of interest in John's accounts of his history. Thus he grows up "without knowing of his father or his mother and what mighty happenings brought his conception" (p. 256), and his "eyes do no' light when he hears of Mr. Abram and forty for forty" (p. 257). James Creary's acceptance and embracing of the values of European society is clearly posited by Reid as the cause of his lack of appreciation of his history and his race: when John tells his nephew of his history, "he does no' want to listen to me, for he has got a wife to his bed who is of the English" (p. 261). Indeed, the prosperous James Creary out-Englishes the English, without heeding the admonition of that old folk proverb that his uncle calls to his attention: "The higher monkey climbs, the more he exposes his underpart" (p. 258). Thus we are not surprised when he sits silently by as his wife refuses to allow their baby to receive John's traditional gift, a neckguard, exclaiming, "I will not have these barbaric customs in this house!" (p. 264)

On the other hand, Garth, even from his infancy, shows an appreciation for his folk heritage, for when John shows the neckguard to him, "Nice it is to see how shine comes to his eyes." And despite his mother's efforts to restrain him, the infant "[gets] a finger on the chain" (p. 264) and continues to tug at it until he succeeds in taking it from John's finger. We know, of course, that James Creary is too far lost to bring any light to his son; and thus we recognize it as the work of providence that he and his wife are destroyed by smallpox and John rescues his grandnephew, Garth. John frequently looks at this child and thinks, "Bro', for true is Davie, this" (p. 266). That this is indeed another Davie is affirmed by the child's appreciation of his history: "Much of his happy times comes when we take him into the mountains and tell o' things dead and gone. That time such a way his eyes light up, and Timothy and me must talk and talk'' (p. 273). From the time he is a young child, Garth not only reads but he also relies upon the experience of his elders to help him interpret and assess what he discovers in books. Thus his uncle must help him judge the characters of Gordon and Bogle: ''We have been taught in our history classes that Gordon and Bogle were devils while Eyre was a saint who only did what he did because it was necessary. You knew both Gordon and Bogle. Were they as bad as painted?'' (p. 277) Even after Garth finishes law school, ''he . . . will no' open his chambers till he can serve his 'prenticeship with older Benchers who can teach him of their experience. Garth is a wise one who has learnt that knowledge o' things to come is no' spoilt by learning of the past'' (p. 277).

As Garth sets out to try to improve the caliber of life for his people, we constantly see parallels to the problems that challenged his grandfather Davie and Bogle and Gordon: extreme poverty, a lack of economic and political strength, and cruel exploitation by the rich and the powerful. When Garth attempts to expound his people's grievances to the Corporation officers, he too is ignored and humiliated, much as Bogle was at Morant Bay, and, again as at Morant Bay, the anger and the frustrations of the crowd lead to a riot. The difference in the present situation, however, Reid emphasizes, is that Garth is a leader who has learned from the mistakes of the past and therefore has a power that his foreparents at Morant Bay did not have to save his one hundred imprisoned followers: ''Through tangled woodlands o' many old books he has gone a-search for the matter that will make his hundred see light again. He is gone a-walk through musty old books, seeking for the marks what generations o' freemen ha' made for us to walk by; marks that tell us why we are free who live under the Jack. Everytime he stumbles on a mark I see him nod his head like he is saying *thankie* to the men o' ancient times'' (p. 303).

Reid stresses the point that, despite the fact that Garth is a London-educated lawyer and a wealthy businessman, he remains a man of the people and never loses his sense of race and identity. Unlike his father, Garth never forgets where his ''navel-string is buried'' (p. 276), and there remains his fidelity. Thus, at the end of the novel, we rejoice with John Campbell at such a leader, from such a lineage: ''My boy is thundering in the finish of his race. Mighty things ha' gone into his conception. He is leading his people to the promised land that his father's father had reached for'' (p. 368).

Throughout his career, Vic Reid has continued to write with the goal of helping Jamaicans, particularly young Jamaicans, to know themselves through an awareness of their rich and heroic history. In keeping with this goal, he wrote three novels especially for young readers: *Sixty-Five* (1960), which treats the Morant Bay uprising; *The Young Warriors* (1967), which focuses upon the Maroons; and *Peter of Mount Ephraim* (1971), which is based on the Daddy Samuel Sharpe slave rebellion of 1831. *The Jamaicans* (1978), which treats the valiant struggles of the 17th century Jamaican guerrilla Juan de Bolas to preserve the freedom and dignity of his people, was motivated by the novelist's recognition that Jamaicans needed to know this aspect of their history. Reid told me, "It is really sickening to know that so *few* people know anything of Juan de Bolas."

The Jamaicans focuses upon a band of escaped slaves who, under the leadership of de Bolas, establish a mountain stronghold above Guanaboa Vale and reach a truce with the Spaniards, who in return for not attempting to dislodge them are spared raids upon their haciendas. These guerrillas, who derive their sustenance and protection from the land, are well nigh invincible when fighting in the jungles, "where the leaves and trees immediately around you knew your presence, and shared your secret with you, because you had become one of them, and would even suborn the rest of the forest that hid your enemy" (p. 127; quotation and those following from *The Jamaicans*, 1978 ed.). The alien Europeans (the occupying Spanish and the imperialistic British) have no such relationship with the land, and thus, despite their advantage in terms of weapons and men, they find themselves at the mercy of the Blacks whenever they venture into the jungles. When the Black warriors enter battle, they are also inspired and emboldened by their glorious history. Old Miguel often reminds his countrymen of the valiant deeds of five generations of mountain soldiers who had been "from the earliest landings of their African ancestors, fighting their way from the coast into the high country, linking up with and leading the few remaining Arawak Indians [in battle against the colonizers]" (p. 201). Thus, as the guerrillas prepare for the most crucial battle of their career, the band's elder, Old Miguel, reminds Juan de Bolas that the outcome of battle depends not only on "bullets and legs" but also on the spirit of the people, which must be strengthened by having the poet/griot *"speak each night. . . . He must tell and retell the story of our past, until all our young men know it as they know their mother's teats"* (pp. 201–02).

The bravery, ingenuity, and intelligence of the Black Jamaican guerrillas is frequently contrasted to the cowardice, incompetence, and ignorance of the White Europeans. The behavior of all the Whites, ranging from Ezekiel Tubbs (the servile, cowardly Cockney soldier, captured and enslaved by the guerrillas, who "had a natural talent for obeying orders" [p. 181]), to Don Christobal Arnaldo de Ysassi (the gullible Spanish governor, who foolishly reveals strategic information and practically invites attack and defeat), reinforces the point that Juan and other guerrillas make when comparing themselves to Europeans: "We are so much the worthy ones" (p. 198). Indeed, as is so strikingly illustrated in the behavior of the Coromantee girl Kedela (the only woman on de Bolas's council), even the women are superior: "[Kedela] was as much warrior as Juan and the others, and Old Miguel had said to the priest that theirs must be the only race in which the women fought shoulder to shoulder with the men. . . . Our women were warriors in Africa even then. Why did God so specially bless us . . . in the fine women he gave us?" (pp. 211–12). De Bolas's friend Pablo contends that because the guerrillas have adopted the Spanish language and religion and because they have been "befriended" by the Spanish governor they owe an allegience to the Spaniards in their battle with the English for sovereignty over Jamaica. However, de Bolas, recognizing that the English are winning the war, determines that the guerrillas' goal should be to win the respect of whichever European power prevails. Thus, to force the conquering English to recognize the desirability of negotiating with them, de Bolas and his men audaciously attack and destroy the powerful English stronghold at St. Jago (Spanish Town). They win an easy victory over the English, who are consequently forced to deal with them on their own terms. Pablo regards Juan de Bolas's new alliance with the English as traitorous, however, and thus the two brave warriors are thrust into mortal combat, thereby effecting what no European ever could—the destruction of the two bravest and most indestructible of the guerrilla heroes. Reid suggests that their deaths are symbolic for the future of Jamaica, for in their final embrace they become one: as Old Miguel observes, "If they see now, they will know they are one, . . . they know they are neither African, nor Spanish, nor English, but of the Jamaican earth" (p. 265).

Though Reid's second novel, *The Leopard* (1958), is set outside of Jamaica (in Africa), it too was motivated by a need to give more balance to history. When I asked the novelist what inspired him to write *The Leopard*, he exclaimed, "Sheer anger! I was angry because the Western press and the writers were treating the Mau-Mau as if they weren't human beings, as if they were sheer *animals*." Thus Reid set out, as he does in preparing all of his novels, to ground himself thoroughly in the history and folklore of the area and period he planned to treat. The result is a spellbinding work, which not only provides a more sympathetic view of the Mau-Mau uprisings, but also establishes Reid as a novelist of the chase par excellence.

Set in Kikuyu land in Kenya, *The Leopard* focuses on a young African warrior, Nebu, and his pursuit of a White victim. Through flashbacks during this chase we learn that several years ago, when Nebu was absorbed in the fervor of a tribal dance performed solo to the accompaniment of the rains and the winds (which were his drums and pipes), his White mistress had walked into the room and, overwhelmed with lust for the naked native servant, she had incited him to the act that led to her pregnancy and death, apparently at the hands of her husband, who was deranged by his wife's delivery of a "grey" child. Though Nebu's White quarry is much more adept than most Whites in maneuvering in the forest, the African finds it easy to follow and overcome him because ultimately he betrays himself through some foolish act. Frequently Nebu is led to conclude that "the pink one ahead is a fool as all the pink ones are fools" (p. 24; quotation and those following from *The Leopard*, 1972 ed.). The African, on the other hand, is protected by and adept in this beautiful land. When he runs into the bush, "the bush was waiting and drew him in with a hundred thousand green arms in heat for him" (p. 52). Indeed, as Reid informs us, "the land was a book you learned to read" (p. 25), and "the black knew each inch of the land as a lion cub knew the tits" (p. 68). Thus Nebu easily overtakes his foe and would have killed him with no difficulty had he not been briefly stunned to discover that his prey is Bwana Gibson, his former master whom he had wronged. His shock and his guilt slow his reactions, and though he delivers a mortal blow, Gibson is allowed the time to bring his rifle up and shoot his assailant. Before he dies, Gibson reveals that he has been hunting Nebu for the last ten years and taunts, "This time I brought your son so that he could watch you die" (p. 40). The wounded Nebu then sets out to take his crippled son back to Nairobi, but they are stalked by a leopard. The son, scheming to bring about the death of the "nigger" father whom Gibson has taught him to despise, ultimately causes his own death as well as Nebu's (indirectly). Without minimizing the violence of the Mau-Mau uprisings, Reid helps us to see the humanity of all concerned, presents a positive vision of the African warrior, and gives us a sense of traditional Africa, while at the same time commenting upon the complexity of the problems resulting from colonialization.

Reid has recently completed two works: *Nanny-Town*, a novel based on Nanny, a priestess-warrior who led the Blue Mountain Maroons against the English and forced them into signing a treaty which gave her people autonomy (1983), and *The Horse of the Morning*, a biography of N. W. Manley, who was clearly the prototype for Garth of *New Day* (scheduled for publication soon). He is presently working on a novel, *The Naked Buck*, which will be more contemporary in its setting and will focus on ordinary Jamaicans, including the Rastafarians, who though they may not be "necessarily heroic in the accepted term . . . [are] people who are determined to use their folk intellect, and their folk understanding, and their own historical precedence to find a place for them[selves] in this world" (interview). Portions of *The Naked Buck* were published in 1983 in *Focus*.

CRITICAL RECEPTION

Since Vic Reid's first novel, *New Day*, appeared in 1949, it has been hailed as a landmark in West Indian literature. Gerald Moore writes, 'It was with *New Day* that a new generation of West Indian writers really began the task of breaking free from the colonial cocoon and flying with wings of their own in a distinctly tropical sky" (*The Chosen Tongue*, 1969, p. 6). Peter Abrahams claims that *New Day* "marked the beginning of the emergence of a whole new school of Jamaican and West Indian novelists" ("Foreword," *The Independence Anthology of Jamaican Literature*, ed. A. L. Hendricks and Cedric Lindo [Kingston: The Arts Celebration Committee of the Ministry of Development and Welfare, 1962]). And Mervyn Morris notes, "*New Day* was the first West Indian, and remains the only Jamaican, novel in which the language of narration is a dialect" (Introduction to *New Day* [London: Heinemann, 1973]).

Despite the recognition of the importance of *New Day* in Caribbean literature, the novel has not been without its censurers. Debate about the novel generally centers around the accuracy of Reid's history, his reproduction of dialect, and the validity of his political stance. In his essay, "The Historical Foundation of *New Day*" (1949), H. P. Jacobs details inconsistencies and variations in the novel regarding events and personalities. Kenneth Ramchand (*An Introduction to the Study of West Indian Literature*, 1976) attacks the novel for its unimaginative treatment of actual historical figures, its inadequacies in historical understanding, and its "discontinuous story-line" (p. 39). In his introduction to the Heinemann edition of *New Day*, Morris responds to Ramchand's argument, contending that the book is "fiction, not history" and presenting a detailed analysis of the various ways in which the book is "an intricate whole."

One of the most frequently noted attributes of *New Day* is its language, which has been both praised and damned. Hailing the novel as "a liquid, lyrical thing of wondrous beauty," Zora Neale Hurston praises the reproduction of "the colorful idiom of the island. It is rich to luxury in the figures and sayings of the island. The speech, the attitudes, the geographical descriptions are as Jamaican as a mouthful of ackee in season" ("At the Sound of the Conch Shell," 1949, p. 4). Ramchand describes Reid's dialect as successful invention and concludes that "on the whole . . . Reid's experiment is a successful one" (*The West Indian Novel*, 1970, p. 101). R. B. LePage ("Dialect in West Indian Literature," *Journal of Commonwealth Literature* 7 [July 1969], 1–7; reprinted in Baugh, *Critics on Caribbean Literature*, 1978, pp. 123–29), suggests that Reid's language "had a very literary flavour and, for me at least, failed to carry conviction." Louis James charges, "[Reid] created a *patois* more concentrated and precise than the vernacular, but he also cut it off from the variation, the acerbity, the vigour that exists in the spoken word" (*Islands in Between*, 1968, p. 66). Morris, conceding that the novel is "narrated in a modified version of Jamaican speech," concludes that "the narrator's language seems appropriate enough from an old middle-class Jamaican who has, for part of his life, been in close contact with a rural peasant community" (Introduction, *New Day*).

The political vision of the author is the grounds for the attack on *New Day* by Selwyn R. Cudjoe (*Resistance and Caribbean Literature*, 1980), who insists that while Reid recognizes the need of the Jamaicans to determine their own destiny and to resist oppression, he "fails to perceive the traumatic reorganization in political and social relations that must take place if self-government is to mean anything at all" (p. 148). Sylvia Wynter expresses similar concerns about the political philosophy of the novel, suggesting that the third part of the novel "fails by ignoring the fact that a change in the superstructure of the plantation, a new Constitution, even Independence, were changes which left the basic system untouched" ("Novel and History, Plot and Plantation," 1971, p. 102). Within a basically laudatory critique that praises Reid's achievement in conveying a "rooted sense of identity within a lived landscape" (*The West Indian Novel*, p. 123), Michael Gilkes charges that Garth's assertion of nationhood built upon racial harmony is misleading since "the real gulf is finally not one of race or politics, but of class." He continues, "Garth's boast that 'in our island we have proven that race is skin shallow' is largely a political expedient, ignoring the deeper division of class which his brother Davie . . . had implicitly recognized" (p. 122).

The Leopard has not received the extensive critical attention that has been accorded *New Day*. The most useful studies of *The Leopard* are Gregory Rigsby's introduction to the 1971 Collier edition, Mervyn Morris's introduction to the 1980 Heinemann edition, where Morris calls attention to the differences between the British and American editions of the novel, Mark Kinkead-Weekes " 'Africa'—Two Caribbean Fictions" (1973), Ramchand's treatment in *The West Indian Novel and its Background*, and James's treatment in *The Islands in Between*.

Reid's works are also considered in Griffiths, *A Double Exile* (1978); King, *West Indian Literature* (1979); Van Sertima, *Caribbean Writers* (1968); Lamming, *The Pleasures of Exile* (1960); and Harris, *Tradition the Writer and Society* (1973).

HONORS AND AWARDS

Vic Reid has received several honors, including a Silver Musgrave Medal (1955), two Canada Council Fellowships (1958 and 1959), the Mexican Escritores Award (1959), a Guggenheim Fellowship (1960), a Gold Musgrave Medal (1978), the Order of Jamaica Award (1980), and the Norman Manley Award for Excellence in Literature (1981).

BIBLIOGRAPHY

Works by Vic Reid

New Day. New York: Knopf, 1949; London: Heinemann, 1950, 1973; Kinston: Sangster's, 1970; Chatham, N.J.: Chatham Bookseller, 1972.

The Leopard. London: Heinemann, 1958; New York: Viking Press, 1958; New York: Collier, 1971; Chatham, N.J.: Chatham Bookseller, 1972.

Sixty-Five. London: Longman, 1960.

The Young Warriors. London: Longman, 1967.

Peter of Mount Ephraim. Kingston: Jamaica Publishing House, 1971.

The Jamaicans. Kingston: The Institute of Jamaica, 1976, 1978.

Nanny-Town. Kingston: Jamaica Publishing House, 1983.

The Horse of the Morning: A Life of Norman Washington Manley. Kingston: Caribbean Authors, 1985.

Studies of Vic Reid

Davies, Barrie. "Neglected West Indian Writers. No. 2. Vic Reid. The Leopard." *World Literature Written in English* 11 (November 1972), 83–85.

Hurston, Zora Neale. "At the Sound of the Conch Shell." *New York Herald Tribune Weekly Book Review*, March 20, 1949, p. 4.

Jacobs, H. P. "The Historic Foundation of *New Day*." *The West Indian Review* (Kingston) 1 (May 14, 1949), 21–22; 1 (May 21, 1949), 10–11; 1 (May 28, 1949), 18–19.

James, Louis. ''Of Redcoats and Leopards: Two Novels by V. S. Reid.'' In *The Islands in Between*, 1968, pp. 64–72.

Kinkead-Weekes, Mark. '' 'Africa'—Two Caribbean Fictions,'' *20th Century Studies* 10 (December 1973), 37–59.

Morris, Mervyn. Introduction to *The Leopard*. London: Heinemann, 1980.

———. Introduction to *New Day*. London: Heinemann, 1973.

Ramchand, Kenneth. ''History and the Novel: A Literary Critic's Approach.'' *Savacou* 5 (June 1971), 103–13.

Rigsby, Gregory. Introduction to *The Leopard*. New York: Collier, 1971.

Wynter, Sylvia. ''Novel and History, Plot and Plantation.'' *Savacou*5 (June 1971), 95–102.

See also General Bibliography: Allis, Cudjoe, Gilkes, Griffiths, Harris, Hughes, King, Lamming, Moore, Ramchand (1970, 1976), and Van Sertima.

JEAN D'COSTA

Jean Rhys (1890–1979)

Critics at three corners of the triangular trade lay claim to Jean Rhys. In England scholars read her as "British woman writer," painter of grim urban settings and social subtypes, catching time, place, mood, and the values that upheld a fading imperial world: England after Victoria, before Hitler. To American critics her work speaks mostly of woman-as-victim, although they recognize her insight into British society. In the Caribbean Rhys is the exponent of the "terrified consciousness" (Kenneth Ramchand, *The West Indian Novel and its Background*, 1970, p. 223) of the ruling class. For all three groups, Rhys presents problems of classification which disguise problems of interpretation and acceptance. How can the author of "Let Them Call It Jazz," the creator of Christophine, and the satirizer of Hester Morgan be sincerely British? It is permissible to mock from within, but surely not to stand outside wanting to be Black, hating "being white and getting like Hester" (*Voyage in the Dark*, Penguin, 1980, p. 62), hating the faces "like . . . blind rabbit[s]" (p. 19), faces "the colour of woodlice" (p. 23). Then, too, Rhys is not Everywoman's feminist: the Rhys heroine is devoured as greedily by other women as by men. Caribbean readers, more concerned with class, race, and history than with the politics of sex and gender, may well question the significance of Mr. Mackenzie, or of René the gigolo.

Rhys's life does much to confuse interpretations of her work. By her own admission, she wrote "everything" that mattered in her life into her fiction: how tempting, then, to use that life to explain the art or, worse, to use the art to document the life. Rhys critics have tried both and have mired themselves in speculation and error. In her will she left instructions that no biography be written of her, instructions that led her literary executor, Francis Wyndham, aided by Diana Melly, to publish a selection of Rhys's letters so as to let her speak of her life in her own voice. *The Letters of Jean Rhys* (1984) illuminates the quality and movement of the writer's life, but hardly resolves the difficulty of how and where to place her work.

A reader new to Rhys usually puzzles over her viewpoint: looking both ways across the Channel and the Atlantic, she seems "for" and "against" both perspectives. Her inside–outsider's treatment of England, France, and the Caribbean gnaws away at comfortable ethnocentrisms. Her characters play out the pathologies of exploitation as lovers, as siblings, as neighbors, as whole social groups. Looking for some kind of familiar ground, the reader tries to fit Rhys into available models of contemporary fiction, and fails. Rhys's style and narrative techniques set her apart. She belongs to no recognizable school; she fits into no ready-made slot. Inevitably, the reader yields to speculations about the writer's history, seeking the answers to these puzzles in her work. Using the novels as guide to their creator leads the unwary into perilous interpretations.

The danger of misconstruing Rhys's life has lessened with the publication in 1984 of two works: Elgin W. Mellown's *Jean Rhys: A Descriptive and Annotated Bibliography of Works and Criticism*—an essential tool for Rhys scholarship—and the volume of letters mentioned above. The latter, when read in conjunction with Rhys's *Smile, Please: an Unfinished Autobiography* (1979), steers one away from many of the errors of fact which have haunted Rhys scholarship. *Smile, Please* sketches Rhys's early life and ends in 1939 with the briefest outline of her early career as a writer. *The Letters of Jean Rhys*, helpfully annotated, document the years 1931 to 1966, while Mellown's introductory essay offers a clear overview of Rhys's life and works.

Yet even among these seemingly definitive works, discrepancies arise: Was Rhys's first husband Jean Lenglet or Jean Langlet? Did her father die in 1908 or 1909? Trifles all, one might say, yet such details emphasize the warning Rhys herself made: the life is nothing, the art is all. One could go further and say that the art consumes the life and that the surviving fragments of bald fact should never be seen as anything other than, at best, a map for a vanished landscape.

BIOGRAPHY

The bald facts of her life are soon told. Born in 1890 on the British West Indian island of Dominica, Ella Gwendolen Rees Williams (later Jean Rhys) was the daughter of a Welsh doctor, William Rees Williams, and his White Dominican wife, Minna Williams (née Lockhart). Rhys was the fourth of five children: two older brothers left for school in England while Rhys was very young; her elder sister went to live with an aunt in St. Kitts, passing out of Rhys's life; and the younger sister was her junior by seven years. The family lived in Roseau but made frequent visits to the Lockhart plantation, "Geneva."

On this estate lived Rhys's maternal grandmother and a beloved great-aunt,

Jane Woodcock (*Smile, Please*, pp. 26–28). *Wide Sargasso Sea* (1966) draws on their reminiscences of Dominica in the mid–19th century. Unfortunately, a famly quarrel split the Lockharts and separated the child from this refuge of love and beauty, perhaps contributing to the intense longing with which the adult would later write about the vanished domain of childhood.

Rhys's life in Dominica followed the conventional pattern of the small White upper class. Yet the conventional was not a blind, unvarying system in colonial Dominica, with its blend of French and English Creole, its mixture of cultures, and its memories. Rhys went to a convent school where Whites were the minority; she was conscious early of the ambivalences in color-class relationships, of shade prejudice, of "outside" children fathered by White men; and she was brought up to be "a lady," an "English lady," using the speech, dress, and manners of a country she had never seen. Her autobiography reveals a strong identity with Dominica and an early sense of the unrealness of England. From this came her odd double vision of the White metropolitan world, a vision bred into the colonial, the Creole.

Few hard facts emerge to speak of her relationships with her family. Her autobiography suggests that Rhys was attached to her father and in awe of her mother. After her departure from Dominica in 1907 at the age of sixteen, details concerning her family are scarce indeed. Rhys went to England with a sister of Dr. Rees Williams, attended the Perse School in Cambridge and the Academy of Dramatic Art (later RADA) in London. Accounts differ as to how long she spent in either school, but within two years her father's death left her without support, and rather than return to Dominica, she joined a touring theater company as a chorus girl. Her first two years in the "Mother Country" were strange and unsettling, and in this mood she read *Jane Eyre*.

Rejecting as false Charlotte Brontë's portrayal of Rochester's mad Jamaican wife, Rhys was undergoing that cross-cultural shock familiar to those who cross between the colonial and the metropolitan worlds. The contrast between the two marked her deeply: gray cities, snappish landladies, the weekly bath ordered days in advance, the new rules of speech, dress, and conduct. One curious reaction was that her "love and longing for books completely left [her]" (*Smile, Please*, p. 90).

In her autobiography Rhys outlines her first love affair: the older man, conventional and kind; the naive girl, deeply in love, and quite unready for the break which came in 1913. After a lonely Christmas, Rhys moved to new rooms, where, suddenly, she began to write down—as if possessed—"everything that had happened . . . in the last year and a half" (p. 104). Three and a half thick black notebooks later, she had composed what would eventually become *Voyage in the Dark* (1934). Her ex-lover helped to support her for six years more while she worked at odd jobs on the stage, or as a mannequin, and, during the war, in a canteen.

Little else can be traced of those years. In 1917 she met a Dutch songwriter and journalist, Jean Lenglet (or Langlet). After a brief acquaintance, Lenglet proposed and left for Holland. Rhys speaks in *Smile, Please* of her intense relief at joining him in 1919 and ceasing to be the pensioner of her former lover (pp. 106–14). The notebooks went with her, although she did not look at them "for seven years."

This Biblical span of time brought marriage, motherhood, poverty, and travel and confronted Rhys with her life-work: writing. In the first three years of their marriage, the Lenglets moved between Amsterdam, Paris, Vienna, and Budapest. Rhys taught English in a French family, Lenglet for a while worked with the Inter-Allied Commission in Vienna, but they were never financially secure. In 1920 Rhys bore a son, William, who died three weeks later; then came a daughter, Maryvonne, in 1923. There were no other children.

Other events now shaped the writer's fortunes. While seeking a publisher for Lenglet's work, Rhys came in touch with Ford Madox Ford, who was shown drafts from the black notebooks. Then Lenglet's arrest in France in 1923 for offences against currency regulations led to his imprisonment and extradition to Holland, and Rhys lived for a while with Ford and his common-law wife, the Australian artist Stella Bowen. The plot of Rhys's first novel draws on her affair with Ford. His patronage launched Rhys's career: her first sketches entitled "Vienne" appeared under the pen name "Jean Rhys" in *TransatlanticReview* (1924), Ford's journal.

Stella Bowen's description of Rhys in her memoirs, *Drawn from Life* (1940), makes a useful commentary on Rhys the woman and the writer. This closeness of life and art has tempted some critics to reconstruct Rhys the woman from what many see as the composite heroine of her first four novels. Yet life proves to be more complex than art. Rhys heroines do not publish books. Aided by Ford, Rhys brought out *The Left Bank and Other Stories* (1927). Ford's preface praises her technical skill and her insight into the "underdog." Their affair was by then over, but its shape is preserved in Rhys's next work, *Postures* (now *Quartet*, 1928): Marya Zelli falls into the hands of the Heidlers, those good Samaritans, while her husband is in prison. Marya's affair with H. J. Heidler forms the center of the work. Later both Jean Lenglet (pen name Edouard de Nève) and Ford based novels on the same material, with Rhys the translator and promoter of Lenglet's novel, *Barred* (1932). She also translated Francis Corco's novel *Perversité* (1928), wrongly attributed to Ford by the publisher.

On a visit to London in 1927, she had met a publisher's reader, Leslie Tilden Smith, whom she married in 1932 after her divorce from Lenglet. Her daughter, Maryvonne Lenglet, remained in Holland, visiting her mother during school holidays in the gray city to which Rhys had once vowed never to return, the city of Julia Martin, outcast. Rhys's second novel, *After Leaving Mr Mackenzie* (1931), moves between London and Paris and was completed in a Paris hotel where Rhys went alone to write: its heroine, Julia Martin, is the archetype of the unwanted, placeless human garbage cast up by great cities, living in cheap hotels, an embarrassment to the respectable. The novel was composed in the very settings which it presents.

Rhys's life was now centered on writing, and she was a strict craftswoman. Witness her reworkings of the black notebooks to create the White West Indian heroine of *Voyage in the Dark* (1934). But the crowning work of this period—and a great novel by any measure—was *Good Morning, Midnight* (1939). Its mood and date are symbolic: Sasha Jensen, revisiting her past in the dark, mocking streets of Paris, symbolizes a bitter and alienated world on the brink of darkness.

In the short years between her second marriage and the coming of war, Rhys visited Dominica with Leslie Tilden Smith (1936). She had not seen her home for some thirty years, yet her only letter from Dominica (*The Letters of Jean Rhys*, pp. 28–30) speaks with a passion of identification seemingly at odds with the creator of Sasha Jensen, the displaced person of London and Paris. Rhys's insight into placelessness and loss of identity derives from her Dominican origins: such is the paradox of belonging without owning, or of owning without belonging, that grants an understanding of exile and loss.

At this period Rhys was at work on the story of the first Mrs. Rochester. The idea had been with her since she read Brontë's novel in 1907, predating in conceptual terms all of her other work. Shortly after the sudden death of Leslie Tilden Smith in 1945 Rhys wrote: "I should like to finish [the novel]—partly because Leslie liked it, partly because I think it might be the one book I've written that's much use" (*Letters*, p. 39). His death was a great blow: she was now cut off from the world of publishing and writers. Despite good reviews in the 1930s, her books were out of print, forgotten; yet her obsession with the transformation of experience into literary art did not vanish. Rather, it survived to torment her.

Rhys was now a woman in her mid-fifties, shortly to be a grandmother. Her letters show her anxiety for her daughter and her ex-husband in Holland, both of whom were members of the Resistance and were imprisoned, Lenglet in a concentration camp. In 1947 Rhys married George Victor Hamer, Max, a cousin of Leslie Tilden Smith's. The Hamers had little money: their lives were made up of moving from one set of inconvenient lodgings to another. Soon Hamer became involved in a case of fraud, and Rhys was charged by a neighbor with assault. She spent five days in the hospital of the Holloway Prison for observation and was discharged. Hamer, however, was sentenced in 1950 to three years' imprisonment, of which he served two. Rhys moved to be near him, living upstairs in a pub: the Maidstone period was harsh, unsettled.

In those desolate years came the first "discovery" of Rhys. She saw and at once replied to an advertisement in *The New Statesman and Nation* of November 5, 1949, inquiring after her whereabouts. The actress Selma Vaz Dias was putting on a dramatic adaptation of *Good Morning, Midnight* and needed Rhys's permission. In this way began an association between the two women which would both help and hinder the writer. The production of her novel pleased and encouraged Rhys. Again she fell into obscurity; her contact with Selma Vaz Dias broke down, but not her devotion to the first Mrs. Rochester.

Writing in rented rooms in the cold and damp of English winters took its toll. The Hamers moved first to Cornwall and later to Devon. Helped by her brother, Colonel Rees Williams, Rhys strove to find the stability and peace which would enable her to complete her work and, in her words, "earn death." In 1956 she replied to yet another advertisement in *The New Statesman and Nation*: Selma Vaz Dias and the BBC were seeking permission to broadcast *Good Morning, Midnight* as a radio play. So great was Rhys's obscurity that many, then and later, thought her dead.

Selma Vaz Dias's "In Quest of a Missing Author" (*Radio Times*, May 3, 1957) attracted public attention. Encouragement now came to Rhys not only from Selma Vaz Dias but from Diana Athill of André Deutsch, Ltd., whose introduction to *Smile, Please* sheds light on Rhys's life and craft. Both Athill and Francis Wyndham—editor, critic, and long an admirer of Rhys's work—took part in the struggle to complete *Wide Sargasso Sea*, the story of Brontë's lunatic.

The creation of this novel deserves full study for it represents far more than the efforts of an ill and aging writer to put her thoughts together. Rhys experimented, redrafted, and cut again constantly. Her health slowed her, but her real labor was the shaping of artistic truth, that which transcends historical truth. She called it "a demon of a book" which "never leaves me" (*Letters*, p. 158). She wrote it as a dramatic monologue for Selma Vaz Dias and in 1959 spoke of having written it "three times" (*Letters*, p. 172). In the seven more years that passed before its appearance, Rhys suffered a severe heart attack (1964) and Max Hamer's health broke down. He died in 1966, shortly before the appearance of *Wide Sargasso Sea*.

At this point Wyndham and Melly end their edition of Rhys's letters. Apart from what it shows of Rhys herself, the volume is even more valuable for its illumination of the creative process. For further knowledge of Rhys's art and of her last years scholars must draw on interviewers such as Marcelle Bernstein, Mary Cantwell, John Hall, and Hannah Carter. The acclaim of *Wide Sargasso Sea* brought her—late—the attention she deserved. Her earlier work was reprinted and passed into the realm of students and scholars. The friendship of Athill, Wyndham, Melly, and David Plante (who helped her edit her autobiography) brought her comfort. She published two other collections of stories as well as the autobiography and died in 1979.

MAJOR WORKS AND THEMES

Rhys's fiction belongs, as she did, to worlds whose mutual understanding has "the feeling . . . of . . . things that . . . couldn't fit together" (*Voyage in the Dark*, 1969 ed., p. 67). The dissonances of seemingly different worlds inform the Rhysian novel, finding coherence in her art: in order to read Rhys adequately, the reader must be alive to her use of class structures, of colonialism and the metropolis seen from within and without, of love and sex defined by money, race, and gender, of exile as a human universal, and of the solitary, observing, experiencing self. All of her work is charged with a sense of belonging in many places at once: the Paris of Sasha Jensen is a reflex of the London she fled. *Wide Sargasso Sea*, Rhys's most famous work, asserts the necessity of accepting many worlds in one or of enduring the tragic consequences of denial.

Denial, rejection, alienation: these are the major themes of Rhys's work. Ford Madox Ford recognized her portrayal of wretchedness in *The Left Bank and Other Stories*: "Hunger" speaks ironically of common human misery, while "La Grosse Fifi," with its *crime passionel*, its seedy boardinghouse, and its evocation of the painfully beautiful and the indifferently sordid, points the way in which Rhys's talent would grow. Her spare, controlled style, her extreme care with diction, her gift for speech patterns, and her striving for form are all evident in her first collection.

Behind this early work, of course, lie the black notebooks entitled "This Is My Diary" (*Smile, Please*, p. 104). Even without seeing this 1914 manuscript, a reader of Rhys could assume that that exercise shaped her perceptions of the many barriers that wall us off each from the other. Rhys was very aware of point of view not merely as an artistic device but as a terrible function of the human condition. Marya Zelli in *Quartet* (1928) is keenly aware of the qualitative differences between her viewpoint and that of Lois Heidler, the suffering wife-procuress of Marya's lover, H. J. Heidler. Narrated in the third person from Marya's viewpoint, the novel occasionally produces a transparent double vision by suggesting divergent views:

> "It seems such a pity to smash up all our plans for you, just because H. J. imagines that he's in love with you—for the minute." [Lois] went on in a reflective voice: "Of course, mind you, he wants things badly when he does want them. He's a whole hogger."
>
> "So am I," Marya told her. "That's just why I must go off."
>
> The other made an impatient and expressive gesture, as if to say: "D'you suppose that I care what you are, or think or feel? I'm talking about the man, the male, the important person, the only person who matters." (1973 ed., pp. 63–64)

Sex, gender, money, and status are factors which govern viewpoint in both the individual and the social group. Rhys's next novel shows the divisive effects of these on lovers, friends, and family. *After Leaving Mr Mackenzie* (1931) tells Julia Martin's story of futile wandering in the back streets of London and Paris. Middle-aged, fading, timid, Julia has been discarded by her "cautious" lover, Mr. Mackenzie; her encounters with Mackenzie, with Horsfield (a kinder version of the "cautious" man), and her visit to her family in London make up a chilling odyssey. After their mother's funeral, the hostility latent between Norah, the conformist, repressed, dutiful sister, and Julia, the black sheep, bursts out:

> "You're an extraordinary creature," said Norah. She enjoyed seeing her sister grow red and angry, and begin to talk in an incoherent voice.
>
> Julia talked on and on, answering the yellow gleam of cruelty in Norah's eyes.

"People are such beasts, such mean beasts," she said. "They'll let you die for want of a decent word." (1980 ed., pp. 97–98)

Much of Rhys's work explores the ranges of cruelty which derive very simply from viewpoint and self-interest, those insurmountable barriers. In *Quartet* and *After Leaving Mr Mackenzie* Rhys the White Creole may seem far away, but her extraordinary ability to depict fine shades of discrimination—be they sexual, generational, familial, or social—comes from a peculiar sensibility which finds full expression in her next heroine, also a White West Indian, in *Voyage in the Dark* (1934).

Anna Morgan's voyage begins with her childhood in the West Indies: "the sun . . . terrible, like God" (*Voyage*, 1980 ed., p. 63), "Miss Jackson Colonel Jackson's illegitimate daughter—yes illegitimate poor old thing" (pp. 138–39), "the still palms in the churchyard" (p. 37). The action opens in England with Anna, a chorus girl in a third-rate touring company, meeting an older man with whom she has an affair. Her passive gaze assesses her lover Walter, cautious and respectable; his handsome, calculating cousin Julian with eyes like "high, smooth unclimbable walls" (p. 147); her stepmother, Hester Morgan, the model of ladylike English snobbery; the other chorus "girls"—each hoping for a man with money; and the many drab landladies in those "houses all exactly alike [in] the streets going north, south, east, west, all exactly alike" (p. 152). Without the support of a man, Anna can find no place in this world, no peace, no identity, no future. When the affair ends, Anna falls into anomie: "You feel peaceful, but when you try to think it's as if you're face to face with a high, dark wall. Really all you want is night" (p. 120). The original version sent to Constable ended with Anna's death after a back street abortion, but the editor rejected this, and, after weeks of agonizing, Rhys added the last four sentences that save Anna's life and compel her "to start all over again" (p. 159).

The respectable world has no place in it for the Marya Zellis, the Julia Martins, the Anna Morgans. Brought up as "ladies," educated but unqualified, unemployable, they are types very familiar to the prewar West Indian world: women born into a social position deriving from family, from inherited money, but never from themselves. Failing in the competition for husbands, they pass from one keeper to another. Such education as they have serves to intensify their insight into their humiliations. It is useless to try to dismiss them as dated or as the exaggerated caricatures of a morbid imagination. Rhys's heroines disturb because they invade our thin self-confidence founded on money, training, class, race—all of those determinants of viewpoint.

The monstrous effects of viewpoint dominate Rhys's two great novels, *Good Morning, Midnight* (1939) and *Wide Sargasso Sea* (1966). Each is structured so as to enhance the role of viewpoint through the perceptions of the individual protagonist. The earlier novel, using a modified stream-of-consciousness technique, plunges the reader into the consciousness of sensitive, emotionally scarred Sasha Jensen. Visiting the Paris of her youth, she also visits herself of then and now, mocked, rebuked, threatened, and embraced by the settings of the past. Her dealings with René the gigolo, René her alter ego, exemplify the exquisite reaches of cruelty to the other and to the self. The resonance of cruelty between individuals and groups reaches its height in the case of the first Mrs. Rochester, Brontë's lunatic on whom Rhys had meditated for decades.

All of Rhys's work on alienation, rejection, and denial, all of her insight into conflicts of class and culture, and all of her skill in conveying the vulnerability of the single psyche find full expression in the double narratives of Antoinette Cosway and the young Englishman whom she marries. A study of dislocation and insanity, the novel permits—demands—the double interpretation of Antoinette as sane, the young husband as mad, and vice versa. The opening first-person narrative presents Antoinette Cosway's childhood and adolescence: the early death of her father, the Emancipation Act which brings bankruptcy and the open hostility of the freed slaves, the rejection of Antoinette's French Creole mother by Jamaican society, and the utter loneliness of "Coulibri," the estate gone ruinate, wild. These make up the child's first impressions. Loneliness and rejection come early: her mother has no interest in her; Tia, her only friend, sees her across the barriers of race and class; even Christophine, the Black woman from Martinique who is closest to her, is a figure of awe and terror. Joy and horror intersect her world: gold and silver ferns, the parrot in flames, Aunt Cora's bright patchwork quilt, her mother's horse dead beneath the frangipani tree. Such is the youth of Rochester's bride.

His first-person narrative takes over halfway through the novel, showing her on their honeymoon as she appears to a man of very different background, equally starved for acceptance and love. The sum of their mutual insecurities proves too much. Distrusting herself, Antoinette fails to win her husband's trust when she gives herself to him. Distrusting his instincts, the young husband misunderstands and comes to fear himself, his wife, the servants, the Creole society, the landscape itself. Hate overwhelms them both. For the husband, external controls take the place of communication. If her spirit eludes him, at least her body shall be secure in a prison of his choosing. In the solitary attic of Thornfield Hall, she will be denied forever all that fed her spirit. Or so he thinks. For it is there, in that place which is no place, that Antoinette dreams her recurrent dream for the last time: "Then I turned around and saw the sky. It was red and all my life was in it. . . . Now at last I know why I was brought here and what I have to do" (*Wide Sargasso Sea*, 1980 ed., pp. 153–56).

Rhys's development of Brontë's minor character fuses together the worlds which lie across the wide Sargasso Sea, at the three corners of the triangular trade. Her vision unites their conflicts: no longer can we see the northern landscape as separate and apart from the tropical. The crisis of identity which shatters Antoinette Rochester's sanity recoils upon the master of Thornfield Hall, left with a semblance of sanity but within, "thirst," "longing," and ultimately, "nothing." The cross-cultural conflict which informs this tragedy transcends parochialisms of place and time to show us spiritual murder and spiritual suicide:

''We'll see who hates best. But first, first I will destroy your hatred. Now. My hate is colder, stronger, and you will have no hate to warm yourself. You will have nothing'' (p. 140). Laying this curse on Antoinette, the young husband commits his double crime: hate for the other is death for the self.

Indifference, studied and unstudied cruelty, the thwarted desire for love, and guilts sexual, familial, racial, and social form the dark side of Rhysian fiction. Setting them off are her evocations of utter honesty, beauty, desire, and the unquenchable urge to go beyond fear and darkness. The last works which came from her hands were *Tigers Are Better-Looking* (1968), a collection of stories which includes her favorites from *The Left Bank*; *My Day* (1975), three familiar essays; *Sleep It Off, Lady* (1976), a story-cycle uniting all aspects of her psychic history; and *Smile, Please: an Unfinished Autobiography*, in 1979, the year of her death. The collection of letters published in 1984 reinforces our image of a sensibility tortured by joy and pain, by the promise of beauty and the certainty of emptiness, and by a courage that could look upon this human condition and tell the truth.

CRITICAL RECEPTION

Critical approaches to Rhys reflect the special interest of her three main audiences. While this is inevitable, Rhys's work demands a complex reading which recognizes both the peculiar nature of cross-cultural experience in her native Caribbean and the focal role of this in Rhys's perceptions. In his *Introduction to the Study of West Indian Literature* (1976), Kenneth Ramchand addresses the question of where Rhys ''belongs.'' Noting that ''the many-sidedness or objectivity of a work of art'' (p. 98) renders it open to a wide range of interpretations, Ramchand disposes of those who would limit readings of Rhys to any single cultural set. Her complex and subtle vantage point creates the apparent division of audiences and certainly has played no small part in the anxiety of critics to claim or reject her.

Rhysian criticism has shifted ground over the years. In the 1930s reviewers tended to follow the lead of Ford Madox Ford, but, while praising her acute style, some saw her work as merely sordid. The novel, one must remember, is a bourgeois artifact and should not be used against its sponsors. At least, not before they signal permission. Rhys was ahead of her times. Useful and influential insights into her work came later from Francis Wyndham, A. Alvarez, Wally Look Lai, John Hearne, Kenneth Ramchand, Walter Allen, and Elgin W. Mellown. Writing in the late 1960s and 1970s, these critics and others developed the concept of the composite heroine shown at different stages of life and began to trace the interrelationship of the writer and her female protagonists. They also raised the question of Rhys's literary identity and began to assess the cross-cultural resonances of her work. Elgin W. Mellown's recent bibliographical study provides a useful summary of Rhys criticism; he lists the adaptations and translations of her work and adds extremely helpful notes on her life and work.

Four book-length studies of Rhys exist: Louis James, *Jean Rhys* (1978); Thomas Staley, *Jean Rhys: A Critical Study* (1979); Peter Wolfe, *Jean Rhys* (1980); and Helen Nebeker, *Jean Rhys: Woman in Passage* (1981). Of these Staley and Wolfe provide the fullest overviews of Rhys's craft. Staley enlarges on Rhys's indebtedness to Ford, shows her early stories as a quest for artistic focus, and praises the emergence of an "original voice and tone" (p. 36) in *Quartet*. Placing her firmly in a modernist tradition, Staley carefully differentiates Rhys's art from the bourgeois feminine aesthetic of such writers as Virginia Woolf and Dorothy Richardson. Yet Staley misreads Rhys's literary development by interpreting *Voyage in the Dark* as a new departure after the two earlier novels, not then knowing of the black notebooks of 1914 or of the version entitled *Susie Tells*, which Mrs. George Adam showed to Ford (*Letters*, p. 65). Errors such as these were inevitable prior to the appearance of new biographical and bibliographical material, and, such is the complexity of Rhys's artistic history, other errors will doubtless continue to arise. Less explicable is Staley's view of the heroine of *Wide Sargasso Sea* as "hollow," her character "covered over by the mysterious and exotic qualities Rhys gives to her" (p. 115).

Problems of careless reading and of biographical error also arise in James and Wolfe. Wolfe's treatment of *Wide Sargasso Sea* includes minute misreadings which cast doubt on his interpretations: Pierre, the little crippled brother, does not die "while Coulibri burns"; the family is not stoned "as they flee Coulibri" (p. 140). A single stone is thrown at the Black groom helping them to their horses. The only other stone is cast by Tia, and, most important of all, the burning parrot is not a "contrivance [smuggled in] to spare [Antoinette] from further hurt" (p. 140): it is a preternatural spectacle of sacrificial pain and horror (echoing the transfigurative death scene of Flaubert's "Un Coueur Simple") which will recur at the climax of Antoinette's last dream.

Myth is the focus of Helen Nebeker's study of sexuality and psychology in Rhys. Some of her readings are strained, as in her uncertainty about Anna Morgan's virginity and whether Anna kisses Walter's hand "in gratitude for the experience or for the money" (p. 60). A simpler explanation is Anna's childlike desire for bonding to this father-lover. Nebeker analyzes the social roles of men and women through the myths and institutions of Victorian patriarchy, relying heavily on Freudian theory. Again, useful insights into the temporal complexities of such works as *Good Morning, Midnight* must stand against extraordinary nonsenses such as the equation of Maudie Beardon's name with woman-as-siren (p. 52).

Other aspects of Rhys—her controlled narrative innovations, her deliberate choice of both literal and figurative imagery, and her selection of detail—are discussed by Mellown, Wolfe, and others. Wally Look Lai ("The Road to Thornfield Hall," 1968), Dennis Porter ("Of Heroes and Victims: Jean Rhys and *Jane Eyre*," 1976), and Michael Thorpe ("The Other Side: *Wide Sargasso Sea* and *Jane Eyre*," 1977) argue the connections between Brontë and Rhys in ways that add usefully to Nebeker's comments, while the sociosexual dimensions of the Rhys heroine, leading to the tragedy in *Wide Sargasso Sea*, are put in historical context by Louis James and Cheryl Dash ("Jean Rhys," 1979). Both James and Dash insist upon the complexity of Rhys's Caribbean experience and its distance from the narrow stereotypes of island life which influence many readers.

The variant approaches to so complex and subtle a writer show how much each approach has to gain from the others. Rhys's works offer much to the analysts of society, of sexuality, of the psyche, of British imperial history, of Anglo-European letters, and of the Creole societies with their instinctive knowledge of power and exploitation and their paradoxical attachment to the islands of their exile. The study of Rhys the writer has only begun.

HONORS AND AWARDS

A grant of three hundred pounds per annum was made to Rhys by the Royal Literary Fund in 1966. In 1967 she was awarded an Arts Council Bursary and the W. H. Smith Literary Prize.

BIBLIOGRAPHY

Works by Jean Rhys

The Left Bank and Other Stories. London: Cape, 1927; New York: Harper, 1927.

Postures. London: Chatto and Windus, 1928 (as *Quartet: a Novel*, New York: Simon and Schuster, 1929;) London: Deutsch, 1969; New York: Harper & Row, 1971; Harmondsworth: Penguin, 1973, 1977, 1981, 1982; New York: Vintage Books, 1974; New York: Perennial Library, Harper & Row, 1981.

After Leaving Mr Mackenzie. London: Cape, 1931; New York: Knopf, 1931; London: Deutsch, 1969; Harmondsworth: Penguin, 1971, 1977, 1980; New York: Harper & Row, 1972, 1982; New York: Vintage Books, 1974; New York: Harper & Row, 1982.

Voyage in the Dark. London: Constable, 1934, 1936; New York: Morrow, 1935; London: Deutsch, 1967; New York: Norton, 1968, 1982; New York: Popular Library, 1975; Harmondsworth: Penguin, 1969, 1975, 1978, 1980.

Good Morning, Midnight. London: Constable, 1939; London: Deutsch, 1967; New York: Harper & Row, 1970; Harmondsworth: Penguin, 1969; New York: Vintage Books, 1974; New York: Perennial Library, Harper & Row, 1982.

Wide Sargasso Sea. London: Deutsch, 1966; New York: Norton, 1967, 1982; Harmondsworth: Penguin, 1968, 1969, 1970, 1975, 1976, 1977, 1979, 1980; New York: Popular Library, 1973, 1975.

Tigers Are Better-Looking, with a Selection from The Left Bank. London: Deutsch, 1968; Harmondsworth: Penguin, 1973, 1977, 1981, 1982; New York: Harper & Row, 1974; New York: Popular Library, 1976.

My Day. New York: Frank Hallman, 1975.

Sleep It off, Lady. London: Deutsch, 1976; New York: Harper & Row, 1976; New York: Popular Library, 1978. Harmondsworth: Penguin, 1979, 1980, 1981.

Smile, Please: An Unfinished Autobiography. London: Deutsch, 1979; New York: Harper & Row, 1979 [Mellown notes small but significant revisions in the American edition (p. 115)]; Harmondsworth: Penguin, 1981, 1982; Berkeley: Donald S. Ellis/Creative Arts, 1983.

Jean Rhys Letters 1931–1966, ed. Francis Wyndham and Diana Melly. London: Deutsch, 1984; and as *The Letters of Jean Rhys*. New York: Viking, 1984.

Translations by Jean Rhys

Carco, Francis. *Perversity*. Trans. Ford Madox Ford [Wrongly attributed to Ford by the publisher]. Chicago: Pascal Covici, 1928.

De Nève, Edward. *Barred*. London: Harmsworth, 1932.

Studies of Jean Rhys

Allen, Walter. "Bertha the Doomed." *New York Times Book Review*, June 18, 1967, p. 5.

Allfrey, Phyllis Shand. "Jean Rhys: A Tribute." *Kunapipi* 1 (1979), 6–22.v.

Alvarez, A. "The Best Living English Novelist." *New York Times Book Review*, March 17, 1974, pp. 6–7.

Athill, Diana. Foreword to *Smile Please*. New York: Harper & Row, 1979.

———. "Jean Rhys and the Writing of *Wide Sargasso Sea*." *The Bookseller*, August 20, 1966, pp. 1378–79.

Bernstein, Marcelle. "The Inscrutable Miss Jean Rhys." *Observer Magazine*, June 1, 1969, pp. 40–42, 49–50.

Bowen, Stella. *Drawn from Life: Reminiscences*. London: Collins, 1940.

Brathwaite, Edward. *Contradictory Omens*. Monograph. University of the West Indies, Mona, Jamaica, 1974, pp. 33–38.

Braybrooke, Neville. "Jean Rhys." In *Contemporary Novelists*, ed. James Vinson. London: St. James Press; New York: St. Martin's Press, 1972, pp. 1161–65.

Campbell, Elaine. "Apropos of Jean Rhys." *Kunapipi* 2 (1980), 152–57.

———. "Jean Rhys, Alec Waugh and the Imperial Road." *Journal of Commonwealth Literature* 14 (August 1979), 58–63.

Cantwell, Mary. "A Conversation with Jean Rhys." *Mademoiselle* 79 (October 1974), 170–71, 206, 208, 210, 213.

Carter, Hannah. "Fated to Be Sad: Jean Rhys Talks to Hannah Carter." *Guardian*, August 8, 1968, p. 5.

Casey Fulton, Nancy J. "Jean Rhys's *Wide Sargasso Sea*: Exterminating the White Cockroach." *Revista Interamericana Review* 4 (Fall 1974), 340–49.

———. "Study in the Alienation of a Creole Woman: Jean Rhys's *Voyage in the Dark*." *Caribbean Quarterly* 19 (September 1973), 95–102.

Dash, Cheryl M. L. "Jean Rhys." In *West Indian Literature*, ed. Bruce King, 1979, pp. 197–209.

De Nève, Edouard. "Jean Rhys, romancière inconnue." *Les Nouvelles littéraires* 880 (August 26, 1939), 8.

Descriptive Bibliography of the University of Tulsa Jean Rhys Collection. N.d. See Mellown, *Jean Rhys*, 1984, p. 159, for details.

De Souza, Eunice. ''Four Expatriate Writers.'' *Journal of the School of Languages* [Jawaharlal Nehru University] 4 (Winter 1976–77), 54–60.

Dias, Selma Vaz. ''In Quest of a Missing Author.'' *Radio Times*, May 3, 1957, p. 25.

Dick, Kay, ''*Wide Sargasso Sea*.'' *Sunday Times*, October 30, 1966, p. 50.

Ford, Ford Madox, ''Preface: Rive Gauche.'' In Jean Rhys, *The Left Bank and Other Stories*. London: Cape, 1927.

Gardiner, Judith Kegan. ''Rhys Recalls Ford: *Quartet* and *The Good Soldier*.'' *Tulsa Studies in Women's Literature* 1 (Spring 1982), 67–81.

Greene, Sue N. ''Six Caribbean Novels by Women.'' *Nieuwe West-Indische Gids* 58 (1984), 61–74.

Hall, John. ''Jean Rhys.'' *Guardian*, January 10, 1972, p. 8.

Harris, Wilson. ''Carnival of Psyche: Jean Rhys's *Wide Sargasso Sea*.'' *Kunapipi* 2 (1980) pp. 142–50.

Hearne, John. ''The *Wide Sargasso Sea*: A West Indian Reflection.'' *Cornhill Magazine*, no. 1080 (Summer 1974), 323–33.

James, Louis. *Jean Rhys*. London: Longman, 1978.

Jones, Angela. ''Voodoo and Apocalypse in the Work of Jean Rhys.'' *Journal of Commonwealth Literature* 16 (August 1981), 126–31.

Kappers-den Hollander, Martien. ''Jean Rhys and the Dutch Connection.'' *Maatstaf* (The Hague) 30 (1982), 30–40.

Look Lai, Wally. ''The Road to Thornfield Hall.'' *New World Quarterly* 4 (Crop time 1968), 17–27. See also *New Beacon Reviews*, Collection One. Ed. John La Rose. London: New Beacon, 1968, pp. 38–52.

Luengo, Anthony. ''*Wide Sargasso Sea* and the Gothic Mode.'' *World Literature Written in English* 15 (April 1976), 229–45.

Mellown, Elgin W. ''Character and Themes in the Novels of Jean Rhys.'' *Contemporary Literature* 13 (Autumn 1972), 458–75; also in *Contemporary Women Novelists*, ed. Patricia Meyer Spacks. Englewood Cliffs, N.J.: Prentice-Hall, 1977, pp. 118–36.

———. *Jean Rhys: A Descriptive and Annotated Bibliography of Works and Criticism*. New York: Garland, 1984.

Miles, Rosalind. *The Fiction of Sex: Themes and Functions of Sex Differences in the Modern Novel*.'' London: Vision, 1974, esp. pp. 96–106.

Naipaul, Vidia S. ''Without a Dog's Chance.'' *New York Review of Books*, May 18, 1972, pp. 29–31.

Nebeker, Helen E. ''Jean Rhys's *Quartet*: The Genesis of Myth.'' *International Journal of Women's Studies* 2 (May-June 1979), 257–67.

———. *Jean Rhys, Woman in Passage: A Critical Study of the Novels of Jean Rhys*. Montreal: Eden Press Women's Publications, 1981.

Nielsen, H. and F. Brahms. ''Retrieval of a Monster: Jean Rhys's *Wide Sargasso Sea*.'' In *Enigma of Values*, ed. K. H. Petersen, and A. Rutherford. Aarhus, Denmark: Dangaroo Press, 1975, pp. 139–62.

Packer, P. A. ''The Four Early Novels of Jean Rhys.'' *Durham University Journal* 71 (June 1979), 252–65.

Plante, David. ''Jean Rhys: A Remembrance.'' *Paris Review* 76 (Fall 1979), 238–84; reprinted in David Plante. *Difficult Women: A Memoir of Three*. New York: Atheneum, 1983.

Porter, D. "Of Heroes and Victims: Jean Rhys and *Jean Eyre*." *Massachusetts Review* 17 (Autumn 1976), 540–52.

Staley, Thomas. *Jean Rhys: A Critical Study*. London: Macmillan, 1979; Austin: University of Texas Press, 1979.

Thieme, John. " 'Apparitions of Disaster': Brontean Parallels in *Wide Sargasso Sea* and *Guerrillas*." *Journal of Commonwealth Literature* 14 (August 1979), 116–32.

Thomas, Clara. "Mr Rochester's First Marriage: *Wide Sargasso Sea* by Jean Rhys." *World Literature Written in English* 17 (April 1978), 342–57.

Thomas, Ned. "Meeting Jean Rhys." *Planet* (August 1976), 29–32.

Thompson, Irene. "The Left Bank Aperitifs of Jean Rhys and Ernest Hemingway." *Georgia Review* 35 (Spring 1981), 94–106.

Thorpe, M. "The Other Side: *Wide Sargasso Sea* and *Jane Eyre*." *Ariel* 8 (July 1977), 99–110.

Tiffin, Helen. "Mirror and Mask: Colonial Motifs in the Novels of Jean Rhys." *World Literature Written in English* 17 (April 1978), 328–41.

Williams, Angela. "The Flamboyant Tree: The World of the Jean Rhys Heroine." *Planet* (August 1976), 35–41.

Wolfe, Peter. *Jean Rhys*. Boston: Twayne, 1980.

Wyndham, Francis. "An Inconvenient Novelist." *Tribune*, no. 721 (December 15, 1950), 16, 18.

———. Introduction to *Wide Sargasso Sea*. Harmondsworth: Penguin, 1968.

———. Introduction to *The Letters of Jean Rhys*. New York: Viking/Elisabeth Sifton Books, 1984; London: Deutsch, 1984 (as *Jean Rhys: Letters 1931–1966*).

See also General Bibliography: Allis, Herdeck (1979), Hughes, and Ramchand (1970, 1976). Full, annotated listings of Rhys criticism can be found in Mellown (1984). The *MLA* bibliographical indexes list Rhys under *two* headings: "English Literature X: Twentieth Century" and "English Literature II: Australia, Canada, etc.," in which the West Indian list is included.

ROLAND E. BUSH

Garth St. Omer (1931–)

BIOGRAPHY

Biographical facts about Garth St. Omer are very difficult to come by. He is a sensitive, self-protective artist who feels very strongly that his work must stand on its own merits and speak for itself apart from any extraliterary authorial commentary or biographical intrusions from misguided critical assaults. However, based on a survey of published facts and information culled from the author's own nonfictional writings and comments (made while graciously denying me a formal interview), the following is a brief overview of relevant biographical data.

Garth St. Omer was born in 1931 in Port Castries, the capital of St. Lucia, the unnamed but unmistakable setting of his major works. The earliest stages of the author's education were received in St. Lucia. During the 1950s St. Omer was among a small but influential group of artists whose work would eventually attract international attention to that tiny volcanic island of the Lesser Antilles, located between Martinique (to the north) and St. Vincent (to the south). (The group included Dunstan St. Omer, a painter, and Roderick and Derek Walcott, twin brothers and gifted poets and dramatists.)

Upon completion of his studies in St. Lucia, St. Omer transferred to the University of the West Indies, Mona, Kingston. There he studied from 1956 to 1959, majoring in French and Spanish. In 1959 St. Omer was graduated with a B.A. in French literature. Since then he has traveled extensively. Following a period of study in France, he moved to Africa, where he wrote and taught in

Ghana during the mid–1960s. It is generally thought that most of his early works were written during this period (although I was unable to confirm this in my discussion with the author). Like some of his peripatetic protagonists, St. Omer has returned periodically to St. Lucia before departing again for other parts of the world.

In the early 1970s St. Omer moved to New York, following a sojourn in London. It was during this period that he undertook studies for the doctor of philosophy in comparative literature, the final requirements of which were completed at Princeton University in August, 1975. In the same year St. Omer moved to California. He currently lives and teaches in Santa Barbara, California, and has recently completed the manuscript of his first novel set in North America.

MAJOR WORKS AND THEMES

Garth St. Omer is a writer of emotionally powerful and intellectually compelling short narratives. Generically, his works are all novellas. They combine the compression characteristic of the short story with the greater development of theme, character, and event typical of the novel; and about all of them, there is the tone of the 20th century's dominant narrative mode—the confessional.

From his earliest published novella, *Syrop* (1964), to his most recent, *J-, Black Bam and the Masqueraders* (1972), St. Omer's works reveal a familiar complex of themes, conflicts, and even characters, consistently developed, elaborated upon, modified, and deepened effectively through an ever-increasing technical control and formal sophistication. Organized in a manner comparable to the connected narratives of Faulkner, Joyce, Proust, and Mann, his works constitute a trenchant, interrelated, multivolumed commentary on the existential dilemmas inherent in colonial and post-colonial life in the West Indies. Progressing in a style which tends to replace chronology and external reference with duplication and internal associations as formal determinants, these slim volumes continue uniquely to mine the fundamental themes of exile, identity, and alienation implicit in the entire body of Caribbean writing.

Syrop is St. Omer's earliest novella and the first work to be published outside the Caribbean. This story, with its classical overtones of man's untimely but inevitable meeting with fate, is chronologically, stylistically, and thematically the best introduction to St. Omer's art. It contains many motifs employed by the writer in later (and longer) works: madness, sibling rivalry, intergenerational conflict, religion, illegitimacy and its social responses, exile and return, success, and responsibility for oneself and others. Graced by a subtly symbolic pattern of imagery, highly descriptive language, and an astute manipulation of point of view and temporal sequence, *Syrop* dramatizes the brief and ironic passage of a young boy into manhood, achieved on the very day of his death. In this tale of a divided house in which rejection, guilt, and the explosive violence of internalized frustrations characterize family and social relationships, life as imprisonment and death as a release are pervasive elements.

The story opens with a description of a static setting for reader/viewer to contemplate. It is an isolated and impoverished fishing community on a small, undeveloped Windward Island. The village is separated from the main town by large drainage canals, where children play, "guiding their small boats with long sticks from the concrete banks," unconcerned that the canals are "filled with a black oozing sediment and there is, always, a very foul smell" (p. 139). In this putrid atmosphere, the principal character, Syrop, has grown to adolescence, nursing his blind father, Deaies, since his mother's death twelve years earlier and his brother's imprisonment four years after that.

The action begins at dawn on the day before Lescaut, Syrop's brother, imprisoned for committing manslaughter during a drunken brawl, is scheduled to be released and also on the eve of the Feast of St. Peter and St. Paul, "patron saints" of this village of fishermen. The coincidence of these two events—the exile's return and the community's celebration of its most important annual religious feast day—constitute the story's basic plot device, developed in an almost contrapuntal fashion. The seven episodes of the novella alternate from third-person dramatic exchanges between Deaies and his children to the first-person interior monologues of each successive character introduced. Those of Deaies reveal profoundly the sources of the old man's suffering—disappointment with an anguished and inexorably "unlucky" life to which he has finally resigned himself as he awaits death; disappointment with his daughter, Anne, now a prostitute; and disappointment with his eldest son, Lescaut, whose imminent return to the community now totally dominates his younger son's thoughts.

For Deaies Syrop is the family's only hope. The old man's pride in the young boy's strength of character and will enables him to endure what remains of his wasted life. Syrop has matured early. Through hardship, misfortune, and early intimacy with death, he has quickly become a man. However, in spite of Deaies's awareness of his son's development, he sees an ominous sign in the coincidence of events. Lescaut's shameful return, if not Anne's disgrace, will surely mar the feeling of achievement and pride he and his younger son were to experience as a consequence of Syrop's participation in the ceremony and his formal acceptance into manhood by the men of the village: "Not to be able to go to Mass tomorrow with the others will be a great disappointment to Syrop. But he will have to live with his disappointments as I have learnt to do so with mine. And if he dies then it were better for him not to have this privilege at all than to have and in the having to be disgraced by a brother and a sister" (p. 149). In these thoughts, revealing the father's decision to prohibit his son's involvement in the procession, we observe a foreshadowing of doom which reflects the pervasive tone of fatalism characteristic of St. Omer's writing. For mingled with a tenacious desire for change, for a better future, St. Omer's characters nonetheless carry within them a heightened sense of the tragic potentialities of life. And any expressions of hope emerge more often than not with a bittersweet taste conditioned by experience.

When Anne, pregnant and in a vindictive mood, visits the old man and abuses him, verbally and physically, Syrop comes to his father's defense. In the struggle, the unborn child she carries is fatally injured. Defeated, disowned, and physically beaten, she curses her father and brother and departs to find solace in a local tavern, where she later hears of her brother's tragic death. Although shaken, Anne is not completely surprised, however. Earlier she, too, has reflected on human fate. Prompted by the awareness of the fetus now "rotting" in her womb, she has already confronted the reality of death: "*La mort?* What is death? Sometimes I think I prefer to die than to live as it is for me to live. I am sure that it is better there" (p. 166). And numbed more by the weight of her life and the alcohol she consumes in order to endure it than by the news of Syrop's death, Anne staggers away to claim her brother's disfigured body.

Earlier, excited about Lescaut's return, Syrop had decided to celebrate his brother's arrival with a homecoming breakfast. To get enough money he had joined some older boys diving for coins tossed into the water by tourists. As the ship prepared to leave, Syrop, unlucky and "beginning to be desperate" (p. 179), noticed a group of sailors lingering at the rail of the ship. As the propeller started to turn, the other boys swam away. Concentrating his eyes and thoughts on the sailors, Syrop began a silent prayer: "Oh God, I have not asked for anything before this. I did not ask You to have my name on the board today. I only ask for this; and now the ship is leaving" (p. 180).

When one of the sailors drops a coin near the stern of the ship, Syrop impulsively dives after the shining object. "Then he saw it and under the surface his hands closed upon it and, at that moment, he was happier than he remembered he had even been. Then he began to surface" (p. 181). Unable to fight the strong pull of the propeller, however, he is drawn, head first, into the powerful blades. As if it were an offering to a chthonic deity, the coin falls from Syrop's mouth as he is sucked into the sharp, whirring blades and rolled repeatedly in and out of the water.

Anne's arrival on the wharf produces an effusive mixture of grief and anger as she taunts life and mocks human fate before the unrecognizable form of her brother's "mangled" body. But consistent with the sense of the inevitable which permeates the narrative, Deaies, speaking to the nephew with whom he will now go to live, stoically accepts this painful reminder of the human situation—this brotherhood of death: "After, Ti-Son, when you take me home again, you must tell them I say they must not feel sorry for me because it is really nothing and could happen, even as it happened to me today, to anyone of them" (p. 185).

It is a dramatization of such poignant recognitions of the absurd that makes St. Omer's short narratives hauntingly unforgettable. For in one sweeping blow, two events of hope and expectation for a young boy on the threshold of manhood are both negated by the capriciousness of an unknown god. In Syrop's pleas for mercy, we observe the transformation of an apparent act of divine intervention into an ironically (and profanely) twisted random event. The juxtaposition of the young boy's prayer and the swiftness with which the blades decapitate him leave little doubt about the nature of the universe into which he was thrown.

We are thus prepared for the irrational and apparently meaningless world of the subsequent novellas and for the characters who, like it or not, find themselves caught in the web of an inescapable fate.

In *A Room on the Hill* (1968) we have an illustration of the tragic dilemmas faced by St. Omer's characters. The people in this story are caught in physical and, in particular, psychic situations in which transcendence or, closer to St. Omer's ironic religious echoes, salvation evolves from an anguished awareness comparable to but significantly different from the absurd consciousness of existential anti-heroes. It originates instead in a much deeper psychic and cultural source of conflict and confusion.

A Room on the Hill is the story of John Lestrade, an intellectual, who, like Camus' Clemence in *La Chute*, has witnessed a suicide without responding to the last-minute cries for help. However, in contrast to Camus' novel, in which the anonymity of the victim maintains a certain degree of distance between him and the protagonist, John Lestrade is an intimate friend of the deceased, whose death plagues him by revealing the emptiness and inauthenticity of his own life. And just as Stephen had seen in the earlier death of Desmond, a childhood friend, the "seed of his own death . . . and been fascinated by it" (p. 58), so, too, Stephen's demise provokes Lestrade's terrifying awakening to his own spiritual death-in-life, to his own sleepwalking among the living.

This repeated image of Lestrade's somnambulistic existence, in fact, emerges as the emblematic metaphor of island life. In one of the many recollections which constitute most of the events in the narrative, John remembers an evening with Stephen as the two watched from a balcony above the "automatons" file by below in a predictable procession. At that moment Lestrade perceives a connection between Stephen, himself, and the "robots" who walk by unseeing and unseen: "There was a key in his back as there were keys in the backs of all the inhabitants of the island. And those keys, it was the island itself that manipulated them" (p. 51). Unable to impose self-exile and oppressed by the "poisonous air of the island," John Lestrade, like Jean Clemence, seeks refuge in isolation.

The title of the work refers to John Lestrade's decision following Stephen's drowning to remove himself physically (and emotionally) to a "room on the hill." In isolation he searches his memory and exhumes "corpses of his old self, probing with the scalpel of his new awareness" (p. 37). And although he later discovers that Stephen's death "far from being an act of despair might have been one of revolt" (p. 119), he nonetheless continues to experience feelings of self-loathing and guilt. This guilt is dramatized in his contacts with other islanders: Miriam, Stephen's former girlfriend, by whom he is subsequently rejected; Anne Marie, Derek's abandoned lover, who is killed in an automobile accident shortly after Derek's return to the island with his English wife; and Harold, a boyhood friend, returned to the island as a barrister. In each relationship we see him "clinging to the security of his little world of self-blame as if he were afraid to leave it" (p. 75). Even when Harold reveals Stephen's confessional letter explaining his intention to drown himself in response to his father's callous squandering of his savings, John Lestrade resists the truth and recognizes "only shame and regret for what his death showed me of myself" (p. 79).

John Lestrade needs the self-lacerating pain of his guilt. Ironically, he exists in a state of suffering partly because that defines his specialness. His pain and depression are real, and really self-destructive. He has become the target of his own unconscious malignance. And although Lestrade takes pride in the clarity with which he begins to see reality, the reader may seriously question the reality and certainty of that clarity. For like the protagonists of Camus' short novels, *La Chute* and *L'Etranger*, he is not always the most reliable, conscious witness to his own emotional and psychic dilemmas. Indeed, we begin to feel that John Lestrade, like Jean-Baptiste Clemence, confronts his own cowardice and confesses his own guilt so that he may judge others: "He had often sat and watched the acceptance, by young men and women, of their life on the island, their mediocre, as it seemed to him, empty life. He had ceased to be sure whether the contempt he had felt for them was born of their acceptance or of his inability to be like them" (p. 97). The need for such judgments appears, at first, to derive from the discrepancy between reality and his youthful desires for "achievement." With his mother's death, he is relieved of the weight of that ambition, but the absence of responsibility to self appears to set him adrift in a sea of guilt and self-recrimination.

However, in spite of this and the ample echoes of existentialists from Dostoyevsky ("Isn't it disgusting how easily we adjust?", p. 21) to Camus and Sartre ("You know . . . people are hell?" p. 80), the source of his suffering and disease is not confined to the vague metaphysical longings of typical existentialist anti-heroes or to frustrated hopes of economic "success." Instead, St. Omer repeatedly links John's feelings (and those of other characters) of fear, anguish, unworthiness, and personal impotence and confusion to the insidious influence of the Catholic Church. The narrative is filled with telling juxtapositions which underscore this point: the fishermen returning in their boats, identified by names such as "God Will Provide," "Hope," and "In God We Trust" while John Lestrade looks on, reads the large letters, and becomes aware simultaneously of the odors of fresh fish, the sea, and "the smell of filth" (p. 26); or, later, when John Lestrade, remembering his mother praying beneath "faded pictures of Saints," "small images of Christ and the Virgin Mary," describes them as all grimy and covered with the "accumulated dust and the excreta of flies" (p. 29). Moreover, the island, we learn, is "virtually a Roman Catholic Stronghold" (p. 165), and more than a few islanders have departed for the seminary only to return "broken in body and spirit" (p. 181) and ill equipped for all but the ravages of rum and complete disillusionment.

The pervasiveness of this influence appears most dramatically in the events surrounding Anne Marie's funeral. St. Omer devotes all of the penultimate chapter to a detailed description of the ironic circumstances. Killed in a car accident, Anne Marie, the "illegitimate" offspring of a White father and his maidservant, is denied a proper church burial. From the vicar general her friends learn, amid the clamor of a band of masqueraders celebrating discovery day ("the discovery of the island by Columbus, the Genoese"), that "the Church does not waiver on this point" (p. 160). Suppressing their anger and frustration over the timidity with which the vicar's pronouncements are met by Anne Marie's other friends, John, Derek, and Harold decide upon an unofficial ceremony. On the road to the cemetery the "unauthorized funeral" is interrupted by the parade of masqueraders who had been performing earlier in front of the church. When this group is concurrently joined by the parallel procession of Old Alphonse, the shoemaker, recently released from the lunatic asylum and leading a large and joyous group of children, the contrast and conflict of traditions—and,therefore, identities—is established. For Alphonse symbolizes the antidote to the schizophrenia of the culture. His is, in the words of Aimé Césaire, "the madness that unchains itself," that sets itself free (*Cahier d'un retour au pays natal* [Paris: *Présence africaine*, 1971], p. 73). The banner of the madman's procession—"MARY MUST COME BACK"—dramatizes poignantly the nature of "the keys" that manipulate the "robots": the sin, guilt, and fear of Catholicism and other colonial remnants which permeate the social fabric and engender the "paralysis" (John's word) which precludes the possibility of self-interested action. Alphonse and the children represent a tradition far more authentic than that espoused by the imported representatives of a neocolonial institution. For the problem is to discover and to assert the self. But the true experience of self is impeded by the psychological and cultural dictates of an antagonistic religious authority that stands in the way of authentic development. "He knew what made Gods possible. And religion too. They gave the lie to reality" (p. 119). The effect, says John, is to foster "a race of imitators" (p. 107). Indeed, throughout all this we are always aware of that fundamental issue which St. Omer develops consistently and without equivocation: the need for awareness and authenticity. And the need to awaken—a recurrent activity in the narrative—is no less a psychological and cultural imperative than a political one.

In *Shades of Grey* (1968), *Nor Any Country* (1969), and *J-, Black Bam and the Masqueraders*, St. Omer's last three published volumes, the pervasive presence of religion in relation to his characters' search for authentic identity is emphasized by the uniformly consistent method which describes their experiences. *Shades of Grey* is actually composed of two novellas. The first, "Lights on the Hill," is the story of relationships between Stephenson, a twenty-eight-year-old intellectual loner who has left the island on scholarship (only to discover upon his return that his alienation has been intensified by his educational experiences); Thea, his lover, who is eight years younger than he; and Eddie, a close and envied friend. Cynical, restless, dissatisfied, confused, and obsessed with his marginality, Stephenson is incapable of making a commitment to Thea that might compromise the freedom of his aimless search for self-identity. Thus, ambivalence suffices for love. Stephenson, like John Lestrade, feels emotionally paralyzed by the circumstances of his life. He chooses the role of spectator, for he recognizes only two possibilities of action: "Some people played games, others watched them" (p. 115). Added to the isolation he feels as a mulatto—"In the country they called him *'ti beche'* and in the town, when they had wished to hurt, 'white nigger,' " (p. 116)—is a personal sense of failure and the envy he feels for Eddie as one of those "people who have achieved something" (p. 21). However, Eddie's death by lightning—one which in its effect parallels the suicide of Stephen in *A Room on the Hill*—reveals to him the futility of the desire for achievement. The climax of the story is Stephenson's subdued recognition of his individual anonymity: "He was, could only have been, a spectator, supported by no weight of tradition or lineage" (p. 117). And the same loud shout from the lunatic asylum which opens the novella closes it, suggesting its importance as a prefiguration of Stephenson's fate.

St. Omer intensifies the psychological penetration of the treatment of this theme of identity and its ultimate religious expansions in the accompanying narrative. As a counterpoint to the pessimistic note upon which the first novella concludes, "Another Place, Another Time," the second story, ends with a positive act of self-affirmation and awareness. The protagonist becomes aware of himself as a product of history amid a welter of pernicious colonial influences.

The narrative recounts the childhood of Derek Charles (a friend of John Lestrade's in *A Room on the Hill*), who, like Stephenson, discovers that the only escape from the island's painful, sordid syndrome of broken families, poverty, and hopelessness is an exile which accompanies the pursuit of education and which, paradoxically, brings with it an experience of isolation and alienation that is equally painful to bear. Derek, like Stephenson, is self-divided and becoming increasingly distanced from the society which encroaches daily upon his hopes for authentic development. Derek is fortunate enough to win an island scholarship to study abroad, however, and it is his face-to-face meeting with the White priest/headmaster prior to his departure that concludes the story and brings into focus the essential conflicts of the novella. For when the headmaster requests that he return to the island as a teacher, Derek consciously recognizes the basis of his earlier "distrust and suspicion" (p. 218) of the clergy. And as he reflects upon his ancestors' emergence from servitude and images of his mother's sacrifices for his education, memories of the priests' earlier condemnations of Carnival assume a new significance. As he looks at the Irish priest—St. Omer's historical irony is obvious—and reflects on the disparity between the "infinitely more comfortable" living conditions of the priests and the conditions of those for whom they had ostensibly martyred themselves, "a sudden picture of colonial seediness" (p. 222) forms in Derek's mind. That St. Omer's perception of organized religion is one that sees it other than as a source of harmony or unity is clear: it is a disruptive element that creates the drama which is at the heart of all his works.

The irreverence implied in the ironic ending of *Syrop* and the identification of religion's historically subversive role in *A Room on the Hill* are indicative of the extent to which religious or, more generally, philosophical issues are characteristic of St. Omer's stories. Moreover, the consistent repetition of narrative apparatus—the means by which the story is presented—is even more noticeable. In other words, Garth St. Omer, by his very choice of genre as well as his selection of techniques within the chosen genre, interweaves form with his most fundamental perspectives. For the novella is distinguished from the novel and the short story by its tendency to concentrate upon traditional philosophical problems. It usually dramatizes, as Howard Nemerov has noted, conflicts between appearance and reality, freedom and necessity, or madness and sanity, but all of these are but aspects of the most frequently addressed problem: identity. This theme, Nemerov suggests, is "pervasive to the point of obsession" ("Composition and Fate in the Short Novel," in *Poetry and Fiction: Essays* [New Brunswick, N.J.: Rutgers University Press, 1963], p. 236). However, it is not only in the theme of identity (and the necessity of authentic behavior) that St. Omer's works embody important aspects of the novella tradition; the narratives also demonstrate the structural conventions and stylistic devices of the genre and, as a group, reveal an effective internal cohesiveness.

George Lukács, the theoretician of narrative forms and critic often cited by St. Omer, has noted (with regard to the paradoxical nature of the genre's dual allegiance to the subjective and objective) that the novella's method of representing reality differs from that of longer forms. In contrast to longer narratives in which "totality" is more a manifestation of content or subject matter, in shorter forms like the novella there is a greater concentration on the internal, organizational conventions of narrative (*Theory of the Novel* [Cambridge: MIT Press, 1971], p. 80). In St. Omer's works we see this not only in the compression and material economy typical of the genre (e.g., a limited number of characters and actions) but also in the repetitive imagery that shapes the form of development in his works. The structure is one of the repetition of motifs (i.e., images, metaphors, characters, and even situations) around the central fictional issues of the relationship between alienation and authentic identity. Two such motifs are the automaton figure (i.e., the unawakened, unaware sleepwalker of the islands) and the image of the canals—the ubiquitous rivers of filth which cumulatively effect a transformation of the tourists' image of the Caribbean as a tropical Paradiso into an ironic inversion of Dante's Inferno with all of its subterranean religious echoes. The recurrence of these elements is as crucial in the novellas' theme and structure as are the authorial intrusions or the statements and actions of characters. For St. Omer's fictive structure relies on the barest minimum of realistic, external detail and depends instead on a continuous series of symbolic images, all designed to dramatize the main concerns of the novellas.

Because short fiction focuses on the ambiguity and inconclusiveness of life, according to Lukács, there is a correspondence between the forming principles and the vision of life or "perspective" that the genre offers. In St. Omer's works this correspondence is manifested in two ways: first, in the compositional conception underlying his narratives; and, second, in the form or pattern of his plots.

The organizational method employed by St. Omer in his novellas reflects an attempt to evoke an awareness of the whole in each narrative. It is a compositional conception which, in its intention of totality, establishes an organic relationship between individual volumes; that is, each novella becomes "associated" with those that precede and those that follow. This is achieved through the repetitions mentioned above (i.e., characters, themes, locales, imagery, and even tone). The protagonists of St. Omer's fiction, for example, are usually presented with psychological "doubles" (in order to emphasize how the characters are invaded from both the outside and the inside) and are presented as if fully developed. Since we have seen them before, it avoids the necessity for "over-elaboration of individual character" found in the conventional narrative genres. In this way, St. Omer approximates the kind of "epic and revolutionary novel of associations" described by Wilson Harris, whereby the "characters are related within a personal capacity which works in a poetic and serial way so that a strange jigsaw is set in motion" (*Tradition the Writer and Society: Critical Essays*, 1967, p. 38).

The correspondence between perspective and form is further reinforced by the open-ended nature of the plots. With this method of concluding his narratives, St. Omer emphasizes the ambiguity and inconclusiveness of life and also underscores the interconnectedness of the novellas; that is, the sense of inconclusiveness, the absence of a definite or certain resolution of conflict(s), functions as narrative interstices of a multivolumed work and also helps to sustain the anticipation of future installments. Moreover, along with the use of duplication and internal associations, this characteristic ending effects a style in which internal elements assume a greater importance than chronology and external reference. This is seen very clearly in the last two published volumes, *Nor Any Country* and *J-, Black Bam and the Masqueraders*.

Perhaps the best way to conclude a discussion of Garth St. Omer's work is to emphasize, using the author's own words, the serious purpose which motivates his artistic efforts: "The person who sets out to become a writer out of an anticipatory sense of the glamour of his occupation, instead of being impelled by an overwhelming need to say something which seems important and needing to be said, is not likely to do much more than provide entertainment for his readers" ("The Writer as Naive Colonial: V. S. Naipaul and *Miguel Street*," *Carib* 1 [1979], 9).

CRITICAL RECEPTION

It was not until the appearance of *Syrop* in 1964 that St. Omer garnered serious critical attention. Edward Brathwaite (in a thoughtful review) identifies this novella as "one of the finest bits of writing in this genre to have come out of the West Indies so far." Its depiction of impoverishment he describes as "accurate" and "pitiless," and "its climax—an illustration of Camus' absurd—is almost unbearable in the impersonality and compassion of its art." Brathwaite laments that St. Omer was forced to change the "marvelous mixture and flavor" of St. Lucia's patois and English narrative in the original in order to please the publisher's desire for what in the end amounted to a "translation of the creole" (Review of *Syrop*, 1964, p. 68).

Michael Gilkes sees in St. Omer's work, in contrast to Derek Walcott's (the St. Lucian with whom he is most often compared), an "uncompromising" and "bleak" vision which, in its portrayal of people caught in a "colonial mesh of poverty, guilt, and self contempt," goes farther in its "depressing fatalism" than even the works of V. S. Naipaul. It is the "trauma of exile and return," notes Gilkes, which generates the thematic trajectory of St. Omer's works, for they center on "the Sargasso-like condition of existence from which escape, exile, is a logical step, and to which return is an act of courage leading to masquerade, madness, suicide" (*The West Indian Novel*, 1981, p. 109). Gordon Rohlehr ("Small Island Blues," 1969) praises St. Omer for a "controlled nostalgic prose of reminiscence" (p. 27), detecting stylistic influences and thematic parallels with the early works of James Joyce. Rohlehr perceives a Joycean vision of human fate: St. Omer's characters, like those of Joyce, "are constantly dreaming of escape, but are incapable of the effort of will demanded, and finally surrender to the tedious limbo around them" (p. 24). Says Rohlehr, "He has fashioned a careful, tightly economical prose and an almost bleak detachment, which matches the cramped narrowness of the society, and the taut spareness of the lives he describes" (p. 24). John Thieme ("Double Identity in the Novels of Garth St. Omer," 1977) is slightly more emphatic about this point: "For St. Omer, like Naipaul, West Indian life is all too often poisoned by its mimetic quality and colonialism is primarily a psychological condition" (p. 95). St. Omer's characters, argues Thieme, "inhabit a world in which psychic division is the normal state of human personality" (p. 95). And the use of "minor characters as foils to his protagonists" (along with the *döppleganger* motif) Thieme considers a "principle of characterization" in his works. St. Omer's, he writes, is an "art of contrasted characters" (p. 88).

A recurrent focus of critical attention is on the issue of male–female relationships. Edward Baugh ("Since 1960: Some Highlights," 1979) sees the typical St. Omer protagonist as one who is afflicted by the "will to meaning," which is negated, paradoxically, by an "absurd" world the more he seeks meaning. His ambivalences toward that world are ironically revealed in his relations with the women who, fascinated by the "aristocracy of his anguish," open themselves to him only to invite his anger and self-deprecation with them and himself. It is here that "the battle of the sexes," writes Baugh, receives "a frightening reality. Sex as a weapon and snare is seen as a leading component of the web of frustrations and meaninglessness, both a factor of, and a momentary, unsatisfactory release from, the pressures of 'small-island' society" (p. 85). Recognizing a similarity between the "hyper-consciousness" of St. Omer's male characters and the kind of consciousness typical of the anti-heroes of existentialist literature, Pamela Mordecai ("The West Indian Male Sensibility," 1982) suggests that the affinity also extends to the area of male–female relationships. It is the "obsession" with success or "distinction" in the protagonist of St. Omer, she writes, "coupled with the absence of an example of decent affection between man and woman, that leads him into the unsatisfying labyrinth of his relationships with women" (p. 639). And those relationships reveal the inherent impossibility of breaking out of the solipsistic world of self, of creating the possibility of community. In Mordecai's words: "If the definition of the existentialist condition in the metropole is the impossibility of an encounter between self and another self-as-self, in the West Indian situation [exemplified by St. Omer's characters] the impossibility of receiving the woman-as-self and the related re-entry into community may well be the predicament" (p. 641).

The absence of distance between author and characters has been the basis for attacks on St. Omer's work. Jacqueline Kaye sees in St. Omer's narratives plots which reveal "egoism and self-absorption" and a "lack of objectivity." This "distilled subjectivity," she insists, makes it "difficult for the reader to feel sympathy with St. Omer's characters" ("Anonymity and Subjectivism in the Novels of Garth St. Omer," 1975, p. 50). Gerald Moore expresses similar concerns about a "lack of distance" and concludes that the similarities in tone, theme, atmosphere, and characterization suggests to him that St. Omer is a writer "desperately in need of an entirely new subject" ("Garth St. Omer," 1972, p. 1191).

As late as 1977, however, Bruce King could still decry the dearth of critical response to St. Omer's work. Observing that the publication of four novels by a house as "reputable" as Faber and Faber normally elicits appreciable interest, King praises St. Omer as "an unusual talent who, regardless whether he develops into a major novelist, deserves attention" ("Garth St. Omer: From Disorder to Order," 1977–78, p. 67).

HONORS AND AWARDS

Garth St. Omer has been the recipient of several awards, including a Ford Foundation Grant and a Fellowship from the Department of Comparative Literature, Princeton University.

BIBLIOGRAPHY

Works by Garth St. Omer

Syrop. In *Introduction Two: Stories by New Writers*. London: Faber and Faber, 1964, pp. 139–87.

A Room on the Hill. London: Faber and Faber, 1968.

Shades of Grey. London: Faber and Faber, 1968.

Nor Any Country. London: Faber and Faber, 1969.

J-, Black Bam and the Masqueraders. London: Faber and Faber, 1972.

Studies of Garth St. Omer

Baugh, Edward. "Since 1960: Some Highlights." In *West Indian Literature*, ed. Bruce King, 1979, pp. 78–94.

Brathwaite, Edward. Review of *Introduction Two*. *Caribbean Quarterly* 10 (March 1964), 68–69.

Gilkes, Michael. "Garth St. Omer." In *The West Indian Novel*, 1981, pp. 102–15.

Kaye, Jacqueline. "Anonymity and Subjectivism in the Novels of Garth St. Omer." *The Journal of Commonwealth Literature* 10 (August 1975), 45–52.

King, Bruce. "Garth St. Omer: From Disorder to Order." *Commonwealth Essays and Studies* 3 (1977–78), 55–67.

Moore, Gerald. "Garth St. Omer." In *Contemporary Novelists*, ed. James Vinson. New York: St. Martin's Press, 1972, pp. 1084–86.

Mordecai, Pamela C. "The West Indian Male Sensibility in Search of Itself: Some Comments on *Nor Any Country*, *The Mimic Men*, and *The Secret Ladder*." *World Literature in English* 21 (Autumn 1982), 629–44.

Rohlehr, F. Gordon. "Small Island Blues: A Short Review of the Novels of Garth St. Omer." *Voices* (Port of Spain) 2 (September-December 1969), 22–28.

Thieme, John. "Double Identity in the Novels of Garth St. Omer." *Ariel* 8 (July 1977), 81–97.

See also General Bibliography: Allis, Herdeck, and Hughes.

DARYL CUMBER DANCE

Andrew Salkey (1928–)

BIOGRAPHY

Andrew Salkey was born in Colón, Panama, on January 30, 1928, of Jamaican parents. When he was two years old he was taken to Jamaica, where he was raised by his grandmother and later his mother, who returned home after the birth of his brother. His father remained in Panama, where he worked first in the Canal Zone for the Americans and later became a reasonably successful entrepreneur, hiring fishing boats and managing a general store and a tenement building which he purchased. He diligently supported his family, but from afar, his existence being confirmed for his son by the monthly check that he religiously sent. The first time Salkey recalls meeting his father was when the thirty-two-year-old author returned to Jamaica on a Guggenheim in 1960.

Growing up in a culture with a strong oral tradition, the young Salkey was early enamored of the folk tales of Jamaica, especially the Anancy tales, which his grandmother and others used to tell him. He was educated at St. George's College and Munro College in Jamaica, after which he went to England (in 1952) and did a B.A. in English literature at the University of London. In London he taught English language and literature and Latin and worked as a broadcaster, interviewer, and scriptwriter for the BBC.

Salkey has served on the editorial board of several magazines, including *Caliban*, *New Letters*, and *Savacou*, of which he was a founding editor. Since 1976 he has been teaching at Hampshire College in Amherst, Massachusetts. The novelist is married and has two sons.

MAJOR WORKS AND THEMES

Andrew Salkey is one of the most prolific of the Caribbean writers, having written five novels, eight children's novels, four volumes of poetry, a collection of short stories, and two travel books and having edited nine anthologies of West Indian literature.

Though the quest for identity and the need for revolution are probably the major themes that permeate most of his work, the style and tone of the treatment and development of these themes and the nature of the world in which they are developed vary greatly as the novelist moves from one genre to another. After *A Quality of Violence* (1959) his later adult novels generally focus on a weak, aimless, lost, ineffective middle-class young man, for all intents and purposes fatherless, unable to determine who he is and what he wants, struggling in a world that is basically corrupt, racist, evil, and absurd. They end in despair. Most of his children's novels focus on a brave, strong, rational young child (usually a boy), growing up in a stable and hard-working family (headed by a strong male figure), bravely and rationally facing problems stemming from natural disasters (drought, hurricanes, earthquakes) or political oppression. They confirm our faith in the common man. His poetry is very romantic and also political. It focuses on the beauty of the West Indies as place, on the love and attraction this homeland retains for its children in exile (this latter is an especially dominant theme in *Away*, 1979), on the historical and political reality of the area, and on the beauty, strength, and heroism of the Caribbean people. Generally the poems reinforce the need for revolution. They inspire a kind of romantic optimism. His travel books, diaries of his visits to Georgetown and Havana, give him an opportunity to reflect upon and comment on the political, economic, sociological, and cultural situations of Cuba and Guyana. He left Cuba optimistic about the future of that revolution.

Salkey's first novel, *A Quality of Violence*, focuses on a rural Jamaican parish during the drought of 1900, in which many of the villagers turn to a Pocomania cult for relief. Within this cult, voodoo-inspired rituals lead to the sacrifice not only of animals but human beings as well. Early in the novel, the original leader of the cult, Dada Johnson, and a rival whip each other to death in a flagellation ritual designed to exorcize the evil spirits that produced the drought. Such violence repeats itself over and over, even among children in the community, until the novel ends with the death of Dada's widow, Mother Johnson, who had ferociously struggled for leadership of the cult after her husband's death and who, once her designs on leadership were thwarted, no less forcefully provokes her own crucifixion: as the people stone her, she yells, "Kill me, yes. Kill me, you stinking, dirty Judas people, you. Kill me!" Salkey concludes, "Then, for the first time that night, she relaxed, and waited" (1978 ed., p. 206).

Salkey's later novels deal with urban, middle-class, presumably more sophisticated central figures, but the bitter conflicts and the innane cruelties that characterize many of the relationships in his earlier novel continue. The major characters of his next four novels are all young men from middle-class Jamaican families who have been raised by powerful mothers toward whom they are very ambivalent and who for all intents and purposes have no father (two fathers live away from home in Panama and Cuba, one father is dead, and the other simply hates his son). We are forced to infer in each case that this absence of a father has some impact on the son's doomed quest for identity. In *Escape to an Autumn Pavement* (1960), all that Johnny Sobert knows of his father is an airmail letter from Panama: "A father is a force. . . . But when an airmail envelope means a father's presence, then there's bound to be a problem later on. Much later, maybe. For child and mother" (1970 ed., p. 77).

The names of these young men, as well as the background, personality, plights, and characteristics that they share, compel comparisons. Jerry Stover (*The Late Emancipation of Jerry Stover*, 1968) and Johnny Sobert have the same initials (one wonders whether it is supposed to be significant that the first initial is J), and their last names consist of a combination of the same letters with the exception of the "t" and "b" (Salkey's use of different combinations of the same letters to force us to recognize similarities occurs again in his satire of the Kirby-Rybik regimes in Kingston [*The Late Emancipation of Jerry Stover*]). The obvious implications of names like Catallus, Heartland, Stover (striver?), and Sobert (sober? He works in a bar.) are not without their inescapable irony. Nor can the unlikely association of Salkey's weaklings with figures such as Jesus (the Js) and Malcolm X be ignored.

These young men, who are confused and bewildered about their racial identity, their national identity, and even their sexual identity, are generally caught up in a series of adventures, apparently designed to help them find themselves, to forge an identity. Often, as in *The Adventures of Catallus Kelly* (1969), the protagonist is involved in an almost ritualistic set of adventures, beginning with his exposure to White racism, including some exposure to homosexuality, and moving to his return to the Black community and his quest for African roots. Ultimately these quests are futile for Salkey's young seekers after self. Generally they find that Whites are racist; indeed, the White woman with whom Catallus has an affair is the author of a blatant Black hate book. In the most extended treatment of the quest among homosexuals, Johnny Sobert, miserable in his heterosexual relationships, is comfortable only with the homosexual Dick, but he is never able to admit his homosexuality and consumate his love. Rather he in essence begs other people to tell him whether he is a homosexual, for like the typical male persona in Salkey's novels, he cannot *himself* determine what he is—or indeed admit and accept what he is. Whatever group of their own people they try to relate to eventually proves disappointing: in *Escape* Johnny regards the middle class as "malformed" (p. 145); in *The Late Emancipation of Jerry Stover* Jerry finds the Black middle class to be blind escapists, the Black political leaders to be empty, corrupt politicians, and the Rastas to be foolish "child-like" dreamers (1968 ed., p. 140). Malcolm Heartland finds the Black revolutionaries with whom he becomes involved to be pawns manipulated by others; they reveal themselves to be selfish, callous, and exploitative in their relationships with others: they routinely sexually exploit their women and have no qualms about killing anyone who gets in their way. Their goals are never clear; their *modus operandi* was, as Malcolm considered it, ''all so trumped up . . . spurious, melodramatic, self-dramatizing fantasy . . . like a third-rate show of modish entertainment . . . totally unreal'' (*Come Home, Malcolm Heartland*, p. 145). The quest for self in Africa is no more productive: as Johnny Sobert concludes, ''Africa doesn't belong to me! There's no feeling there. No bond'' (*Escape*, p. 48).

The isolation of Salkey's lost individuals is exacerbated by the fact that they are unable to relate meaningfully to other human beings across racial, cultural, or class lines. Many of his young Black men strive to develop relationships with White women, ironically lending credence to the claim in the racist hate literature that Fiona reads to Johnny, ''One of the chief reasons for the blacks pouring into Britain is their desire to mate with the white women of our country'' (*Escape*, p. 134). Salkey notes that a student whom he met in Havana wanted to know whether he could come to London and ''get a White woman *too* (*Havana Journal*, 1971, p. 43; italics added). The Black woman lover of Malcolm Heartland accuses, ''Every one of you, every single Black man, in this blasted country, . . . prefers a white woman to one of his own'' (*Come Home, Malcolm Heartland*, p. 63). Indeed, Johnny Sobert recognizes that his motivation for coming to London may have been to get a White woman: he reflects, ''Respectable people are married people. Shade's the thing. Could very well be the reason for my coming to England where I can get a girl a million shades lighter than myself'' (*Escape*, pp. 77–78). Salkey tells us that Catallus Kelly had ''an eye for what his generation of immigrants called 'white pussy' '' (*Catallus Kelly*, p. 136). Larry, another West Indian immigrant who is reasonably successful in London, notes in reference to his blond companion, ''Oh, she! Just a piece-a-excess-profit-tax, old man. You got to arrange a show every time, you know. The public expect it of you. And who am I to let down my vast public?'' (*Escape*, 117; this passage recalls the previously quoted selection which Fiona read to Johnny which also noted that the Black sought the White woman for ''prestige''). We are frequently reminded, however, that these relationships are futile, empty, self-defeating gestures to find self and fulfillment. Clearly, often the White woman is no more than a necessary accoutrement to confirm that the man has symbolically achieved success. At other times she seems to be a symbol against whom he can direct his anger toward the society she represents and thereby achieve some revenge and retribution. Johnny Sobert's White lover, Fiona Trado, tells him that her previous African paramour ''wanted me only as a sort of beating-stick for the white man's plunder of Africa'' (*Escape*, p. 42). Conversely, some of these Black men are merely pawns for the White women to indulge their fantasies of Black sexuality. Clearly that is the case with the relationship between Catallus and his Fascist paramour, who despises Blacks and writes crude and incendiary racist propaganda tracts. Just as obvious is the fact that Johnny feels victimized in his relationship with Fiona, whom he actually hates, who causes him to feel a sense of a loss of his identity, and whom he recognizes is merely "using" him (*Escape*, p. 125); he reflects upon their love-making: "All this for free, from me without love. From me without my permission, only submission" (p. 126).

Salkey's protagonists' aspiring, snobbish, middle-class backgrounds apparently also make it impossible for them to achieve any kind of meaningful relationship with people from the lower classes. Jerry Stover, for example, frequently makes love to his family's maid Miriam, but only when he is drunk—obviously when he is sober, he prefers to retain class distinctions. When she informs him that she is pregnant, he stifles a desire to laugh and gives her some money for an abortion. Further, even though Jerry seems sympathetic toward the lower-class Rastas, he regards them as inferiors and never comprehends their plans for revolution, nor does he have any faith in their envisioned revolutionary society.

Thus, unable to relate to people in any meaningful way, unable to find any avenue through which they can satisfactorily express themselves, unable to determine who they are, Salkey's lost middle-class seekers inevitably settle for seeking and asserting themselves through desperate, meaningless, uninhibited, often violent and perverted sexual acrobatics. Their lives, marked by incessant sexual activity, often described explicitly and titillatingly, might best be characterized through a phrase from *Catallus* as "a riot of fornication" (p. 82). Sex inevitably seems the only conscious option for action of which they are capable—even when they are "involved" in other apparent options such as Black power movements, political involvement, Rastafarian activity, and the like. Inevitably the field for action ends up the bed (or the car seat, the floor, whatever—the setting for copulation is often not a consideration among Salkey's characters).

Given the meaningless ritual of self-discovery that we witness with Salkey's protagonists, the emptiness of their beings, the inanities of their world, we are not surprised that there is nothing to discover and no meaningful world in which to discover it. We are neither surprised nor disappointed then in the outcomes of their quests: Catallus Kelly returns to Jamaica and is committed to an insane asylum; Johnny Sobert, still unable at the end of the novel to acknowledge his love for Dick or to end his brutalizing relationship with Fiona, is last seen agonizing over the fact that both of them are waiting for him to come to them. At the conclusion of *The Late Emancipation of Jerry Stover*, most of Jerry's cohorts (they are called the Termites) have been killed by a landslide, and our last view of Jerry is of him aimlessly wandering through the streets of Lower Kingston. Finally, Malcolm Heartland (who, though weak, is notable among Salkey's characteristically passive characters in these novels for taking *some* action on his own—he at least makes a decision to return to Jamaica and appears to be making some efforts to work toward it) meets his death as a result of his involvement with the Black revolutionaries.

Unlike the lost, weak, undirected sons in Salkey's novels, the mothers are strong, determined women who know what they want, consistently strive for it, and attempt to give some direction to the lives of their sons. In these novels and in a few other instances in Salkey's works, there is, however, the implication that the power, strength, and domination of the women contribute to the ambivalence and emasculation of the men and are thus destructive.

These conflicting views of women are represented even in *Anancy's Score* (1973), the tales which Salkey has created based upon the popular Anancy of African and New World tales. Salkey takes the traditional trickster and places him in a modernized, urbanized setting. In his "How Anancy Became a Spider Individual Person" Salkey invents an etiological tale explaining how Anancy got certain characteristics: here Salkey makes the wife a bossy Eve, given to tongue lashing and nagging Anancy, and ultimately succumbing to the temptations of the snake and tricking Anancy into eating the apple. It is she who is responsible for the cunning ways of Anancy, the bad, and the male is responsible for the "goodness of the poet-person" in him (p. 27). In several of these tales, Anancy, like the principals in Salkey's novels, is noted for his callous victimization and sexual exploitation of women. Like Dada Johnson of *A Quality of Violence*, an Obeah man and a confidence trickster who "treated" women in his back yard ("The table is a sort of altar of office, and it give the whole thing a look of hospital work," he boasts [p. 39]), Anancy plays whatever role is convenient to achieve his ends (minister, root doctor, whatever), pretending to help women at the same time he is thinking about seducing them. In "Anancy, the Sweet Love-Powder Merchant," for example, a distraught wife consults Anancy for help with her husband: "As Anancy handing over the love stuff [potion] with one hand, he collecting two mash-up ten shilling notes with the other, and if he could produce a third hand, it would've been straight up Sally dress taking a feel" (p. 54).

On the other hand, in the children's stories, in the poetry, and occasionally elsewhere, the strength of the woman is presented as a positive and constructive force, and women are held up as objects of respect and admiration rather than of disdain and exploitation. In *Havana Journal* (1971), Salkey notes, "*because of the curiously limp and uneven contribution of the man, the woman in the West Indies, wherever she may have come from, has, of necessity, to be the only natural revolutionary in West Indian society*" (p. 91). In *Drought* (1966) he writes, "The strength of the people of Naim was rooted in the morale and resourcefulness of its women.... The men and the boys owed their over-all security to the unassuming and unsung strength of their womenfolk" (p. 31). In the historical and romantic poem *Jamaica* (1973), which Salkey labored over for twenty-one years as he painstakingly studied, analyzed, synthesized, and subsumed the history of his country, he chooses a woman as the major symbol, Caribbea, obviously representing the Caribbean. And here in counterbalance to the futility and nihilism characterizing the treatment of the lost Caribbean man in his novels is the optimism inspired by the possibility of the return of the new Caribbean man to Caribbea, who is mother, guide, and savior, the one who prepares the path "on which your new men may walk" (1973 ed., p. 49). Here is the hope for revolution as, inspired by Caribbea, men are encouraged to "own up to weself," embrace their own traditions and "fuck the nex' man" (p. 14), develop pride, reject old advice, and "plan for change!" (p. 84).

CRITICAL RECEPTION

Given the prolific output of Andrew Salkey, it is surprising that he has received very little extended critical consideration. He is mentioned in most (though by no means all) surveys and studies of Caribbean literature, but in most cases there is little more than passing notice. The appearance of his books has been regularly observed in British, American, and Caribbean periodicals, such as the *Times Literary Supplement*, the *New Statesman*, the *Sunday Gleaner*, and *The Listener*. Some reviewers and later critics have praised his skill, characterization, and promise. Graham Hough in his review in *The Listener* called *A Quality of Violence* "a vigorous, imaginative and quite unusual novel" (October 22, 1959, p. 698). Anthony Boxill concludes his review of *Escape to an Autumn Pavement* with the observation, "It is an interesting book because the author has taken a serious problem and handled it with subtlety" ("The Emasculated Colonial," *Présence africaine* [3rd Quarterly 1970], p. 149). Kenneth Ramchand acclaims Salkey's strength in *Quality* to be his exploration "of the irrational element in human existence" (*The West Indian Novel and its Background*, 1970, p. 129). Marie Richardson calls *Quality* "an interesting first novel" which "seems to start and finish out of the blue, but the characters are very much there" ("New Novels," *New Statesman* 58 [October 10, 1959], p. 487). While the anonymous *TLS* reviewer of *The Late Emancipation of Jerry Stover* objected that "in places, [the novel] is over-elliptical; there is at times a certain skimpiness of characters, and whether the final social implications are valid is problematical," he concludes, "But altogether a worthy addition to this interesting novelist's growing reputation" (February 15, 1968, p. 149).

Other reviewers and later critics have objected to the dialect, the nihilism, the violence, and the sex in Salkey's works. Donald E. Herdeck says his dialect is weak (*Caribbean Writers: A Bio-Bibliographical-Critical Encyclopedia*, 1979, p. 186), and he quotes Sylvia Wynter, who asserts, "The use of the Jamaican dialect . . . is Mr. Salkey's bugbear. The moment he touches the dialect his artistic skill lapses, and the use of dialect which he employs in order to justify the use of dialect, is highly fraudulent" (*Caribbean Writers*, p. 186). The anonymous reviewer of *Escape* in the *Times Literary Supplement* notes that the novel "is superficially accurate enough, but there is a note of artificiality about a good deal of the dialogue, the style and some aspects of the situation" (July 15, 1960, p. 445). Sandra Pouchet Paquet laments the fact that Salkey's portrayal of Pocomania is limited to portraying it as a "black art," stressing "the cult's potential for violence and irrational action rather than its framework of authentic religious beliefs" ("The Fifties," in *West Indian Literature*, ed. Bruce King, 1979, p. 73). David Haworth complains, "The hero of Andrew Salkey's new novel [*The*

Adventures of Catallus Kelly] is *also* preposterously athletic sexually'' (''New Fiction: Fathomless Moments,'' *New Statesman* 77 [February 14, 1969], p. 230; italics added). Wilson Harris decries the ''triumph of all meaninglessness'' in *Quality* (*Tradition the Writer & Society*, 1973, p. 25).

One of the most extensive essays treating Salkey is Bill Carr's ''A Complex Fate: the Novels of Andrew Salkey'' (1968). Carr insists that *Quality* cannot be simply interpreted in ''mid-twentieth century rationalist terms: free enquiry (Parkin) versus the brute pressures of the mob'' (p. 102), but concludes that it is a ''fable on the conflicting possibilities—Mother Johnson or Brother Parkin—that ultimately make up the Jamaican consciousness'' (p. 104). Carr discusses *Escape to an Autumn Pavement* as ''a classic exposition of the tense polarities of middle-class West Indianness when these are dramatized in an alien setting'' (p. 106).

The most extensive treatment of the children's novels is C. R. Gray's ''Mr. Salkey's Truth and Illusion'' (1968), in which he argues that those novels are all too often unrealistic, nostalgic, and romantic. He observes some promising progression in the books and maintains the hope that ''some really excellent books for children will come from Mr. Salkey's pen'' (p. 53); but overall he concludes that the children's novels are not successful. They have too much ''misleading nostalgia and sentimentality'' (p. 53); the language is false and bookish (''[Salkey] prefers to pretend that his characters have no trace of their environment in their language'' [p. 51]); and he ''falsif[ies] his characters and . . . contrive[s] such tenuous reasons to hold his plots together'' (p. 54). Gray remains reluctant to recommend these books for Jamaican children until they are ''prepared to separate the wheat from the chaff'' (p. 54).

HONORS AND AWARDS

Andrew Salkey has received numerous grants and awards, including the Thomas Helmore Poetry Prize for *Jamaica* (1955); a Guggenheim Award for *A Quality of Violence* (1960); a Deutscher Kinderbuchpreis Award for *Hurricane* (1967); a Sri Chinmoy Poetry Award (1977); and a Casa de las Americas Prize for Poetry for *In the Hills Where Her Dreams Live* (1979).

BIBLIOGRAPHY

Fiction by Andrew Salkey

A Quality of Violence. London: Hutchinson, 1959; Nendeln/Liechtenstein: Kraus Reprint, 1970; New Beacon, 1978.

Escape to an Autumn Pavement. London: Hutchinson, 1960; Nendeln/Liechtenstein: Kraus Reprint, 1970.

The Late Emancipation of Jerry Stover. London: Hutchinson, 1968; Harlow, Essex: Longman, 1982.

The Adventures of Catallus Kelly. London: Hutchinson, 1969.

Anancy's Score [short stories]. London: Bogle-L'Ouverture, 1973.
Come Home, Malcolm Heartland. London: Hutchinson, 1976.

Poetry by Andrew Salkey

Jamaica. London: Hutchinson, 1973; London: Bogle-L'Ouverture, 1983.
In the Hills Where Her Dreams Live: Poems for Chile, 1973–1980. Havana: Casa de las Americas, 1979; Sausalito, Calif.: Black Scholar Press, 1981.
Land. Sausalito, Calif.: Black Scholar Press, 1979.
Away. London: Allison and Busby, 1980.

Children's Novels by Andrew Salkey

Hurricane. London: Oxford University Press, 1964, 1979; Harmondsworth: Puffin Books, 1977; New York: Penguin, 1977.
Earthquake. London: Oxford University Press, 1965, 1979; New York: Roy, 1969.
Drought. London: Oxford University Press, 1966.
Riot. London: Oxford University Press, 1967, 1973.
Jonah Simpson. London: Oxford University Press, 1969; New York: Roy, 1970.
Joey Tyson. London: Bogle-L'Ouverture, 1974.
The River That Disappeared. London: Bogle-L'Ouverture, 1979.
Danny Jones. London: Bogle-L'Ouverture, 1980.

Travel Books by Andrew Salkey

Havana Journal. Harmondsworth: Penguin, 1971.
Georgetown Journal: A Caribbean Writer's Journey from London via Port of Spain to Georgetown, Guyana, 1970. London: New Beacon, 1972.

Anthologies by Andrew Salkey

West Indian Stories. London: Faber and Faber, 1960, 1968.
Stories from the Caribbean. London: Paul Elek Books, 1965, 1972; New York: Dufour, 1968.
The Shark Hunters. London: Nelson, 1966.
Caribbean Prose: An Anthology for Secondary Schools. London: Evans, 1967.
Island Voices: Stories from the West Indies. New York: Liveright, 1970.
Breaklight: An Anthology of Caribbean Poetry. London: Hamish Hamilton, 1971; Garden City, N.Y.: Doubleday, 1972; Garden City, N.Y.: Anchor, 1973.
Caribbean Essays: An Anthology. London: Evans, 1973.
Writing in Cuba since the Revolution: An Anthology of Poems, Short Stories, and Essays. London: Bogle-L'Ouverture, 1977.
Caribbean Folk Tales and Legends. London: Bogle-L'Ouverture, 1980.

Studies of Andrew Salkey

Carr, Bill, "A Complex Fate: The Novels of Andrew Salkey." In *The Islands in Between*, ed. Bruce King, 1979, pp. 100–08.

Gray, C. R. "Mr. Salkey's Truth and Illusion." *Jamaica Jouurnal* 2 (June 1968), 46–54.

See also General Bibliography: Allis, Brown, Griffiths, Harris, Herdeck, Hughes, James, Moore, Ramchand (1970), and Van Sertima.

IAN D. SMITH

Dennis Scott (1939–)

BIOGRAPHY

Dennis Scott was born into a middle-class family in Kingston, Jamaica, and received his education at Jamaica College, where he became headboy while it was still a boarding institution. The ensuing years found him entering the University of the West Indies, Mona, then leaving to teach at Presentation College, Trinidad, returning to Jamaica to teach at Kingston College and his alma mater Jamaica College before finally going back to university, where he graduated with a first class in English. While at UWI he was the assistant editor of *Caribbean Quarterly*. Soon after, he went to Athens, Georgia, on a Shubert Playwrighting Fellowship, 1970–71 (where he wrote the "Black Mass" sequence in *Uncle Time*), and later received a Commonwealth Fellowship to undertake a special diploma course in education at Newcastle-Upon-Tyne, England. He returned to teach once again at Jamaica College before becoming director of the School of Drama at the Cultural Training Centre, Kingston. This latter post allowed him to marry his two loves, teaching and drama. Having resigned from the School of Drama, Scott is presently a visiting professor of directing at the School of Drama at Yale, where he recently directed a well-received production of *A Raisin in the Sun*.

His award-wining production of Trevor Rhone's *Smile Orange* (1972) initiated an invitation extended to Scott to participate in the annual National Playwrights Conference in the United States; 1983 marked Scott's ninth year in this venture. An offshoot of this was Scott's adaptation of *Sir Gawain and the Green Knight*, commissioned by the O'Neill Center for the National Theatre of the Deaf in 1977.

Scott describes his family background as being a very happy experience, with permissive parents allowing him to read whatever he wanted. This "heat and comfort of home" is consciously contrasted to the coldness of experience of the "closed universe of a boarding institution" (interview with Ian D. Smith, Kingston, Jamaica, June 23, 1983). In this cold public world of the boarding school, Scott explains, he learned to use language as defense and to manipulate; that is, he used language to structure the environment he wanted. This was to be of signal importance for Scott as a poet. The warm family experience, on the other hand, accounts partly for Scott's interest in relationships, which he sees as "loyalties and contracts between people" and, in particular, the familial bond (interview). The importance of human and social bonds cannot be lost on the reader of Scott's poetry or those who have read or seen the plays. In addition, the pattern of conflict between "cold" and "hot," which results in an ability to master and control, can be clearly seen in the dialectical tensions which structure the poems.

Scott maintains that theater has been his first love, being fostered early in primary and high schools by way of involvement in skits, concerts, and the drama club. Not of least importance was Scott's wide reading (he notes that at age twelve he had read all of Shakespeare), supported by his strong sensitivity to a storytelling tradition and the theatrical qualities he finds in the native oral traditions. For him a narrative element is primordial in art, and he avers that all his poems tell stories, for which he offers a definition: "a story contains a situation which consists of people acting towards each other in a specific environment" (interview). We understand that for Scott the narrative structure is a prerequisite for treating human relations.

Travel to the United States at seventeen and a tour of the West Indies at about age twenty exposed him to the world outside the Caribbean, on the one hand, and allowed him to become aware of the commonalities that the people of the region share, on the other. These travel experiences united with other elements to focus Scott's attention on relationships between people in the peculiar social contexts in which they evolve. He points out that he developed a social consciousness rather late, owing in part to his secure background, which did not promote an adequate exposure to societal ills. It has been for him a process of self-discovery: "Nobody explained this to me when I came" ("Sentry," *Uncle Time*, p. 11).

Having been a dancer for many years Scott left to give more attention to directing. He explains that he got tired of being on stage, being part of an "organization," whereas as director he found it more exciting to be able to organize elements (interview). This propensity to "organize" permits an insight into Scott's care and craft as a poet: the deft choice of word, the correct image, the superb control of form, are all part of this desire to organize elements in a profoundly meaningful whole. In this context, it is perhaps interesting to note that Scott also sees his early Episcopalian/Anglican background (he is now agnostic) as furnishing him with a sense of form and ritual.

Scott's diverse career interests as dancer, playwright, poet, teacher, critic, actor, and director attest to an untiring intellect which pursues ways of understanding the environment and communicating back to it. In the course of this mutual education, that unremitting, unsentimental, precise intellect continues to make a substantial contribution to Jamaican and West Indian culture.

MAJOR WORKS AND THEMES

As the opening poem in the collection *Uncle Time*, "Bird of Passage" defines the rite of passage that the poet-persona undergoes in realizing his poetic calling. Using the Icarus myth as a frame of reference, Scott announces a determined commitment to the task of poet; for in this instance the "bird is not really / dead. Yet" (p. 3). Moreover, the symbolic scenario of the difficult but assertive flight to freedom away from the island of imprisonment and the scorching sun becomes a paradigm for the nature of experience in the Scott world. Gradually, then, the notions of commitment, struggle, danger, pain, and patience, implicit in the bird symbol, evolve out of this dialectical vision of the price "we must pay / to be complete" ("Lemonsong," *Dreadwalk: Poems 1970–78*, p. 16).

"Portrait of the Artist as a Magician" adumbrates the artist/poet in the process of carefully trying to define himself through his art: "He painted the ball / first, balancing on it himself / . . . / and in his hands mirrors" (*Uncle Time*, p. 10). At a given moment, he attempts to negate the picture by painting it all white, but it is too late; once the process has begun it takes on a vigorous autonomy: "But the ball began to roll." In that "magical" moment, the creative unconscious usurps the control of the too rational mind. Like a vacuum that nature abhors, the archetypically conceived creative unconscious constantly threatens to invade in this drama of the inner world of the poet's mind: "On certain days / the old house thunders open, the field / shivers its flat side like damp horses" ("Precautionary Measures," *Uncle Time*, p. 9). Yet, there are moments when the poet-persona yearns to escape from the "stone tomb" of the rational mind and the superficial level of existence to the wildly vital world represented by cats, "those sovereigns / melting past my window." Then, he attests, "something wild in me wakes / wants to be free, my nails scratching / the cold bed's iron" ("Because of the Cats," *Uncle Time*, p. 15).

For this surrender to the unconscious mind Scott finds a parallel in the surrender to love "without deceit." As "Diary" informs us, both "break a man open / so clean / not a hair on the skin of the child inside is wounded" (*Dreadwalk*, p. 42). In this descent into the self beyond the surface response of the "skin," "The starfish of our hearts / become dry and sharp / when we take off our bodies sometimes, / going into the sea" ("The Compleat Anglers," *Uncle Time*, p. 24). It is significant that Scott perceives one dimension of experience in terms of another for it represents his way of trying to understand and define the process of living. This method produces a multivalence in the poetry as in a given poem we see different strata of meaning become fused in one symbolic action.

Common to the poems is a surrealistic style, the use of Jungian archetypes of the self, and a psychoanalytical context of examination that determine the peculiar nature of the poetry. Also present are images of a painful though necessary self-analysis that leads one back to a clearer perception: ''Against that immaculate surgery there is no appeal'' (''Diary,'' *Dreadwalk*, p. 42). Tacitly, Scott extends this paradigm to include the experience of the reader in a moment of comprehension; like the unbidden unconscious, the ''poem cuts us off from ordinariness / with its iced mouth, truth'' (''Chillsong,'' *Dreadwalk*, p. 7). A result of this constant awareness of the psychic and emotional life is that, even in instances where we do not expect it, Scott manages to convey a strong and sometimes frightening insight into the inner world of the personae.

One area that the creative unconscious forces the poet to confront is death and mortality. ''Sentry'' uses the image of the soldier on duty keeping watch against the enemy: ''It is forbidden to sleep on guard, / in the dreamshadow you can't see them limping along, / covering their basket like mouths'' (*Uncle Time*, p. 11). These are the ''reapers,'' the mighty triumverate of mortality, age, and death, of whose power the persona is initially ignorant. However, he begins to notice their inescapable tyranny, ''the muscles softening'' and the ''young faces pinched / off at the base, breaking like shy stalks.'' These images evoke the extreme vulnerability of merely being human and throw into relief the surrealistically conceived conclusion: ''In the stone gardens of my mind / there are old men with fingers like scissors, / snip, snip. Harvesting heads.''

This disturbing picture of the old man Death and the fragmented psyche of the persona finds an analogue in the title poem, ''Uncle Time.'' Time with its inevitable end in death becomes personified as a primevally cynical being washing his foot in the sea, ''quiet-like wid 'im sea-win' laughter'' (p. 32). Here Scott fuses archetypal symbols of time—sea, sand, land—with Jamaican dialect to achieve a unique perception which is identifiably local but universally threatening: ''Watch how 'im spin web roun' yu house, an, creep / inside; an' when 'im touch yu, weep.''

Death becomes an enemy precisely because it negates life, that which Scott champions rigorously in the poems. Death is not only an event but grows into a metaphor that describes all activities that are noncreative. Negation of the active life of the mind is a kind of death; so is the lack of awareness of one's self and place in society, with particular reference to the dislocated Black in a historical perspective, and the estranged urban poor in a more sociopolitical context; and the absence of love in relationships which reduce it to physical lust and surface attractions. This conflict between 'life'' and ''death'' is another manifestation of the dialectical vision that subtends the action of the poetry.

Of singular importance to Scott is the experience of being West Indian. As a primary step, he examines the need to concern ourselves with those problems that are a part of our historical legacy. The persona of ''Homecoming'' discovers that "again, again these / hot and coffee streets reclaim / my love" (*Uncle Time*, p. 6), while the dead ancestors who have become "All Saints" communicate across the chasm of death to the present generation via memory. Like Orestes chased by the Furies, "We leave the city / pursued by memories / drawn towards the pocked hill" (*Uncle Time*, p. 35). There "we rehearse / their acts of endurance, / we perform / their freedom" (*Uncle Time*, p. 36). Taking the form of a litany, and reinforced by ecclesiastical images, this call for a responsibility to our heritage equates itself with the devotion to a religious vocation.

However, Scott remains aware that the history of the region cannot be simplified as "this place has possessed us / all who came / victor and victim / its possession" (*Uncle Time*, p. 36). Thus "Pages from a Journal, 1834" recounts the haunting effect of memory from the perspective of an Englishman returning home after emancipation: "the hills are woodcut wild, / inked at my heart / and hard to erase" (*Uncle Time*, p. 33). The opening words, "So, goodbye to dark," become heavily ironic as he understands that "the past permits / no unchaining" (p. 34); that the "dark" memories have an equally great claim on him as on the ex-slaves. Similarly, Scott contrasts perspectives in the "companion pieces," "Farmers' Notebook" and "Epitaph"; one recounts the decapitation and burning of a White woman, the other the brutal hanging of a slave. Both poems produce a cathartic effect in the reader through the direct probing of our consciences: "when the field furls out later / . . . / will you forget that / thick flesh here, grown / soft and nourishing?" ("Farmers' Notebook," *Uncle Time*, p. 40).

Although an indictment of the system of slavery is never absent, it is Scott's insistence on seeing history from varying perspectives that becomes significant. Through this technique of shifting perspectives he reveals not only the commonality that both victor and victim share but also the idea that the relationship between them is one of dynamic tension. Hence the image of the "Prism" is used in "Black Mass: Recessional" to describe this: "[the prism] is full, it explodes, containing us all / into the constant ceremonies of our living" (*Uncle Time*, p. 51).

"No Sufferer," which concludes *Uncle Time*, turns our attention to the plight of the urban poor and the poet's identification with them. Though he may not be a "sufferer" in comparable material terms, there is a poverty they share "when my wit / ratchets, roaming the hungry streets / of this small flesh, my city" (p. 53). This may be too neat a conceit, but the main point remains that the poet is dedicating his creative endeavors to the cause of the socially alienated. The closing words, "acknowledge I," speak of the self-assertion of both a poetic consciousness and a Black consciousness symbolized in "I."

At this point the essential distinction between Scott's two collections can be made. Whereas the emphasis in *Uncle Time* is on history and racial conflict, *Dreadwalk* concentrates on the present-day condition of the urban "sufferer." It also experiments more profoundly with the linguistic and conceptual possibilities of "I." "I," as popularized by the Rastafarians, serves to identify its members, operating both as a proper noun and an object pronoun. For them this is a linguistic way of throwing the self into relief. Having its provenance in this group where Black awareness finds its vigorously assertive manifestation, "I" also becomes a generic noun in Scott referring to a progressive Black outlook.

In this light "Dreadwalk" presents itself as a noteworthy choice as title poem. It narrates the meeting of a persona and "blackman" who represents firsthand knowledge of the kind of oppression meted out to the "children." The latter have been removed by a nameless force "like sand from the quarry" (p. 39), another symbolic scenario that reenacts the social privation that results in their total loss of self. The Jungian stone of the self, having pulverized to sand, suffers a further loss by being denied a place in the social quarry. It is the song of this existential annihilation that the blackman articulates: "blackman came walking I / heard him sing" (p. 39).

These opening lines introduce explicitly the ambiguous function of "I" as first person narrator and as generic name for "blackman." The semantic effect of the interchangeability of personae gained through the lineation becomes further exploited because there is no punctuation. Given these initial ambiguities, Scott explores the linguistic continuum between dialect and "Standard English" in a way that accommodates all these subtle variations. In virtually any given line one can sense the language shifting back and forth, in an almost autonomous way, from one idiolect to another. In fact, the fluidity of the linguistic shifts come to symbolize the learning process of the narrating persona; in other words, he learns the language he has to sing.

"Dreadwalk" may be the most radical example of Scott's play with shifting voices, but "I-song" depends also on this need to identify speakers. In the opening section the now adult persona speaks of an old friend who has died: "I does most of his dying privately" (p. 33). In the second section it is the voice of the dead person who speaks of the lesson imparted to the adult persona as a child: "And the boy I hit to make him listen. He learned / how Time hammers suddenly" (p. 33). Given the connotations of social deprivation associated with "I," the weighty fact of his mortality only serves to complicate this persona's sense of nonbeing; a knowledge so painful that "I" withdraws into himself, "dying privately."

Although the voice of "I" speaks in the second section of the poem, in a curious way it is the narrator who actually writes. This ambiguous situation is rendered in a line which precedes the verbal entry of "I" into the poem: "I writes this with it" (p. 33). Recalling Rimbaud's "je est un autre"—I is an other—in its grammatical deviation and ultimate meaning, this line attempts to articulate the *possession* of the narrator by the "spirit" of "I." Thus in yet another "magical" moment I's knowledge of a terrible existential fate aggravated by social alienation is reborn in the narrator. It becomes evident that the possession described here provides an elaboration, in a different context, of the way the creative unconscious controls the poet and leads to illumination.

"And it's true" along with "Neighbours" underscores the social indictment made by focusing on the real source of suffering: a lack of social responsibility—

the charity of brotherhood in its practical and fundamental sense. Yet, in typical fashion, Scott offers a different perspective in "Lemonsong," which engages the question of responsibility to one's neighbor in the context of social revolution. Sitting under the lemon trees of Moncada, symbolic site of the Cuban revolution, a pensive father expresses fear that his sleeping son will heed to the voices of the dead revolutionaries—the voices of history—"who desire / only that we keep safe / what they have won" (*Dreadwalk*, p. 18). It is not that the father considers commitment to social freedom undesirable, but faced with the possibility of having to witness the sacrifice of the life of a loved one, a natural fear causes hesitation: "can no house stand / without such sour sacrifice, without / the whisper of bullets in the hand?" (p. 17). Thus paternal responsibility enters into conflict with social duty.

It is to Scott's credit that while he examines a more radical stance of political selfhood, at the same time he invests the whole with a more personal and emotionally charged tone. The love poems also extend the range of tone in this personal dimension, but there is a unique quality that arises out of the fusion of the public/social with the private chiefly in poems that establish the father/son—adult/child dialogue as a formal and thematic device. With this in mind we can begin to appreciate the full tonal and emotional range of "All Saints," where the adult ancestral voices dialogue with the modern generation in the youth of its independence, as well as "Dreadwalk" and "I-song," where the mature social consciousness of "I" is imparted to the intellectually and experientially innocent.

Scott's willingness to reexamine the isues from different points of view and to make plain the dialectical tensions results in a "poetic density" that is characteristic of his work. This achievement is significant as Scott's evolution as a poet can be understood as a movement away from the early tendency to a "lyrical" style to a deliberate search for a linguistic spareness that attains maximum effect.

A passage from "The Dumb-School Teacher" describes accurately the way Scott's language functions: "Words had shapes / changeable as / aspects of the truth" (*Uncle Time*, p. 18). Words not only accumulate dual and triple meanings but also possess the revealing power of irony. "Neighbours" opens: "Squatted. Stiff like / a snackbox in my window's / frame, his cardboard house" (*Dreadwalk*, p. 13). If we read this passage as a set of run-on lines, a visual parallel is being drawn between the squat claustrophobic house and a cardboard box. If we stop at "Stiff like," this phrase reads "in a stiff manner" with a colloquial pun on "Stiff" as a dead body. Not only is the house a moribund place, but, by virtue of a transferred epithet, it is suggested that the man in the house is also "dead," his meager existence denying him a full humanity. The ominous phrase further suggests, in prophetic manner, his physical death. Equally notable is the truncated rhythm of the opening line, which hints at something unpleasant to come, while evoking the strained tone (also suggested by "Stiff") in which the narrator speaks. By placing "window's" at the end of the line, it achieves special focus, directing us to see the persona looking through the window at the destitution of the neighbor at a safe and comfortable distance, not wanting to be involved. Thus, by astute lineation and use of rhythm, a trenchant social critique is engaged. Further, as the various meanings surface, there is a corresponding uneasy shifting of tones. Like so much of Scott's poetry, the language is sinewy, supple, and void of linguistic luxury without sacrificing the emotional resonance of the whole.

This wry, ominous, ironic, dangerous tone becomes a characteristic feature of style, which is thrown into relief when lines are significantly set off from the rest of the poem. In this way a temporal hiatus is imposed in the moment of our reading, thus increasing our awareness of a dramatic pause, which highlights what is to follow in a theatrical manner. Such is the full effect of the conclusion of "Endgame," for example, which sharpens our sensitivity to the tonal and semantic accretions that occur in the simple phrase, "Black to move" (*Uncle Time*, p. 47), given in the context of a surreal game of chess.

Scott also attempts to gain linguistic control by building the poems on a central conceit, as in "Hunt," where the haunting memory of a lover is conceived in terms of a woman stringing a needle. In such a case, as with "Resurrections," the poem achieves a metaphysical—in a stylistic sense—dimension. An extension of this technique is the use of literary and mythical allusions as a structuring and expository device. "Apocalypse dub" draws on the Biblical myth of the Horsemen of the Apocalypse to dramatize hunger, disease, and murder as the harsh realities that will lead to a social cataclysm. "At that frail and absent evening house" seems to fuse images from *The Glass Menagerie*, "The Lady of Shallot," and the fairy tale "Sleeping Beauty" to create a female persona—a bird-woman—who becomes a symbol of the fragility of human existence. "Birdwalk" uses the metrical pattern of the nursery rhyme "Sing a song of sixpence" to reveal both the injustice suffered by the maid, Gatta, at the hands of her middle-class employers as well as her dream for an eventual escape from this latter-day slavery, symbolized by the blackbird of freedom, "walking through she head." Not only do these allusions communicate a broader frame of emotional and semantic reference for the reader, they also allow Scott to concentrate on how far he can pare away at language without losing in poetic effect.

The breadth of allusion confirms a Scott axiom which holds that all experiences are valid; because these literary and mythical references have become part of the cultural heritage of the region, they can be effectively used to explore the human condition as known in the West Indies. This compounding of European-American forms and icons with specifically local ones results in a complex perspectivism in any given poem. There is not only a satisfying textual richness but an equally profound poetic experience for the reader. In a similar way, Scott's attitude to language means that he exploits the range of speech open to him, which leads to subtle linguistic effects. After all, "A poem has to sing" ("Poem:," *Dreadwalk*, p. 46), and all forms must be considered in the quest to communicate positive and socially regenerative values.

CRITICAL RECEPTION

Since Scott's intervention in the West Indian literary scene, critics, in their attempts to identify his work, have sought to place him in a recognizable category. This had led to seeing him as an inheritor of the continuing legacy of Walcott and Brathwaite: "Methodically, he is similar to Walcott in that his personal corrosions extend into this wider cultural problem; ideologically, he is similar to Brathwaite in that he has evolved to a kind of Third World consciousness/acceptance" (Anthony McNeill, "Dennis Scott, Maker: Part I, 'Journeys,' " 1971, p. 49). However, Edward Baugh, hoping for a finer distinction, senses in the work of these two more established writers a "determining colonial past and background," whereas Scott, like McNeill and Morris, who "have all attained their poetic majority in post-independence Jamaica," focuses more on the "matter of here and now; we are now on our own" ("Since 1960: Some Highlights," in *West Indian Literature*, ed. Bruce King, 1979, p. 87). However, Scott's unique qualities have solicited critical attention mostly in the direction of his use of language.

Victor Questel notes that Scott has managed to "produce both a new style and sound in West Indian poetry," but maintains, "The problem about *Uncle Time*, though, is that Scott is finally more concerned with the technique and style he has evolved" ("*Uncle Time*: A Pointer of the Shape of Things to Come," 1976, p. 6). Mervyn Morris notes that there is a performance element in the poetry, that they are "usually aware of an audience" (Introduction to *Uncle Time*, p. xvii). However, his conclusions serve to modify the implications of Questel's: "All his poems are graceful and intelligent; the finest persuade us that they are deeply felt" (p. xvii).

Other critics extend this performance metaphor to discuss the poetic quality and significance of his work. Gordon Rohlehr identifies a dialectic of self and other, one that is best resolved for him in "Dreadwalk": "Scott's 'Dreadwalk' moves like a painstakingly choreographed dance in which the dancers, Self and Other, poet and his double, feel their way around mutual mistrust, menace and uncertainty, towards a reconciliation which is neither escapist nor sentimental" ("The Problem of the Problem of Form: The Idea of an Aesthetic Continuum and Aesthetic Code-Switching in West Indian Literature," 1983). Baugh develops a similar thesis, giving attention to the love poetry: "The quality of a solemn dance, of ritual, runs through Scott's work whether the theme be violence or praise. In Scott's love poems, this dance of He and She, moving apart or together, takes on the quality of wordless, slow-motion explosions of marvel" (p. 90).

It is generally recognized that Scott's "Uncle Time" created a pioneering role for itself in using dialect for serious poetry. At the same time this raises the question of the importance of dialect/vernacular in his poetry and invites considerations of the underlying assumptions of his attitude to the European and native traditions in literature. Questel notes accurately that in *Uncle Time*, "Rather than talk about the dual tradition the Caribbean writer has to draw on, Scott demonstrates how one can tame both the tradition and the terrain in order to produce significant poetry'' (p. 6). Morris in his introduction to *Uncle Time* develops by simply pointing out that Scott has written a variety of poems: ''Accepting that what he knows is what he is, he has written a wide range of poems, some of which will be faulted by a too narrow West Indianism for seeming to bear no distinctive marks of Scott's Jamaican origins, and a few of which may—because of their local language and reference—be imperfectly received by readers unarmed with a knowledge of our Jamaican context'' (p. xviii).

By way of conclusion we quote Lloyd Brown, who elucidates the mutual productivity that exists between the poet and the source from which he draws to forge a peculiar style: ''Ras' lot and that of the folk have given birth to distinctive styles and forms that now sustain the art and vision of the poet. Finally, however, the poet's relationship with the folk and their art is not merely parasitic; . . . his indebtedness to the styles and forms of the folk constitute[s] a tribute to their collective vitality and, individually, to their personal resiliency'' (*West Indian Poetry*, 1978, p. 171).

HONORS AND AWARDS

In addition to Jamaican Festival Commission bronze and silver medals awarded for poetry, and several Best Director awards, Scott has been the recipient of a Shubert Playwrighting Award (1970), a Commonwealth Fellowship (1972), the International Poetry Forum Award for *Uncle Time* (1973), the Commonwealth Poetry Prize (1974), the Silver Musgrave Medal (1974), and the Prime Minister's Award for contribution to art and education (1983).

BIBLIOGRAPHY

Works by Dennis Scott

Uncle Time. Pittsburgh: University of Pittsburgh Press, 1973.
Sir Gawain and the Green Knight. New Orleans: Anchorage Press, 1978.
Dreadwalk: Poems 1970–78. London: New Beacon Books, 1982.

Studies of Dennis Scott

Brown, Stewart. ''New Poetry from Jamaica.'' *New Voices* 3 (1975), 48–50.

McNeill, Anthony. ''Dennis Scott, Maker: Part 1, 'Journeys.' '' *Jamaica Journal* 5 (December 1971), 49–52.

Questel, Victor. ''*Uncle Time*: A Pointer of the Shape of Things to Come.'' *Tapia* 6 (June 1976), 6–8.

Rohlehr, Gordon. ''The Problem of the Problem of Form: The Idea of an Aesthetic

Continuum and Aesthetic Code-switching in West Indian Literature.'' UWI Interdepartmental Conference 3, St. Augustine, Trinidad, May 19, 1983.

Smith, Ian. ''Language and Symbol in the Poetry of Dennis Scott.'' *Carib*, no. 1 (1979), 27–38.

See also General Bibliography: Allis, Baugh (1971), Brown, Hughes, and King.

SANDRA POUCHET PAQUET

Samuel Dickson Selvon (1923–   )

BIOGRAPHY

Samuel Dickson Selvon was born on May 20, 1923, in South Trinidad. He grew up in San Fernando and attended Naparima College there. He received no formal education after high school. His parents could not afford it, and he had no ambition to pursue the professional life of a lawyer or a doctor or even a writer. Selvon wanted to write music, and then he wanted to be a philosopher. His writing career evolved as a matter of course out of a talent for writing essays that became evident while he was still at school.

Selvon's father's family had come to Trinidad from India. His mother was half-Indian and half-Scottish; her father was a Scotsman who owned a coconut estate in Icacos, South Trinidad. Yet it was Selvon's mother, not his father, who spoke fluent Hindi and urged her son to take the extra class in Hindi offered at school. Despite her efforts, Selvon recalls that he grew up largely unconscious of race and ignorant of Hindu religious and cultural rituals. His sense of identity was shaped primarily by the cosmopolitan values of his racially mixed environment and the colonial experience. His school companions were Indian, African, Chinese, European, and various combinations of these. His parents never required that he grow up to be Indian, and he matured without fear of Creolization. "By the time I was in my teens," Selvon wrote in the *Trinidad Express* (September 23, 1979, p. 2), "I was a product of my environment, as Trinidadian as anyone could claim to be, quite at ease with a cosmopolitan attitude, and I had no desire to isolate myself from the mixture of races that comprised the community.''

During World War II Selvon joined the local branch of the Royal Naval Reserve. He worked on mine sweepers and torpedo boats as a wireless operator from 1940 to 1945. He read widely while he was in the navy, and it was at this time that he discovered his ambitions to write about the Trinidad landscape and peasant life as he knew it. This was partly inspired, he recalls (interview with Daryl Cumber Dance, February 1980), by the English writer Richard Jeffreys, who wrote a great deal about the English countryside and peasant life in England: ''When I first started to write I transposed that feeling and love that this writer seemed to me to have for nature, I transposed that into Trinidad and saw myself in a way as a kind of local Richard Jeffreys, who was going to try to get all of the physical aspects of the island and the beauty, the natural beauty of the island, I was going to be the one to write that sort of thing.''

After the war, Selvon worked as a journalist in Trinidad from 1946 to 1950. He was a subeditor of the *Guardian Weekly*, a magazine published by the *Trinidad Guardian*. This was an important job for Selvon. Not only did his journalistic training serve him well as a writer but, as subeditor of one of the few outlets for young writers in Trinidad, it put him in touch with the ambitions of other aspiring writers like Errol Hill, Cecil Herbert, Cecil Grey, Ian Roach, Clifford Sealey, Barnabus Ramon-Fortune, and George Lamming. Selvon was also writing poems and short stories at this time; some of these were published in *Bim* and others were sold to the BBC.

Selvon married for the first time in 1947 and started a family. But he was restless and feared the cramping influences of life on a small island. In 1950 he left for London in search of wider horizons. He traveled on the same ship as George Lamming, Barbadian poet and novelist, who had been living in Trinidad.

In London, Selvon first stayed at the Balmoral Hostel along with many other West Indians from other islands, as well as Africans and Indians. This was a formative experience for Selvon. His life at the Balmoral inspired characters and situations in numerous short stories as well as *The Lonely Londoners* (1956), his very successful novel about emigrant life in England.

On first arriving in London, Selvon found that he could not get a permanent job as a journalist as he had hoped. He was not a member of the National Union of Journalists, and he could not become a member without a permanent job. With some difficulty he secured a job as a civil servant at the Indian Embassy in London. He wrote and published his first novel, *A Brighter Sun*, while working there. With the publication of *A Brighter Sun* in 1952, Selvon's writing career was off to a promising start. He was able to get more free-lance work from English newspapers and magazines and was working on another novel when he fell ill with tuberculosis and was hospitalized for fifteen months. But Selvon was encouraged by the reviews and sales of his first novel and the free-lance work available to him. In 1954, after his release from the hospital, Selvon resigned from the Indian Embassy to become a full-time writer.

Sam Selvon lived in England for almost three decades before moving to Calgary, Alberta, in 1978. He has published ten novels, one collection of short stories, numerous articles, radio plays, and television and film scripts. He has received many awards and honors and traveled to the Caribbean whenever the opportunity presented itself. He was there in 1963, 1968, 1969, and 1979. Selvon currently resides in Calgary, Alberta, with his second wife, Althea Nesta Daroux. He has three children.

MAJOR WORKS AND THEMES

After more than thirty years in Great Britain and Canada, Selvon is essentially a writer-in-exile, but paradoxically, what distinguishes Selvon as a writer is his continuing Caribbean focus: "I am always going to be writing as Caribbean man," says Selvon in his interview with Daryl Cumber Dance. Like other major writers of the English-speaking Caribbean, among them Wilson Harris and Derek Walcott, Selvon is committed to the idea that Caribbean man, whatever his ancestry, possesses a distinct sensibility and potential. Living in the Caribbean, Selvon explains, "you become Creolized, you not Indian, you not Black, you not even White, you assimilate all these cultures and you turn out to be a different man who is the Caribbean man." For Selvon, as for Walcott and Harris, the loss of Old World traditions is no cause for despair, but an opportunity for rebirth and renewal.

Selvon's views on Caribbean man, his sense of shared sensibility, his elation in finding himself part of the New World landscape—all reflect Selvon's early experience of life in Trinidad. Selvon recalls that he was raised without racial or ethnic fetters, that he was far more interested in American movies than in learning Hindi, that his sense of community extended beyond the boundaries of race and religion. Being part Indian and part Scottish is not important to his sense of self. "They don't really interest me," he explains to Dance, "ancestry and going back and tracing things like that." For Selvon, his roots are not India and Scotland but the canefields and cacao estates of Trinidad. His disaffection with history as a creative force does not lead, as is popularly supposed, to confusion and despair, but to a sense of identity that is rooted in the landscape of his birth. "This island is my shadow," says Selvon, "and I carry it with me wherever I go" (Conference on East Indians in the Caribbean, University of the West Indies, St. Augustine, September 1979).

Selvon is most commonly perceived as a folk poet, and the reasons are clear. Selvon writes primarily about the predicament of the working-class majority in the Caribbean, agricultural and urban. He knows them intimately and has striven consistently to capture the essence of their experience in the structure and design of his fiction. He knows their language and uses it appreciatively and well; he was a pioneer in the use of a modified dialect as the language of consciousness and the language of narration as well. He understands both the colonial reality and myths with which the Caribbean is burdened. He is sensitive to the divisive cultural and economic pressures that push Caribbean citizens into exile and undermine them at home. But he also understands and admires the resilience of spirit that characterizes them and the physical and cultural phenomena from which they draw strength. In "The Folk in Caribbean Literature" (1972), Gordon Rohlehr writes that Selvon "bridges the gap between oral and scribal traditions" (p. 8) in the English-speaking Caribbean. Sensitive to folk forms through which the community records, organizes, and directs its own experience, Selvon's fiction remains essentially true to the working-class experience he describes, whether in terms of idiom, ideology, or landscape.

Selvon's ten novels and short stories roughly divide into those set in London and those set in Trinidad, those that explore the attractions and frustrations of West Indian emigrant life, and those that explore the psychic dangers that beset Caribbean life at home and the potential sources of strength with which they might be resisted. Selvon's ideal of Caribbean man never was conceived in terms of an ideal society. He describes the lurking menace as well as the promise of the Caribbean landscape. His perception of the Caribbean as the beginning of something new is informed by his understanding of the Caribbean's bitter history of migration and slavery.

Selvon was always committed to describing the realities of Caribbean life beyond the local color, the nostalgia, and the sensationalism that frequently characterize the peasant novel. As early as *A Brighter Sun* (1952), Selvon was mapping the sociological contours of the Trinidad landscape as he described an agricultural way of life devalued by creeping urbanization, the inequities of the plantation system, education, and a variety of foreign influences, whether derived from the U.S. military bases established during World War II or from the different values of those who returned from abroad impressed with the way the rest of the world lived. But because Selvon's response to the Caribbean landscape is neither the despair nor the cynicism of a V. S. Naipaul, this is also a novel whose counter theme is the beauty and idealism of Caribbean man.

The hero of *A Brighter Sun* is the newly married son of an agricultural laborer who leaves his family in the sugar cane belt to settle in a suburban village much closer to the city. He moves from a closed Indian community to a multiracial one. As Selvon conceives it, these changes in personal status and environment push an innocent and ignorant young Tiger to a new understanding of his environment and of his responsibilities as a citizen. Tiger and his young wife, Urmilla, discover a new sense of community within the framework of Trinidad's larger multicultural society: "Why I should only look for Indian friend? What wrong with Joe and Rita? Is true I used to play with Indian friend in the estate, but that ain't no reason why I must shut my heart to other people. Ain't a man is a man, don't mind if he skin not white, or if he hair curl?" (1971 ed., p. 48). Movement away from the isolated racial exposure of their childhood in the sugar belt is a positive step for Tiger and Urmilla in this novel, though the condescension Tiger acquires to an agricultural way of life is to be the cause of much grief and turmoil in the sequel to this novel, *Turn Again Tiger* (1958).

In *Turn Again Tiger*, Selvon returns Tiger and Urmilla to the canefields of their childhood. They rent out their home in Barataria and go reluctantly to the estate village of Five Rivers, where Tiger is to help his father supervise an experimental cane project. For both Tiger and Urmilla, this step back into their agricultural past is a learning experience that allows Selvon to explore the tensions between the sugar estate culture of their childhood and the urbanization they experience in Barataria. Tiger's new literacy and growing economic and cultural independence in Barataria set him apart in the agricultural community of Five Rivers.

Tiger's return to the canefields, in a subordinate role to his father, sharing his father's house, assisting him as a timekeeper, allows him to come to terms with his roots in the plantation system to which his father was indentured (and which programmed his father's life and expectations and those of an entire community). Frustrated by his father's values and expectations, Tiger confronts and destroys the icons of the past that confine his spirit and inhibit his growth. He challenges the humiliations imposed by his father's authority as head of their joint household and foreman (not supervisor as Tiger was led to believe) of the cane project in a brutal fight with the old man; he burns the books that leave him directionless and disconnected from his peasant origins; and he destroys the specter of White superiority taught by a colonial history and reinforced by the hierarchy of the plantation system in a violent sexual encounter with the White wife of the White supervisor of the cane project. With these three icons shattered, Tiger frees himself from the burden of shame with which he regarded his peasant and colonial history. The theme is renewal and rebirth as Tiger moves from scorn of his father's subservience to the White supervisor and of his dependence on cane to admiration of his father's hard-earned expertise; from alienation and disconnection to a position of leadership and community responsibility in Five Rivers; from rejection to understanding and respect for the life-sustaining rhythms of planting and harvesting that are the heart of the peasant experience. Tiger becomes psychically whole in Five Rivers. The novel's final statement is one of faith in the creative thrust of peasant life that has not only survived the anguish of an exploitative colonial history but moves beyond it.

In subsequent novels about Caribbean life, Selvon is no longer sure that his ideal of Caribbean man will be realized. *I Hear Thunder* (1963) reflects Selvon's disappointment over the failure of community evident in the collapse of the West Indian Federation and in the racism that polarized Guyana and spilled over into Trinidad as well. The confidence and faith of the earlier novels takes second place to a concern with mapping the divisive elements in the society, among them, race, education, money, and inherited colonial values. The theme is estrangement among old friends, between son and mother, between a successful son of the soil and his folk roots. The plot revolves around Mark, son of a washerwoman, who returns home as a doctor with a White wife, to claim his place in Trinidad society.

The Plains of Caroni (1970) once again targets the sugar industry and its dependents. The novel examines the conflict between sugar workers and company management over mechanization of the industry. The conflict reflects the failure of community that afflicts the whole society. University-educated Romesh is isolated in his approval of the new harvester. His family's money and his education give him a very different relationship to cane, unlike those who perceive their livelihood and power as dependent on the old plantation methods of planting and harvesting. The novel is satirical, but the irony is indulgent rather than condemnatory. The satirical voice is so intimate and so at ease with the language, the landscape, and the culture described that it acquires the disquieting power of the calypso, targeting and mirroring the society's foibles and limitations. One senses the calypsonian's delight in a memorable turn of phrase, in the witty encapsulation of some commonplace prejudice that captures the tone and nuance of society's way of looking at itself.

In *Those Who Eat the Cascadura* (1972), Selvon examines the cultural climate that preceded independence in the Caribbean. The novel is set in Sans Souci, a rural village that is economically dependent on a cacao estate owned and managed by an Englishman, Roger Franklin. Sans Souci is an isolated village, divorced as we are told from "the birthpangs of a people moving from subjugation" (p. 27). This allows Selvon the chance to examine in the fictionally appropriate context of the estate village the structure of that life and the hierarchy of values that organizes and sustains a colonial relationship. Selvon explores a quality of indoctrination that is both racial and colonial, an indoctrination that leaves its victims "unaffected by any thought of freedom from the white man's grip" (p. 28). "It's more than racial," Selvon explains, "I mean it goes right back to the whole concept of being colonized, of the feeling that White is supreme, of looking up towards the White man as if it is a goal to be attained" (interview).

Simply told, the plot evolves around a passionate and doomed love affair between Franklin's English guest, Garry Johnson, and Franklin's unacknowledged daughter in the village, Sarojini. The love story of Garry and Sarojini unfolds as a fated occurrence given the context of cultural and psychic dependence that accompanies the economic dependence of this village on the expatriate. Garry and Sarojini are characterized in terms of their class and status so that their love affair is a commentary on a wide range of social and political themes.

The inequities in the relationship between the great house and the village are always an issue in the novel, and Selvon makes the reader aware of this in a variety of ways. The poverty and insecurity of the villagers are powerfully contrasted to the order and stability represented in the great house Franklin occupies. A hurricane might devastate the villagers' homes, but Franklin's house is built to weather such storms. While Franklin is cast as responsible and dedicated to making the estate productive and competitive, it is also clear that he feels a limited responsibility to the village community. They are totally dependent on a fairmindedness and a generosity that he simply does not possess. By the end of the novel he is entertaining plans to amalgamate his property with that of a local White landowner, and there is no evidence that he has given any thought to the impact this will have on the estate village. Yet Franklin is supported by an environment that accepts his authority and privilege without question. Eloisa, his housekeeper, watches over him jealously in return for the privilege and security vested in her proximity to him. Kamalla, with whom he secretly simulates rape and assault on a regular basis, has only one regret, and that is that no one knows the privilege she feels as the one selected to be his whore. To his overseer Prekash, who boasts more schooling than anyone else in the village, Franklin is the model of appropriate conduct.

The psychic dangers portrayed in the villagers' dependence on Franklin are potentially devastating, and Selvon makes us feel and know this. But this is not a novel of despair. *Those Who Eat the Cascadura* is extraordinarily alive in its description of the lushness and fragility of the cacao estate and its environs and the sympathetic chords that sustain the village as a community. There is a strong sense of the continuance of life as Eloisa, Franklin's old housekeeper, sternly but not unsympathetically, tries to get Sarojini back on track again, with the old formula for bringing a West Indian folk tale to an end: "What happen done and finish with. Mr. Johnson is a *big* white man what living in England, and he was only here on holiday, and the two of you like one another, and now he gone back to England. Crick crack, monkey break my back, wire bend and the story end" (p. 128). A vision of paradise ends here, but all is not lost. The rhythm of life Selvon describes has its restorative undercurrents, however prosaic. As Eloisa directs, "Best make yourself busy, girl, instead of sitting down there like a poor-me-one. The yard want sweeping" (p. 128).

The social and political awareness and the broad range of sympathies that characterize Selvon's treatment of Trinidad's landscape and people are also evident in his treatment of emigrant life in *The Housing Lark* (1965) and in the recently completed trilogy: *The Lonely Londoners* (1956), *Moses Ascending* (1975), and *Moses Migrating* (1983). These novels are an important record of the rigors of emigrant life in Britain that spans some twenty-seven years, a record that testifies to Selvon's own resilience as a Caribbean writer through long years of exile.

Writing from the point of view of the newly arrived emigrant in *The Lonely Londoners*, Selvon reveals that their expectations are high. The emigrant is part of a community that shares a common predicament and a common language. He is sustained by a sense of Caribbean identity as he lays claim to the metropolis in expected fulfillment of his status as a colonial. At the center of *The Lonely Londoners* is the experience of the group, "the boys," as they are referred to repeatedly, though Moses Alloetta emerges as their natural leader by virtue of his experience and superior skills at spinning a yarn or ballad. Survival for the emigrants rests on a sense of shared community, on a sense of style and wit and courage that is defined in a variety of adventures the emigrants share and in the lyric power of the modified Trinidadian dialect which Selvon makes the language of narration in this novel. But the emigrants' expectations of a better life in Britain are ill conceived, and at the end of *The Lonely Londoners* Moses, despite the good times, sees a forlorn shadow of doom hanging over the emigrant community: "As if, on the surface, things don't look so bad, but when you go down a little, you bounce up a kind of misery and pathos and a frightening—what? . . . As if the boys laughing, but they only laughing because they fraid to cry, they only laughing because to think so much about everything would be a big calamity" (1972 ed., p. 126). Lonely and anxious, Moses dreams of writing a best-seller, of becoming a literary giant and escaping the drudgery of the workplace.

The tone of *The Lonely Londoners* is essentially comic in its peception of the ironies of emigrant life in Britain. But in Selvon, laughter expresses the resiliency and resourcefulness of the emigrant who characteristically is able to laugh both at the absurdities in his environment and at himself; it is a necessary feature of his survival. As Selvon explains in an interview given to Peter Nazareth in 1979, "The comedy element has always been there among black people from the Caribbean. It is their means of defence against the sufferings and tribulations that they have to undergo" (pp. 423–24).

In the sequel, *Moses Ascending*, the Caribbean emigrant is transformed by his experience abroad. Moses, the central figure in *The Lonely Londoners*, now owns a dilapidated house in Shepherd's Bush, and this radically alters his perception of himself in relation to Britain and his fellow emigrants. Fictionally his house has a symbolic power similar to V. S. Naipaul's *A House for Mr Biswas*. An interesting association when one considers that Moses, like Naipaul's Kripalsing in *The Mimic Men*, is writing his memoirs. Like Kripalsingh, Moses' language mirrors the emigrant's emotional and cultural investment in English society, the lurking nostalgia for the Caribbean, the instinct for survival, the wit that masks defeat. The obvious differences between the two novels suggest that Selvon's might be read as a satiric commentary on Naipaul's novel.

Unlike *The Lonely Londoners*, in *Moses Ascending* the group has dissolved into a single voice, representative maybe, but the isolated voice of a man on his own and wanting it that way. His comrades of the past have been replaced by tenants, among them, a White Man Friday, illegal Asian immigrants, and unknown to him, a Black Power organization. Moses is not in control for long. The terms of his survival are clearly defined in his struggle to occupy the top floor of his dilapidated house. Struggling for ascendancy amid "leaks and cracks and other symptoms of dilapidation which infested the house" (p. 10) are older emigrants from the Caribbean, a new generation of militant Black Britons, Asian immigrants, and working-class Whites. Survival now rests on a resourcefulness and wit that is fueled by radical racial politics and English working-class culture rather than the sense of adventure and enterprise that characterizes the emigrant community of *The Lonely Londoners*. The tone of laughter is also changed. The "kiff-kiff" laughter of the earlier novel becomes the self-flagellating irony of a man who uses irony to obfuscate reality and limit self-awareness.

In *Moses Migrating*, Selvon returns Moses to the Caribbean landscape. Moses goes reluctantly, afraid of any experience that might alter his status as British citizen. He flirts with the idea of marrying a local beauty and settling down, but he settles for the rogue's role of abandoning her and returning to Britain. Moses projects himself as a purveyor of British culture and values. His transformation is complete. Laughter no longer represents pain or even confusion, just vacancy and at times embarrassment. Moses and his band of carnival tourists are the targets of unrelieved satire in the novel. Selvon's disgust with Moses shows. Meanwhile, his own commitment to the Caribbean remains strong. As he tells Daryl Cumber Dance: "If I have an axe to grind, it is this, that I would always, always show why this thing [Caribbean unification and racial Creolization] isn't working and try to show why it should win. This would be a very wonderful thing if all this mixture of races throughout the Caribbean could learn to have a common identity."

CRITICAL RECEPTION

Since the publication of *A Brighter Sun* in 1952, Selvon has been reviewed favorably as innovative in his use of dialect and among the most entertaining of Caribbean writers. But serious appreciation of Selvon's merits as a writer has been slow in coming, and there is as yet no book-length study of his accomplishments. Among the most useful contributions to an understanding of his work are those by Edward Brathwaite, Kenneth Ramchand, F. Gordon Rohlehr, Michel Fabre, and Peter Nazareth.

Edward Brathwaite, West Indian poet and historian, was among the first to try to define the folk sensibility that distinguishes Selvon's writing. In "Sir Galahad and the Islands" (1975) Brathwaite draws heavily on Selvon to make a statement about the impact of migration on the West Indian folk sensibility. In "The New West Indian Novelists: Part One" (1960), Brathwaite isolates three different and complementary aspects of Selvon's folk sensibility: the East Indian peasants of Trinidad; Selvon's "racy humorous celebration of Trinidad's city-slickers"; and a lyrical soul-searching. Much criticism of Selvon is built on Brathwaite's initial assessment.

Writing on "The Folk in Caribbean Literature" (1972), F. Gordon Rohlehr analyzes the texture of Selvon's fiction in the context of specific folk forms. This essay provides a concrete basis for the often repeated claims that Selvon is a folk poet. Rohlehr writes convincingly that Selvon "bridges the gap between oral and scribal traditions" in the English-speaking Caribbean.

Kenneth Ramchand has also written appreciatively about Selvon's folk sensibility but with a different emphasis in mind. Ramchand is generally careful to describe Selvon's use of dialect as evidence of the writer's considerable sophistication. In his excellent study, "*The Lonely Londoners* as a Literary Work" (1982), Ramchand writes: "The language of *The Lonely Londoners*is not the language of the people or of any one stratum of the society; it is a careful fabrication; a modified dialect which contains and expresses the sensibility of the whole society" (p. 650). An important earlier statement on Selvon's use of dialect appears in Ramchand's *The West Indian Novel and its Background* (1970). His study of *A Brighter Sun* as a peasant novel in *An Introduction to the Study of West Indian Literature* (1976) explores the merits of this novel in relation to Edgar Mittelholzer's *Corentyne Thunder*.

In "Samuel Selvon and the West Indian Literary Renaissance" (1977), Frank Birbalsingh attempts an evaluation of Selvon's work from *A Brighter Sun* to *Moses Ascending*. But Birbalsingh takes his cue from V. S. Naipaul and is inclined to dismiss Selvon's later work as repetitive and uninspired. A more worthwhile general study is Michel Fabre's "Samuel Selvon" (In *West Indian Literature*, 1979). Fabre is particularly interested in how Selvon has molded Caribbean folk traditions into a recognized literary form. He has written two other essays on the subject: "The Queen's Calypso: Linguistic and Narrative Strategies in the Fiction of Samuel Selvon" (1977–78) and "From Trinidad to London: Tone and Language in Samuel Selvon's Novels" (1979).

In "The Clown in the Slave Ship" (1977), Peter Nazareth links Selvon's complexity with his use of humor. He finds Selvon one-dimensional and predictable when he writes without humor. The merits of one Selvon mode as opposed to the other needs to be debated more fully, but this is an excellent point of departure.

HONORS AND AWARDS

Samuel Selvon has received many honors and awards, including two Guggenheim Fellowships (1954 and 1968); a Travelling Scholarship from the Society of Authors, London (1958); a Trinidad Government Refamiliarization Scholarship (1962); and a Trinidad and Tobago Humming Bird Medal for work in Caribbean literature, 1969.

BIBLIOGRAPHY

Works by Samuel Selvon

A Brighter Sun. London: Wingate, 1952; London: Longman, 1971.
An Island Is a World. London: Wingate, 1955.
The Lonely Londoners. London: Wingate, 1956; London: Longman, 1972.
Ways of Sunlight. London: MacGibbon & Kee, 1957; London: Longman, 1973.
Turn Again Tiger. London: MacGibbon & Kee, 1958; London: Longman, 1978; London: Heinemann, 1979.
I Hear Thunder. London: MacGibbon & Kee, 1963.
The Housing Lark. London: MacGibbon & Kee, 1965.
A Drink of Water. London: Nelson, 1968.
The Plains of Caroni. London: MacGibbon & Kee, 1970.
Those Who Eat the Cascadura. London: Davis Poynter, 1972.
Moses Ascending. London: Davis Poynter, 1975.
Moses Migrating. London: Longman, 1983.

Studies of Samuel Selvon

Birbalsingh, Frank. "Samuel Selvon and the West Indian Literary Renaissance." *Ariel: A Review of International English Literature* 8 (July 1977), 5–22.

Brathwaite, Edward. "Jazz and the West Indian Novel." *Bim* 11 (January-June 1967), 275–84; 12 (July-December 1967), 39–51; 12 (January-June 1968), 115–26.

———. "The New West Indian Novelists: Part One." *Bim* 8 (July-December 1960), 208–10.

———. "Roots." *Bim* 10 (July-December 1963), 10–21.

———. "Sir Galahad and the Islands." *Bim* 7 (July-December 1957), 8–16.

Davies, Barrie. "The Sense of Abroad: Aspects of the West Indian Novel in England." *World Literature Written in English* 11 (November 1972), 67–80.

Fabre, Michel. "From Trinidad to London: Tone and Language in Samuel Selvon's Novels." *Literary Half Yearly* 20 (January 1979), 71–80.

———. "Moses and the Queen's English: Dialect and Narrative Voice in Samuel Selvon's London Novels." *World Literature Written in English* 21 (Summer 1982), 385–92.

———. "The Queen's Calypso: Linguistic and Narrative Strategies in the Fiction of Samuel Selvon." *Caribbean Essays and Studies* 3 (1977–78), 69–76.

Macdonald, Bruce F. "Language and Consciousness in Samuel Selvon's *A Brighter Sun*." *English Studies in Canada* 5 (Summer 1979), 202–15.

Nazareth, Peter. "The Clown in the Slave Ship." *Caribbean Quarterly* 23 (June-September 1977), 24–30.

———. Interview with Sam Selvon. *World Literature Written in English* 18 (November 1979), 420–37.

Paquet, Sandra Pouchet. Introduction to *Turn Again Tiger*. London: Heinemann, 1979.

Ramchand, Kenneth. "*The Lonely Londoners* as a Literary Work." *World Literature Written in England* 21 (Autumn 1982), 644–84.

———. "Sam Selvon Talking: A Conversation with Kenneth Ramchand." *Canadian Literature* 95 (Winter 1982), 56–64.

Rohlehr, F. Gordon. "The Folk in Caribbean Literature." *Tapia*2 (December 17, 1972), 7–8, 13–15; 2 (December 24, 1972), 8–9.

See also General Bibliography: Allis, Cudjoe, Gilkes, Hughes, King, Lamming, Moore, and Ramchand (1976, 1979).

LLOYD W. BROWN

A. J. Seymour (1914–)

It has become fashionable in some quarters to characterize Arthur J. Seymour as a ''transitional'' writer (Edward Baugh, *West Indian Poetry 1900–1970: A Study in Decolonisation*, 1971, p. 7). To repeat the standard cliché, all figures are, technically, figures of transition, and in this broad sense there is no real ground of dissatisfaction with the label. But, unfortunately, the tendency has been to apply the label to the Guyanese poet with more than a touch of condescension: Seymour is, allegedly, a member of the ''old'' school of innocuous, colonial poetry in West Indian literature, one whose works share nothing of significance in common with the more ''progressive'' writers of the contemporary Caribbean. However, no one who is really familiar with the Seymour opus over the past forty-seven years ought to take such judgments seriously, though they seem, unfortunately, to be more popular than they deserve. Seymour's early work does reflect the sensibilities of an older, colonial generation whose response to their society was a far cry from the vigorous protests and intense creativity of the post-war generation. But those early works hardly define all of Seymour's output since then. Over succeeding decades he has lent his voice to the themes of post-war nationalism and post-independence self-appraisal which have dominated West Indian literature for the last thirty-five years. In the process the reader may detect significant shifts from an earlier, neo-Victorian derivativeness to an imaginative blending of folk and traditional literary forms, the kind of blending which one has come to expect in the ''progressive'' mainstream of current West Indian poetry.

In short, Seymour is not so much a ''transitional'' poet, in the patronizing sense of the term, as he is a *representative* poet, one whose lengthy career reflects quite accurately the major developments and shifts in the region's literature for nearly half a century. In this sense he is one of very few writers in the West Indies, in any genre, whose work is an important mirror not only of his personal development but of West Indian poetry as a whole. This factor alone makes his work a prerequisite subject for anyone who wishes to grasp the impact of the region's modern history on the evolution of its literature. But since Seymour has never limited his literary activities to the writing of poetry, his contributions to the region's literary history must be weighed in other ways as well—particularly the roles he has played in fostering the literature, as anthologist, critic, and editor during those crucial post-war years when the idea of creating or criticizing West Indian literature was taken seriously only by a handful of believers like himself. And he has managed to do much of this on his own, publishing most of his work at his own expense, in Guyana, while pursuing a career as a local civil servant and while finding additional time for a variety of public appointments. Guyana's durable "man of letters" has carved a significant niche for himself in West Indian literature and therefore deserves special study.

BIOGRAPHY

Arthur James Seymour was born on January 12, 1914, in Guyana. He graduated from high school (Queen's College), and like his father before him joined the civil service in 1933, first as an unpaid volunteer, than as a member of the Bureau of Publicity and Information. As a civil servant his appointments have included the head of Information Services and deputy chairman of the Department of Culture, and for two years (1962–64) he was information officer at the central secretariat of the Caribbean Organisation in Puerto Rico. Between the Puerto Rican appointment and the deputy chairmanship at the Department of Culture he also worked in the local bauxite industry (Demerara Bauxite Company) as community relations officer, then as public relations officer. He has been retired from public service since 1979.

Throughout that career Seymour pursued another career of sorts, as activist, organizer, and leader on a wide variety of community and cultural groups, among them the Boys' Brigade, Tourist Committee, International P.E.N. Club, library committees, Caribbean Conservation Association, and the Guyana National Trust. Given his activist bent it is not surprising that a great deal of this "other" career focused on organizing and directing events or forums related to literature and the other arts. He was the founder and editor of *Kyk-over-al*, one of the leading literary magazines of its time (1945–61) in the English-language Caribbean. This was a period in which local interest in the region's literature was minimal, and given the severely limited readership then, as now, for literature in general, Seymour's publication was one of the rare outlets for young West Indian writers, several of whom have emerged since then as the major voices of the literature. Another Seymour project performed a similar service, the Miniature Poets series

(1951–53). The poetry pamphlet series featured, among others, Wilson Harris, Martin Carter, Ellsworth McG. Keane, Harold Telemaque, Philip Sherlock, Wordsworth McAndrew, and Frank Collymore. Two later projects went beyond literature: he was involved, as literary coordinator, with the first Caribbean Festival of the Arts, held in Guyana in 1972; and for more than a year he edited the *Bulletin* of the Institute of Creative Arts (1977–78). Seymour's literary energies have often taken him abroad, on lectureships and poetry readings in other Caribbean territories, in Brazil, the United States, and West Germany.

MAJOR WORKS AND THEMES

Like so many of the poetry pamphlets to follow during the next forty-odd years, Seymour's earliest collections of poetry are representative of their times. Both *Verse* and *Coronation Ode*, published in 1937, reflect the pre-nationalist temper, or colonial quiescence, which was to be shaken in many quarters by the burgeoning nationalism of the 1940s. As the title of *Coronation Ode* suggests, young Seymour's themes are predicated on a certain loyalty to British Empire and British sovereign, and his sense of poetic form is rooted in the conventions of the European literary classics. In turn, the first major collections, both published in the 1940s, articulate the contemporary urgency of a West Indian identity—*Over Guiana Clouds* (1944) and *The Guiana Book* (1948).

The new note in Seymour's poetry is linked with a theme which has become fairly standard in many writers from Guyana. On the one hand, language and a common colonial experience encourage and intensify a sense of close identity with the West Indian islanders to the north. But on the other hand, this shared West Indian heritage and identity is articulated through the *continental*, rather than the island, landscape. The effect is persuasively ambiguous, both emphasizing the Guyanese integration with the West Indian experience and delineating the distinctive, continental setting of Guyanese history and aspirations. On the whole Seymour's landscape painting is moving away from the insipidly ornamental word pictures which so many earlier authors (and minor contemporaries) borrowed in their own derivative way from the most banal elements of English Romantic verse. As in the case of his nationalist contemporaries in both prose and poetry, Seymour's nationalist landscape is effectively symbolic at its best; the continental dimensions of his South American setting encourage a sense of limitless possibilities for Guyanese mainlander and West Indian islander alike; but at the same time the landscape bears the signs of limitations and ugliness, the unlovely heritage of the colonial past.

The poem "Carrion Crow" in *Over Guiana Clouds* is a striking example of this ambiguity. Ethereally beautiful in flight, the vulture is a revolting and awkward creature close up, on the ground. It is a symbol of striking paradoxes that are inherent in Caribbean history with roots of slavery and colonialism counterbalanced by a persistent, cultural vitality. The bird's appearance and flight are therefore symbols of both promise and limitation, death and creativity, ugliness and beauty. While the carrion crow embodies these cultural and historical paradoxes, the diversity of the landscape itself reflects the social mosaic of Seymour's culture. Hence the various sources of West Indian ethnic groups and the diverse historical are all merging into a harmonious order in "Patterns."

This perception of history as harmonious creation continues in *The Guiana Book*, where it is also integrated with the poet's own self-awareness as artist. That is, the perceived creativity in West Indian history as a whole is being duplicated on a microcosmic level by the poet's own artistic design. In reading poems like "There Runs a Dream" and "Kyk-over-al, " one is struck by a carefully, self-consciously contrived sense of *poetic* design which both describes and symbolizes the poet's subject (Caribbean history) as a harmonious pattern of cultural survival and vitality which has been, paradoxically, derived from the destructive heritage of the past. Here, and in "Tomorrow Belongs to the People," the transforming imagination of the poet is analogous to the culture's collective energies. Indeed, it is more than an analogy, it is a microcosm.

The effectively self-conscious emphasis on the poet's imagination as microcosm is even more pointed when Seymour's immediate subject is West Indian folklore and folk art, for then the poet integrates his own themes and form with the constructs of folk art—themselves the living expression of the historical heritage which the poet celebrates or deplores. In "Slaves," for example, the folk art forms are the religious songs that are the heritage of Black slavery, songs in which the "humming" of slaves—their "heart-music"—become integral parts of Seymour's own language, retaining, in the process, their peculiar blend of pathos and resilient strength. In "Drums" the sound and rhythm of the instrument is both an insistent echo of a historical continuum (Africa to the Caribbean present) and the fundamental rhythm of a poem which insists on the need to grasp and accept that historical continuum in its entirety without colonial or racial self-hatred. By a similar token the rhythm of dancers in "West Indian Dance" and the wild shadows of the dancers themselves all become poetic images with which Seymour describes the grotesque and destructive history from which these beautifully proportioned and vital folk art forms evolved. This is a technique and this is a theme which persist through much of Seymour's later poetry. In *Black Song* (1971), for example, steelband players who create their instruments and their music from metal junk ("Steel Band") are, in their own way, reenacting that perpetually creative principle which Seymour attributes to the area's cultural history.

As a work like "Steel Band" indicates, much of the achievement of the 1940s and 1950s continues into the poems of the 1970s—even after allowance is made for the overall unevenness of the corpus as a whole. Since the early 1970s the familiar themes of cultural creativity have been integrated with the retrospectiveness, and introspectiveness, of the older man. *Song to Man* (1973) continues to celebrate history as renewal and re-creation. The vigorous promise which the poet marks in his contemporary West Indies is both the harbinger of a hoped-for future and a reminder of a historical vigor. But there is a more insistently personal note here, one seldom heard in earlier volumes. "One Name" chronicles the mature lover's memories in a manner that is pointedly analogous to recollections of the group's historical experience. The intense self-scrutiny which has marked so much of post-independence West Indian literature is present here, bringing to Seymour's work the subdued, even somber mood which one often finds in Seymour's contemporaries.

Given the widespread disillusionment with the failed promises of nationhood and with a demoralizing sense of stasis, one expects to find this kind of mood in much of the contemporary literature. The fact that Seymour apparently shares it is yet another indication of the representative nature of his poetry from one generation to another. Somberness in Seymour's later poetry is often linked with the older man's preoccupation with aging and death. In one sense the poems of *Italic* (1974) are easily perceived in the context of the earlier, ebullient works on history as achievement and creativity: "Italic," "Handshake," and "Images Before Easter" are all based on the fundamental cycle of life-death-life of the earlier poems. But in the collection as a whole it is death or deterioration which seems to dominate the atmosphere of the cyclical theme.

"Images Before Easter," one of the best of Seymour's later works, is a fine example of the introspective, highly personal context within which all of this unfolds—a private introspectiveness which is comparable with the much more celebrated "confessional" poetry of Derek Walcott, whose early work once found an outlet in Seymour's *Kyk-over-al*. As in Walcott, Seymour's West Indian simultaneously explores body, self, and culture in multiple levels of self-analysis. The longest journey, the poet muses, is both private ("into one's self") and allegorical, a metaphor of the West Indian's cultural self-exploration. The connection which Seymour exposes here is more than rhetorical, for the act of defining and discovering one's deepest self is inevitably a process of cultural discoveries. And given the diverse nature of the West Indian's cultural origins, these discoveries are likely to be not only local, or regional, in terms of Caribbean culture per se, but also global: "Each island and each continent / Has its ground in my being / Everything passes into itself through me" (*Italic*, pp. 15–16). Altogether, the poem is a remarkably economical and compact statement of the kind of complex insight which, in an *occasional* work like this, places Seymour on the same level with the *consistently* superior work of Derek Walcott: one plunges deeper into one's private self to affirm complicated relationships with a regional culture (and with the world outside which has contributed to that culture from all the continents); private self-exploration is simultaneously cultural identification and universal affirmation. The private Self becomes the microcosm of All. The Whole confirms the peculiarities of the individual persona and the specifics of local culture.

CRITICAL RECEPTION

Critical reception of Seymour's poetry has trended to be sparse. Edward Baugh offers some detailed but relatively brief comments in *West Indian Poetry 1900–*

1970 (1971). But the critic simply dismisses the poetry as "transitional" and old-fashioned. The study predates some of Seymour's more ambitious work in the 1970s but fails to discover those strengths which are evident in the earlier volumes like *Over Guiana Clouds* or *The Guiana Book*. Donald E. Herdeck's *Caribbean Writers: A Bio-Bibliographical-Critical Encyclopedia* (1979) is even less useful in this regard. Baugh does note Seymour's invaluable contributions to the literature, as editor. Lloyd Brown, in *West Indian Poetry* (1978), offers a relatively detailed outline of Seymour's major themes, with particular emphasis on Seymour's contributions to the tradition of cultural nationalism in modern West Indian poetry.

Also of interest is the 110-page bibliography of Seymour's works, prepared by the National Library of Guyana in 1974 in honor of his sixtieth birthday. It includes translations of his works and anthologies in which his poetry appears.

HONORS AND AWARDS

Seymour was awarded the Golden Arrow of Achievement, by the government of Guyana for services to literature in 1970.

BIBLIOGRAPHY

Works by A. J. Seymour

Autobiography

Growing up in Guyana. Georgetown: Author, 1976.
Pilgrim Memories. Georgetown: Author, 1978.
Thirty Years a Civil Servant. Georgetown: Author, 1982.

Anthologies

Kyk Anthology of West Indian Poetry. Georgetown: Author, 1952.
Kyk Anthology of Guianese Poetry. Georgetown: Author, 1954.
Themes of Song. Georgetown: Author, 1961.
My Lovely Native Land (with Elma Seymour). Port of Spain: Longman Caribbean, 1971.
New Writing in the Caribbean. Georgetown: Caribbean Festival of the Arts, 1972.
Independence Ten: Guyanese Writing, 1966–1976. Georgetown: Author, 1978.
A Treasury of Guyanese Poetry. Georgetown: Author, 1980.

Literary Criticism

A Survey of West Indian Literature. Georgetown: Author, 1950.
Caribbean Literature. Georgetown: Author, 1951.
Edgar Mittelholzer: The Man and His Work. Georgetown: National History and Arts Council, 1968.
Introduction to Guyanese Writing. Georgetown: Author, 1971.
The Making of Guyanese Literature. Georgetown: Author, 1980.
Studies in West Indian Poetry. Georgetown: Author, 1981.

Poetry

Coronation Ode. Georgetown: Author, 1937.
Verse. Georgetown: Chronicle, 1937.
More Poems. Georgetown: Author, 1940.
Over Guiana Clouds. Georgetown: Standard, 1944.
Sun's in My Blood. Georgetown: Standard, 1945.
Six Songs. Georgetown: Author, 1946.
The Guiana Book. Georgetown: Author, 1948.
We Do Not Presume. Georgetown: Author, 1948.
Leaves from the Tree. Georgetown: Master Printer, 1951.
Water and Blood. Georgetown: Author, 1952.
Ten Poems. Georgetown: Argosy, 1953.
Three Voluntaries. Georgetown: Author, 1953.
Selected Poems. Georgetown: Author, 1965.
Monologue. Georgetown: Author, 1968.
Patterns. Georgetown: Author, 1970.
Black Song. Georgetown: Author, 1971.
I Anancy. Georgetown: Author, 1971.
Passport. Georgetown: Author, 1972.
Song to Man. Georgetown: Author, 1973.
A Bethlehem Alleluia. Georgetown: Author, 1974.
Italic. Georgetown: Author, 1974.
Love Song. Georgetown: Author, 1975.
Mirror. Georgetown: Author, 1975.
Religious Poems. Georgetown: Author, 1980.

Studies of A. J. Seymour

Brown, Lloyd W. "The Guyanese Voice in West Indian Poetry: A Review of Arthur J. Seymour." *World Literature Written in English* 15 (April 1976), 246–52.

Dolphin, Celeste. "The Poetry of A. J. Seymour." *New World (Fortnightly)* 1 (April 1965), 31–39.

McLeod, A. L. "Tradition and Transition: A. J. Seymour and the Poetry of Guyana." *ACLALSB* 6 (November 1982), 42–54.

See also General Bibliography: Allis, Baugh (1971), Brown, Herdeck, Hughes, and McDowell.

DARYL CUMBER DANCE

Michael Thelwell (1939–)

BIOGRAPHY

Michael Thelwell was born into a well-known Jamaican family on July 24, 1939. His father, the late Morris Thelwell, was a member of the House of Representatives during the 1940s; his mother, Vic Thelwell, is a retired secretary of the All-Island Jamaica Cane Farmers Association; and his brother Richard was permanent secretary in the Ministry of Mining and Natural Resources during the Manley administration. Thelwell's father died when the children were quite young, and their mother supported them as an officeworker. Thelwell describes their economic and social status thusly: ''[After my father's death] we were in point of fact quite poor in terms of what Mr. Nixon called his cash flow, but the fact is because it was a class based society . . . we had a certain *position* in what I suppose one might term the Jamaican middle-class—and we had a certain amount of credit and by scrimping along, we lived in genteel poverty'' (interview with Daryl Cumber Dance, Amherst, Massachusetts, December 9, 1979; later quotations from Thelwell are from this source).

As a member of the Kingston middle class, Thelwell was not much exposed in his home to the folklore that came to be one of his major interests and an important element in his writing. However, his family had rural roots, ''and in the country [among] the peasants the folklore is a kind of, a medium of communication and entertainment and exchange. And that's when I really learned a lot about duppy stories and Anancy stories, and riddles and that kind of stuff.'' Even in Kingston, though his family had nothing to do with Pocomania churches, barnyards, or the like, "I found that fascinating and used to hang around those neighborhoods, those poor neighborhoods where these things took place just to observe them, [including] the Rastas. I had a lot of friends among what the Jamaican middle class would refer to as the poorer class."

After attending small private preparatory schools, Thelwell studied at Jamaica College. He later completed a B.A. in English literature at Howard University in 1964, and an M.F.A. at the University of Massachusetts, Amherst, in 1969.

While at Howard, Thelwell became involved in the Civil Rights movement and served as director of the Washington office of the Student Nonviolent Coordinating Committee (SNCC) from 1963 to 1964, and as director of the Washington office of the Mississippi Freedom Democratic Party from 1964 to 1965. Several of his short stories focus on his experiences demonstrating in Washington, D.C., and throughout the South during this period, which he describes as "one of the more significant experiences of my life—on a number of levels. . . . [For one thing] the experiences in the South led me to a much clearer view and perception of the realities of the society which produced me; and the next thing that was significant—I think I have probably written as much about the American South as I have about Jamaica."

From 1969 to 1975, Thelwell chaired the W. E. B. Du Bois Department of Afro-American Studies at the University of Massachusetts, Amherst. He continues in that department as associate professor of literature.

MAJOR WORKS AND THEMES

Before the appearance of his well-received novel, *The Harder They Come* (1980), Thelwell's short stories focused on the Civil Rights movement in America and portrayed the fear and agony, the pain and suffering, the humiliation and pride, the humor and ludicrousness of people caught up in situations involving efforts to integrate restrooms, organize voter registrations, and the like.

Those early works reinforce his rather unconventional vision of his role as a writer. He feels no compulsion to produce works; he does not regard writing as a means of personal self-expression: "As far as I'm concerned writing by Black writers has to be historically and culturally very purposeful and very pointed. [The role of] the Black writer at this time . . . is largely to reclaim and define our culture for ourselves. . . . All my fiction attempts in certain ways—with perhaps not as much success as I'd like—to use the cultural resources, the cultural traditions, the linguistic traditions . . . and to selectively mine these resources, which [are] the legacy of the Black writer, and weld them into literary forms." Given his philosophy, when Grove Press approached him and asked him about writing a novel based on the Perry Henzell and Trevor Rhone film *The Harder They Come* (the first feature film made in Jamaica), Thelwell was pleased for the opportunity to write a work which offered an opportunity to make a relevant political statement while also giving a meaningful introduction to Jamaican life and culture: "I wanted the book not to be a book about Jamaica; I wanted it to be a Jamaican book, a product and an artifact of the culture itself."

Thelwell is eminently successful in achieving his goal. *The Harder They Come* is as Jamaican as saltfish and ackee. Every aspect of the Jamaican landscape, people, and culture is forcefully and dramatically represented in this novel. There are moving pictures of the magnificent Jamaican countryside (the lush mountainsides, the clear cool waters with their coral reefs, etc.); the squalid, brutal Kingston slums (the bustling marketplaces), the poverty-striken and violent dungle, the scheming street urchins, the Sufferers, the prisons, the corrupt policemen, etc.); as well as the retreats of the wealthy (the rich Jamaicans hiding in their castle-like enclaves protected by guard dogs and high fences, and the American tourists frolicking on beaches and boogying at clubs which exclude the natives). There are captivating accounts of folk practices and rituals, many of them, like the meticulously reproduced Nine Night celebration, derived from Africa. The sounds and rhythms of Jamaica are apparent throughout the novel. The author's superb rendering of Jamaican dialect and his brilliant reproduction of the folk speech invite comparison with masters such as Samuel Selvon and Vic Reid.

The novel recounts the adventures of Rhygin, a Jamaican gunman whose 1948 exploits have become legendary. Thelwell provides a detailed account of Rhygin's childhood in the Jamaican countryside, where he grows up in a traditional and stable community that reinforces a sense of history, place, culture. There he is taught by his grandmother and others in the community, "Bwai—you a somebody. You come from some whe' . . . from decent people dem. . . . And you raise up decent, to know what right an' to have manners" (p. 110). The idyllic scenes of country life so memorably portrayed at the beginning of the novel are already beginning to be disturbed by the ominous signs of the encroaching disruptive elements of the city, which even then we sense will one day destroy, not only Rhygin, who is psychologically headed for the city from the moment we meet him, but also the land and the people who remain behind. As anticipated, at his first opportunity, like many before him, Rhygin migrates to the city, a place characterized by crime, violence, poverty, and dislocation. The forewarning that this move will inevitably lead to Rhygin's destruction is inescapable. A neighbor had earlier warned him (and us), "Town people dem *different*, different bad" (p. 110); and Thelwell has provided a memorable parable of a frightened parakeet who in his panic darts from his safe hiding place where a flock of birds huddled together. The bird realizes his error and attempts to return to his "community," but it is too late, and he is snatched away by a menacing hawk. Ivan's grandmother reinforces the lesson of the event: "You think is hawk kill that parrot? . . . We see ol' hawk *ketch* 'im. But is *'fraid kill* 'im. If 'im did stay ina the guava trees wid the rest of 'im generation dem, the hawk never coulda catch 'im" (p. 42).

When Ivan ventures into Kingston, a variety of hawks set upon him, beginning with street urchins who rob him, malicious churchmen who cruely abuse him, corrupt law officials who visit all manner of injustice upon him, businessmen who appropriate his music, and so on and on. No wonder then that having lost faith in the church, the family, the free enterprise system, the justice system, and most of mankind, he is driven to a life of crime. His involvement in the ganga trade finally leads him to a shootout with policemen, one which ends in his death—*and* his immortalization. His bravado is captured in songs and children's games. The novel closes as one boy in Trench Town gulley faces a posse:

> "Bram, Bram, Bram!" He leapt from cover, guns blazing.
>
> The posse returned fire. "You dead!" the sheriff shouted. "Cho man, you dead!"
>
> "Me Ah Rhygin!" the boy shouted back. "Me can' dead!"
>
> He again swept the posse with withering fire before dancing back under cover. His clear piping voice sang out tauntingly, "Rhygin was here but 'im jus' disappear." (pp. 391–92)

It is not simply Rhygin (or even individuals) who is destroyed by the city, with its industrialization, capitalism, and assorted corrupting American influences (for Thelwell makes the culpability of all of these elements clear), but the culture and the land itself. Industrial waste is a blight destroying the once beautiful land. When Ivan returns some years after his migration to his rural paradise, he thinks he is hallucinating when he notes "a discordant, unnatural presence, stark against the green hillsides," and he inquires about what it is: " 'Progress,' the man said, not looking at him. 'Industrial waste—from de bauxite plant' " (p. 313). When he returns to the beautiful beaches where he had frolicked as a child, they are the exclusive domain of White American tourists, who entertain themselves by demeaning once proud islanders. Ivan sees one of his childhood heroes grinning ingratiatingly and posing for a tourist couple:

> He nodded vigorously and his white teeth flashed in the sunlight. Then, still grinning, he retreated to the end of the raft, flexed his muscles, and struck a pose. It seemed practiced. His powerful muscles bunched and stood out but the posture was distorted, one of servility, the power leashed, controlled, displayed, and his face was a mask of ingratiating, slightly stupid amiability.
>
> "Beautiful," the woman said, laughing, and aiming her camera. . . .
>
> So the change was not in the river. What had happe[ne]d to the solitary, reserved giant they had called River King, and of what lineage and family was the grinning buffoon who had his place? (p. 319)

CRITICAL RECEPTION

The early reviews of *The Harder They Come*, which was widely reviewed in the United States, England, and the Caribbean, were nothing short of raves. Reviewers applauded the book's "realism," "authenticity," and "fascination." They labeled it "compelling reading," "universal," "a classic," even "baad." Most reviewers commented on the authenticity and the richness of the langauge, the compelling descriptions of the Jamaican landscape, and the extensive use of

Jamaican folklore. Even then-Prime Minister Michael Manley issued a release from Jamaica House applauding the "authenticity and . . . realism that make it compelling reading" (quoted in "Novel on 'Rhygin,' " *Sunday Gleaner*, May 21, 1980, p. 3). Gerian Steve Moore acclaimed it "probably the most important novel about the Caribbean since the publication of George Lamming's *In the Castle of My Skin* ("The *Black Scholar* Book Reviews," 1980, p. 91).

A few critics attacked Thelwell for his romanticization of and sentimentality about certain aspects of Jamaican life. Lloyd W. Brown acknowledged the appeal of Thelwell's portrait of rural Jamaica and his focus on the cultural pride of his villagers but suggested that Thelwell was guilty of oversentimentalizing rural Jamaica. Thelwell's greatest failure, Brown suggested, was his evasion of some of the crucial critical questions regarding Jamaica's urban problems and his too facile implication that the Jamaican elite are largely responsible for those problems. Even worse, Brown continued, was Thelwell's glorification of criminal brutality and sexual prowess: "The Caribbean writer or radical intellectual who confuses this type of power with 'greatness' or revolutionary action is simply replaying the Caribbean man's ancient ritual of impotence. Rather than challenging the status quo, he is merely pandering to it" ("*The Harder They Come*: Beyond the Reel Thing," 1981, p. 185).

HONORS AND AWARDS

Michael Thelwell's short stories "Direct Action" and "Community of Victims" received honorable mention in the *Story Magazine* Short Story Contests in 1963 and 1964, and his "The Organizer" received first prize in that contest in 1967. Thelwell received the National Foundation on the Arts and the Humanities award for the essay "Notes from the Delta" in 1968. He was a Fellow of the Society for the Humanities at Cornell University in 1969, and he was the recipient of a 1969–70 award from the Rockefeller Foundation.

BIBLIOGRAPHY

Works by Michael Thelwell

The Harder They Come. New York: Grove Press, 1980.

Studies of Michael Thelwell

Brown, Lloyd D. "*The Harder They Come*: Beyond the Reel Thing." *Freedomways* 21 (Third Quarter 1981), 180–85.

Dahlin, Robert. "Michael Thelwell" (interview). *Publishers Weekly* 217 (April 4, 1980), 6–7.

Moore, Gerian Steve. "The *Black Scholar* Book Reviews." *Black Scholar* 4 (January–February 1980), 91–92.

EDWARD BAUGH

Derek Walcott (1930–)

BIOGRAPHY

Derek Alton Walcott was born in Castries, St. Lucia, on January 23, 1930. His sense of vocation as poet was in his own opinion fostered by a feeling of having been destined to complete the work of his father, Warwick Walcott, who died in his thirty-fifth year, when his son was one year old, and who had practiced poetry, drawing, and watercolor painting in a small way as an avocation. Derek Walcott is himself an accomplished painter. He owes his sense of inherited artistic talent not only to his father but also to his mother, Alix, a former schoolteacher, who, in his boyhood, was an active member of a small, middle-class cultural group well known for its amateur theatricals. His twin brother, Roderick, is also a distinguished playwright.

Walcott's genius showed itself early and caused him to be regarded as something of a prodigy by his schoolmates at St. Mary's College, a high school for boys in Castries. His first published poem appeared in *The Voice of St Lucia* when he was fourteen. At eighteen, and with the financial help of his mother, he published his first volume, *Twenty-Five Poems* (1948). In the following year (1949) a long poem, *Epitaph for the Young*, appeared, and in 1950 the St Lucia Arts Guild, which he had helped to found, produced his important first play, *Henri Christophe*.

The mentor who fostered more than any other the young Walcott's artistic gifts was Harold (Harry) Simmons (1914–66), a family friend. Simmons, a painter and folklorist, not only gave the youth painting and drawing lessons but also gave him access to his library of poetry and art books as well as to his collection of classical records. Simmons combined a sophisticated, wide-ranging artistic curiosity with a passionate, pioneering interest in the folkways of his native land. In his own combination of allegiances to island and to world, Walcott has been true to the spirit of his master.

In love with St. Lucia though he was, the young Walcott, on the threshold of maturity, had to answer the call of wider horizons. At just the right moment of his career, the British awarded him a Colonial Development and Welfare Scholarship to the University College of the West Indies in Jamaica. He enrolled in 1950 and was graduated three years later with a B.A. in English, French, and Latin. He stayed on for another year as a graduate student in education. In 1952 he had published another small collection, *Poems*, at his own expense, and early in 1954 the student drama society presented *Henri Christophe*, designed and directed by Walcott himself.

After leaving university, he worked variously for the next three years, 1954–57, as teacher (The Grenada Boys' School, St. Mary's College, and Jamaica College) and feature writer and literary critic for *Public Opinion*, a Jamaican weekly. In 1959 he settled in Trinidad, which he was to make his home for the next twenty-two years, and soon founded the Little Carib Theatre Workshop, which later became the Trinidad Theatre Workshop. This has been one of the great works of his life. The excellent company of actors which he forged, in difficult circumstance, became a natural extension and vehicle for his talents as playwright and director. Unfortunately, this collaboration came to an end in 1976, when he broke with the Workshop.

The last two major plays of his which the Workshop performed under his direction were the musicals *The Joker of Seville* and *O Babylon!* The music for both was composed by the American Galt MacDermot, who had done the music for the Broadway hit *Hair*. Walcott's friendship and collaboration with MacDermot is one facet of his increasing involvement with the United States in recent years. In the late 1970s he began to do teaching stints at Yale and Columbia Universities. From before that time he had made creatively rewarding friendships with some notable American poets, including Robert Lowell. Latterly, one of his closest friends has been the brilliant Russian poet exiled in America, Joseph Brodsky. Since 1981, Walcott has been teaching creative writing at Boston University. But he returns to the Caribbean at every opportunity, to produce his plays and to refresh his creative roots.

MAJOR WORKS AND THEMES

Plays

Walcott attained his majority as a dramatist with *Dream on Monkey Mountain* and *Ti-Jean and His Brothers* (*Dream on Monkey Mountain and Other Plays*, 1970). *Henri Christophe* (1950), *The Sea at Dauphin*, and *Malcochon* (*Dream *on Monkey Mountain and Other Plays*) had been significant steps leading to this peak. *Henri Christophe*, while still an apprentice piece of a stilted, borrowed grandeur, marked the beginning of Walcott's dramatic quest for a Caribbean hero figure. He tells us that he was attracted to this story from the Haitian Revolution, because "they seemed to him then, those slave-kings, Dessalines and Christophe, men who had structured their own despair. Their tragic bulk was massive as a citadel at twilight. They were our only noble ruins" (*Dream on Monkey Mountain and Other Plays*, p. 12).

With *The Sea at Dauphin* (first produced in 1954) and *Malcochon, or Six in the Rain* (first prodcued in 1959), Walcott abandoned the obviously "heroic," historical protagonist for a more original kind of hero figure, one which would more naturally allow him scope for exploring West Indian society and predicament as well as for exploiting the imaginative possibilities of his native landscape and forging a West Indian dramatic idiom. The protagonists of these plays, fisherman (*Dauphin*) and woodcutter (*Malcochon*), are both eloquently embittered advocates for the dispossessed and the socially outcast against the power of state, church, and law.

Dauphin and *Malcochon* were one act plays. In the full-length *Ti-Jean* and *Dream*, the movement begun in the shorter works was brought to fulfilment. Ti-Jean, the poor peasant boy, and Makak, the degraded, self-despising charcoal burner from Monkey Mountain, develop the image of the folk hero not only by the degree to which their portrayals subsume a large sweep of Black and West Indian history but also in the fact that each in his own way effects a revolution in his circumstances, thereby ensuring his stature as communal exemplar.

Ti-Jean is based on a skillful combination of St. Lucian folk tale and a St. Lucian form of folk theater of the streets. It tells the story of the three sons of a poor, widowed peasant woman, who take up, each in turn, a challenge issued by the Devil. Whoever succeeds against the Devil will get his heart's desire; whoever fails will be devoured. This fable about man's never-ending struggle with evil becomes a statement about the history of the Black man of the Diaspora. The Devil is also Papa Bois, the Old Man of the Woods in Caribbean folklore, and the White Planter, on whose estate generations of Blacks have slaved and been dehumanized. The youngest son, Ti-Jean, succeeds through humility, love, and "manwit." In his moment of triumph, achieved on the brink of despair, he learns "what a man is" (p. 162).

Makak, too, has to earn painfully his true manhood, a creative and un-self-conscious sense of self. In order to do this he has to redeem the Black colonial psychosis. In his purgatorial dream, he overcomes not only the temptation to revenge but also the "rage for whiteness that does drive niggers mad" (p. 228). He finds psychic wholeness and becomes, like Ti-Jean, a light for his people.

Both *Ti-Jean* and *Dream* made orginal and theatrically exciting use of West Indian music. In *The Joker of Seville* (first performed in 1974), *O Babylon!* (first performed in 1976), and *Marie LaVeau* (first performed in 1979) Walcott pursued the musical form, but with an increasing penchant toward the conventional format of the Broadway musical. *Joker* (in *The Joker of Seville and O Babylon!*, 1978) is based on Tirso de Molina's *El Burlador de Sevilla* and Roy Campbell's English translation of it, *The Trickster of Seville*. Tirso's story of the amatory adventures of Don Juan seemed to Walcott to lend itself easily to cultural adaptation: "The wit, panache, the swift or boisterous elan of [Tirso's] period, and of the people in his play, are as alive to me as the flair and flourishes of Trinidadian music and its public character" (*The Joker of Seville and O Babylon!*, pp. 3–4).

But from behind the mask of the bacchanal, Walcott shoots satirical barbs against the hypocrisy and cruelty of conventional morality and attitudes toward sexuality. *Babylon* also challenges institutionalized authority, this time in the form of an exploitative capitalism. The action centers in social conflict, between the "sufferers" (Rastafarians) of the Kingston ghetto and a mafia-type alliance between a corrupt man-of-the-people, the Reverend Deacon Doxy, and "foreign investors / called the New Zion Construction Company" (p. 174), for whom he is the necessary lackey and go-between. It is a conflict between Jah Rastafari and Babylon (the police, big business, middle-class prejudice against the poor). It is the neocolonial, post-independence version of the old story of Black dispossession.

In *Remembrance* (first performed in 1977) and *Pantomime*(first performed in 1978), Walcott eschewed the musical form and also returned to exploring the cultural and psychological aspects of the West Indian colonial experience. In this latter regard, Albert Perez Jordan and Jackson Phillip, the Black protagonists of *Remembrance* and *Pantomime*, respectively, are "progressions" on Makak and Ti-Jean.

Jordon is a retired primary school teacher of the old school, one who had instilled into his students respect for the British Empire and a love of English literature. He now finds himself living, sadly, beyond his time, scandalized by the impatient, revolutionary spirit of a new generation which would seem to be sweeping aside all of the past and the values which had formed him. His dilemma is highlighted by the seemingly senseless death of his son in the "February revolution," the Trinidadian Black Power uprising of 1970. Walcott depicts Jordan's inner uncertainties and contradictions with a complex blend of sympathy and criticism. The portrayal is enhanced by an equally subtle and strong depiction of Jordan's wife, the long-suffering but outspoken Mabel. She is the fullest, most sensitively and unsentimentally realized female character in Walcott's drama to date.

The only two characters in *Pantomine* are male: Harry Trewe, an Englishman and sometime actor on the English music hall stage; and Jackson Phillip, a Trinidadian waiter and sometime calypsonian. Their thespian identities make them fit agents for an examination of the themes of identity, role playing, and the shifting ground between appearance and reality. The setting is Trewe's small hotel in Tobago, Robinson Crusoe's island according to legend. It is the off-season, and the hotel is closed. Jackson has been kept on, to wait on Trewe and, doubling as handyman, to make what little repairs are necessary. Here then, in this claustrophobic, isolated setting, is the prototypical Crusoe–Friday situation.

The action is motivated by a comic reversal of the Crusoe–Friday roles. The serious purpose of this reversal involves an exposure of the cultural and racial arrogance that supported the adventures of the colonizer. The relationship between Trewe and Jackson teeters on the edge of violent collapse, but they eventually win through, to the point where they can deal with each other frankly and with mutual respect, as "man to man," rather than as Prospero to Caliban, White to Black, master to servant.

MAJOR WORKS AND THEMES

Poetry

In a Green Night: Poems 1948–1960 (1962) confirmed the promise of Walcott's earlier volumes of verse, and its variety of themes spanned many of the concerns that were to recur in his subsequent work—death, love, transience, the loss of religious faith, the commitment to the Word of Art, his love of the islands, his deep sense of place, the grim legacies of West Indian history, his concern for "the black, the despairing, the poor" (p. 33), the violence of man. But, in spite of the accomplished technique and ringing eloquence, the collection as a whole remains more promise than fulfilment. The truly adult poet is, however, already making his presence felt, in the extent, for example, to which "A Careful Passion," which records the end of a dangerous love affair, differs from the other love poems in the book, which, for all their bittersweet eloquence, remain essentially at the level of the decorative-nostalgic.

The development which took place between *In a Green Night* and *The Castaway and Other Poems* (1965) can be illustrated by reference to the treatment of landscape in the two collections. In the first, landscape is predominately benign and pastoral, marking the poet's simple identification with a loved place. The second collection modifies and complicates the paradisal vision by an unflinching acknowledgment of the inhospitable and problematic aspects of Caribbean landscape and climate, these in turn providing telling metaphors for a bleak, unromantic scrutiny of self and society.

The figure of Robinson Crusoe provides a unifying persona, an image which accommodates a variety of related themes having to do with alienation and the need for relationship and community, desolation and emptiness on the one hand, and the challenge to create, to fill the void, on the other hand. For example, the West Indies is seen, like Crusoe, as shipwrecked and lost but not without possibilities both metamorphic and Edenic.

Scrutiny of the harsh truths of separations and deprivations of one kind or another continues in *The Gulf and Other Poems* (1969), and the history of violence that has attended some of these rifts becomes an increasingly central concern. The title poem takes a bird's-eye view, from a jet flying over the Gulf states, of America and its racial problem and the fact that man never seems to learn from the violent lessons of history. It issues a warning: "The Gulf, your gulf, is daily widening" (p. 29).

In his next book of poetry, *Another Life* (1973), Walcott looks back across the gulf of years in an attempt to "fix" and define, as much as to celebrate the other, lost life of his childhood and youth in St. Lucia. At the same time, he is concerned to show how the man he is grew out of the youth he was. The autobiographical instinct of his poetry is here given its head. A major impulse is to see the story of his life as reflecting the history of the West Indies, so the poem's more public themes include the clash of cultures in the making of the region, the search for a liberating idea of history, and the fatal neglect of the artist by a philistine society. The poem is also a speculation on the nature of memory and the problematic relationship between the actual and the ideal.

Sea Grapes (1976) is a collection of lyrics which reflect the arc of ideas that the narrative of *Another Life* had traced. There is a movement from the disillusioned view of a brash, tawdry, tourist-oriented Caribbean to a reconnection with stregthening roots, the virtues of a "small-islander's simplicities" and "life not lost to the American dream" (p. 10); from the anger and bitterness, the invective of the explicitly political poems like "The Lost Federation" and "Parades, Parades" to the essentially religious affirmation of reverence for life and of the capacity to endure in poems like "The Harvest," "Earth," and "To Return to the Trees."

Some of the emotional resonance of the affirmation in *Sea Grapes* comes from the poet-persona's intimations of age, his ability to be happy "that fine sprigs of white are springing from [his] beard" (p. 92). The aging hero, or the man of action whose life is mostly behind him, is a dominant figure in *The Star-Apple Kingdom* (1979). These male protagonists all exemplify the notion of the hero—whether poet, politician, Hindu holy man, or adventurer—as being inevitably lonely. The volume features two long poems, "The Schooner *Flight*" and "The Star-Apple Kingdom," each of which takes a critical look at the socio-political situation of the post-colonial West Indies against the background of the region's colonial history. The view is cynical, bleak, despairing, but set over against these factors are the protagonists' capacity for concern, perseverance, and the courage of their ideals.

In *The Fortunate Traveller* (1981), Walcott's anxiety for the Caribbean, for "these islands of the blest, / cheap package tours replaced / by politics, rain, unrest" (p. 19), is integrated, in the long title poem, into a global concern for the poor of the earth and an anticipation of a violent justice that could well assert itself if the rich nations fail to answer the plea for mercy. The structuring of this collection into three sections headed "North," "South," and "North" not only suggests the idea of the North–South dialogue among nations, First World and

Third World, but also makes explicit a recurrent movement in Walcott's work, between poems which are about/set in the Caribbean ("South") and ones which are about/set in metropolitan countries ("North").

Walcott's imagination continues to shuttle between South and North (especially New England, where he has been living of late) in his latest book, *Midsummer* (1984). This sequence of numbered, sonnet-like lyrics constitutes a single, widely ranging rumination on well nigh all the themes that have preoccupied him, centering on exile of one kind or another, the never-ending quest for "home," and the reconciling and transcendent power of the imagination. In the end he comes back, as he always does, to "the midsummer sea, the hot pitch road, this grass, these shacks that made me" (LIV). And while the sense of separation can never be finally appeased, there is enough to be thankful for: "though no man ever dies in his own country, / the grateful grass will grow thick from his heart" (LIV).

CRITICAL RECEPTION

The high critical acclaim which Walcott has steadily come to enjoy is nowhere more unreservedly expressed than in an appreciation by Joseph Brodsky, which was featured in the *New York Review of Books* (1983). There has been high praise too in reviews by other major poets such as Seamus Heaney and Louis Simpson. Indeed, the most unstinting admiration has been expressed by fellow poets rather than by critics.

Brodsky specifically addresses the question of regionalism, berating those who speak of Walcott as "a West Indian poet" or "a black poet from the Caribbean" and arguing that a "mental and spiritual cowardice [is] obvious in the attempts to render this man a regional writer" (p. 39). Brodsky's praise will no doubt fuel the controversy that Walcott attracts, since it may be seen as further evidence of Walcott's accessibility to being appropriated by the White critical establishment and further cause for questioning his West Indian relevance.

Here the question of language becomes important. Brodsky cites "the unwillingness of the critical profession to admit that the great poet of the English language is a black man" (p. 39). The sociopolitical implications of a judgment such as this are highlighted when Carole Rodman asks Walcott whether, when he was writing *Dream on Monkey Mountain*, he saw himself "as an English poet who happened to be black, or a black who might have to give up being an English poet lest he betray his race" (Selden Rodman, *Tongues of Fallen Angels*, 1974, p. 245).

Whereas West Indian critics on the whole, and understandably, have a special interest in those poems in which Standard English is modified or replaced by Creole, Helen Vendler regards Walcott's Creole as a distraction, arguing that "a macaronic aesthetic, using two or more languages at once, has never yet been sustained in poetry at any length" ("Poet of Two Worlds," 1982, p. 26). But Seamus Heaney sees the Creole poem "The Schooner *Flight*" (*The Star-*

Apple Kingdom) as "epoch-making" because in it Walcott has "found a language woven out of dialect and literature, neither folksy nor condescending, a singular idiom evolved out of one man's inherited divisions and obsessions" ("The Language of Exile," 1979, p. 5). This view is to be seen as strengthening, rather than subverting Heaney's claim that "Walcott possesses English more deeply and sonorously than most of the English themselves" (p. 8).

Calvin Bedient and D. S. Izevbaye also clarify sensitively the notion of Walcott as an English poet. Bedient observes: "It can be no small privilege and excitement to 'represent' in 'English' poetry the language of calypso and by way of identifying the collectivity that authenticates him [Walcott] as a poet with a people" ("Derek Walcott, Contemporary," p. 37). Izevbaye argues, "Walcott's skill in creating new meanings out of old, that is, the creation of a new language based on his commitment to standard English and a mythohistoric interpretation of West Indian identity, is a central part of Walcott's achievement" ("The Exile and the Prodigal: Derek Walcott as West Indian Poet," 1980, p. 78).

The sonorousness as well as the "divisions and obsessions" mentioned by Heaney call attention to other areas of critical focus. The tension in Walcott between a penchant for the sonorous, the richly wrought line, and a professed yearning toward a "plain" style, "the style past metaphor" (*The Gulf and Other Poems*, p. 67), has been noted as a leading factor in his search for his own style. (See, for example, Edward Baugh, "Metaphor and Plainness in the Poetry of Derek Walcott," 1970). The sonorousness has been seen by some critics as a weakness and self-indulgence. Denis Donoghue speaks of an "impression of rhetorical excess [which] arises from Walcott's poems" ("Themes from Derek Walcott," 1977, p. 95). This kind of criticism has also been leveled at the plays.

Vendler exemplifies a major concern of Walcott criticism when she identifies dividedness as his "agenda" (p. 23). Some critics, such as Victor Questel, tend to read the dualisms in very personal-psychoanalytical terms, quick to explain Walcott's writings as projections of psychological "hang-ups" engendered by his personal history. So Questel sees the author of *Dream on Monkey Mountain* as failing to distance the major characters sufficiently from himself. Where Questel often sees Walcott's dualities as fraught with contradiction and confusion, other critics like to see them more as strengths than as weaknesses. And Mervyn Morris observes: "Although so much of [Walcott's] own writing explores and dramatises divisions within himself, the thrust is usually towards reconciliation, acceptance, compassion" (*West Indian Literature*, ed. Bruce King, 1979, p. 146).

To Lloyd Brown the dualities are an integral factor in "the complex vision of the poet's persona" (*West Indian Poetry*, 1978, p. 118), and critics like Brown and Robert Hamner find themselves having to stress the essentially and easily overlooked positive in Walcott's work: "The bleakness of Walcott's vision of the gulf is proportionately offset by his faith in the individual capacity to create a fulfilling identity and role from the void of the gulf" (Brown, 1978, p. 130). "The meticulous honesty with which he attends to the somber aspects of life attests not to a morbid pessimism but to a profound faith in the undying worth of things in themselves'' (Hamner, *Derek Walcott*, 1981, p. 106).

HONORS AND AWARDS

Derek Walcott is a Fellow of the Royal Society of Literature (England, 1966) and an Honorary Member of the American Academy and Institute of Arts and Letters (1979). He was made an Officer of the British Empire in the Queen's Birthday Honors (St. Lucia List) for 1972, and was awarded the Gold Hummingbird Medal of Trinidad and Tobago in 1979 and an Honorary D.Litt. by the University of the West Indies in 1973. His numerous other awards include Rockefeller Foundation Fellowship in Theater (1958), Eugene O'Neill Foundation-Wesleyan University Fellowship for Playwrights (1969), Guggenheim Fellowship (1977), Welsh Arts Council International Writers Prize (1980), John D. and Catherine MacArthur Prize (1981), Guinness Award for Poetry for ''A Sea-Chantey'' (1961), Borestone Mountain Poetry Award for the best poem of 1963 (''Tarpon'') and of 1976 (''Midsummer, England''), Royal Society for Literature Award for *The Castaway* (1966), Obie Award for the most distinguished Off-Broadway play, *Dream on Monkey Mountain* (1971), the Jock Campbell New Statesman Award for *Another Life* (1974) and the *American Poetry Review* Award (1979).

BIBLIOGRAPHY

Works by Derek Walcott

Plays

Henri Christophe: A Chronicle in Seven Scenes. Bridgetown, Barbados: Advocate, 1950.

Harry Dernier: A Play for Radio Production. Bridgetown, Barbados: Advocate, 1952.

Ione: A Play with Music. Caribbean Plays, no. 8. Kingston: Extra-Mural Department, University College of the West Indies, 1957.

Drums and Colours: An Epic Drama. *Caribbean Quarterly* (Special issue) 7 (June 1961).

Dream on Monkey Mountain and Other Plays. New York: Farrar, Straus and Giroux, 1970; London: Cape, 1972. Includes *The Sea at Dauphin*, *Malcochon*, and *Ti-Jean and His Brothers*.

The Joker of Seville and O Babylon! New York: Farrar, Straus and Giroux, 1978; London: Cape, 1979.

Remembrance and Pantomime. New York: Farrar, Straus and Giroux, 1980.

Poetry

Epitaph for the Young. Bridgetown, Barbados: Advocate, 1949.

25 Poems. Port of Spain: Guardian Commercial Printery, 1948; Bridgetown, Barbados: Advocate, 1949.

Poems. Kingston: City Printery, 1951.

In a Green Night: Poems 1948–1960. 1962; London: Cape, 1962; 1969.

Selected Poems. New York: Farrar, Straus and Giroux, 1964.

The Castaway and Other Poems. London: Cape, 1965, 1969.

The Gulf and Other Poems. London: Cape, 1969, 1974.

The Gulf. New York: Farrar, Straus and Giroux, 1970.

Another Life. New York: Farrar, Straus and Giroux, 1973; London: Cape, 1973; Washington, D.C.: Three Continents Press, 1982.

Sea Grapes. New York: Farrar, Straus and Giroux, 1976, 1977; London: Cape, 1976.

The Star-Apple Kingdom. New York: Farrar, Straus and Giroux, 1979, 1980; London: Cape, 1980.

The Fortunate Traveller. New York: Farrar, Straus and Giroux, 1981; London, Faber and Faber, 1982.

Selected Poetry. Selected, annotated, and introduced by Wayne Brown. London: Heinemann, 1981.

Poems of the Caribbean. New York: Limited Editions Club, 1983.

Midsummer. New York: Farrar, Straus and Giroux, 1984; London: Faber and Faber, 1984.

Interviews with Derek Walcott

''Walcott on Walcott'' (interview with Dennis Scott). *Caribbean Quarterly* 14 (March-June 1968), 77–82.

''We Are Still Being Betrayed'' (interview with Raoul Pantin). *Caribbean Contact* (July 1973), 14, 16; (August 1973), 14, 16.

''Conversation with Derek Walcott'' (interview with Robert Hamner). *World Literature Written in English* 16 (November 1977), 409–20.

''An Interview with Derek Walcott'' (interview with Edward Hirsch). *Contemporary Literature* 20 (Summer 1979), 279–92.

''Reflections Before and After Carnival'' (interview with Sharon Ciccarelli). In *Chant of Saints*, ed. Michael S. Harper and Robert B. Stepto. Urbana: University of Illinois Press, 1979, pp. 296–309.

Studies of Derek Walcott

Baugh, Edward. *Derek Walcott: Memory as Vision: Another Life*. London: Longman, 1978.

———. ''Metaphor and Plainness in the Poetry of Derek Walcott.'' *The Literary Half-Yearly* 11 (July 1970), 47–58.

———. ''Painters and Painting in *Another Life*.'' *Caribbean Quarterly* 26 (March-June 1980), 83–93.

———. ''The Poem as Autobiographical Novel: Derek Walcott's *Another Life* in Relation to Wordsworth's *Prelude* and Joyce's *Portrait*.'' In *Awakened Conscience*, ed. C. D. Narasimhaiah. New Delhi: Sterling, 1978, pp. 226–35.

———. ''The West Indian Writer and His Quarrel with History.'' *Tapia*, February 20, 1977, pp. 6–7; February 27, 1977, pp. 6–7, 11.

Beckman, Susan. ''The Mulatto of Style: Language in Derek Walcott's Drama.'' *Canadian Drama* 6 (Spring 1960), 71–89.

Bedient, Calvin. "Derek Walcott, Contemporary." *Parnassus* 9 (Fall-Winter 1981), 31–44.

Breiner, Lawrence. "Tradition, Society, the Figure of the Poet." *Caribbean Quarterly* 26 (March-June 1980), 1–12.

Brodsky, Joseph. "On Derek Walcott." *New York Review of Books*, November 10, 1983, pp. 39–41.

Brown, Lloyd. "Dreamers and Slaves: The Ethos of Revolution in Walcott and Leroi Jones." *Caribbean Quarterly* 17 (September-December 1971), 36–44.

Brown, Wayne. Introduction to *Selected Poetry*. London: Heinemann, 1981.

Burton, R.D.E. "Derek Walcott and the Medusa of History." *Caliban* 3 (1980), 3–48.

Colson, Theodore. "Derek Walcott's Plays: Outrage and Compassion." *World Literature Written in English* 12 (April 1973), 80–96.

Donoghue, Denis. "Themes from Derek Walcott" (Review of *Sea Grapes*). *Parnassus: Poetry in Review* 6 (Fall-Winter 1977), 88–100.

Fabre, Michael. " 'Adam's Task of Giving Things Their Names': The Poetry of Derek Walcott." *New Letters* 41 (Fall 1974), 91–107.

Figueroa, John. Review of *Another Life*. *Bim* 15 (June 1975), 160–70.

———. "Some Subtleties of the Isle: A Commentary on Certain Aspects of Derek Walcott's Sonnet Sequence, *Tales of the Islands*." *World Literature Written in English* 15 (April 1976), 190–228.

Goldstraw, Irma E. *Derek Walcott: An Annotated Bibliography of His Works*. New York: Garland, 1984.

Hamner, Robert D. *Derek Walcott*. Boston: Twayne, 1981.

———. "Derek Walcott's Theater of Assimilation." *West Virginia University Philological Papers* 25 (February 1979), 86–93.

———. "Mythological Aspects of Derek Walcott's Drama." *Ariel*8 (July 1977), 35–58.

Heaney, Seamus. "The Language of Exile" (Review of *The Star-Apple Kingdom*. *Parnassus: Poetry in Review* 8 (Fall-Winter 1979), 5–11.

Hill, Errol. *Derek Walcott*. London: Macmillan, 1984.

Ismond, Pat. "Breaking Myths and Maidenheads!" *Tapia*, May 18, 1975, pp. 4, 5, 9; June 1, 1975, pp. 6–8.

———. "Walcott Versus Brathwaite." *Caribbean Quarterly* 17 (September-December 1971), 54–71.

Izevbaye, D. S. "The Exile and the Prodigal: Derek Walcott as West Indian Poet." *Caribbean Quarterly* 26 (March-June 1980), 70–82.

King, Lloyd. "Derek Walcott: The Literary Humanist in the Caribbean." *Caribbean Quarterly* 16 (December 1970), 36–42.

Lane, M. Travis. "At Home in Homelessness: The Poetry of Derek Walcott." *Dalhousie Review* 53 (Summer 1973), 325–38.

Morris, Mervyn. "Walcott and the Audience for Poetry." *Caribbean Quarterly* 14 (March-June 1968), 7–24.

Questel, Victor. "Dream on Monkey Mountain in Perspective." *Tapia*, September 1, 1974, pp. 2–3; September 8, 1974, pp. 6, 7, 10; September 15, 1974, pp. 6–7; September 29, 1974, pp. 5–8.

———. "The Horns of Derek's Dilemma." *Tapia*, March 25, 1973, pp. 4–5.

———. "Walcott's Major Triumph" [*Another Life*]. *Tapia*, December 23, 1973, pp. 6–7; December 30, 1973, pp. 6–7.

Rodman, Selden. "Derek Walcott." *Tongues of Fallen Angels*. New York: New Directions, 1974, pp. 233–59.

Rohlehr, Gordon. "Withering Into Truth: A Review of Derek Walcott's *The Gulf and Other Poems*." *Trinidad Guardian*, December 10, 1969, p. 18; December 11, 1969, p. 17; December 13, 1969, p. 8.

Stewart, Marian. "Walcott and Painting." *Jamaica Journal* 45 (May 1981), 56–68.

Trueblood, Valerie. "On Derek Walcott." *American Poetry Review* 7 (May-June 1978), 7–10.

Vendler, Helen. "Poet of Two Worlds" (Review of *The Fortunate Traveller*). *New York Review of Books*, March 4, 1982, pp. 23, 26–27.

Walmsley, Anne. "Dimensions of Song: A Comment on the Poetry of Derek Walcott and Edward Brathwaite." *Bim* 13 (July-December 1970), 152–67.

Wieland, Jim. " 'Making Radiant the Moment': Notes Towards a Reading of Derek Walcott's *Sea Grapes*." *ACLALS Bulletin*, 5th ser., no. 3 (December 1980), 112–21.

See also General Bibliography: Allis, Baugh (1971, 1978), Brown, Herdeck, Hughes, James, Moore, and Ramchand (1976).

ENID E. BOGLE

Eric Walrond (1898–1966)

Eric Walrond and Claude McKay, two prominent writers of the Harlem Renaissance, turned to their native Caribbean homeland for their inspiration. But while McKay continued to write extensively after his initial successful work, Walrond's literary creativity after his highly acclaimed *Tropic Death* (1926) virtually ceased. Except for a few essays that surfaced in the 1930s in Marcus Garvey's *The Black Man*, no creative work exists of Walrond, hailed in the 1920s as one of the most brilliant of the younger generation of Negro writers. Perhaps equally baffling and crucial to a full understanding of Walrond is his reconciliation with Marcus Garvey in London a decade after they had traded heated arguments and Garvey had publicly denounced Walrond. Yet Garvey had not denied Walrond's talent as a writer; in fact, despite Walrond's ideological differences with others, no one disputes his brilliance—his prodigality of talent perhaps—but never his ability.

BIOGRAPHY

Eric Derwent Walrond was born in Georgetown, British Guiana—now Guyana. At an early age he migrated with his mother to her native Barbados. Young Walrond attended St. Stephen's Boys School, known for its vigorous and challenging curriculum, and although sheltered by his genteel mother, Walrond roamed the countryside, admiring the landscape and learning the rural customs. Soon, however, he was uprooted again when his mother decided to join her

Guyanese husband in the Canal Zone, where he had gone to seek employment. Here Walrond continued his education in public schools and with private tutors, becoming fluent in Spanish.

Walrond's first job was as secretary and stenographer at the Cristobal Health Department. Later, he began a two-year stint as a reporter for the British subsidized *Panama Star and Herald* and, according to Robert Hill in *The Marcus Garvey and the United Negro Improvement Association Papers* (vol. 1, 1983, p. 182; hereafter *MGUNI Papers*), Walrond also assisted his uncle H. N. Walrond in publishing the *Workman*. When Walrond arrived in New York in 1918, he was repeatedly denied employment despite his impressive background as a reporter and publisher. Eventually he attended City College of New York (1922–24) and Columbia University (1924–26). While in college he worked as an associate editor of *The Weekly Review*, a short-lived journal, and served briefly as an associate editor of a Negro publication, *The Brooklyn and Long Island Reformer*.

Walrond worked also at the British Recruiting Mission, but he is more readily remembered as associate editor for Marcus Garvey's *Negro World* (1921–23) and business manager for the Urban League's *Opportunity: Journal of Negro Life* (1925–27). It is not quite clear how deeply committed Walrond was to the Garvey movement, for in attacking and condemning the literature of those who "prostituted their intelligence, under the direction of the white man, to bring out and show up the worst traits of our people" (quoted in *MGUNI Papers*, vol. 1, p. liv), Garvey singled out and castigated Claude McKay and Eric Walrond. Walrond's association with *Opportunity* provided him with the literary exposure he needed; he was a friend of Langston Hughes; he was invited to many of the distinguished "gatherings"; he was a member of the Eclectic Club—a sophisticated artistic group—and according to Arthur P. Davis, Walrond was the "rage" of the early and mid–1920s (interview with Enid Bogle, Washington, D.C., June 5, 1984).

Those who associated with Walrond found him compelling and forthright, often sensitive in his writings to the conditions around him, particularly as he articulated the aspirations and problems of the Negroes in the 1920s. His early essays published in a variety of magazines and newspapers such as *New Republic*, *Independent*, *Dearborn Independent*, *Crisis*, *Current History*, *Negro World*, *The Saturday Review of Literature*, and *Opportunity* attest to the range of his political and literary convictions. In these essays he recorded his anger with racist America. His frequent reviews of plays and books displayed his literary tenets and at times his biting and passionate wit. Walrond was uncompromising in his belief that the responsibility of a good writer went beyond propagandism. At the same time he felt that an artist should not be locked into conformity. When for instance in Wallace Thurman's *Infants of the Spring* (New York: Macauley, 1932) a character suggests that writers return to their racial roots and cultivate a healthy paganism based on African traditions, Cedric Williams, the satirized Walrond, champions the right of the artist to "pursue his own individual track . . . choosing his own path. If indeed a writer is inclined to use African traditions, then so be it'' (pp. 239–40).

Tropic Death, published in 1926, is a culmination of the author's literary tenets. Its success helped Walrond to receive a John S. Guggenheim Foundation Fellowship. He left New York on yet another journey and traveled throughout the Caribbean to collect material for a ''series of novels and short stories of native life in the West Indies . . . [with the intent of] weaving into them a considerable amount of legends, folktales, pleasant songs and voodoo myths abounding in the region'' (quoted in Ramchand, ''The Writer Who Ran Away: Eric Walrond and *Tropic Death*,'' 1970, p. 74).

There is much uncertainty about Walrond's whereabouts and activities after he left New York. Hill claims that Walrond returned to the United States in June, 1929, but that he left again in 1932 for London (p. 182). Robert Bone in *Down Home: A History of Afro-American Short Fiction from Its Beginnings to the End of the Harlem Renaissance* (New York: Putnam, 1975) claims that according to the publisher's files, Walrond completed a history of the Panama Canal called ''The Big Ditch'' before leaving New York and that he ''travelled throughout Europe, lived in France for several years, then settled in London'' (p. 176). In London with his second wife, Walrond lived the life of an imposing English gentleman. But more important, he renewed his relationship with Garvey, who by then had been deported from the United States but who continued championing the cause of the Negro in his speeches, but mostly in *The Black Man*, which he edited and published. That Walrond became a Garveyite remains undocumented; what is certain, however, is that Walrond published numerous essays in *The Black Man*. One can only speculate that the reconciliation was prompted by their similar goal to voice the dilemma of the Negro everywhere. Walrond's ''The Negro in London,'' ''The Negro in the Armies of Europe,'' ''The End of Ras Nasibu,'' ''Fascism and the Negro,'' ''The Negro Before the World,'' and ''On England'' attest to the scope of his political concerns and his obsession with the plight of ''the Negro.''

Yet these essays in *The Black Man* seem a meager output for a writer as talented as Walrond. Missing is his literary preoccupation while in France. John Hearne, Caribbean novelist and critic, comments on the association that Walrond must have had with the ''Movement'' in France, but he, too, is puzzled that no record documents what might have been an ''interesting'' period (interview with Enid Bogle, University of the West Indies, Mona, July 2, 1984). Still missing, too, is the draft of the project for which he received the Guggenheim Fellowship. In his letters to the Foundation, Walrond confessed that he had had his ''ups and downs'' and that his quest for security in a world in which nothing is stable led him astray, but indicated that he was determined to produce something which would in some small measure justify the confidence which the Foundation so generously reposed on him (quoted in Ramchand's report of a letter written to Mr. Henry Allen Poe in 1940, p. 74). Walrond died in 1966 without fulfilling his promise. Seemingly his only essay associated with the Caribbean after he received the Guggenheim Fellowship is "Can the Negro Measure Up?" prompted by his visit to Guadeloupe and honoring Henri Gregoire, the 18th century priest of peasant origin, champion of the cause of Negro liberty (*The Black Man* 11 [August 1937], 9).

MAJOR WORKS AND THEMES

Tropic Death (1926), a collection of ten short stories dedicated to Casper Holstein and republished posthumously in 1972 with a dedication to his daughters Jean, Dorothy, and Lucille, presents Walrond's treatment of the traditions and customs of his native Caribbean. He singles out for particular attention the atrocities that those who seek a better life endure when they are uprooted. The milieu of each story corresponds with places Walrond visited as a young man. That this environment provides the source for his book is not surprising, for as early as 1923 in his review of de La Torre's painting, Walrond stressed the importance of environment to the artist, stating: "In every artist's life, it is inexorable that environment play a determining part" (*Crisis* [September 1923], p. 169).

Throughout the collection, Walrond creates vivid pictures of the life and activities of the migrant laborers. Bone suggests that Walrond may have developed his technique of close observation and unflinching realism from Balzac. He suggests further that Walrond's comment about de La Torre—that were he a literary artist, he would be a combination of Balzac, Pierre Loti, Lafcadio Hearn, Joseph Conrad, and de Maupassant (p. 169)—might be an acknowledgment of his own aesthetic and major influences. From de Maupassant he may have developed his clinical detachment and comic irony; from Conrad, the shaping of the atavistic implication of his art; and from Lafcadio Hearn and Pierre Loti, the animating myth (Bone, "Eric Walrond," 1975, p. 186).

The overriding image throughout the stories is that of horrible death—whether by forces of nature, supernatural means, or man against man. In "Drought" the starving Beryl dies because she supplements her diet by eating marl. Fire of unknown origin burns Mr. Poyer to death in "Panama Gold," and in "Wharf Rats" a ferocious shark stalks and subdues young Philip as he dives for coins thrown overboard by the tourists. Death in "Vampire Bat" and "Black Pin" is caused by supernatural rather that natural forces. Walrond uses Obeah, a popular folk belief, as its agent. So deadly is the instrument that conveys the Obeah that when redirected to its sender "it took the life of animal and plant that was in its path and left [Zink Diggs] petrified by the stove, the white clay pipe ghostly in her mouth. Even her eyes were left sprawling open, staring at the cat, likewise dead" ("Black Pin," *Tropic Death*, 1926, p. 182). In "Black Pin" the characters are aware of the power of Obeah and use it accordingly, but in "Vampire Bat," Captain Bellon Prout ridicules their superstitions and pays the utmost price. The morning after he rescued what in the night he thought was an abandoned, naked Negro baby, his lifeless body was found alone in his cabin.

The ''Yellow One,'' ''Subjection,'' and ''Palm Porch'' record death from still another means: physical harm caused by man's inhumanity to man. In ''Yellow One,'' La Madurita's harmless association with the Cuban cook on board a vessel from Honduras to Jamaica contributes to the hatred between a coal black Negro and a Cuban, who like her is a mestizo. They scuffle and in the melee La Madurita is trampled to death. In ''Subjection'' a United States marine in Panama hunts and shoots a Negro worker whose only crime is his verbal defense of a fellow worker being whipped by the overseer. The drunken English vice consul in ''Palm Porch'' was probably beaten to death. His behavior at Miss Buckner's ''establishment'' threatened to embarrass the ''aristocratic'' owner and her male customers. Later, his corpse was removed, and no one seemed concerned about his fate.

''Tropic Death,'' the title story, captures the death image in seemingly the most painful way. It details the agony of Sarah Bright and her son who journey to Panama in search of her husband, as did Walrond and his mother. They reside in Bottle Alley, where their comfortable life in Barbados is replaced by one of poverty, noise, and disease. Not only is the physical environment hostile and depressing, but the father's ineffectiveness and offensive behavior are also disappointing. Yet the saddest and most disturbing scene is the parting, when the father develops leprosy and leaves the hospital and his family for the inevitable death in a leper's home.

In ''White Snake'' Walrond presents death of another kind—not of a human being but of a snake. Set in the forest of Guyana, ''White Snake'' is a frightening tale of the experiences of Seenie, a Black servant girl ostracized by the villagers because she is pregnant. Seenie takes refuge in a deserted hut in Waakenham, a thinly populated area on the dense Essequibo coast. One night, she falls asleep nursing her son, Water Sprout. Half-awake she hears him crying away from her, when allegedly she is nursing him on the bed. Suddenly the sucking stops; she awakens fully and races across the room to him. Six hours later they find the fresh dead body of a bloating milk-fed snake.

That Walrond depicts death in such gruesome forms seems to be no accident; he is painfully aware of the plight of the laborers, but he chooses not to be a social protester. Instead he presents horrendous images and allows the stories to speak for themselves. His detachment is broken only once when at the end of ''Subjection'' after the marine kills the Negro worker Walrond writes satirically: ''In the Canal Record, the Q.M. at Toro Point took occasion to extol the virtues of the Department which kept the number of casualties in the recent labor uprising down to one'' (p. 158). But in the other stories, Walrond's concern is to present the atrocities of the colonial system coupled with the dangers of a natural environment—the very natural environment that also gives comfort to two servant girls. In ''White Snake'' the foliage brings barbaric peace to Seenie's soul, and in ''Wharf Rats'' Maffi, after work, disappears in the dark to dream on the beach, as she gazes at the stars and the sea.

Besides focusing on the agents of death, Walrond presents other life-threatening circumstances. For instance, men who labor in the quarries or at the canal suffer indignities as their Black families are "herded in box car huts in murky tenements." They endure physical pain, registered in Ballet's "young perspiring back cricking in upward swing," or in men "using picks swung by gnarled hands" or "moaning men jogging with drills on their backs, pounding the unexplored jungle." And they are hungry—"scally ragamuffins dart after boxes of stale cheese and crates of sun-sopped iced apples that were dumped into the sea" (p. 69). Thus whether Walrond writes of the plantation system ("Vampire Bat") or industrialization ("Subjection," "Panama Gold," "Wharf Rats," "Palm Porch"), whether the laborers are in Barbados or Panama, they suffer excruciating pain.

Walrond also presents the problem of color that inevitably occurs in a colonial system where the closer one's color approximates that of the ruling White the more "benefits" he obtains. No wonder then that the mulatto Miss Buckner ("Palm Porch") would have liked to be White and is disgusted with four of her daughters, who, by not marrying Whites, married beneath them. Ella, too, denigrates Mr. Poyer's Blackness ("Panama Gold"). Hubigon despises Jota because he is yellow-skinned and gains entry to places that are closed to Black Americans. Even the girls in ports show more attention to the yellow-skinned sailors than to the Black ones. And, of course, Alfred is attracted to "La Madurita" and hopes to take her back to Jamaica to brag to his friends ("Yellow One").

Walrond captures, too, the importance of religion despite the prevalent practice of Obeah. The Plymouth Brethren religion ("Wharf Rats" and "Tropic Death") is a source of strength to the migrant families, although a harsh faith in which to rear hemmed-in peasant children. Sarah Bright turns to the church when she is distraught and is consoled by her son, who tells her not to cry for "God will provide for us" (p. 250). La Madurita in her confused state relies on her religion—"de Laud will provide" (p. 64). Coupled with the religion is the fervent belief in Obeah. Enraged by Marva and Philip's behavior, Maffi vows to put an end to it. "Ah go stop ee, oui. . . . This very night" (p. 95), she vows diabolically. And although Walrond does not identify her method of working Obeah, when the story ends, Philip ("Wharf Rats") is swallowed by the chop-licking man-eating shark and Maffi, humming an Obeah melody, has peace come to her at last.

The mother–son bond is given ample treatment in *Tropic Death*; in fact, the treatment of children generally is an important segment of Walrond's presentation. In "Tropic Death," Sarah Bright clings to her son. She leaves the girls with relatives in Barbados, but she takes young Gerald with her to Panama. She becomes overly protective, and like Seenie and Water Sprout, a special bond develops between them. The bond seems to be stronger when the fathers relinquish their paternal obligations, a not uncommon situation in the Caribbean.

April Emptage raises her children without any mention of a father (''Black Pin''), and for Miss Buckner's children, the ''less said of their father, the better'' (''Palm Porch,'' p. 126).

But there are families in which the father is present, even though his importance as head of household varies. Alfred St. Xavier Mendez (''The Yellow One'') is lazy; he prefers to wait until he arrives in Jamaica to discuss the inadequate accommodation aboard the ship, rather than assert himself like others do, including his wife, to get food and water for his child. Coggins Rum (''Drought'') tries to control his children; his daughter Beryl's death is not his fault—she was ''hard ears.'' Mr. Oxley (''Tropic Death'') assumes his fatherly responsibility, contending that men who do not support their family ''muss be got de heart uv a brute'' (p. 251); Jean Baptiste and Boyce (''Wharf Rats'') are religious men who are strict with their children—Jean Baptiste keeps at the head of his bed a greased cat-o-nine-tails, which he is prepared to use if warranted.

In *Tropic Death* Walrond presents a kaleidoscopic view of the disillusions and aspirations and human interaction of the Caribbean people, focusing on the problem of migration and its attendant problems.

CRITICAL RECEPTION

The publication of *Tropic Death* in 1926 was a personal triumph for Walrond, who up to this time had published only a number of essays, reviews, and vignettes on several topics. The book received high critical acclaim. While the majority of Walrond's contemporaries wrote of life in Harlem, Walrond turned to his early environment for his source. Robert Herrick's review in *New Republic* (November 10, 1926) speaks of the significance of *Tropic Death*, distinguishing it from contemporary fiction because of its ''virgin working of a rich new field''—the laborers of the Black West Indies—and the faithful rendition of their experiences by one who writes from direct involvement. Herrick commends Walrond, whose ''dramatic presentation of character in dialogue, in a vernacular so literal as not always to be readily intelligible, is masterly convincing,'' adding, ''The African temperament, modes of thought, have never been more exactly interpreted in language'' (p. 332). Sterling Brown in *The Negro in American Fiction* (New York: Atheneum, 1937) lauds Walrond for his familiarity with the ''diverse West Indian dialects'' (p. 154), although he claims that at times the ''prose is somewhat overwritten, sometimes too oblique for clarity.'' Brown praises Walrond for his handling of the material, for like Toomer, Walrond stresses the ''tragedy and pain in his milieu rather than the joy of living'' stressed by the Harlem school. Brown sees *Tropic Death* as ''unapologetically naturalistic,'' aimed to make the reader ''see, to give him a sense impression of a unique interesting world'' (p. 155). Hugh M. Gloster in *Negro Voices in American Fiction* (1948) concurs with Brown on the naturalistic approach of *Tropic Death*, adding that each story portrays man as a helpless animal impelled primarily by instinct and controlled mainly by capricious forces'' (p. 181). According to W. E. B. Du Bois, *Tropic Death* is a human document of great significance and great promise (*Crisis* 33 [January 1927], 152).

But it was not all praise for Walrond. Herrick writes that in *Tropic Death* Walrond is "careless of composition, as the younger writers of the day often are, disdaining unity and coherence in their effort to seize a deep reality" (p. 366), but that he creates pictures and characters easily, and for concise irony not even de Maupassant surpasses Walrond in his conclusion of "Subjection" (p. 366). Robert Bone in *Down Home* agrees that the quality of the collection is uneven but acknowledges that the "stronger tales in *Tropic Death* must be counted among the most effective of the Harlem Renaissance" (p. 195). Kenneth Ramchand ("The Writer Who Ran Away") contends that Walrond's *Tropic Death* should be reclaimed from North America because it is "one of the startling treasures in the lost literature of the West Indies" (p. 67).

With *Tropic Death* Walrond adds a new dimension to the writings of the Harlem Renaissance, focusing on Black people outside of the United States. As he takes us through the Caribbean, we are presented not with the usual traditional lore and beauty of the Tropics but with the venomous experiences that seem inescapable for those who migrate. Walrond reveals his obsession with migration, not only within the Caribbean, but also to and within the United States. His aim was to present the plight of Black people, and he was successful. It is regrettable that the potential exhibited in *Tropic Death* did not explode in other creative endeavors.

Walrond's *Tropic Death* is also discussed in Kenneth Ramchand, *The West Indian Novel and its Background* (1970), Richard Barksdale and Kenneth Kinnamon, *Black Writers of America* (New York: Macmillan, 1972), Michael Hughes, *A Companion to West Indian Literature* (London: Collins, 1978, 1979); Benjamin Brawley, *The Negro Genius* (New York: Dodd, Mead, 1937, 1966); J. Saunders Redding, *To Make a Poet Black* (Chapel Hill: University of North Carolina Press, 1939), and Alain Locke, *The New Negro: An Introduction* (New York: Boni, 1925).

HONORS AND AWARDS

Eric Walrond received several prizes for his early fiction in *Negro World and Opportunity*. He was a Zona Gale Scholar at the University of Wisconsin in 1928, but his most significant award was the John Simon Guggenheim Memorial Foundation Award, which he received in 1928.

BIBLIOGRAPHY

Works by Eric Walrond

Tropic Death. New York: Boni and Liveright, 1926; New York: Macmillan-Collier, 1972.

Studies of Eric Walrond

Bone, Robert. "Eric Walrond." In *Down Home: A History of Afro-American Short Fiction from Its Beginnings to the End of the Harlem Renaissance*. New York: Putnam, 1975, pp. 171–203.

Gloster, Hugh M. "Eric Walrond." In *Negro Voices in American Fiction*. Chapel Hill: University of North Carolina Press, 1948, pp. 181–83.

Hill, Robert, ed. *The Marcus Garvey and the United Negro Improvement Association Papers*. 2 vols. Berkeley: University of California Press, 1983.

Martin, Tony. "The Defectors—Eric Walrond and Claude McKay." In *Literary Garveyism*. Dover: Majority Press, 1983, pp. 124–38.

Ramchand, Kenneth. "The Writer Who Ran Away: Eric Walrond and *Tropic Death*." *Savacou* 2 (September 1970), 67–75.

See also General Bibliography: Allis, Herdeck, and Ramchand (1970).

VICTOR J. RAMRAJ

Denis Williams (1923–)

Denis Williams' reputation as a writer rests on two novels, *Other Leopards* (1963) and *The Third Temptation* (1968), and a handful of short stories. He has done far more work as a painter and considers himself more an artist than a writer. He has also been involved in recent years in archaeology, a field he considers to be "as exciting as writing novels" (interview with Victor J. Ramraj, Georgetown, Guyana, September 8, 1984). He still writes off and on, and perceives himself as having a "bifocal perception," capable of both the scientific inquiry demanded of archaeology and the imaginative vision required of painting and writing (interview). His novels and short stories reveal a significant talent, and though he may be known more as a painter and an archaeologist, his fiction has earned him a secure place in any survey of Caribbean literature.

BIOGRAPHY

Denis Joseph Ivan Williams was born on February 1, 1923, in Georgetown, Guyana, to Joseph Williams (a merchant) and his wife Isabel (née Adonis). He was educated in Georgetown, earning his Cambridge senior school certificate in 1941. Though interested in writing, he wanted to become a painter, and in 1946–48 he attended the Camberwell School of Art in London as a British Council scholar. On graduation, he stayed in London and followed a career as a painter, lecturing at the Central School of Fine Arts and tutoring at the Slade School of Fine Arts. He had several successful one-man exhibitions at Gimpel Fils Gallery. Of his London experience, Williams has ambivalent feelings. He admits that it was "not only formative, but to a degree even determinative." However, he adds, "given the circumstances and the day, acceptance on this level was in fact far the most unacceptable, indeed probably the most humiliating, of choices open to the Colonial artist" (*Contemporary Authors*, vol. 93–96 [Detroit: Gale Research, 1980], p. 556).

The ten years in Britain were followed by ten years in Africa. He spent the first five years in Sudan (the setting of *Other Leopards*) as lecturer in the Khartoum School of Fine Arts, and subsequent years in Nigeria as lecturer at the School of African Studies, University of Ife (1962–66), and the School of African and Asian Studies, University of Lagos (1966–78). In both places Williams studied African art and classical antiquity and developed a strong interest in archaeology. He was occupied as well with his own personal search for identity and ancestry. His African experience made him realize that though he has African roots, Africa was not home. He was aware also that he could not avoid Europe in Sudan and Nigeria; European culture permeated both places. Consequently, it was not difficult for him while absorbed with examining his African identity to write *The Third Temptation*, a novel influenced by the French New Novel and set in Wales (the home of his first wife) that has nothing to do with his African experience.

Uncomfortable in Europe and Africa, Williams felt he should return to his own "primordial world," the interior of Guyana (interview). He lived from 1968 to 1974 in the Mazaruni area of the Guyana hinterland, writing and painting and researching the Amerindians' tribal art, particularly their petroglyphs. He described this as a "tremendous" period of his life, one free of "twentieth-century anxieties" (interview). He recalls with pride building his own house, acting as midwife when his wife gave birth, and having no library, no books other than a perennial subscription to *The New Statesman*, through which he "kept up with language" (interview). While here, he painted what he considers one of his finest paintings, *The Majestas*, a portrait of Christ, using leaves reflecting various degrees of light for His face. He also began working on a novel, *The Sperm of God*, in which he examines the "mongrel, polyglot society" of the New World, where, unlike the Old, there is no "purity of sperm" (interview). These ideas appear in his book *Image and Idea in the Arts of Guyana* (1970) and his short story "The Sperm of God" (*New Writing in the Caribbean*, ed. A. J. Seymour [Georgetown: Caribbean Festival of the Arts, 1972]).

Eventually, for his children's sake, Williams left his primordial haven for Georgetown. For the last ten years he has held several administrative positions with the government of Guyana. He was director of art in the Ministry of Education and founding principal of the E. R. Burrowes School of Art. His most recent position indicates his interest in archaeology (in which he obtained an M.A. in 1979 from the University of Guyana): he is currently director of the Walter Roth Museum of Anthropology. He still intends to complete *The Sperm of God*—his first novel set in the Caribbean—on which he has been working sporadically for the last sixteen years.

MAJOR WORKS AND THEMES

Lionel Froad, the protagonist of *Other Leopards*, refers to the title halfway through the novel when distinguishing between individuals who are absolutely sure of themselves and their causes and others who are burdened with uncertainties and doubts: "Some leopards think they have no spots simply because they have no mirrors. Others manage to know, somehow" (p. 88; quotation and those following from *Other Leopards*, 1983 ed.). Froad is an "other leopard," tormented by ambivalence and inner conflict. Like the author, he is a Guyanese educated in Britain, and he has come to Johkara, a fictional version of Sudan, ostensibly to work as an archaeological draftsman for an English scholar, Hughie King, but essentially to find his roots and identity. What he has discovered when the novel opens is that he is a divided man, caught between two worlds, to neither of which he feels he belongs. It is the illustration rather than the resolution of this predicament which is the central concern of the novel—though an ambiguous resolution is offered in the last two pages.

The protagonist, an intelligent, contemplative individual, examines his dilemma with poetic intensity and insight. The first two pages underscore his duality. He has two names: "I am a man, you see, plagued by these two names, and this is their history: Lionel, the who I was, dealing with Lobo, the who I continually felt I ought to become" (p. 19). Lionel is the Westernized part of his psyche, while Lobo is the ancestral: "All along, ever since I'd grown up, I'd been Lionel looking for Lobo. I'd felt I ought to become this chap, this *alter ego* of ancestral times that I was sure quietly slumbered behind the cultivated mask" (p. 20). He is tormented by not belonging, wanting "to be committed, happy. Like everybody else" (p. 20). Ambivalent and vacillating, he is overcome by "involuntary paralysis" (p. 20). Williams employs two images, one traditional and the other new, to point up Froad's duality of mind: the awareness of his divided nature strikes him while he is standing on a bridge in Kutam Bridge, Johkara. Johkara, in the Sudanic belt of Africa, is itself dichotomized; it is not "quite sub-Sahara, but then not quite desert; not Equatorial black, not Mediterranean white. Mulatto. Sudanic mulatto, you could call it. Ochre. Semi-scrub. Not desert, not sown" (p. 19).

If Lobo is portrayed as Lionel's alter ego, so, on one level, is Hughie. In fact, both Lobo and Hughie represent antithetical characteristics at odds in Lionel's psyche. Lobo represents the "swamp and forests and vaguely felt darkness" (p. 20); Hughie the cerebral, the disciplined, the ordered, the rational, the conscious, and the inquiring—qualities Lionel both admires and despises. Lionel's relationship with Hughie is characterized by this ambivalence. Despite Hughie's condescending treatment of him for his inability to be more methodical and even-tempered, Lionel is "fond of him" (p. 83), and he admits "liking Hughie's cold intelligence; clear apart mind" (p. 116). The metaphorical, psychological oneness of the two is suggested by several images of marriage and lovers. On one occasion, Lionel states, "I sometimes felt Hughie could read my thoughts.

. . . In some things it was like we were married'' (p. 133). And at the end of the novel, when Lionel tries to rid himself of this burdensome part of his psyche by killing Hughie, Hughie appears to be an understanding participant: ''So fast it was as though he was greedy for the screwdriver; he came hungrily into it, like we were lovers understanding this inevitable moment'' (p. 211).

The rejection of this part of Lionel's psyche takes place after he has already discarded his other alter ego, Lobo. This occurs on his discovering the true nature of Amanishakete, the Queen of Meroe during the 1st century B.C., who, he wanted to believe, could prove his ancestry to be noble and dignified. Before visiting the archaeological site where statues of her were unearthed, Lionel has to endure the mocking of Amanishakete by Hughie—who significantly states of a gold figurine of the queen, ''Pity she has no head'' (p. 135)—and he more than ever wants to ''prove Amanishakete . . . and myself into existence. We had no being otherwise; not in Hughie's eyes'' (p. 136). When he does see the statues of the Queen, she is shown flogging a group of slaves. Lionel cannot help but see her as ''cruel, gross, ugly. . . . She knew hate and Law. No trace of love and care. She was a spreading desert'' (p. 155). He feels humiliated by his ''own past'' (p. 155) and knows he now has to join Hughie in condemning himself, rejecting any hope of finding solace in an ancestral identity.

Earlier Froad is startled when he recognizes a sketch of Amanishakete in an archaeological volume to be ''the image, pure and simple and shatteringly original, of Eve'' (p. 103). Eve is the daughter of the Chief, a domineering Black Christian missionary who, like Froad, is from Guyana. She has married a Muslim against her father's wishes and, when the novel opens, has fled her husband's home with their baby. Froad, who eventually becomes her lover, sees her initially as a kindred spirit. She, who addresses him not as Lionel but strictly as Lobo, is compared to the gloom of forest floors and dark, silent rivers and is considered ''raw earthy, nearer to the natural state'' (p. 91). She is a true descendant of Amanishakete. Unlike Lobo, she is not reluctant to commit herself to Africa, associating readily with the various Muslim, Ethiopian, and Sudanese pockets, participating in a *zaar* ceremony, and dancing at the Tigrinya wedding. In commenting on Amanishakete's society, Hughie dismisses it as a fringe culture with no connection with its parent and with no germinal influence itself, and he terms it a ''faecal culture'' (p. 52), a phrase Froad does not forget. Later, when Eve, the contemporary image of Amanishakete, is rejected by Froad, Williams pervasively employs fecal images: as Froad, furious at Eve for lying about being pregnant, goes in search of her, he is surrounded by scavengers emptying latrine buckets in their carts, and he stealthily gains entrance to the place she is visiting through a latrine at the rear of the building.

Eve is a foil to Catherine, Hughie's Welsh secretary, with whom Froad is intimately involved. Together they constitute one of the many polarized pairs tugging at Froad. Though Catherine—who calls him exclusively ''Lionel''—is sincerely concerned about his emotional welfare, he is wary of her, perceiving her to be in Hughie's camp. Caught between the two women, and experiencing ambivalent feelings toward both, he becomes—as in all situations—passive and paralyzed and is unable to readily make love to either unless he is forced into violence—the only form of expression of will displayed by him.

Froad is caught too between opposing political causes. On the one hand are the Christian Blacks of the South, who are bent on secession; on the other are the governing Muslim Arabs of the North, who oppose them. Eve's father, the Chief, and Mohammed, a spokesman for the Arabs, persuade him to write in support of their respective causes, one appealing to Froad's Christian upbringing, the other to his Pan-African sentiments. Both ironically phrase their appeal similarly: the Southerners will trust him, they say, because he is "a Christian Negro interested in the future of Africans in Africa" (pp. 58 and 65). In neither does he see any true humanity or true devotion to Africa. But feeling obligated to choose, he vacillates and procrastinates for the longest while. In the end, when he acts in support of the Northerners, he does so on impulse, and his article is published belatedly after a *coup d'état*.

Williams' solution to Froad's predicament takes the form of ambiguous symbolism. After stabbing Hughie, Froad flees to a Johkara jungle. He strips himself of clothing, daubs himself with mud, and eventually perches on a tree. From this position, at the end of the novel, he watches a light approaching in the distance and wonders whether it is Hughie coming after him or whether it is the dawning of a new day; and, if it is Hughie, is he going to be kind or cruel? The symbolic implication of all this is that, unable to accept or choose one thing over the other (like Eve in her uncritical assimilation of Africa, Catherine in her decision to return to Wales, and the Chief in his acquiescence to deportation), Froad rejects all aspects of his tormented psyche and goes through various stages of devolution until he reaches the primordial state from which, in his "own time" (p. 222), he could begin to evolve organically, naturally. The ending is not pessimistic. On the contrary, the images and phrasing suggest a sense of rebirth. What form the rebirth will take is not clear. It could be a repetition of what he has experienced before; it could be a fresh start.

To convey Froad's cultural and racial dichotomy, Williams employs a number of African as well as Christian and classical allusions and images. A prominent motif in the latter part of the novel is the Zagreus myth. Williams effectively uses it to point up the various elements tugging at Froad. Zagreus, the product of an illicit union between Persephone and Zeus (in the form of a serpent), is pursued by the Titans, set on him by the jealous Hera. To survive, Zagreus has to assume many disguises, but eventually he is torn apart by the Titans. Froad perceives himself to be similarly of an illicit union and needing disguises and cunning to survive. He, who almost is torn apart by the Muslim women at the *zaar*, wonders whether Zagreus need have perished. Catherine sees no parallel between Zagreus and Froad since she feels that while Zagreus accepts his fate of the hunted, Froad is a creature of selfish protest, in love with his "Burden" (p. 164). The Chief believes Zagreus has to perish because he does not pit himself against evil, that is, the Titans, and because he breaks with his people.

Hughie feels the myth has significance only insofar as it underlines that "opposition is the fundamental attitude of being for *homo sapiens*" (p. 170). Though Froad disagrees with these interpretations of the Zagreus myth, he cannot reject them. They continue to haunt him, augmenting his inner turmoil.

Williams' portrayal of Froad's divided life does not reflect a simple dialectic pattern. The antitheses are recognizable, but equally evident are the various gradations between the two poles and the varying emphases on these gradations and on the different forms of paralysis—which make it difficult to provide an easy schema of the novel without doing it an injustice. Williams further complicates the novel (and perhaps slightly blurs the focus) by shifting between considerations of Froad's generic problems of racial identity and his personal conflicts, particularly in the second part of the novel. As is indicated in the epigraph from Ptolomy—"Some things happen to mankind through more general circumstances and not as a result of an individual's natural propensities"—Williams is exploring the effects of larger historical and racial issues on the individual. In the first part, the characters clearly have generic functions; their individuality is submerged; they converse about politics, race, and culture; personal conflicts are not incisively or centrally examined. Hughie and Lionel talk about African antiquity; Catherine and Lionel about whether he yearns to be White; the Chief and Lionel about politics; even Lionel and Eve, whose marriage is disintegrating, talk more about cultural differences than about personal problems. However, the characters are given enough individuality to make them flesh and blood and become more so placed in a graphically and sensuously depicted setting. In the second part, which illuminates the last sentence of the epigraph from Ptolomy—"For the lesser cause always yields to greater and stronger"—Williams imparts a bit more individuality to the characters, who, such as Hughie, talk of their personal experiences with lovers and parents. The protagonists, however, have already been set apart by the "greater and stronger" racial and cultural factors, and this makes attempts at deep personal relationships difficult.

Williams's other novel, *The Third Temptation*, was written while he was in Nigeria studying African classical art and searching for his African roots. The novel, however, surprisingly has little or nothing to do with Africa or racial identity. Williams, in fact, is concerned less with themes than with formal and technical experimentation, based on the narrative theories of the *Nouveau Roman* school, particularly as advocated by its chief exponent, Alain Robbe-Grillet and as illustrated by Robbe-Grillet's *Jealousy* (1957). Like Robbe-Grillet, Williams in *The Third Temptation* employs multiple and apparently chaotic time sequences and points of view, avoids cause-and-effect narration and structuring, and minimizes the importance of meaning. The novel is a difficult one, and it makes demands on the reader for which he may or may not feel amply compensated.

Despite Williams's avoidance of narrative chronological progression, it is possible to unravel some of the various time sequences and shifting points of view and trace a plot, though this perhaps defeats what Williams is attempting to do in deliberately twisting and disjointing the narrative flow. The novel is set in a Welsh seaside resort, Caedmon, on a summer day. The central incident is the accidental death of a young man at a busy intersection. The young man himself is just barely portrayed; Williams focuses on the responses of certain individuals to the accident, concentrating on a period of three hours: Joss Banks (a middle-aged businessman), Sean (his friend), a constable directing traffic, a young girl with a beach ball, a pregnant woman, and an attractive blonde, Chloë.

Of the observers, Joss is the most important. His preoccupations and recollections at the time of the accident provide the novel with a tenuous narrative framework. Joss, a retired printer, recalls seducing Bid, the wife of a young artist, Lawrence Henry Owen, known as LHO, who was employed in his printery as a designer. LHO, faced with his wife's betrayal, committed suicide (described from his point of view in a scene which constitutes a prologue to the novel). Joss married Bid but was haunted by LHO's suicide and his subsequent murder of Titch, another employee, who made unsavory comments on Joss's relationship with Bid. Joss sold his printery, and in the current time sequence it is evident that he and others have not forgotten what he has done. Other incidents in the different time frames may have bearing on Joss's experience, but we become aware that—as Joss himself observes—certain details are perhaps "without point or purpose, without core or meaning" (p. 57).

Williams is particularly interested in experimenting with "point of view." He employs a modified version of Robbe-Grillet's *je-néant* or the "absent I." The main character perceives himself both in the first and third person, with the shifting from one to the other arbitrarily done. A number of other points of view are given, including those of statues, portraits, and faces on billboards. Certain incidents and scenes are returned to and presented in a mixed, altered way depending on the consciousness employed. Williams underscores these multiple viewpoints through the pervasive presence of mirrors and reflections. The true nature of an individual, Williams suggests, could only be established by this multiplicity of perceptions:

> This much must be added; persons pursuing their business along Sweeley Street, their business or their pleasure, pay no attention to the projection of their actions, their activities, their movements, upon the visual fields. Naturally. It is as though from the sanctum of the insulated "I" all the world were thought to be blind; as though this "I" were not itself constantly multiplied on a thousand moving retinas, each from a different angle, and thereby modified. Yet all is motion, reflection, modification, multiplication. Sweeley Street as it were observing Sweeley Street. (p. 91)

Supplementing the various points of view of the novel, Williams makes us conscious of how he, as a painter-novelist, perceives the setting. He draws attention to angling and framing (reminding us of Robbe-Grillet's complementary cinematic approach), and to the colors, hues, shadows, shapes, sizes, perspectives, and distances of particular scenes. His verbal paintings illustrate the observation made by the artist LHO about "the displacement of chiaroscuro by pure chromatics" (p. 65) in contemporary art.

In his portrayal of Joss Banks and the other characters, Williams attempts to capture their sensory, emotional, and mental experiences, to show what during a short concentrated period they see, hear, touch, imagine, and remember. In addition, however, Williams is making a statement about power, as is indicated by the title and the several references to the third (according to Matthew, the second according to Luke) temptation of Christ, wherein He is offered power by Satan. Joss, who had used his position of authority to take away another man's wife, comes to realize as his life deteriorates the ambiguous nature of power: it is both evil and divine, and one could be both its practitioner and its victim.

CRITICAL RECEPTION

While *Other Leopards* has had a favorable and wide critical reception, *The Third Temptation* has attracted little attention. Perhaps this is either because the later novel, set in Wales and peopled by British characters, is not considered a Caribbean novel proper, or because its *Nouveau Roman* form makes it a bit too demanding and inaccessible.

One of the first critics to recognize *Other Leopards* is Louis James, who describes the novel as "a powerful study" which examines the West Indian's "metaphysical and political" response to Africa (*The Islands in Between*, 1968, p. 7). A year after, Gerald Moore, emphasizing the political, describes the novel as "a harsh but necessary book" (*The Chosen Tongue*, 1969, p. 124). Mark Kinkead-Weekes's comparative study of Vic Reid's *The Leopard* and *Other Leopards* offers the first extended study of the novel, examining fairly incisively the thematic as well as the stylistic and technical. He draws attention, for instance, to the importance of form and voice: the narrator's "voice is always aware of the end it has come through before it begins" ("Africa—Two Caribbean Fictions," 1973, p. 58). Other critics have compared the novel with Reid's *The Leopard* as well as with O. R. Dathorne's *The Scholar Man*: for instance, Wilfred Cartey, in "The Rhythm of Society and Landscape" (1966); and Dathorne, in *The Black Mind: A History of African Literature* (1974). More recently, Edward Baugh, in an introduction to the 1983 Heinemann edition of the novel, says that it resists "reduction into any simple, unequivocal solution or message" and that this "can prove exasperating to the reader" (p. v). Baugh provides a comprehensive account of the political and psychological issues, paying special attention to Froad's West Indian sensibility.

Two points have been emphasized by many critics. The first is the author's brilliant verbal paintings of the setting. As James says: "Williams . . . gives us his painter's vision of Africa. . . . And it is this vivid artist's vision that opens the door to Africa as an area of the mind" (pp. 7–8). The second is the complexity of the novel and the difficulty of capturing its richness in a simple schema. Baugh puts it this way: "Indeed, *Other Leopards* is, like its protagonist, suspicious of our hankering after certainties and absolutes" (p. v); and James states:

"The book manages to avoid the neat clichés of the European intellectual world against the passion of Africa" (p. 8).

The ambiguous ending of the novel has attracted the attention of almost all critics. Moore sees Froad as regressing toward infantilism and offers a fascinating interpretation of Froad stealthily entering the house (where Eve is visiting) through the back lavatory. He sees it as "undisguised imagery of anal re-entry to the womb of infancy" (p. 123). He sums up the novel as a "record of personal failure, but it is a failure of the kind necessary to understanding" (p. 125). For Michael Gilkes, "climbing the tree is a symbolic act, for the tree . . . represents a hollow pillar of light by which the shaman climbs up to heaven or down to the underworld" (*The West Indian Novel*, pp. 143–44). He sees Froad as an Ariel figure freed from the intellectual bondage of Hughie-as-Prospero. For James, the "pressures of finding an identity have driven Froad . . . into the 'castle of his skin,' rejecting possession by either Africa or Europe. However agonizing this position, it is the true point of discovery" (p. 10). Baugh says that what Froad comes to accept is that he is a divided man, adding that it "may seem a let-down to the reader that Froad has taken as many pages to recognise what the reader might have been able to tell him from the outset; but what is important is that Froad does now recognise it" (p. ix). And Kinkead-Weekes sees the ending as "a mordant exposure of what it means to be 'uncommitted' and without 'identity' " ("Africa—Two Caribbean Fictions," p. 57).

HONORS AND AWARDS

Denis Williams has received several awards for painting, including second prize in the *London Daily Express* Painters Under Thirty-Five Competition (1955) and first prize in the Guyana National Theatre Mural Competition (1976). The government of Guyana honored him with the Golden Arrow of Achievement (1979). For his work in archaeology and anthropology, he has received grants from such institutions as the International African Institute (1965) and the Smithsonian (1973).

BIBLIOGRAPHY

Works by Denis Williams

Other Leopards. London: New Authors, 1963; London: Heinemann, 1983.

The Third Temptation. London: Calder and Boyars, 1968.

Giglioli in Guyana 1922–1972 [Biography]. Georgetown: National History and Arts Council, 1970.

Image and Idea in the Arts of Guyana. Georgetown: National History and Arts Council, 1970.

Icon and Image: A Study of Sacred and Secular Forms of African Classical Art. London: Allen Lane, 1974; New York: New York University Press, 1974.

Studies of Denis Williams

Baugh, Edward. Introduction to *Other Leopards*. London: Heinemann, 1983.

Cartey, Wilfred. "The Rhythm of Society and Landscape." *New World* (Guyana Independence Issue) (1966), pp. 97–104.

Dathorne, O. R. *The Black Mind: A History of African Literature*. Minneapolis: University of Minnesota Press, 1974, pp. 446–47.

Harris, Wilson. "Denis Williams." *Kaie*, no. 4 (July 1967), 21–22.

James, Louis. Introduction to *The Islands in Between*. London: Oxford University Press, 1968, pp. 7–10.

———. "Or the Hopeful Dawn" (Review of *Other Leopards*). *Public Opinion*, June 18, 1965, pp. 14–15.

Kinkead-Weekes, Mark. "Africa—Two Caribbean Fictions." *Twentieth-Century Studies*, no. 10 (1973), 37–59.

Review of *Other Leopards. Times Literary Supplement*, July 19, 1963, p. 521.

Rowe-Evans, Adrian. Review of *Other Leopards. Transition*3, no. 10 (1963), 57–58.

Seymour, A. J. "The Novel in Guyana." *Kaie*, no. 4 (July 1967), 59–63.

Times Literary Supplement, Review of *Other Leopards*, July 19, 1963, p. 521.

See also General Bibliography: Allis, Gilkes, Herdeck, Hughes, Moore, and Ramchand (1970, 1976).

ARTHUR DRAYTON

Francis Williams (1700–1770)

So little is known of the 18th century Jamaican poet Francis Williams that a case must presumably be made for his inclusion here. Such a case is best made in terms of his uniqueness, for he is the only writer of the 18th century Anglophone Caribbean known for a certainty to be Black. Moreover, although only one of his poems is available to us, a Latin ode preserved in Edward Long's *A History of Jamaica* (1774), he emerges from it as the only English-speaking poet of that time to deal with the peculiar predicament of being Black, educated, and a writer. His was an era when creative writing in the region was more or less reticent about the horrors of slavery as well as the constraints, legal and customary, inflicted on free Blacks. He therefore stands out in his readiness to make his and his people's grievances the subject of his work; and in baring his soul as he did, he disclosed his predicament writ larger than he could himself have suspected. In this respect, therefore, he would bear comparison with his American counterpart and contemporary, Phillis Wheatley; and in his emotions he anticipates her successors, George Moses Horton and Countee Cullen, and some of the *angst* to be found in Black poetry closer to our own time.

BIOGRAPHY

The third son of John and Dorothy Williams, Francis was born circa 1700 and was to become famous as a protégé of the Duke of Montagu. But his family history would have played no small part in propelling him toward this destiny.

Freed from slavery, his parents were already a *cause célèbre* early in the century. In 1711 a bill was introduced in the British House of Commons:

> for enabling John Williams (a free Negroe of the Island of Jamaica) his wife and children, bred up in the religion of the Church of England, and naturaliz'd, to be witness in civil causes; and that no slave might be witness against them; and to provide, that they on all occasions, in the said island, and other her Majesty's plantation, may be tried by a jury, as other her Majesty's subjects are to be tried. (Anon., *The Importance of Jamaica to Great Britain*, n.d.)

No doubt partly because of his family history and partly because he was evidently very intelligent, Francis was selected by the Duke of Montagu (of whom Ignatius Sancho was an even more illustrious protégé) to receive a higher education in England. It was an experiment on the part of the duke "to discover, whether, by proper cultivation, and a regular course of tuition at school and University, a Negro might not be found as capable of literature as a white person." Williams more than fulfilled the duke's expectations. He distinguished himself at Cambridge University in mathematics and the classics. He also earned himself a reputation as a writer of verse. But on his return to Jamaica an attempt to make him a member of the Governor's Council was blocked. He opened a school in Spanish Town, a township some fifteen miles from Kingston and the former capital under Spain, where he taught reading, writing, Latin, and mathematics.

MAJOR WORKS AND THEMES

The poem by which Francis Williams is known is a Latin ode to George Haldane, governor of Jamaica in 1759. Edward Long's account suggests that he was also the author of other poems; and although Long is characteristically skeptical, he mentions that the song, "Welcome, Welcome, Brother Debtor," very popular in England in the 1730s and 1740s, was also ascribed to him. It is therefore probably worth mentioning that this song appeared in no fewer than four English poetical miscellanies: *The Vocal Miscellany* (1738); *The Nightingale, Containing a Collection of 422 of the most Celebrated English Songs* (1738); *The Merry Companion, or Universal Songster* (1742); and *A New Academy of Compliments: Or, The Lover's Secretary* (1743).

Dedicatory odes were not uncommon in the British Caribbean at that time. Indeed, the first known "book" printed in Jamaica was such an ode, *A Pindarique Ode on the Arrival of His Excellency Sir Nicholas Lawes* (1718). Odes and other kinds of verses given over mainly to praise and flattery of personages both great and small satisfied two urges: they allowed lesser talent to take advantage of the indulgent neoclassical doctrine of *imitatio*; and they facilitated purveyors of fashionable *vers de société* in the consensual pretence that theirs was a polished, civilized way of life. Francis Williams parts company with these practitioners to the extent that he imparts an edge to the conventional niceties.

What might be merely formulaic in other hands becomes charged in his. Beneath the hyperbolic surface lie the nightmare realities of the Black experience in particular and the slave society in general:

Under your leadership *all that had been perpetrated ill-advisedly*is now vain, never to recur in your presence. So all the people, not to mention the *lesser throng*, may see that you have relieved them of *the yoke that would have clung to their necks* and *the evils* which this innocent isle had formerly *suffered with grievous torment*. (Emphasis added)

Nor will his heightened consciousness allow him to be content with the vagueness of generalities. The humility of the conventional disclaimer only thinly conceals an affirmation of his common humanity and his people's and therefore an indictment of White racism:

It is not for me, warrior dear to Mars! to extol the deeds of generals: Minerva forbids an Aethiop to do. . . . We live under the sun which drives a fire-bearing team; all eloquence deserts our hearts. Receive this then, bathed with much soot, from a mouth that tries to sing. Its power comes from the heart, not the skin. *Established by a powerful hand, (for the bountiful Creator gave the same soul to all living beings, nothing withheld), virtue itself is innocent of color, as is wisdom. There is no color in the pure mind, none in art.* (Emphasis added)

But Williams's revolutionary universalistic claim, as the late West Indian historian Elsa Goveia aptly described it, must not distract us from an equally important, equally relevant aspect of the poem, namely, the fact that this proto-West Indian revolutionary intellectual had not entirely escaped conditioning by his times. The suggestion that the sun-drenched Tropics are not congenial to creativity may be a conventional disclaimer, but it is also suspiciously close to Caribbean self-rejection, an inferiority complex of which White "West Indians" were the progenitors but not the sole cultivators. Nor could it be by accident that in pressing his credentials as a cultivated human being he shifts from the universalism of art and humanity to a rationalization that quietly accepts Whiteness as norm, anticipating William Blake's lefthanded liberal sentiments by some thirty years: "Nor let it be a cause for shame that you bear a white body beneath a black skin."

Francis Williams was a curiosity for detractors like Long: for the serious student of slave societies and of the literature of the Black experience he is a prototype as both affirmer and victim. Like Phillis Wheatley he did not escape the snares of racism unscathed; but unlike her he was willing and able to use 18th century poetic traditions to affirm man's uncontestable common humanity, to protest racism, and to recognize his moral superiority over his socially ordained superiors.

CRITICAL RECEPTION

In *A History of Jamaica* Edward Long devotes about eleven pages to Francis Williams (pp. 475–85), and he remains our only extensive source of information. Other contemporary writers referred to him briefly. Among these David Hume the philosopher stands out in a foreshadowing of Long's racist detractions. In a 1753–54 appendage to his essay "Of National Characters," Hume stated quite frankly: "I am apt to suspect the Negroes to be naturally inferior to the Whites"; a few sentences later Francis Williams is made to fit in this Procrustean bed: "In Jamaica, indeed, they talk of one Negro as a man of parts and learning; but it is likely he is admired for slender accomplishments, like a parrot who speaks a few words plainly" (quoted by Wylie Sypher, *Guinea's Captive Kings: British Anti-slavery Literature of the 18th Century* [Chapel Hill: University of North Carolina Press, 1942], pp. 52–53).

Long's extended remarks amount to a racially motivated vilification and an equally tendentious commentary on the ode, "to prove an inferiority of Negroes to the race of White men." As Locksley Lindo has pointed out in "Francis Williams: a 'Free' Negro in a Slave World" (1970, p. 75): "Though his readers, white men who were profiting from the institution of slavery, were always a sympathetic audience, Long slants his comments in such a way as to leave no doubt as to the verdict he wishes his readers to bring in" (p. 75).

Locksley Lindo's article rescues Francis Williams' ode from Long's distortions by providing a more faithful translation and setting it in its contemporary neo-classical context and the larger frame of Greco-Roman literature. Drawing attention to "Long's weakness as a Latin scholar or his prejudice or both," Lindo shows how Williams drew on two different treatments of the elegiac couplet, the Catullan and the Ovidian. Using Ovid's couplet-bound sense unit for his basic metric pattern, the poem occasionally breaks out into the sustained Catullan periodic style, in one instance over as many as three couplets. These variations coincide with the edged expression of joys and hopes and the statement of his revolutionary principle. Thus Williams clearly intended meter and rhythm to point to "what is for him and for us the crux of the matter." Lindo also identifies various ways in which Williams was indebted to Roman precedents and suggests that, far from being guilty of "scarcely allowable" excesses, as Long had charged, he was often more restrained and pragmatic than were the Roman models which he imitated.

In "West Indian Consciousness in West Indian Verse: A Historical Perspective" (1970), Arthur D. Drayton accords to Francis Williams an honored place in the development of a West Indian consciousness. He is seen as the inheritor of a family reputation in the struggle for civil liberties and human dignity, legal and constitutional at first, now literary. The ode is rooted in 18th century neo-classical tradition, but the poet knows how to interpose the realities of the Black experience. The ode as accomplishment contains both affirmation and dilemma, the poet's experience is both personal and communal, and the implications clear for the Caribbean and beyond, for Francis Williams' time and for some two hundred years more.

BIBLIOGRAPHY

Studies of Francis Wiliams

Drayton, Arthur D. ''West Indian Consciousness in West Indian Verse: A Historical Perspective.'' *Journal of Commonwealth Literature* 9 (July 1970), 66–68.

Lindo, Locksley. ''Francis Williams: A 'Free' Negro in a Slave World.'' *Savacou* 1 (June 1970), 75–80.

Long, Edward. *A History of Jamaica*. London: T. Lowndes, 1774.

See also General Bibliography: Brown.

VICTOR L. CHANG

Sylvia Wynter (1928–)

BIOGRAPHY

Sylvia Wynter was born on May 11, 1928, to Jamaicans Percival Wynter and his wife Lola Maude, née Reed, then resident in the Holguin Oriente Province of Cuba. At age two she returned to Jamaica with her parents and was educated at the St. Andrew High School for Girls. In 1946 she was awarded the Jamaica Centenary Scholarship for Girls, which took her to King's College, University of London, to read for the B.A. honors in modern languages (Spanish) from 1947 to 1949.

She was awarded the M.A. in December of 1953 for her thesis edition of a Spanish Golden Age *comedia* ''A lo que obliga el honor'' by Marrano Antonio Enríquez Gómez. The work was praised as being a scholarly work of real importance in a crucial and relatively unexplored field. Thus, from very early, her work prefigured two of Sylvia Wynter's later major areas of interest: drama and criticism.

Between 1954 and 1959 she traveled through Europe, living in Norway, Sweden, Italy, and Spain. She met and married a Norwegian pilot, Captain Isachsen, and had a daughter, Annemarie, with him. In these years also, she went into the world of the theater—acting, dancing, and writing.

Some time in 1958 she met the Guyanese novelist, Jan Carew, who was to become her second husband. She had read and commented favorably on his poems on the BBC Overseas Programme, ''Caribbean Voices.'' She was herself then writing for BBC-TV and Radio and had done a version of Federico García

Lorca's *Yerma* for them, translating it into the Jamaican vernacular and transposing it to a Jamaican setting. She was to return to another Lorca play later in her career, *The House of Bernarda Alba*, adapting it as she had *Yerma*, and titling it "The House and Land of Mrs Alba." In her adaptations, then, she fused her interest in drama, her study of Spanish, and her deep involvement with the indigenous folk culture of her people, which were to be continuing aspects of her best work.

In collaboration with Carew, she wrote several pieces for the BBC (as well as for the commercial ITV), including an adaptation of Guyanese Martin Carter's "The University of Hunger," broadcast in 1961 and 1962 as "The Big Pride." More importantly, she completed "Under the Sun," a full-length play for stage which was bought by the Royal Court Theater. The play was also broadcast in a radio version by the BBC-Third Programme and by radio stations in the United States, Denmark, Canada, and Jamaica. This is the earliest genesis of the novel that was to be published by Jonathan Cape in September, 1962, as *The Hills of Hebron*.

The couple, with the two children Annemarie and Christopher, spent March to July, 1962, in the then riot-torn British Guiana, where Sylvia taught Spanish for two terms at Queen's College. At the end of July, the family left Guyana for Jamaica, where, according to a newspaper interview (*Daily Gleaner*, August 9, 1962), they intended to live pemanently, with the feeling that now Jamaica had attained independence, they had to "help create new values, new cultural images . . . project new Jamaican images."

Their optimistic aim was "to form a Jamaican professional theater company" because the country needed "a truly indigenous theater." This deep and abiding interest in drama and the native culture, already noted, accounted largely for Sylvia Wynter's creative output in the next few years. It led her to write and direct a musical, *Shh, It's a Wedding*, to her involvement with the Spanish Town Folk Theater's 1962 production of *Miracle in Lime Lane*, to an adaptation in 1965 of Roger Mais' *Brother Man*. In that year, too, she wrote the historical pageant, *1865—A Ballad for a Rebellion*, and collaborated with Alex Gradussov in 1970 on the Jamaican Pantomime for that year, *Rockstone Anancy*. Her continuing interest in drama led to a 1979 publication of her play for schools, *Maskarade*, and a translation of Francisco Cuevas's *Jamaica Is the Eye of Bolivar*.

By 1963 the Carews had separated, and Jan had gone to Canada. (The marriage was to end in July 1971.) After a break of nearly ten years, Sylvia Wynter returned to the academic world in October, 1963, when she was appointed assistant lecturer in Hispanic literature at the Mona campus of the University of the West Indies. She was to remain continuously at the university until September, 1974, with a year's secondment in 1965 to the JLP government to write *Ballad for a Rebellion*, and again in 1969–70 to write a biography of Sir Alexander Bustamante, the first prime minister of an independent Jamaica and one of the country's National Heroes.

Sylvia Wynter embarked in 1967 on what could be described as the second phase of her career. She began to write critical articles "in order to establish a 'critical space,' a new dimension for criticism" in the West Indies (unpublished letter, UWI, Mona). Her reviews and articles would seek to fuse her interest in Afro-Caribbean culture, her academic interest in Latin American writing, and her conception of the role of the creative writer in the West Indies.

She was invited by the Department of Literature at the University of California at San Diego to be a visiting professor for 1974–75, and she left Jamaica in September of 1974. It was a journey from which, like so many other West Indian writers before her, she was not to return. She resigned from the University of the West Indies, effective April, 1975, and continued at San Diego for another year as the coordinator of the Literature and Society Program.

Sylvia Wynter became chairperson of African and Afro-American Studies, and professor of Spanish in the Department of Spanish and Portuguese at Stanford University in 1977. It is a position she presently holds, and thus—in the words of John Figueroa—she has now joined "the long list of talented West Indians who have found it necessary or expedient to leave the West Indies to work and make their contribution elsewhere" (Donald Herdeck, *Caribbean Writers: A Bio-Bibliographical-Critical Encyclopedia*, 1979, p. 228).

MAJOR WORKS AND THEMES

Sylvia Wynter's most significant and valuable contribution to West Indian literature has been twofold, consisting of literary criticism and her only novel, *The Hills of Hebron* (first published in 1962, and reissued in 1984, by Longman). Indeed, it can be said that her concerns as a critic, a West Indian writer, and a female writer, are all reflected in the novel. Her criticism alone would ensure her a place in the history of West Indian writing. Beginning in 1967, she published a series of articles and book reviews that would open, in her own words, "a new dimension for criticism" (unpublished letter, UWI, Mona).

In 1968 and 1969 she had published in two parts the monumentally titled "We Must Learn to Sit Down Together and Talk About a Little Culture: Reflections on West Indian Writing and Criticism" (hereafter cited as "Little Culture"). This was occasioned by her desire to express her disagreement with several works of criticism emerging from the University and to articulate what she saw as the radical difference between what she termed "acquiescent" criticism versus "challenging" criticism. For her, the "acquiescent" critic pretended to take an objective stance outside of the historical process which had molded his point of view. This "pretended objectivity and detachment" in fact resulted in a distorted perspective which merely served to bolster the status quo. The "challenging" critic, on the other hand, accepted and was aware that his point of view was molded by this historical process, and this awareness—Wynter felt—could lead to creative insights that could help to initiate conscious change. She expanded further on this in 1973, when in a note on her critique "Creole Criticism," she wrote, "Creole criticism . . . is merely English literary criticism rehashed in brown or black face" (unpublished document prepared for the Spanish Department, UWI, Mona). Her attacks were wide-ranging and, at times, savage, aimed particularly at the work of W. I. Carr and Louis James (then lecturers in the Department of English at Mona) as well as at the work of Wayne Brown, John Hearne, Cameron King, and Mervyn Morris. As far as Wynter was concerned, all theses critics were too quick to come to terms with the "brilliant myth" of Europe as the "super culture which embraces all other cultures, and obliterates as it absorbs" ("Little Culture II," p. 31). In being enchained by this cultural myth, such "acquiescent" critics reflected and paralleled "the inauthenticity of the University and its society." Worse yet, since these critics were also the educators, Wynter felt that "the hostility that the West Indian writer meets with from University students comes directly from the concept of literature sold to them by [such] educators" ("Little Culture I," p. 31). Moreover, what she found is that the critics she examined almost all failed to understand that "when the creative instinct is stifled or driven into exile the critical faculty can survive only as maggots do—feeding on the decaying corpse of that which gives it a brief predatory life" ("Little Culture I," p. 26). The writing of criticism in the University had become like a "branch plant" industry, with the interpreter replacing the writer and the critic displacing the creator.

Sylvia Wynter's second major piece of literary criticism, "Creole Criticism: A Critique" (1973), reflected her belief that the folk culture represents "the only living tradition in the Caribbean" and that it is only by "drawing from, by feeding from [the West Indian peasant] that a truly national literature could begin" (p. 20). Indeed, it was that personality through "the re-invention of its culture against impossible odds, that made the West Indian novel possible." She also saw the culture of the folk as a kind of "guerrilla resistance against the market economy," and she posited the existence of a pervasive "African heritage which has been the crucible of the cultural deposits of the immigrant peoples" (p. 14). It was this recognition which motivated, in large measure, her attack on Kenneth Ramchand because she saw his mission as being "to negate, destroy, diminish, disguise the African centrality in the cultural dynamic of the Caribbean peoples" ("Creole Criticism," p. 13). In opposition to this, she celebrated and emphasized the importance of the folk culture in such essays as "Jonkonnu in Jamaica" (1970), "Novel and History: Plot and Plantation" (1971), and "One Love: Aspects of Afro-Jamaicanism" (1972). In "Jonkonnu," for instance, she set out to prove the existence of "a pervasive African-descended folk culture in Jamaica, one that had . . . acted as a principle of revolt and a form of cultural resistance to the cultural superstructure brought by the colonizer" (unpublished document prepared for the Spanish Department, UWI, Mona).

From the viewpoint of the 1980s, when we have such magisterial and insightful criticism as Gordon Rohlehr's book on Brathwaite's poetry, *Pathfinder*, and Bruce King's collection of critical essays on *West Indian Literature* (1979), the controversy and heat generated by Wynter's articles in the 1970s, seem out of proportion. But her work was crucial because she was the first to articulate, and focus on, the problem, and she was ideally suited for it, being a creative writer herself, academically trained in literary criticism, and educated in the metropole. She was also an agitator, a stimulating lecturer, and a polemical writer who presented papers at numerous conferences expressing her point of view.

Whether West Indian criticism would have inevitably come of age and shed its dependent role is difficult to say. There is little doubt, however, that she helped to hasten the process by her provocative and stimulating articles.

In *The Hills of Hebron* (1962) Wynter turned her attention to the folk culture which had always absorbed her in her literary adaptations as well as her literary criticism and accounted in part for her interest in the work of Lorca. He too had grown up amid "a rich folk tradition," and his plays "recreated rhythms and cadences of speech familiar to the people" ("An Introductory Essay to an Adaptation of Federico García Lorca's *The House of Bernarda Alba*, and an Extract from the Adapted Play, *The House and Land of Mrs Alba*," 1968, p. 49). Before she adapted Lorca's play, she examined, she says, "the play in the original in order to identify the social, historical and economic determinants of the characters and their society" (p. 49).

To a certain extent, this was exactly the approach she brought to her own work and though at heart the novel is a kind of *roman à clef*, Wynter invests it with so much of her concerns that the medium is too freighted with the message. This has led one critic to complain that there is an "abundance of political, racial and other abstractions, sometimes provocative, often somewhat ill-sorted. . . . The writer is first a thinker and then a story-teller" (Karl Sealy, Review of *The Hills of Hebron*, 1963, p. 292).

The story is concerned primarily with the fate of the revivalist group, the New Believers of Hebron, after the death of their founder, Moses Barton. Their present leader, Obadiah Brown, had vowed not to touch his wife Rose for a year and a month until the next hurricane had passed. But now, Rose is obviously pregnant, and Miss Gatha, widow of the founder of Hebron who wants the eldership for her son Isaac, denounces them both. To the community it seems the land is stricken with drought as a punishment from God for this broken vow. We learn that Rose has, in fact, been raped, and though the rapist's identity is not revealed until late in the novel (p. 248), we can guess long before the end that it is Isaac who returned, bitter and disillusioned, to steal the money box and disappear forever from Hebron. The ordeal has taught the Brethren and Obadiah an object lesson, and they have moved toward a recognition that religious fervor is not enough and that isolationism is no answer to the problem of poverty. Indeed, salvation lies in creative labor rather than in the worship of an abstract God. As Obadiah says: "The first thing we are going to do, starting tomorrow, is to build a good road, a broad road out into the world" (p. 281). The novel ends with Miss Gatha cradling Rose's child "to her withered breasts" in a gesture of peace and reconciliation, while the drought is broken by an equally symbolic rain.

As has been noted, Sylvia Wynter invests the novel with so much that the messages tend to overwhelm the story. Indeed, it could be said that almost all of the concerns of the West Indian writer are demonstrated here. Her ironic attacks range from a criticism of the alienating effects of a colonial education on Black students to a scathing look at the would-be politicians who "calm and smiling, would don the robes of office abandoned by their former masters, would echo firmly their platitudes and half-truths and compromises and subtle distortions, would make themselves counterparts of the men whom ostensibly they had overthrown" (p. 235). She attacks the period of slavery during which "the ghosts of dark millions" had perished, "coffined in the holds of ships, so that some could live to breed more slaves" (p. 53), as well as the period of colonial rule. She does not spare either the revivalist cults or the Rastafarian religion that looks to Ethiopia for salvation when "Mussolini beat the hell out of the conquering Lion of Judah and not even there the black man is free" (p. 271). She protests, too, against police brutality, the corruption of the established church, the discrimination of Whites against Blacks, the fickle nature of the masses, the oppression of women by men, and so on. Most of all, she stresses the theme of betrayal in all its aspects: the betrayal of wife by husband (as in the case of Moses and Gatha), of master by slave, and slave by fellow slave (as in the case of Cato), of mother by son, of community by prophet, of dream by harsh reality.

In spite of this weakness, however, and the rather drawn-out and episodic nature of the work, *The Hills of Hebron* achieves some fine effects. One of these is in the area of language. Wynter employs Standard English for her main narrative, but she subtly shapes the speech of her characters to echo the Creole patterns and rhythms and the pervasive influence of the King James version of the Bible. Thus she talks about "birthing our sons," and Obadiah's speech has an archaic and poetic ring to it: "Remember back with me, Brothers and Sisters, remember back one year and one month, this same time, this quiet hour, this cool time, this dark time, before the sun burst bright on us" (pp. 12–13). Miss Gatha claims: "My son never once looked at a woman to lust after her unseemly" (p. 21), and Gee describes how "the moonlight jumped off the road and I could hear ghosts breathing out fire and smoke and my heart did catch up my mouth" (p. 32). Her descriptions, too, have that vivid metaphorical quality one associates with Jamaican Creole speech. The sun is seen "curved over the land like a machete blade" (p. 105), and a rainbow is described in awe: "Look at the arch and the sweep of it, the blue, the green, the scarlet flame, the lizard tongue of it" (p. 41). Elsewhere we are told, "the curiosity of the congregation blazed up like fire through a heap of cane trash" (p. 23).

The book is also rich in Biblical echoes and allusions, not only in the names like Hebron, Moses, Obadiah, Ananias, and Isaac, but also in near paraphrases. Like the original, this Moses is "to lead the people . . . out of bondage into the Promised Land" (p. 105), and in his first vision, "the bush flamed orange and green fire . . . and the ground on which I was standing . . . was holy, holy, ground"

(p. 107). The coconut palms were "as innumerable crucifixions against the sky" (p. 55), and "their past had vanished like Elijah, riding in his chariot of fire" (p. 11). The Angel of Death "has flown his bat-wings far away from us" (p. 12).

Though the novel's chief character is Elder Obadiah Brown, this could be said to be a woman's novel. It is the women who seem to demonstrate the strengths and enduring qualities of the folk culture, the women who provide support and sustenance for their men. Moses would never have survived without the help of Liza, Kate, and Gatha. The range of peasant experience is displayed, too, in the women, whether it is Aunt Kate, or May May, or the ambitious, embittered Miss Gatha. It is a woman who pecipitates the crisis in Hebron, but it is also the women who provide continuity and survival through the children they bear. It is through the women, too, that Wynter captures all the pathos, longing, suffering, and ignorance of the working class. Moreover, the women are projected as the ones who are really in touch with the spirit world, whether it is May May, who is a genuine mystic, or Sue, who was "born with a veil over her face" and therefore has second sight.

Wynter is very successful, too, in depicting the rural Jamaican landscape and in evoking the settlement of Hebron in both good and bad times. By numerous references to Jamaican flora—like ackees, mangoes, breadfruit, Jerusalem candles—and to fauna like the peeniwallies (fireflies), iguanas, and john crows, she lends the novel an air of authenticity. At times, she succeeds in fusing elements of the natural with the symbolic so that the star-apple tree assumes symbolic significance when associated with Miss Gatha because "the star apple is a mean fruit, the meanest one of all . . . it would rather stay on the tree branch and wither away than drop down like any other fruit" (p. 80). The carrion crow which perches on the topmost limb of the guinep tree in Miss Gatha's yard is symbolic, since she waits, too, to reap the benefits of death.

Wynter uses epigraphs to the four sections of the novel not only to point out the protest nature of what she is writing but also to locate the action within a spiritual sphere and to establish the continuity of the African heritage. Thus, she uses quotations from an Amazulu account of the initiation of a diviner as well as an incantation of Boukman, the Haitian prophet who advocates: "Throw away the god of the whites who has so often caused us to weep" (p. 103). She also quotes from Dostoevsky and again locates the novel in the context of a continuing search for God: "With every people, at every period of its existence, the end of the whole national movement, is only the search for God" (p. 253).

There is little doubt that Wynter's portrait of Moses Barton, the deluded founder of the Brethren who dies in a self-inflicted crucifixion, is modeled on the figure of Alexander Bedward (1859–1930), the Jamaican folk hero and leader of a messianic cult movement which attracted thousands of followers from all over Jamaica at the beginning of the century. Like Bedward, Moses promised his followers he would fly to heaven and, when he failed to do so, was "tried on a charge of lunacy, convicted, and sent to the Mental Hospital" (p. 118). However, the vast array of the other characters are Wynter's own creation, and they are carefully and interestingly differentiated not only in their ages but in their individual traits, whether it is Brother Hugh, "a short man with a paunch and a great self-importance," or Sister Sue, with her "narrow slanted eyes, embedded like chips of black quartz in her full cheeks" (p. 16), or Gee, with her "long neck set well back on her shoulders, and high young breasts" (p. 43).

Wynter brought to the novel, too, her dramatic expertise and knowledge, and many of the scenes in the novel have this sharp, dramatic quality, none better than in the opening confrontation in the church between Miss Gatha and the others, when Rose's pregnant state is revealed and we are faced with the mystery of who is responsible. The conflicts between the characters are clearly etched and convincingly realized. The scene is carefully orchestrated to lead to the climax, when the apron drops from Ann's fingers and she backs away and "the congragation saw the clear rising of Rose's stomach" (p. 25). Wynter ends the scene with a rapid change of tone: "The bubble of the morning's celebrations was shattered and the fragments went spinning away like the mist in the morning light" (p. 25).

The novel is, in a sense, about the paradoxical triumph of failure. As Wynter has observed, "Their failure is important. The failure of the men and women in West Indian novels is a witness to the impossible odds against which they are pitted" ("Little Culture I," p. 31). Only by writing about it can we realize and appreciate the tremendous odds against which these people struggled and recognize that, in Naipaul's words, "to have survived was a triumph." Thus Sylvia Wynter succeeds in depicting real and believable characters, who are not reduced "to a non-self, assimilated to ugliness, sin, darkness, immorality" ("One Love," p. 75) but are "unofficial opposed alternative 'human' [selves] whose humanity survives" (p. 73).

CRITICAL RECEPTION

Sylvia Wynter's work has not yet been given the kind of sustained critical scrutiny that it deserves. The single most significant piece of recognition for her critical work comes from Edward Brathwaite, himself a creative writer, critic, teacher, and cultural historian. In his "The Love Axe/1: Developing a Caribbean Aesthetic, 1962–1974" (1977), he accords her "Reflections on West Indian Writing and Criticism" very high praise. It is, he says, "one of our great critical landmarks: a major essai in literary ideas" (p. 101). Tacit recognition has been given also by Edward Baugh, who included an excerpt in his *Critics on Caribbean Literature* (1978), and by John Hearne in his *Carifesta Forum* (1976).

Similarly, little attention has been paid to *The Hills of Hebron*, apart from brief reviews in *Time*, *Freedomways*, *Bim*, and *TLS*. Kenneth Ramchand in his *The West Indian Novel and its Background* (1970) makes a few slighting references to it as "an overloaded work by a West Indian intellectual anxious to touch upon as many themes as possible" (p. 41). In his review in *Bim*, Karl Sealy praises the "author's insight into and delineation of character" as "extraordinary and sure,'' but complains that the novel ''caricatures the religious conflicts of a backward people.'' The most recent review by Herma Diaz, however, sees the novel as one of ''great profundity.'' She, too, notes that the author is ''inclined to use some of her characters as mouthpieces for her views'' and that in the story ''everyone is a loser.'' There is no doubt that *The Hills of Hebron* is a flawed first novel, but its achievements are considerable and should be recognized.

BIBLIOGRAPHY

Works by Sylvia Wynter

The Hills of Hebron. London: Jonathan Cape, 1962; New York: Simon and Schuster, 1962; London: Longman, 1984.

''An Introductory Essay to an Adaptation of Federico García Lorca's *The House of Bernarda Alba*, and an Extract from the Adapted Play, *The House and Land of Mrs Alba*.'' *Jamaica Journal* 2 (September 1968), 48–56.

''We Must Learn To Sit Down Together and Talk About a Little Culture: Reflections on West Indian Writing and Criticism, Part I.'' *Jamaica Journal* 2 (December 1968), 23–32; Part 2, *Jamaica Journal* 3 (March 1969), 27–42.

''Jonkonnu in Jamaica: Towards the Interpretation of Folk Dance as a Cultural Process.'' *Jamaica Journal* 4 (June 1970), 34–48.

School Edition and Adaptation of *Black Midas* by Jan Carew. London: Longman, 1970.

Jamaica's National Heroes. Kingston: National Trust Commission, 1971.

''Novel and History: Plot and Plantation.'' *Savacou* 5 (June 1971), 95–102.

''One Love: Aspects of Afro-Jamaicanism.'' *Caribbean Studies* 12 (October 1972), 64–99.

''Creole Criticism: A Critique.'' *New World Quarterly* 5 (1973), 12–36.

Rody and Rena, the Sea Star Readers (with Annemarie Isachsen). Kingston: Jamaica Publishing House, 1975.

Jamaica Is the Eye of Bolivar (Translation of a play by Francisco Cuevas). New York: Vantage Press, 1979.

Studies of Sylvia Wynter

Baird, Keith E. Review of *The Hills of Hebron*. *Freedomways* 3 (Winter 1963), 111–12.

Brathwaite, Edward K. ''The Love Axe/1: Developing a Caribbean Aesthetic, 1962–1974.'' *Bim* 16 (July 1977), 53–56; Part 2, *Bim* 17 (December 1977), 100–06.

Charles, Pat. Review of *The Hills of Hebron*. *Bim* 9 (January-June 1963), 292.

Diaz, Herma. Review of *The Hills of Hebron*. *Sunday Gleaner Magazine*, August 12, 1984, p. 5.

Panton, George. ''Bedward in New Guise.'' *Sunday Gleaner*, July 22, 1962, p. 1.

Ramchand, Kenneth. *The West Indian Novel and its Background*. London: Faber, 1970, pp. 41–42, 121–23, 127–29.

Review of *The Hills of Hebron*. *Time* 80 (August 11, 1962), 69.

Review of *The Hills of Hebron*. *Times Literary Supplement*, no. 3161, (September 28, 1962), 75.
Sealy, Karl. Review of *The Hills of Hebron*. *Bim* 9 (January-June 1963), 292.
See also General Bibliography: Allis, Herdeck, and Hughes.

General Bibliography

Allis, Jeannette B. *West Indian Literature: An Index to Criticism 1930–1975*. Boston: G. K. Hall, 1981.

Baugh, Edward. *West Indian Poetry 1900–1970: A Study in Cultural Decolonisation*. Kingston: Savacou, 1971.

———, ed. *Critics on Caribbean Literature*. London: Allen & Unwin, 1978.

Brown, Lloyd W. *West Indian Poetry*. Boston: Twayne, 1978.

Cudjoe, Selwyn R. *Resistance and Caribbean Literature*. Athens: Ohio University Press, 1980.

Gilkes, Michael. *The West Indian Novel*. Boston: Twayne, 1981.

Griffiths, Gareth. *A Double Exile: African and West Indian Writing Between Two Cultures*. London: Marion Boyars, 1978.

Harris, Wilson. *Tradition the Writer & Society: Critical Essays*. London: New Beacon, 1973. (Orig. publ. 1967.)

Herdeck, Donald E., ed. *Caribbean Writers: A Bio-Bibliographical-Critical Encyclopedia*. Washington, D.C.: Three Continents Press, 1979.

Hughes, Michael. *A Companion to West Indian Literature*. London: Collins, 1979.

James, Louis, ed. *The Islands in Between: Essays in West Indian Literature*. London: Oxford University Press, 1968.

King, Bruce, ed. *West Indian Literature*. London: Macmillan, 1979.

Lamming, George. *The Pleasures of Exile*. London: Michael Joseph, 1960.

Maes-Jelinek, Hena, ed. *Commonwealth Literature and the Modern World*. Liège, Belgium: Revue des Langues Vivants, 1975.

McDowell, Robert E. *Bibliography of Literature from Guyana*. Arlington, Tex.: Sable, 1975.

Moore, Gerald. *The Chosen Tongue*. London: Longmans, Green, 1969.

Niven, Alastair, ed. *The Commonwealth Writer Overseas: Themes of Exile and Expatriation*. Liège, Belgium: Revue des Langues Vivants, 1976.

Ramchand, Kenneth. *An Introduction to the Study of West Indian Literature*. Kingston: Nelson Caribbean, 1976.

———. *The West Indian Novel and its Background*. London: Faber and Faber, 1970.

Van Sertima, Ivan. *Caribbean Writers: Critical Essays*. London: New Beacon, 1968.

Index

Contributors

HIMANI BANNERJI, a native of India, is a Ph.D. student at the University of Toronto and a Lecturer at York University in Toronto. Her essays and reviews have appeared in a variety of journals in Canada, India, and Africa. She is the author of a book of poetry, *A Separate Sky* (1982), and a forthcoming volume of short stories.

EDWARD BAUGH is Chairman of the Department of English at the University of the West Indies, Mona, Kingston, and the author of *West Indian Poetry 1900–1970: A Study in Cultural Decolonisation* (1971) as well as numerous articles on West Indian literature. He edited *Critics on Caribbean Literature* (1978).

HAROLD BARRATT, originally from Trinidad, is Chairman of the Department of Languages, Letters and Communication at the University College of Cape Breton, Sydney, Nova Scotia. He holds a doctorate in Renaissance drama and teaches Shakespeare, the literature of the Caribbean, and short fiction. He has published several essays in a variety of journals.

ENID E. BOGLE, Lecturer in English at Howard University, was born in Jamaica. She is a graduate of Shortwood Teachers' College, Howard University, and the Catholic University of America. She is the co-author of "An Annual

Bibliography of Afro-American, African and Caribbean Literature for the Year 1976" (*CLAJ* 21 [September 1977], 100–57) and soon to be published essays on Louise Bennett, Nanina Alba, and the Jamaican Christmas Pantomime.

ANTHONY BOXILL was born in the West Indies and educated there and in Canada. Since 1966 he has taught courses in Commmonwealth Literature at the University of New Brunswick. He is the author of *V. S. Naipaul's Fiction: In Quest of the Enemy* and of several articles on West Indian literature.

LLOYD W. BROWN, a Jamaican, is currently Professor of Comparative Literature at the University of Southern California. He is the author of *Bits of Ivory: Narrative Techniques in Jane Austin's Fiction* (1973), *West Indian Poetry* (1978), and numerous essays and articles on English, West Indian, and Black American literature. He also edited *The Black Writer in Africa and the Americas* (1973).

ROLAND E. BUSH was born in Philadelphia, Pennsylvania, and received a Ph.D. in Comparative Literature from the University of Southern California. He teaches courses in Hispanic Literatures, Literature and the Other Arts, and mythology at California State University in Long Beach. His articles and reviews have appeared in a variety of journals.

ELAINE CAMPBELL is Assistant Professor of English at Regis College in Weston, Massachusetts. She wrote the introduction for Virago Press's new papercover edition of Phyllis Shand Allfrey's *The Orchid House* (1982) and is co-editing a two-volume, multi-genre anthology of writing by women from the Caribbean Basin for Three Continents Press. Her doctoral dissertation on West Indian fiction will be published by Commonwealth Press under the title *Eden's Exiles*.

VICTOR L. CHANG, who has taught in Canada, the United States, and England, is presently a Lecturer in English at the University of the West Indies, Mona. Currently, he is working on a book on Edgar Mittelholzer for Heinemann, as well as on a novel which plans to explore the Jamaican Chinese experience.

RHONDA COBHAM is a graduate of the University of the West Indies and of St. Andrew's University, Scotland, where she presented a doctoral thesis on Caribbean literature in 1982. She has contributed articles to a variety of books and journals and wrote the introduction to the New Beacon edition of Alfred Mendes's *Black Fauns* (1984). She now lives in Germany and teaches in the African Studies Program of the University of Bayreuth.

EUGENIA COLLIER, a native of Baltimore, Maryland, teaches Afro-American literature and creative writing at Howard University. She has published articles, poems, and stories in various publications. Her play, *Ricky*, has been produced in Chicago and Baltimore. She has completed a novel and is beginning a second.

DARYL CUMBER DANCE, a native Virginian, is Professor of English at Virginia Commonwealth University in Richmond. She is the author of two collections of folklore (*Shuckin' and Jivin': Folklore from Contemporary Black Americans* [1978] and *Folklore from Contemporary Jamaicans* [1985]) and several articles on Afro-American and Caribbean folklore and literature.

KWAME DAWES, like his father, novelist Neville Dawes (treated in this anthology), was born of Jamaican parents temporarily living in Africa. Kwame Dawes was born in Accra, Ghana, and moved to Jamaica in 1971. He is presently completing the requirements for a master's degree in West Indian Literature at the University of the West Indies in Kingston, where he also works as a tutor in philosophy. He has written and produced several award-winning plays and has published poetry and essays.

JEAN D'COSTA, a native of Jamaica, is now Associate Professor of English at Hamilton College in Clinton, New York. She is the author of four children's novels (all set in Jamaica), a critical study, *Roger Mais* (1978), and numerous articles and essays. See also Joyce Johnson, "Jean D'Costa," in this volume.

ARTHUR DRAYTON is Chairman of the Department of African Studies at the University of Kansas and Professor of African Studies and English. He formerly taught at the University of the West Indies and the University of Ibadan, Nigeria. The author of several articles and encyclopedia entries on West Indian literature, he is currently working on "Essays on Literature and Society in the Black World."

NORVAL "NADI" EDWARDS, a native of Jamaica, is a candidate for the M.Phil. at the University of the West Indies, Mona, where he is a Teaching Assistant in English.

ROBERT D. HAMNER, Professor of English and Humanities at Hardin-Simmons University in Abilene, Texas, taught at the University of Guyana in 1975–76 on a Fulbright Fellowship. He is the author of *V. S. Naipaul* (1973), *Critical Perspectives on V. S. Naipaul* (1977), and *Derek Walcott* (1981), as well as numerous articles on West Indian literature. He is presently editing essays on Joseph Conrad as a Third World writer and on Derek Walcott.

DAVID INGLEDEW completed a B.A. in English Literature and History at the University of the West Indies in Mona and a master's in English at Queen's University, Ontario, Canada. His thesis was titled "The Dark Divide: A Study of the Novels of John Hearne.'' He taught on the high school level for one year and is currently working in industry in Jamaica.

JOYCE JOHNSON is Jamaican. She did undergraduate work at the University College of the West Indies, Jamaica, and postgraduate work at the University of Toronto and McGill University. She formerly taught at the University of the West Indies and now lectures at the College of the Bahamas in Nassau.

BRIDGET JONES was born in England and educated at Cambridge University. She taught French at the University of the West Indies, Mona, from 1964 to 1982. At present she is living mainly in England. She has published articles on French Caribbean literature, especially Léon Damas, and a few poems.

LEOTA S. LAWRENCE teaches Caribbean and Afro-American literature in the English Department at Howard University, where she received her Ph.D. in 1976. She has published articles on Caribbean literature in several journals and is presently working on a book-length study of ''The Women in Caribbean Literature.''

MARK A. McWATT is a lecturer in English and West Indian literature at the Cave Hill (Barbados) campus of the University of the West Indies. He has published articles and reviews on West Indian literature.

BRYANT MANGUM received a Ph.D. in American literature from the University of South Carolina. Since 1971 he has been a member of the English Department at Virginia Commonwealth University, where he teaches courses in modern and contemporary American literature. He has published articles on F. Scott Fitzgerald, Ernest Hemingway, Stephen Crane, and Kurt Vonnegut, Jr., and is working currently on a book-length study of Fitzgerald's short stories.

CAROL P. MARSH received her early education in Bermuda. She is a Phi Beta Kappa graduate of Howard University, where she also earned the M.A. and Ph.D. degrees. She has published in the *CLA Journal* and *The Dictionary of Literary Biography*. She has taught at the Berkeley Institute in Bermuda, Howard University, the University of the District of Columbia, and Morehouse College. She is currently Assistant Professor of English at Georgia State University.

PAMELA C. MORDECAI edits the *Caribbean Journal of Education* for the School of Education, University of the West Indies, Mona. She has written on Caribbean literature and developed curriculum materials in language arts for the Caribbean. Her poetry is represented in various journals and anthologies, including *Jamaica Woman* (1980), which she co-edited with Mervyn Morris.

DAPHNE MORRIS is a former member of the Department of English at the University of the West Indies, Mona. She wrote the introduction to the Heinemann edition of Roger Mais's *The Hills Were Joyful Together* (1981).

MERVYN MORRIS, a native of Jamaica, teaches in the Department of English at the University of the West Indies, Mona. He is the author of four volumes of poetry and numerous critical essays. See also Pamela Mordecai, "Mervyn Morris," in this volume.

IAN H. MUNRO was born in Canada and received his Ph.D. from the University of Texas at Austin. He has taught at the University of Texas, Western Illinois University, Bayero University College in Kano, Nigeria, and Wuhan University in Wuhan, China. At present he is Associate Professor of English at William Jewell College in Liberty, Missouri. He has published articles on George Lamming and articles, reviews, and interviews on African, Caribbean, and Commonwealth literatures.

EVELYN O'CALLAGHAN is a Jamaican graduate of the National University of Ireland and Oxford University, where she held a Rhodes scholarship. A Lecturer in English at the University of the West Indies, Barbados, she has written reviews and articles on West Indian literature.

SANDRA POUCHET PAQUET is a native of Trinidad and Tobago. She currently teaches Afro-American, Caribbean, and African literature at the University of Hartford, Connecticut. She is the author of *The Novels of George Lamming* (1982) and is presently writing a critical study of the novels of Samuel Selvon.

KENNETH RAMCHAND, a Trinidadian, is a Senior Lecturer in English at the University of the West Indies, St. Augustine. He is the author of *The West Indian Novel and its Background* (1970), *An Introduction to the Study of West Indian Literature* (1976), and numerous essays on Caribbean literature. He edited *West Indian Poetry: An Anthology for Schools* (1971), a volume of poetry; *West Indian Narrative: An Introductory Anthology* (1980); and *Best West Indian Stories* (1982).

VICTOR J. RAMRAJ, who is originally from Guyana, is an Associate Professor of English at the University of Calgary, Canada. He edited the Caribbean issue of *A Review of International English Literature* and is the author of *Mordecai Richler* (1983) and scholarly papers on Canadian and Commonwealth literature published in Caribbean, European, and North American journals.

WILFRED D. SAMUELS is an Assistant Professor of English and Black Studies at the University of Colorado at Boulder. Progeny of Jamaican parents, he received his Ph.D. degree in American Studies/Afro-American Studies from the University of Iowa. He is the author of several critical articles, scholarly expositions, and book reviews.

REINHARD W. SANDER has taught in the United States, Nigeria, England, and Jamaica and is at present a lecturer in African and Caribbean literatures at Bayreuth University, West Germany. He wrote his Ph.D. thesis on early West Indian literature, a revised version of which will be published by Greenwood Press. He has edited *Kas-Kas* (1972), *An Index to Bim* (1973), *From Trinidad* (1978), and *Der Karibische Raum zwischen Selbst- und Fremdbestimmung* (1984).

IAN D. SMITH was until 1983 an Assistant Lecturer in the Department of English at the University of the West Indies. Presently he is enrolled in a doctoral program at Columbia University in New York.